Rules of the Game

The complete illustrated encyclopedia of all the sports of the world

The complete illustrated encyclopedia of all the sports of the world

Rules of the game

by the **Diagram Group**

St. Martin's Press
New York

Diagram Visual Information Ltd

Editor **Sylvia Worth**
Research editors **Sullivan Services**

Art director **Richard Hummerstone**
Designers Jo Gait, John Seabright, Ian Wood
Art staff Jeff Alger, Darren Bennett, Graham Blake, Trevor Bounford, Paul Buckle, James Dallas, Brian Hewson, Bob Ho, Elly King, Susan Kinsey, Pavel Kostal, Lee Lawrence, Paul McCauley, Kathleen McDougall, Helen Roberts, Jane Robertson, Graham Rosewarne, Tim Scrivens, Rupert Shaw, Dino Skeete, Sylvia Tan.

Contributors H Amery, D Berwick, N Berwick, F Bill, L Caddell, A Fawcett, J P D Grint, David Heidenstam, B Horne, J Jellinek, M Ling, B McIntosh, Paulin Meier, Ruth Midgley, A T H Rowland-Entwistle, J Rowland-Entwistle, M Tyler, J Walker, J Weatherall, M Winfield.

Proof readers Austin H Guest, Susan Pinkus.
Indexer Susan Bosanko

Typesetting by Bournetype, 3 Yelverton Road, Bournemouth, Dorset, U.K.

Library of Congress Cataloging-in-Publication Data

Rules of the game : the complete illustrated encyclopedia of all the sports of the world / by the Diagram Group.
    p.   cm.
    Includes indexes.
    ISBN 0-312-11940-2 (pbk.)
    1. Sports—Rules.   I. Diagram Group.
[GV731.D52   1995]
796—dc20   94-36062
                                              CIP

First Revised Paperback Edition: January 1995
10 9 8 7 6 5 4 3 2 1

Acknowledgements

The authors and publishers wish to extend their warmest thanks to the many sports associations, equipment manufacturers, and other organizations without whose kind and generous assistance this book could not have been compiled. Unfortunately, it is not possible to name them all individually, but special thanks are owed to:

The government tourist offices of France, Spain and Switzerland
Steve Allison (jiu jitsu)
Simon Arron (motor racing)
Christ Aston (crossbow archery)
E Ayling & Sons Ltd, Racing Blade Specialists (rowing)
R Bamber (crossbow archery)
Peter Bayer (biathlon)
Don Berliner (aerobatics)
John L Bishop (golf)
James Black (aerobatics)
Otton Bonn (canoe sports)
David Brown (golf)
Nancy Clark (speedball)
Colin Clemett (table tennis)
Mr R A B Crowe (rugby union)
Danny Cullinane (athletics)
Stanley I Fischler (ice hockey)
Brian Forter (canoeing)
Michael R Heuer (aerobatics)
Keo Holdings (surfing)
Stuart Houghton (softball)
Danny Hughes (mountain running)
Fred Inch (flat green bowls)
Barbara James (athletics)
David Kersey (motorcycle racing)
Dieter Krickow (modern pentathlon)
Leon Paul Equipment Co Ltd (fencing)
Graham C Lester (lacrosse)
Olympic yacht class organizations (yachting)
Lindy Nisbett (athletics)
Rita Overend (lacrosse)
Edwin Phelps, Racing Boatbuilder and Waterman to Queen Elizabeth II (rowing)
Wally Rauf (luge tobagganing)
John Roche (equestrian sports)
Chloe Ronaldson (roller skating)
Rudolph Sablo (weightlifting)
Salter Bros Ltd (rowing)
G Sambrooke Sturgess (yachting)
Silva Compasses (London) Ltd (orienteering)
Cyril A Sinfield (athletics)
Per Sjohult (canoe sailing)
Don Stamp (target and field archery)
Rolf Thiede (canoe polo)
Tony Thornley (orienteering)
Berny Wagner (athletics)
Cliff Webb (windsurfing)
Peter Wells (canoeing)
John White (gymnastics)
Irene B Williams (synchronized swimming)
F Wilt (athletics)
Benjamin Wright (figure skating)
Albert Woods (canoeing)
Tony Yorke (cycling)

Foreword

Rules of the Game, which was first published in 1974, has become established as the authoritative digest of the official laws and rules of the major sports of the world. In 1977 **Rules of the Game** was presented by the American Booksellers Association as a gift for the White House Home library.

The continuing aim of this book is to assist the reader in understanding the world's major sports, and in so doing to increase his/her enjoyment as a spectator or player. We have retained all of the features which have made **Rules of the Game** the valued companion of the sports enthusiast, but the whole work has been thoroughly revised to take account of recent changes to rules of play.

For years the most comprehensive book on sports designed for general use, it has now been brought fully up to date to include some of those sports which have increased in popularity in recent years. Hang gliding, freestyle skiing, running game target shooting, windsurfing and jiu jitsu are included.

The method of presentation is predominantly visual, every effort having been made to explain in pictures the complex features of the sporting activities. The guidelines of the book are the official international rules and laws published by the governing sports bodies for each of the sports included in the book. Full copies of the rules of individual sports may be obtained from the appropriate sports governing body, listed on page 310.

We have used both imperial and metric units of measurement throughout the book. For instance, all diagrams of playing areas show both sets of units. In the body of the text, however, the measurements quoted are those laid down by the international governing sports body within that particular sport. Where both imperial and metric measurements are specified, both are quoted.

The original structure of the book, which is such that sports of a similar nature are grouped together, has been retained. As an additional aid there is a double index. The groups of sports are first presented in the contents, and on page 317 each particular sporting activity appears in alphabetical order.

Different features of each sport are described, including major objectives: playing area and equipment; timing and scoring; rules and regulations; participants and officials; playing procedure; and misconduct and its consequences. Those sports that appear in the Olympic calendar carry its symbol beneath their title.

This book could not have been compiled without the cooperation and personal involvement of so many international sports authorities. Their help and the consistent enthusiasm of the editorial team have, we hope, produced a book that will ignite in the reader a lasting understanding and enjoyment of sporting activities and the international sporting arena.

In a work of this scale – over 150 sports, 2000 illustrations and 250,000 words – we have aimed at maximum accuracy, and hope that this goal has been achieved in the interest of furthering a broadened and more precise understanding of the **Rules of the Game.**

The following international and national sports organizations (listed by sport in the order in which they are given in this book) gave advice and approval before publication.

Athletics
International Amateur Athletic Federation
British Amateur Athletic Association
Athletic Congress of the USA
Mountain running
International Committee for Mountain Racing (ICMR)
Orienteering
British Orienteering Federation
International Orienteering Federation
US Orienteering Federation
Modern pentathlon
Union Internationale de Pentathlon Moderne
The Modern Pentathlon Association of Great Britain
United States Modern Pentathlon Association
Triathlon
British Triathlon Association
Triathlon Federation USA
International Triathlon Union, Canada
Gymnastics
British Amateur Gymnastics Association
Fédération Internationale de Gymnastique
Trampolining
The British Trampoline Federation Ltd
Fédération Internationale de Trampoline
Weightlifting
The United States Weightlifting Federation Inc
International Weightlifting Federation
British Amateur Weightlifters' Association
Boxing
Amateur Boxing Association of England
International Amateur Boxing Association (AIBA)
British Boxing Board of Control
Wrestling
Fédération Internationale de Lutte Amateur
English Olympic Wrestling Association
United States Amateur Wrestling Foundation
Judo
International Judo Federation
Karate
World Union of Karatedo Organizations
Kendo
Zen Nihon Kendo Renmei
Aikido
Aikido World Headquarters
British Aikido Association
Jujitsu
British Jujitsu Association
Fencing
Fédération Internationale D'escrime
Amateur Fencing Association
Horseshoe pitching
National Horseshoe Pitchers' Association of America
Darts
British Darts Organization Limited
Archery
National Archery Association of the United States
The Grand National Archery Society
IAU Field Division TK
Internationale Armbrustschutzen Union
National Crossbowmen of the USA
National Field Archery Association (USA)
Fédération Internationale de Tir à l'Arc
Shooting
International Shooting Union
National Rifle Association of America
National Rifle Association (UK)
The Clay Pigeon Shooting Association
The National Small-Bore Rifle Association (UK)
Billiards, snooker and pool
The Billiards and Snooker Control Council
Billiard Congress of America

Skittles
Amateur Skittles Association
Ten pin bowling
Fédération Internationale de Quilleurs
American Bowling Congress
British Tenpin Bowling Association
Canadian 5 pin bowling
Canadian 5 Pin Bowlers Association
Bowling
British Crown Green Bowling Association
English Bowling Association
Boules
Fédération Française Du Sport Boules
Curling
US Curling Association
Croquet
The Croquet Association
Golf
Professional Golfers' Association of America
Court handball
World Handball Council
United States Handball Association
Rugby fives
Rugby Fives Association
Jai alai (pelota)
National Association of Jai Alai Frontons
US Amateur Jai Alai Players' Association
Squash
United States Squash Racquets Association
The Squash Rackets Association
International Squash Rackets Association
Paddleball
National Paddleball Association (USA)
Badminton
The International Badminton Federation
Badminton Association of England
United States Badminton Association (USBA)
Lawn tennis
The International Tennis Federation (ITTF)
Lawn Tennis Association
Table tennis
The International Table Tennis Federation
English Table Tennis Association
United States Table Tennis Association
Volleyball
Fédération Internationale de Volleyball (FIVB)
United States Volleyball Association
Basketball
Fédération Internationale de Basketball (FIBA)
English Basketball Association
National Basketball Association, USA
Netball
The International Federation of Netball Associations
All England Netball Association Ltd
Korfball
International Korfball Federation
British Korfball Association
US Korfball Federation
Team handball
Internationale Handball Federation
British Handball Association
US Team Handball Federation
Speedball
AAHPER Speedball Committee (USA)
Gaelic football
Cumann Luthchleas Gael
Australian rules football
Victorian Football League (VFL)
American football
National Football League
Canadian football
Canadian Football League
Rugby
International Rugby Football Board (IRFB)
London Society of Rugby Football Union Referees
The British Amateur Rugby League Association (BARLA)

Soccer
Fédération Internationale de Football Association (FIFA)
The Football Association Ltd
United States Soccer Federation
Baseball
British Baseball Federation
National Baseball Congress
International Baseball Association
Softball
National Softball Federation
Amateur Softball Association of America
Rounders
National Rounders Association
Cricket
Marylebone Cricket Club
Lacrosse
United States Women's Lacrosse Association Inc
English Lacrosse Union
All England Women's Lacrosse Association
US Inter Collegiate Lacrosse Association
International Lacrosse Federation
Roller hockey
Fédération Internationale de Roller Skating
National Roller Hockey Association of England
Field hockey
Fédération Internationale de Hockey
The Hockey Association
Hurling
Gaelic Athletic Association (Eire)
Shinty
Camanachd Association
Ice hockey
National Hockey League
Bandy
Svenska Bandyförbundet
Swimming and synchronized swimming
Fédération Internationale de Natation Amateur (FINA)
Amateur Swimming Association
Unites States Swimming
Water polo
Fédération Internationale de Natation Amateur (FINA)
Amateur Swimming Association
Diving
Fédération Internationale de Natation Amateur (FINA)
Amateur Swimming Association
United States Diving
Surfing
International Surfing Association
British Surfing Association
US Surfing Federation
Water skiing
International Water Ski Federation (IWSF)
British Water Ski Federation
American Water Ski Association
Rowing
Fédération Internationale Des Sociétés D'Aviron (FISA)
Amateur Rowing Association
The United States Rowing Association
Canoe sports
International Canoe Federation
British Canoe Union
Yacht racing
International Yacht Racing Union
US Yacht Racing Union (USYRU)
Powerboat racing
Union International Motornautique
American Powerboat Association
UK Offshore Boating Association
Windsurfing
Professional Boardsailors Association
US Boardsailing Association
Skating
International Skating Union
Canadian Amateur Speed Skating Association

Skiing
Fédération Internationale de Ski
The British Ski Federation
United States Ski Association
Biathlon
Internationale de Pentathlon Moderne et Biathlon
British Ski Federation
Skibob racing
Skibob Association of Great Britain
Fédération Internationale de Skibob
Luge tobogganing
Fédération Internationale de Luge de Course (FIL)
Canadian Amateur Bobsleigh and Luge Association
Bobsleigh racing
British Bobsleigh Association Ltd
Fédération Internationale de Bobsleigh et de
  Tobogganing
Pigeon racing
Royal Pigeon Racing Association
Sled dog racing
International Sled Dog Racing Association Inc
Greyhound racing
The National Greyhound Racing Club Ltd
American Greyhound Track Operators' Association
Horse racing
International Racing Bureau Ltd
The Jockey Club of Great Britain
The Jockey Club, USA
Harness horse racing
Harness Horsemen International
Show jumping
Fédération Equestre Internationale
The British Show Jumping Association
American Horse Shows Association
Dressage
Fédération Equestre Internationale
BHS Dressage Group
American Horse Shows Association
Three-day event
Fédération Equestre International
The British Horse Society
American Horse Shows Association
Polo
The Hurlingham Polo Association
Roller skating
Fédération Internationale de Roller Skating
National Skating Association of Great Britain
United States Amateur Confederation Roller Skating
Cycle racing
British Cycling Federation
US Cycling Federation
Motor cycle racing
Fédération Internationale Motocycliste (FIM)
Auto Cycle Union (ACU)
American Motorcyclist Association (AMA)
Gliding
Soaring Society of America
British Gliding Association
Hang gliding
British Hang Gliding Association
Air racing
Formula Air Racing Association
International Formula One (USA)
Aerobatics
International Aerobatics Commission
British Aerobatic Association
Royal Aero Club of the United Kingdom
National Aeronautique Association of USA
Sport parachuting
United States Parachute Association
British Parachute Association
Ballooning
Balloon Federation of America
British Balloon and Airship Club

Athletics

10 athletics arena;
   Olympic events
12 running events; relay
   events
14 steeplechase; hurdle
   events; marathon
15 walking events
16 javelin
17 shot put
18 discus
19 hammer
20 high jump
21 pole vault
22 long jump
23 triple jump; decathlon
   and heptathlon
24 cross-country running;
   mountain running
25 orienteering
26 modern pentathlon
28 triathlon

Gymnastics

30 equipment
31 women's artistic,
   women's vault
32 women's asymmetric
   bars; beam
34 women's floor exercises
36 men's artistic, men's
   floor exercises
38 men's rings
39 men's vault
40 men's pommel horse
41 men's parallel bars
42 men's horizontal bar
43 rhythmic gymnastics
44 sports acrobatics
45 trampolining
46 weightlifting

Combat

48 boxing
50 wrestling
52 judo
54 karate
56 kendo
58 aikido
60 jiu jitsu
62 fencing

Stick and ball

164 baseball
168 softball
170 rounders
172 cricket
176 lacrosse
179 roller hockey
180 field hockey
182 hurling
184 shinty
186 ice hockey
192 bandy

Water

194 swimming
196 synchronized
   swimming
198 water polo
200 diving
202 surfing
204 water skiing
206 rowing
208 canoe sprint racing
210 canoe slalom racing
211 wild water racing
212 canoe polo
213 canoe sailing
214 yacht racing
218 Olympic yacht classes
222 offshore yacht racing
224 windsurfing
226 powerboat racing

Winter

228 speed skating
229 short track speed
   skating
230 figure skating
234 skiing
236 skiing: Alpine
237 skiing: downhill racing,
   Alpine combined event
238 skiing: slalom
240 skiing: giant slalom and
   super-G
241 freestyle skiing
242 ski jumping
243 ski flying
244 skiing: Nordic cross-
   country
245 skiing: Nordic
   combined event
246 biathlon
248 skibob racing
250 luge tobogganing
252 bobsleigh racing

Target

64 horseshoe pitching
65 darts
66 target archery
68 field archery
69 crossbow archery
70 rifle shooting
73 running game target shooting
74 rapid fire pistol shooting
75 free pistol shooting
76 clay pigeon shooting: Olympic trench
78 clay pigeon shooting: skeet
79 clay pigeon shooting: down-the-line

Target ball

80 English billiards
82 carom billiards
84 snooker
86 pool
89 skittles
90 tenpin bowling
92 Canadian 5 pin bowling
94 flat green bowls
97 crown green bowls
98 boules (boccie)
101 curling
102 croquet
104 golf

Court

108 court handball
110 rugby fives
111 jai alai (pelota)
112 squash
114 paddleball
116 badminton
118 lawn tennis
120 table tennis

Team

122 volleyball
124 basketball
128 netball
130 korfball
132 team handball
135 speedball
138 Gaelic football
140 Australian rules football
144 American football
151 comparison of college and professional American football
152 Canadian football
155 comparison of American and Canadian football
156 rugby union; rugby league
160 soccer (Association football)

Animal

254 pigeon racing
255 sled-dog racing
256 greyhound racing
258 horse racing
260 harness horse racing
264 show jumping
268 dressage
271 three-day event
274 polo

Wheels

278 roller skating (speed); roller derby
279 roller skating (artistic)
280 cycle racing
282 motorcycle racing
284 motorcycling: drag racing, sprint, speedway, ice racing
286 motorcycling: moto cross
287 motorcycling: trials, grasstrack racing
288 motor racing: circuit racing (single-seater)
290 motor racing: circuit racing (sedan and sports car), drag racing
292 motor racing: stock car racing, rallying
293 motor racing: hillclimb, slalom, autocross, rallycross, hill trial
294 karting

Air

296 gliding
299 hang gliding
300 air racing
303 aerobatics
306 sport parachuting
308 ballooning

309 sports information bodies
310 governing sports bodies
317 index of sports
318 index

Athletics

Athletics comprises a wide range of events and demands a variety of different skills from its participants. There are two broad categories of athletics events – track and field. Track programs are made up of sprint, middle distance, distance, relay, hurdle and walking events. Field programs include throwing events and jumping for distance and height. Also Marathon and long distance walking events take place outside the stadium on roads.

Maximum inclinations For running and jumping events the maximum inclinations are 1:100 in the lateral direction and 1:1000 in the running direction.
For throwing events the maximum inclinations for the runways are 1:100 in the lateral direction and 1:1000 in the running direction; throwing fields have a maximum inclination of 1:1000.

Direction of running All races are run with the competitors' left hands toward the inside of the track.
Lanes All lanes are of uniform width.
Finish All races should end at the same point.

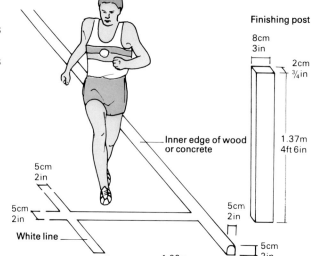

Finishing post

8cm
3in

2cm
¾in

Inner edge of wood or concrete

1.37m
4ft 6in

5cm
2in

5cm
2in

White line

5cm
2in

5cm
2in

1.22m
4ft

STANDARD 400m TRACK

General rules for field events Competitors compete in the order drawn by lot. Unless competing in a simultaneous track event, a competitor missing his turn in a field event is not permitted to take the trial so missed.
A competitor who unreasonably delays a trial is liable to have that trial disallowed and recorded as a fault.
After a second delay in a competition, he shall be debarred from further trials though credited with any performance made up to that time.

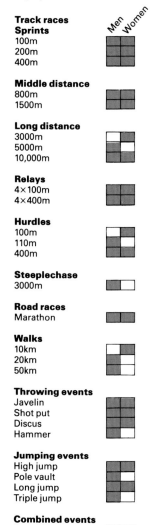

Olympic athletic events

Track races
Sprints
  Men Women
100m
200m
400m

Middle distance
800m
1500m

Long distance
3000m
5000m
10,000m

Relays
4×100m
4×400m

Hurdles
100m
110m
400m

Steeplechase
3000m

Road races
Marathon

Walks
10km
20km
50km

Throwing events
Javelin
Shot put
Discus
Hammer

Jumping events
High jump
Pole vault
Long jump
Triple jump

Combined events
Decathlon
Heptathalon

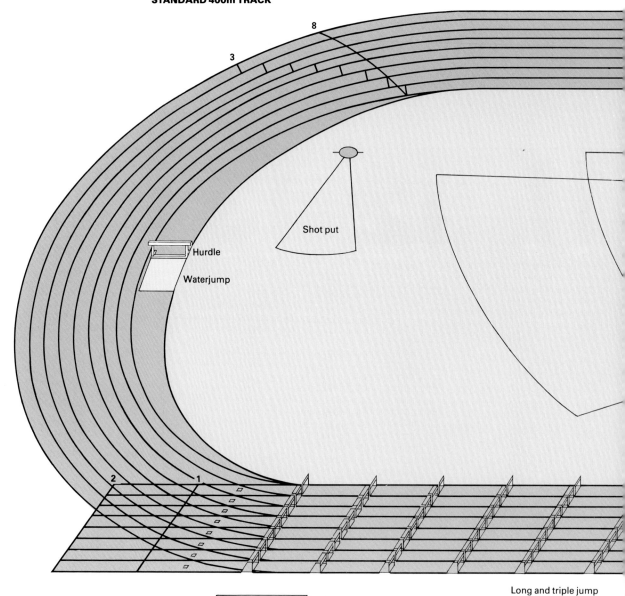

Shot put

Hurdle

Waterjump

Long and triple jump

The referee may award a substitute trial to any competitor hampered in the course of a trial.
Fingers must not be taped together, but the use of tape to cover injuries will be allowed if the referee is satisfied on medical or other evidence that the tape is necessary.

Starts
1 100m and 100m hurdles
2 110m hurdles
3 200m
4 400m
5 800m
6 1500m
7 3000m steeplechase
8 3000m and 5000m
9 10,000m

Dress Clothing must be clean, non-transparent, even when wet, and designed and worn so as not to cause offense.
Numbers Competitors must wear numbers. In the high jump and pole vault competitors may wear one number on either their back or their front. Competitors in all other events must wear numbers on both their back and front.
An adhesive number for side of shorts may also be required, if photo finish is used.

Footwear Competitors may compete in bare feet or with shoes on one or both feet. Styles of footwear vary for different events, but all must conform to certain general specifications:
a maximum of eleven spikes is permitted;
spikes must not project more than 9mm except in the high jump and javelin, where a maximum of 12mm is accepted (non-synthetic surfaces allow a maximum length of 25mm);
all spikes shall have a maximum diameter of 4mm and may be of any thickness except in the high jump, where the heel maximum is 19mm and the sole, 13mm.

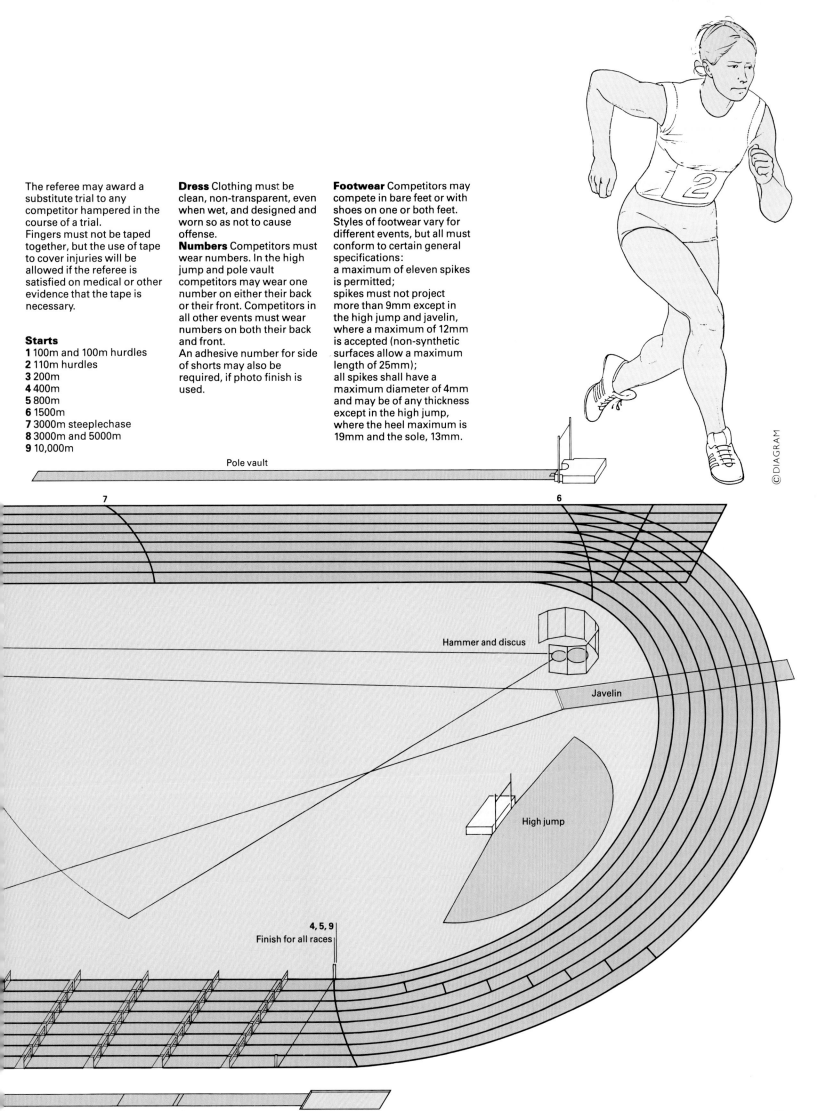

© DIAGRAM

Pole vault

7

6

Hammer and discus

Javelin

High jump

4, 5, 9
Finish for all races

Running events

The Olympic Games include individual track events run over distances ranging from 100m to 10,000m.

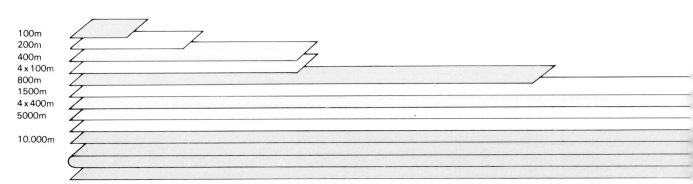

100m	
200m	
400m	
4 x 100m	
800m	
1500m	
4 x 400m	
5000m	
10,000m	

Distances are measured from the edge of the starting line farthest from the finish to the edge of the finish line nearest the start.

Heats Preliminary rounds (heats) are held when there are too many competitors for a satisfactory single-round competition.
Only in circumstances approved by the referee may a competitor take part in a heat other than that in which his name appears in the program.

The start In all races run wholly or partly in lanes the start shall be so staggered that the distance from start to finish shall be the same for each competitor.
In all races not run in lanes the starting line shall be curved so that wherever it occurs on the track all the runners can cover the same distance in the race.
The starter in his own language gives the commands, "on your marks" and "set" in races up to and including the 400m and "on your marks" in all longer Olympic races.
The pistol is then fired when the competitors are all steady in position.

False starts It is a false start if a competitor:
fails after a reasonable time to comply with the command "set";
starts before the pistol is fired.
Competitors are recalled by a pistol shot after a false start.
The competitor(s) responsible must be warned. Competitors are disqualified after causing two false starts, or three in the decathlon or heptathlon.

Lanes All the individual races shorter than 800m are run completely in lanes.
Also run in lanes are the first bend of the 800m and the first three turns of the 4 x 400m relay.
Lanes are decided by lot. Any competitor who leaves his lane shall be disqualified, with the following three exceptions, if in these cases he does not gain advantage or obstruct another competitor:
(i) if a competitor is forced out of his lane;
(ii) if a competitor runs out of his lane in a straight;
(iii) if a competitor runs outside the outer line.
Marks may be placed on or beside the track only for relay races.

800m
a Staggered start
b End of section run in lanes (first lap)
c Finish (second lap)

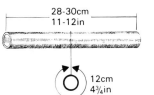

Running direction

Relay events

Events There are four Olympic relay events: men's and women's 4×100m, and men's and women's 4×400m.
Procedure Each of the four team members runs one stage of the race.
A baton is carried in the hand and transferred in the take-over zone from one runner to the next. If dropped, the baton must be picked up by the competitor who dropped it.

Composition of teams Substitutions may only be made from the list of athletes already entered for the meeting, whatever the event.
A team may change its running order.
No competitor may run more than one stage in a race.
The relay baton is a smooth, circular, hollow tube made of rigid material in one piece. It must weigh not less than 50g (1.75oz).

Lanes 4×100m relay races are run entirely in lanes.
In races up to 4×200m, members of a team other than the first runner may commence running not more than 10m outside the take-over zone.
In 4×200m races the first 2 stages as well as that part of the third leg up to the exit

28-30cm
11-12in

12cm
4¾in

Shoes with a maximum of eleven spikes in the sole are worn for track running events.

Pistol Races are started by the report of a pistol or similar apparatus, fired upward into the air.

Starting blocks may be used in individual races up to and including 400m and by the first runner in relay races.

They must be constructed entirely of rigid materials. They may be adjustable, but must be without springs or any other device whereby the athlete might obtain artificial assistance. Athletes in the "set" position must have both hands in contact with the track.

Leaving the track Any competitor who voluntarily leaves the track or course may not then continue running in a race.

Obstruction A competitor who jostles, runs across, or otherwise obstructs another competitor is liable to disqualification.

After a disqualification the referee may order the race to be re-run or, in the case of a heat, permit any affected competitor to compete in the next round.

Assistance No person except an official timekeeper shall indicate intermediate times to a competitor.

Track competitors will be disqualified for receiving any other assistance from persons within the area, but coaching may be given from the spectating area.

The finish Competitors are placed in the order in which any part of their torso (as distinguished from the head, neck, arms, legs, hands, or feet) reaches the vertical plane of the edge of the finish line nearest to the start.

(Competitor (**a**) is the winner in the finish illustrated *right*.)

Timing Fully automatic timekeeping equipment is used for the Olympic Games and most other major meetings. Otherwise timing is by timekeepers using stopwatches.

Times are taken from the flash of the pistol to the moment when the competitor's torso reaches the finish.

Individual and relay races up to and including the 1500m are timed to $\frac{1}{10}$ sec.

Longer races are timed to $\frac{1}{5}$ sec, but recorded as multiples of $\frac{2}{10}$ sec.

Fully automatic electric times shall be regarded as the official time and are timed to $\frac{1}{100}$ sec.

Ties In a tie for first place in a final the referee decides if it is practicable for those tying to run again.

If a tie in a heat affects qualification for the next round, the tying competitors run again, only if it is impracticable for both to qualify.

All other tied results stand.

© DIAGRAM

from the first bend will be run entirely in lanes.

In 4×400m races the first lap as well as that part of the second lap up to the exit from the first bend will be run entirely in lanes.

All competitors may break from their lanes immediately they have passed the exit from the first bend. The position of the teams at the start shall be retained at each take-over zone. After lanes have ceased to be used, runners can move to an inner position on the track as incoming team members arrive, provided this can be done without fouling. In events where the first part of the race is run in lanes, the competitors, after completing this part, are free to take up any position on the track.

After handing over the baton competitors should remain in their lanes until the course is clear to avoid obstruction to other competitors.

a Staggered start
b First take-over zone
c Second take-over zone
d Third take-over zone
e Finish

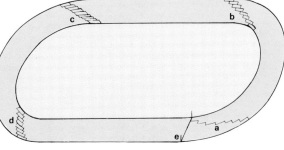

10m 11yd   Take-over zone 20m 22yd

Steeplechase

The Olympic steeplechase is a men's event run over 3000m. It comprises 28 hurdle jumps and seven water jumps. Competitors may jump, vault, or stand on the hurdles. The hurdles numbered (3) and (4) are positioned after the competitors have passed by on the first lap. Competitors run outside the water jump on the first lap.

Steeplechase hurdles have a base on either side and must weigh 80–100kg (176½–220½lb). They are positioned across the three inside lanes.

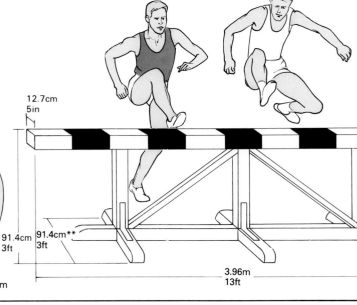

Hurdle events

Olympic hurdling events are held over 110m and 400m for men and over 100m and 400m for women. In addition, the decathlon includes a 110m hurdles and the heptathlon a 100m hurdles race.

All hurdling events are run in lanes, and there are ten hurdles in each lane.

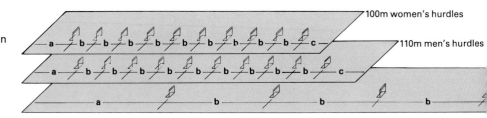

Hurdles are made of metal with the top bar of wood. They are designed so that a force of 3.6–4kg (8lb–8lb13oz) applied to the center of the top edge of the crossbar is required to overturn them. The height of the hurdles varies with the length of the race and the age and sex of the competitors.

Disqualification A hurdler will be disqualified if he: trails a foot or leg below the plane of the top of the bar of the hurdle at the instance of clearance; jumps any hurdle not in his own lane; deliberately knocks down any hurdle with his hand or foot.

Height of hurdles
h=0.838m (2ft 9in) 100m women
h=1.067m (3ft 6in) 110m men
h=0.914m (3ft) 400m men
h=0.762m (2ft 6in) 400m women

Marathon

The marathon is 42.195km (26mi 385yd) long. The start and finish are usually in the arena, but the rest of the race is run on made-up roads.
Distances, in kilometers and miles, are displayed to the competitors along the route. Competitors must leave the race if ordered to do so by the medical staff.

Refreshments Approved refreshments may be taken at official refreshment stations, sited at about 11km (7mi) and then at every 5km (3mi). No other refreshments are allowed. Additional sponging points, supplying water only, are provided midway between the refreshment stations.

The water jump is the fourth jump in each lap. The water jump hurdle stands the same height as the other hurdles, but is sunk into the ground.

Disqualification A steeplechaser will be disqualified if he:
steps to either side of the jump;
fails to go over or through the water;
trails his foot or leg below the horizontal plane of the top of the hurdle.

12.7cm
5in

91.4cm
3ft

70cm
2ft 3½in

3.66m
12ft

3.66m
12ft

Concrete
Track surface (matting on non-synthetic surfaces)

100m women's hurdles: a=13m, b=8.5m, c=10.5m
110m men's hurdles: a=13.72m, b=9.14m, c=14.02m
400m hurdles a: 45m, b=35m, c=40m

400m hurdles

b — b — b — b — b — b — b — c

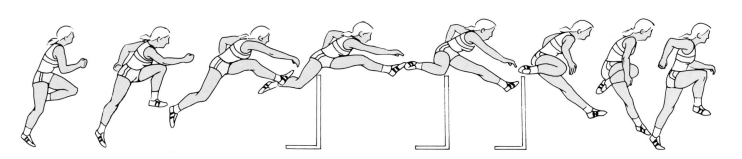

Walking events
◯◯◯◯

The events most often included in international competitions are the 20km and 50km road walks for men, and the 10km road for women.
Track events are 20,000m and 50,000m for men and 5000m and 10,000m for women.

Action Walkers must maintain unbroken contact with the ground. Thus the rear foot (**r**) must not leave the ground before the advancing foot (**a**) has made contact. The leg must be momentarily straightened, while a foot is on the ground.

Refreshments Approved refreshments may be taken at official refreshment stations in walking races exceeding 20km.
Stations are sited at 10km and then every 5km.
No other refreshments are allowed.
Additional sponging points, supplying water only, may be provided at points after 20km.

Disqualification A competitor is entitled to one caution, signaled with a white flag, before being disqualified, signaled with a red flag.
Action is taken against a competitor after the independent recommendation of three judges, or two judges if one is the chief judge.

In track races a disqualified competitor must immediately leave the track. In road races he must immediately remove his number.
If immediate notification is impracticable, competitors may be disqualified immediately after a race ends.

© DIAGRAM

15

1

Javelin

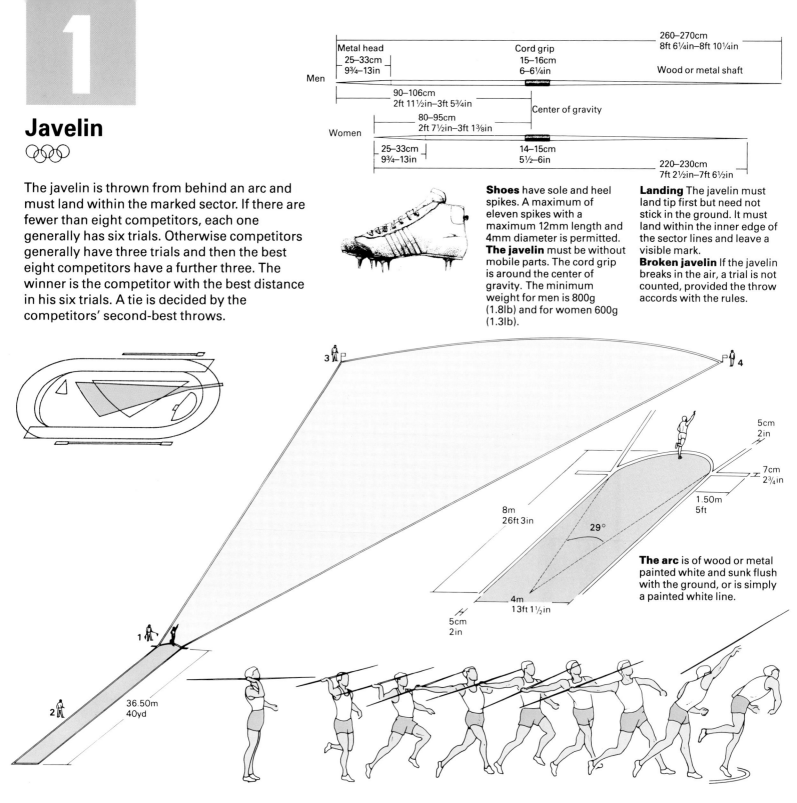

	Metal head		Cord grip		260–270cm 8ft 6¼in–8ft 10¼in	
Men	25–33cm 9¾–13in		15–16cm 6–6¼in			Wood or metal shaft
		90–106cm 2ft 11½in–3ft 5¾in		Center of gravity		
		80–95cm 2ft 7½in–3ft 1⅜in				
Women						
	25–33cm 9¾–13in		14–15cm 5½–6in			
				220–230cm 7ft 2½in–7ft 6½in		

The javelin is thrown from behind an arc and must land within the marked sector. If there are fewer than eight competitors, each one generally has six trials. Otherwise competitors generally have three trials and then the best eight competitors have a further three. The winner is the competitor with the best distance in his six trials. A tie is decided by the competitors' second-best throws.

Shoes have sole and heel spikes. A maximum of eleven spikes with a maximum 12mm length and 4mm diameter is permitted.
The javelin must be without mobile parts. The cord grip is around the center of gravity. The minimum weight for men is 800g (1.8lb) and for women 600g (1.3lb).

Landing The javelin must land tip first but need not stick in the ground. It must land within the inner edge of the sector lines and leave a visible mark.
Broken javelin If the javelin breaks in the air, a trial is not counted, provided the throw accords with the rules.

The arc is of wood or metal painted white and sunk flush with the ground, or is simply a painted white line.

Practice throws Before any throwing event two practice throws in the arena are permitted only from or near the circles or scratch line.
Implements must always be returned by hand either in practice or during the competition.
Throwing action The javelin must be held at the grip. It must be thrown with one hand only over the shoulder or the upper part of the throwing arm. It must be neither slung nor hurled. The competitor is not permitted to turn his back to the arc after preparing to throw and before discharging the javelin. A throw is a foul if the competitor touches with any part of his body the arc or scratch lines or the ground beyond them.
In the course of running up to throw a competitor may not cross either of the parallel lines forming the runway.
The competitor must not leave the delivery area until the javelin has landed, when he must leave from behind the arc and scratch lines.

Judging A white flag indicates a fair throw and a red flag a foul.
At least two judges should keep a record of all trials and check recordings at the end of each round.

Measurement A throw is measured from the nearest mark made by the head of the javelin (**a**) to the inner edge of the circumference of the arc (**b**). Measurement is along a line from the mark and through the center of the radius of the arc (**c**). Distances are recorded to the nearest even unit of 2cm (1in) below the distance thrown.

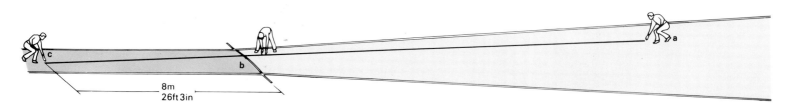

Shot put

OOOOO

The shot is put from a circle and must land within the marked sector. If there are fewer than eight competitors, each one generally has six trials. Otherwise competitors generally have three trials and then the best eight competitors have a further three. The winner is the competitor with the best distance in his six trials. A tie is decided by the competitors' second-best throws.

The shot is made of solid iron, brass or any metal not softer than brass, or a shell of such metal filled with lead or other material. It must be spherical in shape and smooth-surfaced. The minimum weight for men is 7.26kg (16lb) and for women 4kg (8.8lb).

110-130mm
4⅜-5⅛in

95-110mm
3¾-4⅜in

Shoes are without spikes since a concrete surface is recommended for within the circle.

The circle is bounded by a white-painted band of iron, steel or wood. Concrete is recommended for the surface within the circle. There is a raised stopboard for this event.

11cm
4⅜in

40°

10cm
4in

5cm
2in

75cm
2ft 6in

2.135m
7ft

5cm
2in

© DIAGRAM

Judging A white flag indicates a fair throw and a red flag a foul.
At least two judges should keep a record of all trials and check recordings at the end of each round.

Putting action The competitor must begin his put from a stationary position within the circle. Only one hand may be used and throughout the putting action this hand must not be dropped below its starting position. The shot must not be brought behind the line of the shoulders.
A put is invalid if the competitor, after commencing his action, touches with any part of his body the top of the stopboard (**s**) or the ring bounding the circle, or the ground outside (**g**). He is permitted to touch the inside of the stopboard or ring. The competitor must not leave the circle until the shot has touched the ground, when he must, standing, leave from behind the dividing line.

Interrupting a trial Provided there has been no infringement, a competitor is permitted to interrupt during a trial, provided the competitor does not exceed the maximum time for a given trial.
When interrupting a trial, the competitor may lay down his shot. He must then restart from a stationary position.
Landing The shot must land within the inner edge of the sector lines.

Measurement takes place immediately after each trial. Puts are measured from the nearest mark made by the shot to the inner edge of the ring bounding the circle. Measurement is along a line from the mark and through the center of the circle. Distances are recorded to the nearest 1cm (¼in) below the distance put.

g

s

s

Discus

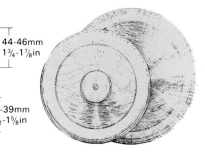

The discus is thrown from a circle and must land within the marked sector. If there are fewer than eight competitors, each one generally has six trials. Otherwise competitors generally have three trials and then the best eight competitors have a further three. The winner is the competitor with the best distance in his six trials. A tie is decided by the competitors' second-best throws.

The discus A smooth metal rim is permanently attached to the body of the discus, which is made of wood or other suitable material. A weight is secured in the center. Minimum discus weights are 2kg (4lb 6.5oz) for men, and 1kg (2lb 3.2oz) for women.

Holding the discus The most usual method is illustrated. Fingers must not be taped together.

Shoes without spikes are worn for discus and hammer events.

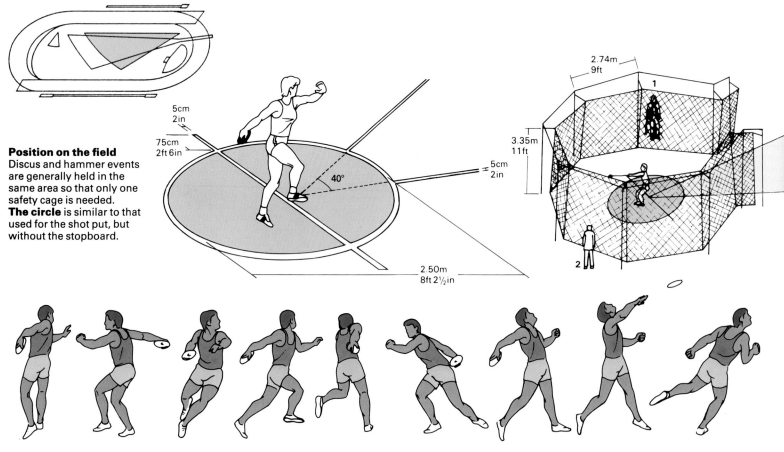

Position on the field
Discus and hammer events are generally held in the same area so that only one safety cage is needed.

The circle is similar to that used for the shot put, but without the stopboard.

Throwing action The competitor must begin his throw from a stationary position. He may hold the discus as he wishes and use any throwing technique. His throw is a foul if, after commencing his action, he touches with any part of his body either the top of the ring bounding the circle or the ground beyond it. This rule remains in force while the discus is in flight.
At the end of the throw the competitor must, from a standing position, leave the circle from behind the dividing line.

Interrupting a trial
Provided there has been no infringement, a competitor is permitted to interrupt a trial, provided the competitor does not exceed the time given for the trial. When interrupting a trial, the competitor may lay down his discus. He must then recommence his action from a stationary position.

Landing The discus must land within the inner edge of the sector lines.

Judging Five judges are needed. Judges (1) and (2) watch on their own side for infringements within the circle. (Their positions are reversed for left-handed throwers.) Three judges are needed in the field since the landing area is unpredictable.

Measurement A throw is measured from the nearest mark made by the discus (a) to the inner edge of the ring bounding the circle (b). Measurement is along a line from the mark and through the center of the circle (c). Distances are recorded to the nearest 2cm (1in) below the distance thrown.

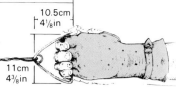

117.5-121.5mm
3ft 10¼in-3ft 11¾in

10.5cm
4⅛in

11cm
4⅜in

Hammer

110–130mm
4⅜–5⅛in

The hammer is thrown from a circle and must land within the marked sector. As in other throwing events some competitors may be eliminated after three trials. The winner is the competitor with the best distance in his six trials. A tie is decided by the competitors' second-best trials.

Hammer glove A right-handed competitor should wear a glove on his left hand.

The hammer The spherical head is of any metal not softer than brass, or has a shell of such metal filled with lead or other material. The head is attached by a swivel to the handle, which is a single length of steel wire with a diameter of 3mm (⅛in).

The grip may be a single or a double loop but must not have hinging joints. Neither the handle nor the grip must stretch appreciably during throwing. The minimum weight for a complete hammer is 7.260kg.

5cm
2in

75cm
2ft 6in

40°

5cm
2in

2.135m
7ft

Cage For safety reasons the circle for the hammer and discus events is shielded by a netting cage with a metal frame.

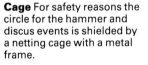

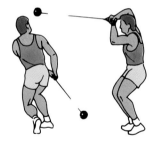

Judging Hammer throwing is judged by five judges. Positions and responsibilities are as for discus throwing.
Throwing action The competitor must begin his throw from a stationary position, when he is permitted to rest the head of the hammer on the ground inside or outside the circle. The head of the hammer may also touch the ground during preliminary turns or swings (**a**).
A throw is a foul if, after commencing his action, the competitor touches with any part of his body either the top of the ring bounding the circle or the ground beyond it (**b**).

The competitor must not leave the circle until the hammer has landed, when he must, from a standing position, leave from behind the dividing line.
Landing The hammer must land within the inner edge of the sector lines.
Broken hammer A trial is not counted if the hammer breaks during throwing or flight, provided the throw was made in accordance with the rules. Nor is it counted a foul if the broken hammer caused the competitor to lose his balance and infringe the rules.
Interrupting a trial As in other throwing events, provided there has been no

infringement, a competitor is permitted to interrupt a trial, provided the competitor does not exceed the time given for the trial. He must not, however, interrupt a trial during which the hammer head has touched the ground during the preliminary swings or turns.
Measurements A throw is measured from the nearest mark made by the head of the hammer to the inner edge of the ring bounding the circle.
Measurement is along a line from the mark and through the center of the circle. Distances are recorded to the nearest 2cm (1in) below the distance thrown.

©DIAGRAM

High jump

⊙⊙⊙⊙⊙

The high jump is made over a crossbar between rigid uprights. The crossbar is raised after each round, and competitors remain in the competition until eliminated by three consecutive failures.

Judging Two or three judges ensure that the apparatus and landing area are in order and that all jumps are correctly made.

Shoes Heel spikes and plastic heel cups are recommended when jumping for height.

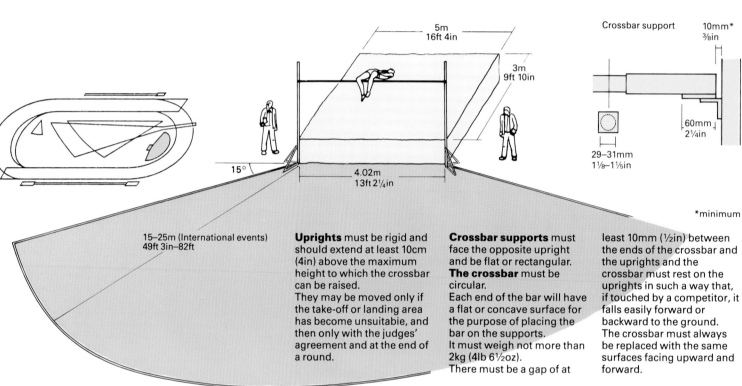

Fan The IAAF recommended size is illustrated

15–25m (International events)
49ft 3in–82ft

Uprights must be rigid and should extend at least 10cm (4in) above the maximum height to which the crossbar can be raised.
They may be moved only if the take-off or landing area has become unsuitable, and then only with the judges' agreement and at the end of a round.

Crossbar supports must face the opposite upright and be flat or rectangular.
The crossbar must be circular.
Each end of the bar will have a flat or concave surface for the purpose of placing the bar on the supports.
It must weigh not more than 2kg (4lb 6½oz).
There must be a gap of at

least 10mm (½in) between the ends of the crossbar and the uprights and the crossbar must rest on the uprights in such a way that, if touched by a competitor, it falls easily forward or backward to the ground. The crossbar must always be replaced with the same surfaces facing upward and forward.

Run-up The length of run-up is unlimited. The minimum length of the runway is 15m. Markers may be placed for run-up and take-off, but may not be placed in the landing area.
Markers must be supplied or approved by the organizers.
Procedure Starting heights for each round are

announced by the judges before the event begins. The minimum height the bar is raised for each round is 2cm.
Competitors may start jumping when they wish and choose whether to attempt any subsequent height. Elimination occurs after three consecutive failures,

regardless of the height at which they occur.
Failures A jump is counted a failure if the competitor: takes off from two feet (**1**); touches the ground or landing area beyond the plane of the uprights without first clearing the bar (whether or not he makes a jump);

knocks the bar off the supports (**2**) (even if he has landed before the bar falls). If he touches the landing area with a foot in the course of a jump and in the opinion of the judge no advantage is gained, the jump should not for that reason be considered a failure.

Measurements are made perpendicularly from the ground to the lowest part of the upper side of the bar. New heights are measured before jumping begins, and heights are remeasured after jumping if a record is to be established.

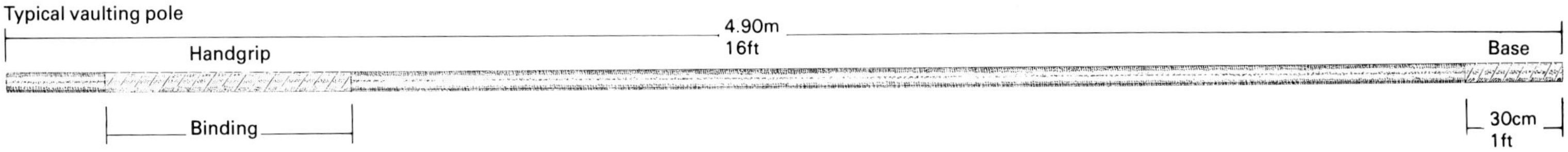

Typical vaulting pole

	4.90m / 16ft	
Handgrip		Base

Binding

30cm / 1ft

Pole vault

ooooo

Competitors use a flexible pole to vault a crossbar between two uprights. The crossbar is raised after each round, and competitors remain in the competition until eliminated by three consecutive failures.

4.3–4.37m / 14ft 2in–14ft 4in

5m / 16ft 4in

5m / 16ft 4in

Pole A competitor may use his own pole. A pole may be of any material, but must be smooth-surfaced. It may be of any length or diameter. Typical dimensions are

shown. Bindings, except at the foot of the pole, should be smooth and must not exceed two layers of adhesive tape of uniform thickness.

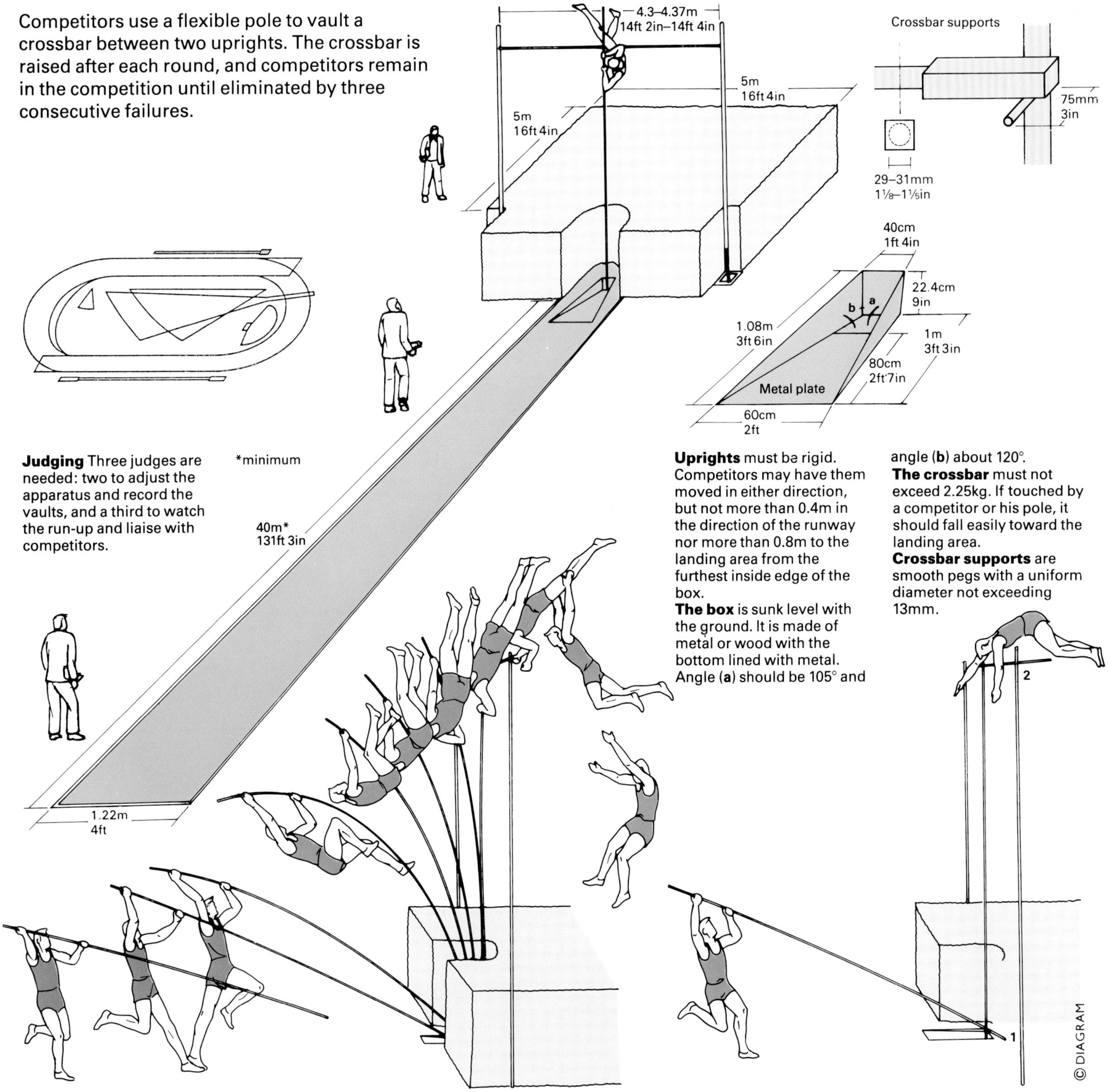

Crossbar supports

75mm / 3in

29–31mm / 1⅛–1⅕in

40cm / 1ft 4in

22.4cm / 9in

1.08m / 3ft 6in

1m / 3ft 3in

80cm / 2ft 7in

Metal plate

60cm / 2ft

Judging Three judges are needed: two to adjust the apparatus and record the vaults, and a third to watch the run-up and liaise with competitors.

*minimum

40m* / 131ft 3in

1.22m / 4ft

Uprights must be rigid. Competitors may have them moved in either direction, but not more than 0.4m in the direction of the runway nor more than 0.8m to the landing area from the furthest inside edge of the box.
The box is sunk level with the ground. It is made of metal or wood with the bottom lined with metal. Angle (**a**) should be 105° and

angle (**b**) about 120°.
The crossbar must not exceed 2.25kg. If touched by a competitor or his pole, it should fall easily toward the landing area.
Crossbar supports are smooth pegs with a uniform diameter not exceeding 13mm.

2

1

© DIAGRAM

Run-up The minimum length of the runway is 40m. Marks may only be placed alongside the runway.
Procedure Starting heights for each round are announced by the judges before the event begins. The minimum height the bar is raised for each round is 5cm. Competitors may start

vaulting when they wish and choose whether or not to attempt any subsequent height. Elimination occurs after three consecutive failures regardless of the height at which they occur. Competitors are permitted to place a substance on their hands or on the pole in order to obtain a better grip, but the use of tape on the hands

or fingers is not allowed, unless for first aid reasons.
Failures A competitor fails, if he:
1) touches the ground, including the landing area beyond the vertical plane through the upper part of the stopboard with any part of his body or with the pole, without first clearing the bar;

2) knocks the bar off the supports;
3) after leaving the ground places his lower hand above the upper one or moves the upper hand higher on the pole.
It is not counted as a failure if a competitor's pole breaks.
Measurements are made perpendicularly from the ground to the lowest part of

the upper side of the bar. Heights are measured before each round and after a vault, if a record is to be established.

Long jump

Competitors leap from a take-off board into a sand landing area. If there are fewer than eight competitors, each one generally has six trials; otherwise competitors generally have three trials, and then the best eight competitors have a further three. The competitor with the longest jump in his six trials is the winner. A tie for first place is decided by the competitors' second-best jumps.

1.22m 4ft

45m 147ft 6in

Take-off line
Take-off board
Plasticine indicator

20cm 8in
10cm 4in
10cm 4in

1.22m 4ft

Support bracket

9m* 29ft 6in

1m 3ft 3in

2.75m* 9ft

Judging There are four judges. Judge (**1**) watches for failures (no jumps); he has two flags, one red and one white. Judges (**2**) and (**3**) measure the jump after judge (**3**) has marked it. Judge (**4**) calls up competitors and clears the runway.

*minimum

Landing area The sand in the landing area should be moistened before the competition begins. It must be raked level with the take-off board before every jump.

The take-off board is made of wood and sunk level with the runway. The edge of the board nearest to the landing area is the take-off line. Immediately beyond this is a tray of Plasticine or some similar soft substance for recording foot faults.

Run-up The length of the run-up is unlimited. Marks may not be placed on the runway, but may be placed alongside it. Marks may not be placed beyond the take-off line.

Take-off A failure is counted if a competitor touches with any part of his body the ground beyond the take-off line or take-off line

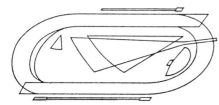

Take-off board | Plasticine indicator

extended. This rule applies whether he makes his jump or merely runs up without jumping. Long jumpers may not use weights or grips.
Landing It is a failure if a competitor when landing: touches the ground outside the landing area nearer to the take-off than the nearest break in the landing area; after a completed jump walks back through the sand; employs any form of somersaulting.

Measurements A jump is measured from the nearest break in the landing area made by any part of the competitor's body (**m**). Measurement is up to the take-off line and at right angles to it. Distances are recorded to the nearest 1cm below the distance jumped.

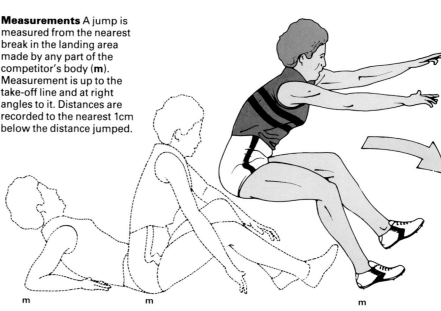

m   m   m

Triple jump

The triple jump comprises a hop, step and jump sequence. As in other field events some competitors may be eliminated after three trials. The winner is the competitor with the best distance after six trials. A tie is decided by the competitors' second-best trials.

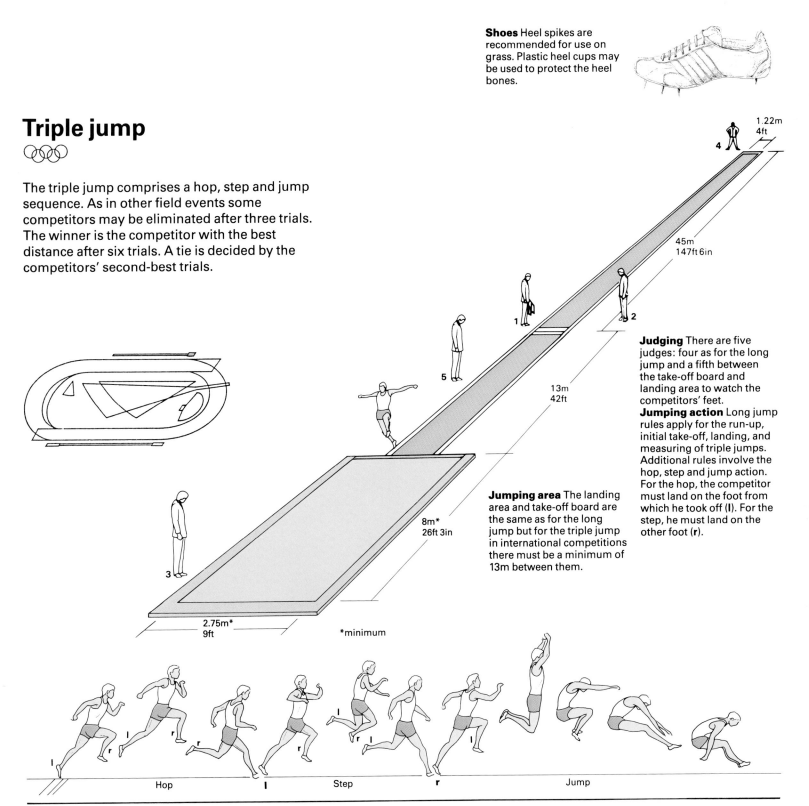

1.22m
4ft

4

45m
147ft 6in

13m
42ft

Judging There are five judges: four as for the long jump and a fifth between the take-off board and landing area to watch the competitors' feet.

Jumping action Long jump rules apply for the run-up, initial take-off, landing, and measuring of triple jumps. Additional rules involve the hop, step and jump action. For the hop, the competitor must land on the foot from which he took off (**l**). For the step, he must land on the other foot (**r**).

Jumping area The landing area and take-off board are the same as for the long jump but for the triple jump in international competitions there must be a minimum of 13m between them.

8m*
26ft 3in

2.75m*
9ft

*minimum

Hop   **l**   Step   **r**   Jump

Decathlon and heptathlon

Combined events competitions are made up of a number of events. The decathlon is a men's competition of ten events and the heptathlon a women's competition of seven events. Competitors score points for their performance in each event.

Order of events Events are held in the set order listed. A competitor is considered to have withdrawn from the competition if he fails to take part in any event.
The order of competing is drawn before each event.

Rules IAAF (International Amateur Athletic Federation) rules generally apply for each event. Exceptions are that competitors are allowed only three trials in each field event and that three false starts in a track event result in elimination without points from that particular event.

Scoring is according to IAAF tables. Points are awarded not for placings, but for achieving set times, heights, and distances. In a tie, the competitor with most points in the majority of events wins. If the tie remains, the person with most points in any one event wins.

Decathlon

First day		Second day	
A	100m	**F**	110m hurdles
B	Long jump	**G**	Discus
C	Shot put	**H**	Pole vault
D	High jump	**I**	Javelin
E	400m	**J**	1500m

Heptathlon

First day		Second day	
A	100m hurdles	**E**	Long jump
B	High jump	**F**	Javelin
C	Shot put	**G**	800m
D	200m		

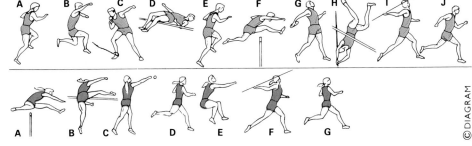

© DIAGRAM

Cross-country running

Cross-country races are governed more by local conditions than detailed rules. But, generally, cross-country running is a winter sport in which individuals and teams compete over courses through the countryside. The first runner to complete the course is the winner; and team performances are determined by the aggregate placings of individual team members.

Course For major events the courses should be confined to open country, fields, heathland and grassland. A limited amount of plowed land is allowed. Woodland sections must be clearly marked. Roads should be kept to a minimum. There should be no high obstacles, deep ditches, dangerous ascents or descents, thick undergrowth or any other excessively difficult obstacle. Artificial obstacles should only be used when absolutely necessary. The competitors should be allowed an unrestricted run for the first 1500m (1 mile).

Markings The course should be clearly marked with red flags on the left and white flags on the right. Flags should be visible from 125m (140yd).

Distances The recommended international distances are:
senior men: 12k (about 7½ miles);
junior men: 8k (about 5 miles);
senior women: 6k (about 3¾ miles);
junior women: 4k (about 2½ miles).
Distances vary in national and local races.

Competitors For local and national races runners may compete individually or in a team; a race may include both competitions.
For international events runners must enter as part of a team.

Teams The regulations for teams, reserves and number of runners to score can differ. The IAAF cross country team championship ruling, which may be a standard guide, is as follows: For men's races teams of not more than 12 competitors can be entered. Not less than 6 nor more than 9 of these shall be allowed to start, of whom 6 will score for the team.
For women's races, junior men's and junior women's, teams of not more than 8 competitors and not less than 4 can be entered. Not more than 6 of these shall be allowed to start, of whom 4 will score for the team.

Assistance Competitors may not receive assistance or refreshment during a race.

Start Races are started with a pistol shot. A 5-minute warning may be given, if there is a large number of competitors.
Stations are provided and the members of each team line up behind each other at the start of the race.

Team scoring After the race the placings of the scoring members of each team are added together. The team with the lowest aggregate is the winner.
If there is a tie, the team whose last scoring runner finished before the other team's last scoring runner is award the higher place.

Officials for major events should include: a referee, a judge, a timekeeper, a starter, clerks of the course, pointsmen, umpires, funnel judges and funnel controllers, result recorders and assistants.

Dress Competitors wear starting numbers on their chests and backs. Running shoes are chosen depending on terrain and can be with or without spikes.

Mountain running

This sport is concentrated in hilly or mountainous areas of the world, where facilities for other types of sports may be scarce.
Traditions vary from country to country depending on the type of terrain but with the advent of a world cup competition in 1985, held each year since in a different country, rules for international competition have been developed.
These rules ensure that the sport remains based on running and not mountaineering, involving rock climbing and scrambling.

Courses All courses must avoid dangerous ascents or descents. For international competition courses must be clearly marked with flags, although many local competitions do not take place over a marked course. In these cases runners are required to pass through checkpoints (usually mountain summits) and to find their own way between checkpoints. Short races are mostly marked.

Distances vary from 1 to 25 miles and vary in height climbed.

Uphill only There are two types of mountain race, of which this is the first. This is predominant in Alpine regions.

Up and down races are the second type. These are usual in the UK.

Dress Normal athletic clothing is worn, but specially developed mountain shoes are often worn. Protective clothing is worn as dictated by weather conditions.

Result The first runner to complete the course is the winner. Course records are not considered important because of the widely varying weather conditions in which the events may take place.

Orienteering

Orienteering is a sport in which individuals or teams compete on foot in forests or rough countryside. Competitors reach the finish by way of a number of control points located through the use of a map, a compass and the application of navigational skills.

Orienteering map

Map Specially drawn maps are used for orienteering. The course is overprinted on the map or printed on mastersheets for competitors to copy onto their own map at the start of the race.
For major competitions, the map scale is 1:15,000 or 1:10,000.
Competitors are also given the out-of-bound areas and any special information relevant to the course. Smaller events require the competitor to have a map case in which to secure his map, and a red pen with which to plot the course.

Course Orienteering courses vary considerably according to the nature of the competition and the age group catered for. They are usually in heavily wooded areas or heavily contoured open moorland.
Lengths of courses vary with the different classes. The usual direct line length for senior elite competitions is about 12-14 km and for the youngest classes 2-3 km. Competition areas are closed for a period before events so that no competitor can gain unfair knowledge of the terrain.

Officials Orienteering needs a number of officials, the most vital of whom is the course planner. He is totally responsible for the planning of the course and the general outline of the competitive area. A controller checks his decisions. Officials and timekeepers must be present at the start and finish of the event. There is usually an official at each control point in international events to take intermediate times.

Control points The number of control points varies with the length of the course and type of competition.
Score orienteering competitions, which present random route choice with a time limit, have roughly twice as many control points

Safety Some organizers require competitors to carry a whistle for use in an emergency, particularly if the area of competition is mountainous or exposed

Control marker

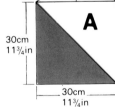

30cm
11¾ in

30cm
11¾ in

as point orienteering competitions.
A control marker consists of a three-sided prism, each side of which is a 30cm square divided diagonally with the upper half white and the lower half orange. Each control is numbered to allow correct identification.

Control card Each competitor is issued with a control card, which he stamps when he reaches a control point and which is used to calculate start, finish and elapsed time.

Compulsory tracks or paths are marked by white and orange/red tape or flags.

Dress The choice of clothing is entirely free, provided it gives full body and leg protection against possible

cuts and abrasions. Nylon orienteering suits and tracksuits are most usual. Studded athletics shoes are the most suitable footwear. For international events starting numbers are worn on the chest.

The start Competitors are started at 1-2 minute intervals to prevent following. There is usually an assembly area, from which competitors walk through to the start.

The finish is usually in an open area with facilities for time display and announcements.

Duration varies with the type of competition. Most events end only when the course is completed. Score events have a time limit.

Compass An orienteering compass should have:
1 transparent base plate
2 rotating compass housing
3 orienteering lines
4 direction marker
5 magnifying lens
6 distance marker
7 safety cord

Orienteering compass

© DIAGRAM

Scoring In point orienteering (a straight race around a circuit of control points), relay orienteering (in which the circuit is completed by a team of participants) and line orienteering (where the complete route is shown) the competitor or team with the fastest time wins. Team scores are obtained by adding together the times of the team members. Score orienteering is performed to a strict time limit (usually 1-1½ hours). In that time competitors visit as many controls as possible. Each control has a points tariff, varying from 5 to 50 points. Controls are deployed in such a way that competitors have to decide whether to

visit many low-scoring controls or a few high-scoring ones. The competitor or team with the highest aggregate tariff score is the winner, but penalty points are deducted for every minute by which a competitor exceeds the time limit. There are no bonuses for finishing early.

Misconduct Competitors are disqualified if they miss a control (except in score orienteering) or if they stamp their control card incorrectly. The competitor must conduct himself in a sporting manner and must not try to gain information from spectators or other competitors before or during the event.

Modern Pentathlon

The Modern Pentathlon is an Olympic event comprising fencing, swimming, shooting, cross-country and riding contests. Individual and team classifications are based on points awarded for competitors' performances in each of the five disciplines. Teams have three members. The Modern Pentathlon is open for both men and women in Club, National, International and World Championships but only open for men in the Olympic Games.

Classification The points scored for each discipline are added together to give the final classification.
Only competitors who start in all five disciplines will be considered.
A competitor who withdraws or is eliminated from one of the five disciplines may remain in the competition but will receive 0 points for that discipline.
The team classification is obtained by adding together the points obtained by the three team members.
Ties In the event of a tie the competitor or team with the highest number of wins in the different disciplines wins the event. If there is still a tie, in international events the diciplines are valued in order:
fencing, swimming, shooting, running, riding.
Participants Nations may enter four competitors, but only three actually take part in the competition.

Rules Modern Pentathlon events are governed by the rules of the UIPMB (Union Internationale du Pentathlon Moderne et Biathlon) and of the international governing bodies of the five disciplines involved.
Order The event takes place over four or three days in the following order:
1) fencing;
2) swimming;
3) shooting;
4) cross-country running;
5) riding.
Swimming and shooting are held on the same day. The riding can be over one or two days.
Draw A draw to determine the order of participation takes place the day before the start of the fencing.
The other four events have a reverse order start.
Doping control
Competitors are subject to doping control at any time. The penalty for doping is disqualification.

Substitution A competitor can be replaced if he withdraws due to injury from the fencing competition.
The replacement starts in the swimming with 0 points for the fencing.
Substitution is not permitted at any later stage in the event.

RIDING
Horses One horse is provided for every two competitors, plus one reserve for every eight competitors. All horses are carefully selected to ensure equality between them.
The course is 600m long with fifteen obstacles including a double and a triple combination.
Obstacles may not exceed prescribed dimensions:
a straight fence may not exceed 120cm in height;
a water jump may not exceed 300cm in width;
a spread fence may not exceed 120cm in height and 150cm in width;
an oxer (equal bars) may not exceed 120×130cm.
The course is inspected by a jury two days before the competition. This is the last opportunity for changes to be made to the plan of the course or to any obstacle. Competitors may view the course on the day before the competition.

Scoring Competitors can receive a maximum of 1100 points – for a clear round in the time allowed (1min 43sec). Penalty points are deducted as follows:
for each commenced second above the time allowed, 2 points;
for a knockdown or a horse's foot in the water, 30 points;
for a fall of the horse, rider or both, 60 points;
for a refusal (each time), 40 points;
Any disobedience leading to the knocking down of an obstacle will be penalised by extra penalty points as follows:
if at a single obstacle or part A of a combined obstacle, 10 points;
at part B of a combined obstacle, 15 points;
at part C of a combined obstacle, 20 points.

© DIAGRAM

FENCING

Area Fencing pistes with all-copper mats, measuring 2m×14m.

Equipment Epees approved and inspected by the FIE (Fédération Internationale d'Escrime).
Electrical touch recorders are used.

Dress must conform to international fencing regulations. National colors must be worn on the opposite arm to the weapon.

Bouts All fencers meet each other aiming for one touch; coup doubles are not counted. There must be at least 20 bouts in total. If there are less than 21 competitors, a second go around must take place. One bout lasts 2 minutes. If there is no decisive touch, the bout counts as a loss for both competitors (double defeat).
If a competitor is eliminated in the fencing, all his bouts are disregarded.

Scoring Winning 70% of the bouts yields a total of 1000 points.
Points are gained or lost for each victory above or below this percentage; these points are calculated by dividing 1100 by the number of bouts.
In the event of a tie, a deciding bout must be held to determine the fencing winner, but the number of points scored is not affected.

SHOOTING

Pistols The caliber must be 5.6mm (0.22). The maximum size is 300mm by 150mm by 50mm, with a 5% tolerance in one direction. The maximum weight is 1.26kg.

Ammunition Bullets must be made of lead or a similar soft, homogeneous substance.

The target is a circle with a 50cm diameter, black with a white edge. It is divided into six scoring zones.

Shooting distance is 25m.

Procedure Four series of five shots are fired by each competitor. (A practice series of five shots may be taken before the first series.) Competitors must not raise the shooting arm more than 45° from the vertical line before the target turns to face the shooter.
All commands are given in English.

Scoring Maximum target points of 200 are obtainable. This is worth 1270 Penthalon points.
A target score of 182 points will earn an athlete 1000 Pentathlon points and each target point is worth plus or minus 15 scoring points.

SWIMMING

The pool must conform to the standard approved by FINA (Fédération Internationale de Natation Amateur).

Race 300m for men and 200m for women, freestyle. Competitors are divided into heats according to the current standings and the number of lanes.
The starting signal is a pistol shot.
Injured competitors may start in the water.

Scoring Pentathlon points are awarded on a "par" basis, with the men earning 1000 points for a swim of 3min 54sec. The women's 1000-point mark is at 2min 40sec. Each 0.5sec under or over these times gains or loses 4 points.

CROSS-COUNTRY RUNNING

The course is 4km for men and 2km for women. It is marked with white tape and with signposts marked by pairs of flags, red on the left side and white on the right.

Viewing On the morning of the cross-country competition, competitors view the course and are given a contour map.

Dress Competitors must wear their team colors and their starting number on their chests and backs.

Procedures Competitors start at intervals of 30sec.

Scoring For men completing the course in 14min 15sec there are 1000 points. Every second faster or slower than this time gains or loses 3 points. For women completing the course in 7min 40sec there are 1000 points. Every second faster or slower than this time gains or loses 5 points.

Triathlon

Triathlon is a three-part sport consisting of swimming, cycling and running.
The three stages are competed as a continuous event without a rest. The triathlon originated in the USA during the 1970s with the Hawaii "Iron Man" contest. There are both individual and team events.

Triathlons are contested over varying distances. There are three internationally recognized distances:
Short course
Swim 1.5km (0.93 miles)
Cycle 40km (24.9 miles)
Run 10km (6.2 miles)
Long course
Swim 2.5km (1.55 miles)
Cycle 80km (49.7 miles)
Run 20km (12.4 miles)
Iron man
Swim 3.8km (2.4 miles)
Cycle 180km (112 miles)
Run (Marathon) 42.195km (26.2 miles)

The courses are usually a circuit with the start, finish and transition area in the same place. However, the start and finish can be in different places with two transition areas. The course should be clearly marked.
Competition timing begins when the competitor has begun swimming and ends when the competitor has reached the finish after the running.
Transition time, ie time for changing clothing and equipment from one section to another, is included in the total competition time.

Officials A triathlon is organized by a race director, who may have a deputy and assistants. The race referee ensures competitors keep to the rules. There should be 8 timekeepers and 8 recorders, transition judges, a safety officer, rescue canoeists and rescue power boat crews. There are separate swim, cycle and run officials, marshalls to direct competitors on the cycle and run courses and draft busters to ensure drafting does not occur. Funnel judges check the placing of competitors at the finish.

Transition area Between sections competitors change from swimming kit into cycling kit and collect their bicycles from racks usually numbered in race order. At the end of the cycling section the bicycles are returned to the racks in the transition area and competitors may change into separate running kit. Cycling is not allowed in the transition area.

SWIMMING
The start All competitors start with an audible and visual signal at the same time either from the shore or in shallow water. Except on entering and leaving the water, the competitor should swim at all times.
The course Buoys mark the course every 50m and a lead boat acts as a guide 25m ahead of the leading competitor.
Clothing Colored swim caps with the competitor's number are worn, a swim costume (this may be a triathlon suit designed for wearing for all sections of the event) and swimming goggles. It is optional to use a wet suit with a thickness of no more than 3mm. Buoyancy aids are prohibited.

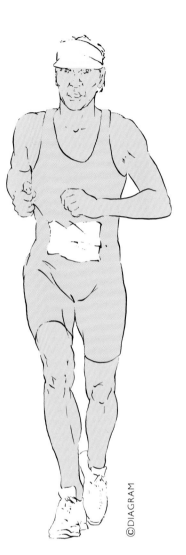

Safety Colored caps are worn to identify swimmers in the water, and canoes and powered safety craft patrol the course. Swimmers raise one hand to be rescued. Events will not be held if water temperatures are too low.

Disqualification A swimmer is disqualified if he:
does not follow the course;
does not comply with rules on clothing and equipment;
proceeds with aid from the sea bed or bottom of a pool or with aid from a line or boat; or
exceeds the time limit designated for the swimming section.

CYCLING

Transition The cycle section starts immediately after the swim and the competitor has changed to cycling clothing.

Course Usually takes place on public asphalted roads. All sand and grit should be removed from the curves. Competitors must follow the rules of the road.

The bicycle Lightweight racing cycles with derailleur gears are used. These must be in roadworthy condition. Low profile machines are permitted but not machines with wind reducing protective shields.

Clothing A triathlon suit or cycling shorts and suitable shirt are worn with cycling shoes or running shoes. A race number is attached to the rider's back and a helmet is compulsory.

Drafting It is not permitted to be paced by another rider or by a car and riders must keep a minimum distance of 5m behind the rider in front and when overtaking must move out by at least 2m. Race officials, known as draft busters, patrol the course to ensure this rule is not infringed.

Disqualification A cyclist can be disqualified for:
drafting;
not following the rules of the road;
not wearing a helmet; or taking refreshment other than at an official refreshment station.

RUNNING

Transition The running section starts after the competitor has racked his bicycle. A change of shoes and clothing may take place.

Course Running usually takes place on public roads and streets.

Clothing Running shoes, shorts and vest or triathlon suit are worn with the race number attached at the front.

Disqualification A runner may be disqualified, if he is paced or receives assistance.

Finish The running section finishes in a finishing funnel, which marks the end of the race.

2

Gymnastics

⚭⚭⚭

Gymnastics encompasses many forms of human movement and dance. Competitive gymnastics is divided into four separate disciplines: women's artistic gymnastics, men's artistic gymnastics, rhythmic gymnastics and sports acrobatics. Each discipline has its own specific requirements in terms of apparatus, style of performance and judging criteria.

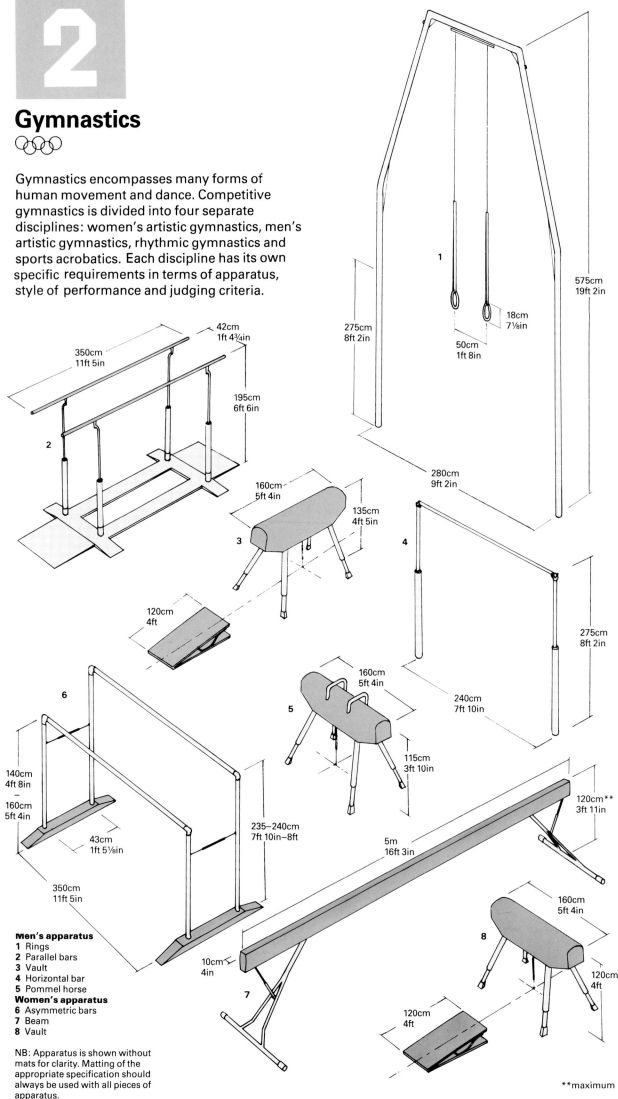

Men's apparatus
1 Rings
2 Parallel bars
3 Vault
4 Horizontal bar
5 Pommel horse
Women's apparatus
6 Asymmetric bars
7 Beam
8 Vault

NB: Apparatus is shown without mats for clarity. Matting of the appropriate specification should always be used with all pieces of apparatus.

Equipment
Men gymnasts compete on the floor, pommel horse, rings, vaulting horse, parallel bars and horizontal bars. Women compete on the vaulting horse, asymmetric bars, beam and floor. Competitors perform compulsory and optional movements on each apparatus. There are separate titles for the team competition, individual combined events competition, and the individual events competitions.

Officials Four judges score each event independently, supervised by one superior judge (two in the men's individual finals).
Compulsory exercises are set for a period of four years. They are designed to test the gymnast's control and mastery of specific skills.
Voluntary exercises give the gymnast the opportunity to display his/her own area of expertise.
Scoring The highest and lowest scores of the four judges are discarded and the middle two are averaged to give the recorded score. Each exercise is scored from 1 to 10, with deductions of whole, half, and one-tenth points.
In some events there is a starting score with a possible bonus (awarded for risk, virtuosity, and/or originality) to create a maximum of 10 points. Basically, gymnasts are penalized for general faults (such as lack of assurance or elegance) and for faults specific to the apparatus. Exercises and movements are officially defined and graded in terms of difficulty. Some exercises are required to contain sections of specified difficulty.
Team competition The six members of each team perform a compulsory and an optional exercise on each apparatus. The five highest scores are added to give the team total (maximum points: men 600, women 400.)
Individual combined events (all-round) competition The 36 leading gymnasts in the team competition perform an optional exercise on each apparatus.
(Maximum points: men 60, women 40.)
Individual events competitions The eight competitors with the highest total on each individual apparatus from the team competitions compete again for the individual apparatus title. The maximum score for both men and women is 10.

Women's artistic gymnastics

The apparatus used in women's competitive gymnastics comprises vault, asymmetric bars, balance beam and the floor. The exercises required are specific to the individual pieces of apparatus. The gymnast may be required, depending on the level of the competition, to perform both compulsory and voluntary routines on each piece of apparatus.

©DIAGRAM

WOMEN'S VAULT
The horse for the women's vault is 120cm high. The springboard is placed in line with the short axis of the horse.

The gymnast performs one compulsory vault and then two optional vaults. For the optional vault the best mark awarded counts. The requirements of the individual vault and the maximum mark possible are presented in the FIG Code of Points. All vaults are graded A, B, C or D for difficulty and are also divided into eight groups by type. The gymnast must display the number of the vault she is about to perform.

Phases The vault is divided into four phases for purposes of evaluation:
1) first flight phase;
2) support/strike phase;
3) second flight phase;
4) landing.
The run up is not evaluated. All vaults must be performed with the support of both hands on the horse. The vault illustated (*above*) is the compulsory exercise specified by the FIG for 1989-1992; it is the Yamashita with a half turn (180°) in the second flightphase.
The optional vault may not be the same as the compulsory vault.

Scoring Each judge scores the vault by making deductions from a maximum possible of 10 points.

The following are examples of possible deductions for error in the women's vault as laid down by the FIG:
if an optional vault does not correspond to the number displayed by the gymnast;
if the body position is at fault in the first flight phase;
if the arms remain bent in the support phase.

Example of women's compulsory vault 1989-1992
1 a strong powerful run up combined with efficient use of the Reuther board;
2 strike the horse in the stretched position;
3 with a strong thrust from the horse pike at the hips;
4 complete 180° turn about the long axis prior to landing.

Examples of previous years' compulsory vaults

Compulsory vault 1972
1 quarter turn in 1st flight;
2 contact and thrust;
3 quarter turn in 2nd flight;
4 landing.

Compulsory vault 1981–1984
1 stretched 1st flight;
2 handspring;
3 full turn about longitudinal axis during 2nd flight;
4 landing.

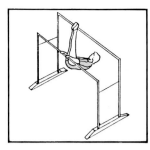

WOMEN'S ASYMMETRIC BARS

The asymmetric bars consist of two wooden or fiber glass bars placed parallel to each other but at different heights above the mats. The lower bar is 155cm above the floor and the upper bar is 235cm above the floor. Each competitor first performs the current compulsory exercise as laid down by the FIG. The elements comprising the compulsory exercise are of the same general kind as for the optional exercise.

The most important features of the exercise are:
a) upward swings or circular swings;
b) movements from swing to handstand;
c) turns around the longitudinal axis of the body (pirouettes);
d) turns around the short axis (saltos);
e) counter, grip change, and flight elements;
f) Hecht elements;
g) kips.

The exercise should form a continuous and harmonious whole without stops or interruptions. Only four consecutive elements may be performed on the same bar; the gymnast must then change bar, touch the other bar or dismount.

The following are examples of possible deductions for error in the women's asymmetric bars exercise: monotony in rhythm; fewer than 10 elements; dismount not corresponding to the exercise's level of difficulty.

Compulsory exercise 1989–1992

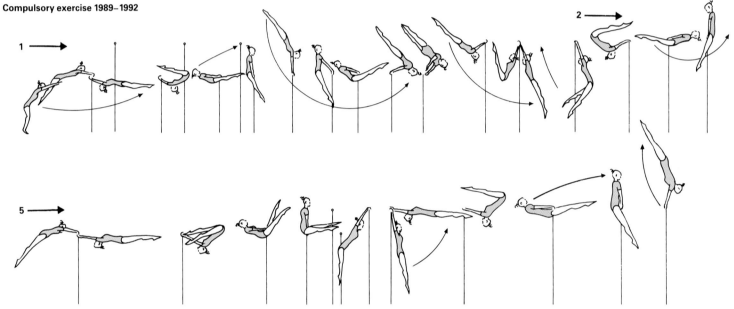

WOMEN'S BEAM

The balance beam is suede covered, 5m × 100cm. Each competitor first performs the current compulsory exercise as laid down by the FIG.

The gymnast is required to perform a balanced routine of movements which lasts between 1 minute 10 seconds and 1 minute 30 seconds.

The timing begins when the gymnast's feet leave the floor and ends when they return to the floor. If she falls she may resume within 10 seconds.

The gymnast must make use of the entire length of the beam

Each competitor also performs an optional exercise composed of elements chosen by herself, within guidelines. The following element groups must be included:
a) acrobatic elements, with and without a flight phase in the forward, backward, or sideways movement;
b) acrobatic strength elements;
c) gymnastic elements, such as turns, leaps, steps, runs, and balance elements in sitting, standing, or lying positions;
d) dance steps.

Compulsory exercise 1989–1992

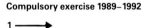

Example of compulsory asymmetric bars exercise 1989-1992
1 from stand facing the bars, float upstart, lay away clear hip circle backwards with Hecht ½ turn to catch upper bar, swing backward;
2 straddle legs forward to upstart on high bar, lay up to handstand, ½ turn;
3 swing down between the bars, swing forward with ½ turn;
4 underswing with legs together and ½ turn with flight over the low bar to catch the low bar in momentary support;
5 glide forward, straddle upstart to sit on low bar. Catch the high bar long upstart, lay away;
6 clear hip circle backward to handstand;
7 longswing between the bars to salto straight with full turn dismount to land.

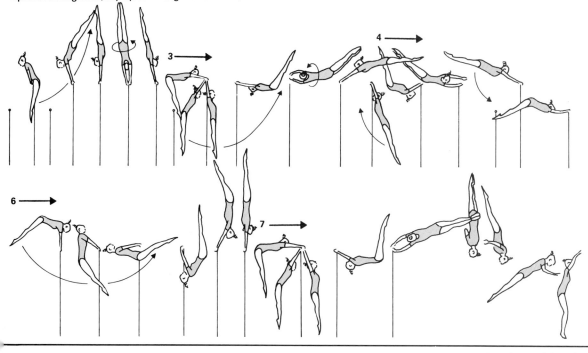

©DIAGRAM

The following are examples of possible deductions for error in the women's beam optional exercise:
monotony of presentation;
monotony in direction of movement;
omission of an acrobatic series;
supporting a leg against the side of the beam;
more than three pauses.

Example of compulsory beam exercise 1989-1992
1 from stand straddle press to handstand. Lower legs to side sitting position;
2 raise legs while making a ¼ turn to a sitting position, extend left leg and stand on right leg. Step forward, chasse step ½ turn;
3 cartwheel with ¼ turn, back flip, sissone jump to land on one leg, immediate roll backwards to shoulder stand;
4 roll forward to one legged stand while swinging the other leg to needle stand;
5 Arabesque. Step, step, stretched jump forward with arch. Cross step with ¼ turn, continue turning to complete ½ turn;
6 backward walkover without flight to one leg, lower leg to the beam. Return to high balance stand;
7 Step forward, handspring forward with flight to land in stand, skip steps with changes of arm position, step with ½ turn;
8 step forward, split leap, full turn, change leg step with ⅛ turn. Lower body to forward scale;
9 step sequence with turns to end facing the end of the beam;
10 circle arms while making ½ turn to face along the beam;
11 step forward, running steps, Arab spring, backward salto straight with full turn dismount to land.

33

WOMEN'S FLOOR EXERCISES

The floor exercise is performed on a 12m × 12m specially sprung matted area. The women's floor exercise is performed to music.

Each competitor first performs the current compulsory exercise as laid down by the FIG. The elements comprising this exercise are of the same general kind as for the optional exercise.

Each competitor also performs an optional exercise composed of elements chosen by herself within guidelines.

The exercise should last from 1min 10sec to 1min 30sec.

The musical accompaniment may consist of taped orchestral music or taped or live piano music.

The gymnast must incorporate the following elements into her routine:
a) acrobatic elements;
b) acrobatic strength elements;
c) gymnastic elements, such as turns, leaps, steps, runs, arm swings, and balance elements in sitting, standing, or lying positions;
d) dance steps.

The following are examples of possible deductions for error in the women's floor exercise as laid down by the FIG:
lack of high points;
monotony in presentation;
elements of exaggeratedly theatrical character;
stepping outside the floor area;
lack of a series with two salto high points or a double salto.

Example of women's compulsory floor exercise 1989-1992

1 arms lowered and body wave;
2 round off, back flip, back flip, salto backward straight with full turn;
3 chasse step, body wave, ½ turn to sit back into backward roll to split leg handstand;
4 1/4 turn and chasse step, 11/4 spin with leg held behind and slide down into splits;
5 swing rear leg forward, roll over, sit up and Valdez to stand;
6 two spring jette, ½ turn and kick;
7 three running steps, change leg split leap, jump with full turn, upward jump with change of feet;
8 step and lunge, 1/4 turn and hop backward, join feet and split jump travelling backward, join feet and ½ turn. Step, join feet, upward jump, split leap;
9 free cartwheel, back flip, layout backward salto with split leg to land on one knee;
10 stand and chasse step forward, lunge, ½ turn, three running steps and sideways jump, side gallop;
11 ¾ turn with leg behind, step back and ½ backward walkover, body move back, forward and walkout;
12 step and full spin with split leap from it. Join feet together and body wave;
13 step with ¼ turn and make full spin. Jump legs alternately to side, step and show attitude position. Lower leg and arms and then show attitude position again;
14 three steps into the corner with ½ turn, running step into round off, back flip, piked Arabian salto to one leg, walkout into Tinsica;
15 step and reverse spin, step forwards into finishing position.

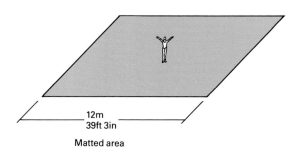

12m
39ft 3in

Matted area

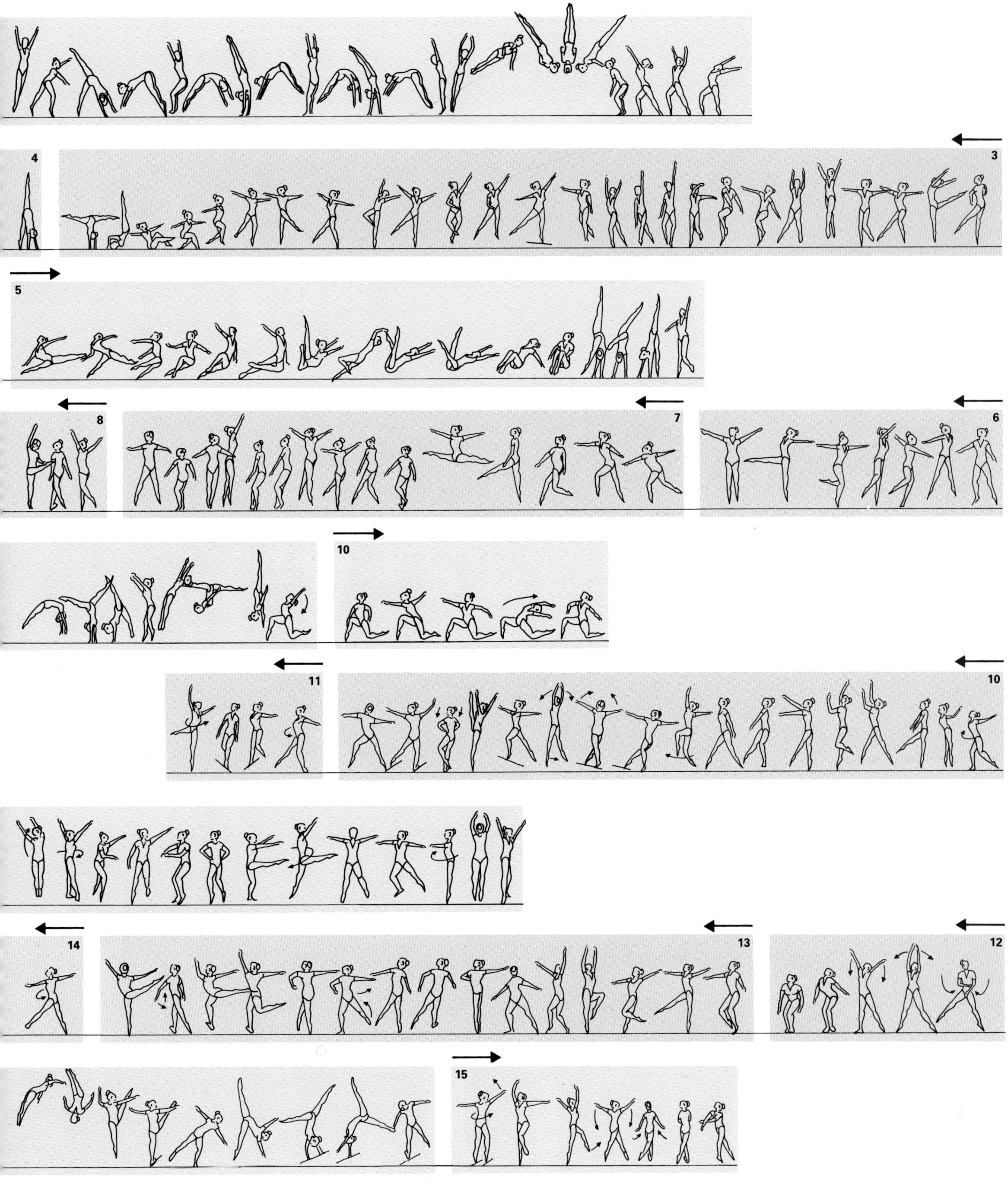
4
3
5
8
7
6
10
11
10
14
13
12
15

Men's artistic gymnastics

Six pieces of apparatus are used in men's artistic gymnastics: floor, side or pommel horse, rings, vault, parallel bars and the horizontal or high bar. The gymnast may be required to perform both compulsory and voluntary exercises on all six pieces of apparatus.

1 ⟶

MEN'S FLOOR EXERCISES

The floor area used is the same as that used by women. However, the exercise is not performed to music.

Each competitor first performs the current compulsory exercise as laid down by the FIG. The movements comprising this exercise are of the same general kind as for the optional exercise.

The exercise should last between 50 and 70 seconds.

Voluntary exercises must form a harmonious and rhythmic whole; they should consist of acrobatic jumps connected with acrobatic and gymnastic elements (eg handstands) elements of flexibility, strength and balance.

The gymnast must incorporate the following into his routine:
a) three different acrobatic connections;
b) one strength part;
c) one static element of balance on one arm or one leg.

All available floor space must be used.

The following are examples of deductions laid down by the FIG:
running paces in excess of 3 steps;
stepping out of the floor area;
for too long or too short a performance.

Example of a men's voluntary floor exercise

1 round off;
2 back flip;
3 full twisted double back salto;
4 fall with half turn, straddle clip to back support;
5 front support, lift leg through to splits, lift out to stand;
6 tucked front salto step out, handspring piked front salto;
7 fall to front support, turn to sit, full lever lift to handstand, pirouette, lower feet to floor;
8 round off piked side salto;
9 forward roll single leg lift to handstand, straight leg forward roll;
10 Y balance;
11 round off, back flip, double tucked back salto.

8 ⟶

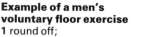

12m
39ft 3in

Matted area

10 ⟶   **11** ⟶

2 ⟶   3 ⟶   4 ⟶

← 6   ← 5

← 7

9 ⟶

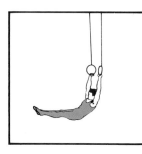

MEN'S RINGS

Each competitor first performs the current compulsory exercise as laid down by the FIG. The elements comprising the compulsory exercise are of the same general kind as for the optional exercise.

The exercise on rings should be composed of strength, swing, and held parts in about equal proportions.

The exercise should contain:
a) one handstand executed from swing;
b) one handstand executed with strength;
c) one static held part and one optional held part.
The held parts should be held without swinging of the rings.
The following are examples of possible deductions for error laid down by the FIG:

if the additional strength part does not correspond to the general difficulty of the exercise;
if swing, strength and hold parts are not properly distributed;
if there is no handstand, or if the handstand does not correspond to the general difficulty of the exercise.

Example of voluntary rings exercise

1 from hang straight body lift to inverted hang, kip to support swing to top plant;
2 lower and swing forward to forward uprise;
3 straight body, straight arm lift to handstand;
4 swing backwards through hang, Homma salto to swing in support to handstand;
5 forward giant circle to handstand;
6 swing forwards to double straight salto dismount.

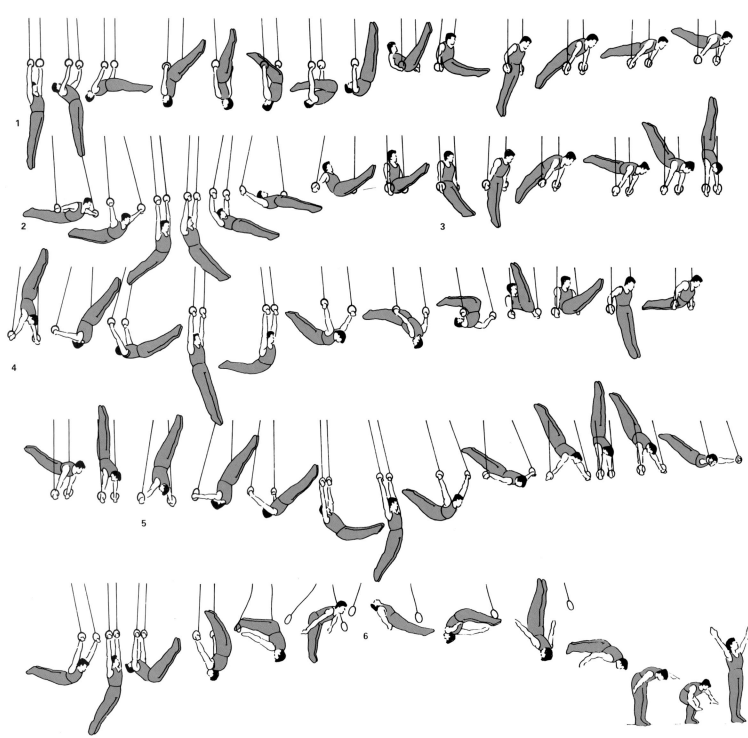

MEN'S VAULT

Men use the same vaulting horse as women except that it is set at a height of 135cm. The springboard is placed in line with the long axis of the horse. The competitors must select a vault from the list of tariffed vaults in the FIG Code of Points; these are listed according to type and graded according to difficulty.

Approach The maximum length for the approach is 25m.

The vault begins with a run and take off from both feet and is executed with a brief support phase on the horse with both hands or with one hand.

Flight The gymnast is required to attain a height of 1m above the horse and a distance of 2m from the horse during the flight from the horse

In all competitions only one attempt at the compulsory and optional vault is permitted.

The vault shown is the straight Tsukahara (named after the Japanese gymnast who first performed it).

Scoring
The scoring system is the same for compulsory and optional vaults with a maximum score of 10 points in both cases.

Each type of vault is awarded a tariff according to its level of difficulty, with all vaults having a base score. Deductions are made from the base score for technical

faults and for errors in form. The following are examples of deductions laid down by FIG:

if the run exceeds 25m;
if the gymnast deviates from the line of the long axis of the horse during the flight phases;
if the arms are bent when they should be straight.

Example of a men's voluntary exercise: Tsukahara

1 jump from the board with quarter turn;
2 continue turning to complete a half turn with strong thrust from hands;
3 one and quarter backward salto in straight position.

Yamashita with ½ turn

1 jump with forward rotation from the board;
2 thrust from the hands with an extended body then vigorously fold into a 'piled' position;
3 extend the hips into a straight position while simultaneously making a half turn around the long axis of the body;
4 landing.

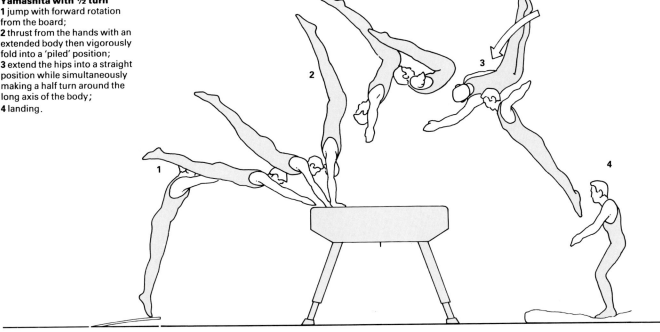

MEN'S POMMEL HORSE

Each competitor first performs the current compulsory exercise as laid down by the FIG. The elements comprising the compulsory exercise are of the same general kind as for the optional exercise.

A competitor performs a voluntary exercise composed of elements chosen by himself in accordance with certain guidelines.

All three parts of the horse must be used.

The exercise must comprise:
a) different types of circular and pendulum swing in various positions of support on all parts of the horse;
b) at least two scissor type connections;
c) an element performed on one handle only.

Double leg circles must predominate in the performance.

The following are examples of possible deductions for error laid down by the FIG:
if one part of the horse is not used;
if there is a marked tendency to use one part of the horse;
if there is no scissor part.

Example of voluntary pommel horse exercise
1 direct Stockli "B" out;
2 circle in side support;
3 Schwaben flank;
4 Wendeswing forward with ½ turn;
5 Russian Wendeswing forward with o turn;
6 Czechkehre on the end;
7 Kreiskehre forward onto handles;
8 Thomas flair (x 2);
9 front shear (scissor);
10 front shear with ½ turn;
11 pendulum swing;
12 backshear;
13 double leg circle;
14 Czechkehre;
15 double leg circle;
16 Czechkehre back travel out;
17 Chaguinian.

MEN'S PARALLEL BARS

The parallel bars are two wooden laminated bars placed parallel to each other and at the same height. Each competitor first performs the current compulsory exercise as laid down by the FIG. The elements comprising the compulsory exercise are of the same general kind as for the optional exercise. Each competitor also performs an optional exercise composed of elements of his choice, within certain guidelines. The gymnast is required to perform movements of support, hang, swing and balance. The exercise should be performed above and below the bar and include turns about the long axis with static holds and strength parts.

The following are examples of possible deductions laid down by the FIG: if more than three pronounced hold parts are included.

Example of a voluntary parallel bars exercise

1 long upstart, back straddle to front support;
2 under somersault to handstand;
3 swing forwards, Stützkehre;
4 backward longswing;
5 swing forwards, Stützekehre;
6 underswing to upper arm support;
7 back uprise straddle cut to half lever;
8 straddle lift to handstand;
9 swing forwards, Stützkehre;
10 swing forwards, tucked double backward salto, dismount.

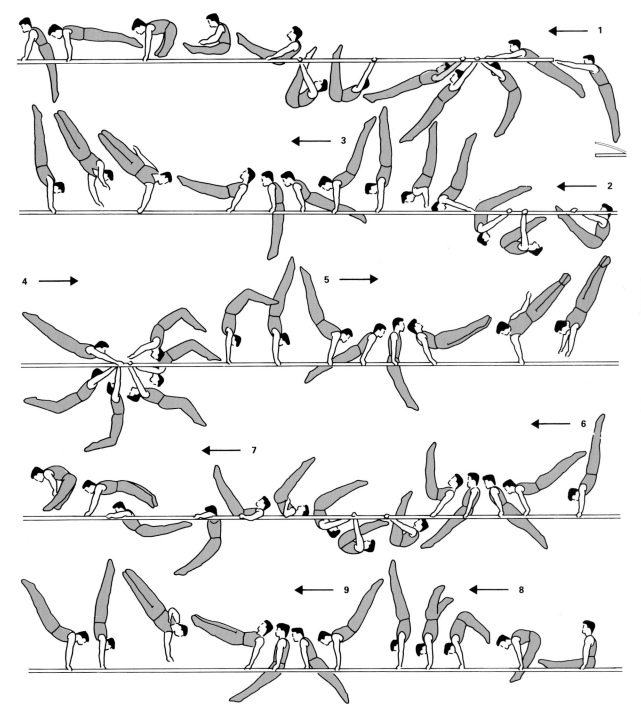

© DIAGRAM

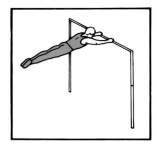

MEN'S HORIZONTAL BAR

The horizontal or high bar is made of high tensile steel. Each competitor first performs the current compulsory exercise as laid down by the FIG. The elements comprising the compulsory exercise are of the same general kind as outlined below for the optional exercise.

Each gymnast performs an optional exercise composed of elements chosen, within guidelines, by himself. The exercise should consist entirely of swinging elements without interruptions. It must include:

a) forward and backward giant swings;
b) movements close to the bar;
c) elements with turns around the long axis;
d) flighted elements which recatch on the bar.

The following are examples of possible deductions laid down by the FIG:
for the inclusion of hold or strength parts;
for omitting one of the minimum requirements;
if the exercise is not concluded with a proper dismount.

Example of a compulsory horizontal bar exercise (1989-1992)

1 from overgrasp cast half turn to mixed grasp, sliding forwards change to undergrasp;
2 Endo circle;
3 forward long swing, squat in dislocate; to
4 Elgrip swing hop change to undergrasp;
5 forward giant to top change;
6 giant circle backwards;
7 giant circle backwards with blind change;
8 forward giant circle, to Voronin hop;
9 swing forward, hop to undergrasp, kip to handstand;
10 forward giant circle with half turn and reach under to cross hand grip;
11 cross hand giant swing change grip to overgrasp;
12 backward giant swing;
13 double tucked backward salto dismount.

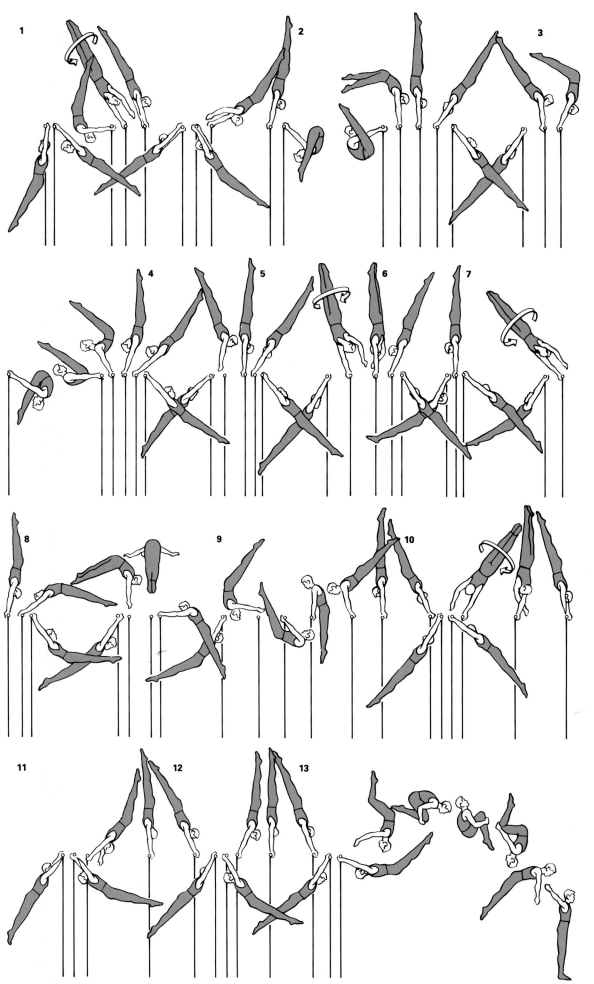

Rhythmic gymnastics

Rhythmic gymnastics is all floorwork performed to music with or without small hand apparatus. Gymnasts work with ropes, hoops, balls, clubs and ribbons; they may perform individually or in groups. There is a time limit on both individual and group exercises and gymnasts are judged on their performance in body movements and certain elements of movement with each specific item of apparatus.

Individual exercises
There is a time limit of 1-1½ min. All exercises with or without apparatus must include:
a) Fundamental groups of body movements:
jumps and leaps;
balances;
pivots;
flexibility.
b) Other groups of body movements:
various methods of travelling; skips and hops;
swings and circles;
turns;
waves.
Apparatus must not be gold, silver or bronze in colour. (Junior gymnasts may work with apparatus proportionate to their size.)
Rope of hemp or similar synthetic material without handles and proportionate to the size of the gymnast.
a) Fundamental groups of movement:
jumps or leaps;
skips or hops;
b) Other groups of movement:
swings, circles, rotations, figure eights, throws.
Hoop of wood or plastic. Interior diameter: 80-90cm. Weight: 300g min.
a) Fundamental groups of movement:
rolls on floor or body;
rotations;
b) Other groups of movement:
swings, circles and figure-eights;
passing through or over hoop
throws.
Ball of rubber or similar synthetic material. Interior diameter: 18-20cm. Weight: 400g min.
a) Fundamental groups of movement:
throws;
active bouncing;
free rolls over body or on floor;
b) Other groups of movement:
circles, spirals, figure-eight movements.

Clubs of wood or synthetic material. Length: 40-50cm. Weight: minimum of 150g for each club.
a) Fundamental groups of movement:
small circles with clubs;
mills;
rotations of clubs during flight of apparatus;
b) Other groups of movement:
throws;
asymmetric movements;
swings, circles;
tapping.
Ribbon comprising a stick attached to a ribbon. The stick shall be made of wood, plastic or fiber glass. Length: 50-60cm. Diameter: 1cm max at the widest part. The ribbon shall be of satin or similar material. Length: 6m. Width: 4–6m. Weight: minimum of 35g.
a) Fundamental groups of movement;
snakes in different planes;
spirals in different planes;
swings, circles in different planes;
b) Other groups of movement:
figure eights;
throws;
small tosses.
Group work
There is a time limit of 2–2½min.
Groups of 6 gymnasts perform together using either:
a) 6 pieces of identical apparatus; or
b) 3 pieces of one type of apparatus and 3 of another, eg 3 hoops and 3 ropes. The judges assess gymnasts on the basis of body movement elements and specific apparatus elements in addition to exchanges of apparatus and changes of formation of the gymnasts.

Rope

Hoop

Ball

Club

Ribbon

© DIAGRAM

Sports acrobatics

Sports acrobatics is the only sport form of gymnastics to have a separate international governing body. The International Federation for Sports Acrobatics (IFSA) was founded in 1973 and regulates all aspects of this branch of gymnastics.

Sports acrobatics comprises two main sections: tumbling and group work. Unlike artistic gymnastics there are no compulsory exercises to be performed.

Women's trio balance routine

Competition area
Pair and group exercises are performed on a gymnastic floor area of 12 × 12m. Tumbling is performed on a special sprung track. The approach run must be a minimum of 10m, the track 25m and the landing zone 5m.

Events The following events are included in sports acrobatics competitions:
a) tumbling for women;
b) tumbling for men;
c) men's pairs;
d) women's pairs;
e) mixed pairs (one man/one woman);
f) women's trio;
g) men's four.

Pair and group work
There are 2 basic routines for pair and group work – balance and tempo routines. The combined routine contains elements from both these categories.
All routines with the exception of men's four balance are performed to music. They must be integrated into a smoothly choreographed presentation of less than 20 minutes for balance and tempo routines and 3 minutes for combined routines.

The balance routine
consists of elements without a flight phase; pyramids; handstands; balances; individual elements; choreographic and combination movements. The men's four balance routine consists of one or two pyramids being built and held for four seconds. Since the formations involve great height there is no music and a safety mat is allowed.

The tempo routine
consists of elements with a flight phase; turns; somersaults; including at least 2 elements where the partner is caught; individual elements; choreographic elements and a tumbling series.

The combined routine
consists of a minimum of 5 pair and group elements, at least 2 of which are balance elements and at least 2 tempo elements. There is a minimum of three individual elements.

Scoring
In all routines the following are evaluated:
difficulty;
composition;
execution;
general impression; time of balances (that they are held for long enough).
The final mark for an exercise is reached by deducting marks for any faults in these areas.

Tumbling
Three tumble runs are performed – one consisting of somersaults without twist, one with somersaults with twist, and a run combining elements from both categories.

The straight run must have at least 3 somersaults – a double somersault is considered as 2 somersaults and a triple as 3 somersaults. Somersaults with 180° or more are not permitted.

The twisting run consists of a minimum of one somersault with at least 360° twist.

The combined run must have a minimum of one somersault without twist and one somersault with a minimum of 360° twist.

Scoring
In all tumble runs the following are evaluated:
difficulty;
general impression;
composition;
execution.
The final mark for an exercise is reached by deducting for any faults in these areas.

Mixed pair tempo routine

Men's four balance routines

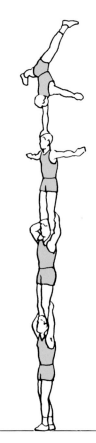

Trampolining

There are trampoline competitions for individuals, teams of five, and synchronized pairs. Each type of competition includes compulsory and voluntary routines of ten movements each. Marks are awarded for execution and difficulty; the judges deduct points for form breaks, loss of rhythm, loss of height, and lack of synchronization, from the maximum mark of 10.

Frame height: 0.95–1.05m; length of bed: 3.60–4.30m; width of bed: 1.80–2.15m; width of webbing: 6–12mm.

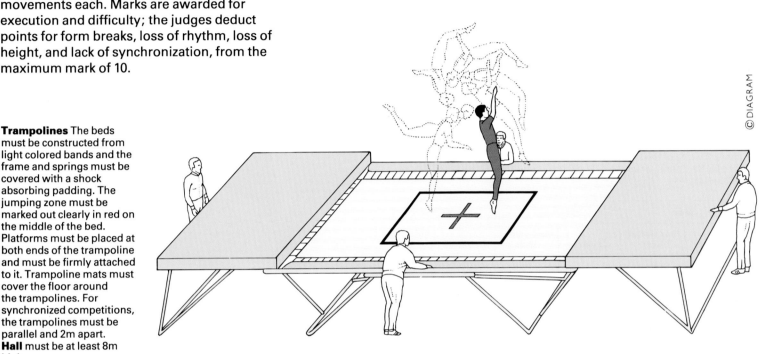

© DIAGRAM

Trampolines The beds must be constructed from light colored bands and the frame and springs must be covered with a shock absorbing padding. The jumping zone must be marked out clearly in red on the middle of the bed. Platforms must be placed at both ends of the trampoline and must be firmly attached to it. Trampoline mats must cover the floor around the trampolines. For synchronized competitions, the trampolines must be parallel and 2m apart.
Hall must be at least 8m high.
Dress Leotard and long gymnastic trousers for men. Leotard for women. Trampoline shoes. Spotters must wear track suits and gym shoes.
Officials One referee; five judges for execution, two for difficulty; and three for synchronized jumping; chief recorders; assistants; arbitration jury comprising a member of the organizing committee, the president of the technical committee, the referee, and two judges.
Spotters are compulsory at each side of the trampoline to ensure the safety of competitors. They are forbidden to speak to competitors; 0.3 of a mark is deducted each time this rule is disregarded.
Individual competitions The ten best competitors in a preliminary round go forward to a final round. The preliminary round comprises one compulsory and one voluntary routine. The final comprises one voluntary routine.
Team competitions Teams have 3–4 members, all of whom perform one compulsory and two voluntary routines. Team scores are obtained by adding a team's three best scores for each routine.

Synchronized competitions Pairs of competitors perform the same routine simultaneously. Synchronized competitions comprise a compulsory, voluntary and final in the same way as individual competition.
Routines Compulsory and voluntary routines each consist of ten elements. Second attempts at routines are permitted only if the jury decides that a competitor was obviously disturbed (eg by faulty equipment or spectators).
Warming up Two hours' training on the competition apparatus is allowed before the competition starts. Competitors are also allowed one practice routine of 30 seconds each before each round for which they have qualified.
Start The referee signals after the competitor is on the trampoline. Competitors may make as many preliminary jumps as they wish before starting the first element.
Required posture In all positions except straddle jumps, the feet and legs should be kept together and

the feet and toes pointed. Depending on the requirements of the movement, the body should be tucked, piked or straight. In the tucked and piked positions, the thighs should be close to the upper body. In the tucked position, the hands should touch the legs below the knees. The arms should be straight and held close to the body wherever possible. In multiple somersaults with twists, the tuck and pike position may be modified during the twisting phase.
Repetition If a jump is repeated in the voluntary routine, there is no score for the degree of difficulty of the repeat.
Multiple somersaults with twists in the first, middle, and last phase have the same degree of difficulty; they are regarded as different jumps (not repeats). Skills having the same amount of rotation but performed in the tucked, piked and straight positions are considered to be different jumps.
Degree of difficulty Marked in tenths of a point from 0.1. All jumps without rotation have no degree of

difficulty. Other jumps are rated on the principle:
90° somersault, 0.1;
360° somersault, 0.4;
180° twist, 0.1;
360° twist, 0.2 points.
In skills combining somersaulting and twisting, the difficulty values are added together for twisting somersaults. Piked and straight somersaults without twists are awarded an extra tenth of a point for difficulty.
Interruption A routine is interrupted if:
a competitor does not perform the compulsory routine in the written sequence;
the elasticity of the bed after landing is not used for the immediate continuation of the next movement and a break is caused;
any part of the competitor's body touches the frame or the suspension system during the routine;
the competitor is physically helped by a spotter;
the competitor leaves the trampoline during the routine due to insecurity;
the sequence of jumps in a synchronized competition is different.
After an interruption, the referee tells the judges what

the maximum mark should be. The routine is only judged to the point of interruption.
End of routine A routine ends with both feet on the trampoline after the tenth element. The competitor may then make one more jump in a stretched position. If he fails to land on his feet after the tenth movement, he is judged to have made an additional movement, for which 1 point is deducted. The competitor must stand upright for at least 3 seconds after landing, or 1 point is lost for insecurity.
Result The winner is the competitor or team with the highest total of points. Competitors with equal marks in individual and synchronized competitions are given the same placing. In team competitions places are shared in a tie.
Scoring The highest and lowest marks of the execution judges are disregarded and the middle three marks are added together. The score for execution is added to the difficulty mark and in synchronized competition this total is added to the mark for synchronization.

Weightlifting

Competitors attempt to lift a weighted bar by two different methods: the snatch and clean and jerk. In each type of lift, each competitor makes a maximum of three attempts to lift the bar. There are individual and team classifications for the snatch and the jerk, and for the total weight of the competitor's best performances in the two types of lift.

Dress The competitor must wear a one-piece (leotard type) costume. A short sleeved, collarless, T-shirt may be worn under the costume. Trunks may be worn over the costume. The maximum width of the belt worn may be 120mm at its widest point.

Categories Lifters are grouped into categories. There are 10 categories for men, 9 for women, and 7 for veterans. The maximum body weight for each category is given in the table.

Men		Women		Veterans	
Category	Max weight limit	Category	Max weight limit	Category	Max weight limit
	kg		kg		kg
1	52.0	1	44.0	1	60.0
2	56.0	2	48.0	2	67.5
3	60.0	3	52.0	3	75.0
4	67.5	4	56.0	4	82.5
5	75.0	5	60.0	5	90.0
6	82.5	6	67.5	6	100.0
7	90.0	7	75.0	7	+100.01
8	100.01	8	82.5		
9	110.0	9	+82.51		
10	+110.01				

Boots The maximum height permitted on the upper part of the shoe measured from the top of the sole is 130mm. The sole cannot project from the shoe by more than 5mm at any point.

Bandages are allowed on the wrists, knees, hands, fingers and thumbs. Alternatively, leather wrist straps and elastic knee caps may be worn. Plasters on the fingers are allowed, but cannot cover the tip of the fingers. No bandages are allowed on the elbows, the torso, the thighs and the shins.

Competitors Competitions are organized for men or women. In major championships each country may enter a team of ten athletes and two reserves spread over the different categories. In women's major championships each country may enter nine women and three reserves. A competitor may compete only in one weight division. The athletes compete within the categories established by the rules, according to their bodyweight. The IWF recognizes three main age groups: junior (up to and including 20 years of age); senior; and veteran (over 40 years of age).

Platform All lifts must take place on the competition platform, 4m square. The platform may be made of wood, plastic or any solid material and may be covered with a non-slippery material. The height must be between 50–150mm.

Weighing-in begins 2 hours before the start of the competition and lasts 1 hour. Weighing-in takes place in the presence of three appointed referees, one official from the lifter's team and the competition secretary.

Lifting order A number is drawn for each athlete entered. This number is retained by the athlete throughout the competition, even if he/she moves to a higher category. The lot number decides the order of the weigh-in and the order of lifting during the course of the competition.

Duration After being called, a competitor is allowed 1½ minutes before making an attempt. After 30 seconds a warning signal is heard. If at the end of the 1½ minutes the competitor has not raised the barbell from the platform to make his/her attempt, this attempt is declared "no lift" by the three referees.

When a competitor attempts 2 lifts in succession, he/she is allowed 3 minutes for the succeeding attempt. After 2 minutes a warning signal is heard. If at the end of the 3 minutes the competitor has not raised the barbell from the platform to make the attempt, this attempt is declared "no lift."

Officials In international competitions these consist of a jury, competition secretary, technical controller, referees and doctors on duty.

Referees There are three referees whose task is to ensure that the equipment and the lifts are correct. The chief referee must be positioned not less than 6m from the center of the platform. He signals the end of each lift by ordering the lifter to replace the barbell.

The jury, composed of category 1 referees from the participating countries, ensures that the technical rules are applied. It can correct refereeing mistakes.

The timekeeper ensures that lifters make their attempts within the time allowed.

Judging The three referees decide whether a lift has been performed correctly. They announce their decision (usually by lights) after the lifter has replaced the barbell on the platform. If the majority approve the lift (white lights), it is a "good lift;" otherwise (red lights) it is a "no lift."

Scoring The snatch and the jerk places are won by the competitors lifting the heaviest weights in each of these lifts. There is also a combined winner – the competitor lifting the heaviest combined weight in the snatch and the jerk. If a tie occurs, the lighter competitor is ranked first. The final classification of the competitors is calculated in accordance with the total weight lifted by adding the best results accepted by the referees. The classification of teams is calculated by adding the points allocated to each competitor. Team points for each lift (snatch and clean and jerk) are allocated to a team as well as for the total. When two or more competitors obtain the same result at a competition where they registered at the same bodyweight, the competitor who reached the result earlier in the course of the competition is classified before the other one(s). In the case of a tie in the classification of teams, the team having the largest number of first places is classified first.

Zero in the snatch does not eliminate a competitor from the championship. He/she will be allowed to continue in the jerk. Similarly, a competitor who has been successful in the snatch but has a zero in the clean and jerk is qualified for the snatch but not the jerk, or total.

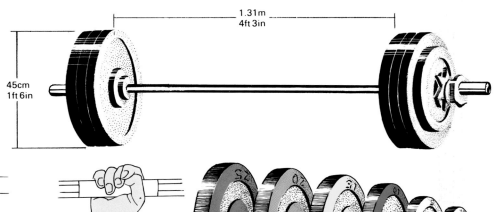

Weights Only disc barbells may be used. The barbell and collars together weigh 25kg.

1.31m / 4ft 3in

45cm / 1ft 6in

The grip

The discs are marked with their weights. They are loaded on the barbell with the largest inside and the smallest outside. They are locked onto the bar with a collar. The discs weigh 25kg (red); 20kg (blue); 15kg (yellow); 10kg (green); 5kg (white); 2.5kg (black); 1.25kg (chrome); 0.5kg (chrome); 0.25kg (chrome).

The grip Hooking is permitted; the competitor covers the last joint of the thumb with the fingers of the same hand at the moment of gripping the bar.

The snatch

The jerk

Lifting In a competition, weights must be lifted using two methods: the snatch and the clean and jerk. A lifter is allowed three attempts in each type of lift. If he succeeds at a weight in one attempt, he progresses to a heavier weight for his next lift.

A lifter states in advance the weights that he intends to attempt, assuming he succeeds at each attempt; but these selections can be changed during the competition.

During competition for a particular lift, the bar is made progressively heavier, and lifters take their turns when it reaches the weights they wish to attempt. Once it has been lifted by any competitor at a particular weight, it cannot then be made lighter. In general, the bar's weight is increased by any multiple of 2½kg.

Two hand snatch The bar is placed horizontally before the lifter's legs.
The lifter grips the bar, palms down, and pulls it in a single movement from the ground to the full extent of both arms vertically above his head, while splitting or bending the legs.
The bar must pass along the body with a continuous movement.
After the weight is fully extended above his head, the lifter is allowed unlimited time to adjust his position (the "recovery"). He must then become motionless, with his arms and legs extended and his feet on the same line. The referee signals for the bar to be replaced.
Prohibitions The lifter must not:
pause during the lift;
turn his wrists over until the bar has passed the top of his head;
extend his arms unevenly or incompletely; or
finish with a press-out.

Two hands clean and jerk
The clean The bar is placed horizontally before the lifter's legs.
The lifter grips it palms down, and brings it in a single movement to the shoulders, while splitting or bending the legs.
He may then rest the bar on his collar bones, his chest, or on his fully bent arms.
The lifter must not:
during the clean in the squat or split position, touch his knees or thighs with his elbows or upper arms;
let the bar touch his trunk before it touches his shoulders;
place the bar on his chest before the elbows are turned over.
The recovery The lifter is allowed unlimited time before the jerk to return his feet to the same line and straighten his legs.
He may also:
lower the bar onto his shoulders if it is causing inconvenience;
withdraw his thumbs or unhook from the bar;
change the width of his grip. These adjustments may not be part of the clean or the jerk.

The jerk The legs are bent and then the arms and legs are extended so as to bring the bar to the full stretch of the arms vertically extended.
The lifter may make another recovery before becoming motionless. Then the referee signals for the bar to be replaced.
Any apparent jerking movement must be completed. Any apparent effort from the shoulders, if the lift is not completed, will constitute a "no lift;" this includes lowering the body or bending the knees.

No lift In either the snatch or the jerk the lift is invalid and a "no lift" is declared:
a) for pulling from the "hang;"
b) if the bar reaches the knees in an unfinished attempt;
c) for a pause during the extension of the arms;
d) for finishing with a press-out;
e) if oil or grease is used on the thighs to help the bar to slide;
f) if any part of the body other than the feet touches the floor;
g) if the lifter replaces the bar before the referee's signal to do so;
h) if, after the referee's signal, the lifter drops the barbell;
i) if the lifter leaves the platform during any part of the lift;
j) if the arms are bent or extended during the recovery;
k) if the arms are extended unevenly above the head.

© DIAGRAM

Boxing

Boxing is an ancient sport but in its modern form, as basically defined by the Marquess of Queenberry in the 1860s, two boxers contest a bout of limited duration using only their gloved hands to land scoring blows on the target area of their opponent. Bouts are decided on points or by stoppage.

The ring Most contests are held in a three or four roped ring. The floor must be canvas over an undercover of felt or rubber.
The maximum ring dimensions are 20ft square; minimum dimensions are 16ft square for amateurs and 14ft square for professionals. There must be at least 1ft 6in floor space beyond the ropes.

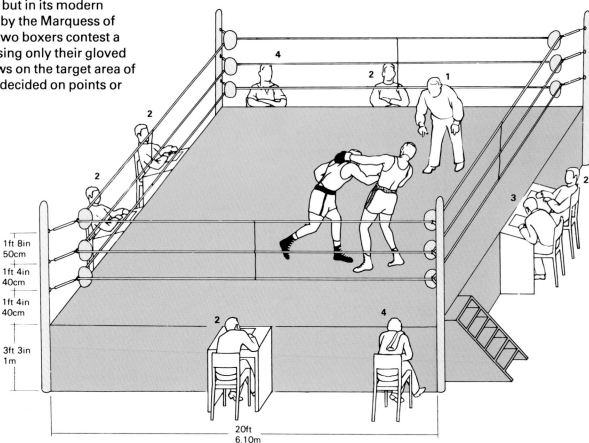

1ft 8in
50cm

1ft 4in
40cm

1ft 4in
40cm

3ft 3in
1m

20ft
6.10m

Weigh in Amateur boxers must weigh in, naked, on the day of the contest. Professionals must weigh in at 11.00am for afternoon tournaments or at 1.00pm for evening tournaments. (Licenses are issued only after very strict medical examination.)

Officials In both amateur and professional contests there are:
1 a referee, who is responsible for controlling the bout;
2 judges, who score the contest (5 in amateur and 3 in professional boxing);
3 a timekeeper;
4 an official second and 1 assistant second to aid the boxer in the intervals between rounds (up to four seconds are allowed in professional contests).
In amateur boxing there is also a scoring jury, whose duty it is to supervise the work of the officiating panel of judges.

Referees In Great Britain professional bouts are scored only by the referee; elsewhere the referee acts as one of three judges.
The referee is always responsible for:
looking after the boxers in the ring;
administering cautions when necessary;
controlling the corners;
giving the count;
stopping the contest when necessary.
Seconds must leave the ring when ordered by the referee. They must not coach during a round. They are permitted certain medical equipment for treating cuts and injuries.

Weight categories	Amateur (AIBA)		Professional (WBC)	
	lb	**kg**	**lb**	**kg**
Light flyweight	106	48	108	49
Flyweight	112	51	112	51
Bantamweight	119	54	118	53.5
Featherweight	126	57	126	57
Junior lightweight	–	–	130	59
Lightweight	132	60	135	61
Light welterweight	140	63.5	140	63.5
Welterweight	148	67	147	66.6
Light middleweight	156.5	71	154	70
Middleweight	165	75	160	72.5
Light heavyweight	179	81	175	79
Cruiserweight	–	–	195	88.5
Heavyweight	201	91	+195	+88.5
Superheavyweight	+201	+91	–	–

AIBA (International Amateur Boxing Association)
WBC (World Boxing Council)

Scoring
Bouts can be won:
on points;
by a count-out (for a count of 10 seconds);
on a stoppage by the referee;
by the opposition being unable to continue (retirement);
on a disqualification.
Points decisions Each round in a contest is worth a fixed number of points to the winner.
In amateur boxing the winner of a round receives 20 points, and his opponent proportionately fewer. When boxers are equal in merit, each receives 20 points. Auxiliary points (three of which make up one point) are awarded for scoring blows. At the end of the contest auxiliary points may be awarded for attack, defense, leading off or for style.
In a dual match, two clubs or two nations may agree to a draw decision when the majority of the judges scored the competition equally.
Similar principles apply in professional boxing. The maximum number of points for a round is 10 in most countries.
Points are awarded for attack, defense, showing initiative, and for style. If scores are equal at the end, the bout is declared a draw. (To score, all blows must be delivered with the knuckle part of the closed glove and must land on the target area.)

Gloves 8oz gloves are worn by amateurs up to 148lb and professionals. Amateur boxers over 148lb wear 10oz gloves.

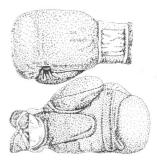

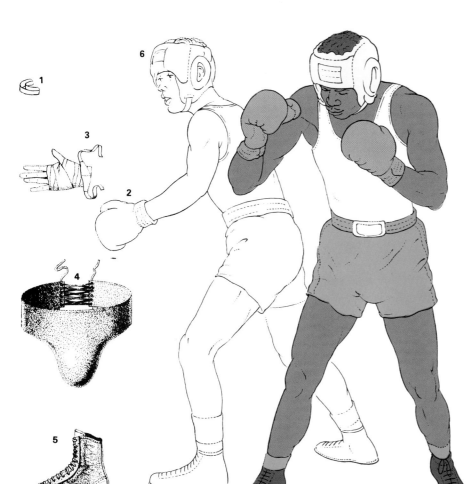

Fouls Punching on certain areas outside the target is illegal – eg below the belt (**1**), the back of the neck (**2**), and in the kidneys (**3**).
Pivot or backhanded blows are also fouls, as is hitting with the butt of the hand (**4**), the wrist, or the elbow (**5**). It is illegal to hit continually with the inside of the glove (**6**).
Too much body contact is also against the rules, such as butting (**7**), careless use of the head, shouldering, and wrestling.
Other fouls include:
persistently ducking below the waistline (**8**);
failing to step back from a clinch when ordered to "break";
hitting on the break;
deliberately punching an opponent on the floor or when he is falling (**9**);
holding onto the ropes with one or both hands for defense or attack;
not trying to win.
The referee may rule as a foul any act that he considers to be outside the rules. Fouls are punished by a warning – with consequent loss of points.
Persistent misconduct leads to disqualification.

Equipment for amateur and professional boxers:
1 gumshield (mouthpiece)
2 gloves
3 tape
4 protector
5 boots
6 headguards (amateurs only)

Tape On each hand amateurs are allowed up to 8ft 4in of 2in soft dry bandage or up to 6ft 6in of Velpeau dry bandage. Professionals are allowed, on each hand, up to 18ft of 2in soft bandage, or 9ft (below middleweight) or 11ft of 1in zinc oxide tape. Tape must not be put over the knuckles.

Dress Amateurs wear shorts and vests; professionals wear only shorts. Boots are worn.

Duration In competitive amateur boxing:
contestants in the open (senior) category box three 3-minute rounds;
intermediate class contestants usually box three 3-minute rounds;
novices box three 2-minute rounds.
Professional title contests are over twelve 3-minute rounds;
title eliminator contests are over ten or twelve 3-minute rounds;
other contests are over six 2-minute rounds, or six, eight, or ten 3-minute rounds, depending on the experience of the contestants.
(There is a 1-minute break between rounds in all contests.)

The bout The referee first calls the boxers together to ensure that the rules are understood. The boxers then shake hands.
(In professional contests the handshake is repeated at the start of the final round; amateurs must shake hands at the start of the third round.)
During the bout boxers must obey all the referee's instructions.
At the knock-down, the standing boxer is ordered to a neutral corner, and the referee takes up the count. If the fallen boxer rises, the count is over (though in amateur and some professional contests there is a mandatory count of eight). The boxers then continue.

In both professional and amateur boxing, if a boxer is given a count at the end of a round, the count must continue either to eight or, if he is unable to resume, to ten, before the gong is sounded for the end of the round.
The referee has the power to end the contest if he judges that one boxer is unfit to continue.
The referee raises the winner's hand when the contest is over.
Standing count In amateur boxing a boxer who receives one of a series of hard punches may still be standing upright and yet be counted. (This rule was introduced to better protect amateur boxers against physical damage.)

1

2

3

4

7
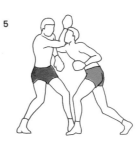

5

8

6

9
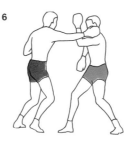

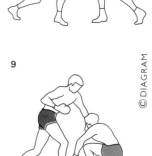

©DIAGRAM

Wrestling

Wrestling is an ancient sport with two modern Olympic styles: freestyle and Greco-Roman. (Contestants may not use their legs in Greco-Roman wrestling.) Contestants take part in a series of elimination rounds. Only the first three winners from each pool qualify for the final. Placing is by a system of classification points.

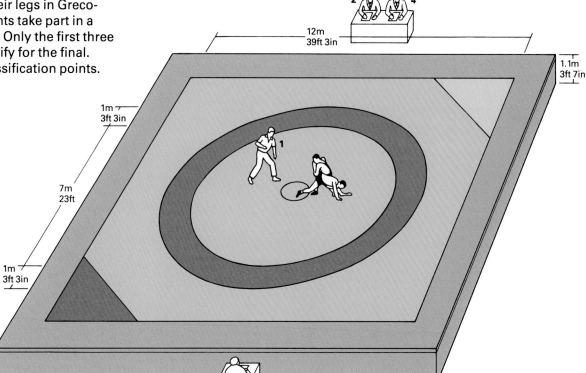

The mat for international contests has a circular contest area 9m in diameter. There is a center circle 1m in diameter. The two diagonal corners of the mat are marked in red and blue. If the mat is on a platform, it must be no more than 1.1m high.

Dress Tight-fitting, one piece, red or blue singlet, undergarment and handkerchief. Light knee-guards are permitted; bandages only when prescribed by a doctor. Shoes must not have heels, nailed soles, rings or buckles. Covering the skin with oils or grease is forbidden. Wrestlers must be clean-shaven unless their beards are several months old. Fingernails must be cut short.

Officials:
1 referee
2 mat chairman
3 judge
4 mat controller (timekeeper)

Mat chairman is the chief official. Only he communicates with the judge and referee. He indicates decisions by raising a wrestler's color.

Start of bout Wrestlers shake hands in the center of the mat, are inspected, and return to their corners until the referee's whistle. Each round starts in the standing position (**1**).

Wrestling on the ground Wrestling may continue if a wrestler is brought to the ground. The wrestler underneath may counter his opponent and get up (**2**) with hands and knees at least 20cm apart. He may change position only when the referee has blown his whistle after the uppermost wrestler has made first contact by placing both hands on the other's shoulder blades.

Referee wears white, with a red armband on one arm and a blue armband on the other. His duties are to: start, interrupt, and end bouts; warn or caution wrestlers; indicate points scored and falls; inspect wrestlers at the start of each bout; and stop a bout by making a T sign to the timekeeper if wrestlers are injured. He must not make untimely interventions or obstruct the view of officials or the public if a fall is likely.

Judge raises his baton with the appropriate color to declare points and gives a score sheet to the mat chairman when a bout ends.

Duration The duration of the bout is 5 minutes without a break. The timekeeper announces the time every minute. At the end of the bout, the timekeeper rings the bell and the referee then blows his whistle; no action is valid between the bell and whistle.

If a wrestler is forced to halt for any reason beyond his control, the referee stops the bout; the bout ceases if interruptions exceed 2 minutes.

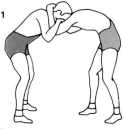

Standing position

The uppermost wrestler must not resume by jumping on his opponent. A wrestler who has brought his opponent to the ground must be active; if both wrestlers are passive they must resume in a standing position.

Kneeling position

Placing in danger A wrestler is placed in danger (of a fall) when he goes beyond 90°, with his back turned to the mat, and resists with the upper part of his body. Examples occur when a wrestler: forms a bridge (**3**) to avoid a fall;

The bridge

rests on his elbows to keep his shoulders off the mat; is lying on one shoulder with the other shoulder 90° beyond the vertical line; is turned with his chest or stomach to the mat to create a placing in danger position after his upper body has passed through 90°.

The fall

The fall (**4**) Both shoulders must be in contact with the mat. A fall is signaled by the referee striking the mat with his hand and blowing his whistle.

Category	Weight limits	
	lb	kg
Light flyweight	105.8	48
Flyweight	114.6	52
Bantamweight	125.6	57
Featherweight	136.7	62
Lightweight	149.9	68
Welterweight	163.1	74
Middleweight	180.7	82
Light heavyweight	198.4	90
Heavyweight	220.4	100
Heavyweight plus	286.6	130

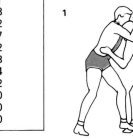

Wrestling on the edge of the mat If the wrestler who is underneath is within the limits of the mat (even if one competitor has both legs, and the other one or both legs off the mat), the bout continues for as long as the wrestling takes place within the confines of the mat.
If either wrestler executes a hold outside of the limits and so puts himself and his opponent off the mat, the bout must be interrupted and resumed standing in the center of the mat.
If the head and shoulders of the wrestler underneath go off the mat, the bout must be stopped.

Termination of bout A bout is terminated when: both shoulders of a wrestler simultaneously touch the mat when his opponent is in control (fall);
when a 15 point differential in score occurs (technical superiority);
at the conclusion of 5 minutes wrestling and one wrestler has a point advantage;
sudden death overtime is used to decide a winner when the bout ends in a draw with equal points having been scored. The first point scored wins the match; there is no time limit;
when a third caution is given to a wrestler, he is disqualified.

Scoring a bout
One point is scored for: bringing an opponent to the mat with no back exposure;
moving from the underneath to the uppermost position in control;

applying a correct hold without causing an opponent to touch the mat with his head or shoulder.
Two points are scored: if an opponent is put in a rolling fall from *par terre*;
if an opponent rolls from side to side to form a bridge using the elbows and shoulders.
Three points are scored for: taking an opponent from the standing position to an immediate position of danger.
Five points are scored for: a high amplitude throw to an immediate position of danger.
The final is contested by the last three contestants. If any finalists have not met in previous rounds, they must take part in a final bout. If they have met in previous rounds, the penalty points for such bouts are carried forward and they do not meet again.
The results The competition is won by the finalist with the least penalty points. If two finalists have equal penalty points, the winner is the contestant who defeated the other.
If three finalists have equal penalty points, in both the final and during earlier bouts, they are rated by the number of falls, wins on points, and draws. If the tie is still unbroken, the winner is the wrestler with least cautions in the final.
If none of these tie-breaking procedures produces a result, the competition is declared drawn.

Fouls The laws forbid:
1 stepping on an opponent's feet;
2 touching an opponent's face between his eyebrows and mouth;
3 gripping the throat
4 forcing an elbow or knee into an opponent's stomach or abdomen;
5 gripping the mat edge;
6 pulling an opponent's hair, flesh, ears, private parts, or costume;
twisting his fingers or toes; brawling, kicking, throttling and pushing;
applying holds liable to endanger life, fracture limbs, or torture into submission;
bending an opponent's arm more than 90°;
head holds using both hands;
scissor grips by the legs to an opponent's head or body;
speaking to a wrestler during a bout;
forcing an opponent's arm behind his back at less than 90°;
lifting an opponent from a bridge to throw him onto the mat (a bridge must be pressed down, but not collapsed by pushing in the direction of the head).
A wrestler applying a hold from behind, in the standing position, with his opponent's head turned down, may only throw the opponent to the side and must ensure that part of his own body, other than his feet, touches the mat before his opponent's body.
A double head-hold (double Nelson) is permitted, but

must be applied from the side and the legs must not be used against an opponent's body.
Greco-Roman wrestling also forbids:
seizing an opponent's legs; gripping an opponent with the legs;
using the legs to push, lift or exert pressure when they are touching an opponent's body.
Passive obstruction is: continually obstructing an opponent's holds;
continually lying flat on the mat;
willfully running off the mat; holding both an opponent's hands.
Cautions are given for: passive obstruction (after a verbal warning);
lack of sportsmanship; infringements and fouls; failing to heed the referee; arguing with the judge or mat chairman.
When the referee cautions a contestant, he raises one arm.
After two cautions, the mat chairman co-opts the controller to assist him.
A competitor loses the bout if he receives three cautions (for which there must be a majority decision of three, including the mat chairman and controller).
Disqualification A contestant may be disqualified from an entire competition for a serious offense or for being disqualified twice for passivity.

Penalty points The result of a bout is converted into classification points using the official table.
Elimination Contestants are eliminated after 2 losses. Elimination rounds continue until only three wrestlers remain in each pool.

Classification points – positive scoring system		
Result of the bout	Winner's points	Loser's points
Fall	4	0
Technical superiority (15-point margin)	4	0
Injury default or withdrawal	4	0
Forfeit (loser eliminated)	4	0
Disqualification for misconduct	4	0
Superiority (12–14 point margin)		
Loser has technical points	3.5	0.5
Loser has no technical points	3.5	0
Decision (1–11 point margin)		
Loser has technical points	3	1
Loser has no technical points	3	0
Disqualification for passivity		
Winner leads by 12–14 points	3.5	0
Winner has scored technical points	3	0
Winner has not scored technical points	2	0
Both wrestlers disqualified for passivity	0	0

Judo

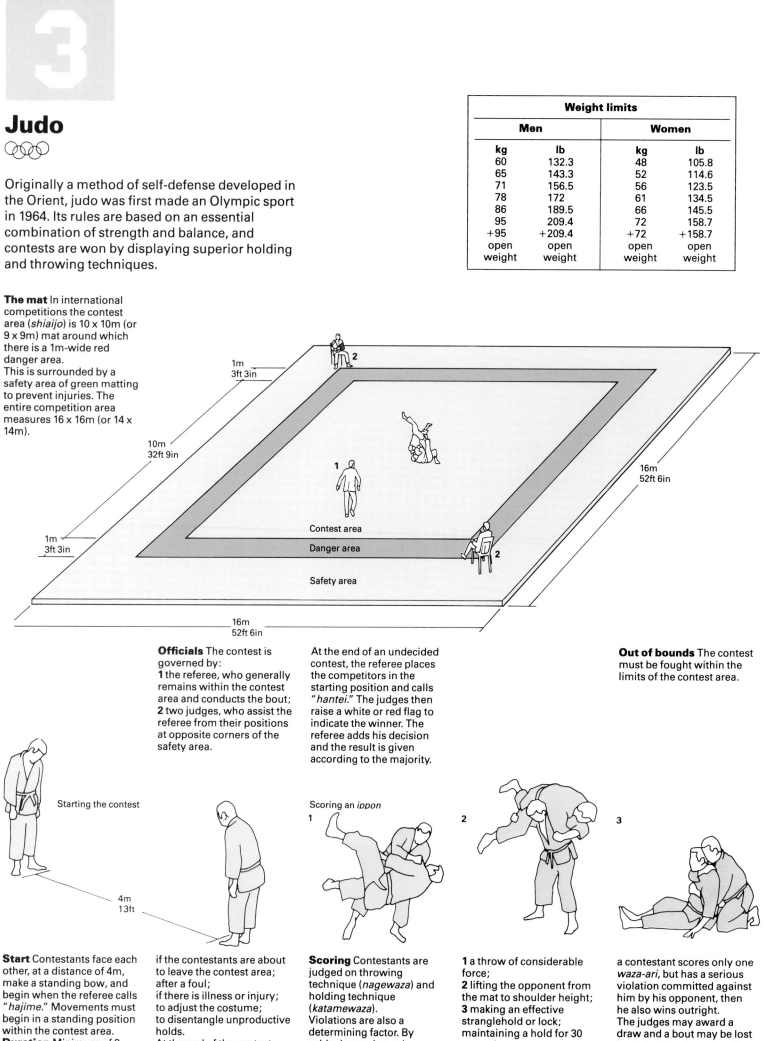

Originally a method of self-defense developed in the Orient, judo was first made an Olympic sport in 1964. Its rules are based on an essential combination of strength and balance, and contests are won by displaying superior holding and throwing techniques.

Weight limits			
Men		Women	
kg	lb	kg	lb
60	132.3	48	105.8
65	143.3	52	114.6
71	156.5	56	123.5
78	172	61	134.5
86	189.5	66	145.5
95	209.4	72	158.7
+95	+209.4	+72	+158.7
open weight	open weight	open weight	open weight

The mat In international competitions the contest area (*shiaijo*) is 10 x 10m (or 9 x 9m) mat around which there is a 1m-wide red danger area.
This is surrounded by a safety area of green matting to prevent injuries. The entire competition area measures 16 x 16m (or 14 x 14m).

1m
3ft 3in

10m
32ft 9in

1m
3ft 3in

16m
52ft 6in

16m
52ft 6in

Contest area

Danger area

Safety area

Officials The contest is governed by:
1 the referee, who generally remains within the contest area and conducts the bout;
2 two judges, who assist the referee from their positions at opposite corners of the safety area.

At the end of an undecided contest, the referee places the competitors in the starting position and calls "*hantei*." The judges then raise a white or red flag to indicate the winner. The referee adds his decision and the result is given according to the majority.

Out of bounds The contest must be fought within the limits of the contest area.

Starting the contest

4m
13ft

Scoring an *ippon*

1

2

3

Start Contestants face each other, at a distance of 4m, make a standing bow, and begin when the referee calls "*hajime*." Movements must begin in a standing position within the contest area.
Duration Minimum of 3 minutes and maximum of 20, arranged in advance. The contest may be temporarily halted, on the call of "*matte*":

if the contestants are about to leave the contest area;
after a foul;
if there is illness or injury;
to adjust the costume;
to disentangle unproductive holds.
At the end of the contest competitors return to their starting places, face each other and make a standing bow after the decision.

Scoring Contestants are judged on throwing technique (*nagewaza*) and holding technique (*katamewaza*).
Violations are also a determining factor. By achieving an *ippon* (one point) a competitor wins outright. *Ippon* is awarded for:

1 a throw of considerable force;
2 lifting the opponent from the mat to shoulder height;
3 making an effective stranglehold or lock; maintaining a hold for 30 seconds.
If the contestant just fails to make an *ippon*, he may be awarded a *waza-ari*. Two *waza-ari* equal one *ippon*. If

a contestant scores only one *waza-ari*, but has a serious violation committed against him by his opponent, then he also wins outright.
The judges may award a draw and a bout may be lost by default. In the event of injury, illness or accident, the referee and judges decide on the result.

Dress The costume (*judogi*) is white or off-white. The jacket (**1**) must be long enough to cover the thighs and have a minimum reach to the fists when the arms are fully extended downward. The body of the jacket must be wide enough to cross over at the level of the bottom of the rib-cage with a minimum overlap of 20cm (7.8in).

The trousers (**2**) must be long enough to cover the legs.

The belt (**3**) fastens the jacket at the waist and is long enough to go twice round the body. It is tied with a large square knot and its ends are about 15cm (6in) long.

A white or red sash distinguishes contestants.

Groundwork Contestants may apply ground techniques (*ne-waza*):
if the attacker moves directly into *ne-waza* after throwing his opponent;
when one contestant falls;
when *ne-waza* follows a successful stranglehold or lock in the standing position;
after any skillful technique that does not qualify as a throw;
or in any other situation in which a contestant falls to the ground.

Fouls It is forbidden to:
1 sweep an attacking opponent's supporting leg from the inside (although it is permissible to hook his instep);
2 attempt to throw an opponent by entwining a leg around his leg (*kawazu-gake*);
3 fall back deliberately when an opponent is clinging to the back and when either contestant controls the other's movements;
4 adopt an excessively defensive attitude either physically or by not attacking;
5 pull the opponent down in order to start groundwork;
6 take hold of the opponent's foot or leg in order to change to *ne-waza*, unless exceptional skill is shown;
7 put a hand, arm, foot, or leg directly on the opponent's face or to take his *judogi* in the mouth;
maintain, while lying on the back, a leg hold around the opponent's neck when he manages to stand, or to position the knees to lift him up;
apply joint locks (*kansetsu-waza*) except at the elbow joint;
endanger the opponent's spine or neck;
lift an opponent who is lying on his back off the mat in order to drive him back onto the mat;
break back fingers;
intentionally go outside or force the opponent to go outside the contest area;
continuously hold the opponent's costume on the same side with both hands, or the belt or bottom of the jacket with one hand;
seize the inside of the sleeve or bottom of the trousers;
continuously stand with fingers interlocked with the opponent's;
deliberately disarray the costume;
wind the belt around the opponent;
disregard the referee;
make derogatory remarks or gestures;
do anything contrary to the spirit of judo.

1

2

3

4

5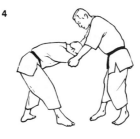

6

7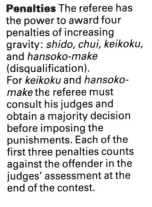

Penalties The referee has the power to award four penalties of increasing gravity: *shido, chui, keikoku,* and *hansoko-make* (disqualification).
For *keikoku* and *hansoko-make* the referee must consult his judges and obtain a majority decision before imposing the punishments. Each of the first three penalties counts against the offender in the judges' assessment at the end of the contest.

©DIAGRAM

Karate

Karate is a practical, empty-handed fighting technique, a formal method of physical and mental training, and a competitive combat sport. Contests of sport karate are held as sparring matches, in which some karate techniques are not permitted and only a few used very often. To avoid injuries all punches, blows, strikes, and kicks are controlled and pulled back before contact.

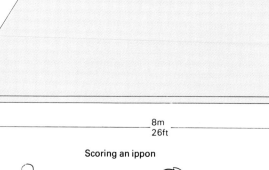

Match area A flat, 8m-square surface without obstacles.
Officials
1 a referee;
2 a judge;
3 an arbitrator;
4 timekeeper(s), record keeper(s) and caller-announcers.
The referee conducts the match (including announcing the start, the suspension, and the end of the match); awards points; imposes penalties and issues warnings.
He may extend the duration of a match when necessary. The referee gives all commands.
When the judge signals an effective technique, the referee considers the signal and gives a judgement.
The judge assists the referee. He takes part in consultation with the referee and arbitrator when invited. The judge carefully observes the actions of the contestants and signals to the referee an opinion in the following cases:
when an *ippon* or *waza-ari* is observed;
if a prohibited act and/or technique is committed (or about to be);
when an injury or illness of a contestant is noticed;
when either or both of the contestants have moved out of the competition area.
The arbitrator oversees the operation of the match and the actions of the referee and/or judge and, when requested, he may express an opinion to the referee. He supervises and directs the timekeeper.
Procedure The referee and judge take up their positions. The contestants stand facing each other with their toes to the starting line and bow to one another.
On the referee's call of "*shobu sanbon hajime*," the match begins.
Halting the match The referee stops the bout on the call of "*yame*" when a

Target area

Scoring an ippon

scoring technique is seen. The contestants take up their original positions. The referee identifies the relevant score and awards *waza-ari* or *ippon*. The referee then restarts the bout by calling "*tsuzukete hajime*." When a contestant has scored *sanbon* during a bout, the referee calls "*yame*" and orders the contestants back to their standing lines as he returns to his. The winner is then declared and the bout is ended at this point.
Temporary halts The referee may temporarily halt the match when:
both or either of the contestants are out of the area (or when the judge signals an exit);
the referee orders the contestant to adjust his *gi*;

the referee or judge notices that a contestant has contravened the rules or appears about to do so;
the referee considers that one or both of the contestants cannot continue with the bout owing to injuries, illness or other causes;
a contestant seizes his opponent and does not perform an immediate effective technique (the referee will separate them);
one or both contestants fall or are thrown and no effective techniques are immediately forthcoming.
No score If the match ends with no *ippon* scored, the winning decision is given by *hantei* (the referee consults with the judge to arrive at a decision).

Competitions may be divided into the team match and the individual match.
In team matches each team must have an odd number of contestants. The contestants are all members of a team. There are no fixed reserves. The fighting order can be changed for each round but, once notified, it cannot then be changed.
Team matches may be organized in one of two ways:
a) individual contestants are paired off for fights and the winning team is the one with the most individual winners;
b) a winning individual continues to meet new opponents from the other team until he is defeated.
In both cases, ties are broken by the greater number of *ippons*, then by the greater

number of *waza-ari* and wins by decision.
Fouls and disqualifications count as *ippons*. If a tie still remains, then a deciding bout is held.
Deciding bouts, if held, are between one chosen representative from each team.
In the event of a continuing tie, there is an extention ("*encho-sen*"). If the tie persists, each team selects a further representative, and so on, until a decision is obtained.
If there is no decision after a bout of an individual match, an extension is fought.
In the event of a tied "*encho-sen*" in an individual bout, the majority decision of the panel will be announced by the referee.

Dress Contestants must wear a white karate-gi. One must wear a red belt on top of the belt, the other a white belt. Each competitor must wear an identification sign such as a number on the chest or the back. Approved mitts are compulsory. Gum shield, boxes and soft shin pads are allowed.
Protective or safety devices may only be used if permitted by the referee council.

Duration A match usually lasts 2–3 minutes, but this may be extended to 5 minutes. Stoppages for injury or inquiry are not included in the match time. The timekeeper signals with a gong or buzzer at the end of the match and 30 seconds before the end.

Winning To win a bout it is necessary;
a) to be the first contestant to score three *ippons* or 6 *waza-ari*, or a combination of the two totaling *sanbon*;
b) for the other contestant to be disqualified;
c) to be awarded the bout by decision of the referee and judge.

Disqualification may be due to repeated fouls after warning. It may also be imposed if the contestant:
fails to obey the referee;
becomes so excited that he jeopardizes the smooth running of the bout;
acts in a dangerous manner and deliberately violates the rules concerning prohibited behavior;
breaks rules with malicious intent; or
breaks match rules in some other way.

No score

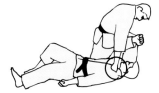

Scoring is by using recognized competition karate techniques in good form, on the permitted scoring area on the opponent's body. Actual physical contact is strictly limited and is not required for scoring. Light contact is permitted on the body. Only very light contact is permitted on the face and head.
To score, the technique must have the potential to penetrate deep into the target.
Excessive physical contact always results in disqualification.
Ippon (one point) is awarded for a blow that is struck with: good form, correct attitude, strong vigor, *zanshin* (constant alertness of mind),

proper timing, and correct distancing.
Blows may be thrusts, snaps, hits or kicks.
Waza-ari (half point) is awarded for a blow that is less correct but still effective – if, for example:
the opponent is moving away from the blow;
the blow is slightly off target;
the blow is delivered from an unstable position.
A full point is still given for less powerful blows if:
the attack was delivered just at the moment when the opponent began to move toward the attacker;
the attack was delivered just at the moment when the opponent was thrown off balance by the attacker;
a combination of effective

blows was applied;
the opponent had lost his fighting spirit and turned his back on the attacker;
the attack was delivered on defenseless parts of the opponent.

Not ippons An *ippon* is not awarded if an attacker fails to deliver a blow the moment he has seized or thrown his opponent.
If two opponents score simultaneously, neither point is counted.
Scoring techniques delivered simultaneously with the end of time signal are counted, as are techniques delivered if an attacker is inside the match area but his opponent outside it.

Victory by decision In the absence of a *sanbon* score, or of a defeat caused by a foul or disqualification during the bout, a decision is taken on the basis of the following considerations:
whether there have been any *ippons* or *waza-ari* awarded;
the attitude, fighting spirit and strength shown by the contestants;
the superiority of tactics and techniques.

Protests A contestant's team officer may protest against a decision by appealing to the arbitrator, who then consults the referee and judge.

Injuries If a contestant is badly hurt it is usually because a foul has been committed against him by

Penalties Every fighter who contravenes the rules is warned or penalized. The nature of the penalty is announced by the referee after consultation with the referee panel. Warnings may be imposed for attempted minor infractions of the rules. Warnings may also be imposed for the first instance of any minor infractions.
Keikoku is imposed for minor infractions for which a warning has previously been given in that bout, or for infractions not sufficiently serious to merit *Hansoku-chui*. A *waza-ari* is added to the opponent's score.
Hansoku-chui is usually imposed for infractions for which a half point penalty has previously been given in that bout. An *ippon* is added to the opponent's score.
Hansoku is imposed following a very serious infraction. It results in the opponent's score being raised to *sanbon*.
Shikkaku is disqualification from the tournament, competition or match. The opponent's score is raised to *sanbon*.

Fouls The following are fouls:
1) direct attacks to the body other than the arms and legs;
2) dangerous techniques, such as blows to the eyes or testicles;
3) dangerous throws;
4) persistent attacks directly on the shin;
5) direct attacks to the hips, knee joints, or insteps;
6) unnecessary grabbing, clinching, or body crashing;
7) excessive moving out of the match area, or moves wasting time;
8) ignoring contest rules;
9) unsporting behavior.

his opponent. The opponent is disqualified and the injured contestant wins the match
If a contestant refuses to continue, or requests permission to quit after a minor injury is the loser. He loses the contest if he requests permission to quit for reasons other than injury.
If an injury is not the responsibility of either contestant, or if both competitors are injured simultaneously and both are responsible, the bout is awarded to the contestant who has amassed the most points at the time. If the point score is equal, then the referee consults with the judge to obtain a decision.

© DIAGRAM

Kendo

One of the traditional Japanese martial arts, kendo is presented as a modern competitive sport. Two contestants, wearing protective armor, fight with bamboo swords. Footwork is vital – kendoka use short, fast, gliding steps, and sometimes a jump for counter attacks.

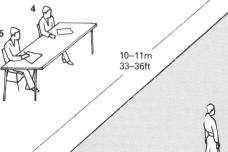

10–11m
33–36ft

10–11m
33–36ft

Effective cut or thrust

No effective blow

Cannot judge

Interrupt the match

Area A smooth, wooden-floored square area, usually 10×10m or 11×11m. The center is marked with a cross or circle, the boundary with lines 5–10cm wide. Two starting lines are also marked. Around the boundary is a clear surround space at least 1.5m wide.

Duration 3 or 5 minutes. Extra time if needed for a result: 3 minutes. Interruptions are not included in time.

Officials
One chief (1) and two assistant judges (2) inside the area, two of them "forward" and one "rear." Using red and white flags, these judges control conduct, point out and rule on valid techniques and infringements and, where necessary, decide the victor. Line judge (3). Timekeeper and assistants (4). Scorekeeper and assistants (5).

Signals used by judges in the area:
effective cut or thrust, flag raised diagonally upward in the direction of the scorer;
no effective blow, both flags waved downward in front of the body;
cannot judge, both flags held crossed downward in front of the body, red flag out;
interrupt the match, both flags raised.

Announcements *Men ari* (or *koto, do* or *tsuki ari*): successful scoring technique at the area named;
Yame: interruption;
Nikomme: re-start after one point is scored;
Shobu: re-start after one point each;
Encho hajime: re-start for extra time;
Shobu ari: end of match, a victory;
Hikiwake: a draw.
Contestants are separated:
a) if a contestant falls or drops his *shinai,* and his opponent does not immediately strike an effective blow (re-start at the starting lines);

b) if contestants are in a prolonged hilt-to-hilt with no apparent intention of striking a blow (re-start at the same point).
Procedure Contestants bow, cross *shinai,* and take up starting positions (both standing or both squatting). The match begins on the chief judge's call of *Hajime* and continues until his final call of *Yame.*

Dress
1 *Keikogi* (shirt)
2 *Hakama* (ankle-length "divided skirt")
3 *Hachimaki* (toweling headcloth)

Protective equipment
4 *Men* (mask)
5 *Kote* (gauntlets)
6 *Do* (breastplate)
7 *Tare* (apron)

Shinai Made of equal sections of bamboo, held together by leather and strings at the tip, halfway point, and hilt.
If one *shinai* is used: it must be under 118cm in length and weigh 468gm.
If two *shinai* are used: the longer has a maximum length of 110cm and must weigh 375gm, and the shorter has a maximum length of 60cm and a minimum weight of 265gm.

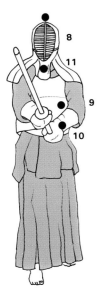

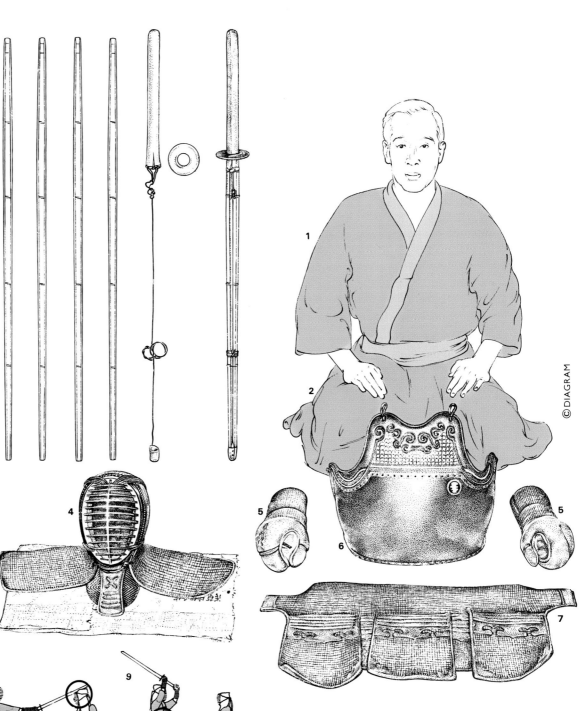

Scoring techniques
Cuts (made with the forward third of the *shinai*); thrusts (with the tip of the *shinai*).

Scoring areas
For cuts:
8 left and right temples;
9 left and right breastplate;
10 left and right wrist (left wrist permitted only when the left hand is at shoulder height or higher;
11 For thrusts: the throat.

Effective techniques One point is awarded for a blow delivered with full spirit and correct form. The vote of one judge is sufficient if the others are undecided. Techniques are still effective if delivered as the opponent drops his *shinai*, steps or falls out of bounds, or as time is called.

Result The winner is the first to score two points, or the contestant with the higher score by the time limit.
In case of equality at time, the judges may declare a draw, award a decision to one of the contestants, or call for extra time. If there is extra time, the winner is the first contestant to score. Team matches may be to one of two systems: pairing or elimination (see karate for details).

Fouls A competitor may not:
place his foot outside the match area;
fall with any part of his body outside the area;
use his *shinai* as a prop to prevent his body from going outside the area;
trip his opponent;
illegally shove or thrust with his *shinai*;
strike or thrust at his opponent's unprotected parts;
grasp his opponent with the hands;
use his *shinai* hilt to break his opponent's grasp of his *shinai* hilt;
grasp his opponent's *shinai* above the hilt after dropping his own *shinai*;
use disrespectful or undignified acts or words.

Penalties Using disrespectful or undignified acts or words results in disqualification for the offender and two points for his opponent.
Other fouls result in a warning, and one point to the opponent after the third foul in a match.

Injuries The match ends if a contestant is injured so that he cannot continue.
If his opponent caused the injury, the injured man wins with one point;
otherwise, the injured man forfeits the match and his opponent is awarded two points.
If a contestant requests an end or halt without sufficient reason, he forfeits the match and his opponent is awarded two points.

Aikido

There are two distinct types of aikido: competitive and non-competitive. The sport described below is a competitive fighting sport, based on an ancient Japanese system of self-defense, and is referred to as *Tomiki* aikido. Force is not met with counter-force but with avoiding action, enabling the defender to take advantage of the attacker's temporary loss of balance to score with a successful aikido technique.

Area At least 9m square, preferably with a surrounding safety area.
Types of competition *Kata* is a formal event. *Ninin dori, tanto randori* and *randori kyoghi* are three types of fighting event.
Dress As for judo. For identification, one contestant wears a red belt (or string or tape at the belt); the other, white. Metal badges and jewelry are prohibited.
Officials For *kata* and *ninin dori,* a minimum of three judges, one of whom acts as senior judge. For *tanto randori* and *randori kyoghi,* one referee in the competition area and two judges positioned outside the area. For all competitions, a recorder and a timekeeper.

9m
29ft 6in

9m
29ft 6in

1 Senior judge
2 Assistant judges
3 Scorer
4 Timekeeper

Terms used in aikido are:
hajime, begin;
soremade, finish (of round or fight);
yame matte, stop (the competitors return to their initial positions and timing is interrupted);
ippon, one point;
tanto ippon, one point for knife strike;

waza-ari, half point;
waza-ari awazette ippon, second half point, making one full point;
hantei, call for score or judgement;
hikkiwake, draw;
chui, warning.

Referee's signals (for *tanto randori* and *randori kyoghi*) are:
ippon, arm raised above the head;
waza-ari, arm raised to shoulder height;
no score, right hand waved from side to side, above the head or in front of the body;
hajime, rapid lowering of the arm from outstretched position in front of the body or above the head;
hantei, right arm raised centrally above the head.
Judges' signals are made with a red or white flag to indicate each contestant. Competitor outside the area: flag pointed to area edge and waved from side to side.

Competitor stayed in the area: flag raised, hand pointed to the area edge. Scoring technique: flag raised.
Did not see: both flags waved in front of legs.
Vote on judgement: red or white flag raised for a win, both for a draw.

KATA
An open competition in which competitors perform any *kata* of their own choice within a time limit of 2–3 minutes. These must consist of aikido techniques. If the *kata* is unlikely to be known to the judges, a written sequence of techniques must be submitted prior to the competition commencing.
Procedure *Tori* and *Uke* enter the area, advance to the center of the mat and bow to *Joseki.* They turn inwards 4m apart and bow. *Joseki* is in a position to the left of *Tori.*
After the completion of the *kata,* they return to their original positions and bow to each other. They turn to face *Joseki* and await the score.

Each judge writes down his/her score which is passed to the senior judge. The recorder announces the total score. *Tori* and *Uke* bow to *Joseki* and leave the area.
Assessment The *kata* is assessed as follows:
the beginning – avoidance, breaking of balance and correct positioning;
the correct performance of the throw or control;
the finish – *Zanshin* and *Ukemi.*
The overall assessment is based on: posture and movement; co-ordination between *Tori* and *Uke*; pace and purpose.
Scoring Each judge scores up to a maximum of 10 points.

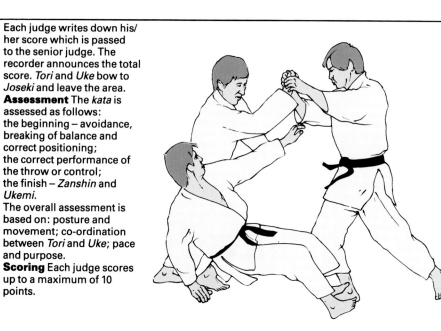

NINIDORI
Three participants work as a team. Each is *Tori* (defender) for 30 seconds while the remaining two take part as *Uke.* The total time is 1½ minutes.
Procedure The team enter the area, advance to the center of the mat in line and bow to *Joseki.*
The first *Tori* takes up position in the center of the mat with *Joseki* to his left and the two *Uke* face *Tori* in a line at a distance of about 2m.
All three bow and the competition commences on the signal *hajime. Yame* is called after 30 seconds. The second and third *Tori* follow the same procedure until completion (*soremade*). The team bow

TANTO RANDORI

Free fighting between two contestants, over two rounds of 2 minutes each. The defender, who is unarmed in the first round, becomes the attacker, armed with a rubber-composition "knife", in the second. The competitor commences the competition with the "knife".

Procedure Competitors take up position in the center, 4m apart. The referee is positioned between the opponents with the first attacker to his right. All three bow to *Joseki* and the competitors then face each other. The attacker collects the knife from the referee, the competitors bow to each other and on *hajime* the contest begins.

Once the referee signals that either the defender or the attacker has scored a point the "knife" changes hands and the roles are reversed. The contest stops at half time (2 minutes) and immediately re-starts with the competitor wearing the white sash as the attacker. At the end of the competition the attacker returns the "knife" to the referee. The referee indicates the winner. The competitors bow to each other, then to *Joseki*, and retire from the area.

Scoring as attacker The target area is the front and rear of the defender from the belt to the shoulder line. A scoring attack must: start from the hip line; be a thrusting movement made after both feet have moved forward;

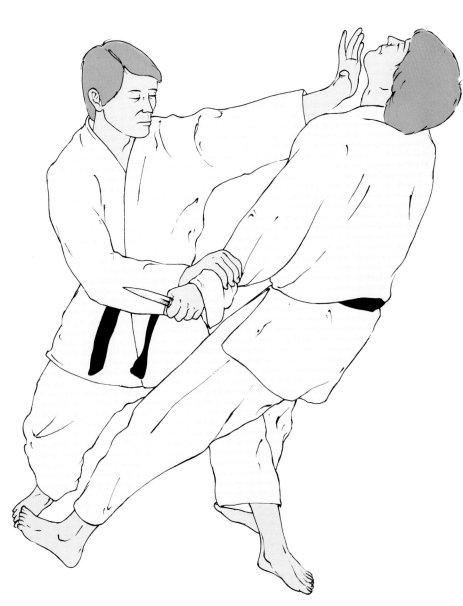

be struck from a proper distance; have the attacking arm fully extended with the knife in the horizontal position at the moment of striking. If the defender falls to the ground during the contest the attacker may score if he strikes immediately and correctly. An attack does not score if it

is deflected by the defender as it hits the target area.

Scoring as defender The defender can score with any skillful aikido technique. One point is scored when the defender performs a correct basic technique. A half-point is scored when the defender makes a successful sacrifice technique; or breaks his opponent's

balance and has control with an aikido lock but the attacker is not taken to the ground. A score is awarded if the attacker drops the "knife" due to a correct defense technique; or if the attacker is thrown out of the area and the defender has been in the area throughout.

Winning If a competitor at any time scores a total of two points, the contest ends and he is declared the winner. If the contest goes to full time, the contestant with the higher number of points wins. If the scores are level at full time, one extension period takes place. If this is indecisive, the winner is the contestant judged to have attempted the most techniques with style.

Fouls Unsporting, dangerous, forbidden, over-forceful, or non-aikido behavior or techniques; grasping the clothing, grappling or preventing action in any other way; disobeying the referee, or stopping and adjusting clothing without his permission; preventing action during the contest; persistently using incorrect attack with the knife; repeatedly stepping outside the area or deliberately forcing an opponent outside the area.

Penalties Fouls make contestants liable to warning, the loss of a half-point or disqualification.

After a score the referee calls *"matte."* Both contestants return to their starting positions. The referee announces *"ippon"* (one point) or *"waza-ari"* (half point) indicating the scorer.

On *"hajime"* the fighting resumes. A technique delivered simultaneously with the end of time scores.

to each other and then face *Joseki* in a line and wait for the total score to be called. Each judge writes down the score which is passed to the senior judge. The recorder announces the total score. The team bow to *Joseki* and leave the area.

Rules The following weapons may be used by the *Uke* for part of the time: *Tanto, Jo, Bokken.*
Attacks must begin one step away from *Tori.*
Only aikido techniques may be used.

Assessment is made on: movement and posture; correctness of technique; variation of attack and defense; speed and stamina; use of competition area; breakfalls.

Scoring As for *kata.*

RANDORI KYOGHI

Aikido free-fighting between two unarmed contestants.

Procedure as for *tanto randori,* except that both competitors are unarmed and compete from *tegatana* position. The competition lasts for 3 minutes, but the fight ends if one contestant scores two full points.

Scoring As for the defender in *tanto randori.*
Competitors attempt to apply techniques or recognized variation of the *randori-no-kata* or counters to these techniques.

After scoring As for *tanto randori.*

Winning The winner is the first contestant to reach two full points. Otherwise the contestant with the higher number of total points at the end is the winner. If these scores are equal, the contestant judged to have attempted the most techniques with style is the winner.

Interruptions, fouls As for *tanto randori.*

© DIAGRAM

Jiu jitsu

Jiu jitsu (ju jitsu) is a traditional Japanese martial art with some early Chinese influences. The modern form of the sport, which has martial and self-defense aspects, is described below. The sport does not meet force with brute strength but rather utilizes psychology, knowledge of anatomy, strategy and skill in movement in order to defeat the opponent. This is achieved by redirecting the opponent's attack and then taking advantage of his loss of balance either to throw, strike, or lock him.

Weight categories for *nage-waza* and *ne-waza*			
Male		**Female**	
kg	**lb**	**kg**	**lb**
under 72	under 159	under 60	under 132
72–85	159–187	60 and over	132 and
over 85	over 187		over

Competition area
Minimum of 12m square with at least a 1m surrounding safety area.
Types of competition
Nage-waza (*tachi-waza*); *ne-waza*; individual demonstration (gauntlet and V-attack).
Competition categories
Individual demonstration event is divided by grade of competitor.
Nage-waza and *ne-waza* are divided into the weight categories shown in the table, as well as by grade.

14m 45ft 11in
12m 39ft 4in
14m 45ft 11in
1m 3ft 3in
1m 3ft 3in
4 or 2
1
2
1
2
1
2
3
3
3
3

1 Senior judge
2 Assistant or side judge
3 Corner judge
4 Timekeeper and recorder

Officials
For *nage-waza* and *ne-waza*, one senior judge in the competition area and two or four corner judges, one timekeeper and recorder. For individual demonstration (V-attack and gauntlet), one assistant judge in the competition area and two to four side judges including one senior judge, one timekeeper (optional) and recorder.
Terms used in jiu jitsu are:
yoi, ready;
hajime, begin;
yame, stop;
matte, used where the judge wants the action stopped, but the positions held;
yoshi, continue;
osaekomi, pinning or hold-down;
toketa, hold-down broken;
ippon, one point/win;
waza-ari, half point;
waza-ari, awazette ippon,

second half point making one full point for win;
hikkiwake, draw;
hantei, call from senior judge for a judgement from corner judges;
chui, warning.
Judges' signals
Senior judge:
hajime, yoshi, hand moved from head height to waist height in front of body once, alternatively, hands at waist height moved inwards once (in *ne-waza* the two contestants may be touched);
yame, hands moved at waist height outwards once or from waist height to above head height once;
matte, both hands outstretched in front of body;
oesaekomi, one hand outstretched from body over contestants;
toketa, one hand waved

rapidly from side to side, palm face down;
waza-ari, arm moved at shoulder height to scoring contestant;
waza-ari awazette ippon, appropriate side arm, moved first to shoulder height then above head height toward scoring contestant;
ippon, appropriate side arm moved in "hands up" position;
hikkiwake, arm moved in cutting action from above head height to shoulder height;
chui, infringing contestant pointed at with straight arm, at eye level.
Corner judge
For a decision the appropriate arm is raised above the head on the winning contestant's side. In *ne-waza* and *nage-waza* corner judges have a red flag

held in the right hand and a white flag held in the left to correspond to the colored belts of the competitors and to their starting positions relative to the senior judge. In the absence of flags the right hand corresponds to red and left hand to white.
NAGE-WAZA
Procedure Competitors bow to each other and to the senior judge. On command *hajime*, competitors attempt to break each other's balance and move into a position to produce a movement which will result in a throw. A successful controlled throw gives a win (*ippon*), and an almost successful throw results in *wazari* being called. If an attempt does not warrant a score, the contestants will be given the command *yoshi* (continue).

Duration is 3 minutes. In the event of no score at the end of this period, then extra time may be given at the discretion of the senior judge.
Scoring
An *ippon* is scored when: the opponent has been thrown, both feet having left the floor, and judged to have landed with at least 50% of the back on the mat.
A *waza-ari* is scored: when the opponent has been thrown, both feet having left the floor, and judged to have landed with less than 50% of the back on the mat; or the opponent has been thrown, one foot having left the floor, and judged to have landed with at least 50% of the back on the mat.
Waza-ari awazette ippon – two *waza-aris* giving one *ippon*.

Dress

Competitors wear a white judo *gi* with appropriate colored belt (*obi*) indicating the standard the competitor has reached. In *ne-waza* and *nage-waza* competition one competitor wears a red belt, one a white belt for identification purposes.

Judges Senior judges wear a white *gi* and *black hakama* (ankle length divided skirt), with sleeveless black over-*gi* and *obi* or over-robe without *obi* (depending on their qualification).
Corner judges wear a white *gi* and black belt and *hakama*.

Fouls It is forbidden to: apply over-forceful dangerous techniques, such as strikes to eyes or testicles;
endanger the opponent's neck or spine;
bend back fingers;
in *ne-waza*, apply locks other than to the arm;
make derogatory remarks or gestures;
disregard or show disrespect to the officials;
exhibit unsporting behavior and do anything contrary to the spirit of jitsu.
A foul may result in;
a private warning by the referee in a quiet voice;
a public warning by the referee in a loud voice (*Chui*);
immediate disqualification by the referee;
disqualification from future competition.

NE-WAZA

Procedure Competitors bow to each other and to the senior judge. They are then told to sit "back-to-back." On *hajime*, they turn and attempt to pin the opponent down on his/her back for 30 seconds.
Alternatively, armlocks or *ajemis* (strangles) may be applied to gain a submission.

Duration is 2 or 3 minutes. In the event of no score at the end of this period then extra time may be given at the discretion of the senior judge.

Scoring

An *ippon* is scored:
by submission (signaled verbally or else by tapping); or
when the opponent is pinned on his back for 30 seconds.
The contest may be stopped by a senior judge in order to prevent possible injury and *ippon* awarded accordingly.

INDIVIDUAL DEMONSTRATION (GAUNTLET AND V-ATTACK)

Procedure *Tori* (defender) bows to side judges then to two lines of *ukes* (attackers) 3m apart who then turn to face inward. *Tori* is given the commands *yoi*, then *hajime* and commences to walk between the two lines of attackers. Attackers attack from front or side with punches, kicks, broken bottle, full bottle, knife, cosh and chain. All weapons are rubber, plastic or wooden. *Tori* then demonstrates appropriate defenses.

After *yame* is called the attackers form in two lines in a "V" shape with the defender at the head of it. On command of *yoshi*, attacks commence from alternate sides in very quick succession. On *yame*, the defender bows to the attackers and to the side judges. The scores are given after all the competitors have finished.

Duration may be either one or two minutes or alternatively when the senior judges have seen a sufficient variety of attacks to enable a score to be given.

Scoring Marks out of 10 are awarded by each judge for style (to include posture, smoothness and use of movement), skill (to include use of mat area, strategy, variation, speed and suitability of defense) and composure (possession of stamina, calmness and awareness under stress conditions). In addition, up to 5 marks may be awarded to individual attackers for quality and intent in attacking, which is added to their gauntlet and V-attack scores to produce a final score.

Fencing

Modern fencing has its roots in the historical traditions of swordsmanship. Two opponents contest an assault or bout using one of three weapons: foil, épée, or sabre.

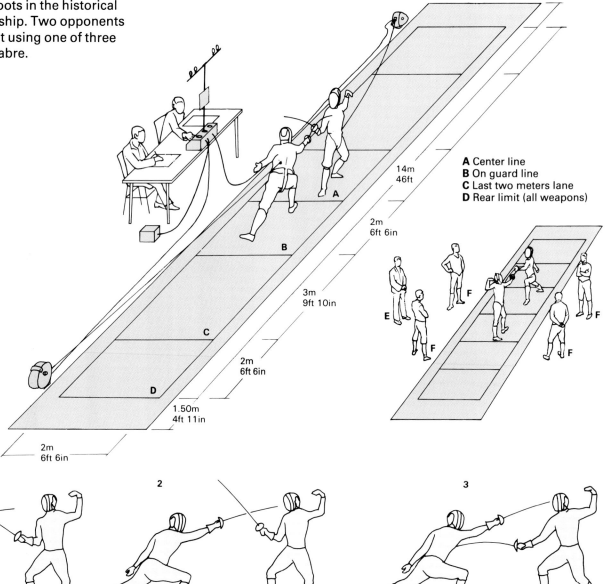

A Center line
B On guard line
C Last two meters lane
D Rear limit (all weapons)

The piste The fencing area must be flat and evenly lit and may be indoors or outdoors. Various surfaces are permitted: wood, linoleum, rubber, plastic and metallic mesh.
The width of the piste is constant, its length is 14m with 2m each end run off.
Officials The president (**E**) controls each bout with the help of four judges (**F**). If electronic apparatus is used he is assisted by only two ground judges. The president and the judges (who must all be amateur) comprise the jury.
Other officials are scorers, timekeepers and electronic equipment supervisors.

Duration of bouts In the preliminary rounds of a competition, the winner is the first person to score 5 hits. The time limit is 6 minutes and the fencers are warned at 5 minutes that there is 1 minute left to fence. If the scores are equal at the end of time, a deciding hit is fenced. If, however, one fencer has more hits than the other, then the fencer with the most hits wins the bout. In the later stages of the competition, the winner is the first person to score 10 hits; in men's events the time limit is 10 minutes and a warning is given at 9 minutes; while in women's events the time limit is 8 minutes and the warning is given at 7 minutes.
A tie in épée, in the preliminary rounds, counts as a defeat for both competitors.
Playing procedure The first fencer called stands with his open side toward the president. The contestants stand facing each other 2m from the center of the piste.
The president orders "*en garde*," asks the competitors if they are ready, then calls "*allez*."
The bout only stops when the president calls "*halte*" which he may do:
after a hit has been given;
at dangerous play;
if a competitor is disarmed;
if a player leaves the piste.
After a valid hit, the contest resumes with both fencers behind the on guard lines. If a hit is invalid, play continues at the spot where fencing was halted.
Hits made before "*allez*" or after "*halte*" is called are annulled.
In non-electric foil and sabre, fencers change ends after one competitor has scored half the possible number of hits.
Attack and defense For a hit to be valid in foil and sabre the fencers' movements must follow the correct phrase. Basically, when attacked a fencer must parry before he can make a riposte. The attacker is the fencer who first threatens the target with his sword arm outstretched (**1**); he remains on the attack until the opponent has parried the attack (**2**).
In the case of a compound attack (several movements made to mislead the opponent), the defending fencer may make a stop hit at his opponent (**3**), provided that hit reaches the target before the final movement of the attack has started.
In simple terms: the phrase must follow the sequence of attack, parry, riposte, counter-riposte. Variations depend on the speed of movement and the line and complexity of the attack.
In épée there is no fencing phrase and no priority of movement. The first to hit his opponent scores one hit.
In all weapons the *flèche* or running attack is allowed.

Scoring To score a hit the fencer has to strike his opponent's target area with the sword point. In sabre a cut with the edge or the top third of the back edge also counts.
The fencer must be on the piste for his hit to count. Hits that land off the target in foil and sabre become valid if the fencer who is hit has taken up an extreme position to avoid being hit on target. A hit off target brings the phrase to an end.
Electronic scoring equipment may be used. Fencers use electronic apparatus that indicates hits on the target area by a system of lights.

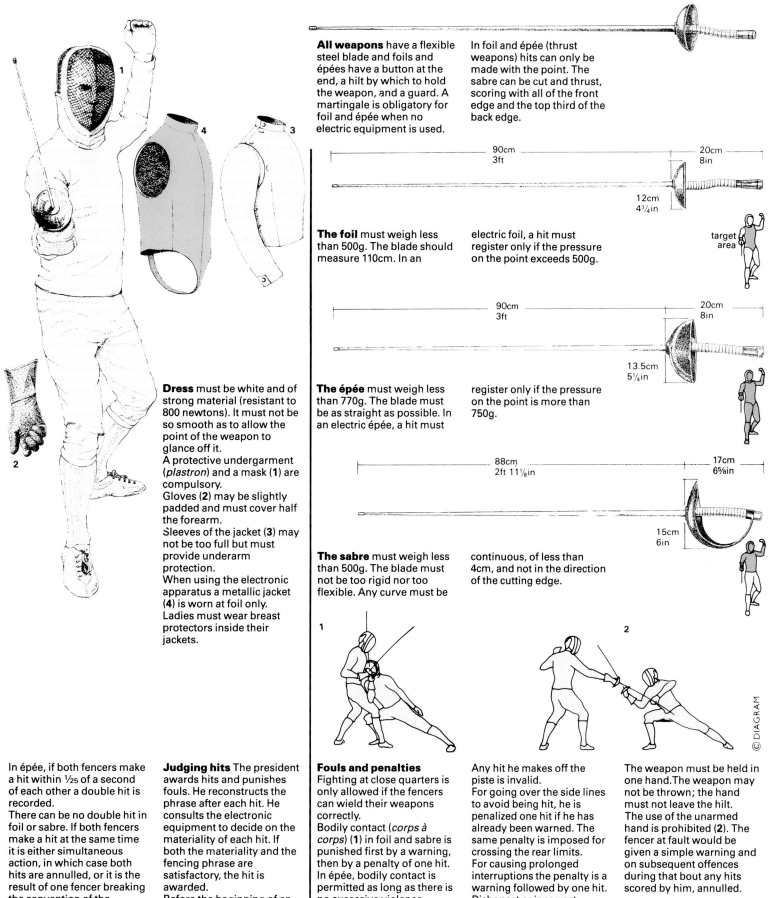

All weapons have a flexible steel blade and foils and épées have a button at the end, a hilt by which to hold the weapon, and a guard. A martingale is obligatory for foil and épée when no electric equipment is used.

In foil and épée (thrust weapons) hits can only be made with the point. The sabre can be cut and thrust, scoring with all of the front edge and the top third of the back edge.

90cm
3ft

20cm
8in

12cm
4¾in

The foil must weigh less than 500g. The blade should measure 110cm. In an electric foil, a hit must register only if the pressure on the point exceeds 500g.

target area

90cm
3ft

20cm
8in

13.5cm
5¼in

The épée must weigh less than 770g. The blade must be as straight as possible. In an electric épée, a hit must register only if the pressure on the point is more than 750g.

88cm
2ft 11⅛in

17cm
6⅝in

15cm
6in

The sabre must weigh less than 500g. The blade must not be too rigid nor too flexible. Any curve must be continuous, of less than 4cm, and not in the direction of the cutting edge.

Dress must be white and of strong material (resistant to 800 newtons). It must not be so smooth as to allow the point of the weapon to glance off it.
A protective undergarment (*plastron*) and a mask (**1**) are compulsory.
Gloves (**2**) may be slightly padded and must cover half the forearm.
Sleeves of the jacket (**3**) may not be too full but must provide underarm protection.
When using the electronic apparatus a metallic jacket (**4**) is worn at foil only.
Ladies must wear breast protectors inside their jackets.

In épée, if both fencers make a hit within 1/25 of a second of each other a double hit is recorded.
There can be no double hit in foil or sabre. If both fencers make a hit at the same time it is either simultaneous action, in which case both hits are annulled, or it is the result of one fencer breaking the convention of the phrase. The president must then decide on the offender and award the hit to his opponent.

Judging hits The president awards hits and punishes fouls. He reconstructs the phrase after each hit. He consults the electronic equipment to decide on the materiality of each hit. If both the materiality and the fencing phrase are satisfactory, the hit is awarded.
Before the beginning of an assault the president must check the electronic equipment to ensure that no false scoring is registered.

Fouls and penalties
Fighting at close quarters is only allowed if the fencers can wield their weapons correctly.
Bodily contact (*corps à corps*) (**1**) in foil and sabre is punished first by a warning, then by a penalty of one hit. In épée, bodily contact is permitted as long as there is no excessive violence.
Ducking is allowed and the unarmed hand may touch the piste, but if the fencers pass each other the president must halt the bout and reposition the contestants. A hit in the act of passing is valid; one made after passing is not.
For crossing the piste limits laterally the fencer loses ground; 1m at foil and 2m at épée and sabre.

Any hit he makes off the piste is invalid.
For going over the side lines to avoid being hit, he is penalized one hit if he has already been warned. The same penalty is imposed for crossing the rear limits.
For causing prolonged interruptions the penalty is a warning followed by one hit. Dishonest or incorrect fencing, intentional brutality, or vindictive actions are punished by a warning. Refusal to obey the orders of the president and other officials is penalized by a warning at the first offense, a penalty hit at the second, and then by exclusion from the competition.

The weapon must be held in one hand. The weapon may not be thrown; the hand must not leave the hilt. The use of the unarmed hand is prohibited (**2**). The fencer at fault would be given a simple warning and on subsequent offences during that bout any hits scored by him, annulled.

© DIAGRAM

Horseshoe pitching

In horseshoe pitching, competitors pitch specially manufactured "horseshoes" at stakes from alternate ends of a court. Although there are two basic methods of scoring, the object in both is to pitch the shoes as near the stake as possible. A game may last for 50 pitches from each player or pair, or until a player or pair scores 40 points.

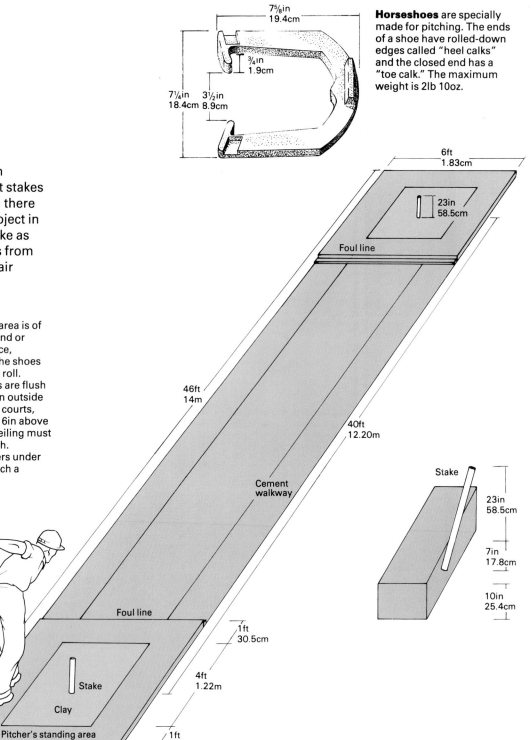

Horseshoes are specially made for pitching. The ends of a shoe have rolled-down edges called "heel calks" and the closed end has a "toe calk." The maximum weight is 2lb 10oz.

Officials A tournament committee organizes the contest.
A referee decides disputes about scores.
Each court has an official scorer.
Contests There are various types of contest.
Two players usually play the best of 11 games.
In tournaments contestants play one game against each of the other players.
Qualifying rounds may be held to divide competitors into classes. Each player may have to pitch 50 or 100 shoes alone. The winners of each class may play each other.

Court The target area is of moist clay, dirt, sand or synthetic substance, prepared so that the shoes will not bounce or roll. Pitching platforms are flush with the ground on outside courts. For indoor courts, they may be up to 6in above the ground. The ceiling must be at least 12ft high. Women and players under 17 years of age pitch a distance of 30ft.

Singles Each player has two shoes and uses the same pitcher's box. Players pitch both shoes in turn at the opposite stake to complete an inning. They then walk to that stake, tally the score, and pitch back toward the first stake.
Doubles Partners separate, one at each stake. Shoes are pitched from one box by two players, then pitched back by the other two. No movement between the boxes is necessary. The partners' scores are added together but the individual records of ringers and shoes pitched should be kept.

Start Players toss a coin; the winner decides who pitches first. If there is more than one game, the choice of starting alternates thereafter.
Pitching The pitcher must stand on one of the pitching platforms. His feet must stay behind the foul line until the shoe has left his hand. His opponent must remain on the opposite side of the stake, either in the rear quarter of the other pitching platform or behind the pitching box, with the toes of one foot touching that platform.
He must not talk, move, or in any other way distract the pitcher. Such an offense incurs a loss of score in that inning.

No player may walk to the opposite stake, or be informed of the position of the shoes before an inning is complete.
Once thrown, shoes may not be moved or touched until the scores have been decided.
Such an offense incurs a loss of score in that inning.
Scoring Shoes must be within 6in of the stake to score.
A shoe that first strikes the ground outside the target area cannot be scored, nor can any shoe thrown from an invalid position. Such shoes may be removed from the pitching box on the request of the opponent.

A shoe landing in the area and breaking is not scored; it is removed and another pitch taken.
A "ringer" is a shoe that encircles the stake so that a straight edge could touch the two prongs without touching the stake.
Three-handed games If two players score a ringer in an inning and the third does not, then his shoes are disregarded.
Cancellation scoring Each ringer scores three points. Each shoe closer than an opponent's scores one point. Innings continue until one player reaches 40 points.
Only the difference between

the scores in each inning counts. If the result of an inning is equal, then no score is recorded.
The scorer in one inning pitches first in the next inning. If no points are scored, the order of pitching alternates.
Count-all scoring Each ringer scores three points and one point is scored for every shoe within 6in of the stake, regardless of the position of an opponent's shoes.
A game consists of 25 innings, 50 shoes being pitched by each player. Ties are broken by pitching an extra inning. The order of pitching alternates.

Darts

Players throw darts at a circular target divided into different scoring areas. Games are played by individuals, pairs, or teams of any number. Players aim to reduce a starting score exactly to zero.

Darts Each player uses three darts. Darts must not exceed an overall maximum length of 30.5cm (12in), nor weigh more than 50g (1.8oz). Darts comprise: (**1**) a sharp point, usually made of steel; (**2**) a barrel, with finger grips, made of metal (usually brass), wood, or plastic weighted with metal; (**3**) a flighted stem which may consist of up to three separate pieces (made of feathers, plastic or paper).

The scoreboard is a slate or black-painted board. Each side's score is recorded in chalk.

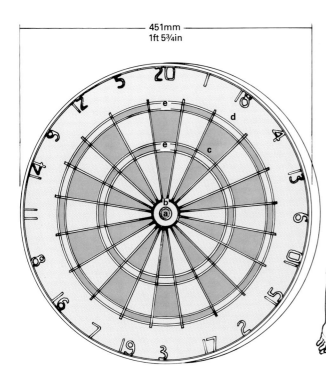

The dartboard is usually made of cork, bristle, or elm, with the divisions and sector numbers marked by wires. Adjacent sectors are differentiated by color. The board is always hung so that the 20 sector is vertically above the bull.

Dimensions of the dartboard
a Bull dia., 12.7mm (0.50in)
b Semi-center dia., 31.8mm (1.25in)
c Double wire to center bull, 170mm (6.69in)
d Treble wire to center bull, 107mm (4.21in)
e Double and treble ring inside width, 8.0mm (0.313in)

Playing area The dartboard is hung on a wall, with the scoreboard to one side. The toe line, 2.37m (7ft 9¼in) from the dartboard, is marked either on a mat or on the floor.

1.73m
5ft 8in

2.37m
7ft 9¼in

Toe-line

Officials Except in some organized championships, a player or spectator acts as scorer, and there is usually no referee.
Starting Each player, or one member of each pair or team, must get a dart in the doubles ring to begin scoring. The starting double is scored, as are darts thrown after it in the same turn.
Turns In singles games, each opponent throws in turn. In pairs and team games, the different sides throw in turn, with members of each side playing in the order established at the start of the game.
The first turn goes to the player, pair, or team that wins the toss of a coin or

gets a dart nearest the bull in a preliminary throw.
Scored throws A throw is invalid if the player is not behind the toe-line when throwing.
Only those darts sticking in the board at the end of a player's turn are scored. Thus darts are not scored if they rebound, stick in another dart, fall from the board, or are knocked out before the player ends his turn. Re-throws are not permitted.
(Also note starting and finishing procedures.)

Scoring Scored throws are deducted from a starting total – usually 301, 501, or 1001.
Darts in the inner bull score 50, and in the outer bull 25. Darts in a sector score according to the sector number – unless they are within the outer (doubles) ring, when they score double the sector number, or the inner (trebles) ring, when they score three times the sector number.
Finishing The game ends with a double bringing the score exactly to zero. If the scores on a player's turn take him past zero, or to one, he goes back to the score before that turn and forfeits any darts remaining in that turn.

OTHER DARTS GAMES
Cricket is a game for two teams of equal size. The team winning the toss of a coin decides either to "bat" or to "bowl." Each player throws one dart in a turn, and turns alternate between the two teams.
When "batting," a team aims to score as many as possible; when "bowling," to "take wickets" by scoring inner bulls.
After five wickets have been taken, the teams change roles.
The team with the highest batting score wins the game.
Football is a game for two players, each throwing three darts in a turn.
A dart in the inner bull "gains control of the ball."

This player can then start scoring "goals" by throwing doubles. He continues scoring until his opponent "takes the ball away" by scoring an inner bull. The first to score ten goals wins the game.
Round the clock is a singles game for any number of players.
Each player throws three darts in a turn. After a starting double, each player must throw one dart into each of the sectors, in order, from 1 to 20. Darts in sectors other than the next one wanted are not scored. First to finish is the winner.
As a variation, players are awarded an extra turn for scoring with the last dart of a turn.

Target archery

In target archery competitors shoot a specified number of rounds. Each round consists of a certain number of arrows shot from prescribed distances. Each arrow that hits the target scores according to its distance from the center.

The field All competitors compete on one field. Men and women are separated by a clear lane at least 10m wide. Buttresses are numbered and pegged securely to the ground. There are one to three (usually two) targets in each lane. Lanes must be clearly marked. The points on the shooting line directly opposite each buttress must be marked and numbered acccordingly.
Archers shoot from a sequence of distances.
Men shoot at: 90m, 70m, 50m, and 30m.
Women shoot at: 70m, 60m, 50m, and 30m.
In club shooting, the target line is usually permanent and the shooting line is moved up at each distance.
Officials These may include:
an organizing committee;
a director of shooting (or field captain) and his deputy;
a scores committee;
scorers (one per target);
a technical commission of at least five members.
Competitors Archers compete as individuals and as teams. National teams comprise three archers.
Scoring generally occurs after 6 arrows at longer distances, and after 3 arrows

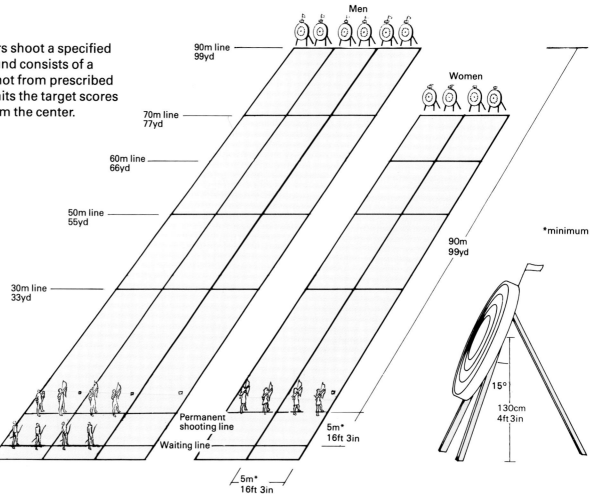

at shorter distances. Archers call their own scores, with other archers in the group verifying. Scores are determined by the position of the arrow shaft on the target face.
An arrow touching two colors or a dividing line scores the higher value.
An arrow passing through the target (**1**), an arrow

rebounding from the target (**2**), or an arrow rebounding from another arrow, will only score if their marks on the target face or arrow can be identified. An arrow embedded in another arrow scores the same as that arrow.
An arrow deflected from another arrow scores as it lies in the target.

Arrows that hit the wrong target after rebounding from the ground do not score.
No archer may touch the arrows or the target face until the scores have been verified.
After arrows have been drawn from the target, all holes are marked.

The target Targets are made of straw ropes stitched together. Target faces are made of paper or other suitable material.
There are two standard circular FITA (Fédération Internationale de Tir à l'Arc) target faces of 122cm and 80cm diameters. They are divided into ten concentric scoring zones of equal width: 6·1cm on the 122cm target face, and 4cm on the 80cm target face. The targets are also divided into five concentric color zones. The 80cm target face is used at 50m and at 30m.
Competitors are drawn for targets. There is a maximum of four (preferably three) archers to each target.
3 FITA international 122cm target face:
a white (outer) 1 point
b white (inner) 2 points
c black (outer) 3 points
d black (inner) 4 points
e blue (outer) 5 points
f blue (inner) 6 points
g red (outer) 7 points
h red (inner) 8 points
i gold (outer) 9 points
j gold (inner) 10 points

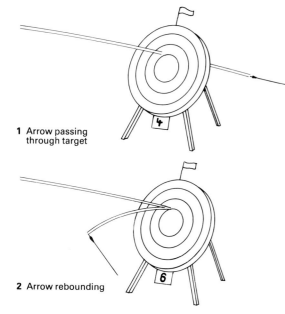

1 Arrow passing through target

2 Arrow rebounding

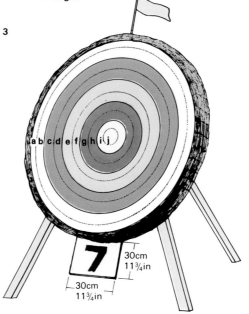

Dress Normal clothing is worn, but it must be close-fitting above the waist to prevent catching the bowstring. The competitor must wear his target number on his back.

Glasses may be worn and binoculars used to spot arrows between shots.

An archer's equipment may include:
1 quiver;
2 arm guard (to protect the arm from the bowstring);
3 leather glove or tab (to protect the drawing hand);
4 draw-check;
5 plunger button (to gain optimum arrow performance).

© DIAGRAM

Arrows are generally of tubular aluminum alloy or carbon tube. Length, weight, and stiffness vary to suit the archer and the bow.

The ideal length is from the base of the thumb to the archer's chin, in the sideways shooting stance. The weight is usually less than 1oz (28g). The stiffness of the spine of the arrow determines (for a given bow) whether it will drift to the left or right. The arrow is not held on the string by the fingers, but the string, at the nocking point, fits into the nock of the arrow. The "serving" at this point is made thick enough for the arrow to hang on to the string. Arrows must be marked to identify the archer.

The bow Any form of bow is allowed except the crossbow. Most advanced archers use composite bows made of laminated glass; or carbon fiber limbs attached to a cast metal or laminated wooden handle.

There is no specified length for a bow. Longer bows are steadier in the hand; shorter bows shoot a faster arrow, less affected by wind.

All bows may be fitted with foresights or bowmarks for range and to compensate for lateral drift. One lip or nose mark is allowed on the string.

Certain attachments, including lenses, prisms, rearsights, mechanical releases, are forbidden for recurve bows.

The draw-weight is the weight of pull at full draw (when the bowstring is pulled back). This is usually between 35–45lb (15.8–20.4kg) for men, and 24–28lb (10.9–12.7kg) for women.

Tournaments A single FITA round may be shot over one or two days, and consists of 144 arrows, 36 arrows at each distance. Distances shot are:
Men: 90m, 70m, 50m, 30m.
Women: 70m, 60m, 50m, 30m.

The longest distance is shot first. If shot over two days, the two longest distances are shot on the first day. A complete tournament is either one or two FITA rounds. At world championships, a single FITA is shot as a qualifier, followed by a Grand FITA knock-out tournament.

Grand FITA The top 24 men and 24 women from the qualification single FITA shoot a match of 36 arrows, 9 at each distance starting at the longest distance. The top 18 archers of each sex from these eighth finals shoot again 36 arrows but starting at the shortest distance and ending at the longest. This constitutes the quarter finals. From the quarter finals, the top 12 men and 12 women enter the semi-finals shot from long distances to short. The grand finals are shot by the top 8 men and the top 8 women from short to long distances. In the event of a tie on score that affects entry to the next bout of 36 arrows or affects awards, there is a shoot-off

of 3 arrows per archer at the last distance shot, repeated as many times as necessary to eliminate the tie. Archers start from scratch score at each of the Grand FITA. There is also Grand FITA for teams, in which 3 archers from each country shoot together on one target as a unit. The system is similar to the individual Grand FITA but 12 leading teams of each sex go forward from the qualification round straight into a grand semi-final, and the leading 8 of those teams go forward to the grand final for teams.

Starting Under the control of the director of shooting (or field captain), each competitor begins each day with six sighting arrows, which are not scored.

Shooting Except for the disabled, shooting is from an unsupported standing position, with a foot each side of the shooting line or both feet on the shooting line. Archers shoot in turn, usually one archer per target. The target group member who shoots first changes with each end. During an end an archer shoots three arrows consecutively, then returns behind the waiting line while other members of the group shoot.

Each archer has a maximum of 2½ minutes for his three

arrows, from the moment he steps up to the shooting line A warning signal is given after two minutes. Twenty seconds is allowed for archers to change details. Arrows shot outside the allotted time entail loss of points. All time signaling is by colored lights or plates, or digital clocks, and sound signals by whistle or similar equipment.

While on the shooting line archers may not receive any information.

An arrow is not regarded as being shot if the archer can touch it with his bow without moving his feet from their position at the shooting line, or if a buttress blows over, in which case another arrow may be shot in its place.

Result Competitions are won by the archer with the highest total score after the prescribed rounds have been completed.

A few competitions under local rules are decided by the most hits or the most golds.

Ties In an FITA round if the score total is tied, the winner is the archer with the greatest number of scoring hits. If a tie persists, the winner is the archer with most tens, and then the most hits scoring nine points. If a tie still persists the archers are declared equal.

Field archery

There are two major types of field archery: freestyle and barebow (or instinctive). Freestyle allows the equipment used in target archery, but barebow forbids any artificial forms of aiming. Both styles use targets of four different sizes located around a course. Under international rules competitors shoot two rounds: the hunters' round and the field round.

The range The targets are set out in sequence over natural terrain in two courses, one course for each round. Each course is of one or two units, of 14 targets each. Direction of shooting and shooting distances vary. Shooting distances are marked by posts. In the field round, 10 targets each have one distance post, and 4 have four posts. In the hunters' round, all have four posts.

Where there are four posts, competitors shoot from all four posts – beginning with the farthest post and gradually approaching the target. In the hunters' round at championship level, competitors are not informed of the measured distances of the posts from the targets.

Dress is as for target archery. In rounds shot over unmarked distances, competitors may not use field glasses or other visual aids; any aids for calculating distances; any memoranda for improving scores.

The bow There are two classes of bow: freestyle and instinctive.

Freestyle includes any bow that may be used for target archery.

Instinctive prohibits any attachments that would aid the aim.

Draw weights tend to be heavier than for target archery.

Arrows are similar to those used in target archery, but may have larger fletches.

Officials are similar to those in target archery. One competitor in each group is target captain, and two are scorers.

Duration A tournament consists of two rounds – a field round and a hunters' round shot on separate days. Each round is of 28 targets (two units, or two circuits of the same unit) and requires 112 arrow shots from each archer.

Shooting Competitors shoot from marker posts driven into the ground. The shooting stance is with both feet behind the post. Competitors move around the course in groups of three to six (preferably four). The field captain assigns the post from which each group will start its round, so that all groups start shooting at the same time, each at a different target.

Within each group the shooting order rotates; members may shoot singly or in pairs – as indicated at each post. Each archer shoots four arrows at each target. Where there is one distance post, he shoots all four arrows from that post. Where there are four distance posts, he shoots one arrow from each post.

An arrow is not considered to have been shot if the archer can touch it with his bow without moving his feet from behind the shooting line.

Scoring Arrows passing through or rebounding off a target can be scored (provided that all arrow holes have been marked previously). Otherwise rules are as for target archery. The accumulated total scores decide the result of competitions. Ties are determined by most targets hit, then by most scoring arrows, then by most arrows in the highest scoring zone (ie spots). If the tie is still undetermined, the archers are declared equal.

The scores are recorded after all the archers in the group have shot their arrows; except on the 30cm face, where scores may be taken after two archers have shot; or on the 15cm face after each archer has shot. The maximum possible score for a target is 20 points, and for a round 560 points.

Targets There are four standard circular target faces: 60cm, 45cm, 30cm, and 15cm in diameter.

In both the field round and the hunters' round, all the faces are divided into an outer ring, an inner ring, and a center circular spot. The inner ring is half the diameter of the outer ring; the center spot is ⅙ the diameter of the outer ring. In the field round, the outer ring and center spot are black and the inner ring is white.

In the hunters' round, both the inner ring and the outer ring are black, with a thin dividing line, and the center spot is white.

Except in FITA championship events, the targets may be drawn on animal figures, but the center spot must always be clearly visible.

Target faces must always be at least 15cm from the ground.

The outer ring scores 3 points; the inner ring scores 4 points; and the center spot scores five points.

Field round target Hunters' round target

The field round: consists of two units each of 56 arrows. Each unit comprises:					
Number of arrows from each distance	Distance	Number of targets	Number of posts for each target	Diameter of target faces	Total arrows
4	15m, 20m, 25m, 30m	4	1	30cm	16
4	35m, 40m, 45m	3	1	45cm	12
4	50m, 55m, 60m	3	1	60cm	12
1	15m, 20m, 25m, 30m	1	1	30cm	4
1	6m, 8m, 10m, 12m	1	4	15cm	4
1	30m, 35m, 40m, 45m	1	4	45cm	4
1	45m, 50m, 55m, 60m	1	4	60cm	4
					Total 56

Shots are mixed to give maximum variety.

The hunter's round: consists of two units each of 56 arrows. Each unit has a total distance of 1480m. Competitors shoot one arrow from each of four different distance posts for each target. These are:				
Number of arrows from each distance	Distance	Number of targets	Diameter of target faces	Total arrows
4	5–15m	2	15cm	8
4	10–30m	4	30cm	16
4	20–40m	5	45cm	20
4	30–50m	3	60cm	12
				Total 56

Beyond these general rules, distances do not have to be notified to competitors.

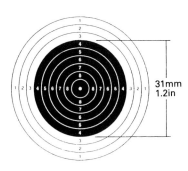

Crossbow archery

There are two major types of crossbow archery – match (traditional style) and field (archery style). Competitions are controlled by the International Armbrust Union (IAU). Match shooting takes place on purpose built ranges equipped with mechanized target transport systems. Field crossbow shooting shares many of the rules of Olympic style target archery and takes place on open sports fields.

MATCH CROSSBOW SHOOTING

Shooting Crossbowmen shoot at individual targets as follows:
10m match: competitors shoot a specified number of shots within 100 minutes in an unsupported standing position;
30m match: competitors shoot in both a standing and kneeling position, 90 minutes being allowed for each position.

International matches consist of:
10m match: 60 shots standing (possible 600 points); 40 shots for women and juniors (400 points);
30m match: 30 shots standing + 30 shots kneeling (possible 600 points).

Dress Competitors wear specialized leather clothes. The use of slings is permitted.

Officials A range officer exercises duties corresponding to those of a range officer in small-bore shooting.

Crossbows Stocks for both match and field events are usually of hardwood and the bow or "prod" produced from glass or carbon fiber composites.
Sights must be non-magnifying, correcting lenses may not be part of the crossbow.

Match crossbows Bow strings are made from steel wire or synthetic fibers. Match crossbows are cocked (loaded) with the aid of a lever. Triggers may be mechanical or electronic action. Crossbows for 10m shooting are scaled down version of 30m equipment.
Max weight:
10m match: 6.5kg
30m match: 10kg

Bolts A match bolt consists of a rounded steel head with a blunt cylindrical point. The tail of the bolt is flightless and may be made of compressed hardwood or high-tensile aluminum tube.

Targets Each competitor has his own mechanized target which returns to him after each shot. The target consists of a wooden holder with a cast lead center. The target faces are made from heavy paper, a circular black aiming mark being printed on a white background.

Sizes of the targets are as follows:
10m match: 31mm diameter aiming mark surrounded by a circular target field of 46mm diameter, bulls-eye (10 zone) = 1mm dia;
30m match: 96mm dia aiming mark surrounded by a circular target field of 120mm dia, bulls-eye (10 zone) = 3mm dia.

© DIAGRAM

FIELD CROSSBOW SHOOTING

Shooting Crossbowmen shoot at individual targets in an unsupported standing position. A competition "round" lasts for a specified number of shots. Bolts are shot in sets or "ends" of 3 bolts, 3 minutes being allowed per end.

International rounds
A championship round (using 60cm target face) consists of:
30 shots from 65m;
30 shots from 50m;
30 shots from 35m;
with a possible score of 900 points.

Dress Competitors wear lightweight sports clothing.
Officials A crossbow field captain exercises duties corresponding to those of a

field captain in target archery.
Bolts may be made from any safe material and may be between 30.4–45.7cm in length. Bolts are usually made of high-tensile aluminum alloy or carbon fiber arrow tubing. They must carry vanes or "fletchings" (usually 3). All

bolts in a set must be identical and clearly marked for identification.
Targets Portable buttresses are made from woven straw, insulation board or polyethylene foam. They may be round or square in shape and are mounted on folding wooden stands. The standard 60cm diameter

archery target face is made from laminated paper. These faces are divided into five concentric colour zones (yellow, red, blue, black and white). Scoring values are: inner "gold" 10 points, outer "gold" 9 points and so on, down to 1 point for the outer white.

Field crossbows Bow strings must be non-metallic and may be made from synthetic fibers. Triggers must be mechanical. Crossbows must be drawn by hand. Electronic devices are not allowed.
Max weight: 10kg.
Max bow tension: 43kg.

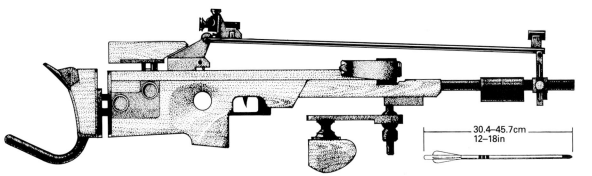

Rifle shooting

ᴏᴏᴏᴏ

Rifle shooting is divided into three basic categories: smallbore, bigbore, and air rifle. These are determined by the type of rifle used, and there are further subdivisions in competition shooting based on the type of shooting position used (prone, kneeling, and standing). The competitor who records the highest score with his total of shots wins the competition.

Range Competitors shoot in line, shoulder to shoulder, and there must be enough space behind them for officials and spectators. The targets are numbered to correspond with the firing points.
Sighting (or practice) targets are clearly marked and may be removed during the competitive shooting.
Outdoor targets are fixed so as to remain stationary even in high winds; wind flags are placed 10m in front of the competitors.
Behind the targets there must be bullet catchers, and an earth wall or adequate dead ground.
Distances are measured from the target face to the firing line, where the competitor may place his forward foot or elbow.
Clocks are used to inform competitors of remaining shooting time.
10m range: indoor or outdoor. The target height is 1.5m above the level of the shooting station and may be adjusted to the competitor's height. The background must be light-colored and non-reflecting. Horizontal deviation from an angle of 90° may not exceed 25cm. The competitor usually changes the targets himself.
50m range: indoor, semi-indoor, or outdoor. The optimum target height above the level of the shooting station is 50cm. Horizontal deviation from an angle of 90° may not exceed 1m.
300m range: the line of targets can be lowered into a covered pit and the range may be surrounded by walls for security. The optimum target height above the level of the shooting station is 3m. Horizontal deviation from an angle of 90° may not exceed 6m.

Teams Shooting teams include a team leader. If a competitor drops out after his first sighting and competitive shots, he may not be replaced.

Officials include:
a jury, in general control;
a chief range officer and his deputies for each event, who supervise shooting;
register keepers, who record shooting;
target and pit officers, who supervise the targets.
Target procedures (50m and 300m events). After firing, the competitor observes the target with a telescope. The register keeper signals to the pit marker, who lowers the target and records the value of the shot. He then raises the target or a new target and signals the score. On some ranges the position and value of each shot is recorded electronically at the butts and transmitted to the starter and register keeper at the firing line by VDU.
Targets are made of non-reflective material that registers shots without excessive tearing or distortion. The size of the target varies with the distance.
Targets are divided into nine concentric circles scoring between 1 and 10 points, the innermost circle scoring 10. Shots breaking the boundary between two scoring zones score the higher value.

Targets
50m distance
smallbore rifle events:
diameter 154.4mm
"bull" diameter 10.4mm

10m distance
air rifle events:
diameter 45.5mm
"bull" diameter 0.5mm

300m distance
big and smallbore rifle events:
diameter 1000m
"bull" diameter 100mm

Shooting ranges are available for training before the competition.
Target and shooting order are decided by lot; an elimination series may be held to reduce the number of competitors per target. Conditions must be as consistent as possible, with special allowances for left-handed competitors.
All events are shot in series of 10 shots, which are not interrupted except for emergencies. If a competition lasts more than a day, all competitors must fire an equal number of shots and use the same positions each day.
Warming up shots are only allowed in smallbore competitions, to warm the rifle before the start of the event.
Sighting shots may be fired before the competition and between each series of shots, and they are included in the shooting time. A new sighting target may be raised at the competitor's request.
In smallbore free and bigbore free competitions, 15 minutes are allowed to change positions.
Shots fired after the time limit has expired are registered as misses, unless the competitor has been allowed extra time.

300m
330yd

50m
55yd

10m
11yd

Bigbore
free and standard
7.62mm

Smallbore
free and
standard
5.6mm

Air rifle
4.5mm

Ammunition
Air rifles: maximum caliber 5.6mm; steel projectiles are forbidden.
Smallbore: lead or similar soft material.
Bigbore: tracer, armor piercing and incendiary ammunition are forbidden.

Rifles
Smallbore free
Maximum weight: 8kg
Maximum caliber: 5.6mm
for rimfire (0.22)
The right-hand grip must not rest on the sling or the left arm.
Maximum length of the hook of the butt end is 15.3cm.
The stock or butt end must not give special support against the body. The butt plate has a maximum adjustment of 3cm.

Smallbore standard
Maximum weight: 5kg
Maximum caliber: 5.6mm
Thumb holes, spirit levels, hand stops, and thumb, palm, or heel rests are forbidden.

Bigbore, free and stardard
Maximum caliber: 8mm
Minimum trigger weight (bigbore standard): 1500g.
Other specifications as for smallbore.

Air rifle
Any compressed air or CO_2 rifle, of conventional appearance and 4.5mm caliber.
Dimensions and prohibited features as for smallbore standard.

Sights No lens, lens systems, or telescopic sights are permitted. Correcting glasses, if needed, may be worn by the shooter.

Air rifle

Smallbore standard

Bigbore

Smallbore free

© DIAGRAM

Course events
Smallbore free: English match 50m
60 shots prone, and 15 sighting shots; or two series each of 30 shots and 10 sighting shots. Duration: full match 120 minutes; half match 80 minutes.

Smallbore free: three position 50m
120 shots: 40 prone, 40 standing, 40 kneeling; and 10 sighting shots for each position. (The 40 shots prone may be combined with the first 40 shots of an English match.) Duration: prone, 90 minutes; standing, 120 minutes; kneeling, 105 minutes.

Smallbore standard 50m
60 shots: 20 prone, 20 standing, 20 kneeling; and 6 sighting shots for each position. Duration: 150 minutes.

Air rifle 10m
60 shots standing, and 10 sighting shots. Duration: 120 minutes.

Bigbore free 300m
120 shots: 40 prone, 40 standing, 40 kneeling; and 10 sighting shots for each position. Duration: prone, 90 minutes; standing 120 minutes; kneeling, 105 minutes.

Bigbore standard 300m
60 shots: 20 prone, 20 standing, 20 kneeling; and 6 sighting shots for each position. Duration: 150 minutes.
Unless each competitor has his own target, the maximum time allowance for a four-man team is:
smallbore free (three positions), 21 target hours;
smallbore standard, 10 target hours;
bigbore standard, 10 target hours.

Misses If a competitor fails to hit a target (the shot is outside the scoring ring), the shot may be repeated with a deduction of 2 points.
If he fires a sighting shot on to another competitor's sighting target, there is no penalty but he is not allowed another shot.
If he fires a sighting shot on to another competitor's competition target, 2 points are deducted and no other shot is permitted.
If he fires a competition shot on to any target of another competitor or on to his own sighting target, he is penalized 2 points. If the shot can be identified or if the shots are of equal value, the respective scores are recorded.
If the shots cannot be identified, both competitors may either repeat the shot or accept the shot with the lower value. If the shot is repeated, it may not score more than either of the two original shots.

Excess shots If a competitor fires too many sighting shots, he is penalized 2 points for each shot.
If he fires too many competition shots, he is penalized 2 points for every excess shot after the first two, which do not incur a penalty.
He must then fire correspondingly fewer shots at the next target.
If there are also too many hits on his competition target (disregarding any from another competitor), his best hits are nullified up to the number of surplus shots.

Accessories

a) Telescopes are permitted to locate shots, but may not be attached to rifles.

b) Compensators and muzzle brakes are prohibited.

c) Slings, with a maximum width of 40mm, may be worn only over the upper part of the left arm and must be connected to the front end of the rifle stock.

d) Palm rests must not extend more than 20cm below the barrel axis.

e) Ground cloths or pads of canvas or other thin material are provided by the organizers.

f) A cylindrical kneeling pad or roll is allowed for the kneeling position, with a length of 20cm and diameter of 12–18cm.

Kneeling position

Prone position

Standing position

Dress Restrictions on material, construction, size, and thickness prevent any artificial support in the different firing positions. Competitors may wear numbers on their backs for identification.

Shooting stations must be level at the front and insulated against vibration. The floor is of earth or gravel, covered to prevent competitors acquiring elbowgrip when shooting in the prone position. Tables used for the prone position must be stable.

The firing point should be equipped with: loading bench, ground cloth, official mat for the prone position, official cushion for the kneeling position, a chair for the competitor, and the register keeper's equipment.

10m ranges must be at least 1m wide. Ground cloths, mats, and kneeling rolls are not required. Targets are collected by the register keeper.

50m ranges are usually 1.6m wide. Competitors are sheltered from the weather. There is a signaling system between the register keeper and marker, and a telephone system between these and the range officers.

300m ranges are normally 1.6m wide, and provide protection from the weather. There is a signaling system between the register keeper and the target pits.

Shooting positions There are three recognized shooting positions:

Prone The rifle is supported by both hands, one shoulder, and a sling. It may touch the competitor's cheek.

Standing Both feet must be on the ground. The left (or right) arm and elbow may be supported on the chest or hip, but slings are prohibited. The rifle is held with both hands, a shoulder and the adjacent chest, and the cheek.

Kneeling The toe of the right foot, the right knee, and the left foot touch the ground. The rifle must be held as in the prone position. The left elbow may rest on the left knee. A sling may be used, also a cushion under the right instep. The reverse positions apply for left-handed competitors.

Extra time If a competitor has to stop shooting for more than three minutes, he may ask for extra shooting time. If he has to stop for more than five minutes, he is also entitled to two extra shots.

If a competitor has to change or repair his rifle, he may be allowed extra shooting time and two sighting shots.

Penalties Infringements may be penalized by:
a warning;
a deduction of two points;
disqualification.
In team competitions a disqualification automatically disqualifies the whole team.

Finals In international events the top eight shooters fire a final 10 shot series which is added to the preliminary score to select the winner.

Running game target shooting

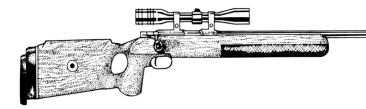

The competitor fires at a moving target (a picture of a wild boar at full stride) on an outdoor range. Competitors are required to shoot at the target in alternate directions both in slow runs and fast runs.

Range The range is outdoor, but the firing point is protected from the weather. The target runs horizontally in both directions across an open area with a constant speed. This area, where the target may be fired upon, is called the "opening." The movement of the target across the opening is called a "run."

The protective walls on both sides of the opening must be of such a height that no part of the target is visible until it reaches the opening. Targets are placed on a trolley or target carrier constructed so that the targets (one running to the left and one to the right) can be alternately shown. The trolley may run on rails, cable or a similar system and is moved by a driving unit which can be regulated accurately for speed.

Target Running game targets depict a running wild boar with scoring rings printed on the shoulder of the animal. The target shows the animal running in left and right directions. Scoring ring values 1 to 10 are clearly printed on the target.

Officials include the chief range officer and his assistants, register keeper and line officer.

Equipment and ammunition The weight of the rifle and sight together must not exceed 5.5kg. The same rifle must be used for slow and fast runs in any event.
For 50m rifles the trigger weight must be not less than 500g.
The trigger pull weight for 10m rifles is unlimited.

Shooting position is standing without support. The use of a sling is not permitted. Until the moment that any part of the target becomes visible in the opening, the shooter must assume the ready position.

Shooting When the shooter has finished his preparation on the range, he must call "ready" before each sighting shot and also before the first shot of the series. The range officer starts the target immediately.
The Olympic program consists of four sighting shots and 30 shots slow, and four sighting shots and 30 shots fast.
In the slow runs, the target crosses the opening in 5 seconds (+0.2 seconds).
In the fast runs, it crosses in 2.5 seconds (+0.1 second).

The run is the time when the target is visible in the opening.

Timing should preferably be done by using an electronic timer.

Misses Every shot prior to the appearance of the competition target is penalized by deducting 2 points from the score. Hits outside the scoring rings are scored as misses. If the shooter does not shoot, the run is scored as a miss. Shots not hitting the target are scored as misses. Skid shots (ricochets) are scored as misses.

10m
11yd

50–52.5m
54yd 2ft–57yd 1ft

©DIAGRAM

73

Ammunition Bullets must be made from lead or a similar soft and even substance.

5.6mm

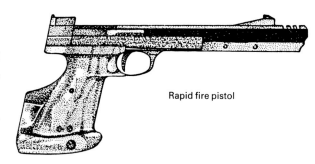

Rapid fire pistol shooting

Rapid fire pistol shooting is sometimes referred to as silhouette shooting. Competitors fire a total of 60 shots at five targets from a distance of 25m. These shots are fired in groups of five, each at different targets that turn simultaneously from a side-on to a face-on position and are exposed for a few seconds.

Rapid fire pistol

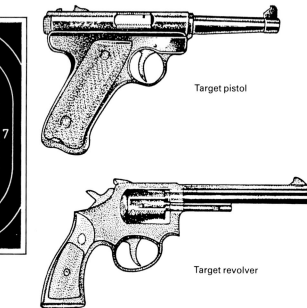

Target pistol

Target revolver

Range A line of targets with revolving silhouettes is placed 25m away from, and parallel to, the firing line.
Targets The targets are placed 75cm apart in groups of five. They appear and disappear simultaneously and are presented face-on for a specified time of 8, 6, or 4 seconds. They turn through 90° at a maximum speed of 0.4 seconds (0.2 seconds in the Olympics and world championships). Each target is black with a white edge of about 1mm width, and is divided into 10 zones, each with a different scoring value of between 1 and 10. The center of the 10-point zone is always between 80cm and 160cm above the level of the firing platform.

Weapons Any type of 5.6mm (0.22 caliber) firearm may be used provided: it is officially approved; the butt is not prolonged to create extra support; the central line of the barrel passes above the upper part of the hand in the normal firing position; the height of the barrel, including all accessories, does not exceed 40mm; its weight, including all accessories, does not exceed 1260g; the weapon fits into a rectangular box with interior measurements of 30cm by 15cm by 5cm. The use of optical lenses is forbidden. No support may be given to the weapon above the hand.

Shooting position The competitor must stand without any kind of support. The weapon must be held in one hand only, so that the wrist may move freely. Shooting must start from the "ready" position. The shooter's arm must point downward at an angle not greater than 45° from the vertical and the arm must remain in this position while waiting for the appearance of the target. When the target begins to face, the shooter may raise the pistol. Leather bracelets and other forms of protection around the wrist are forbidden.
Shooting Every shot fired after the command "are you ready" must be counted. There are 60 shots divided into two courses of 30. Each course consists of six series of five shots, and in each series one shot is fired at each of the silhouettes from the moment they appear face-on until they disappear. A competitor has the opportunity to use a telescope to observe his shots. Before each course, competitors may fire five sighting shots, one at each silhouette.

Duration of each course:
2 series each of 8 seconds;
2 series each of 6 seconds;
2 series each of 4 seconds.
Scoring Each silhouette is divided into 10 sections, scoring between 1 and 10 points. A shot that strikes the demarcation line between two zones will score the higher value. The competitor with the highest total of points wins.
Misfires If the shot does not leave the weapon, the competitor must place the weapon on the table. The referee then decides whether the failure was caused by a misfire or other malfunction. The competitor may be allowed to fire another series of five shots. Should the substitute series score less than the original shots, the latter are counted. Such a procedure is only allowed twice in a course of 30 shots.
If the referee decides that the failure was not due to a misfire or malfunction, the shots that were fired in that interrupted series are cancelled.

Finals In international events the top eight shooters fire a final 10 shot series which is added to the preliminary score to select the winner.

Free pistol shooting

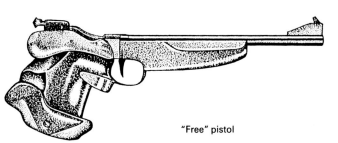

"Free" pistol

In free pistol shooting over 50m, competitors are allowed 60 shots, divided into six series, which must be completed within two and a half hours. The competitor with the highest score wins.

Range Competitors shoot over a distance of 50m.
Targets Each target is a white square. The scoring rings within it are valued from 1 to 10 from the outside inwards. The inner ring is 5cm in diameter. The diameter of each of the other rings is 5cm wider than the one inside it, making the outside ring 50cm in diameter.
Scoring ring values 1–9 are printed in the scoring zones. The 10 point zone is not marked with a number.

Weapons Any type of 5.6mm (0.22 caliber) rimfire firearm may be used provided it is officially approved. The grip of the pistol must not be extended to give extra support to the arm. Optical sights are prohibited.
The firearm used in the free pistol event may only be loaded with 1 cartridge.
Ammunition Any 5.6mm (0.22 caliber) bullet made of lead or other soft material is permitted.

©DIAGRAM

Shooting position The shooter must stand free, without support, completely within the firing point. The pistol must be held and fired with one hand only. The wrist must be visibly free of support.
Bracelets, wrist watches, wrist bands, or similar items which might provide support are prohibited on the hand and arm, which hold the firearm.
Shooting Shooters must be allowed a minimum preparation time of 10 minutes at their allocated

firing points before the beginning of the competition, with the sighting targets visible. No shots may be fired during this preparation time but dry firing is permitted. The 60 shots are divided into six series, and 15 sighting shots are allowed. The target is changed after each series. The competition last 2½ hours.
If the event is divided into two parts, each part must consist of 30 competition shots. The total time for each part is 1 hour 15 minutes.

Misses Shots which are fired before the start of the official shooting time, or which are not fired at all, must be scored as misses. The same applies to shots fired after the end of the official shooting time, unless the chief range officer or the jury has authorized extra time.

a Firing line
b Line of targets

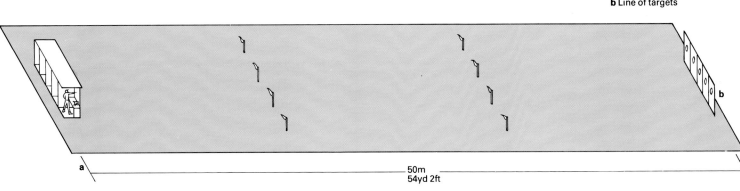

50m
54yd 2ft

Clay pigeon shooting

Clay pigeon shooting now includes 15 types of competition. In all types, competitors with shotguns aim at saucer-shaped clay targets released from traps around the set range. The positions of shooting stations and traps vary with the type of competition.

**OLYMPIC TRENCH
SHOOTING
Shooting range** Five
shooting stations and fifteen
traps. Each shooting station
is a marked square, with a
table or bench on which to
place cartridges, etc. The
traps are in five groups,
three opposite each station.

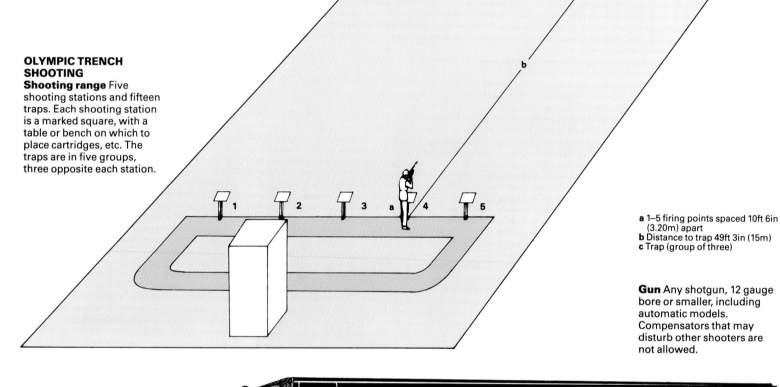

a 1–5 firing points spaced 10ft 6in
(3.20m) apart
b Distance to trap 49ft 3in (15m)
c Trap (group of three)

Gun Any shotgun, 12 gauge
bore or smaller, including
automatic models.
Compensators that may
disturb other shooters are
not allowed.

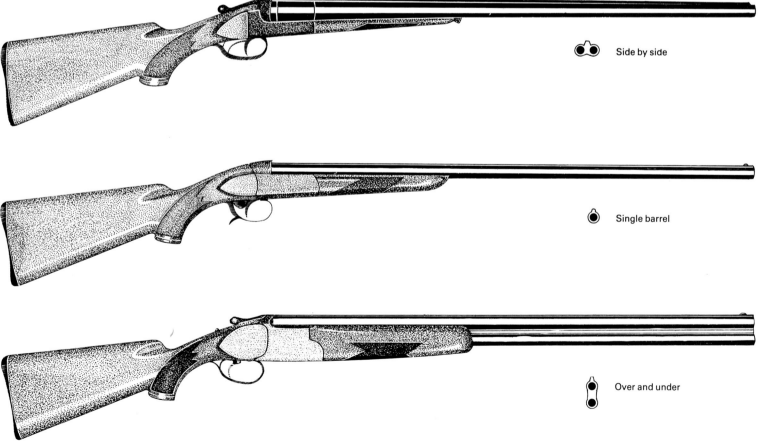

Side by side

Single barrel

Over and under

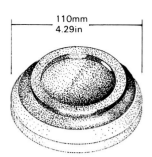

Targets Height 25–27mm; weight 100–110g. The color chosen for a competition must be identical throughout (black, white, or yellow) and clearly visible.

110mm
4.29in

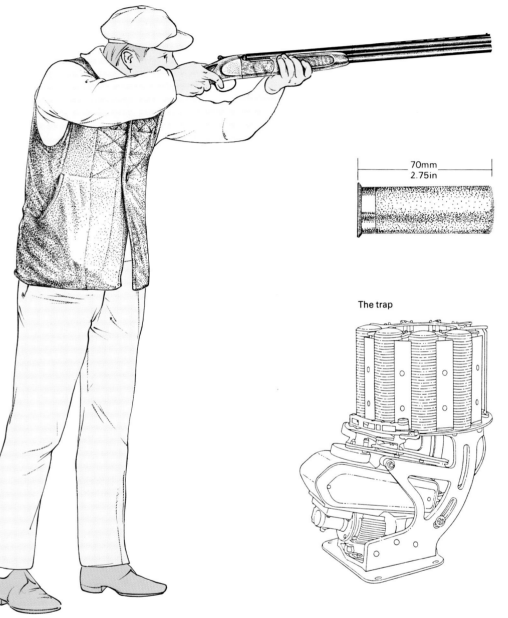

70mm
2.75in

The trap

Ammunition Maximum loaded cartridge length 70mm. Maximum diameter of shot 2½mm (No 6 European or No 7 US). Maximum load of shot 28g. Black powder, incendiary, and tracer cartridges are prohibited.

Traps The three traps in a group are fixed to fire in different directions according to published schemes. At the best angle of elevation targets travel 70–80m measured over level ground. Traps are adjusted each day and then sealed. The center trap of each group is indicated by a line or mark on the roof, visible from the corresponding shooting station.
Pits and screens protect the trap loaders.
Traps are released, electrically or mechanically, by a puller operating where he can clearly see and hear all shooters.
Selector systems conceal from which trap of a group the next target will be released, so that the flight path of a station's next target is unknown to all.

Officials A referee decides hits, misses, and repeat targets. Two assistant referees assist in the scoring. In international competitions, a jury of five controls the competition, and three scorers record misses and misfires. The traps are loaded by trappers and released acoustically.

Shooting is usually in squads of six. The firing order within each squad is decided by ballot each day. Five competitors stand at the shooting stations; the sixth stands ready to take over number 1 station. Each station receives a target; the shooters move to the next station on the right, and the number 5 shooter crosses behind to stand ready for

number 1.
Shooting continues for a round of 25 "birds" (targets) per competitor (ie five birds at each station), though a shorter round can be used for smaller competitions. Shooting may be interrupted by the referee, eg for bad weather or to repair traps. The shooter stands with both feet entirely within the firing box. He loads two cartridges and calls when ready to shoot. The target is thrown immediately. If he misses with the first cartridge, he may shoot at the same target with his second.

Misfires If a gun or ammunition fails, the target is repeated, provided that the shooter:
did not cause the failure;

does not open his gun or touch the safety catch before the referee's inspection;
does not fire his second shot if his first misfired.
Only three misfires per shooter are allowed in a round.
If a first shot has missed, and a second misfired, then on the repeated target the shooter must also miss with his first shot, or the target is lost.
A shooter may change a faulty gun with the referee's permission.

Scoring
A dead target (hit) is one properly thrown and shot at, and visibly broken or reduced to dust.
Competitors may not pick up a target to see if it has been hit.

A lost target (miss) occurs when the target has not visibly broken in the air, according to the referee (even if dust rises).

No bird If the target's timing is wrong (thrown before the shooter's call or not immediately after) and the shooter has not fired at it, a new target is allowed.
If it is irregular in some other way, a new target is allowed whether the shooter has fired or not.
The referee may also allow another target:
if the shooter is materially disturbed;
if another competitor has shot at the same target.
The shot is not scored if a competitor shoots out of turn or before calling.

Ties The three leading places are decided by further 25-bird rounds. Shooting continues until scores differ.

Penalties Competitors breaking rules of conduct or equipment may be warned, fined a number of targets, or disqualified.

World championships
Teams consist of four shooters from each country. The individual contest comprises 200 targets, of which the first 150 also decide the best national team.

Finals In international events the top eight shooters fire a final 10 shot series which is added to the preliminary score to select the winner.

SKEET SHOOTING

Shooting range There are eight shooting stations with two traphouses – the "high house" on the left and the "low house" on the right. From the high house the target emerges at 3.05m above the ground. From the low house it emerges at 1m. Targets must pass through a central area and travel 65–70m in still air (except for UK rules where they must travel a minimum of 50.5m). A timer mechanism releases the target from 0 to 3 seconds after the shooter's call. (Under UK rules the targets are released immediately.)

Targets are the same as for trench shooting.

The traps throw targets at angles that are set within certain limits.

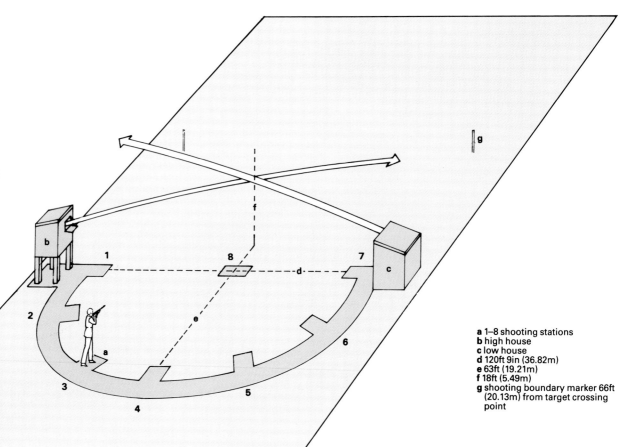

a 1–8 shooting stations
b high house
c low house
d 120ft 9in (36.82m)
e 63ft (19.21m)
f 18ft (5.49m)
g shooting boundary marker 66ft (20.13m) from target crossing point

Firing position   Ready position

Guns throwing wider patterns than those for trench shooting are used.

Ammunition The maximum cartridge length is 70mm. The shot must be spherical, of lead or lead alloy, and 2mm in diameter (max). The maximum load of shot is 28g. Only one type of cartridge may be used by a competitor in a single round. Black powder, tracer, or incendiary cartridges are forbidden. Cartridges must be of normal loading, with no internal changes to give special dispersion.

Officials are as for trench shooting.

Shooting Usually squads of 6 shoot in turn from each station.
At stations 1, 2, 3, 5, 6 and 7 a shooter receives, on separate calls both singles and doubles.
At stations 4 and 8 a shooter receives, on separate calls:
a single target from the high house;
a single target from the low house;
This makes a total of 25 targets for each stage.
The shooter must stand with both feet completely within the shooting box.
At stations 1 and 8 the shooter may raise the gun to his shoulder for a practice aim. On each call, under international rules, the gun must be held in the "ready" position until the target(s) appears. (Under UK rules there is no defined position.) Doubles targets must appear simultaneously, whether immediately on the call or up to three seconds after. The shooter aims first at the target from the nearest house.
Only one cartridge may be fired at any target and only while the target is within shooting bounds. From stations 1 to 7 the target must be within the shooting boundary markers; at station 8 it must be fired at before it crosses the center line.

Scoring The system is the same as for Olympic trench. Only two repeats are allowed for misfires in any round. One repeat is also allowed if the shooter's shooting or gun position was wrong, providing he has not already been warned in the same round.

No bird is allowed for doubles targets if:
both barrels go off simultaneously, providing the first target was hit;
both targets are broken with the same shot (only allowed three times);
the shooter aims for the first and accidentally hits the second (in this case the first is lost, and in the repeat only the second target can score).

DOWN-THE-LINE SHOOTING

Shooting range Five stations, each 36in square, all using a single variable-direction trap.
The trap delivers targets at unpredictable angles, within adjustable limits.
Single-rise shooting Only one target is thrown; the trap is set for it to fall in a defined area.
Double-rise shooting Two targets are thrown simultaneously; the trap is set for them to fall in two separate defined areas.
Targets are the same as for trench shooting.

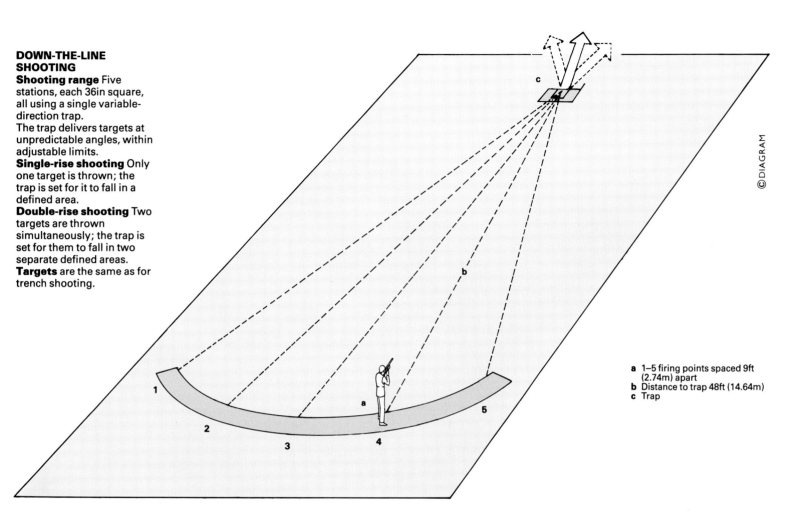

©DIAGRAM

a 1–5 firing points spaced 9ft (2.74m) apart
b Distance to trap 48ft (14.64m)
c Trap

Guns are as for trench shooting. Recoil eliminators are not allowed.
Ammunition is as for trench shooting.
Officials include a referee (whose decision is final), a scorer, a puller, and trappers. There is no jury.
Shooting is normally in squads of five, one at each station. Targets are released at the shooter's call of "pull." Each station receives a target in turn until each competitor has completed an "innings." There are usually five targets per station in a 25-bird "stage." Each shooter then moves to the station at his right. Number 5 moves to number 1.

Scoring Generally, rules are as for Olympic trench, with the following exceptions:
Single-rise shooting "Kills" (hits) are also marked according to which shot hits the target.
Three points are awarded for a first shot kill, two points for a second shot.
Simultaneous shooting of both barrels is not scored – another target is thrown.
Double-rise shooting The shooter may only shoot once at each target.
No birds Additional no birds are declared and two further targets allowed in double-rise shooting if:
only one target is thrown;
a target breaks when thrown;
both targets are broken by one shot;
both barrels discharge simultaneously;
one barrel misfires and the competitor does not fire the other;
the targets are not thrown simultaneously;
the flight of one target is irregular.

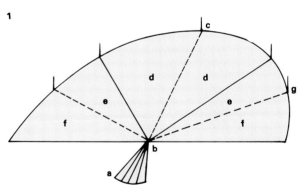

1 Single-rise shooting:

a Firing points
b Trap
c 150ft (45.75m) from trap
d Normal area within which targets are thrown
e Target still allowed
f Target not allowed
g Marker stakes

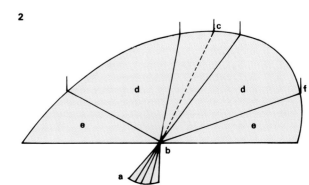

2 Double-rise shooting:

a Firing points
b Trap
c 150ft (45.75m) from trap
d One target to fall in each area
e Target not allowed
f Marker stakes

English billiards

English billiards is played on a special table by two players or pairs. Three balls are used – white, spot white, and red. Players use a cue to propel their cue ball across the table to score points by pocketing balls (hazards) or by hitting both other balls (cannons).

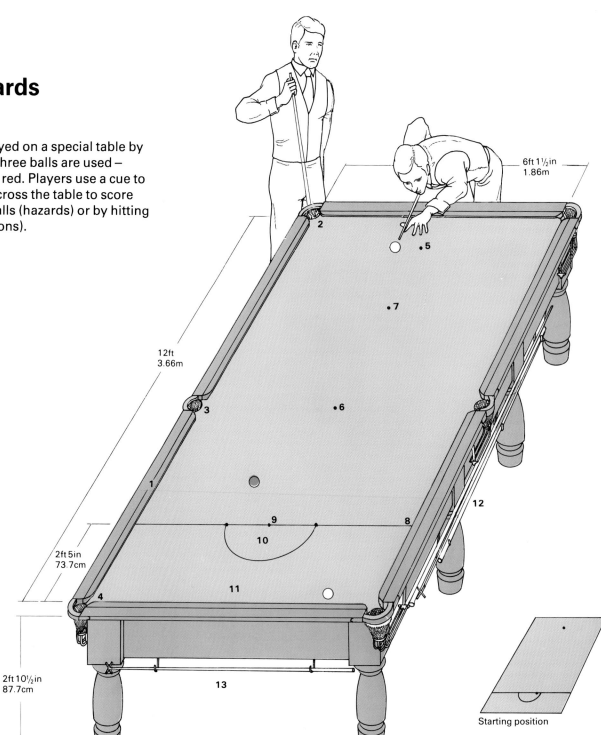

The table is a slate bed, covered with green baize. The dimensions given are those of the standard size table. Scaled down tables are sometimes used.
1 cushion (width 2in)
2 top pocket (width 3½in)
3 center pocket (width 4in)
4 bottom pocket (width 3½in)
5 the spot
6 center spot
7 pyramid spot
8 balk line
9 balk line spot
10 the "D"
11 the balk
12 long butt cue (9ft), half butt cue (7ft), and rest (8ft)
13 half butt rest (5ft)
Lighting Billiard tables must be well lit, and special lighting equipment is normally used.

6ft 1½in 1.86m

12ft 3.66m

2ft 5in 73.7cm

2ft 10½in 87.7cm

Starting position

Balls The white and spot white are the cue balls, one used by each player (or pair of players). The red ball is never touched with a cue; it is only hit by knocking other balls against it.
Officials In tournaments a referee controls the game and is the sole judge of fair play. He may be assisted by the marker, who keeps the score.
Duration Play lasts an agreed length of time, or until one player or side reaches an agreed number of points. A game is known as a frame.
Stringing Players "string" for choice of balls and order of play, ie each plays a cue ball up the table from the "D," and the choice goes to the player whose ball stops

nearer to the bottom cushion. Playing order is kept throughout the game.
Start The red ball is placed on the spot, and the striker places his cue ball at any point in the "D" and plays the first shot.
When his turn is ended, the second player brings his cue ball into play.
When bringing a cue ball into play, no shot may be made directly at any ball within the balk area. If both balls are in this area, the cue ball must strike a cushion outside the balk before it can touch either ball.
Making a shot The striker uses the tip of his cue to hit his cue ball in the direction of another ball. Chalk is applied to the cue to improve contact. The cue

ball must be struck and not pushed; and at the moment of striking, the player must have a foot on the floor. Balls must not to be forced off the table.
Rests Players may use a rest to support the cue for a shot.
Distraction The non-striker must not do anything to distract the striker.
Making a break The shots comprising a player's turn are called a break.
Each time a player scores from a shot he is entitled to another shot. Only when he fails to score does he forfeit his turn. All points scored up to that time are scored for the break.

Balls touching If the striker's ball comes to rest against another ball, the red ball is replaced on the spot. The non-striker's ball, if on the table, is placed on the center spot; if off the table, it is left off, and the striker plays from the "D."
Pocketed balls If the non-striker's cue ball is pocketed during a break, it remains off the table until the break ends.
When the red ball is sunk, it is immediately replaced on the spot. When the cue ball is pocketed, the striker brings it back into play by playing from the "D."
Fouls and penalties A striker who makes any foul shot loses his turn and any score he has made in that break. In addition, he

concedes points to his opponent for the following fouls:
touching his ball more than once in a stroke, one point;
forcing a ball off the table, three points;
not playing out of balk from the "D" correctly, one point;
making a push shot, one point.
The following fouls incur no penalty points:
playing with both feet off the floor;
playing the balls before they are still;
striking the ball with anything but the cue;
playing the wrong ball;
playing out of turn;
playing from outside the "D" when required to play from within it.

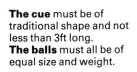

2 1/16 in
5.3cm

The cue must be of traditional shape and not less than 3ft long.
The balls must all be of equal size and weight.

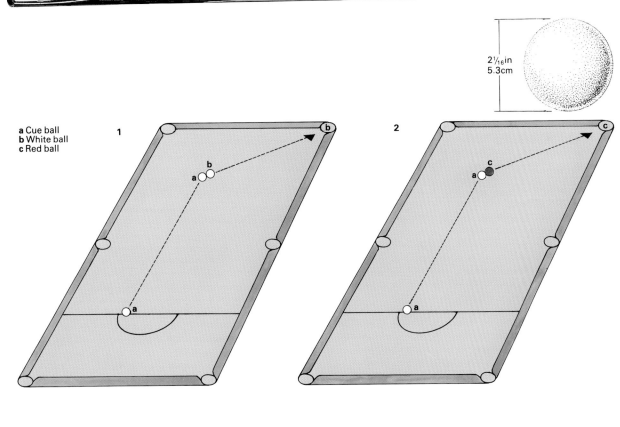

a Cue ball
b White ball
c Red ball

1

2

Scoring The striker scores points for winning hazards, losing hazards, and cannons. All points accumulated in a shot are counted.
Winning hazards Two points if the cue ball hits the other white ball into a pocket (**1**); three points if the cue ball hits the red into a pocket (**2**).

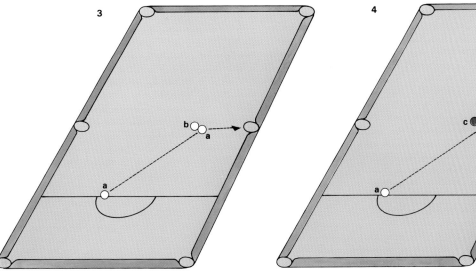

3

4

Losing hazards Two points if the cue ball is pocketed "in off" the white (**3**); three points if the cue ball is pocketed "in off" the red (**4**). Only 15 consecutive hazards may be scored, whether winning, losing, or both.

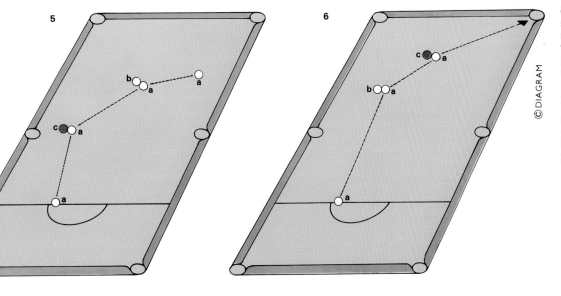

5

6

©DIAGRAM

Cannons Two points are scored when the cue ball strikes both other balls (**5**). If the cue ball goes into a pocket after a cannon, it scores an additional two points if the white ball (**6**), or three points if the red ball, was struck first. 75 cannons may be scored consecutively.
Points to non-striker Two points for all fouls.

Carom billiards

Carom billiards is played on a billiards table with no pockets. It is played with three balls: red, white, and spot white. A carom, scoring one point, is made when the cue ball glances off one object ball on to the other. The first player to reach an agreed number of points wins the game.

The table has a slate base, covered with green baize. There are no pockets. A carom billiards table can be 5ft by 10ft, 4½ft by 9ft, or 4ft by 8ft.
 1 foot cushion
 2 foot string
 3 foot spot
 4 center string
 5 center spot
 6 head string
 7 head spot
 8 head cushion
 9 side rails
10 diamond
11 red ball (first object ball)
12 white object ball
13 cue ball
(Strings are imaginary lines through the spots and parallel to the ends of the table.)

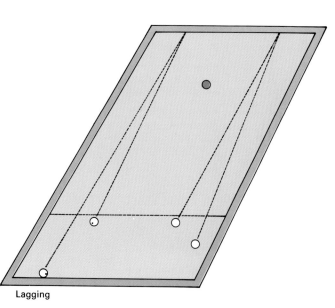

5ft
1.52m

10ft
3.05m

2ft 7in
78.8cm

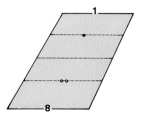

Starting position

Playing order If there are more than two players, the order may be decided by lot. If there are two players or two teams, the order is decided by lagging. In lagging the red ball is placed on the foot spot.
Each player takes a cue ball, and plays it against the foot cushion from behind the head string. One player lags to the right, and the other to the left, of the red ball. Choice of playing order and cue ball goes to the player whose cue ball at the lag comes to rest nearest the head of the table. Cue balls may touch the side rails during lagging.
A player loses the lag if his cue ball interferes with the red ball on the foot spot, or is clearly out of line and

interferes with his opponent's ball.
The lag is repeated if both players are in error or if the result is a tie.
Break shot The break or opening shot is made with the red ball on the foot spot and the white object ball on the head spot. The cue ball is played from the head string, within 6in (center to center) from the white object ball. The cue ball must contact the red ball first.
Rules of play In any shot but a break shot, a player's cue ball may contact either of the object balls first. A player's turn continues until he fails to score, when he also loses one point if his last shot was not a successful "safety."
Officials are a referee and a scorekeeper.

Playing out of turn If the offending player fails to score, it is a foul. The offender loses one point and ends his turn, and the incoming player must accept the balls in position.
If the offending player scores, his opponent must detect the error before a second shot is played. If the error is detected in time, the offender loses one point and ends his turn.
If the error is not detected in time, all points scored count and the player's turn continues until he misses. The offending player must wait for his next turn until all the other players have had a turn, and the new playing order is then retained throughout the game.

Lagging

Cue A carom billiards cue is similar in size and shape to an English billiards cue.
Balls Carom billiards is played with one red object ball, a white ball, and a white ball with two small spots. Each player or side has one of the white balls for a cue ball.

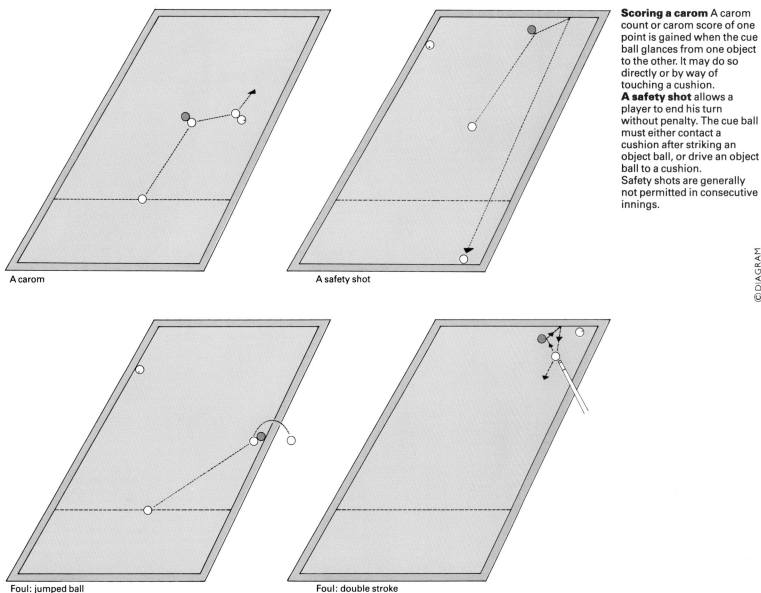

A carom

A safety shot

Foul: jumped ball

Foul: double stroke

Scoring a carom A carom count or carom score of one point is gained when the cue ball glances from one object to the other. It may do so directly or by way of touching a cushion.
A safety shot allows a player to end his turn without penalty. The cue ball must either contact a cushion after striking an object ball, or drive an object ball to a cushion.
Safety shots are generally not permitted in consecutive innings.

© DIAGRAM

Playing from safety It is a foul if a player fails to make an obvious attempt to score on his return to the table after a safety shot. There is a one point penalty and the player loses his turn. Rules on playing from safety continue to apply until the player opens a turn with a deliberate attempt to score. Additional one point penalties are incurred for each infraction.
Kiss shots are all counted, whether they assist in a score or deprive a player of points. The cue ball may kiss from one object ball to another. An object ball already struck by the cue ball may kiss the second object ball either into or away from the path of the cue ball.

Jumped balls If his cue ball jumps off the table, the player loses one point and ends his turn. The cue ball is placed on the head spot or, if it is occupied, on the foot spot. If both are occupied, the cue ball is placed on the center spot.
If the red ball jumps off the table, it is replaced on the foot spot. If the white object ball jumps off the table, it is replaced on the head spot.
Any score made before either or both object balls jump off the table is counted and the player continues shooting.
If all the balls jump off the table, it is a foul.
The offending player loses one point and ends his turn. The incoming player makes a break shot.

Bounce on rail The cue ball remains in play if it bounces onto and rides the rail and then returns to the table. It is treated as a jumped ball if it remains on the rail.
Frozen balls are balls that are touching each other or a cushion.
Frozen object balls remain in play as they are.
If his cue ball is frozen, a player can shoot away from the frozen object ball or have the balls spotted for a break shot. Failure to do either is a foul (resulting in the loss of one point and the end of a turn).
If his cue ball is frozen against a cushion, it may be first played against that cushion.

Fouls All fouls cause the loss of one point and the end of the offender's turn. The following constitute a foul.
Balls in motion: making a shot when any ball is in motion.
Cueing ball: touching the cue ball during "warm up" stroking. The offender may not claim that the touch was his stroke.
Push or shove shot: making a push or shove shot, which is defined as a shot in which the cue tip remains in contact with the cue ball after the cue ball has struck an object ball.
Double stroke: making a double stroke, defined as one in which the cue tip again contacts the cue ball after the cue ball has struck an object ball.

Cue and object ball: touching an object ball with the cue.
Wrong cue ball: shooting the wrong cue ball (the incoming player must accept the balls that are in position).
Foot on floor: not having one foot touching the floor when making a shot.
It is a foul if any player causes interference. The offender loses a point and the incoming player must accept the balls in position. A miscue is not a foul.

Snooker

The game of snooker is played on a pocket billiard table. Fifteen red, six colored, and one white cue ball are used. Points are scored by pocketing balls and by forcing an opponent to give away points through "snookers." It may be played by two persons, pairs, or teams.

Triangle A triangular rack is used to position the red balls for the start of play.

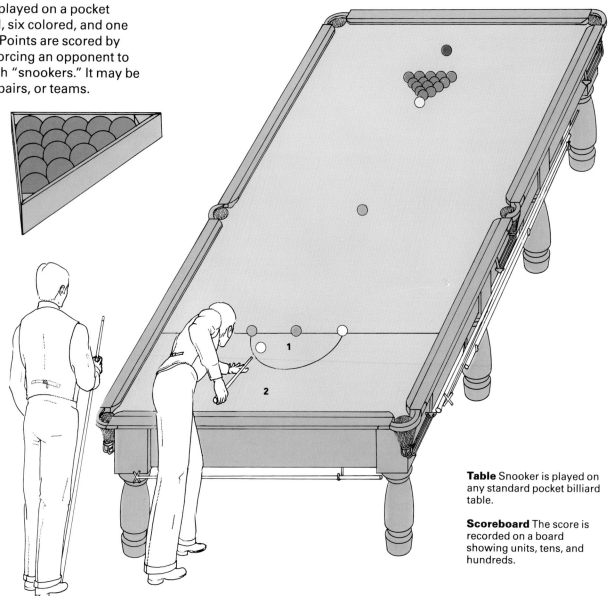

Starting positions The balls are positioned on the table as shown.

Starting play A coin is tossed to decide who will play first. The game begins with the starter playing the cue ball from within the "D" (**1**) at any red ball.

Rules of play The initial stroke of each turn must strike the cue ball against a red, so long as any red remains on the table.

If the striker succeeds in pocketing a red, he scores that ball and continues his break by attempting to pocket any non-red ball: he must nominate which ball he is aiming for and he must hit the cue ball against that ball. If he pockets it, he adds the value of that ball to his score.

Red balls that are pocketed are not replaced on the table; but colored balls are, at this stage, immediately respotted.

The player's break continues:

he plays alternately a red and a nominated colored ball until he fails to score on any stroke. The sum of points in his break is then added to his total score for the game to that stage, after which his opponent attempts a break.

The opponent plays from wherever the cue ball has come to rest. If the cue ball is pocketed at any time, the break ends, and it is next played from the "D." It can be played from the "D" at any ball that is "on," whether in or out of the balk area (**2**).

Play continues in this way until there are no red balls

left on the table. The player pocketing the last red may attempt to pocket any colored ball. If he succeeds, that colored ball is respotted.

Thereafter, the colored balls must be struck by the cue ball and pocketed only in strict ascending order of value; and once pocketed, they are not put back on the table. A break ends when a player fails to pocket the colored ball of lowest value left on the table.

Pairs and teams play as for singles, with turns alternating between the sides, ie a player of one side is followed, at the end of his break, by an opponent. Order of play within a side must remain the same throughout a game.

Duration of play The player with the highest score when all balls are cleared from the table is the winner. When only the last (the black) ball is left, the first score or penalty ends the game – unless this makes the scores equal, in which case the black is respotted and the players draw lots for the choice of playing at the black from the "D." The next score or penalty ends the game.

"On" ball The ball that is next to be struck is referred to as "on."

Respotting balls Red balls are not respotted, even if illegally pocketed. But any colored ball pocketed while there is a red on the table, or illegally pocketed at any stage, is respotted at once

(even during a break).
If the appropriate spot is covered, the ball is replaced on the first available spot in descending order of value, beginning with the black spot.

If all spots are covered, any ball except the black or pink is replaced as near as possible to its own spot, on the top cushion side (ie away

from the "D"), and without touching any other ball. Where there are various equally close positions, preference goes to the one that is also nearest to the top cushion.

The pink or black is replaced as close as possible to its spot, on the side toward the "D" and on the centerline of the table.

Table Snooker is played on any standard pocket billiard table.

Scoreboard The score is recorded on a board showing units, tens, and hundreds.

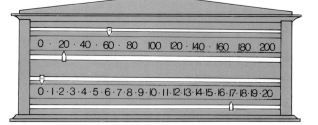

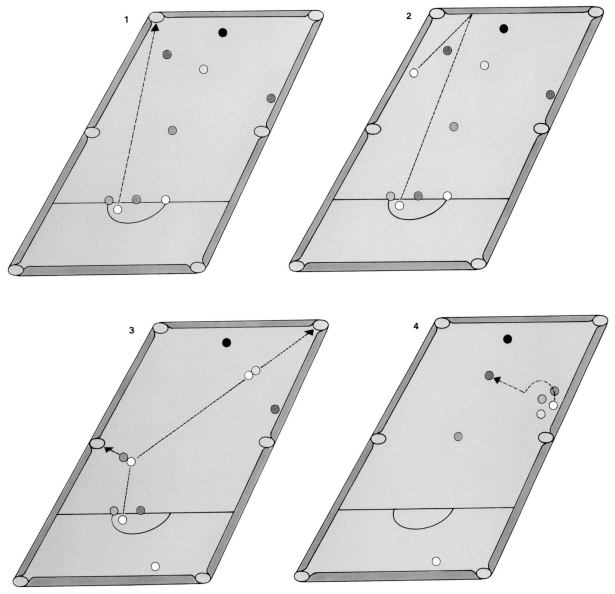

Cues and rests are as for English billiards.

Balls The 22 balls must all be of equal size and weight. English balls are 2$\frac{1}{16}$in in diameter, American 2$\frac{1}{8}$in.

Fouls and penalties After any foul shot, the striker loses his turn and any score that he may have made on that break. His opponent receives the appropriate penalty score, and has the option of playing the balls where they have come to rest or of asking the other player to do so.

The minimum penalty score is four points. The following apply only if they give a higher penalty.

a) For pocketing the cue ball (**1**), missing all balls (**2**), or first hitting a ball which is not "on," the penalty is the value of the "on" ball.

b) For striking simultaneously, or pocketing with one shot (**3**), two balls (other than two reds, or the "on" ball and a nominated ball), the penalty is the higher value of the two balls struck.

c) For forcing a ball off the table, or moving a ball when the cue ball is touching it, the penalty is the value of the "on" ball, or of the ball off the table or moved, whichever is greater.

d) For pocketing the wrong ball, the penalty is the value of the "on" ball, or of the ball pocketed, whichever is greater.

e) For playing with other than the cue ball, or playing at two reds with successive shots, the penalty is seven points.

f) For playing with both feet off the floor, or playing improperly from the "D," the penalty is the value of the "on" ball, or of the ball struck, or of the ball pocketed or improperly spotted, whichever is greatest.

g) For playing the balls before they have come to rest, or before they have been spotted, or when they have been wrongly spotted, the penalty is the value of the ball struck, or pocketed, or of the ball wrongly spotted, whichever is greatest.

h) For playing the ball with anything but the cue, the penalty is the value of the "on" ball, or of the ball touched, whichever is greater.

i) For a push stroke, jump shot (**4**), or playing out of turn, the penalty is the value of the "on" ball, or of the ball struck or pocketed, whichever is greater.

Balls touching If the cue ball comes to rest against another ball it must be played away from that ball without moving it, or the stroke counts as a push shot. If the cue ball is touching an "on" ball, the striker incurs no penalty for missing the "on" ball, or for striking another ball.

Scoring values Snooker balls score as follows:
red, one point;
yellow, two point;
green, three points;
brown, four points;
blue, five points;
pink, six points;
black, seven points.

A snooker A player is snookered when a ball he must not play obstructs a straight line between the cue ball and the ball that is "on." He must attempt his shot, and will be penalized for missing the "on" ball or first hitting any other ball. If he is snookered by an opponent's foul stroke, he may play any ball he nominates. If he pockets it; it is treated as a red, unless all reds are off the table, in which case it is treated as the "on" ball from which he is snookered.

A snooker

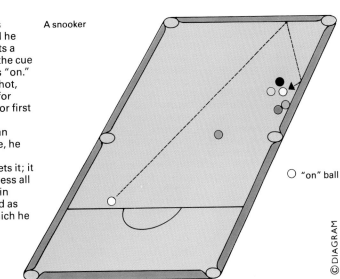

○ "on" ball

©DIAGRAM

85

Pool

Pool is played on a pocket billiard table with one white cue ball and fifteen numbered object balls. It can be played by two individuals, pairs, or teams. Points are scored for pocketing designated balls in designated pockets. The first player or side to reach an agreed number of points wins the game.

The table A slate base, covered with green baize. There are six pockets. Table sizes range from 3½ft by 7ft to 5ft by 10ft; the length is always twice the width.
1 foot cushion
2 foot string
3 foot spot
4 center string
5 center spot
6 head string
7 head spot
8 head cushion
9 long string
10 side rails
11 pocket
12 cue ball
13 object balls
(Strings are imaginary lines through the spots and parallel to the ends of the table.)
Officials are a referee and a scorekeeper.

5ft
1.52m

10ft
3.05m

2ft 7in
78.8cm

Lagging Players "lag" to decide the order of play. The choice goes to the player whose cue ball comes to rest nearest the head of the table after being stroked against the foot cushion from behind the head string. The cue ball may touch the side rails.
The player winning the lag usually chooses to play after his opponent.
Duration A match is made up of an agreed number of "blocks." Each block is played to an agreed point requirement – usually 125 or 150 in title play.
Scoring One point is scored for pocketing a designated ball in a designated pocket. An additional one point is scored for every other object

ball pocketed in the same stroke.
Break shot Starting with his cue ball behind the head string, the opening player must either:
1 drop a called (designated) ball into a called pocket; or
2 drive the cue ball and two object balls to a cushion.
He may shoot directly at the object balls or make the cue ball touch one or more cushions before contact with the balls.
Failure to achieve either objective is a foul, and the player loses two points. At the option of his opponent, he then either ends his turn or, with the balls reframed, is compelled to break again.
Two points are lost for each consecutive failure to meet the break requirements. The

15-point penalty does not apply. If, however, the opening player drives two balls to a cushion and scratches the cue ball into a pocket (**3**), he loses only one point and ends his turn. This scratch counts toward a three scratch 15-point penalty.
When the opening player legally breaks the object balls without pocketing a called ball, the incoming player accepts the balls in position.
Pocketing balls A player must always designate the ball he is aiming to pocket and the pocket in which he is aiming to score.
He must notify the referee, unless his intention is obvious.
In the latter case, the referee

calls the ball and the player must make any necessary correction before striking the cue ball.
Combination, carom, and kiss shots are all legal, and the player need not state the type of shot he intends to employ.
Illegally pocketed balls are spotted on the long string.
Ball bouncing from pocket If an object ball falls into a pocket and then rebounds on to the table, it is not considered pocketed.
If the ball was the called ball, the player ends his turn.
The ball remains in play where it comes to rest on the table.
Continuous play A player may pocket 14 object balls successively. The 15th object ball is left in position on the

table and becomes the break ball. The cue ball is also left in position. The 14 pocketed balls are racked by the referee, who leaves space for one ball at the foot spot apex of the triangle.
The player then continues his turn. If he chooses, he may call and pocket one of the racked object balls. Otherwise, his procedure is to pocket the break ball in a designated pocket and carom the cue ball from the break ball into the triangle of racked object balls. If he is successful his turn continues. If not, rules for misses apply.
A player may continue counting 14 balls, having them reracked, and breaking until he misses, scratches, or scores the required number of points for the game.

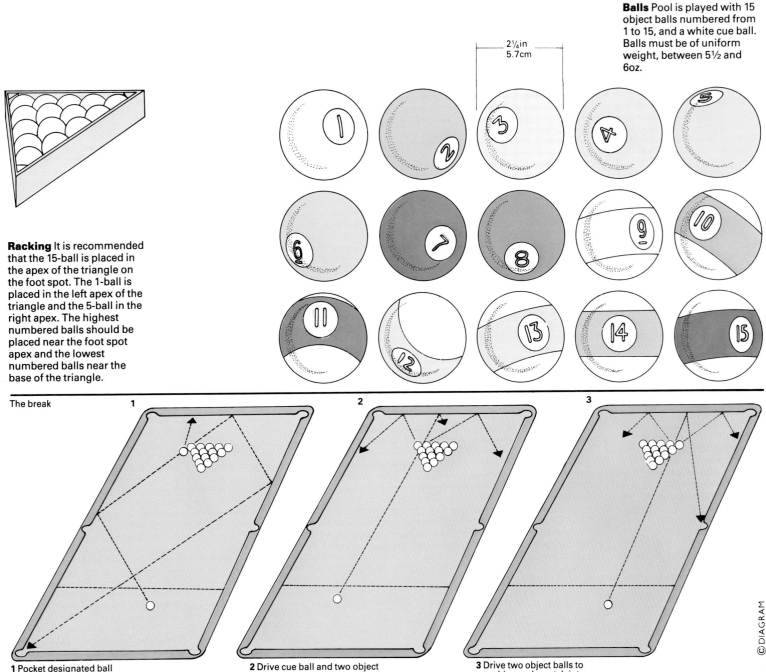

Balls Pool is played with 15 object balls numbered from 1 to 15, and a white cue ball. Balls must be of uniform weight, between 5½ and 6oz.

2¼in
5.7cm

Racking It is recommended that the 15-ball is placed in the apex of the triangle on the foot spot. The 1-ball is placed in the left apex of the triangle and the 5-ball in the right apex. The highest numbered balls should be placed near the foot spot apex and the lowest numbered balls near the base of the triangle.

The break

1 Pocket designated ball

2 Drive cue ball and two object balls to cushion

3 Drive two object balls to cushion and scratch into pocket with cue ball

© DIAGRAM

Interference with the rack
If an unpocketed 15th ball interferes with the racking of the 14 balls, the unpocketed ball is placed on the head spot.
If an unpocketed 15th ball and the cue ball both interfere with the racking of the 14 balls, the 15 object balls are racked and the player has the cue ball in hand.
If the cue ball interferes with the racking of the 14 object balls:
the cue ball is in hand if the break ball is not within the head string;
the cue ball is placed on the head spot if the break ball is within the head string;
the cue ball is placed on the center spot if the break ball

or the 15th ball is resting on the head spot.
In any case of interference with the rack, the player has the option of shooting at a ball in the rack or at the unracked break ball.
If he elects to shoot into the rack, he must either drive an object ball to a cushion, cause the ball to hit a cushion after contacting an object ball, or pocket a ball. Failure is a foul, incurring a one point penalty.
Pocketing the 15th ball
If a player by one stroke legally pockets the 14th and 15th balls of a frame, he scores both balls. The 15 object balls are reframed, and the player continues play from where the cue ball came to rest.

Misses A player's turn ends if he misses the shot called. A miss carries no penalty, provided the cue ball hits a cushion after hitting an object ball, or drives at least one object ball to a cushion or into a pocket. Otherwise, the player has fouled, ends his turn, and loses one point.
Scratching A player may scratch the cue ball into a pocket at the break shot or during continuous play. Scratches are also incurred during safety play on a ball frozen to a cushion, and when a player's cue ball jumps off the table.
At his first scratch, a player ends his turn, loses one point, and has one scratch marked against him on the scoreboard.

This scratch may be removed by pocketing a ball at his next turn, or by playing a legal safety.
If he scratches a second time without removing the first scratch, he ends his turn, loses one point, and has two scratches marked against him.
Three scratch 15-point penalty If a player makes a third scratch in succession a penalty of 20% of the game total is assessed. For example: 100 point game, 20 balls; 150 point game, 30 balls. The player is then required, with the cue ball in hand, to break the balls as at the start of a game.
End of block The first player to reach the point requirement must continue

to play until all but one of the object balls on the table are pocketed.
If he fails to clear the table, his opponent attempts to do so. Whichever player clears the table makes the opening shot in the next block. Subsequent blocks are won by the player who first scores the agreed number of points. But if the winner of the block is behind in total points for the match, play continues until one of the players has a score equal to the point requirement for one block multiplied by the number of blocks played. In the final block, play ends when a player pockets the ball that brings his total to the specified number of points for the match.

Safety play In attempting a safety, a player must either:
1 drive an object ball to a cushion;
2 cause the cue ball to strike a cushion after contacting an object ball; or
pocket an object ball.
Failure is a foul with a one point penalty.
The player need not declare his intention to play safe.
If a player has obviously resorted to safety without declaring his intention, the referee announces "safety" after the balls stop rolling.

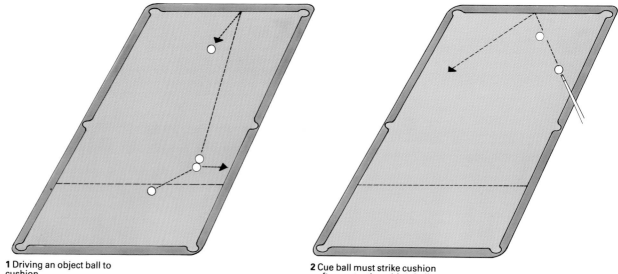

1 Driving an object ball to cushion

2 Cue ball must strike cushion after contacting object ball

Jump shots It is a jump shot if the player causes the cue ball to rise from the bed of the table.
A jump shot is legal if the player causes the cue ball to jump accidentally as the result of a legal stroke, or deliberately, by elevating the butt end of the cue ball in the center or above center.
A jump shot is a foul, with a one point penalty, if the player digs under the cue ball with the tip end of the cue.
Jumped balls If the cue ball jumps off the table, it is a foul. The player ends his turn, loses one point, and has a scratch marked against him. The incoming player has the cue ball in hand.
If the called object ball jumps the table, it is a miss and ends the player's turn. The retrieved ball is spotted.
If a player scores the called object ball and then, as a result of the stroke, causes another object ball to jump the table, he scores the ball legally pocketed. The jumped ball is spotted, and the player continues play.
A ball that comes to rest on a rail is considered a jumped ball. But a ball that returns to the table bed after riding a rail or hitting overhead lighting equipment is not considered a jumped ball and remains in play where it comes to rest.

Balls in motion A stroke is not complete until all balls on the table have come to dead stop.
A stroke made before the balls stop moving is a foul. The offender ends his turn and loses one point. The incoming player can accept the balls in position or insist that conditions prior to the foul be restored.
Object ball within the string If a player has the cue ball in hand and the object balls are within the head string, the object ball closest to the string is spotted on the foot spot. If two balls are equidistant from the string, the lowest numbered ball is placed on the foot spot. The player then plays the cue ball from any point within the head string, shooting at the ball on the foot spot.
Cue ball within the string It is a foul if a player, with the cue ball in hand, fails to shoot from within the head string after a warning from the referee.
The offender ends his turn and loses one point. The incoming player accepts the balls in position and can insist that all balls are positioned as before the foul.
If a head string foul is not detected until a player shoots and scores, he is credited with all balls pocketed and continues play.
If he misses, it merely ends his turn.

Frozen cue ball When the cue ball is in contact with an object ball, a player may play directly at the object ball in contact with the cue ball, provided the object ball is moved and the cue ball strikes a cushion, or provided the object ball in contact with the cue ball is driven to a cushion. Failure to comply with this rule is a foul carrying a one point penalty.
Ball frozen to a cushion A player forfeits one point if he stops the cue ball in front of an object ball frozen against a cushion, whether his cue ball contacts the object ball or not.
When playing such a shot (as a safety measure) the player must either pocket the object ball, cause the cue ball to contact a cushion after striking the object ball, or drive the object ball to another cushion.
Each player is allowed only two legal shots in safety procedure on a ball frozen to, or within a ball width of, a cushion. On the third shot he must either drive the cue ball to a different rail or drive the cue ball to any rail after contact with the object ball.
If a player fails to make this shot correctly, all 15 balls are racked and he must break as at the opening of a game. (Three scratch 15-point penalty rules apply to scratches acquired through safety play on a ball frozen to a cushion.)

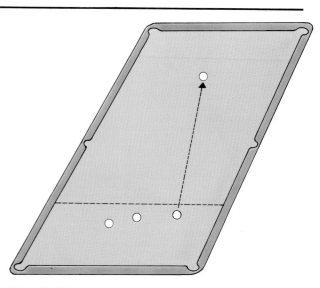

Object all within headstring

Foot on the floor It is a foul if a player makes a stroke with both feet off the floor. The offender ends his turn and loses one point.
Interference by a player If a player accidentally disturbs a ball with any part of his body or clothing, it is a foul. He ends his turn and loses one point.
If a player touches a ball with any part of the cue but the tip, it is declared a deliberate foul. He loses 15 points and must break as at the start of a game.
Outside interference If anyone other than a player disturbs a ball, it must be replaced as near as possible to its position before the intereference.

Time limit on protests If a player considers that his opponent is guilty of a foul, he may ask the referee for a ruling. He must do so before his opponent makes his next stroke.
Disqualification The referee and/or tournament manager may disqualify a player for unsporting conduct.

Skittles

Skittles is a game for an even number of players from two to 24. As a team game it is usually played five a side. The participants roll or throw a ball or a thick, flat disc at nine skittles at the end of an alley and score a point for each one knocked down.

The skittles are made of wood. Different shapes and sizes are used.
The cheese is a thick, flat disc, usually made of *lignum vitae* (a very hard wood). It weighs between 10 and 12lb.

The ball is made of wood or molded rubber, with a diameter of 4½ to 5in.

Rules of play The player must stand with the heel of one foot at least 21ft from the frame. He is allowed one step forward before releasing the cheese or ball. Once it leaves his hand he may take a further pace toward the frame, but he must not cross a line 15½ft from the frame until the cheese or ball has become stationary.
He must stay within the limits of the run until the cheese or ball and the skittles are motionless.
If the cheese or ball hits the side of the alley before hitting the skittles, it is a foul throw. After hitting the skittles, the cheese or ball may hit the side, providing it does not bounce back and hit the skittles again.
Skittles that have been displaced must be repositioned.
Players throw in an agreed order – either from alternate sides or one team at a time – until each participant has completed a chalk.
Officials Competitive matches are played under the complete control of a referee. During a game each team provides a setter-up, who stands near the skittles, though not in direct line with the throws. He sets up the pins at the end of a chalk as well as removing the cheeses or balls after foul throws.

The alley or run is 3ft wide and must be 21ft long from the front of the first plate (on which the front skittle is placed) to the throwing point.
Each skittle weighs between 8½ and 9½lb and conforms to the measurements shown in the diagram.
The skittles rest on circular metal plates 3in in diameter. One plate is the center of the frame, which is the platform for the skittles. The other eight plates are 3in from the edge of the frame and 1ft 10½in from the center.
The frame is 4ft 6in square and made of hornbeam. Behind the frame, at the end of the run, there is a padded area to prevent damage.

Scoring One point is scored for each skittle knocked over. Each player has three throws (often called a chalk), with a maximum score of 27.
If a player knocks down all the skittles before completing his throw, they are set up again.
Three chalks from each player constitute a leg. The scores for each player are aggregated and the side with the higher total wins that leg. A match is the best of three legs.
There is an alternative method of scoring in match play. A chalk is decided by the number of throws needed to knock down all nine skittles, five throws being the maximum number.
A game ends when one team has completed seven chalks. The match is then played over five games. As the winning team is the one with the higher number of chalks, it is possible to lose three of the five games and still win the match.
A floorer (1) occurs when all nine skittles are knocked down by striking the head pin with considerable force at exactly the correct angle.

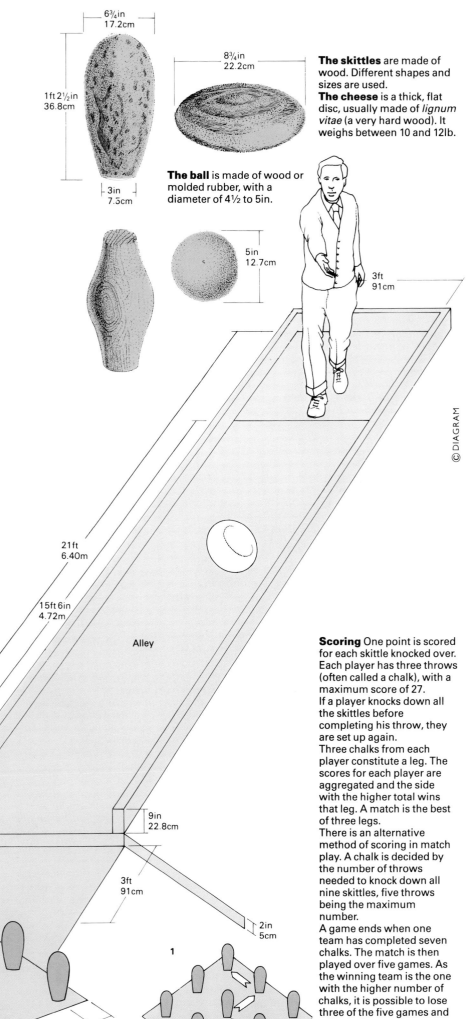

6¾in 17.2cm
8¾in 22.2cm
1ft 2½in 36.8cm
3in 7.5cm
5in 12.7cm
3ft 91cm
21ft 6.40m
15ft 6in 4.72m
Alley
9in 22.8cm
3ft 91cm
2in 5cm
1
Frame
4ft 6in 1.37m
4ft 6in 1.37m.
1ft 10½in 57.2cm

© DIAGRAM

Tenpin bowling

Tenpin bowling may be played by 1 to 5 players, or by teams of up to five a side. A rubber composition or plastic ball is propelled along a lane with the aim of knocking down ten wooden pins that are positioned in a triangle at the end of the lane.

Footwear Bowling shoes have soft soles so as not to scar the approach surface. Ideally, shoes for a right-handed bowler should have leather on the left shoe sole, and rubber tipped with leather on the right sole. Heels are made of hard rubber.

The four-step delivery

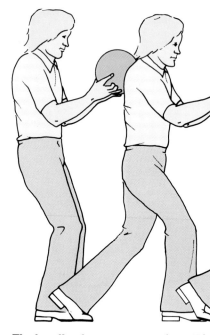

The bowling lane conforms to the measurements shown below.
Gutters run on either side to catch badly aimed balls. The lane's surface is made of either wood or plastic. The first 12ft of all wooden lanes is made of maple, the next 46ft is made of pine and the pindeck is made of maple. At least 15ft must be allowed before the foul line in order to give bowlers sufficient approach space.
Most bowling lanes have automatic machinery to replace the pins and return the ball.
Dress Clothes should be lightweight and allow full freedom of movement.

Rules of play Players take their turn to bowl. A turn is completed when the contestant has bowled a frame.
Fouls The ball must be delivered underarm, so that it runs along the surface of the lane.
The bowler usually employs a four-step delivery.
He must not touch or cross the foul line, even after having sent the ball down the lane. If he does, the foul judge or automatic foul-detecting device will signal an illegal ball. Any pins knocked down by that ball do not score. If the first ball in a frame is a foul, all the pins must be reset. Should they then all be knocked down by a legal second ball, a spare and not a strike is scored.

If the foul ball is the second in a frame, only those pins knocked down with the first ball are counted.
Officials For major competitions a foul judge is appointed, unless the lane is equipped with an automatic foul-detecting device.
Official matches must be played on 2 lanes.

a ball rack/scoring table
b approach area (min. 15ft)
c foul line
d lane (width 3ft 6in)
e guide marks (7ft from the foul line)

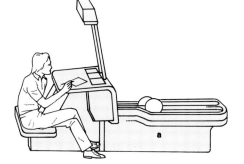

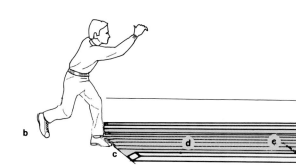

The pins The ten pins are made of maple wood, and are plastic coated. Their weight varies from 3lb 6oz to 3lb 10oz. They stand on spots marked within a 3ft triangle and are numbered from one to ten.

8½in
21.6cm

1ft 3in
38.1cm

The grip Balls have finger holes for gripping. Most bowlers use a three-finger grip.

The ball weighs not more than 16lb. Lighter balls are used by ladies and juniors. The ball measures 8½in in diameter, and is made of a hard rubber composition, plastic or urethane.

© DIAGRAM

Ready for first ball

⊠ Strike

○ First ball

▨ Spare

○○ Second ball

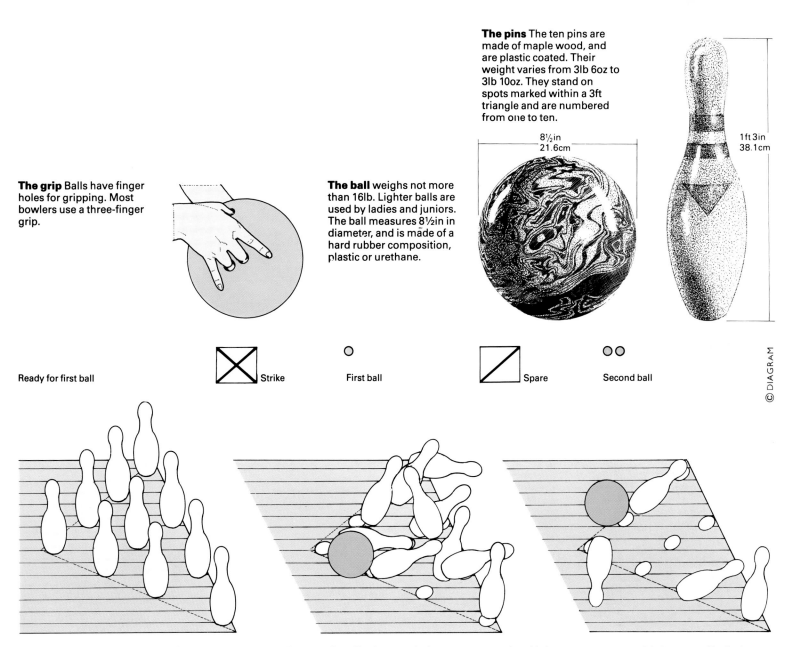

Duration A game of tenpin bowling consists of ten frames.
Every player bowls twice in each frame, unless he knocks down all ten pins with his first ball (a strike). In competitions, matches are decided by the totals of several games.

Scoring The winning player or team has the highest score at the end of ten frames.
One point is scored for every pin knocked over, and a bonus is given for a strike or a spare.

A strike is scored when a player knocks down all ten pins with his first ball of a frame.
A strike scores ten points, plus the score from the next two balls bowled.
If a player scores a strike in his final frame, he is allowed an extra two balls to complete his bonus.
If a strike is achieved in every frame and with both bonus balls, the maximum score of 300 is achieved.

A spare is scored when a player knocks down all ten pins with both balls in a frame. (This includes knocking down all ten pins with the second ball of a frame.)
A spare scores ten points, plus the score from the next ball bowled.
If a player scores a spare in his final frame, he is allowed one extra ball to complete his bonus.

f guide marks (12–16ft from the foul line)
g gutter
h ball return
i visual pinfall guide
j pins

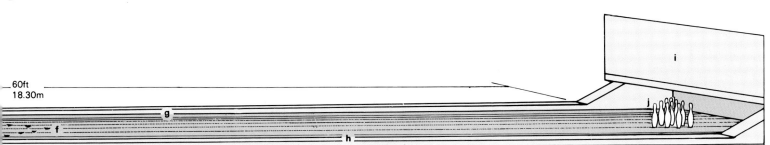

60ft
18.30m

Canadian 5 pin

Canadian 5 pin bowling is played by two players or by two teams of equal numbers. Each player in turn propels a ball at five pins, and points are scored to the value of the pins knocked down.

Officials Competitive matches are controlled by a judge of play. He ensures that the contest is conducted within the rules, and settles any disputes.
Official scorers are appointed for competitions.
Duration One game of Canadian 5 pin bowling consists of ten frames. Each player bowls three balls consecutively in each frame, unless he scores a strike or a spare.
Dress should be lightweight and loose fitting to allow full freedom of movement. Special bowling shoes are worn to provide comfort and the necessary slide.

Fouls A foul is committed if a ball is fairly delivered but any part of the bowler's body or clothing touches any part of the lane, the foul line, or any part of the lane extending beyond the foul line.
If a player knows he has fouled but realizes that his error has not been noticed, he should step onto the foul line so that his transgression may be recorded.
Fouls may be called by:
the foul-line judge;
a foul-detecting device;
a member of one of the opposing teams;
an official scorer.

Fouls

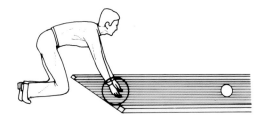

The bowling lane
conforms to the dimensions shown.
a foul line
b lane (width 3ft 6in)
c guidemarks (13-16ft from the foul line)
d channel
e ball returns
f pins

Dead ball No foul is scored when a bowler plays on the wrong lane or out of turn. This is called a dead ball, and the player then takes his proper turn on the correct lane.
Penalties When a player delivers a ball and commits a foul, all the pins knocked down are counted but a penalty of 15 points is deducted from the final score. Any number of fouls may be scored in one game. At the end of the game, a player cannot score less than zero, even if the total number of foul points is greater than the number of legitimate points scored.

The pins are made of plastic or wood, with a strip of rubber around the middle to deaden the force of the ball. They are smaller than those used in tenpin bowling, and measure 12½in in length.

12½in
31.8cm

The grip The ball is held between the thumb and fingers. The fingers are spread out and a space is left between the ball and the palm of the hand.

The ball is made of hard rubber composition. It is 5in in diameter, and has no finger holes.

5in
12.7cm

Head pin

2

3

5

3

2

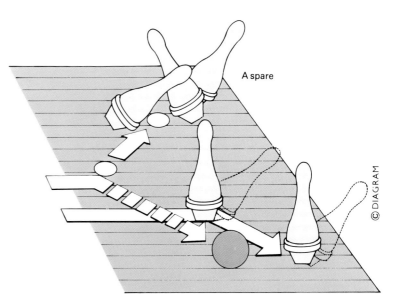

A strike

Scoring Pins have different values. The head pin is worth five points, the two pins immediately behind it are worth three each, and the remaining two pins are each worth two points. A pin counts as being knocked down when it is felled by a fair ball before it leaves the lane surface. Pins do not count as being knocked down if they are felled by a ball that has rebounded off any foreign object in the lane, or the channel.

A strike is scored if a player knocks down all the pins with his first delivery in a frame. The frame is then complete, and the player scores 15 points for that frame plus the score from the first two balls of the next frame(s).
If a player scores a strike in his tenth frame, he is allowed an extra two balls to complete his bonus.
A spare is scored if a player has knocked down all the pins after his first two deliveries in a frame. He scores 15 points for that frame plus the score from the first ball in the next frame. If a spare is scored in the tenth frame, a bonus of one ball is awarded.

A spare

© DIAGRAM

60ft
18.30m

d

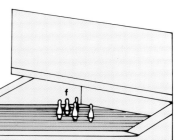

e

f

Flat green bowls

Flat green bowls is played by two players or by two sides of up to four players. Points are scored after each "end" (when all the bowls have been delivered). One point is scored for each bowl nearer to the jack than the opposition's best bowl. Games are decided by ends or by points.

The green is a level grass playing area. Square greens must have sides 33–44yd long (minimum of 40yd for international competitions). Rectangular greens are sometimes permitted, with the same minimum and maximum lengths. The green is bounded by a ditch and bank.

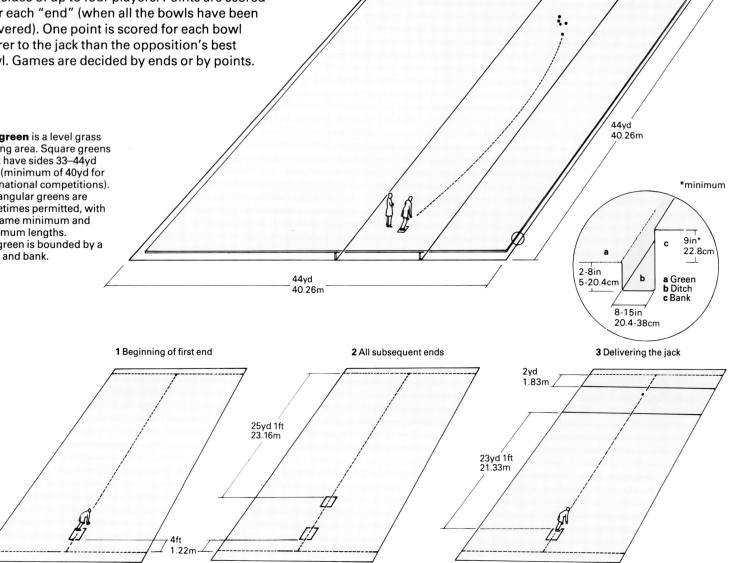

1 Beginning of first end

2 All subsequent ends

3 Delivering the jack

Rinks The green is divided into rinks, 14–19ft wide and numbered consecutively. Rink boundaries are marked by green threads attached to pegs at the rink corners. The center of each rink is marked on the bank at each end by a peg or similar object. White markers on the side banks indicate a distance of 75ft from each end ditch.
Competitions There are various types of competition, such as league or knock-out, and competitors may play individually or in teams. Competitions may be played on one rink or on several rinks.

Teams may be divided into smaller units of one (singles), two (pairs), three (triples), or four (fours), each competing on a different rink.
Officials Games are controlled by an umpire. The score is kept by a marker in singles.
Start Teams draw for rinks. For each rink the winner of the toss decides who bowls first. A trial end in each direction is allowed.
Duration Games are divided into ends, played alternately in opposite directions. Games are played for a specified period of time, a specified number

of ends, or until a specified number of points has been scored by one side.
Play may be interrupted (eg because of the weather) by the umpire or by the mutual consent of the players. Play resumes with the same score, but uncompleted ends are ignored.
Players may not leave the rink for more than 10 minutes.
Placing the mat The mat is positioned at the start of each end and must not be removed until the end is finished.
At the beginning of the first end, it is placed lengthwise

in the center of the rink with its front edge 6ft from the rear ditch (**1**). In all subsequent ends, the front edge of the mat must be not less than 6ft from the rear ditch, and the front edge not less than 75ft from the front ditch, and in the center line of the rink of play (**2**).
Delivering the jack The player to bowl first begins by delivering the jack (**3**).
For a delivery to be valid the jack must travel at least 70ft from the mat.
After delivery, the jack is centered in the rink; if the jack stops less than 2yd from the ditch it is centered 2yd

from the ditch.
If the jack is improperly delivered, an opponent may move the mat in the line of play and deliver the jack, but not the first bowl.
Should the jack be improperly delivered twice by each player it shall not be delivered again in that end, but it shall be centered so that the front of the jack is a distance of 6ft from the opposite ditch and the mat placed at the option of the first to play.
Whoever delivers the valid jack, the players deliver their bowls in the order previously arranged.

94

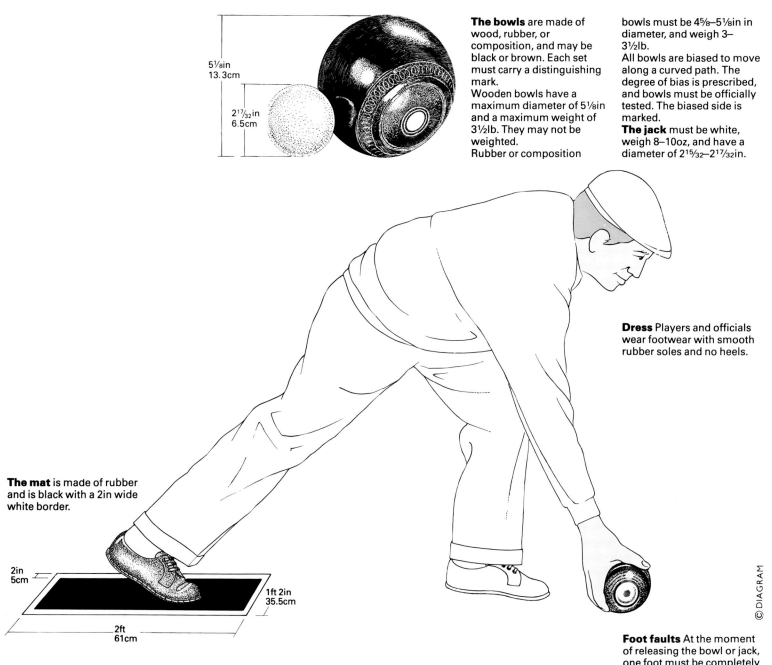

5 1/8 in
13.3 cm

2 17/32 in
6.5 cm

The bowls are made of wood, rubber, or composition, and may be black or brown. Each set must carry a distinguishing mark.

Wooden bowls have a maximum diameter of 5 1/8 in and a maximum weight of 3 1/2 lb. They may not be weighted.

Rubber or composition bowls must be 4 5/8–5 1/8 in in diameter, and weigh 3–3 1/2 lb.

All bowls are biased to move along a curved path. The degree of bias is prescribed, and bowls must be officially tested. The biased side is marked.

The jack must be white, weigh 8–10 oz, and have a diameter of 2 15/32–2 17/32 in.

Dress Players and officials wear footwear with smooth rubber soles and no heels.

The mat is made of rubber and is black with a 2 in wide white border.

2 in
5 cm

1 ft 2 in
35.5 cm

2 ft
61 cm

© DIAGRAM

Correct

Singles Two players each have four bowls, which they deliver alternately.

The score is taken after each end (after all eight bowls have been delivered toward the jack).

Once an end is completed, the players bowl back along the rink for the next end. The winner of one end bowls first in the next end; if the end is tied or void, the same player bowls first in the next end.

The first player to score 25 points wins the game in international matches, world bowls and the Commonwealth Games.

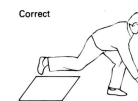

Correct

Pairs Two opposing players alternate until they have bowled two, three, or four bowls each, as previously decided.

Then their teammates alternate until they have bowled the same number. A game lasts for 21 ends. The pair with the higher score wins.

Triples The opposing players play in pairs, bowling alternately. Each player delivers two or usually three bowls. A game usually lasts 18 ends, and the trio with the highest score wins.

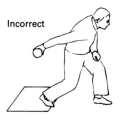

Incorrect

Fours is the main form of bowls.

Each of the four teammates has special duties.

The first player (lead) places the mat, and delivers and centers the jack.

The second player (second) keeps the scorecard, compares it with his opposite number after each end, and gives it to his skip at close of play.

The third player (third) may measure all disputed shots. The fourth player (skip) has charge of the team. He directs his players and may settle disputes with the opposing skip.

Each player has two bowls, which he delivers as in triples.

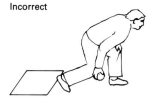

Incorrect

A game lasts for 21 ends. The team with the highest score wins.

Scoring One point is won for each bowl nearer the jack than the opponents' best bowl. If the nearest bowl from each side is equidistant, the end is drawn and is not scored.

The last player may always choose not to play his last bowl in an end.

Either side may claim a maximum rum of 30 seconds after the last bowl has stopped moving to allow all the bowls to settle.

Result Games are won when a side wins an agreed number of points or ends, or by the side with most points after an agreed time.

Foot faults At the moment of releasing the bowl or jack, one foot must be completely on or above the mat. If a player foot faults, he is warned by the umpire. If he continues to foot fault, the umpire may have the bowl stopped and declare it dead. If an invalid bowl disturbs the jack or a valid bowl, the opponent may choose to leave the jack or bowls in position, reset them, or have the end replayed.

Wrong bowl If a bowl is played out of turn the opposing skip may stop it while it is running and have it replayed in its proper sequence.

If a wrong bowl displaces a jack or bowl, the positions may be accepted or the end replayed.

A wrong bowl shall be replaced where it stops with the player's own bowl. If a bowl is delivered out of order and the live bowls and jack have not been disturbed, the opponent bowls two successive bowls.

A player who omits to deliver a bowl may not play that bowl later in the end.

A dead bowl is one that:
stops within 15yd of the mat;
stops completely outside the rink boundaries;
is driven beyond the rink boundaries by another bowl;
finishes in the ditch without having touched the jack on the green;
rebounds from the far bank without having first touched the jack on the green.
All other bowls are live, including "line bowls" on a boundary.
The skips (or, in singles, both players) agree when a ball is dead.
Dead bowls are immediately removed from the rink and placed on the bank.

Dead jack A jack becomes dead if a bowl drives it:
over the bank;
completely over the side boundary;
into a hole or irregularity in the bank;
so that it rebounds within 60ft of the mat.
The end is then void and must be replayed in the same direction.
(A jack remains in play if it rebounds from the far bank onto the rink.)
Damaged jack If a jack is damaged the end is declared dead and a new jack substituted.

Bowls

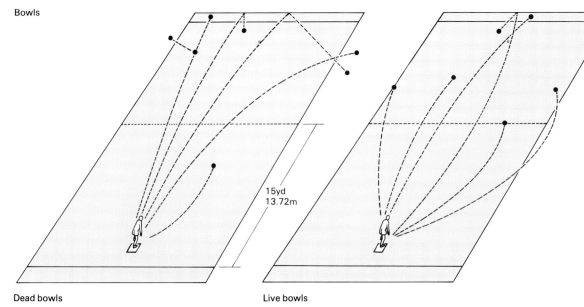

15yd
13.72m

Dead bowls   Live bowls

Jacks

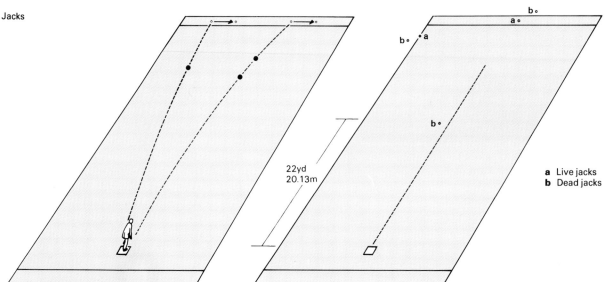

22yd
20.13m

a Live jacks
b Dead jacks

Movement of jack in ditch   Live and dead jack

A toucher is a bowl that touches the jack during its course.
It is not a bowl that first rebounds from the far bank or touches the jack as a result of a subsequent bowl. If the jack is lying in the far ditch, subsequent bowls cannot become touchers. Touchers are immediately marked with a chalk. These marks are removed after each end.
Jack in ditch A jack in the ditch is still live, but may not be moved again except by a previous toucher or by a non-toucher that hits it without leaving the green. If these return the jack to the green it comes back into normal play.
A jack's position in the ditch

may be marked by an object about 2in across, placed above the jack on the top of the bank. (Touchers in the ditch may be similarly marked.)
Displacing bowls and jacks A bowl or jack on the green that is displaced by a non-toucher rebounding from the bank should be restored to its original position by a player of the opposing side.
Players may not disturb a jack, live bowls, or a jack or bowl in motion until the end is completed and scored (except when a bowl is moved for measuring).
If a player disturbs the jack or a bowl, the opposing captain may:
have the bowl or jack

restored to its original position;
accept the new position;
declare it dead (if it is a bowl);
have the end replayed in the same direction.
Boundary jack A jack driven onto the side boundary remains live. Players may play toward it from either side, even though the bowl passes outside the boundary.
A bowl coming to rest within the rink remains live even if it missed the boundary jack (**1**).
A bowl coming to rest outside the rink is dead even if it touched the boundary jack (**2**).
Offenses It is forbidden to: play on the same rink, on the

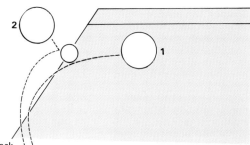

Boundary jack

same day, prior to the competition;
place any object, bowl, or jack on the green for assistance, except for marking a live jack or toucher in the ditch;
distract opponents while they are bowling;
stand less than 1yd behind the end of the mat or in front

of the jack when someone is bowling, except for a skip or third man directing play (the player is not allowed to remain in front of the jack after the bowl is delivered);
change bowls during a game except after an objection or if they have been damaged;
play a bowl out of turn;
play the wrong bowl.

Crown green bowls

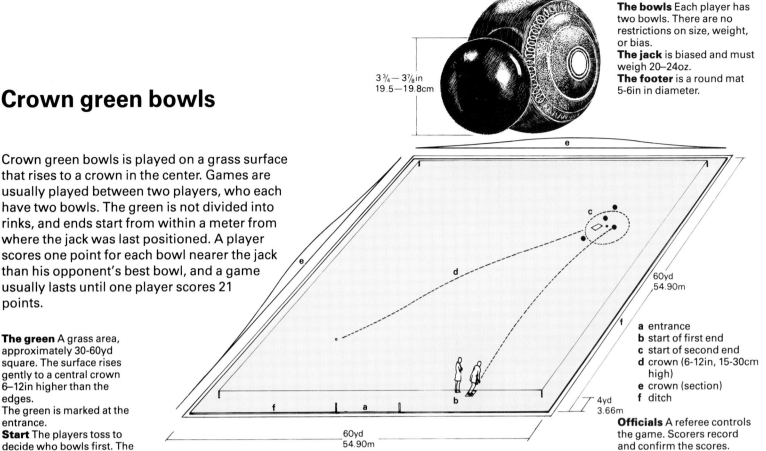

The bowls Each player has two bowls. There are no restrictions on size, weight, or bias.
The jack is biased and must weigh 20–24oz.
The footer is a round mat 5-6in in diameter.

3¾ — 3⅞in
19.5—19.8cm

60yd
54.90m

a entrance
b start of first end
c start of second end
d crown (6-12in, 15-30cm high)
e crown (section)
f ditch

4yd
3.66m

60yd
54.90m

Crown green bowls is played on a grass surface that rises to a crown in the center. Games are usually played between two players, who each have two bowls. The green is not divided into rinks, and ends start from within a meter from where the jack was last positioned. A player scores one point for each bowl nearer the jack than his opponent's best bowl, and a game usually lasts until one player scores 21 points.

The green A grass area, approximately 30-60yd square. The surface rises gently to a central crown 6–12in higher than the edges.
The green is marked at the entrance.
Start The players toss to decide who bowls first. The winner of the toss, or of the previous end, is the leader. For the first end the leader places the footer within 3m of the green entrance and 1m from the edge of the green. For subsequent ends he places it within 1m of the last position of the jack.
The last player in an end carries the footer to the jack. The leader delivers the jack, attempting to "set a mark." A mark is set when the jack stops at least 19m from the footer and has not gone off the green.
If a leader fails to set a mark, the players alternate until a suitable mark is set.
The player delivering the jack must allow the opponent to see which bias the jack is given and watch the course of the jack from near the footer.

Duration A game lasts until one player wins the game by reaching a predetermined number of points (usually 21). If the game is interrupted, the position of the jack is marked for the resumption.
Scoring The player whose bowls are nearest the jack wins the end.
Each bowl nearer than an opponent's best bowl scores 1 point; the maximum score for an end is 2 points. If a player moves the jack or bowls before the score is agreed, the opponent can claim 1 point for each of his bowls in play. No measuring is allowed before an end is finished; bowls and jacks may be disturbed only by the referee.

Delivery A player bowling with his right (left) hand must keep the toe of his right (left) foot in contact with the footer until the bowl or jack has left his hand.
A player must use the same hand throughout the game, for both bowls and jacks.
A player may not move or use the footer until his opponent's bowl has stopped moving. If the footer is moved before an end is finished it must be replaced. A bowl delivered out of turn must be returned and replayed properly.
A bowl or jack that may interfere with another game should be stopped and replayed.
A leader may set another mark if he is unable to

deliver his first bowl because another game is measuring up.
Offenses It is forbidden to: change bowls or jacks during a game (except when damaged); commit unsporting and unfair acts; approach within 1m of an own bowl before it stops;

Officials A referee controls the game. Scorers record and confirm the scores.

Setting a mark

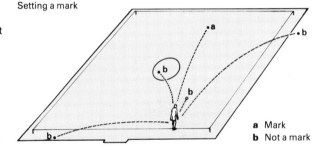

a Mark
b Not a mark

follow a bowl without allowing an opponent an uninterrupted view of its course;
obstruct the view of the jack; stand within the radius of the bowls at the jack end; impede a moving bowl; disturb a bowl that is still.

Moving the jack The jack becomes void if it is struck off the green, and the player who set that mark makes the first attempt to set a new one.
Play resumes from the original footer position if two or more bowls are still to play. Otherwise play resumes from a new position 1m from the edge of the green where the jack went out of play.
An end is void if:
a jack at rest is displaced by an outside cause (including a jack or bowl from another game) and the players cannot agree where to replace it;
a jack in motion makes contact with any person, or with a bowl or jack from another game.

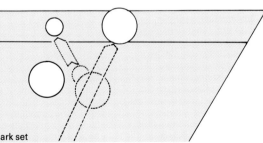

New mark set

Displacing bowls A player who impedes or displaces a still or moving bowl forfeits both bowls in that end.
If a still bowl is displaced by other causes, it must be replaced as near as possible

to its original position.
If a moving bowl is impeded by other causes, it must be played again. (If it is the leader's first bowl he may choose to set a new mark.)

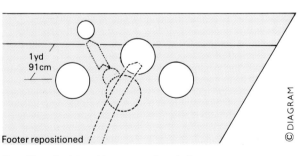

1yd
91cm

Footer repositioned

Dead bowls A bowl is immediately out of play if:
it travels less than 3m from the footer;
it is played or struck off the green;
it falls from a player's hand;
it is placed instead of

bowled;
it is played while the jack or preceding bowl is still in motion;
a player delivers an opponent's bowl by mistake (the bowl is returned to the opponent).

© DIAGRAM

Boules (boccie)

The game of boules, or boccie, is played between two players or teams. Players seek to place their boules nearer to the target jack than their opponents' boules, or to displace their opponents' boules and so improve the position of their own boules in relation to the jack.

The pitch Any type of surface may be used. The lines are traced with a *baguette*; they must be clearly visible and may be retraced if necessary. (Lines must have been challenged before a shot if any allowance is to be made.) The standard pitch length is 27.5m; it may be reduced to a minimum of 24.5m. For international matches, the minimum pitch width is 3m, and there must be end banks at least 20mm high.

Umpire The umpire's decision is final. If he is temporarily absent, any person may settle a question provided both teams first agree to accept his decision.

Scoring When both teams have played all their boules, one team scores one point for each of its boules that is nearer to the jack than the nearest of the opposition's boules.

Delays If a team delays a start or resumption of play, the opposing team receives one point for each 5 minutes, or part of 5 minutes, after the first 10 minutes.
The opponents win when they have 6 points (just from time points or from previous play). If both teams are late, both are penalized.

Throwing the target jack
At the beginning of the game, the right of first throw of the jack is decided by lot; thereafter it belongs to the team that last scored.
The jack is thrown from behind the footline. A throw is valid when the jack comes to rest in the 5m rectangle at the far end; the jack's whole circumference must be within the lines.
If the first throw fails, the same team has the right to try again, provided there was no foul. After two attempts, the opposing team may place the jack in the 5m rectangle (at least 50cm from any line).
If they place it wrongly, they can be asked to move it, but the request must be made before the first boule is thrown.

Types of shot
Une "boule pointée" (a *point*, is a boule thrown, from a standing position, to travel along the ground and stop as near as possible to the jack.
Une "boule portée" is a boule thrown into the air in a parabolic arc and intended to stop as near as possible to the jack.
Une "boule tirée" (a *tir*) is a boule thrown, from a run, into the air in a parabolic arc and intended to displace another object (boule or target jack) on landing.

A Footline
B Out of play line
C Endline

Position of players When the jack is thrown, all other players must stand behind the same footline as the thrower.
If a teammate is out of position, the throw is annulled, and the team loses the right to a second throw – a member of the opposing team then places the jack.
If an opposing player is out of position, the umpire may grant an extra throw. (The penalties are the same if a player stops or deviates a thrown jack.)

Throwing the boule The team that threw the jack throws the first boule (though it need not be the same person who throws). The first opponent then throws.

It is then the turn of the team not winning the point – except that if a thrown boule goes out of play or is annulled, the next throw goes to the other team.
If two opposing boules are at an equal distance from the jack, the team that threw last throws again.
If the tie remains, the other team throws, and so on. When one team has delivered all its boules, the other team continues until all its boules are delivered. The players then measure to decide the score, and then change ends.
If two opposing boules tie for nearest, the end is void and is replayed in the other direction with the same team delivering the jack.

Throwing position Both feet must be behind the footline, except for a *tir* when one foot may be put on the line. The advantage rule is followed after any foul.
Other players must be beyond the footline of the far 5m rectangle. If the pitch allows it they must stand outside the lateral lines but as near alongside them as possible. At the moment of the throw, other players must stand motionless and not stare at the thrower. Teammates of the thrower must not point at lines or objects on or off the pitch. For fouls by opponents, the umpire imposes penalties; for fouls by teammates, the advantage rule applies.

Forms of play The game may be played:
one against one (three or four boules per player);
two against two (two or three boules per player);
three against three (two boules per player);
four against four (two boules per player).

Interfering with the pitch
The throwing team may remove obstacles from the pitch, retrace boundary lines, and smooth or level the surface. They may not create mounds, channels, obstacles, or signs.
After the jack is thrown the pitch may only be touched to mark positions, to efface landing, measuring, and positioning marks, and to mark and efface radius marks for *tirs*. (The umpire may allow the pitch to be leveled if normal play becomes impossible.)
No-one must touch the pitch when a boule is moving.

50cm
1ft 8in

2m
6ft 6in

5m
16ft 3in

12.5m
40ft 11in

5m
16ft 3in

2m
6ft 6in

50cm
1ft 8in

2.5-4m
8ft 2in-13ft

Boule pointée   *Boule portée*   *Boule tirée*

5cm
1ft 8in

50mm
2in

6mm
1/4in

The "baguette" is used for tracing lines and marks, and for measuring and evaluating distances. Both teams' *baguettes* must be identical.

Boules must be made of metal or synthetic material. They must not be nailed, or weighted with lead. They must be 8.8–11cm in diameter and weigh 0.7–1.3kg. Any boule disallowed by the umpire must be replaced.

The jack must be made of wood, and without hobnails, ridges, or lead weighting. It may be colored only to aid visibility under abnormal conditions. An irregular jack must be replaced.

11cm
4 3/8in

3.7cm
1 3/8in

"Points"
A regular "point" is when a boule *pointée* or *portée:*
a) does not go out of play;
b) does not run on more than 1m after displacing a boule or jack on the pitch;
c) does not displace such an object by more than 1m;
d) approaches within at least 2m of the front edge of the far 5m rectangle. (Displacement may be indirect.)
An irregular "point" A *point* is irregular when:
it does not fulfill the conditions to be regular;
a foul has been whistled.
After an irregular *point*, the opponents follow the advantage rule (unless the only irregularity is that the boule *pointée* has run on

more than 1m, in which case the boule *pointée* stays where it is and all other positions may be retained or replaced.
Sideline "point" A *point* landing near a sideline is regular if over half the landing mark is within the line;
othewise all objects are replaced by an opponent and the boule is annulled.
"Tirs"
Designating a target Before making a *tir*, the player must designate one target object (either the jack or an opponent's boule) within the 5m rectangle. If he fails to do this clearly, it is assumed that he has designated the opposition boule nearest to the jack.

Tracing arcs Before a *tir* is made, the opposing team traces arcs with a *baguette:*
a) 50cm in front of the designated target;
b) 50cm in front of any objects within 50cm of the designated target – providing such an arc is also within 50cm of that target. Arcs are normally 15–20cm long, but an arc in front of a designated target may be extended.
Any object that prevents tracing may be temporarily moved.
An arc must be challenged before the *tir* if it is to be ruled invalid.
The umpire will decide in favor of the thrower in cases of doubt caused by unclear or missing lines.

A regular "tir" must fulfill three conditions:
a) the landing point (where it first strikes the ground) must be within 50cm of the designated target;
b) the landing point must be within 50cm of the first object to be struck;
c) the object first struck must be within 50cm of the designated target. (Measurement is to the object's farthest circumference.)
In these cases, a *tir* is regular even if the object first struck is a boule of the thrower's team or if the object is struck before the boule *tirée* touches the ground.
An irregular "tir" A *tir* is irregular when:
it does not fulfill the

conditions to be regular; there has been a foul.
After an irregular *tir*, the opponents follow the advantage rule. If the boule *tirée* is still in play, it may be accepted or rejected. (In disputed cases all marks must be left for the umpire to see. Landing points are judged according to whether or not the outside edge of the relevant arc is broken.)
Special cases
a) If a *tir* is regular and an object is displaced indirectly, the position is accepted even if in front of the landing mark.
b) A *tir* is regular if it touches an object before landing near a lateral line; if it touches the ground before or as it strikes the object, it is regular if the landing mark is within the line (otherwise the boule *tirée* is annulled and all objects are replaced by the opposition).
c) A *tir* is annulled if it comes to rest on the pitch without touching any object.

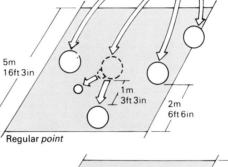

5m
16ft 3in

1m
3ft 3in

2m
6ft 6in

Regular *point*

© DIAGRAM

The *tir* – tracing arcs using a *baguette*

15-20cm
6-8in

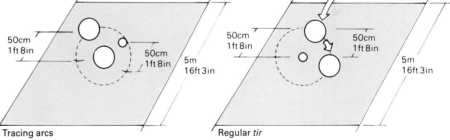

50cm
1ft 8in

50cm
1ft 8in

5m
16ft 3in

Tracing arcs

50cm
1ft 8in

50cm
1ft 8in

5m
16ft 3in

Regular *tir*

Marking objects The position of the jack and all boules must be marked before each throw, using lines at 90° drawn with the *baguette*.
The jack's position is marked by the team that threw or placed it – or if it has been displaced, it is marked by the scoring team.
Measuring is by the team that thinks it has scored; the opponents may verify.
A boule may be temporarily lifted during measuring.
If a measurer disturbs any object:
the opponents score, unless the measuring team is still winning the point after disadvantaging itself;
a moved boule stays in its new position, but a moved jack is replaced.

If objects are disturbed by the umpire, points are considered equal and equidistance rules apply, except that a team scores if it is disadvantaged but still winning the point.
Foul when boule is thrown After a foul by the opposing team, the throwing team may:
a) accept the throw; or
b) reposition the objects and retake the throw.
After a foul by the throwing team, the advantage rule applies.
The advantage rule The opposing team may:
a) accept the position of all objects; or
b) have all objects repositioned.
In either case the fouling

boule may be left in place, or annulled and removed from the pitch.
The inversion rule is applied in cases where:
a) a fouling boule is wholly or partially occupying the former position of another object;
b) under the advantage rule, the opposing team asks for the displaced boules to be repositioned and the fouling boule left in position.
Under this rule the positions of the fouling boule and the displaced boule are simply exchanged.
If the fouling boule partially occupies the former positions of two objects, the team applying the advantage rule chooses which object will be moved.

Misuse of boules
a) The first time a player accidentally plays another's boule, the opposing team puts the correct boule in the position of the boule played in error; the advantage rule applies on subsequent occasions.
b) Deliberately exchanging boules is forbidden, except with the umpire's agreement when a boule is damaged. Both boules are annulled if a player deliberately plays the wrong boule.
c) The opposition wins if a player deliberately delivers too many boules.
d) If the jack is in the 7m rectangle and a player holding a boule enters the rectangle, the carried boule is annulled.

e) Unplayed boules left out of position after a warning will be annulled. Unplayed boules should be in the rack provided or along the side of the pitch allocated to each team.

Playing while boules are moving is a foul and the advantage rule applies.

If the last-played boule touches a moving boule of the same team, the opponents may annul both boules.

If it touches an opponent's boule, the opponents may accept the new position or replay the boule and in either case may accept or annul the last-played boule.

Objects stopped or displaced

a) If during a regular throw, the opponents may reposition or accept the new position of all objects. In either case the thrown boule may be annulled or accepted; or, if the thrown boule was impeded by the opposition, the throwing team may retake the throw.

b) If during an irregular throw, the procedure is as for a regular throw, except that if both teams have fouled, all objects must be repositioned and the thrown boule annulled.

c) A boule impeded by a non-player, animal, or other agency is replayed if within the 7m rectangle; otherwise it is left in position.

Boule out of play A boule is out of play if it crosses a sideline or "out of play" line. Out of play or annulled boules must be placed in the rack or at the far end of the pitch.

Jack out of play The jack is out of play if it crosses any boundary of the 7m rectangle or;

a) if during an end, the jack is replayed in the same direction except that if only one team has still to play it scores as many points as it has boules left to play.

b) if at the last boule, the end is replayed in the other direction with the jack thrown by the team that last threw it.

Out of play – special cases

a) An object is annulled if after a regular or an accepted irregular *point* it touches an object that is out of play.

b) If a *boule pointée* joins a group of objects that are touching and therefore annulled, the *point* becomes irregular and the opponents can either accept the boule *pointée* (in which case the touching objects are annulled) or have the touching objects put back in position and the boule *pointée* annulled.

c) A boule is annulled if it stays on the pitch only because it meets a boule that is out of play or annulled.

d) If an object that was not moving is displaced by an out of play boule returning to the pitch, the object is put back in position. If a moving object is similarly displaced, it is annulled.

(Players may always prevent out of play boules from returning to the pitch.)

e) A boule remains in play if it meets an obstacle overhanging the pitch; a jack goes out of play.

f) If a boule on or near a sideline touches an object on an adjacent pitch, that boule is annulled. Objects are repositioned if they are displaced after the boule contacted the boule on the adjacent pitch. The advantage rule applies to boules displaced before the boule on the adjacent pitch was contacted.

(Boules should not be thrown until all boules on an adjacent pitch are motionless.

Throwers may ask for a boule on an adjacent pitch to be temporarily lifted. All players may attempt to prevent a boule from touching an object on an adjacent pitch.)

Object from another pitch modifying the game.

a) If disturbance occurs during a *point*, any affected object that was previously motionless is repositioned but the boule *pointée* is retaken only if its effect was altered.

b) If disturbance occurs during a *tir*, the umpire may decide that the *tir* was regular or otherwise all objects are repositioned and the *tir* is retaken.

Disturbance by a player

a) If a boule is accidentally disturbed by a teammate of the thrower, the opposition follows the advantage rule.

b) If disturbance is by an opponent, the thrower may accept the situation or have all objects replaced and then retake his boule.

Chance disturbance (by a non-player, animal, or other agency):

a) If a disturbed object modifies the path of a boule *pointée* (by striking against it or being removed from its path), the object is repositioned and the *point* retaken.

b) If at a *tir* the designated object, or any object within 50cm of it, is disturbed, all objects are repositioned and the *tir* is retaken.

c) In case of a disturbance with no apparent cause, a *tir* is treated as regular and a *point* retaken as under case a) of this rule.

Broken jack The umpire decides whether or not a jack is broken. A broken jack is annulled and must be replaced within a time limit fixed by the umpire. Time penalties will be imposed for delays.

Buried jack

a) If the jack is more than half buried after a regular *tir*, the advantage rule applies (ie the opposition can accept the *tir* and have the jack annulled or reject the *tir* and have all objects unburied).

b) If the jack is less than half buried after a regular *tir* or is at all buried after a *point*, it can be unburied by either team at any time unless this would involve permanently moving any boule.

Broken boules The umpire decides whether or not a boule is broken.

A broken boule may be replaced, along with a player's other boules, within a brief time allowed by the umpire. If a broken boule cannot be replaced, the player must continue with one boule fewer.

All effects (even if caused by a splinter) are counted if a boule is broken during a regular throw; the advantage rule applies if the throw was irregular.

Buried boules

a) After a regular *point* any boule that is more than half-buried is unburied and remains in play; any boule that is less than half-buried is left in position.

b) If after a regular *tir* the boule *tirée* is more than half-buried it is unburied and left in position; any other boule that is more than half-buried is annulled. A boule that is less than half-buried is left in position.

c) After an unaccepted irregular *point* or *tir*, any buried boule is unburied and left in its original position.

Repositioning object

a) An object irregularly displaced by a *tir* or *point* is repositioned by the opposition.

b) An object moved accidentally is repositioned by the opposition.

c) A boule moved by chance or with no apparent cause is repositioned by the team it belongs to; a jack is repositioned by the team currently winning the end.

d) If an object is moved deliberately, the offender is excluded from the game and steps are taken to see that the other team does not suffer.

e) When the advantage rule is being applied, the opposition can no longer accept the new situation once they have moved any object nor reject it once they have effected any mark.

f) Unmarked or badly marked objects may not be repositioned by the team that marked them.

Major fouls are:

a) unsporting conduct;

b) irregularly composed teams;

c) infringing competition substitution rules (in case of illness or other serious cause, two substitutes per team are permitted in fours and one in pairs and triples);

d) not making the most of opportunities;

e) deliberately prolonging a match;

f) deliberately stopping or moving an object against the rules;

g) stopping an object that is on the line but not yet out of play;

h) positioning an obstacle to affect a throw;

i) failure to observe a decision by the umpire;

j) agreeing with another player to ignore any rule;

k) fraud;

l) protesting to an opponent instead of the umpire.

Penalties imposed at the umpire's discretion are:

a) warning;

b) temporary or permanent exclusion of players or teams;

c) loss of the game;

d) the awarding of points to the opposing team or the reduction of the offending team's points.

Increasingly severe penalties are awarded for deliberate or persistent fouling.

A team with one or more players excluded may continue with its other players.

Serious indiscipline is penalized by the total elimination of a team; only in this case can penalties affect results already obtained.

Curling

Two teams of four players deliver round stones across a measured length of ice to a marked target area, or "house." One point is scored for each stone inside the house and closer to its center, or "tee," than any opponent's stone.

Stones are round, not more than 36in (91.44cm) in circumference or less than 4.5in (11.43cm) high. They must not weigh more than 44lb (19.96kg) including the handle and bolt.

They are concave on the top and underneath. A bolt through a center hole screws into a goose-neck handle, which is used to deliver the stone.

A dolly is used in some countries to mark the center of the house.

Playing area An area of ice 46yd long, with two target circles or houses 38yd apart. The houses are usually marked by blue outer and red inner circles.
Behind the circles are hacks or crampits – rubber- or metal-covered footholds from which players deliver their stones.

Officials Umpires supervise the measuring at the end of each head, settle disputes, and have the final decision.

Dress is usually informal and gloves are a matter of choice. Rubber-soled shoes or boots are usually worn. A sliding sole is worn on one foot. Spikes on footwear, which would damage the ice, are not allowed.

Competitions There are many national and international competitions, played under the jurisdiction of the International Curling Federation.

Competitors Two teams, compete against each other for the highest score. Each team has four members: lead, number 2, number 3, and the captain, or skip.

Matches Each match consists of a number of ends, usually 10. In the case of a tie, another end is played to break it.

Procedure The two skips agree by lot which team shall deliver the first stone. Each member has two stones, which are played alternately against his opponent.
A team's order of play is decided by the skip and remains the same throughout the match. At the end of each end, the winning rink starts in the next end. An end is considered started when the first player is on the hack and the skip is in position.
Each player must deliver his stone from the hack and release it before crossing the hog line during delivery.

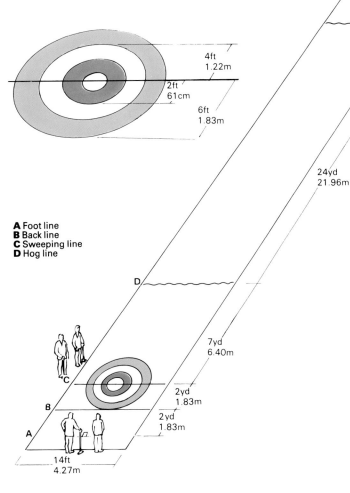

A Foot line
B Back line
C Sweeping line
D Hog line

4ft 1.22m
2ft 61cm
6ft 1.83m
24yd 21.96m
7yd 6.40m
2yd 1.83m
2yd 1.83m
14ft 4.27m

After a stone is delivered the player's side may sweep the ice to the sweeping line. Opposing skips may sweep behind the sweeping line (behind the tee). Sweeping is directed by the skips and must always be to the side. No sweepings must be left in the path of a moving stone. No stone may be substituted for another after a match has started.
If a stone breaks, play continues to the end of that end with the largest fragment. Another stone is used for the rest of the match.
Any stone that finishes on its side or upside down is removed from the ice.
If, during delivery, the handle comes out of a stone, the shot may be replayed.

Any stone that does not pass the hog line is removed, unless it has struck another stone in position.

Penalties
1) Any rink not having three players is disqualified. In the case of illness or accident during a match, the lead plays four stones.
2) If a stone is played from the wrong hack, the stone is removed from the ice.
3) If a player delivers out of turn, his stone is stopped and returned to him.
4) If a player touches a moving stone of his own team, it is removed from the ice. If a stone is touched by a member of the opposing team, it is placed in a position decided upon by the player's skip.

Scoring When all stones have been played, the end is completed and the score taken. The scoring side gains one point for each stone inside the house and closer to its center, or tee, than any stone of the opposing team. Measurements are taken from the tee to the nearest part of the stones.

Brooms or brushes are used in Scotland, elsewhere in Europe, United States and Canada. Whisk brooms are made of corn straw, nylon, flagged polypropylene, or horsehair. On instruction from his skip, each player uses his broom to sweep frost and moisture from in front of the running stone. This helps to keep the stone straight and make it run farther. The skip also uses his broom to direct his team.

© DIAGRAM

Croquet

Croquet is a game for two or four players. The object is to score points by hitting balls with a mallet through a course of hoops and against a center peg. The game is won by the side that finishes the course first with both balls or scores most points in an agreed time.

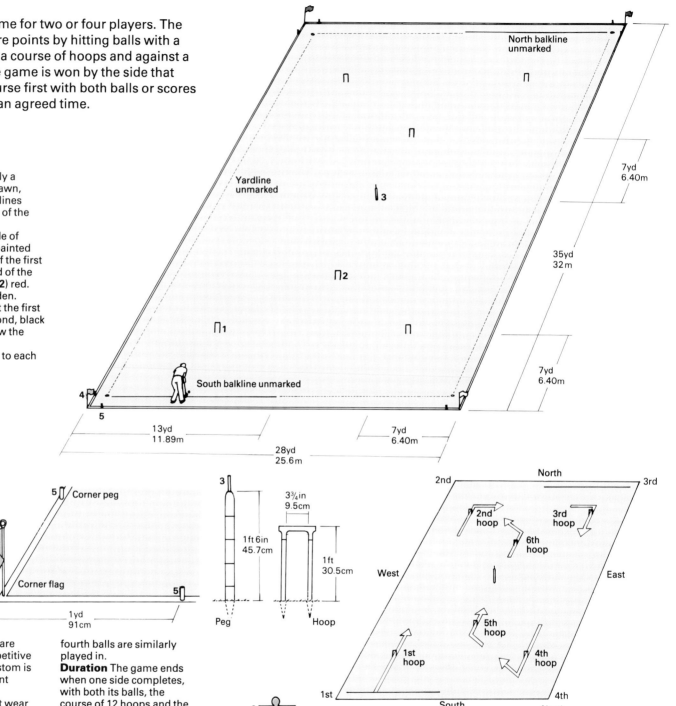

North balkline unmarked

Yardline unmarked

South balkline unmarked

7yd
6.40m

35yd
32m

7yd
6.40m

13yd
11.89m

7yd
6.40m

28yd
25.6m

The court is usually a rectangular grass lawn, bordered by white lines named after points of the compass.
The hoops are made of rounded iron and painted white. The crown of the first hoop (1) is blue and of the last hoop or rover (2) red.
The peg (3) is wooden.
Flags (4) are blue at the first corner, red the second, black the third, and yellow the fourth.
Corner pegs (5) are to each side of the flags.

5 Corner peg

4

1ft
30.5cm

Corner flag

5

1yd
91cm

3

3¾ in
9.5cm

1ft 6in
45.7cm

1ft
30.5cm

Peg

Hoop

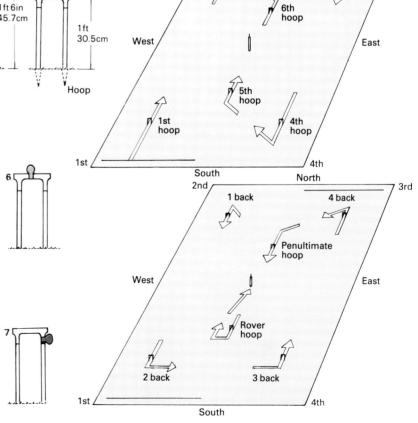

2nd   North   3rd

2nd hoop

3rd hoop

6th hoop

West   East

5th hoop

1st hoop

4th hoop

1st   South   4th

2nd   North   3rd

1 back   4 back

Penultimate hoop

West   East

Rover hoop

2 back   3 back

1st   South   4th

6

7

Officials Referees are appointed for competitive croquet, but the custom is for players to be joint referees.
Dress Players must wear rubber-soled, flat-heeled shoes. White clothing is usual for competitions.
Scoring One point for sending a ball through its next hoop, and one when it strikes the peg at the end of the course. Therefore each ball scores 13, with a maximum of 26 points per side.
Starting play A toss decides who plays first and who has choice of balls. The striker plays either of his balls from a point on either balk line. When his turn ends, his opponent does likewise. The third and

fourth balls are similarly played in.
Duration The game ends when one side completes, with both its balls, the course of 12 hoops and the peg. If there is no winner after an agreed time, the person in play finishes his turn, his opponent has a turn, and then the winner is the side with the most points.
Clips, the color of each ball, are used to indicate the next hoop for each ball. They are attached to the hoop's crown (6) for the first six hoops, and to the upright (7) for the last six. The striker removes his clip after striking a ball through a hoop, replacing it on the correct hoop when his turn ends.

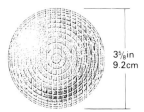

Balls must be of even weight, 15¾–16¼oz. One player or pair takes the blue and the black, the other the red and the yellow.

3⅝in
9.2cm

Mallet It may be any length. The head must be wood, but metal may be used for weighting and strengthening.

The faces, any shape, must be identical and parallel. Only a damaged mallet may be changed during a turn.

Turns alternate throughout the game. Either, but only one, of the side's balls may be used in a turn. Initially, a turn is only one stroke, but extra strokes are gained:
(**a**) by sending a ball through its next hoop – one ordinary shot (a continuation stroke);
(**b**) by making a roquet.

Making a roquet (when the striker's ball hits another) is always followed by a croquet shot and then (unless either ball has been sent out of play) by a continuation stroke.
Each ball may be roqueted only once in a turn unless the striker's ball scores a point by going through a hoop.
If the striker's ball hits two balls in one shot, the roqueted ball is the one hit first.

The croquet shot The striker places his ball alongside the roqueted ball. He then hits his ball and so moves the croqueted ball. It is a foul if the croqueted ball does not at least shake, in which case the balls are replaced and the turn ends.

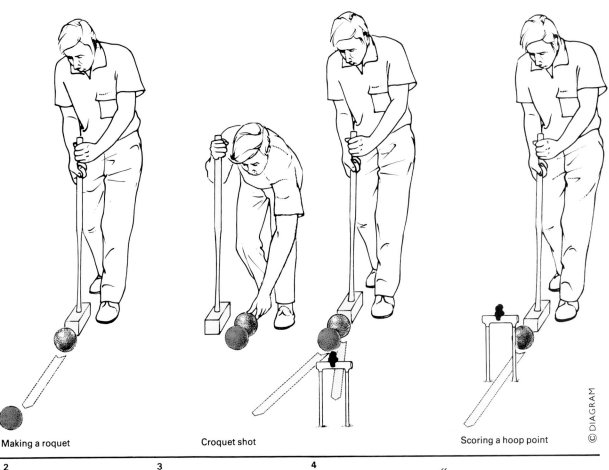

Making a roquet

Croquet shot

Scoring a hoop point

© DIAGRAM

1

2

3

4

In play

Out of play

Foul strokes The striker must not:
touch the head of the mallet with his hand (**1**);
kick or hit the mallet onto the ball (**2**);
rest either the mallet or a hand or arm used in the shot against his leg or foot;
rest the mallet shaft or his hand or arms on the ground;
strike the ball with any part of the mallet but its face;
push or pull his ball when it is touching another, without first striking it distinctly;
hit the ball twice in one shot;
move a stationary ball by hitting a hoop or peg with the mallet;
strike the ball into a hoop upright (**3**) or the peg when it rests directly against it;

touch any other ball with his mallet or any ball including his own with any part of his person;
fail to move the croqueted ball in a croquet shot.
The penalty after a stroke fault (provided it is claimed before the next stroke) is the end of the striker's turn and no point scored.
A ball in hand is a ball that has to be moved:
when any part of it is over the inside edge of the border (**4**);
when it is in the yardline area (the striker's ball is in hand only at the end of his turn; others may be in hand after each stroke).
Balls in hand are to be

placed, before the next stroke, on the yardline at the point where the ball crossed the border.
If two or more balls have to be replaced, the striker decides the order.
Obstacles The striker may move his ball or another if a fixed obstacle outside the court is likely to interfere with his shot.
Any loose impediments (eg leaves) may be moved, and the striker's ball or any ball from which he is taking croquet may be moved from a worn corner spot.
Allowance may be made for damage (eg holes made by a mallet) and any ball may be wiped at any time by the striker.

No player may make guiding marks either on or off the court.
If part of a hoop or of the peg is in a straight line between his ball and all the others, or if part of the peg or hoop will interfere with the mallet in a roquet shot, the player may play his ball from any point on either balk line, provided his opponent was responsible for the ball being so positioned.
Doubles The rules are generally as for singles, with the following exceptions:
turns alternate, but each player takes the same ball throughout;
the striker's partner faces the same penalties as the striker if he contacts a ball

incorrectly;
a player may advise his partner, set his balls for a croquet shot, and indicate the direction his mallet should swing, but he should be well away from him when the stroke is actually made; either player may make a replay if they have received false information.
Handicaps There is an accepted handicapping system, ranging from 20 to minus 3. In singles, one extra turn is given for each unit of difference (called a *bisque*) between players' handicaps. In doubles, half a turn is given for each unit of difference. When taking a half turn (*half bisque*), no point can be scored.

Golf

Golf consists of playing a ball with a club into a series of holes by successive strokes. Players may compete individually or in teams, playing the course together in groups of two, three, or four. The two basic forms of competition are match play and stroke play. In match play the side winning the majority of holes wins the match. In stroke play the winner is the player who finishes with the fewest strokes.

Clubs A player may use a maximum of 14 clubs. He may replace damaged clubs during a round, or add extra clubs if he started with fewer than 14, provided he does not exceed the total. The 14-club rule applies to partners sharing a set of clubs.
There are three types of clubs.

a A "wood" is one with a head that is relatively broad from front to back, and is usually made of wood, plastic, or a light metal. Woods are numbered from 1 to 9 according to shape, and are used for long shots.
b An "iron" has a head that is relatively narrow from front to back, and is usually made of steel; irons are numbered from 1 to 10 and are used for shorter shots; a 3 iron is equivalent to a 4 wood.
c A "putter" is a light metal club used for playing the ball on the putting green.
Each club except the putter has only one striking face. The face may be scored or indented, but may not be shaped or finished in such a way as to cause extra movement of the ball. The length of shaft and the angle of the face of each club vary according to the kind of shot it is designed to play. Steeply angled faces give sharply lifting shots. The grip of the club must not be shaped to fit the hands in any way.

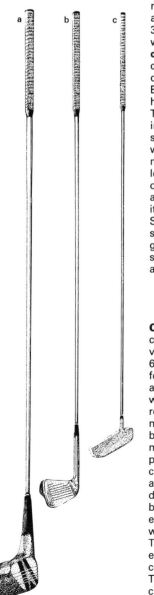

Course A standard golf course consists of 18 holes, varying in length from 100–600yd, and containing the following features:
a) the teeing ground, on which play begins, a rectangular area defined by markers;
b) the fairway, a closely-mown strip along which players aim to hit the ball;
c) the rough, unprepared areas flanking the fairway;
d) hazards, consisting of bunkers or areas of water;
e) the putting green, in which the hole is located. The length and features of each course vary with local conditions and planning. The boundaries must be clearly defined.

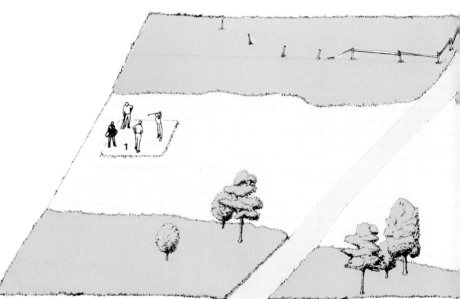

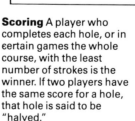

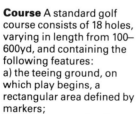

Scoring A player who completes each hole, or in certain games the whole course, with the least number of strokes is the winner. If two players have the same score for a hole, that hole is said to be "halved."
Par is the score that in theory a perfect player would take to complete a hole. Par is calculated on the length of a hole. It ranges from par 3 up to par 5. One stroke under par is a "birdie"; two strokes under is an "eagle"; one over par is a "bogey."
Handicaps are based on the total par score for a course. A man may receive a handicap of up to 24 strokes, and a woman up to 36 strokes.

Match play A hole is won by the side that holes the ball in fewer strokes. (In handicap matches the lower net score wins.) A hole is halved if each side holes out in the same number of strokes. A match consists of a stipulated number of holes. It is won by the side winning the majority of holes, so it can be won before the round is completed.
Three-ball matches: each player plays two matches concurrently.
Best-ball matches: one player plays against the better ball of two, or the best ball of three, players.
Four-ball matches: two players play their better ball against the better ball of their opponents.

Players must play without unnecessary delays. Artificial devices to assist play or strokes, or to measure distance or conditions, are forbidden. A player may ask advice from, or give advice to, only his partner or either of their caddies. He must not ask for or accept physical assistance or protection from the weather.
He may have someone to indicate the line of play to him – on the putting green only the player, his partner or caddie may do so.
Caddies Each player is allowed one caddie to carry his clubs. The caddie may mark the position of the ball.

Stroke play Generally, match play rules apply, but the winner is the player who completes the round or rounds in the fewest strokes. Each competitor has a marker to record his number of strokes on a score card, which the competitor and the marker must sign before it is handed in at the end of the round. In four-ball stroke play two competitors play as partners, each playing his own ball. The lower score of the partners is the score of the hole.
Practice Competitors are not allowed practice strokes during a round, except on the putting green of the hole last played, but practice swings are allowed.

The ball is designed to behave as if it were spherically symmetrical. Its surface is dimpled to improve accuracy and distance of flight. Maximum weight is 1.62oz (45.93g). Minimum diameter must not be less than 1.68in (42.67mm).

If the ball is damaged and unfit for play, another ball may be substituted where the original ball lay. It must be substituted in the presence of the opponent (match play) or the marker (stroke play).
A ball interfering with play may be lifted; it is replaced after the stroke has been made.

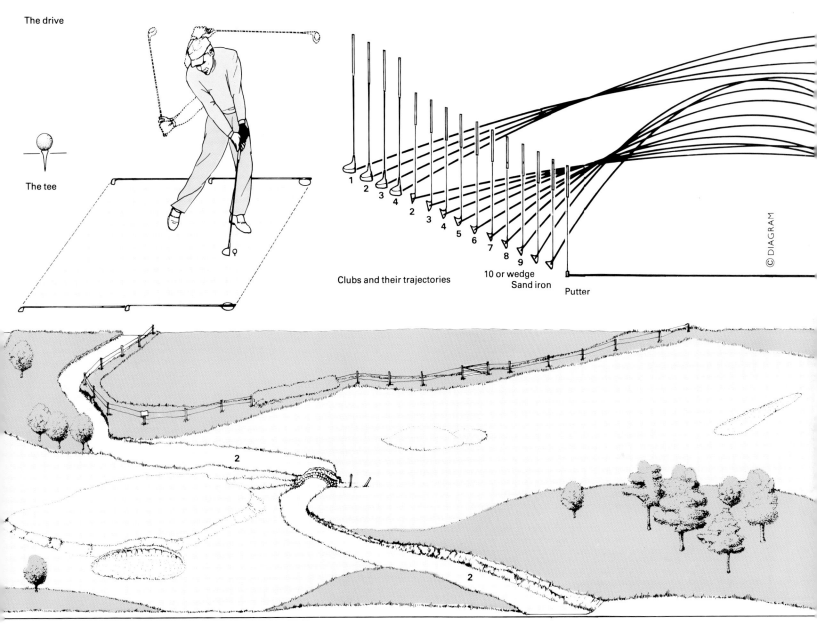

The drive

The tee

Clubs and their trajectories

10 or wedge
Sand iron

Putter

Starting play (1) Each player plays a ball from the first teeing ground. The ball may be played from the ground, from a heap of sand, or on a wooden or plastic tee.
A draw decides who plays first – the "honor." Subsequently, the side that wins the hole takes the honor at the next teeing ground. If a hole is halved the side that last had the honor retains it.
Partners play the ball in any order they choose.
Out of turn In match play if a player plays out of turn, his opponent may require him to replay the stroke, without penalty; in stroke play, the ball is deemed to be in play, without penalty.

Outside tee If the ball is played from outside the teeing ground, in match play the opponent may require it to be replayed from the teeing ground without penalty; in stroke play the player must restart from the teeing ground and incurs a penalty of two strokes. Failure to rectify the mistake is penalized by disqualification.
Off tee If the ball falls off the tee before the stroke, it may be re-teed; if the stroke has been made, it is counted. No penalty is incurred in either case.
Playing the ball The ball must be played as it lies: it must not be deliberately moved or touched. A player must not try to improve his shot by moving, bending, or

breaking anything that is fixed or growing. Nor may he remove or press down sand, loose soil or cut turf. But he may make such adjustments in order to take his stance or swing the club, tee a ball, or repair damage to the green. The player can move loose impediments without penalty unless the impediments or the ball lie in or touch a hazard.
The stroke The ball must be struck with the head of the club – it must not be pushed, scraped, or spooned. A player must not strike the ball twice: if he does the stroke is counted and a penalty stroke is added. The player must not play a moving ball unless it is in water, or moves after the stroke begins.

Order The ball farthest from the hole is played first.
If a player plays out of turn in match play, his opponent may require him to replay the stroke; in stroke play the game continues.
Water hazards (2) are water courses (even when containing no water), or any other areas of water. They include sea, lakes, ponds, rivers, ditches.
A lateral water hazard is one that runs approximately parallel to the line of play. A player may search in water for his ball, and no penalty is incurred by moving it. If a ball lies in or is lost in a water hazard, the player may drop a ball (with a penalty of one stroke) either as near as possible to the point from which the ball was played, or

so that the point at which the ball last crossed the margin or the hazard lies between the ball and the hole.
At a lateral water hazard the player also has the choice of dropping the ball outside the hazard, within two clubs' length of either edge of the hazard and opposite the point at which the ball last crossed the edge of the hazard. The ball must not stop nearer to the hazard than that point. Again, a penalty of one stroke is incurred. A player may make a stroke at a ball moving in water, without penalty, but he must not delay the stroke until the ball is in a better position.

Interference covers any deliberate or accidental act that interferes with the ball while in play.

Wrong ball If a player plays the wrong ball, except in a hazard, he loses the hole (match play) or incurs two penalty strokes (stroke play). In a hazard, strokes at the wrong ball are not penalized or counted, provided the player then plays the correct ball. If the wrong ball belongs to another player, it must be replaced.

Moving ball If a moving ball is accidentally stopped or deflected by any outside agency (a) it must be played from where it lies, and no penalty is incurred.
It is defined as a "rub of the green."
If the ball lodges in anything

that is moving, the player must drop a ball (or place it, if on a putting green) as near as possible to the place where the ball became lodged.

If a ball is stopped or deflected by its owner, his partner, or either of their caddies (b) or equipment, the player loses the hole (match play) or incurs two

penalty strokes (stroke play). If a ball is stopped or deflected by an opponent, his caddie, or their equipment (c), no penalty is incurred in match play and the owner may replay it, or play it as it lies; in stroke play it is reckoned a rub of the green and the ball is played from where it comes to rest.

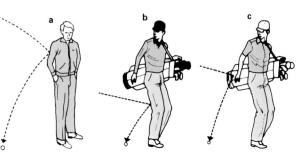

Ball at rest If a ball at rest is moved by any outside agency except the wind, the player must replace it before making his stroke; if he or his caddie moves the ball, there is a one-stroke penalty. If a player moves the ball after addressing it, he incurs one penalty stroke (but there is no penalty if he knocks it accidentally off the tee).
If the ball is moved by an opponent, his caddie, or his equipment, other than during a search, the opponent incurs one penalty stroke in match play; in stroke play the ball must be replaced, but there is no penalty.
If a ball in play and at rest is moved by another ball in motion after a stroke, the

moved ball must be replaced.

Ball on green The rules differ for match play and stroke play.
a) In match play, if an opponent's ball might interfere with the putt, the opponent must lift it. If the ball when played stops where the opponent's ball was, a second stroke must be played before the removed ball is replaced. A player may concede that his opponent would hole out with his next stroke; he may then move the ball before playing his own stroke.

A bunker (3) is an area of bare ground, often a depression, covered with a deep layer of sand.

Long grass and bushes (4) may be moved only to enable a player to find and identify a ball that is lying among them. He is not necessarily entitled to see the ball when actually playing the stroke.

Other obstructions A movable obstruction may be removed; if the ball is moved by so doing, it must be replaced without penalty. If the ball is in or near an immovable obstruction, including casual water (any temporary accumulation of water), ground under repair, or a hole made by a burrowing animal, the player may play the ball as it lies or take relief – that is, lift and drop or place the ball in a new position not nearer the hole.

Dropping the ball is done when the ball has to be repositioned anywhere except on the green, and must be done by the player himself. He must stand erect, hold the ball at shoulder height and arm's length, and drop it (d). Any other method of dropping the ball incurs one penalty stroke.
If the ball touches the player, his partner, caddie or equipment before or after it reaches the ground it is re-dropped without penalty.

A ball must be dropped as near as possible to the point where it lay, but not nearer to the hole.
If a ball is to be dropped in a hazard it must be dropped and come to rest in that hazard.
If a dropped ball rolls into a hazard, out of bounds, or more than two clubs'

lengths from where it struck the ground, or stops nearer the hole than the original position, it may be redropped without penalty. If it rolls into a similar position it may be placed where it first struck the ground when re-dropped, without penalty.

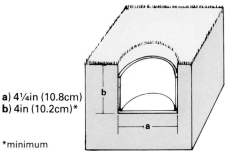

a) 4¼in (10.8cm)
b) 4in (10.2cm)*

*minimum

The hole should be 4¼in in diameter, and at least 4in deep. Any lining must be sunk at least 1in below the surface of the putting green.

In stroke play, if a competitor's ball might interfere with another player's stroke, the latter may ask for it to be lifted. If a player thinks his ball could assist a competitor, he may remove it or play first, without penalty. If a player's ball strikes another on the green, he incurs a two-stroke penalty. He must play his ball as it lies, and the competitor's ball must be replaced.

Lifting A ball to be lifted may be lifted only by the owner, his partner, or another person authorized by the owner. In stroke play, if the ball is lifted (except as provided for in the rules) before holing out, the owner must replace it and incur a one-stroke penalty. He must replace it before he makes a stroke from the next teeing ground or leaves the final green.

Placing The owner, his partner, or either caddie may replace a ball. If a ball fails to remain where it is placed, it can be placed in the nearest spot – not nearer the hole – where it will rest. If the original lie of the ball has been altered, it must be placed in the nearest possible lie similar to the original, not nearer the hole and not more than one club length from the original lie.

Lost or unplayable If a ball is lost or out of bounds – that is, outside the confines of the course – the player may play his next stroke as near as possible at the spot from which he originally played the ball (adding a penalty stroke to his score), except if it is in a water hazard. If the ball was played from the teeing ground, it may be played from anywhere in that area.

If the ball is unplayable the player may play again from the original spot, or drop the ball within two clubs' lengths of where it lay, but not nearer the hole. He incurs a penalty stroke. He is the sole judge whether a ball is unplayable.

He may stand out of bounds to play a ball on the course.

Provisional ball To save time when a ball is out of bounds or lost (except in a water hazard), a player may play another ball from as near as possible to where the original ball was played. This is a provisional ball. He must play the provisional ball before a search begins. Once the provisional ball is played from a point beyond the point where the original ball is likely to be, that ball is deemed lost.

If the original ball is found and is not out of bounds, it comes back into play and the provisional ball is abandoned. A player has five minutes to find his ball. Penalties for infringements are loss of hole in match play, and two strokes in stroke play.

The flagstick

The putting green (5) is the area around the hole specially prepared for putting. A ball on the wrong green must be lifted and dropped off the edge before being played.

The flagstick is centered in the hole to show its position. A flagstick is said to be attended when it is being held. A player may have it held up or removed before and during his stroke. If the ball rests against the flagstick while it is in the hole, the flagstick may be removed. If the ball falls into the hole, the player is deemed to have holed out with his last stroke.

If a ball strikes an attended flagstick, or the person attending it, the penalty in match play is loss of the hole, and in stroke play, two strokes.

The putt The line of the putt must not be prepared, except for the removal of loose impediments, such as stones and leaves. The player may not press anything down with his club, though he may ground the club in front of the ball when addressing it.

If the line of the putt is obstructed by something that cannot be moved, such as casual water or an animal hole, the player may lift the ball and place it in a position to avoid the obstruction – but not closer to the hole. The player may repair any damage to the green caused by the ball's impact, and he may also clean the ball. The line of the putt may be indicated by a partner or a caddie, but must not be marked or touched. The player must not test the surface by rolling a ball. When a ball is in motion after a stroke on the putting green no other ball may be played or touched. If the ball is stopped or deflected by any outside agency, the stroke is canceled; the ball is replaced and played again.

If the ball hangs over the edge of the hole for more than ten seconds, it is deemed to be at rest. If it subsequently falls into the hole a player is said to have holed; with a further stroke added to his score.

Foul putt

Correct putt

© DIAGRAM

Court handball

Court handball is a ball game played by two players (singles) or two pairs (doubles) on a walled court. The ball is struck with a gloved hand in such a way that it is difficult for the opponent to return it. The court may have one, three, or four walls. The four-wall game is the most popular.

The court for the four-wall game must conform to the measurements shown in the diagram.
The lines on the floor must be red or white and 1½in wide.
Officials Each match is controlled by a referee who is, where possible, assisted by a scorer. Larger tournaments are under the overall control of a chairman.
The referee is responsible for:
checking the equipment;
briefly checking that the players are aware of the court regulations;
all decisions during the match;
ruling a player out of the match for unsporting conduct, leaving the court without permission, or reporting late for the start.

Duration The first player or pair to win two games wins the match.
Each player or pair is allowed three 1-minute time-outs in each game. A 5-minute interval is permitted between the first and second games and a 10-minute interval between the second and third.

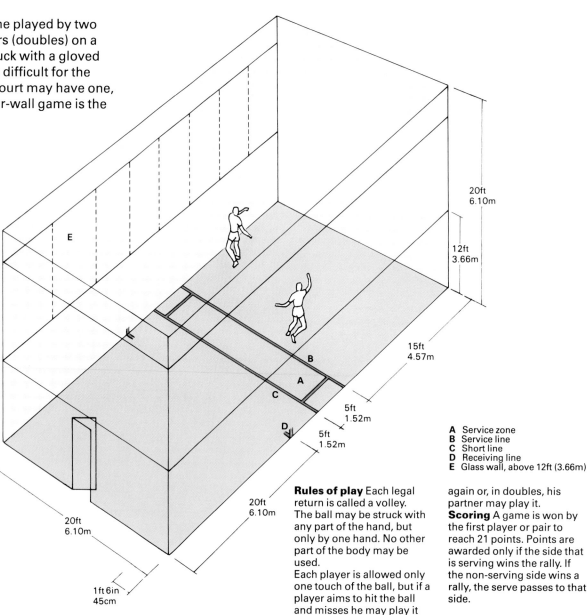

20ft 6.10m

12ft 3.66m

15ft 4.57m

5ft 1.52m

5ft 1.52m

20ft 6.10m

20ft 6.10m

1ft 6in 45cm

A Service zone
B Service line
C Short line
D Receiving line
E Glass wall, above 12ft (3.66m)

Rules of play Each legal return is called a volley. The ball may be struck with any part of the hand, but only by one hand. No other part of the body may be used.
Each player is allowed only one touch of the ball, but if a player aims to hit the ball and misses he may play it again or, in doubles, his partner may play it.
Scoring A game is won by the first player or pair to reach 21 points. Points are awarded only if the side that is serving wins the rally. If the non-serving side wins a rally, the serve passes to that side.

Obstructions or hinders There are two types of obstruction:
dead ball hinders, after which the point is replayed;
avoidable hinders after which the offender is punished by losing a point or the serve.
Dead ball hinders occur when:
the ball passes through an opponent's legs and there is no fair chance of seeing or returning the ball (**1**);
there is any unintentional hindrance that unsights an opponent;
a returned ball, without first bouncing, hits an opponent before striking the front wall;
any body contact with an opponent interferes with the seeing or striking of the ball.

1

2

Avoidable hinders take place when:
a deliberate block is made to prevent a player from reaching the ball (**2**);
a player does not move out of the way to allow an opponent his shot;
deliberate pushing takes place;
a player moves into the path of the ball.

The ball A standard handball is made of blue rubber and weighs 2.3oz. When dropped from a height of 5ft 10in, it should bounce 3ft 6in-4ft at a temperature of 20°C.

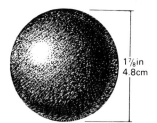

1⅞in
4.8cm

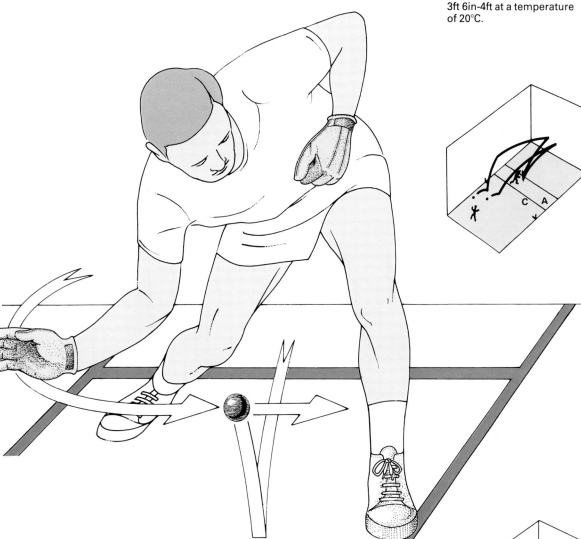

The serve The player or pair to win the toss serves first. Play begins on the call of "play ball" from the referee. The server serves from any position within the service zone (**A**). He must not place any part of either foot beyond the lines around that area. The server bounces the ball on the floor inside the zone, and on the bounce strikes it with his hand or fist against the front wall.
For the service to be valid the ball must rebound and land behind the short line (**C**), whether or not it touches one of the side walls. The player continues to serve until he makes an out serve, or two fault serves in succession.
Service in doubles The server's partner must stand still with his back to the side wall in the service box until the ball has come back past the short line.
Returning the serve The receiver(s) must stand at least 5ft behind the short line, as indicated by the 3in line on the side wall (**D**), until the ball is struck by the server.
If the receiver wants to return the ball before it bounces he must have both feet behind the service zone. But the more usual legal return is to strike the ball on the first bounce. If the ball bounces a second time the server wins a point.
The ball must be returned to the front wall either directly, or after touching one or both side walls.
The return must not touch the floor before hitting the front wall.

Equipment Gloves must be worn. They are light in color, snug-fitting, and made of leather or other soft material. The fingers must not be webbed, and no metal or other hard substances may be worn under the glove.
Surgical gauze or tape may be wound round the hands beneath the gloves to prevent bruising.
Players must change their gloves when they have become so wet as to dampen the ball.
Dress Players must wear white shirts, shorts, socks, and shoes. The costume may bear club insignia.

Service faults come into three categories:
1) dead-ball serves, after which the player takes another serve without penalty;
2) fault serves, two of which result in the service passing to the opponent; and
3) out serves, after which the serve passes straight to the opponent.
Dead-ball serves occur when:
in doubles, the ball hits the server's partner on rebounding from the wall while he is in the service zone and before the ball touches the ground;
the server, or his partner, obscures the receiver's view of the ball.

Fault serves occur when:
the server (**S**) his partner (**P**) steps out of the service zone before the ball has passed the short line;
the ball hits the floor in front of the short line (**1**);
the ball hits a side wall before crossing the short line (**2**), or hits the ceiling;
the ball hits the back wall without first bouncing;
the ball hits the crotch (where the front wall joins the floor) (**3**). A crotch serve into the back wall is allowed.

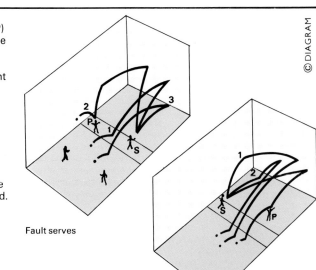

Fault serves

Out serves

© DIAGRAM

Out serves occur when:
the server (**S**) bounces the ball more than three times before serving;
the server aims his hand to serve the ball and misses;
the ball strikes a side wall (**1**), the ceiling, or the floor (**2**) before hitting the front wall;
the ball rebounds and touches the server, or his partner (**P**) while he is out of the service box;
in doubles, the pair serves out of order.

Rugby fives

Rugby fives is a ball game played on a four-walled court by two players (singles) or four players (doubles). The ball is struck with a gloved hand with the object of making it difficult for an opponent to return the ball as it rebounds off the front wall of the court. Points are scored only by the player or pair receiving the serve.

The ball is hard and white, with an inner core of cork and string and an outer skin of leather. Its circumference is 5¾in, and its weight 1½oz.
Equipment Padded gloves are worn on both hands. Players usually dress in white shirts, shorts, socks, and rubber-soled shoes.

The court must conform to the measurements shown in the diagram. The walls of the court should be black and the floor red. The floor has no markings and is made of stone. A wooden board runs across the front wall 2ft 6in from the floor.
Officials The match may be controlled by an umpire, whose decision is final on all incidents.

2ft 6in
76cm

Board

15ft
4.57m

6ft
1.83m

28ft
8.54m

18ft
5.49m

Good service
(as struck with the left hand)

Blackguard

Lets

a

b

Duration The first player to score 15 points is the winner unless the score has reached 14 all. In that event the first to reach 16 is the winner. In a match consisting of more than one game, a three-minute interval is allowed between games.
Scoring Unlike squash or court handball, only the receiver of service can score points. When the receiver wins a rally, he gains a point. If the server wins a rally, he then becomes the receiver.
Starting play Before play begins a preliminary rally is held. The winner becomes the receiver, while the loser serves.
Serving Play starts with the server, or the receiver if requested, throwing the ball so that it first hits the front

wall and then a side wall of his choice (according to whether he is right-handed or left-handed) before falling into court.
After the ball has bounced the server then hits the ball against the same side wall and on to the front wall above the board.
A blackguard is a service that reaches the front wall without hitting the side wall. The receiver may elect to return a blackguard provided that he states that he is going to do so before he hits the ball. He may not however, return a blackguard if he needs only one point to win. If three successive blackguards are served, all untaken by the receiver, then the receiver wins a point.

Returning service The ball may be allowed to bounce off any of the four walls before being returned, as long as it touches the floor only once. The ball may then be struck to hit any number of other walls before hitting the front wall.
Rules of play After the service and its return, the players strike the ball alternately on to the front wall, either directly or after it has hit the side walls. The ball may bounce once before it is struck.
Rallies are won by a player when:
a) his adversary misses the ball, allows it to bounce twice, hits it below the board line, strikes it into the roof, sends it out of court, or directs it on to the floor

before it strikes the front wall;
b) his opponent hits him with the ball when his return would not have gone "up" (ie above the board line);
c) his opponent allows the ball to strike his person before it has bounced;
d) his opponent hits the ball with any part of his body other than the hand or forearm.
Lets The point is replayed when:
a) a player is hit by a return that would have gone "up";
b) a player is impeded in his attempt to return the ball;
c) the striker is hit by the ball after it has bounced;
d) the server, about to serve changes his mind and fails to hit the ball, or calls "no" after striking it.

Doubles The basic rules of singles play all apply. The pair that wins the preliminary rally has the option to receive or serve. The receiver remains "in" until his side loses a rally. Then the first of the opposing pair receives until they lose a rally, after which the second opponent receives until his side loses another rally. The right to receive then passes to the other side. The serving side must change servers every time the opponents score. Only the receiver may return service, unless he or his partner chooses to return a blackguard. If either side plays in the wrong order it must be pointed out before the next rally, otherwise that rally stands.

Jai alai (pelota)

Jai-alai (pelota) is a fast ball game played in a three-walled court (*fronton*) by two players, or by several teams of players. Players attempt to hit a ball (*pelota*) with a wicker basket (*cesta*) against the front wall (*frontis*) so that their opponents will be unable to return it and will therefore lose a point. The game originated in northern Spain. The rules given here are for the game now played in the United States.

The pelota has a hard rubber core, covered with a layer of linen thread and two layers of goatskin. The diameter is 2in and the weight 4½oz.

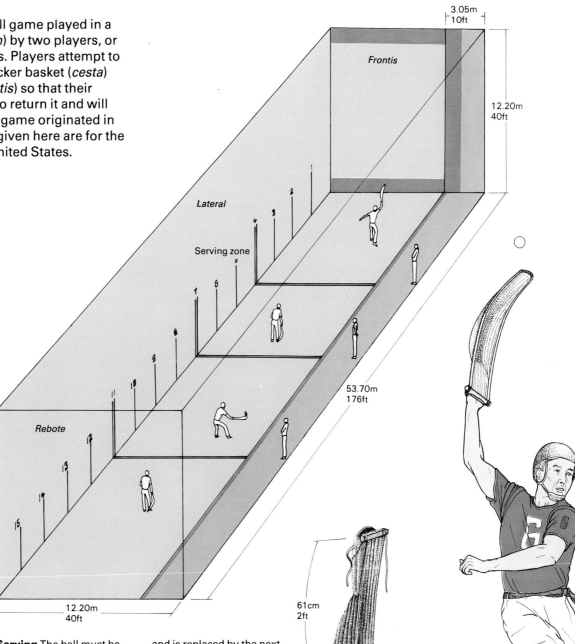

The court has three walls. The front wall is called the *frontis*, the back wall the *rebote*, the side wall the *lateral*.
The *frontis* is made of granite blocks; the *rebote*, *lateral*, and floor are made of gunite, a pressurized cement.
The fourth side of the court has a clear screen through which spectators watch the game.
The court is divided into 15 numbered areas. The serving zone is the space between areas 4 and 7.
Officials There are three judges, standing opposite lines 4, 7 and 11. Officials carry rackets to protect themselves from the ball.
Players The game can be played as singles, doubles or triples.
The *quiniela* (betting) version of the game is played as singles or doubles involving a maximum of eight teams consisting of one or two men.
Scoring A match is played for a number of points ranging from 7–35. Points are gained when the opponent:
a) returns the ball after it has bounced more than once;
b) misses the ball;
c) does not return the ball on to the *frontis*;
d) fails to catch the ball and throw it in a continuous motion.

Serving The ball must be served against the *frontis* so that it returns within the serving zone.
Playing the ball The ball must be caught in the *cesta* and thrown in a continuous motion. It may be returned before it bounces or after it has bounced once.
The ball must be returned to the *frontis* and be played within the green areas on the walls.
Quiniela The first two players or teams begin play with the number 1 side serving.
Play continues until one of the teams loses a point. The losing team then returns to the end of the players' bench

and is replaced by the next team to play (the number 3 side).
The game continues in this way with the winning team always remaining on court, until one side wins the match by scoring the specified number of points. There is a play-off in case of a tie.
Seven-points system In games where eight teams or players are playing for seven points, one point is scored for each win in the first round (ie until all eight players or teams have played once) and two points for each win in subsequent games.

The cesta is a wicker basket made to a player's specifications. It has a chestnut frame, covered with woven reed.
Front court players usually have smaller *cestas* than rear court players.
The player's hand is inserted into a leather glove which is sewn to the outside of the

cesta. A long tape is wrapped around the glove to keep it on the hand.
Dress Players wear white trousers, a colored sash or belt, colored shirt bearing a number, white rubber soled shoes and a helmet.

Squash

Squash is a racket game played in an enclosed court. The object of the game is to keep the ball in play while making it difficult for the opponent to do so. The rules and court dimensions are standard with the exception of the USA and parts of Canada and Mexico.

SINGLES

The court The dimensions of an international court are shown on the large diagram. The small illustration shows an American court.

The board or tin is a strip of resonant material running along the foot of the front wall. It is outside the playing area and makes a distinctive sound when hit.

The walls should be white or off-white and completely smooth. The door of the court should have a flush handle that will not deflect the ball.

Court markings must not exceed 5cm (or 1in in USA) in width and are painted red.

The floor is usually made of hardwood planks laid parallel to the side walls.

Officials The game is controlled by a marker and a referee, who sit in the center of the gallery. The marker calls the play and the score. The referee is in overall charge and decides all appeals. (In the USA appeals are decided by two appeal judges.)

Dress Organizers may specify regulations concerning player's clothing, which must be complied with in their particular tournaments. Otherwise any color clothing is accepted. Non-marking shoes must be worn.

Duration Players are allowed 5 minutes for a warm-up before play begins. A match is the best of five games. Play is continuous except for a 90 second interval between games. In the USA the interval is 2 minutes with a 5-minute interval between the third and fourth game.

Scoring The international singles game is played to 9 points. At 8-all the receiving player may call "no-set" (in which case the game ends at 9 points). The other option is a call of "set 2" (game ends at 10 points). In the USA the game is played to 15 points. At 13-all the receiving player

may choose his call. If the score reaches 14-all without first reaching 13-all, the player reaching 14 first has the option of playing "no set" (game to 15) or "set 2" (game to 16).

Winning points Under international rules, only the server can score points. In the USA both server and receiver can score. A player wins a point, if his opponent fails to make a good return. A return is good, if the ball is returned by the striker onto the front wall above the board and below the out-of-court line, before it bounces twice on the floor. The ball must reach this area without touching the floor and it must not touch any part of the striker's clothing or be hit twice.

If a good return has been made in the direction of the front wall but is deflected by an opponent or his racket (**a**), the striker is awarded the point.

If the ball would not have reached the front wall (**b**), the striker loses the point. If the server fails to keep the ball in play, the service passes to his opponent. If the server wins a point, he keeps the service. If the ball is deflected, when it would have hit a side wall and then the front wall, a let is played.

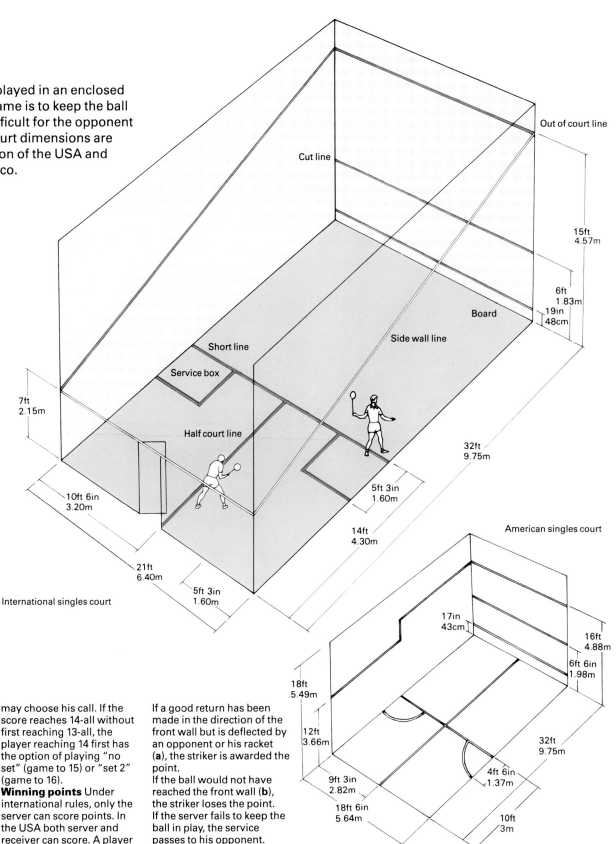

Out of court line

Cut line

15ft
4.57m

6ft
1.83m

19in
48cm

Board

Side wall line

Short line

Service box

7ft
2.15m

Half court line

32ft
9.75m

5ft 3in
1.60m

10ft 6in
3.20m

14ft
4.30m

21ft
6.40m

5ft 3in
1.60m

International singles court

American singles court

17in
43cm

16ft
4.88m

6ft 6in
1.98m

18ft
5.49m

12ft
3.66m

32ft
9.75m

9ft 3in
2.82m

4ft 6in
1.37m

18ft 6in
5.64m

10ft
3m

Deflection
a   **b**

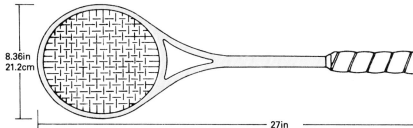

8.36in
21.2cm

27in
68.5cm

The racket The head or shaft must not contain outside edges with a radius of curvature less than 2mm (0.08in). For safety string and string ends must be recessed within the racket head or be covered by a non-marking bumper strip. Damaged rackets should not be used. Strings should be of gut, nylon or substitute material, provided metal is not used. ISRF specification for weight is 255g.

The ball is made of rubber or a composition of rubber and butyl, and must have a matt finish. ISRF specifications are: weight 23.3–24.6g; diameter 39.5–41.5mm.

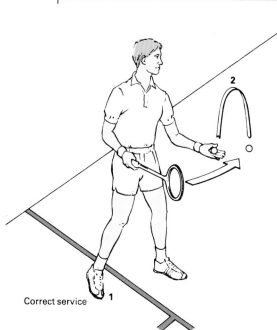

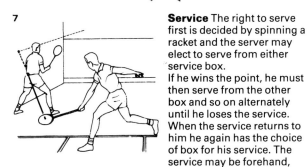

Correct service 1

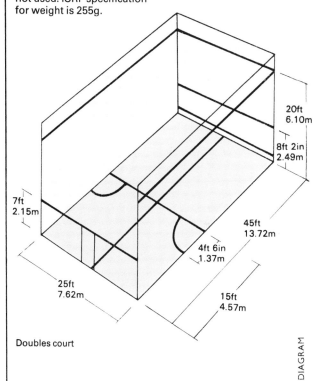

Doubles court

© DIAGRAM

20ft
6.10m

8ft 2in
2.49m

7ft
2.15m

45ft
13.72m

4ft 6in
1.37m

25ft
7.62m

15ft
4.57m

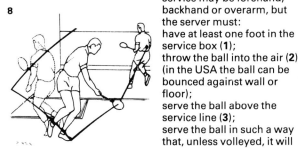

7

8

9

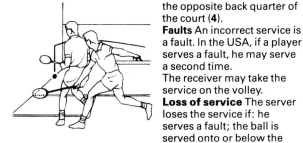

Service The right to serve first is decided by spinning a racket and the server may elect to serve from either service box.

If he wins the point, he must then serve from the other box and so on alternately until he loses the service. When the service returns to him he again has the choice of box for his service. The service may be forehand, backhand or overarm, but the server must:
have at least one foot in the service box (**1**);
throw the ball into the air (**2**) (in the USA the ball can be bounced against wall or floor);
serve the ball above the service line (**3**);
serve the ball in such a way that, unless volleyed, it will return from the front wall to land behind the short line in the opposite back quarter of the court (**4**).

Faults An incorrect service is a fault. In the USA, if a player serves a fault, he may serve a second time.
The receiver may take the service on the volley.

Loss of service The server loses the service if: he serves a fault; the ball is served onto or below the board (**5**); the ball is served out of court (**6**); the ball is served against any part of the court before it hits the front wall; he misses the ball; strikes it more than once; serves on or below the cut line; he touches the ball in any way before it hits the floor twice or his opponent hits it.

Lets are occasions when a rally is replayed. A let is played if:
the ball would have hit a side wall before hitting the front wall, but instead hits an opponent (**7**);
the striker follows the ball around, thus turning before making his stroke, and the ball hits his opponent on its way to the front wall (**8**);
the receiver is not ready to receive service and does not try to play the ball;
the ball strikes any object lying on the floor or is damaged in any way;
the position of the player about to strike the ball makes it impossible for his opponent to avoid being hit or if the striker refrains from making the stroke to avoid hitting the other player (**9**).
It is generally the player's responsibility to claim a let by calling "let please."
If a player misses a stroke completely, he may play another shot provided he can retrieve the ball before it bounces twice.

Obstruction With play taking place in such a confined space, a player must make every effort to give his opponent freedom of movement and full view of the ball.
If the referee considers that a player is making insufficient efforts to avoid obstructing his opponent, he may award that rally to the opponent.

DOUBLES
The game of doubles is a North American invention and specifications for the court originate from the USA.
The ball is hard, not unlike American singles balls, but bouncier.
Rules are the same as for singles, with the following exceptions.

Scoring The game is played to 15 points, with set calls as for North American singles. If the non-serving side wins a rally, a point is added to its score.

Service The two players on the serving side serve one after the other to the receiving side. The first server serves until his side concedes a point and is then relieved by his partner. This order is maintained throughout the match. When a further point is lost, the serve passes to the first player of the opposing pair. When he loses a point, the fourth player takes his turn to serve.

At the beginning of each new game, however, the serving side loses the right to serve after the loss of only one point.
The side winning a game has the choice of serving or receiving at the beginning of the next game.
At the start of each game one player of each pair is designated to receive service in the left-hand court, the other in the right-hand court.
The receiver may not return faulty serves.

113

Paddleball

Paddleball is played by two, three, or four players on a court with one, three, or four walls. A small ball is played against the walls with a paddle (bat). The serving side may win points by serving an ace or winning a volley. The first side to score 21 points wins the game. A match is the best two out of three games.

The court is marked with lines 1½in wide.
The four-wall court has three high walls, a ceiling, and a lower back wall. A line midway between the front and back wall is called the short line (**A**), and in front of it is another line, the service line (**B**). The space between these lines is the service zone (**C**). Each end of the service zone is marked off to form a service box (**D**).
The one-wall court has a 4ft wire fence along the top of the wall. The sidelines are extended beyond the end line at the back of the court to help in judging long balls and serve-outs. The markings are different from those of the four-wall court: the service line is behind the short line. There should be a playing space of at least 6ft around the court.
The three-wall court is similar to the one-wall court, except that the side walls extend as far as the short line.
Officials A referee controls each match, assisted by a scorer.
The referee stands in the center and above the back wall in four-wall courts; on the side near the end of a side wall in three-wall courts; and on the side and toward the front of the court on an elevated platform in one-wall courts.
The scorer keeps a record of play, announces the score after each exchange, and helps the referee generally.
Players A match may be played between two players (singles), by three players (cut-throat), or by four players (doubles).
Dress Players must wear white shirts, shorts, socks, and shoes. Warm-up suits must also be white if worn in a match. A glove may be worn on the hand holding the paddle. Knee and elbow pads of a soft material may be worn.

Duration Matches last for the best of three games. A two-minute interval is allowed between the first two games. A 10-minute interval is allowed after the second game, during which the players are allowed to leave the court.
Time-outs Play is continuous during games except for time-outs. Two time-outs per player or side are allowed in a game. They must not exceed 30 seconds. They may be requested by serving or receiving players. Play may be suspended for 15 minutes for an injured player, but he forfeits the game if he is then unable to continue or is forced to stop again.

Scoring Only the serving player or side scores points. Points are scored when the opposition:
is unable legally to return a serve or volley;
deliberately hinders the serving player or side.
A point is lost if the ball goes out of court, even if it rebounds off the front wall or goes out of play from the first bounce after hitting the front wall.

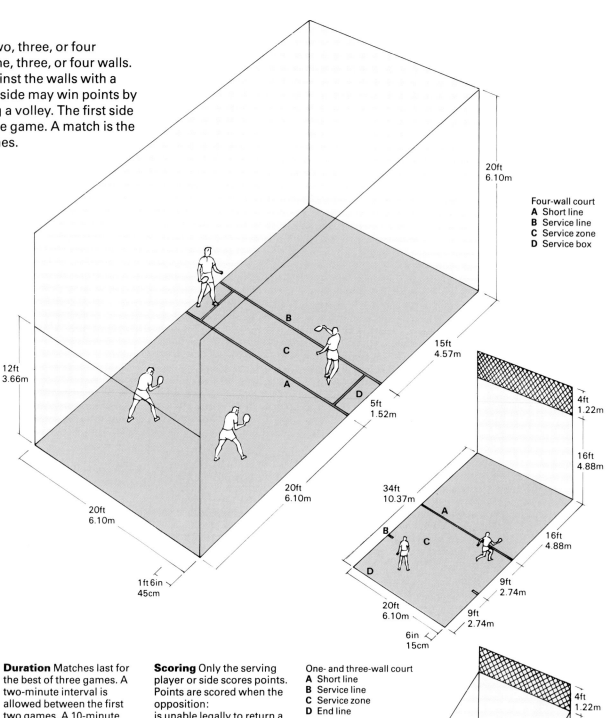

Four-wall court
A Short line
B Service line
C Service zone
D Service box

One- and three-wall court
A Short line
B Service line
C Service zone
D End line

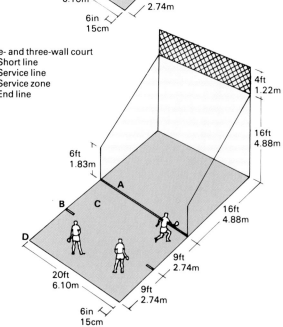

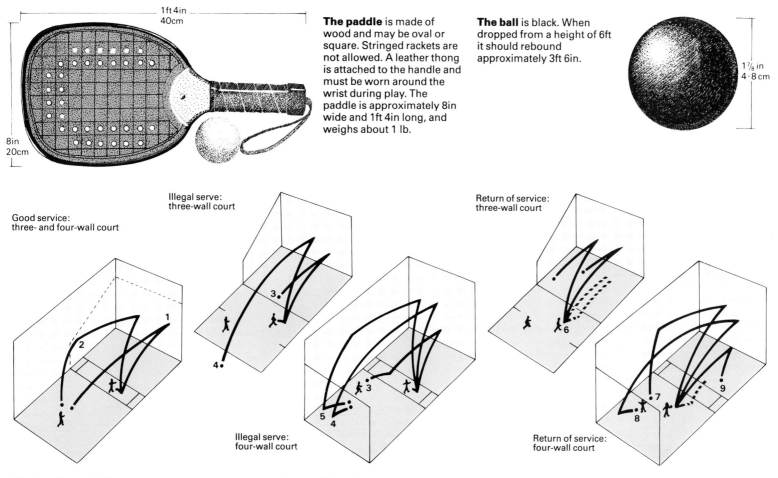

The paddle is made of wood and may be oval or square. Stringed rackets are not allowed. A leather thong is attached to the handle and must be worn around the wrist during play. The paddle is approximately 8in wide and 1ft 4in long, and weighs about 1 lb.

The ball is black. When dropped from a height of 6ft it should rebound approximately 3ft 6in.

1ft 4in
40cm

8in
20cm

1⅞ in
4·8 cm

Good service:
three- and four-wall court

Illegal serve:
three-wall court

Illegal serve:
four-wall court

Return of service:
three-wall court

Return of service:
four-wall court

Playing the ball When returning an opponent's service or shot a player may hold the paddle with one or both hands, but may not switch it from hand to hand. The safety thong must always be around his wrist. He may not hit the ball with his arms, hands, or any part of the body.
The ball may be touched once only; it may be played onto any of the walls.
Service is decided by tossing a coin. The server in the first game also serves first in the third game.
Before each service the server calls the score, giving his own score first. He must not serve until his opponent is ready.
The player may serve from anywhere in the service zone. He may step on a line bounding it, but no part of either foot may be beyond either line of the service zone. The server must remain in the service zone until the ball has crossed the short line.
Method The player drops the ball on the floor within the service zone and strikes it with a paddle on the first bounce so that it hits the front wall (**1**).
The ball must rebound directly behind the short line. In four-wall and three-wall games the ball may touch a side wall first (**2**). In one-wall and three-wall games the ball must rebound within or on the sidelines or the back line.

Illegal serves A serve is illegal if:
the ball hits the floor before crossing the short line (**3**) – a short serve;
the ball rebounds from the front wall to the back wall or over the end line before hitting the floor (**4**) – a long serve;
the ball rebounds to the ceiling before hitting the floor – a ceiling serve;
the ball rebounds from the front wall and hits two or more walls before hitting the floor (**5**);
the ball goes out of court;
the server leaves the service zone before the ball has crossed the short line – a foot fault.

Loss of service A player loses service if:
a) he makes two consecutive illegal serves;
b) he bounces the ball more than twice before striking it when serving;
c) he drops the ball and hits it in the air;
d) he strikes at the ball and misses the serve;
e) he touches his clothes or body with the ball when serving;
f) the serve simultaneously hits the front wall and the ceiling, the floor, or a side wall;
g) the ball hits a side wall before the front wall;
h) the ball goes out of court.
A serve-out is a single action that causes a loss of service.

Return of service The receiver must remain:
in four-wall, at least 5ft behind the short line until the ball is struck by the receiver;
in one-wall and three-wall, behind the service line until the ball passes the short line.
A legally served ball may be returned to the front wall before it bounces (volleying) or after one bounce (**6**).
The ball may touch the side walls (**7**), back wall (**8**), or ceiling, but a return touching the floor and the front wall simultaneously is a bad return (**9**).
When the receiver volleys the ball no part of his body may cross the short line until the return is made.

Obstruction Players must not prevent their opponents from seeing and playing the ball. They must not deliberately hinder an opponent's movements, or make physical contact. The point is replayed if obstruction is accidental. If the obstruction is deliberate the player loses either a point or the serve.

DOUBLES
The doubles game generally conforms to the rules of singles, with some additions.
Service After the first serve-out the service passes to the other side. But thereafter in that game both players of a side are allowed to lose their service before the service passes to the opposition.
Partners' positions
a) In four-wall the server's partner must stand in the service box with his back toward the wall and both feet on the floor until the ball has crossed the short line. If he is not in the proper position it is a foot fault. If he is in a legal position and the ball either hits him before it touches the floor or passes behind him, the serve is replayed.
If he is out of the box and is hit by the ball it is a serve-out.
b) In one-wall and three-wall the server's partner must stand outside the sideline between the short line and the back line until the ball has crossed the short line. If the player is not in this position during a serve it is a foot fault.
If he enters the playing area (ie between the sidelines) before the served ball passes him it is a fault.

© DIAGRAM

Badminton

Badminton is a racket game played by two players (singles) or four players (doubles). A shuttle, generally made of cork and feathers, is hit over a high net that divides a marked court. The object of the game is to hit the shuttle to the floor on the opponents' side of the net. The game derives from the ancient "battledore and shuttlecock."

The court The game may be played out of doors, but it is best played indoors in a draft-free environment. The floor of the court should have a non-slip surface, and is preferably made of wood.
Markings should preferably be in white or yellow. The lines should be 40mm wide. They are included within the overall dimensions of the court.

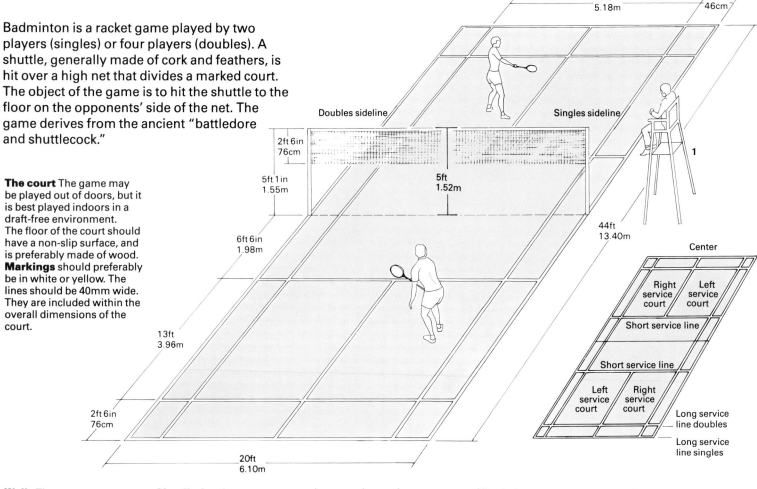

Walls The current recommended space between court and walls for international play is:
wall from base line, 2.3m;
wall from side-line, 2.2m.
Lesser distances are used for club and recreational play. The minimum space recommended is:
wall from base line, 1.5m
wall from side-line, 1.2m.

Ventilation Any system must not move the air.
The net is made of cord with a mesh size of 15–20mm. It is tightly stretched so that its upper edge is flush with the top of the posts.
The posts are firm and placed on the outside boundary lines and should be rigid enough to support the net under tension. If the net is fixed by supports outside the court area, a thin post or strip of material should be fixed to the boundary line and rise vertically to the upper edge of the net.
Officials The umpire (1) is in charge of the match, the court and its immediate surrounds. A service judge and line judges may also be appointed.
If a tournament has an overall referee, players may appeal only on points of law.
Dress may be colored and usually consists of a shirt, shorts, or skirts for women, socks and rubber-soled shoes.
Duration Play should be continuous, though a rest of 5 minutes between the second and third games of a match is allowed in international play.
Changing ends The players change ends after every game and during the third game, when the leading player's score reaches 8 points in a game of 15 points or 6 points in a game of 11 points.

Scoring Only the serving side can score a point.
In doubles and men's singles a game consists of 15 points.
In women's singles a game is 11 points.
A match generally consists of the best of three games.
Setting If both players or sides reach the same score during the last stages of a game, play may be extended by "setting" a new deciding score.
If, for example, the score reaches 13-all in a 15-point game, the first player to reach 13 may choose to "set the game to 5," raising the deciding score to 18 points. If the option to "set" is not taken up at 13-all, or if this score does not arise, it may be taken up at 14-all and set to 3.
In an 11-point game "setting" may take place at 9-all (set to 3) and 10-all (set to 2). The player or side entitled to "set" the game must do so before the next service is taken when the score first reaches the "setting" score.
When the game is "set," the score reverts to 0–0 (love-all) and proceeds to 2, 3 or 5 as appropriate. The final score is recorded as the total number of points scored in the game.

Correct service stroke

Service (toss) The right of service is decided by spinning a racket for "rough" or "smooth," or tossing the shuttle to see, in which direction it lands. The winner has a choice of service or ends. The loser has the other choice.
At the start of a doubles game, the two sides nominate a server and receiver.

Singles The serving court is always decided by the server's score – if it is even, the right-hand court is used; if it is odd, the left-hand court. If the game is "set" the relevant score is the total number of points gained by the server. The shuttle is served into the service court diagonally opposed to the server.

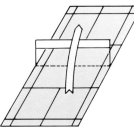

Love or even score

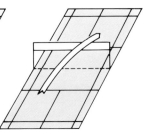

Odd score

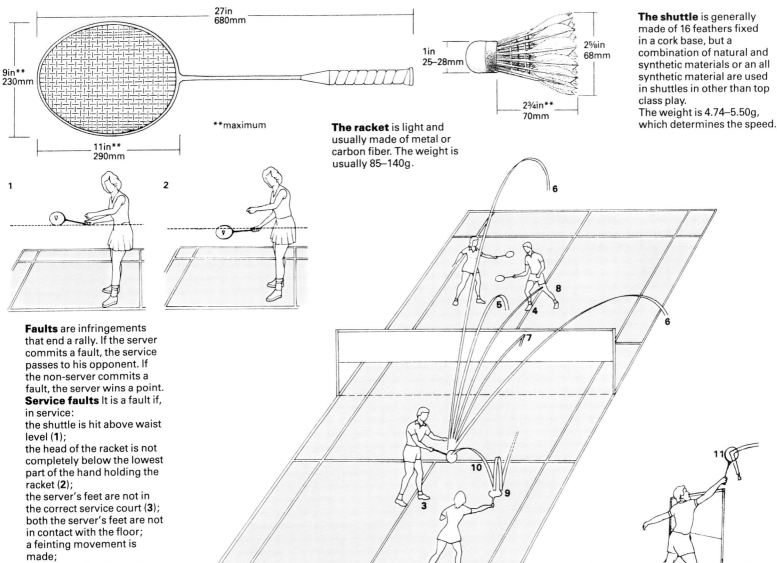

The racket is light and usually made of metal or carbon fiber. The weight is usually 85–140g.

27in 680mm

9in** 230mm

11in** 290mm

**maximum

1in 25–28mm

2⅝in 68mm

2¾in** 70mm

The shuttle is generally made of 16 feathers fixed in a cork base, but a combination of natural and synthetic materials or an all synthetic material are used in shuttles in other than top class play.
The weight is 4.74–5.50g, which determines the speed.

Faults are infringements that end a rally. If the server commits a fault, the service passes to his opponent. If the non-server commits a fault, the server wins a point.

Service faults It is a fault if, in service:
the shuttle is hit above waist level (**1**);
the head of the racket is not completely below the lowest part of the hand holding the racket (**2**);
the server's feet are not in the correct service court (**3**);
both the server's feet are not in contact with the floor;
a feinting movement is made;
the receiver is not standing within the correct service court (**4**);
the receiver moves before the shuttle is struck;
the shuttle lands outside the correct service court (**5**).

General faults It is also a fault if:
the shuttle drops outside the court (**6**);
the shuttle fails to go over the net (**7**);
the player is struck by the shuttle (**8**);
a player hits the shuttle twice with two shots (**9**);
a player and his partner hit the shuttle with successive shots (**10**);
the shuttle is struck before it crosses the net (**11**);
a player touches the net or posts while the shuttle is in play; a player obstructs or distracts his opponent; there is any other transgression of the laws.

Lets A let allows a rally and resulting score to be disregarded. The server restarts the game by serving again from the correct service court. Lets are given by the umpire without appeals made by the players.

Singles Lets in singles are played when the server serves from the wrong court, but only if the mistake is not realized before delivery of the next service.
A let is also played if the server and receiver commit faults at the same moment, or if the shuttle is caught in the net after passing over it, except on service.
A let is also played for any unforeseen or accidental occurrence such as another shuttle coming onto the court or the base of the shuttle completely separating from the rest of the shuttle during a rally.

Doubles Similar let rules apply in doubles games. A let is awarded if a player wins a rally after serving out of turn or from the wrong court or after receiving in the wrong court.

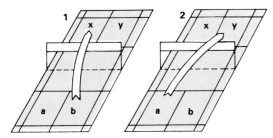

Doubles In doubles the principles of serving are more complicated:
1) If the server (**b**) wins the first point,
2) he then serves into his opponent's left service court from his own left service court; the opponent (**y**) who did not receive on the first point now becomes the receiver.

3) When the serve is lost, it passes to the opponent who was in the right service court at the start of the rally (**x**). After the service has thus changed ends at the beginning of each game, the receiving side (**a, b**) must win two rallies to retrieve it. The first opponent to serve (**x**) does so from alternate courts until he loses a rally.

4) Then his partner (**y**) takes over, serving from the court he occupied at the beginning of the losing rally. He serves from alternate courts until he loses a rally.
5) The service then passes across the net, and both of that pair (**b, a**) serve.

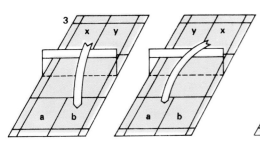

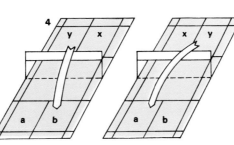

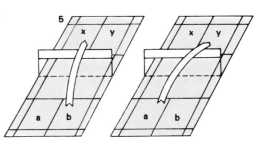

Lawn tennis

Lawn tennis is a racket game in which individuals (singles) or pairs (doubles) compete against each other. The game is played on a court divided by a net. The object of the game is to propel the ball over the net in such a way that it bounces in court and beats any attempt by an opponent to return it.

Court The surface may be grass, a variety of asphalt, wood, porous concrete, or other composition. It is marked out with white lines as shown in the diagram. The lines are included within the limits of the court.

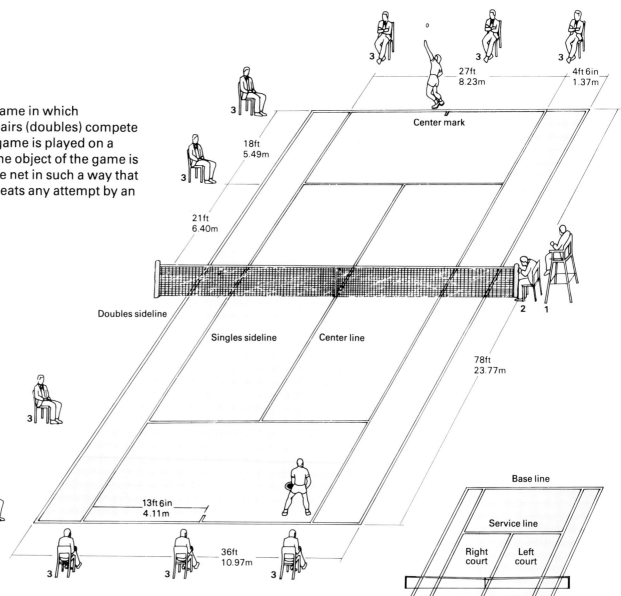

The net is suspended between two posts from a cable covered by white tape. At its center it is kept taut by a vertical strap which is firmly fixed to the ground. The height of the net may be adjusted by a handle attached to one of the posts.
Players Normally men play against men and women against women, except in mixed doubles, where opposing pairs each consist of a man and a woman.
Dress By tradition the shirts and shorts of the men and the skirts, blouses and dresses of the ladies are white, though all professional tournaments with the exception of Wimbledon allow colored clothing. White socks and rubber-soled shoes are worn.

Duration A match lasts a maximum of five sets for men and three for women. A men's match ends when one side has won three sets, and a women's match when one side has won two sets.
Play is continuous, though in certain circumstances and some countries players are allowed a rest of up to 10 minutes after the third set for men and the second for women. This break may be 45 minutes in equatorial countries.
Play is never delayed to enable a player to recover his strength or receive advice.
The umpire may suspend play indefinitely if factors such as crowd disturbance are affecting play.

Officials consist of an umpire (**1**) assisted by a net-cord judge (**2**), linesmen (**3**), and foot-fault judge.
Start of play The choice of service and sides (ends) is decided by the toss of a coin.

Scoring A match is scored in games and sets.
In each game a player begins with no score ("love"). His first point scores 15, his second 30, his third 40, and his fourth wins the game unless there is a "deuce," which is called at the score of 40-all.
After deuce, the next point win is scored as an advantage to the player who won it, and if he wins the following point he wins the game. Should his opponent redress the balance the score returns to deuce, and so on, until the end of the game.
The first player to win six games wins the set, unless each player has won five games, when play continues until one player is two games ahead.
Tie-break To prevent long sets, some tournaments use a tie-break system, which comes into operation when the score reaches six games all.
A player who first wins seven points shall win the game and the set provided he leads by a margin of two points. If the score reaches six points all, the game shall be extended until this margin has been achieved. Numerical scoring shall be used throughout the tie-break game.
In some tournaments the tie-break is not used in a final set, which must be played out in the ordinary way.

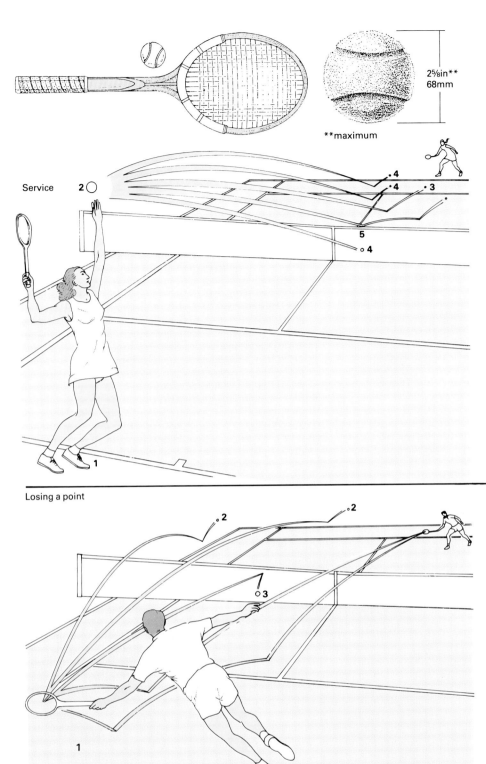

Rackets must be not more than 32in long and 12½in wide; maximum dimensions for the strung hitting surface are 15½in long and 11½in wide. The hitting surface consists of crossed strings connected to the frame and alternately interlaced or bonded where they cross.

2⅝in** 68mm

**maximum

The frames may be made from wood, steel or other compositions.
Tennis balls must be yellow or white. They should weigh 2–2¹⁄₁₆oz (56.7g–58.5g). The outer surface must be uniform and if there are any seams they must be stitchless.

Service

2

Service The server starts play by sending the ball over the net into the service court. He serves from alternate sides, first from behind his right court, and then his left court.
He must serve with both feet behind the base line and within the imaginary continuations of the center mark and side line (**1**).
To serve, the ball must be thrown into the air and struck with the racket before it hits the ground (**2**).
Throughout delivery of service the server must not change his position by walking or running, nor touch with either foot any area other than that behind the base line within the imaginary extensions of the center mark and the side line.

For the service to be good the ball must cross the net without bouncing and pitch into the service court diagonally opposite (**3**). The lines bounding that court are part of its area.
If the server or the service infringes any rule (**4**) a fault is recorded. A second service is then permitted; if that is a fault the receiver gains a point.
It is not a fault if the ball touches the net but still falls into the appropriate court (**5**). This constitutes a "let," and the serve is taken again. A let is also called if the ball is served before the receiver is prepared. The receiver must allow the ball to bounce before he returns it. In the next game the service passes to the receiver.

Losing a point

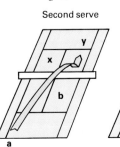

Changing ends Players change ends at the end of the first and third games and any subsequent alternate game in each set.
A change of ends at the end of a set occurs only if the total number of games in that set is an odd number. If the number is even the change takes place after the first game of the new set.
Losing a point A point is lost when the player:
fails to return the ball over the net before it touches the ground twice on his side of the net (**1**);
returns the ball so that it first hits the ground outside his opponent's court, or strikes any object outside that court (**2**);

hits the ball into the net (**3**);
hits the ball twice;
hits the net with his person or racket;
plays the ball before it has crossed to his side of the net;
is hit by the ball anywhere other than on his racket;
deliberately hinders an opponent (a let is played if any hindrance is accidental).
A return is good if it bounces within the court after crossing the net.
The ball may touch the net or cross outside the post as long as it lands in the correct court.
A player's racket may pass over the net after hitting the ball as long as the player did not strike the ball before it crossed the net.

First game	Second game	Third game	Fourth game
First serve	First serve	First serve	First serve

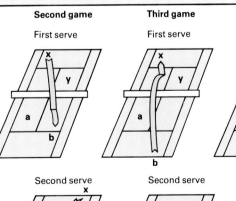

Second serve Second serve Second serve Second serve

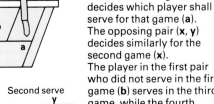

The doubles game is played within a wider playing area. Except for the order of service, the same rules apply as for singles.
Service The pair about to serve in the first game (**a, b**) decides which player shall serve for that game (**a**). The opposing pair (**x, y**) decides similarly for the second game (**x**).
The player in the first pair who did not serve in the first game (**b**) serves in the third game, while the fourth player (**y**) serves in the fourth game. The same order is kept throughout each set.

Receiving The pair about to receive in the first game (**x, y**) decides which player shall receive the first service (**x**). That player then receives all the first services in the odd games of that set. Similarly, the pair due to receive in the second game (**a, b**) makes a choice and the chosen player (**b**) receives the first service in the even games of that set.
In each game partners receive the service alternately. During a rally each pair plays the ball alternately, either partner of each pair being allowed to return the ball.

©DIAGRAM

Table tennis

Table tennis is a game for two players (singles) or four (doubles) and is normally played indoors. Rackets, sometimes called "bats" or "paddles," are used to hit a small, light ball back and forth across a table divided by a low net. The object is to win points by making shots that an opponent is unable to return.

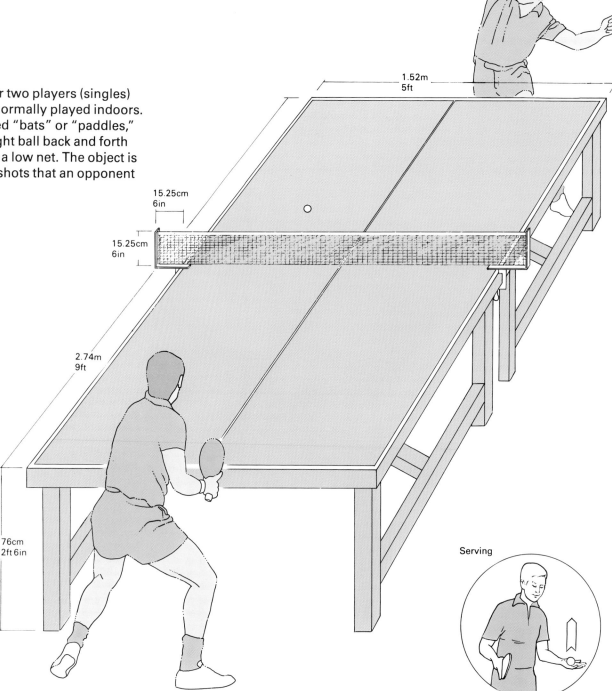

1.52m
5ft

15.25cm
6in

15.25cm
6in

2.74m
9ft

76cm
2ft 6in

Serving

The table may be of any material but is normally of wood. It must give a bounce of about 23cm to a standard ball, when the ball is dropped from a height of 30cm.
The playing surface should be dark-colored, preferably green, and matt, with white marking lines.
A white line, 2cm wide, marks the edges of the table. The sides of the table-top are not considered part of the playing surface.
For doubles, the playing surface is divided into halves by a 3mm white line.
The net, 1.83m long, is suspended across the center of the table by a cord attached to a post at either end.
The playing area is only defined for international competition, where the minimum area required is about 2.75m at each side and 5.5m at ends.
The mimimum height is 3.5m.
Dress Clothing can be of any one or two uniform colors other than white. Match uniform generally consists of shirt, shorts or skirt and flat soled shoes.
Officials Play is controlled by an umpire, whose decision is final on any question of fact.
The racket may be of any size, weight or shape. The blade should be of wood, continuous, of even thickness, flat and rigid. Each side of the blade must be of a uniform dark color, but the two sides need not be of the same color.
In international competitions one side of the racket blade must be red and the other black.
The covering material shall extend up to but not beyond the limits of the blade, except that the part nearest the handle and gripped by the fingers may be left uncovered or covered with any material.

The blade may be covered with;
a) plain, pimpled rubber, with pimples outward, of a total thickness not exceeding 2mm;
b) a sandwich of cellular rubber surfaced with plain, pimpled rubber, with pimples inward or outward, of a total thickness not exceeding 4mm.
(A side not used for hitting is exempted from covering rules.)

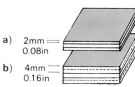

a) 2mm
0.08in

b) 4mm
0.16in

A game is won by the player or pair first scoring 21 points, unless both shall have scored 20 points, when the winner shall be the first to score two points more than the opposition.
A match consists of either the best of three or the best of five games.
Play must be continuous throughout except that either player or pair may claim up to two minutes' rest between the successive games of a match.

Choice of ends and the right to serve or receive is decided by tossing a coin.
If the winner of the toss decides to serve or receive first, the loser has the choice of ends, and vice versa.
The winner of the toss may require the loser to choose first.
In doubles each pair decides which of them is to serve and receive first in the first game.
In each subsequent game the serving pair may choose which of them shall serve first, but the first receiver must be the player who served to him in the previous game.

The ball should be made of celluloid or a similar plastic, white or yellow, with a matt surface. Its weight must be 2.5g.

38.2mm
1½in

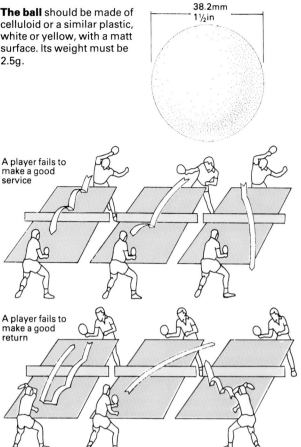

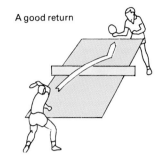

A good service

A good return

Volleying is not allowed

A player fails to make a good service

A player fails to make a good return

Order of play The period when the ball is in play is termed a "rally."

The player who first strikes the ball in a rally is termed the "server"; the second is the "receiver."

A player strikes the ball if he touches it with his racket, held in the hand, or with his racket hand below the wrist. A stroke made with the hand alone, after dropping the racket, is not good; nor is a stroke made by the racket alone after it is dropped or thrown.

In singles, the server must first make a good service, the receiver must make a good return, and then server and receiver make good returns alternately.

In doubles, the server must make a good service, the receiver a good return, the server's partner a good return, the receiver's partner a good return, and so on, in this sequence.

Serving The ball is placed on the palm of the free hand, which must be stationary, above the level of the playing surface and not cupped. The fingers must be kept together, with the thumb free.

The ball is then thrown by hand only, without imparting spin, near vertically upward, so that it rises at least 16cm after leaving the palm of the free hand. The server's free hand must be behind his end line or an imaginary extension of that line from the start of service until he strikes the ball.

On descent the ball is struck to touch the server's court first and then, passing directly over or around the net, to touch the receiver's court. (Around the net is defined as under or around the projection of the net and its supports outside the side line.)

The ball must be struck at the first attempt. At the moment of striking the racket must be behind the end of the table or an imaginary continuation of it. In doubles the ball must touch the right-hand half of the court on the serving side and then the diagonally opposite court or line.

Returning service The ball must be struck to pass directly over or around the net to touch the opponent's court. If the ball in passing over or around the net touches the net or its supports, it is considered to have passed directly, except in service.

The ball must not be allowed to bounce twice before return, nor must it be struck by a player more than once consecutively.

Change of ends The players or pairs change ends after each game and in the last possible game of a match they change ends again when the first one of them scores 10 points. In doubles, the pair receiving at that time change their order. If one player wins every game, the last game may be the second (in a best of 3) or the third (in a best of 5).

© DIAGRAM

A point is lost by a player, if he fails to make a good service or a good return, if the ball bounces twice consecutively on his court, if he strikes it twice consecutively, if he "volleys" it by striking it before it touches his court or if in doubles he strikes it out of the proper sequence. He loses a point also if during play he, or anything he is wearing or carrying, touches the net or moves the playing surface, or if his free hand touches the playing surface.

The ball goes out of play when it touches any object other than the playing surface, the net or its supports, the racket or the racket hand below the wrist, or when the rally is decided in any other way as a point or a let.

A let is a rally from which no point is scored. It occurs when:
a) the ball touches the net or its supports in service, provided the service is otherwise good;
b) a service is delivered when the receiver or his partner is not ready, provided no attempt has been made to return the ball;
c) a player fails to make a good service or return through an accident beyond his control, such as a movement by a spectator or a sudden noise;
d) the ball is broken in play;
e) a rally is interrupted to correct a mistake in playing order or ends;
f) a rally is interrupted to apply the expedite system.

Change of service The service in singles and doubles passes from one player to another after every five points scored, unless both players or pairs score 20 points, when the service changes after every point. In doubles the second server is the player who received first, the third server is the partner of the player who served first, and the fourth server the partner of the player who received first, after which the sequence is repeated until the end of the game.

The expedite system is introduced if a game is unfinished 15 minutes after the start. It then applies to the rest of the game and to all remaining games of the match.

Thereafter, each player serves in turn and if the service and 12 successive strokes of the server are returned by the receiver, the server loses a point. The return strokes of the receiving player or pair are counted out loud, from 1 to 13, by an official other than the umpire.

Volleyball

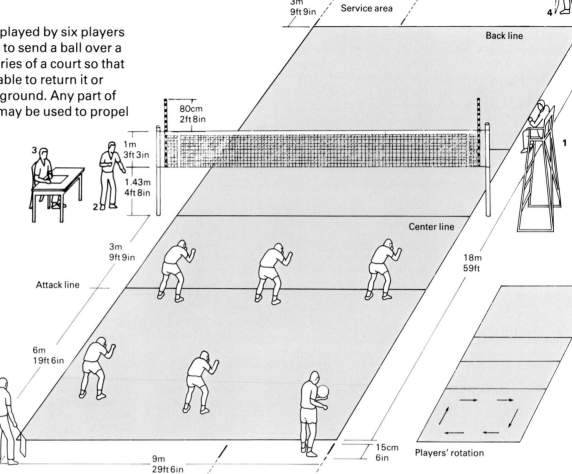

Volleyball is a team game played by six players on each side. The object is to send a ball over a net and within the boundaries of a court so that the opposing team are unable to return it or prevent it from hitting the ground. Any part of the body above the waist may be used to propel the ball.

The court includes the boundary lines, and the ball must clear them completely to be ruled out of court. The attack lines extend indefinitely beyond the side lines.

The net is 1m deep and 9.50m long, made of 10cm-square mesh. Along the top is a double thickness of white canvas with a flexible cable stretched through it. Vertical tapes run down each side of the net, and vertical aerials project above its top.

Temperature Competitive volleyball should not be played when the temperature is below 10°C.

Dress Players wear jerseys and shorts in team colors, with numbers on the back and front of their jerseys. For outdoor play numbered track suits may be worn in cold weather.
Shoes must be light and pliable and without heels; players may obtain permission to play barefoot. Headgear or articles that may cause injury must not be worn.

Officials The game is controlled by:
the first referee (**1**); aided by the second referee (**2**); the official scorer (**3**); and four linesmen (**4**).

Team officials The team coach and captain are responsible for team discipline; they may ask for a time-out or a substitution. At a time-out or substitution the coach must not enter the court, though he may speak to his players.
Captains are the only players allowed to speak to officials. Any dispute over the interpretation of the rules is to be settled on the spot by the referee and the disputing captain. The captain may reserve the right to record a protest after the match.

Positioning At the moment of service the players must take up the positions shown. But once the ball is served they may move anywhere on their own side of the net. Any positional error incurs a fault, and the offender loses all points scored while at error (the opponents retain all theirs).
Correct positions must be resumed when a positional error is spotted.
On the change of service, members of the team that is to serve rotate one position clockwise before serving. The order of rotation must remain constant in each set; it may be changed for a new set if the scorer is informed.

Duration In international competitions a match is the best of five sets.

Intervals The interval between all sets lasts 3 minutes.
Up to 3 minutes are allowed for injury stoppages.
If bad weather, etc, interrupts a game, it may be resumed from where it was halted if on the same court and within 4 hours; otherwise the interrupted set must be replayed.

Ends Before play starts the captains toss a coin for choice of ends or the right to serve first.
Teams change ends after each set unless the next set is the decider, when there is a fresh toss of the coin. In the final set the teams change ends after one side has reached 8 points.

Scoring A match is won by the team that wins 3 sets. Sets are won by the team that first scores 15 points with a minimum lead of 2 points, or play is continued until a 2-point lead is established up to a maximum of 17 points. If teams are tied at 16–16, the first team to score 17 points is the winner.
Whenever a team fails to serve or return the ball or commits any other fault the opposing team wins the rally.
Points are only scored by the serving team winning a rally. If the opposing team wins the rally they win the right to serve without scoring a point.
In the deciding (5th) set, if the opposing team wins the rally, they win the right to serve and score a point.

The serve After the referee's whistle the player in the rear right-hand corner puts the ball into play.
The server stands within the service area and hits the ball with his hand (open or closed) or any part of his arm to send it over the net into his opponents' court. After hitting the ball he may land on the serving line or within the court. The serving team must not distract opponents during the service.
A fault is conceded if the ball touches the net, the net aerial or its imaginary extensions, or a player of the serving team; or if it lands outside the opponents' court.
A player continues to serve until his team commits a fault and a side-out is called. Then the serve passes to the other team. A new set is begun by the team not serving at the end of the preceding set, but the ball must be served by the correct player.

Underarm serve

Tennis serve

Hook serve

Playing the ball

The ball is made of supple leather casing with a bladder, or of rubber or a similar synthetic product. It must be all one color. The circumference must be 65–67cm and the weight 260–280g.

1 Forearm pass
2 A set up
3 A smash

Blocking

Playing the ball Each team may touch the ball up to three times before sending it over the net (**1, 2, 3**). Contact is allowed with any part of the body above the waist as long as the hits are clean and the ball is not held, scooped, or carried in any way.

4 If two or more teammates play the ball at the same moment, it counts as two touches (except in blocking). The ball may be played while the player is in contact with a teammate as long as he is not using him as a prop.

5 If two players go for the same ball but only one touches it, only one touch is counted.

6 When two opponents simultaneously commit a foul, a double fault results and the point is replayed. A hit (except a service) is good if the ball touches the net between the side-markers and drops in court. The ball is out of play if it touches the ground or any object outside the court.

Blocking Blocking is the action of players close to the net to intercept the ball coming from the opponents

by reaching higher than the top of the net.
A collective block is executed by two or three players close to each other. If one member of the composite block is above the height of the net, all members are considered to be so. If the ball touches more than one blocking player this still counts as one block.
Any blocking player is entitled to a second play at the ball. This counts as the first of his team's touches. Blockers may reach over the net, but they must not attempt to touch the ball until the opponent has executed an attack-hit. If two opponents simultaneously touch the ball above the net, the player whose team does not receive the ball as it falls is deemed to have made the last touch. Normal rules of play apply as soon as the ball drops. It is a double fault if the ball is held.
Back-line players may only send a ball from the attack area (or its extended limits) into the opponents' court when it is below net height. From behind the attack line, they may use any

permissible manner to hit the ball into the opponents' court.
Substitution Each team may make six substitutions in each set, but only when the ball is dead and on the request of the captain or coach.
Substitutes must report to the scorer before joining play. While not playing, substitutes must sit with the coaches on the side of the court opposite the referee; they may warm up outside the playing area provided they return to their correct place.
A substitution shall last only the time needed for recording the substitution on the scoresheet and allowing the entry and exit of players.

Anyone playing at the start of a set may be replaced only once. The original player may go back during the same set, but he must return to his previous rotational position.
A substitute who leaves the game may not return in the same set.
A substitute may be replaced only by the player whose position he originally took.
If after six substitutions have been made an injury occurs, the injured player may be replaced.
If after six substitutions, one player is sent off, the team forfeits that set but retains the points it has scored. Play must resume immediately after a substitution.

Fouls A team loses the service or a point if:
a player "spikes" the ball above the opponents' court (**1**);
a player crosses the vertical plane of the net and touches the court or an opponent (**2**);
a player interferes with an opponent's play;
the ball touches the ground;
a team plays the ball more than three times in succession;
the ball touches a player below the waist;
a player touches the ball twice consecutively;
a team is out of position at the service;
the ball is held or pushed;
a player touches the net or vertical aerials (unless the ball knocks the net against him);

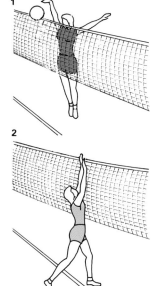

a player crosses the center line when play is in progress;
a back-line player in the attack area returns the ball from above net height;
the ball does not pass over the net between the vertical rods (or their assumed extension);
the ball touches the ground outside the court;
the ball is returned with the use of a teammate as support;
a player receives a penalty card;
a coach or substitute, having been warned, continues the same fault;
a player reaches under the net and touches the ball or an opponent while the ball is on the opponents' side;

the game is persistently delayed;
a substitute joins the play illegally;
a team requests a third time-out after a warning;
a team extends a second time-out beyond 30 seconds;
a team delays a substitution after taking two time-outs;
players leave the court without the referee's permission;
a player intimidates an opponent;
a block is illegal;
a serve is illegal.
Disqualification Persistent misconduct by players, substitutes, or coaches will lead to disqualification for the rest of the set or match.

Time-outs Two 30-second time-outs may be requested in each set, but only when the ball is dead. They may be taken consecutively, or a time-out may be preceded or followed by a substitution. During a time-out the players in play must go to the free zone near their bench.
If a team requests a third time-out, the referee gives a warning and then sanctions any further requests in the same set.

© DIAGRAM

Basketball

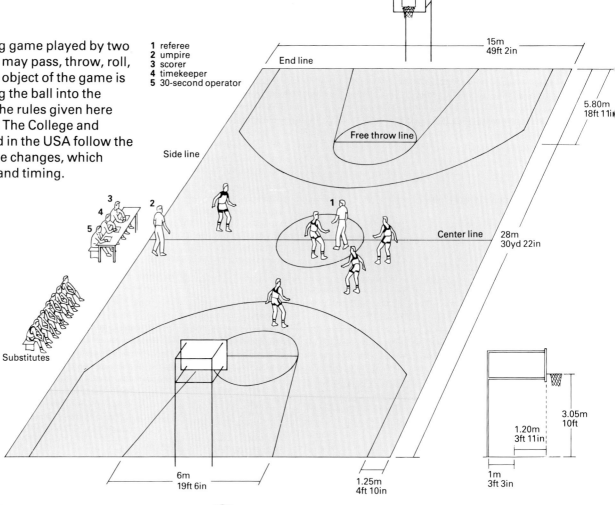

Basketball is a fast, exciting game played by two teams of five players, who may pass, throw, roll, bat or dribble the ball. The object of the game is to score points by throwing the ball into the opposing team's basket. The rules given here are the international rules. The College and Professional games played in the USA follow the same basic rules with some changes, which include court dimensions and timing.

The court must have a hard surface (not grass). Its width may vary by minus 2m and its length by minus 4m, but the proportions must be kept. The ceiling must be at least 7m high. Lighting must be uniform and not hinder players from throwing for a goal.
The distance between the boundary and any obstruction should be at least 2m.
Baskets consist of white cord nets to hold the ball briefly as it drops through. They are suspended from orange metal rings attached rigidly at right angles to the backboards.

1 referee
2 umpire
3 scorer
4 timekeeper
5 30-second operator

End line
Side line
Free throw line
Center line
Substitutes

15m
49ft 2in
5.80m
18ft 11in
28m
30yd 22in
3.05m
10ft
1.20m
3ft 11in
1m
3ft 3in
6m
19ft 6in
1.25m
4ft 10in

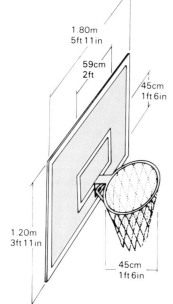

1.80m
5ft 11in
59cm
2ft
45cm
1ft 6in
1.20m
3ft 11in
45cm
1ft 6in

Backboards are made of hardwood or a single piece of equally rigid transparent material with lines and edges to contrast with the background – usually black or white or white on transparent. The supports are bright in color to be easily visible and at least 1m clear of the end lines.

Teams consist of five players and five (in some cases seven) substitutes. Players may leave the court only with official permission except at the end of each half.
Dress Players wear shirts and shorts with basketball boots or sneakers. Shirts carry numbers front and back in contrasting color. Only numbers from 4 to 15 are used.
Coaches inform the scorer of the names and numbers of the players and the captain, and any changes of numbers. The captain may act as coach; if disqualified or injured, he is replaced as coach by the substitute captain. There may also be an assistant coach.
Technical equipment consists of:
a) stopwatches, including game watch and time-out watch;
b) device for administering the 30-second rule, visible to players and spectators;
c) official scoresheet;
d) scoreboard
e) markers, numbered 1-4 in black, 5 in red, to show the number of fouls per player;
f) team foul markers to

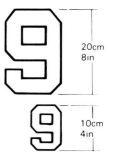

20cm
8in
10cm
4in

indicate when a team has committed the seventh player foul in the half.
Officials are the referee and umpire, assisted by the scorer, timekeeper and 30-second operator. They wear a prescribed uniform. The referee and the umpire divide the court between them, exchanging places after each foul involving a free throw penalty and after each jump ball decision. They use whistles and hand signals to make and explain decisions.
Starting Visitors choose ends. On a neutral court the teams toss up. The teams change ends at half time. Each team must begin with five players on court. The game starts with a jump ball.

Scoring A goal is scored when a live ball enters a basket from above and remains within or passes through. Goals from the field count two points, unless attempted from beyond the 3-point line, when it counts three points. Goals from free throws count one point.
Duration A game consists of two halves of 20 minutes, each with an interval of 10 or 15 minutes. If the score is tied, play continues for as many extra 5-minute periods as necessary to break the tie. Teams toss for baskets for the first period, then change ends for the others.
Forfeited game A game is forfeited if a team:
does not have five players ready 15 minutes after starting time;
is not on court within 1 minute of the referee's signal;
does not have at least two players on court.
If the team, to which the game is forfeited, is ahead, the score stands. Otherwise the score is recorded as 2-0 in its favor.

The ball is spherical and has a leather, rubber, or synthetic case, with a rubber bladder. Its circumference is 75–78cm. It should weigh 600–650g. When inflated, it should bounce between 1.20m and 1.40m on a solid wooden floor if dropped a height of about 1.80m.

Jump ball starts each game.

The referee throws the ball up in the center circle and the opposing players leap up and try to tap it away. The jumpers must stand in the half of the circle nearest their own baskets. The ball is thrown up at right angles to the sideline so that it drops between them. Each player is allowed two taps before the ball touches the ground, a basket, a backboard or another player. The jumpers must remain in position until the ball is tapped. Other players must be outside the circle until the ball is tapped and must not interfere with the jumpers. The toss is repeated if it is a bad one or if both teams violate the rules. A jump ball also occurs if neither team has control, when the ball becomes dead. It takes place in the nearest circle. If the ball lodges on the basket supports, the jump ball takes place from the nearest throw line.

Play The ball may be passed, thrown, batted, tapped, rolled or dribbled, but it may not be carried or kicked. It goes into play, when an official administers a jump ball or free throw or a player is about to throw in.

Live ball The ball becomes alive when a player taps it in a jump ball, when it touches a player on court, when it is thrown in or when it is handed to a free-thrower.

Control A player has control if holding or dribbling a live ball. A team is in control if one of its members has control or the ball is being passed between them. Team control ends with a goal, a dead ball or loss of possession to the opponents.

Dead ball occurs when:
a goal is made;
a violation occurs;
a foul occurs;
on a throw for a technical foul by the coach or his substitute;
at the first of two free throws if it is obvious the ball will not go in the basket;
a held ball occurs;
the ball lodges in the basket supports;
the whistle blows or time expires or the 30-seconds device sounds, unless the ball is on flight for goal.
The ball does not become dead if a foul occurs during an attempt at goal.

Player out of bounds A player is out of bounds if he touches the floor on or beyond the boundary lines (**1**).

Ball out of bounds The ball is out of play when it touches any person or object on or beyond the boundary lines, including the rear of the backboard or its supports. Possession is awarded to the team that did not touch the ball last.

Return to play The player nominated to return the ball stands at the side of the court at the point where the ball went out. He may throw, roll or bounce the ball into court (**2**). No other player may step out of bounds during the throw in. If the ball goes out across the sideline, but between the center line and the end line in a team's attacking half, an official must hand the ball to the player, who is to throw in.

It is forbidden to:
carry the ball into court;
touch the ball in court before another player has done so;
take more than 5 seconds to throw in.

Held ball occurs when two opposing players are both firmly holding the ball (**3**). Officials should not call a held ball too hastily. A player lying on the floor in possession of the ball must have a chance to play it, unless he is in danger of injury.
After a held ball play resumes with a jump ball at the nearest circle.

Dribble occurs when a player, having gained control of the ball, gives impetus to it by throwing, tapping or rolling it and touches it again before it touches another player (**4**) The ball must touch the floor.

The player completes his dribble the instant he touches the ball simultaneously with both hands, or permits the ball to come to rest in one or both hands.

The player may take any number of steps between bounces or when the ball is not in contact with his hand. A second, consecutive dribble is forbidden unless the ball has touched the basket, the backboard or another player or has been batted out of his control by an opponent.

Moving with the ball A player may pivot on one foot – which he must keep stationary on the floor – while stepping once or more than once in any direction with the other foot (**5**). A moving player may stop or dispose of the ball using a two-count rhythm (**6**). The first count (one) occurs as or after he takes the ball when one or both feet touch the ground.

The count of two comes the next time one or both feet touch the ground.

If a player makes a legal stop he may then use only the rear foot as a pivot unless both feet are together.

A player who receives the ball while standing still or comes to a legal stop while holding the ball may lift his pivot foot to jump, but must pass or shoot before one or both feet touch the floor again. If he is going to dribble he must release the ball before lifting his pivot foot.

© DIAGRAM

Interference No player is allowed to touch a basket or its backboard while the ball is in or on the basket.
In attack a player must not touch the ball in its downward flight above the level of the ring, when it is directly above the restricted area, whether during a try for a goal or a pass, until the ball has touched the ring (**1**). No point can be scored. The opponents throw in from the sideline near the place where the violation occurred.
In defense a player must not touch a falling ball above the ring level during an opponent's throw for a goal until the ball touches the ring or will obviously miss (**2**). This applies only to a throw for a goal. If such a violation occurs, the ball becomes dead. The thrower gets one point if it occurs during a free throw, two (or three) if it occurs during a try for a goal. The game is restarted as if a goal had been scored and no violation had taken place.

Shooting for a goal begins with the throwing motion and lasts until the ball leaves the player's hands. On a jump ball neither player has possession, so even if one taps it into the basket, he is not deemed to be in the act of throwing for a goal.

Restart after a goal After a field goal play restarts by a throw in from, or a pass behind, the end line.
The team against whom the goal is awarded takes the throw in. Once a member of the team has the ball, the ball must be released within 5 seconds.

The refereee or umpire handles the ball only to save time. The scoring team must not handle the ball or a technical foul may be awarded against it. Allowance is made for accidental handling.

Time-out The game watch stops when an official signals a violation, a foul, a held ball, unusual delay in getting a dead ball into play, the end of a 30-second period, suspension of play for an injury, or any other official suspension of play.
Charged time-out Each team is allowed two charged time-outs per half, each of 1 minute. They may not be saved up for a subsequent half. One charged time-out is allowed for each extra period of play. The request for a time-out is made by the coach or assistant coach to the scorer, who stops the game, when the ball is dead. A coach may also be granted a time-out if, after a request for a time-out, the opponents score a field goal.

Time-out for injury The officials may order a time-out for injury. The officials must wait for the team in possession to complete its play before signaling time-out unless an immediate stop is necessary to protect an injured player.
Time-in is the resumption of play after a time-out. Play is resumed by a throw in by a member of the team which had control of the ball, by a jump ball, if neither team had control or by a free throw.
The game watch is restarted when the ball is legally tapped in a jump ball or when the ball touches a player on court after a throw in or an unsuccessful free throw.

Substitutes must report to the scorer and be ready to play at once. The scorer signals the substitute's entry, when the ball is dead and the game clock is stopped. The substitute waits for the official's signal before entering the court. A time-out is charged if the substitution does not take place immediately.
After a violation the offending team may field substitutes only if their opponents do so. A player involved in a jump ball may not be replaced.

Thirty-second rule A team must try for a goal within 30 seconds of gaining control of the ball. A new 30 second period does not begin if the ball goes out of bounds and is to be thrown in by the team that had control prior to the ball going out. A period continues if the ball touches an opponent but the team keeps control.
Ten-second rule A team that has possession of the ball in its back court must move it into the front court within 10 seconds. It may not return the ball to the back court.

Three-second rule No player may remain more than 3 seconds in the restricted area between his opponents' end line and free throw line (the lines included) while his team has possession (including throw ins).
This rule does not apply when the ball is in the air during a shot for goal, is rebounding from the backboard, or is dead. An allowance may be made for a player who dribbles in to throw for a goal.

A free throw is taken after a technical foul, or a personal foul on a player in the act of shooting, or after a team has committed 7 fouls in the half.

After a personal foul the fouled player takes the throw. If he is about to leave the field to allow a substitute to come on, he must take the free throw first, unless he leaves because of injury. If the ball is sent into the wrong basket, the throw is taken again. After a technical foul any player may attempt the free throw.

Free throw positions Two opponents must stand in the two places nearest the basket (**1**), with other players in alternate positions outside the free throw lane. The thrower stands immediately behind the free throw line (**2**). Other players can stand where they like as long as they do not interfere with the thrower or the officials, and stay outside the free throw lane until the ball hits the basket, ring, or backboard, or will obviously miss. The ball must be thrown within 5 seconds once it is passed to the thrower.

Free throw violations Generally, after a violation by the thrower's team, or if the ball misses the ring, the opponents are awarded a throw in – unless the throw is given for a technical foul by the coach or a substitute. A violation by opponents is penalized by another free throw. If both teams interfere with the ball before it reaches the basket, a jump ball occurs on the free throw line.

After a technical foul by the thrower has two free throws – unless a jump ball is awarded for a double foul.

coach or substitute, players do not line up. The ball remains in play if the last free throw for a personal foul is missed, unless it goes out of bounds; in that case the opposition takes a throw in from the sideline. If the ball misses the ring and falls on the court, it must be thrown in by the opposition from the sideline opposite the free throw line.

One and one rule When a player commits a personal foul after his team has committed 7 player fouls in a half, any subsequent personal fouls committed by a player, whose team is not in control of the ball, shall be penalized by giving the opponent the opportunity to shoot one free throw. If the free throw is successful, a second free throw shall be taken.

Fouls and violations A violation is an infraction of the rules, penalized by loss of the ball. A foul is an infraction involving personal contact with an opponent or unsportsmanlike conduct, which is recorded as a technical foul against the offender and is penalized by free throws.

After a violation the ball becomes dead and, if a goal is scored, it is not counted. After a foul the official indicates to the scorer the number of the offender.

If a player not shooting is fouled, his team is awarded a throw in near the place of the foul.

If a shooting player is fouled the goal counts if scored and one free throw follows. If the goal is missed, the

Personal fouls A personal foul is a player foul, which involves contact with an opponent whether the ball is in play, alive or dead.

A player shall not block, hold, push, charge, trip, impede the progress of an opponent by extending his arm (**1**), shoulder, hip or knee, or by bending his body into other than normal position, nor use any rough tactics.

A dribbler shall not charge into nor contact an opponent in his path, nor attempt to dribble between opponents or between an opponent and a boundary line, unless there is a reasonable chance for him to go through without

contact. Once a dribbler has head and shoulders past, any subsequent contact is the opponent's responsibility. If a dribbler has established a straight line path, he may not be forced out of that path, but if an opponent is able to establish a legal guarding position in that path, the dribbler must stop or change direction.

Contact with a player in the act of shooting should be penalized (**2**).

Intentional foul is a personal foul deliberately committed by a player (**3**).

Disqualifying foul If a player is guilty of flagrant unsportsmanlike conduct or commits a severe intentional foul (**4**), they shall be disqualified and removed.

Technical fouls

By a player It is a technical foul for a player to: disregard or be disrespectful to an official; use unsportsmanlike tactics, such as offensive language, baiting an opponent, or delaying the game.

Unintentional technical infractions not affecting the game and administrative infractions are not technical fouls unless repeated after a warning.

Any play that continues before a foul is discovered is valid, but a penalty is given on discovery.

The penalty is two free throws for the opposing team.

By a coach or substitute It is a technical foul for a coach or substitute to:

leave his place to follow the action from the boundary line without permission; disrespectfully address officials, assistants or opponents.

The coach may address his team in a charged time-out, if he does not enter the court and the players do not leave it (unless permission is granted). Substitutes may listen, if outside the court. As with players, unintentional infractions are not fouls. The penalty for a technical foul by a coach or substitute is two free throws and possession of the ball to the opponents for a throw in from the mid-point on the side line.

For persistent or flagrant infractions a coach may be banished from the vicinity of

the court, and replaced by the captain or assistant coach.

In an interval Play resumes with a jump ball after two free throws have been taken.

Double fouls When two players foul at the same time a personal foul is charged against each. Play resumes with a jump ball between them.

Multiple fouls When two or more teammates foul against the same opponent at approximately the same time, a personal foul is recorded against each player. The offended player takes two free throws.

If the offended player was shooting, a goal counts if scored and one free throw is awarded.

Five fouls When a player has committed five fouls, either personal or technical, the player must leave the game. A substitute replaces this player.

Seven fouls by team After a team has committed seven player fouls, personal or technical, in a half, all subsequent fouls shall be penalized by the one and one rule.

Right of option When a team has been awarded two or three free throws or the one and one penalty, they may opt not to take the free throws, but to take a throw-in from out-of-bounds at the mid-point of a side line.

Legal guarding position A defensive player has taken a legal guarding position when he is facing his opponent and has both feet on the floor in a normal straddle position.

Netball

Netball is a seven-a-side team game usually played by women. As in basketball, goals are scored by sending the ball through a ring at the opponents' end of the court. Players may pass the ball by throwing it, but they must not run with it. Unlike basketball, players are restricted to certain areas of the court.

The court should have a hard surface. Each goalpost is supported by a socket in the ground, or by a metal base that should not protrude into the court.

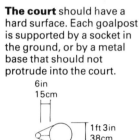

6in
15cm

1ft 3in
38cm

10ft
3.05m

32ft
9.76m

Goal third

100ft
30.50m

Center third

Goal third

33⅓ft
10.16m

50ft
15.25m

Playing positions
1 Goal shooter
2 Goal attack
3 Wing attack
4 Center
5 Wing defense
6 Goal defense
7 Goalkeeper

Starting play

a

b

Officials are:
two umpires (**8**);
two official scorers (**9**);
two timekeepers (**10**).
Umpires must check the court and all equipment before play starts. Each umpire controls half of the court and gives decisions on infringements in that half and the whole of one sideline, though she may be prepared to assist the other if asked. Umpires keep outside the court. Each umpire has a whistle to stop and start play.

Dress Players wear shirts or blouses, skirts or shorts, socks and shoes, which must not be spiked.
Duration A game is divided into four quarters of 15min each. Between the first and second and between the third and fourth quarters there is a 3min interval. Half-time is the mean average requested by the teams up to a maximum of 10min.
Injury time is added to each quarter in which injury occurs.
Up to 5min stoppage is allowed to treat an injured player.

Starting play The captains toss for choice of ends or for the first center pass.
The center (**4**), who is to make the first center pass, takes the ball in the center circle and must pass it within 3sec of the starting whistle. The defending center may not come within 90cm (3ft) of the opposing center and the other players must be within their own areas until the whistle is blown. The first pass must go to a player who moves to arrive in the center third of the court.

Scoring A goal is scored when the ball is sent through the ring by a goal shooter, goal attack or a defender's attempt to intercept a shot at goal.
The shooting player must be wholly inside the shooting circle for the goal to count. Center passes are taken alternately to restart the game after a goal is scored.
Out of play The lines are part of the court and the ball is out of play only if it touches the ground or any object outside them. The ball is also out if it is held by a player standing outside the court (**a**).
Players standing outside the lines cannot jump to play the ball from out of the court (**b**).
The ball is returned to play by a throw in from

immediately behind where it crossed the line.
The team that did not send the ball out of play takes the throw.
The thrower must be alongside her own playing area and must not enter that area until she has released the ball. The throw must be made within 3sec.
If the ball is sent out of play by two opponents at the same moment, play is restarted by the umpire tossing up the ball in the court between the two players opposite where the ball went out.

Ball A size 5 soccer ball is used. It can be made of leather or rubber and must weigh 400–450g.

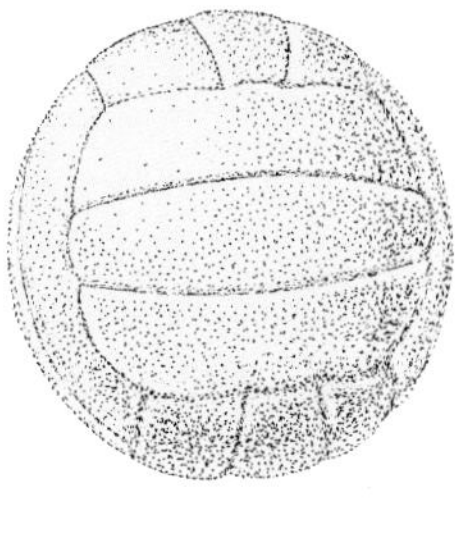

Playing area Each player must remain within the areas illustrated (*right*). Players may change positions only during an interval or after an injury stoppage.

Offside A player is offside if she goes over the boundaries of her area. She may catch the ball over the line, but her feet must remain within the area.

Attack

A
B
C
D
E

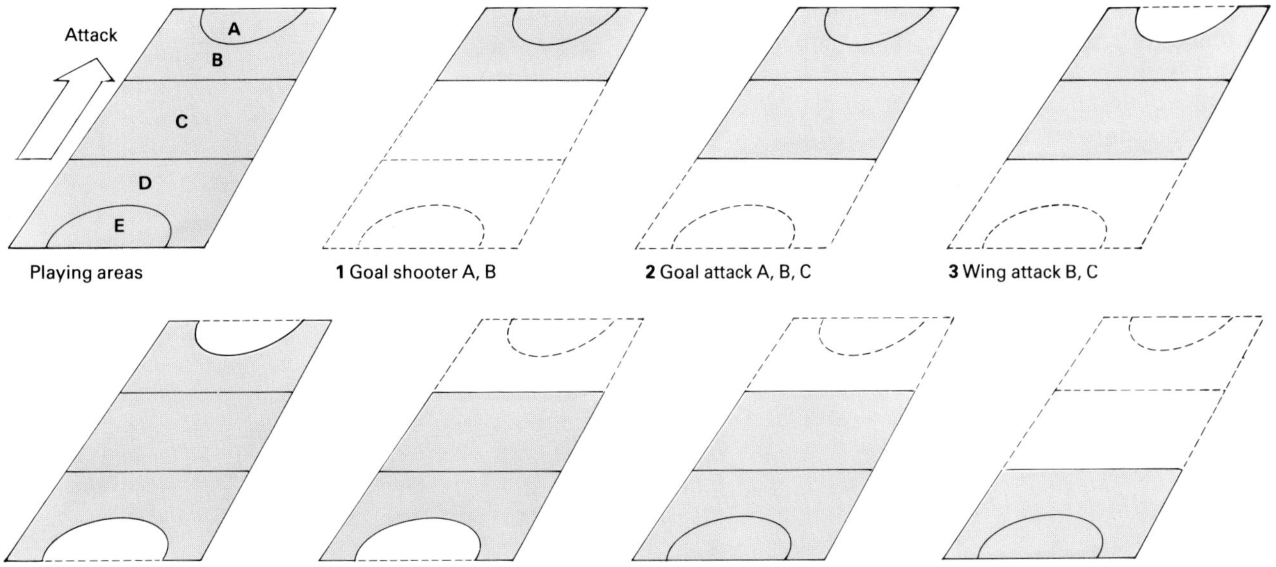

Playing areas

1 Goal shooter A, B

2 Goal attack A, B, C

3 Wing attack B, C

4 Center B, C, D

5 Wing defense C, D

6 Goal defense C, D, E

7 Goalkeeper D, E

Playing the ball

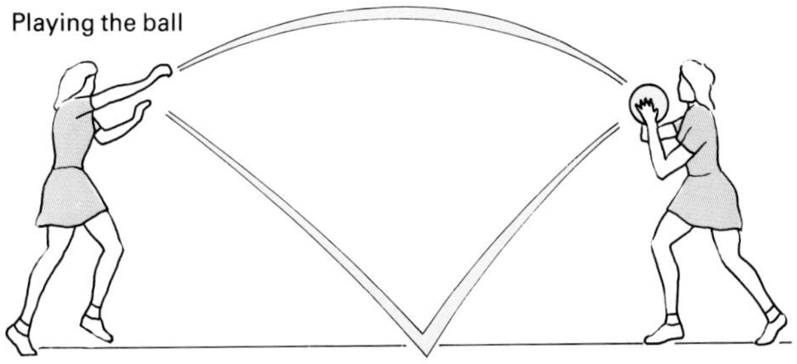

Correct passing   Incorrect passing

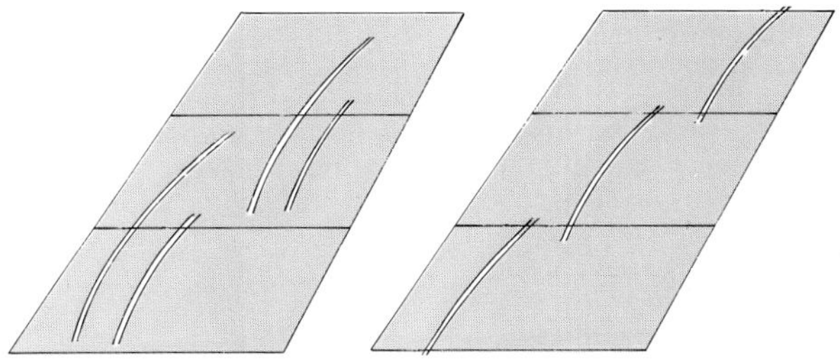

1

2

3

4

5

3ft
91cm

© DIAGRAM

Playing the ball Players may catch the ball in one or two hands, or deflect it to another player.
Having taken possession, they may throw it or bounce it to another player. No player may hold the ball longer than 3sec.
Players may not roll the ball, run with it, throw it in the air and catch it again, bounce it, or drop it and pick it up. They may not deliberately kick it, grab it from an opponent, punch it, or play the ball while they are on the ground.
Players may not use the goalpost as a means of support, not pull at it to keep a shot out of the ring.

Passing A pass must cover a distance that allows a third player to move between the hands of the thrower and receiver.
A pass may not be thrown over a whole third of the court unless it is touched by a player in that third.
Moving with the ball A player may not step with the first foot grounded after catching the ball, but may move the other foot in any direction any number of times (**1**). Pivoting on a foot (**2**) does not count as a step. Hopping is not allowed.

Fouls No player, with or without the ball, may come into physical contact with an opponent in such a manner as to interfere with her play (**3**) or try to knock the ball from a player's hands.
Any player coming closer than 90cm (3ft) to the player with the ball is guilty of obstruction (**4**), though any attempt at interception may be made from outside this distance.
Any intimidating movement is treated as obstruction.
Penalties An offense against the contact and obstruction rules is penalized by:
a) awarding the opponents a penalty pass, if the offense is outside the circle;

b) the option of a penalty pass or a penalty shot, if the offense is inside the circle. In either case the offender must stand beside the thrower and take no part in the play until the ball has left the thrower's hands.
Any other offense results in the award of a free pass from where the infringement took place.
A toss up (**5**) is used to restart play when two opponents commit the same foul simultaneously or when the umpire is undecided about a ruling.

Substitutes Up to three substitutes are allowed in the event of illness, injury or during an interval, but once called into play they cannot be replaced by the original player.

Korfball

Korfball is played by two teams, each with four men and four women. The teams are now positioned within two zones on the pitch. Only in Holland and Belgium is the original three-zone outdoor game still played. Goals are scored by throwing the ball into the opponents' basket. It is essentially a passing game that forbids physical contact, but allows tight marking. The game can be played either outdoors or indoors.

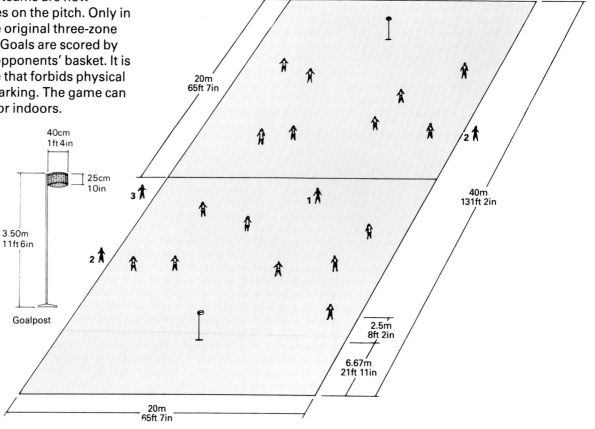

The pitch The dimensions of the pitch are 40×20m (132×66ft) indoors and 60×30m (197×98ft) outdoors, divided into two equal zones.
The field of play is marked out by clearly visible tapes, which must be fixed flat and straight on the ground. A grass pitch is marked by white tapes. Other types are marked with yellow tapes. Flags about 1.5m high may be positioned at the corners but not at the center lines. Spectators are not allowed within 2m of the pitch.
Baskets should be all one color, preferably yellow. The posts are cylindrical, made of wood or metal, and fitted into the ground or a base. Posts must not protrude above the baskets.

Officials

The referee (1) controls the game. He decides the suitability of the pitch and weather; starts, stops, and restarts play; enforces the rules; and settles disputes.

The linesmen (2) judge when the ball is out of play and draw attention to fouls and other infringements. The referee may change his decisions on their advice.
The timekeeper (3) warns the referee before the end of each half.

Teams A team consists of four men and four women; two men and two women are positioned in each zone.
Captains Each team has a captain, who wears a distinctive band on the upper part of his or her left arm. The captain may approach the referee and is responsible for the conduct of his or her team.

Substitutes Two may play for tactical reasons. In case of injury the referee may give permission for further changes.
Dress Teams must wear distinctive uniforms. The players must wear shoes. Players are prohibited to wear objects, which can cause injuries during the game.

Playing areas Every time two goals are scored players move to the other zone. Teams change ends at half time. When moving to the other zone, defenders become attackers and attackers become defenders.

Fouls Players may not:
a) touch the ball below the knee or with the foot;
b) hit the ball with the fist;
c) take possession of the ball when on the ground;
d) run with the ball;
e) avoid passing;
f) dribble;
g) hand the ball to a player;
h) waste time – for example by delaying a pass or free throw or by kicking or throwing the ball away;
i) knock, take or run the ball out of an opponent's hand;
j) push, cling to or hold off an opponent, whether deliberately or not, and even if the opponent does not have possession;
k) excessively hinder an opponent in possession;
l) hinder a member of the opposite sex in throwing or

a player who is already hindered;
m) play the ball or hinder an opponent outside the proper zone;
n) shoot from a defended position;
o) shoot, after cutting past an attacker or from the other zone, a free pass or a throw up;
p) shoot when not playing against a personal opponent;
q) influence a shot by moving the post, or take hold of the post when jumping, running or moving away;
r) violate a free pass or penalty.

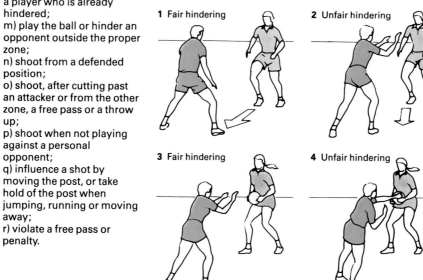

1 Fair hindering

2 Unfair hindering

3 Fair hindering

4 Unfair hindering

Interference (hindering)
Players must not impede the free movements of opponents by physical contact or other forms of obstruction, whether deliberately or not.
A defender may stand in the path of an attacker, but must not extend the arms or legs to prevent him or her from running past nor cause an unavoidable collision.
A player may attempt to influence the direction of a throw or attempt to block the ball provided he or she does not hinder a member of the opposite sex in throwing to someone who is already being hindered.
A player may not hinder an opponent when standing outside his or her own zone.

The ball A number 5 ball, similar to a soccer ball, is used. Its circumference must be 68–71cm and its weight at the start of the game must be between 425g and 475g.

Starting play The home team throws off and chooses the end at which it will shoot. (Captains toss if there is no home team.) Both teams position their players in the different zones.

Duration Two periods of 30 minutes with an interval of 5–15 minutes. Extra time is played for stoppages. The teams change ends at half time.

Throw off To start the game and at the beginning of the second half, the ball is thrown off from the middle of the center line in the attacking zone. After each goal the team that did not score throws off.

Throw up The referee restarts play by throwing the ball up between two opponents if:

Throw off

2.25m
7ft 6in

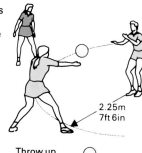

Throw up

a) two opponents seize the ball simultaneously;
b) the ball touches a spectator or an object within the field of play, unless there is no doubt which side would have won possession;
c) neither side is entitled to the ball after an interruption. The referee selects two opponents from the same zone. They must be of the same sex and of similar height.

A free pass is awarded to the other team after an offense or if the ball is sent out of play.
The pass is usually taken where the incident occurred or where the ball went out of play.
It must be taken within four seconds of the referee's

whistle and must be retaken if thrown before the whistle. The players of the opposing team must keep a distance of at least 2.5m until the taker of the free pass moves the ball. The players of the same team of the taker of the pass must keep a distance of at least 2.5m until the ball is brought into play. The ball is brought into play when a player of the opposing team touches it or when a player of the same team as the player taking the free pass touches the ball, while standing at least 2.5m from the spot, at which the pass is taken, or when the ball has traveled at least 2.5m from the place of the free pass. A violation is penalized by a free pass to the opposition;

persistent violations by the award of a penalty.
A goal may not be scored directly from a free pass.
Scoring A goal is scored when the ball passes completely and legally through the opposing team's basket.
A goal is not scored:
if the attackers have committed an offense;
if the ball is thrown through the bottom of the basket and then falls back through it;
if the referee has blown his whistle, except when the offense was committed by a defender and the ball had left the attacker's hand and was out of the defender's reach before the whistle was blown.

Playing the ball Players may use their hands to catch and pass the ball. They must not play the ball with their legs or feet, or with a fist – even if the ball hits the wrist or the back of the hand. They must not play the ball when lying on the ground, unless they fall when in possession.
No player may play the ball outside his or her zone unless he or she plays the ball in the air after jumping from that zone.

1

2

Moving with the ball
Players are not allowed to run with the ball. A player who has stopped with the ball may pivot on one foot. If taking a long throw from a standing position (**1**), it is permissible to place one foot forward and lift the other foot before the ball has left the hands.
A player may jump and land without releasing the ball providing he or she lands in the same position.
A player who seizes the ball when running (**2**) may stop with the ball or may pass it while running provided the seizing and throwing are combined into one flowing movement.
The referee must use his discretion in such cases,

considering the player's pitch, the condition of the pitch, and the need for continuous play, especially in the defense zone.
Passing Players must attempt to pass the ball whenever possible. They must not:
a) deliberately change position without passing;
b) throw the ball with the intention of replaying it;
c) hand the ball to another player (a pass is made only if the ball passes freely through the air or along the ground);
d) dribble the ball, ie tap the ball along the ground and run alongside it.
(If two opponents compete for a ball, one of them may touch the ball several times

before seizing it; this is not a dribble and the player may shoot after playing the ball in this way.)
Out of play The ball is out of play if it:
touches the ground outside the boundary line;
touches a person other than a player or an object outside the playing area.
If the ball is out of play, a free pass is awarded against the team that last played the ball.

---

1 Defended position

2 Defended position
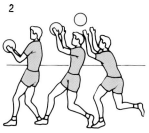

3 Shot from defense zone

4 Cutting
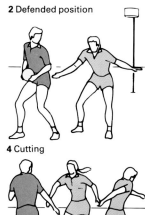

©DIAGRAM

Throwing for a goal Shots at goal are forbidden when the shooting position is defended. It is defended when:
a) the defender is nearer the post than the attacker (**1**);
b) the defender has his or her hand stretched out toward the shooter and is so near the attacker that he or she can touch the attacker without having to bend forward (**2**);
c) the defender faces the attacker and attempts to block the shot (whether the attempt succeeds or not).
A shot at goal may not be made from the defense zone (**3**).
Cutting (**4**) occurs when an attacker runs so close past another attacker that a defender cannot follow the first attacker without the risk

of colliding with the second attacker.
Cutting is not an offense in itself, but it is an offense if the first attacker goes on to throw for goal.
A penalty is automatically awarded for any offense that deprives a team of a chance to score, for example by pushing or preventing a pass to a player with a chance to score.
A penalty may also be awarded for an offense that illegally hinders the attackers.
A player may score directly from a penalty.
A penalty is taken from the penalty spot 2.5m in front of the opponents' post. It must be taken by an attacker.
The player taking the penalty must not touch the ground

between the penalty spot and the post until the ball has been thrown, nor throw the ball until the referee has blown his whistle.
Other players must remain at least 2.5m from the thrower and the post until the ball is thrown and must not interfere with the throw. If an attacker approaches too near the thrower, the defenders are awarded a free pass.
After violation by a defender the penalty will be retaken, if the throw fails to score.
Extra time may be added to each half for a penalty to be taken.

Team handball

Team handball is one of the world's fastest team games. It is played by two sides of seven players and five substitutes. The object is to score the most goals and attackers pass or dribble the ball with their hands until a shooting opportunity is created. When a team loses possession it immediately forms a defensive formation around its goal area.

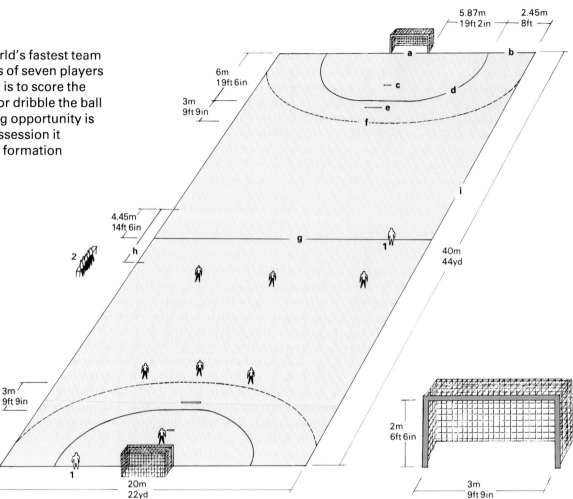

The playing area must be 40m long and 20m wide. Markings are:
a inner goal line
b outer goal line
c goalkeeper line
d goal area line
e penalty line
f free throw line
g center line
h substitution line
i side line
Officials Each game is supervised by two referees (**1**), who are in control of the game. One referee is stationed behind the defense (the goal line referee) the other behind the attack (the court referee). The referees change position as play swings from one end of the playing area to the other.
There is also a scorer and a time keeper.
Teams Each team has up to twelve players (including two goalkeepers), of whom seven (including one goalkeeper) may be in play at any time. Goalkeepers may not play in any other position, though other players may become goalkeepers.
At least five players must be on the court at the start of the game, but at other times play continues if one or both teams have fewer than five players in play.
Substitutes (**2**) may enter the game at any time and as often as required. They need not notify the timekeeper provided the players to be replaced have already left the court. Substitutes must enter from the substitutes' area.

Dress The goalkeeper must be distinguishable from his teammates. Players wear the numbers 1-12 on the backs of their shirts, with the numbers 1 and 12 reserved for the goalkeepers.
Start The captains toss for choice of ends or throw off.
Throw offs are taken from the center, within 3sec of the referee's whistle.
Every player must be in his own half of the court and opponents must be at least 3m from the thrower until the ball has left his hand.

Duration There are two periods of 30 minutes with a 10-minute interval.
Teams change ends after the interval and the game is restarted with a throw off by the other team.
Time may be added on to each period for a free throw or penalty throw.
To achieve a result two extra five-minute halves may be played after a five-minute interval. Ends are changed without an interval.
If score remains a draw, the teams may play two more halves. If they are still drawn, a procedure for shooting five penalties per team may be employed.

Scoring A goal is scored when the whole ball crosses over the goal line between the posts and under the crossbar.
A goal is not scored if the whole of the ball has not crossed the line when an official signals to interrupt the game.
After a goal, play restarts with a throw off from the center by the team that did not score.
A game is won by the team with most goals when play ends.

Body contact In play it is permissible to:
a) use hands and arms to win possession;
b) use the flat of the hand to play the ball from another player (**3**);
c) obstruct an opponent with the body whether or not he has possession (**4**).
It is forbidden to:
1) snatch the ball with one or both hands, or strike it from an opponent's hands;
2) obstruct an opponent with hands, arms or legs;
3) catch an opponent with one or both hands, or handle him roughly by hitting, pushing, running into or jumping into him, or tripping him or by throwing oneself before him;

Body contact
3   4

The ball has an outer casing of colored leather.
For men the weight is 425–475g and the circumference 58–60cm.
For women the weight is 325–400g and the circumference 54–56cm.

Playing the ball

Moving with the ball

Playing the ball A player may:
a) stop, catch, throw, bounce or strike the ball in any manner and in any direction using hands, fists, arms, head, body, thigh or knees;
b) hold the ball for 3sec but no longer;
c) move the ball from one hand to another;
d) stop the ball with one or both hands and then catch it, providing he does not move;
e) pass the ball when sitting, kneeling or lying on the ground.
It is forbidden to:
1) touch the ball more than once unless it touches the ground, another player, or the goal, or is fumbled or passed from one hand to the other;
2) touch the ball with any part of the leg below the knee or with the foot;
3) dive for the ball lying or rolling on the ground, except for the goalkeeper in his own area;
4) deliberately play the ball across the side line or the goal line.

Moving with the ball A player may take only three steps while holding the ball, but he may then stop, bounce the ball with one hand and then take three further steps. If a running or jumping player catches the ball, his steps are not counted until after both feet have in turn or together touched the ground. He may bounce the ball repeatedly with one hand while running with it or standing. Having caught the ball, he is allowed three steps and 3sec to hold it before passing.
He may catch, bounce and catch the ball again when it has touched another player or the goal. There is no limit on the steps between bouncing and recatching the ball.
A player may roll the ball along the ground with one hand.
"Bouncing" only occurs if the player has control of the ball. If the player fails to control the ball when attempting to catch it, he is considered not to have touched it.

4) push or force an opponent into the goal area;
5) deliberately throw the ball onto an opponent, or move it toward him as a dangerous feint.
Goal area Only the goalkeeper is allowed in the goal area.
Any ball that touches or crosses the goal area line may only be played by the goalkeeper.
Any ball that enters and leaves the goal area without being touched by the goalkeeper remains in play.
If a player deliberately plays the ball into his own goal area and the ball does not leave the goal area without being touched, his team will concede:
a) a goal, if the ball enters

the net;
b) a penalty throw, if the goalkeeper touches the ball;
c) a free throw in all other cases.
(Play continues if the ball was not deliberately played into the goal area.)
The goalkeeper (1) may defend the goal in any way, except that he may use his legs below the knees or his feet, only if the ball is moving toward the goal or goal line.
Within his area he is exempt from rules limiting the number of steps or time taken to throw the ball; outside his area he shares the restrictions imposed on other players. A goalkeeper is not penalized for accidentally leaving his area.

A goalkeeper may not play or take the ball into his area or touch the ball outside his area while he is inside it.
Throw in If the whole of the ball passes over the side line a throw in is awarded against the team that last touched the ball. It is taken from where the ball crossed the line.
The thrower must have at least one foot on the side line (2).
If any defender, except the goalkeeper, is the last player to touch the ball before it crosses the goal line outside goal, a throw in is awarded to the attackers. It must be taken from the intersection of the side line and goal line on the side on which the ball went out.

A goal throw is awarded if the whole of the ball crosses the goal line outside the goal, having been last touched by an attacker or by the defending goalkeeper.
It is also awarded if the ball enters the goal direct from a throw off, throw in or goal throw.
It is thrown by the goalkeeper from within his area (3).
The ball is in play again as soon as it crosses the goal area line (4). The goalkeeper must not play the ball again before it touches another player.

Suspension The referees will caution a player guilty of fouls or unsporting conduct. If he repeats the offense, he may be suspended. Suspensions are for 2 minutes.
Substitutes may not be fielded for suspended players, except for the goalkeeper (but another player must then leave the court).
If a player is sent off for a third time, he is disqualified. Particularly serious fouls or unsporting conduct may lead to immediate disqualification.

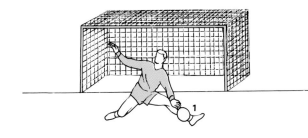

Throw in

Goal throw

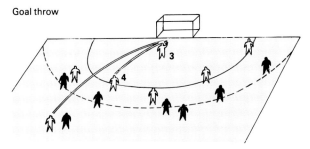

Referee's throw A game is restarted with a referee's throw if:
a) it is halted because both teams infringe the rules simultaneously;
b) it is interrupted without any infringement;
c) the ball hits the ceiling or any object above the floor.
The referee takes the throw where play was interrupted, but if play was interrupted between the goal area line and the free throw line, the referee's throw is taken from the nearest point outside the free throw line.
Players must be shoulder to shoulder with the referee and must not touch the ball until it has reached its apex.

a Area between the goal area line and the free throw line

Free throw

A free throw is awarded to the opponents for:
a) illegally entering or leaving the court;
b) an illegal throw in;
c) illegally playing the ball;
d) deliberately putting the ball out of play;
e) illegal obstruction, tackling or defense;
f) infringements in the goal area by court players;
g) deliberately playing the ball into one's own goal area;
h) infringements by the goalkeeper, except those which incur penalty throws;
i) unsporting conduct.
A free throw may be taken immediately from the spot where the offense occured without the referee blowing his whistle.
If the infringement was committed by a defender between his goal area line and the free throw line, then the free throw is taken from the nearest point outside the free throw line.
If the free throw is delayed the referee will blow his whistle: the free throw must then be taken within 3sec, or a free throw is awarded to the other team. The attackers must not touch or cross their opponents' free throw line before the throw is taken.
When a free throw is to be taken from the free throw line the defenders may stand on their goal area line.
A goal may be scored direct from a free throw.
The ball may be thrown in any direction. The thrower must keep one foot continuously on the ground. He must not touch the ball again until it has touched another player or the goal. Opponents should be 3m away until the ball has left the thrower's hands.

3m
9ft 9in

Penalty throw

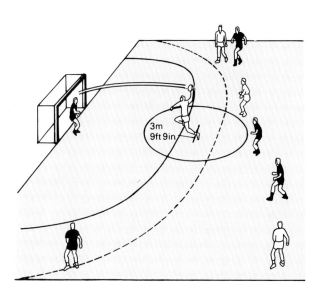

A penalty throw is awarded to the opponents:
a) for fouls anywhere on court, if they destroy a clear chance for goal;
b) if a defender deliberately enters his own goal area for defensive purposes and gains an advantage against an opponent, who has the ball;
c) if a defender deliberately plays the ball into his own goal area and it touches the goalkeeper;
d) if the goalkeeper carries or throws the ball into his own goal area.
The thrower may not cross the penalty throw line before the ball leaves his hand.
He must throw the ball in the direction of the goal and keep one foot continuously on the ground, though the other may be lifted or moved. Both feet must stay behind the line.
The throw must be taken within 3sec of the referee's whistle.
A suspended player is not allowed to take a penalty throw.
The goalkeeper must be at least 3m from the thrower, but he may move about within his area. The throw is retaken if the goalkeeper fouls.
All other players must be outside the area between the free throw line and the goal area line. Opponents must be at least 3m from the thrower until the ball leaves his hand, and they must not attempt to distract him.
If an attacker touches or crosses the free throw line before the ball is thrown: the throw is retaken if a goal is scored;
a free throw is awarded to the defense if the ball strikes the goal or goalkeeper and rebounds outside the area; play continues if the goalkeeper stops or holds the ball.
If a defender touches or crosses the free throw line before the ball is thrown: a goal is scored if valid; otherwise the throw is retaken.

3m
9ft 9in

Speedball

Speedball combines the elements of several team sports, particularly soccer and basketball. The players may kick, throw, and catch the ball; there is no offside rule. Carrying the ball and physical contact are not allowed. There are slight variations between the men's and women's versions of the game.

The ball is an official soccer ball, with a circumference of 27–28in and a weight of 14–19½oz. (A basketball may be used on a small pitch.)

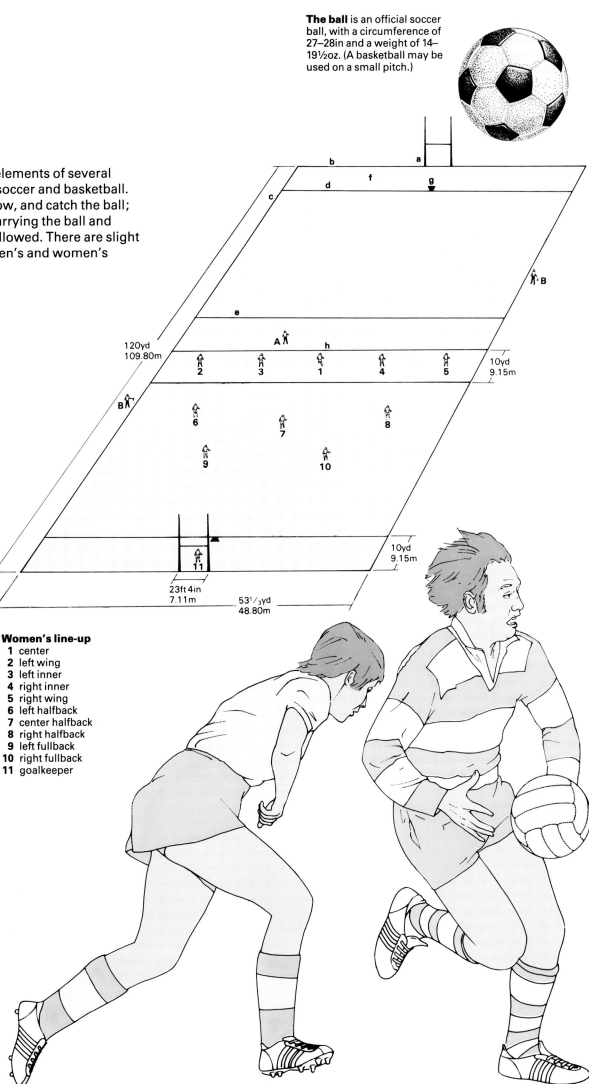

Pitch A full-size pitch is 120yd long by 53⅓yd wide. The various features are:
a goal;
b end line;
c side line;
d goal line;
e restraining line;
f end zone and penalty area;
g penalty kick mark;
h middle line.

Teams There are two teams, each of 11 players.

Substitutes Each team is allowed five substitutes, who may be put into play without limitation after reporting to a linesman. They may go onto the pitch only after the ball is dead.

120yd
109.80m

10yd
9.15m

10yd
9.15m

23ft 4in
7.11m

53⅓yd
48.80m

Men's line-up
1 center
2 left end
3 left forward
4 right forward
5 right end
6 left halfback
7 fullback
8 right halfback
9 left guard
10 right guard
11 goal guard

Women's line-up
1 center
2 left wing
3 left inner
4 right inner
5 right wing
6 left halfback
7 center halfback
8 right halfback
9 left fullback
10 right fullback
11 goalkeeper

Dress Players wear uniforms of jerseys and shorts. Football boots are worn. Dangerous equipment is prohibited.

Officials A referee (A) who is in charge of the game. Two linesmen (B) on opposite sides and in different halves of the pitch, who whistle to indicate fouls, when the ball is out of play, etc.
A scorer, who keeps a record of the game.
A timekeeper who, on the referee's order, excludes time when the ball is not in play.

© DIAGRAM

Duration Each game consists of four quarters lasting 10 minutes. There are intervals of two minutes after the first and third quarters, and 15 minutes after the second.
Extra periods of five minutes are played if the score is tied when the game would normally end.

Time outs Each team is allowed five time outs in a game. Each time out must not exceed two minutes. A team may not request a time out when the ball is in play unless it has possession.
A time out is not charged if requested for the purpose of substituting a player.

Starting play The team that won the toss has the choice of goal or kick off. The loser has the same choice at the start of the second half.
At the start of a half and after a score the game is started with a place kick from the center of the kicking team's restraining line. The ball must reach the opposition's restraining line unless it is touched by another player. The rest of the kicking team must be behind the ball.

Their opponents must be behind their restraining line. Artificial tees may not be used.
Ends are changed for the second and fourth quarters. In the men's game, the ball is then put into play with a punt, drop kick, or pass from the sideline at a point opposite where the ball was in play when the previous quarter ended. It is put into play by a member of the team that last had possession. In the women's game, quarters begin with a restraining line kick off by the team last in possession. Teams also change ends for every period of extra time after the first. Each such period begins with a kick off from the kicking team's restraining line.
After a time out the ball is put in play from the sideline; the team last in possession makes a pass, drop kick, or place kick. The ball must not be put in play nearer to the opposition goal line than where it went out.

Playing the ball The method of playing the ball depends on whether it is an aerial (or fly) ball, or a ground ball.
An aerial ball is one that has been kicked into the air. It remains an aerial ball until it hits the ground.
A loose aerial ball (ie an aerial ball not in a player's possession) may not be kicked (**1**) or kneed. It may be played with the hands and caught (**2**), but not until the kicker's foot has left the ground or the ball has left his foot or leg.
A ball that has been caught may not be dribbled by bouncing on the ground (**3**). It may be dribbled overhead (**4**). An overhead dribble is made by throwing the ball in the air and then running and catching it before it hits the ground. Players are not permitted to make a touchdown by an overhead dribble, nor make consecutive overhead dribbles.

A player who has caught an aerial ball is not permitted to run with it in his hands (**5**). If he catches the ball in the air he may put both feet on the ground. He may make one step in any direction.
A player who has caught an aerial ball may play it to his feet and make a dribble, punt, or drop kick.
A ground ball is one that is stationary, rolling, or bouncing. It may be kicked, headed, or bounced off the body.
It may not be played with the hands, but may be converted into an aerial ball with the feet.
Tackling A player may only guard an opponent who has the ball. He may attempt to play the ball, but must not hold or obstruct the opponent.
If two players are challenging for the ball, they must play the ball and not the man.

A tip off is held if: two players hold the ball simultaneously; there is doubt which side put the ball out of play; there is a simultaneous foul by opponents.
The tip off takes place where the incident occurred, except that it may not be within 5yd of a boundary. The referee or linesman tosses the ball between two opponents, who stand opposite each other, between their own goal and the opponent within an imaginary 4ft circle.
The players attempt to tap the ball to a teammate. They must not tap the ball until it reaches its highest point, nor may they tap it more than twice before it hits the ground or is touched by another player.
If they fail to tap the ball before it touches the ground, the tip off is retaken.
No other player is allowed within 6ft of the tip off.
If the tip off is in the end zone and the ball is caught by an attacker, there is no score although the ball remains in play.

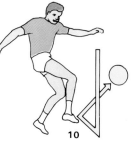

Types of kick
A punt (**9**) occurs when the player drops the ball and kicks it before it touches the ground.
A drop kick (**10**) occurs when the player kicks the ball after it has bounced once.
A place kick (**11**) occurs when the player positions the ball and kicks it while it is stationary.

Scoring The methods of scoring are the same for the men's and the women's versions of the game, but the number of points scored is different.
(If a score is made after the end of period, it is recorded provided the attackers did not give further impetus to the ball after the whistle was blown.)

Men's scoring is by:
a field goal (3 points);
a drop kick (2 points);
a touchdown (1 point);
a penalty (1 point);
an end kick (1 point).
Women's scoring is by:
a drop kick (3 points);
a touchdown (2 points);
a field goal (1 point);
a penalty (1 point).

Drop kick   Field goal

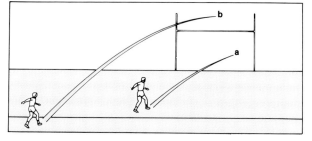

A field goal (**a**) is scored when a ground ball is kicked or legally sent over the end lines between the goalposts and under the crossbar.

A drop kick (**b**) scores when the ball is legally caught and then kicked over the crossbar, providing the drop kick is made outside the defenders' end zone.

5

Converting a ground ball into an aerial ball Players may not use their hands (**6**), but they may use one foot (**7**), or both feet (**8**).

6   **7**   **8**

© DIAGRAM

Out of play A ball is out of play when:
a) it touches the sidelines or the ground outside them;
b) a player with the ball touches a sideline or the ground outside it with any part of his body; or
c) the ball crosses the end line without a score.
A ball that rebounds off the goalposts or crossbar remains in play although a touchdown cannot be scored from it.
The ball is put in play from where it went out. It is returned by either a place kick, a drop kick, a punt, or a pass.
The player returning the ball has five seconds to play it, or it is awarded to the opposition. He must be outside the pitch when he returns the ball, and may not play it again until it has been touched by another player.

Opponents must be at least 5yd from the ball until it is played.
When the ball goes over the sidelines between the end zones it is awarded against the team that last touched it; a goal cannot be scored directly.
If the ball goes across the sideline from a kick off, the opposition kicks it into play from where it went out.
A touchback occurs when an attacker puts the ball over the sideline in the end zone or over the end line without scoring; the defense puts it in play.
A safety occurs when a defender plays the ball over the end line without scoring; the attackers put the ball in play. No score may be made until the ball has passed outside the end zone.

Personal fouls include: kicking; tripping; pushing; holding; blocking; or any unnecessary rough play against an opponent.
Technical fouls include: illegal substitution; taking more than five time outs; unsportsmanlike conduct; more than 11 players from one team appearing on the pitch simultaneously; time wasting.
Violations include: carrying the ball; touching a ground ball with hands or arms; making two successive dribbles; infringements at kick offs, free kicks and penalty kicks; infringements at tip offs; infringements when returning the ball into play; kicking or kneeing an aerial ball unless a player has first caught it.

Penalties vary according to the offense committed.
Personal fouls When a personal foul is committed by a player outside his end zone, a free kick is awarded to the opposition. It is taken either from where the offense occurred or from where the ball was when the foul occurred, whichever is nearer to the offender's goal.
When a player commits a personal foul within his own end zone, two penalty kicks are awarded to the opposition, the first without a follow-up, the second with a follow-up. The fouled player must take the kicks; the ball will be dead after the first attempt.
Technical fouls If a technical foul is committed, the opposition is awarded a penalty kick without a follow-up. Any member of the team may take the kick.

Violations If a player commits a violation outside his end zone, the opposition is awarded a free kick.
If he commits a violation within the end zone, the opposition is awarded a penalty kick, with a follow-up if missed.
Suspension A player may be suspended from the game for unsportsmanlike conduct. A player who commits five personal fouls in a game is automatically suspended.
A free kick may be a punt, drop, or place kick. The ball may be kicked in any direction. It must travel its own circumference. The kicker may not play it again until it is touched by another player. The kicking side may stand anywhere; all opponents must be at least 10yd away from the kicker.

Touch down   End kick   Penalty kick

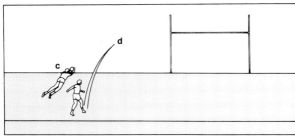

A touchdown (c) may be made by a player who receives a forward pass when in the opposition end zone. The receiver must be completely within the end zone and not be touching any boundary line.

An end kick (d) is scored by legally kicking a ground ball from within the opponents' end zone over the end line outside the goal. (Teams decide before a game whether end kicks are to be scored.)

A penalty kick (e) is scored when the ball is kicked into the goal from the penalty mark after a personal or a technical foul.
Only one defender is allowed in goal, and he must stand on the end line until the ball is kicked.

After some offenses the kicker's teammates are permitted to attempt to score (follow-up) if the kicker misses.
The kicker may not play the ball again until it touches another player; his teammates must be behind the ball.
The opposition (except the goalkeeper) must be outside

the end zone; they may stand on the end line outside the goal.
If there is no follow-up, the ball is dead immediately the kicker misses.
If a team incurs more than one penalty kick with a follow-up for successive fouls or violations, then all but the last kick will be without a follow-up.

Gaelic football

Gaelic football is governed by some of the same rules as hurling, and is played on the same size pitch. Players may catch, fist, and kick the ball, and attempt to score points by getting the ball into the opponents' goal space. The winning team is the one that scores the greater number of points.

Pitch The minimum size of a pitch is 130m by 80m; the maximum size 145m by 90m.

Officials are:
a referee, who controls the game;
two linesmen, one at each side of the field, who change ends at half time;
four goal umpires, one outside each goalpost, who do not change ends.

Teams Each team has 15 players. Three substitutes per team are allowed, but they may only take up their positions during stoppages.

Duration Playing time is usually 70 minutes with a maximum interval of 10 minutes at half time, after which the teams change ends. Playing time for the All Ireland senior finals and semi-finals is 80 minutes.

Start The captains toss for choice of ends. Two players from each side stand in two lines at the center of the field; the other players position themselves behind the 45m lines. The referee then throws in the ball over the heads of the players.

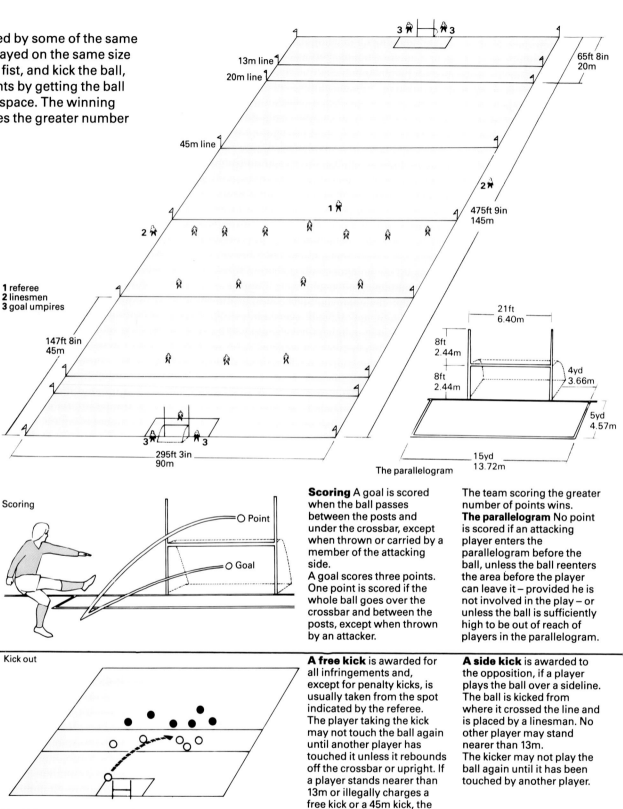

1 referee
2 linesmen
3 goal umpires

The parallelogram

Scoring

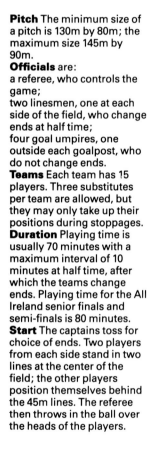

Scoring A goal is scored when the ball passes between the posts and under the crossbar, except when thrown or carried by a member of the attacking side.
A goal scores three points. One point is scored if the whole ball goes over the crossbar and between the posts, except when thrown by an attacker.

The team scoring the greater number of points wins.

The parallelogram No point is scored if an attacking player enters the parallelogram before the ball, unless the ball reenters the area before the player can leave it – provided he is not involved in the play – or unless the ball is sufficiently high to be out of reach of players in the parallelogram.

Kick out In a kick out from goal, the ball is kicked from the ground within the parallelogram.
All opponents must be outside the 20m line; all defendants other than the kicker and goalkeeper must be outside the 13m line.
After a score the ball is kicked out from the 20m line; no player may stand nearer than 13m until the ball is kicked.

Kick out

Free kick

A free kick is awarded for all infringements and, except for penalty kicks, is usually taken from the spot indicated by the referee. The player taking the kick may not touch the ball again until another player has touched it unless it rebounds off the crossbar or upright. If a player stands nearer than 13m or illegally charges a free kick or a 45m kick, the opposing team is awarded a free kick from where he stood or charged. If he charged from within the parallelogram, a penalty kick is awarded to the other team.
If a player other than the kicker kicks a placed ball, he is sent to the sideline.

A side kick is awarded to the opposition, if a player plays the ball over a sideline. The ball is kicked from where it crossed the line and is placed by a linesman. No other player may stand nearer than 13m.
The kicker may not play the ball again until it has been touched by another player.

The ball weighs 320–425g and has a circumference of 69–74cm.

Dress Players wear shirts, shorts, and socks in their team colors, and football boots.

Playing the ball A player may:
kick the ball;
fist the ball;
pass the ball from hand to hand;
strike the ball with his hands when it is off the ground;
hop (bounce) the ball with one or both hands.
The goalkeeper, when he is within the parallelogram, may pick the ball off the ground with his hand or fist it up from the ground.
A player may not:
throw the ball;
hold the ball longer than it is necessary to pass it;
hold the ball for more than four steps, or tip the ball (bounce it on the hand).
A player other than the goalkeeper may not play a ball that is on the ground with his hands, unless he was knocked to the ground with the ball – in which case he may fist it away.
Tackling A player may charge an opponent shoulder to shoulder.
If a player who is being fairly charged deliberately turns so as to make the charge come from behind, that charge will not be termed a foul.
A goalkeeper may not be charged within the parallelogram unless he has the ball or is obstructing an opponent.

Fisting the ball

Passing the ball

A 45m free kick is awarded to the attacking side when a defender plays the ball over the end line. It is taken on the 45m line opposite where the ball crossed the line.
A penalty kick If a defender commits a foul inside the parallelogram, a penalty kick is awarded to the attacking team from the center of the 13m line.
All players other than the kicker and goalkeeper must stand outside the 20m line.

45m free kick

13m
42ft 8in

Penalty kick

1

2

Fouls A player may not:
push, kick, trip (**1**), hold, strike, or jump at an opponent; obstruct a player with his hand or arm (**2**) even if he is not actually holding him;
reach from behind a player who has the ball;
charge a player from behind;
charge or interfere with an opponent who is not playing or moving to play the ball.
Interference If anyone other than a player prevents the ball from crossing a sideline, a sideline kick is awarded against the last player to have touched the ball.
A goal, point or 45m kick is awarded if the ball is similarly prevented from scoring or crossing an endline.

© DIAGRAM

Australian rules football

Australian rules football is played on a large oval pitch between two teams, each of 18 players. The teams try to score goals (six points) through the center posts, or behinds (one point) through the outer posts. The ball may be kicked or punched (handballed), but it may not be thrown.

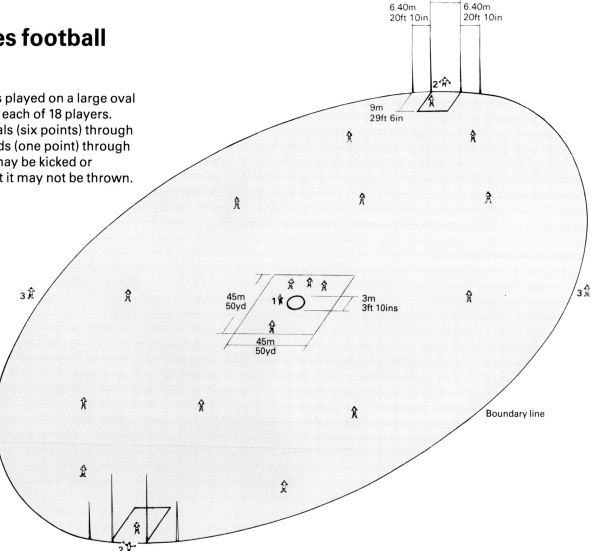

Pitch An oval grass pitch should be 110–155m wide and 135–185m long.

Officials A match is controlled by a field umpire (1), two goal umpires (2), two boundary umpires (3), and two timekeepers. The officials ensure that the ball is kept in play and that the game is played in accordance with the laws.

Teams consist of 20 named players, two of whom are the interchange players (substitutes).

Interchange At any time during the match one of the players not then taking part in the match may be interchanged with one of the participating players. The interchange player may not normally enter the field until the player he is replacing has left it, unless this player cannot be immediately removed from the field due to serious injury.
Players must leave and enter the playing ground through the interchange area during the match.

Start The captains toss for choice of ends. At the start of each quarter and after a goal the field umpire blows his whistle and bounces the ball in the center circle. (He may throw the ball in the air if the ground is unsuitable.) No player may enter the circle and, until the ball touches the ground, only four players per team are allowed inside the square.

Start of play

Duration A game lasts four quarters, each of 25 minutes playing time. Teams change ends after each quarter. A maximum of 3 minutes is allowed between the first and second quarters; 15 minutes at half-time; and 5 minutes between the third and fourth quarters.
The timekeepers sound a siren at the end of each quarter. Play ceases when the field umpire blows his whistle to indicate that he has heard the siren.
Time on may be added when there has been an undue delay, for example in getting the ball when it is out of play.

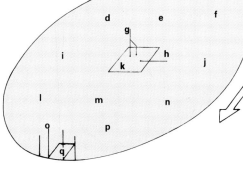

Playing positions
a full back
b right full back
c left full back
d right half back
e center half back
f left half back
g followers (two)
h rover
i right center (wing)
j left center (wing)
k center
l right half forward
m center half forward
n left half forward
o right full forward
p left full forward
q full forward

Bouncing the ball The field umpire bounces the ball:
a) at the start of each quarter;
b) after a goal;
c) when there is doubt over which player has taken a mark;
d) when a player kicking off from behind kicks off from outside the kick-off lines;
e) in scrimmages;
f) when the ball has been bounced and has gone over the goal line, behind line or boundary line, without having been touched by any player;
g) when a player claims a mark, the ball having been touched, and retains possession when held by an opponent, if the field umpire is satisfied the player has not heard his call "play on";
h) when the goal umpire cannot see whether the ball crossed the goal line.

The ball is of hide with a rubber bladder inside. It is normally provided by the home team. The ball may only be changed with the consent of both captains. A standard ball weighs 454–482g and has a short circumference of 57cm and a long circumference of 74m.

Dress Players wear jerseys, shorts, socks and studded boots.

Scoring The team scoring the most points wins; if the score is equal, the game is a draw.

A goal (6 points) is scored when an attacker kicks the ball over the goal line between the goalposts (the center posts) without it touching either the posts or another player.

A behind (1 point) is scored:
a) when the ball goes between the goalposts without fulfilling all the conditions for a goal to be scored;
b) when the ball touches or passes over a goalpost;
c) passes over a behind line without touching a behind post;
d) when the ball is kicked or carried over the behind or goal line by a defender.
If a ball touches or passes over a behind post, it is out of play.
When a player is kicking at goal from a mark or free kick, the kick must be on a direct line through the mark to the center of the goal line.

Scoring after time is allowed if:
a) the ball was in transit before the first siren;
b) the player was awarded a free kick;
c) the player took a mark before the siren.
Scoring is not allowed after time if the ball was touched and assisted in transit or if it touched any player below the knee.

Kick off After a behind, unless a free kick has been given, the defending side kicks the ball from within the kick-off lines.
No opponent is allowed within 10m of those lines. The ball must be kicked clear of the hands and feet, but does not have to be kicked over the kick-off line.

Playing the ball A player may kick the ball, but may not throw it; he may pass the ball with the hands only by handballing (punching) it. A player may hold the ball until he is held by an opponent. Players are allowed to tackle an opponent who has the ball (as permitted by the laws), or block opponents near the ball but not in possession.

Running with the ball A player may run with the ball, but he must bounce or touch it on the ground at least once every 10m.
If, when running with the ball, a player hits it over an opponent's head and catches it, he must bounce or touch it on the ground, or pass it, within 10m.

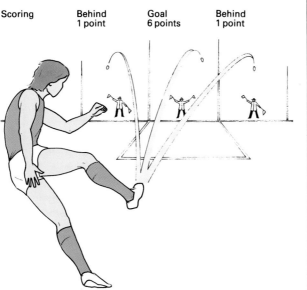

Scoring	Behind 1 point	Goal 6 points	Behind 1 point

Running with the ball

10m
33ft

A mark is awarded when a player catches and holds the ball directly from the kick of another player at least 10m away (**1**). (The ball must not have been touched before the mark.)
A mark is also awarded if the ball strikes an official but is caught by another player before it touches the ground. The player who made the mark is allowed an unhindered kick from anywhere behind where he marked. Only one opponent is allowed to stand at a mark and no other player is allowed within a 10m semicircle behind the mark. If an opponent "crosses the mark" when a player successfully kicks for goal, the goal is awarded; if no goal is scored the player may make another kick. A mark is allowed if it was made by a player before the ball crossed the boundary. It is also allowed on a goal line.

Holding the ball (**2**) A player in possession of the ball, when held by an opponent firmly enough to stop him or retard his progress, must dispose of the ball by kicking or handballing it. Failure to do so within a reasonable time allowed by the field umpire is penalized by a free kick. If the player in possession is forced to lose the ball (eg, by being swung off balance), play continues.
Handball (**3**) A player may pass the ball with the hands only by holding the ball in one hand and hitting it with the clenched fist of the other hand.

Awarding free kicks A free kick is awarded to the nearest opponent of a player who;
a) infringes at a center bounce;
b) unduly interferes with the bouncing of the ball by the field umpire;
c) deliberately interferes with an umpire during the progress of the match;
d) interferes with an opponent when the ball is out of play or is more than 5m away;
e) deliberately holds back or throws an opponent who has kicked or handballed the ball;
f) trips (**6**) or kicks (or attempts to trip or kick) or slings an opponent;
g) is guilty of dangerous kicking when not in possession;
h) strikes or attempts to strike an opponent with his hand or arm, or deliberately with his knee;
i) seizes an opponent below the knee or above the neck (including the top of the shoulder) (**7**);
j) charges an opponent;
k) pushes an opponent from behind (**8**), except when legitimately going for a mark;
l) pushes an opponent in the face (**9**);
m) pushes an opponent who is in the air for a mark;
n) infringes the rules on holding the ball;
o) handballs the ball incorrectly;
p) throws or hands the ball to another player while the balls is in play (**10**);
q) infringes the rules on running with the ball;
r) deliberately kicks or forces the ball out of bounds without it being touched by another player;
s) when kicking off from a behind, kicks the ball out of bounds without another player touching it;
t) kicks the ball out of bounds without it first touching the ground;
u) interferes with an opponent while the ball is

Holding the man (4) A player may hold an opponent who is in possession of the ball, but must allow him a reasonable chance to dispose of the ball by kicking or handballing it. If the player in possession is forced to lose the ball (for example, by being swung off balance), play continues.

Checking (5) A player with the ball may be tackled with the hip, chest, shoulder, arms, or open hands. A player without the ball may be pushed in the chest or side in the proper manner in accordance with the laws, providing the ball is within 5m of him.

Out of play To be out of play the ball must be completely outside the boundary line. The field umpire must be informed, and, unless a free kick has been awarded, the ball is returned to the position in the field where it went out. If, after a mark or free kick, the player does not put the ball back into play from outside the boundary line, the ball is returned to the field at the point where the original mark or free kick took place. If a defender, kicking from behind the goal line or behind line, hits a post, time and another kick are allowed.

Throw in When the ball is over the boundary line, the boundary umpire may be directed by the field umpire to throw the ball over his head toward the center of the field. It must travel between 10 and 15m at a minimum height of 10m.

out of bounds;
v) deliberately wastes time.
Taking a free kick A player may take a free kick from any point behind where it was awarded.
No other player may be within 10m and only one opponent is allowed at that distance.
The field umpire will allow play to continue if a free kick would benefit the offending side.

If an opponent deliberately delays a free kick or a mark, it may be advanced a maximum of 50m toward the offending team's goal. If the offending team commits another offense before the free kick is taken, the kick shall be taken where the second offense occurred, if that is to the disadvantage of the offending team.

If the offense was against a player who had disposed of the ball, his team may take the kick from:
a) where the ball touched the ground;
b) where the ball was caught;
c) where the ball was marked;
d) where the ball went out of play;
e) where the offense occurred.

Scoring from a free kick If an offense by an opponent occurs during a successful kick at goal, the goal will count. If a behind is scored, another kick is awarded. If an attacker commits an offense during his team's kick for goal, no points may be scored and a free kick is awarded to the opposition. If a player is fouled immediately after a score

and "all clear," another free kick is awarded where the offense occurred. There may then be another score before the ball is bounced in the center circle or kicked off.
Suspension The field umpire can caution offenders and report them to the controlling body, which may suspend them from further matches.

© DIAGRAM

143

American football

In American football two teams with 11 players on the field attempt to score points by field goals passed through the upright goalposts or putting the ball behind their opponents' goal line in an approved manner. The winning team is the one that scores the greater number of points.

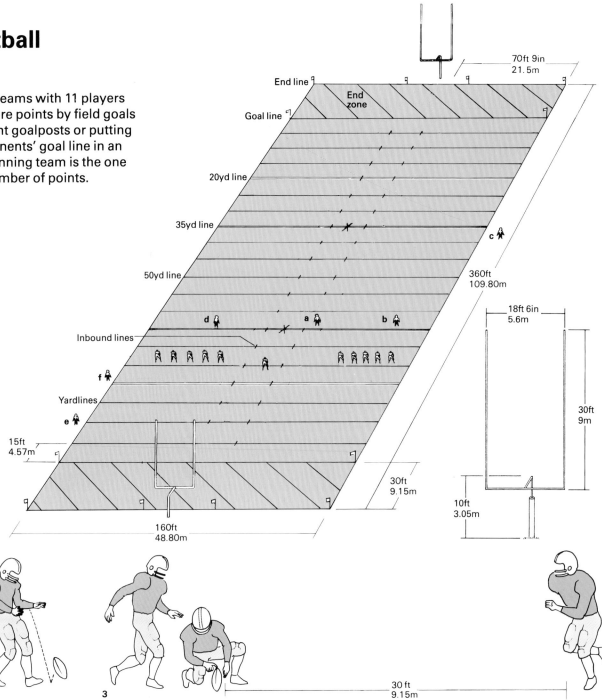

The field The area between the end lines and sidelines is the field of play.
The field is divided between the goal lines by parallel yardlines, 5yd apart. These are intersected by short inbound lines 70ft 9in from each sideline. Between the inbound lines there are marks at 1yd intervals. All measurements are made from the inside edges of the lines. Sidelines and end lines are out of bounds; goal lines signify the start of end zones. No benches or rigid fixtures are allowed within 5yd of the sidelines.

Kick offs

Officials have individual functions, but they are equally responsible for signaling and recording fouls. They all wear uniforms, including a white cap with a visor, and carry a whistle and a flag. The officials are:
a) the referee, who is the chief official in control of the game;
b) the umpire, with special responsibility for equipment and the scrimmage lines;
c) the linesman, who operates on one side of the field and changes sides at half time. He has special responsibility for offsides and encroachment into the neutral zone, or across the line of scrimmage, the chain crew, and covering his side zone;

d) the field judge, with special responsibility for kicks from scrimmage, forward passes across the defensive end line, and similar loose balls;
e) the side judge and back judge, who operate on the same side as the line judge, 13–15yd deep, and have to check the number of defensive players at a snap and the eligible receivers of a pass on their side of the field;
f) the line judge, who operates on the opposite side to the linesman and has special responsibility for timing, recording team time-outs, winning the toss, the score, illegal movements behind the scrimmage line, illegal shifts and illegal covering on his side.

Teams Each team fields 11 players, one of whom is the captain. No team is allowed more than 40 players in uniform.
Substitution Unlimited substitution is allowed. But substitutes are only allowed on the field when the ball is dead (not in play).
Disqualified players and players requiring more than the permitted time out for injury or repairs must be substituted. Players must leave the field on their own side between the end lines.
Starting play The captains toss 30 minutes before the start for choice of kicking off or receiving the kick off, or selecting which end his team will defend first. For the second half the captain who lost the toss chooses

between those three privileges.
Goals are changed at the end of the first and third periods, but possession and the relative position of the ball etc remain unchanged. Play is started on or between the inbound lines, with a kick off (free kick) from:
a) the 35yd line, at the start of each half and after a field goal or try for extra point;
b) the 20yd line, after a safety with a free punt.
Kick offs may be taken in one of the following ways:
1 the ball may be drop kicked;
2 another player may hold the ball for a place kick.
A punt kick, when the ball does not touch the ground, is only permitted from the 20 following a safety. During

kick off, all players must be in bounds.
The kicking team, except for the kicker and the holder of a place kick, must be behind the ball; the opposition must be at least 10yd away.
The ball must travel across the opposition line unless touched by an opponent. It should not go out of play. After a kick off (or any other free kick), if the opposing team gains possession it may advance with the ball; if the kicking team gains possession the ball is dead and is put in play again from where it was recovered.

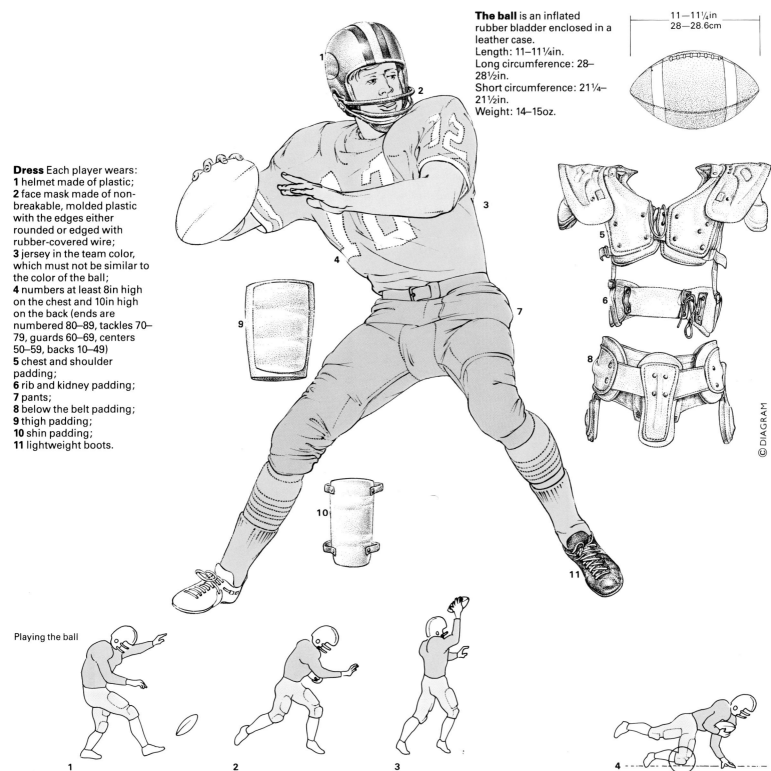

The ball is an inflated rubber bladder enclosed in a leather case.
Length: 11–11¼in.
Long circumference: 28–28½in.
Short circumference: 21¼–21½in.
Weight: 14–15oz.

11—11¼in
28—28.6cm

Dress Each player wears:
1 helmet made of plastic;
2 face mask made of non-breakable, molded plastic with the edges either rounded or edged with rubber-covered wire;
3 jersey in the team color, which must not be similar to the color of the ball;
4 numbers at least 8in high on the chest and 10in high on the back (ends are numbered 80–89, tackles 70–79, guards 60–69, centers 50–59, backs 10–49)
5 chest and shoulder padding;
6 rib and kidney padding;
7 pants;
8 below the belt padding;
9 thigh padding;
10 shin padding;
11 lightweight boots.

© DIAGRAM

Playing the ball

Duration There are 60 minutes' actual playing time, divided into four quarters, of which two comprise a half. Playing time excludes stoppages and other interruptions. There is a 2-minute interval between the periods of each half; only an incoming substitute may enter the field. There is a 15-minute interval at half time.

Overtime period If the game ends in a tie a 15–minute sudden-death period is played. The kick-off is determined by the toss of a coin. The game is won by the first team to score in the extra period. If there is no score, the tie stands.

Team time-outs Each team is allowed three time-outs per half. A time-out lasts 1½ minutes, and 3 minutes are allowed to repair equipment. A time-out is not charged to a team if a player is injured, unless:
he does not leave the game for one play;
he receives unauthorized assistance from the field;
the injury occurs in the last 2 minutes of a half;
a player confers with the coach on the sideline.
Otherwise, a team time-out is at the captain's request. During the last 2 minutes' play a fourth time-out is only allowed in order to remove an injured player.

Subsequent time-outs for injuries are penalized by 5yd.
The same conditions apply in the last 2 minutes of the first half if the score is equal or if the team in possession is behind.

Playing the ball Players may kick, carry, and throw the ball (**1**, **2**, **3**) subject to certain restrictions, such as the number of forward passes allowed.
They may not bat or punch: a loose ball toward the opponents' goal line;
a loose ball in an end zone;
the ball when a player has possession.
A pass in flight may be batted in any direction by the defending side; but the offensive side may only bat such a ball to prevent the other team intercepting the ball.
If the player with the ball touches the ground with any part of his body except his hands or feet, or with any part of the ball, the ball is dead (**4**).

A team in possession is allowed 30–45 seconds to put the ball into play.
A down is a period of action starting from the moment the ball is put into play and ending when the ball becomes dead (goes out of play).

Scrimmage Each team provides a line of at least seven players who stand on either side of the ball and parallel to the goal line. The line of scrimmage for each team is a line passing through the end of the ball nearest a team's own goal line.

The area between the scrimmage lines is the neutral zone.

The remainder of the team, except for the player who receives the snap, must be at least 1yd behind the scrimmage line.

The snap is a backward pass through the legs of one of the players in the line, which puts the ball into play. The snap must be one quick and continuous action. The snapper may not slide his hands along the ball before grasping it, nor move his feet or lift a hand until after the snap. Other players must be stationary at the moment the ball is snapped. No player may enter the neutral zone or move toward his opponents' goal line at a snap.

The snap must be to a player not on the scrimmage line unless the ball touches the ground, in which case play continues as after any other backward pass.

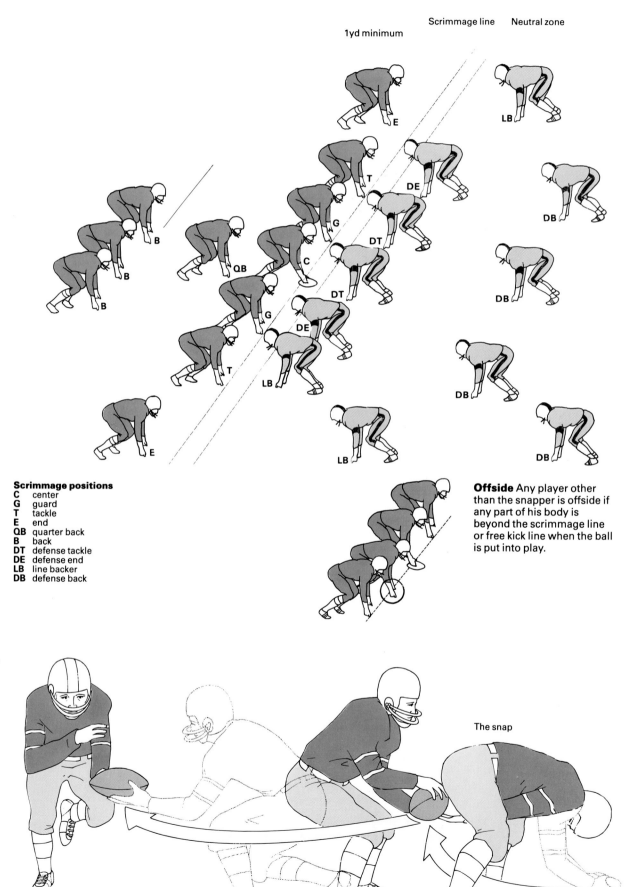

Scrimmage line   Neutral zone

1yd minimum

Scrimmage positions

C	center
G	guard
T	tackle
E	end
QB	quarter back
B	back
DT	defense tackle
DE	defense end
LB	line backer
DB	defense back

Offside Any player other than the snapper is offside if any part of his body is beyond the scrimmage line or free kick line when the ball is put into play.

Moving with the ball
When a team has possession, it is allowed four downs in which it has to advance 10yd to the necessary line or to the goal line.

If it advances that distance while still in possession, it is allowed another four downs. If it does not advance 10yd the ball is awarded to the opposition from the point at which it became dead.

The snap

Fair catch When the ball is in flight from a kick, an opposing player may claim the right to catch the ball by raising one hand at full arm's length above his head and waving from side to side. He is then entitled to field the ball without being impeded or tackled.
If he catches the ball, it becomes dead at that spot. The captain of the team awarded a fair catch must choose to put the ball into play with a snap or free kick. The player is not allowed to advance with the ball after signaling for a fair catch.

Backward pass A runner may make a backward pass at any time. A teammate may catch the pass or recover the ball after it touches the ground in an advance. If an opponent catches the pass, he may also advance; but if he recovers it after the ball has touched the ground he gains possession but cannot advance.

Fumble If a runner fumbles the ball, play continues if either team recovers it, whether or not it touches the ground. If the ball is deliberately fumbled forward, it is an illegal forward pass.

Forward pass The team in possession is allowed one forward pass during each play from a scrimmage, providing the passer (**1**) is behind his line.
Any other forward pass by either team is illegal, and is a foul if made by the passing team. If an illegal pass is intercepted, play continues. All the opposing players are eligible to receive a forward pass, but only those of the passer's team who are on the ends of the scrimmage line (**2**) (except a center, guard or tackle), or are standing at least 1yd behind that line (**3**) may receive the ball.
If an opponent touches the ball, all the passing side is eligible to receive the ball.
The ball at any forward pass becomes dead if it:
goes out of play;
hits the ground;
hits a goalpost or crossbar.

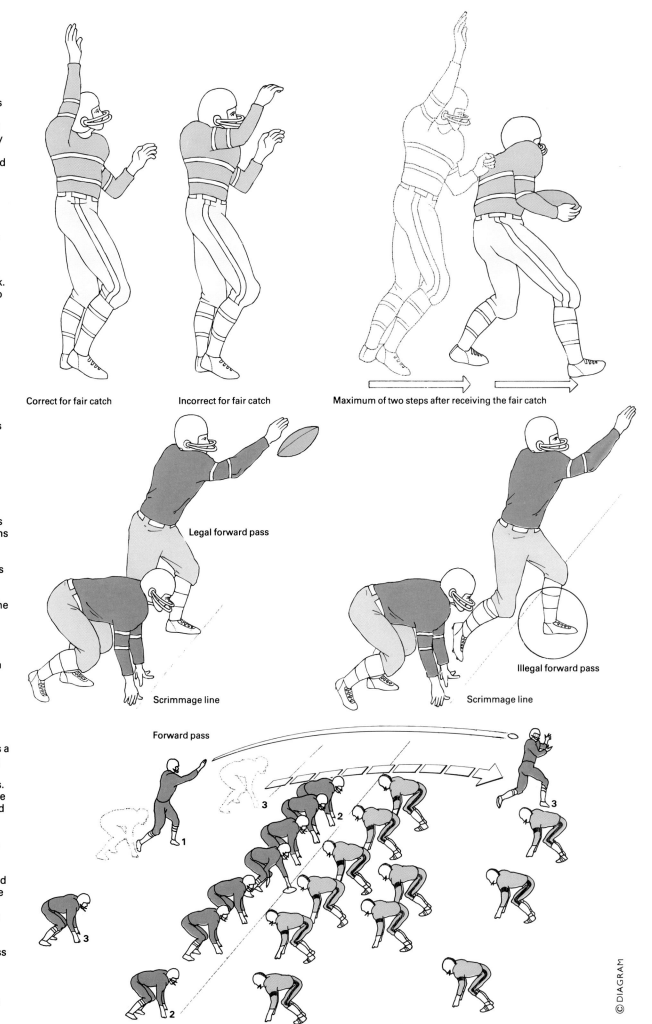

Correct for fair catch

Incorrect for fair catch

Maximum of two steps after receiving the fair catch

Legal forward pass

Scrimmage line

Illegal forward pass

Scrimmage line

Forward pass

Scoring

Touchdown (6 points) occurs when a player carries the ball to the opponents' end zone and crosses the goal line with the ball, or recovers a loose ball on or behind the opponents' goal line. It may be awarded if prevented by a foul.

Extra point (1 or 2 points). After a touchdown the scoring team is allowed an attempt to score either 1 or 2 additional points from a scrimmage taken between the inbound lines and at least 2yd from the opponents' goal line. One point may be scored from a kick; two points may be scored by a run or a pass into the end zone. As soon as the opposition touches the ball it is dead.

Field goal (3 points) occurs when a player kicks the whole of the ball through the opponents' upright goalposts, without it touching the ground or any of his own players, from a place kick or drop kick after a scrimmage, or from a free kick after a fair catch. After a missed field goal attempt, the ball is returned to the spot of the kick.

Safety (2 points) occurs when a team sends the ball into its own end zone and it becomes dead in its possession, or out of play behind its goal line. It is also awarded if a team in possession commits a foul behind its goal line.

The touchdown

Out of play

1 When the ball is kicked out of play, other than from a free kick, it is awarded to the opposition for a scrimmage at the inbounds spot.

2 If the ball goes out of play between the goal lines from the kick-off, without being touched by an opponent, it is kicked off after a 5yd penalty or taken at the 35yd line by the receiving team; it is the receiving team's choice.

3 If a player with the ball runs out of play, his team restarts play with a scrimmage at the inbounds spot.

4 If the ball is fumbled or passed backwards out of play between the goal lines, the side last in possession restarts play with a

scrimmage at the inbounds spot.

5 If the ball is passed forward out of play, the team restarts with a scrimmage from where the ball was passed out of play. If there is a penalty on this play it is enforced at the same spot.

6 If the ball is passed, kicked, or fumbled out of play behind the goal lines by the opposition, the defending team snaps from its 20yd line, between the inbounds lines.

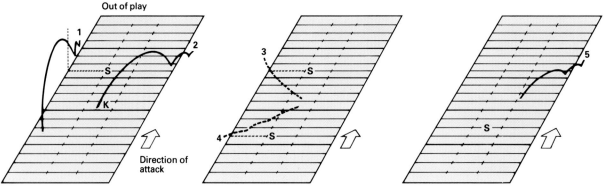

Out of play

Direction of attack

——— Flight of ball
S Scrimmage or snap
K Kick

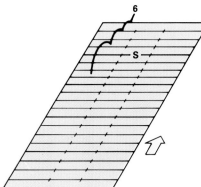

Tackling is the use of hands or arms by a defensive player in an attempt to hold the runner (the player in possession of the ball) or throw him to the ground.

Blocking is the use of the body above the knees by a defending or an attacking player in order to obstruct an opponent.

The hands must be cupped or closed and kept inside the elbows and not outside the body of either player. Arms may be extended to push. A blocker may push in front, but not clamp down on, hang on or encircle an opponent. Players may block an opponent at any time, provided this does not interfere with a pass, a fair catch, a kicker or a passer and provided it is not too rough. A wide receiver may not be cut down by a block below the knees. A wide receiver may not return to the line of scrimmage to block below the waist (crack back block).

A defensive player may not tackle or hold any opponent except the runner, although he may use his hands or arms to remove or evade a blocking opponent.

Once a receiver is 3yd downfield from the line of scrimmage, he can be hit only once by any defender.

An offensive player is allowed to assist the runner by blocking opponents, but he may not:
push or lift the runner;
cause a teammate to obstruct an opponent;
grasp or tackle an opponent with his hands or arms.
If an offensive player is trying to recover the ball after a backward pass or fumble, he may use his hands or arms to remove an opponent.

The runner may ward off opponents with his hands or arms.

Tackling

Blocking

©DIAGRAM

Fouls Players may not strike
with their fists (**1**);
kick or knee a player (**2**);
strike the head, face or neck
of an opponent with the
side, back or heel or the
wrist or with the forearm,
elbow or clasped hands;
block an opponent and strike
him with the forearm or
elbow;
hit an opponent above the
knee with a foot (**3**);
hit or trip an opponent
below the knee (**4**);
tackle a player, who is
obviously off the field;
fall on a prostrate player (**5**)
or on a runner after the ball
is dead (piling on);
grasp an opponent's face
mask.
A defensive player may not:
use his palms above an
opponent's shoulders
except during an initial
charge at a line;
run into a kicker unless
blocked into the kicker (**6**);
throw the runner to the
ground when the ball is
dead;
run into a passer after the
ball has left his hand.
A runner may not advance
after any part of his body
(other than his hands or feet)
has touched the ground
(crawling).
Players must not behave in
an unsportsmanlike manner.
Penalties Infringements are
penalized by one or a
combination of the
following:
loss of a down, when the
team loses that one of its
downs;
loss of yards, when the team
concedes 5yd, 10yd, or 15yd;
Disqualification A team
may be penalized by the loss
of yards for offenses by its
coaches, who may also be
disqualified.

1

2

3

4

5

6

COMPARISON OF COLLEGE AND PROFESSIONAL AMERICAN FOOTBALL

A summary of the major rule differences between the games played by colleges and professionals is given below.

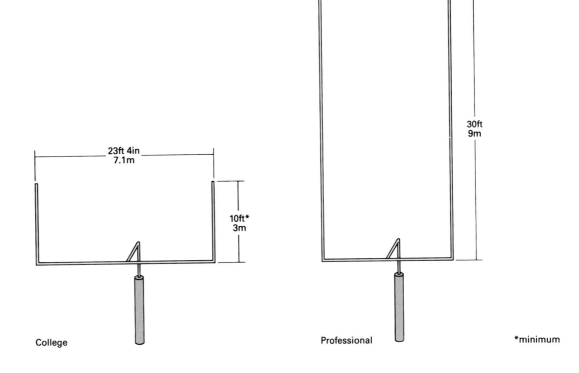

18ft 6in
5.6m

30ft
9m

23ft 4in
7.1m

10ft*
3m

College

Professional

*minimum

Goalposts The goalpost width between uprights is 23ft 4in in college football; in professional football the width between goalposts is 18ft 6in.

The field for the college game has the same overall dimensions as that for the professional game, but the inbounds lines in college football are only 53ft 4in in from the sidelines, and the goal line is the equivalent of the end line on the professional field. In professional football the inbounds lines are 70ft 9in in from the sidelines.

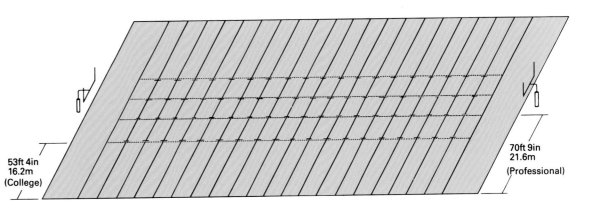

53ft 4in
16.2m
(College)

70ft 9in
21.6m
(Professional)

Ball The ball used in professional football is all leather; colleges may use a rubber or composition-cover ball if agreed beforehand. The dimensions of the ball specified for use in college football are similar to those specified for use by professional players, except that the short circumference must be 21–21¼in compared to 21¼–21½in in professional football.
Officials number 5–6 in college football and 7 in professional football.
Kick off In professional football players kick off from the 30yd line. College players kick from the 40yd line.

If the game ends after 4 periods in a tie score in college football the result of the game is a tie. In professional football a sudden death overtime period of 15 minutes is provided. Whichever team scores first is the winner.
Spot the ball Colleges spot the ball for the conversion attempt at the 3yd line. In professional football the ball is spotted on the 2yd line.

Fumbles The college rule on fumbles is that when a fumble touches the ground, only the team that has fumbled can advance the ball. In professional football a fumble may be picked up and advanced by any player on either team.
If the fumble is caught in the air the rules for both college and professional football permit either team to advance the ball.
Holding an opponent The penalty awarded for holding an opponent is 10yd in college play and 15yd in professional football.

Inbounds In college football the player must have one foot inbounds at the time of the catch. The rules of professional football require that both feet are inbounds while in possession of the ball.
Player on the ground A professional running back or receiver, with the ball, may continue to run after he slips to the ground without being tackled. In college football the runner may not advance if any part of his body except his hands and feet touches the ground.

Missed field goals in professional football result in the ball being returned to the point where the kick was made (line of scrimmage). Colleges return missed field goals to the 20yd line.
Uniformed players Colleges may have as many players in uniform as they wish for a home game, 90 or more, and travel with 60 or more. The squad limit in professional football is 45.

Canadian football

Canadian football is very similar to American football but is played on a larger field with 12 players in a team. Other major differences are that: three downs are allowed to gain 10yd; there is no fair catch; there is an extra means of scoring (a rouge); and a greater number of distances are used to penalize offenses and restart play.

The field The area between the goal lines and sidelines is the field of play. It is divided between the goal lines by parallel lines 5yd apart. These lines are intersected by short lines 24yd from the sidelines (hash marks). The boundary lines are outside the field of play.

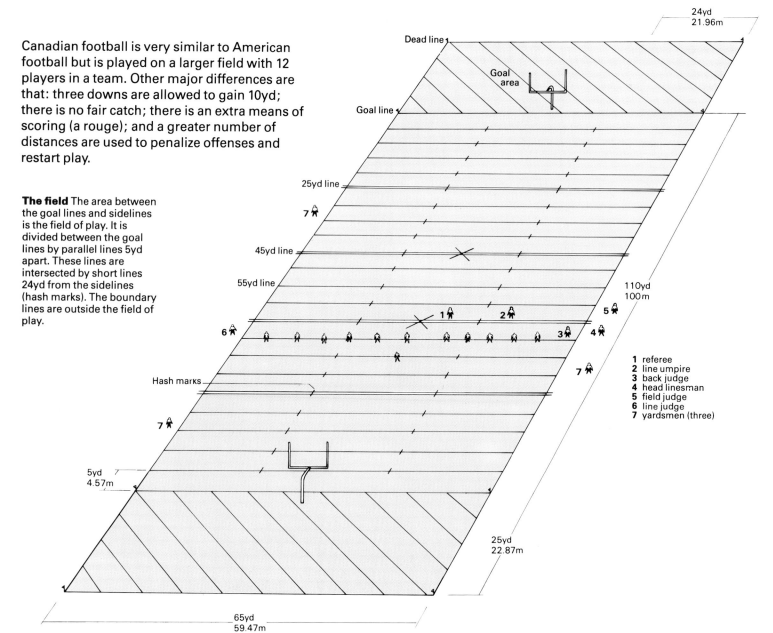

1 referee
2 line umpire
3 back judge
4 head linesman
5 field judge
6 line judge
7 yardsmen (three)

The field officials have individual functions, but are equally responsible for the conduct of the game; any of them may stop the game for a foul.
The referee is the chief official in control of the game. The line umpire has special responsibility for scrimmage lines.
The back judge has special responsibility for players of both teams behind the scrimmage line of the team not in possession.
The head linesman supervises the yardsmen, records downs, checks substitution, and covers the scrimmage line and his sideline.
The line judge has duties identical to those of the head linesman except for yardsmen and downs.
The sideline officials are: the downsman, who indicates the forward point of gain and loss after each play;
three yardsmen, equipped to assist in measurements, two on one sideline and the third on the opposite sideline;
the timekeeper, who has to notify field officials when a period or half is about to end;
the scorer, who records the score and substitutes.
Teams Each team fields 12 players, one of whom is the captain. Substitutes may enter the field at any time when the ball is dead. A replaced player must go directly to his team bench.

Starting play Either the captain of the visiting team or the one that wins the toss may choose to kick off, receive the kick off or choose the goal he wishes to defend. For the second half the other captain has the choice of these.
Goals are changed at the end of the first and third periods. At the start of the second and fourth periods play continues at a point corresponding exactly to where it was in the other half when that period ended.
Play is started between the hash marks from:
the 35yd line, at the start of each half or after a touchdown with a kick off (the conceding team may insist that the scoring team kicks from its 35yd line after a touchdown);
the 35yd line, with a kick off or scrimmage, by a team that concedes three points;
the 25yd line, by the conceding team after a safety touch or a rouge, with a scrimmage (except in the last three minutes of a half, when it must kick off following a safety touch).

Kick offs The players of the kicking team must be behind the ball, except the player holding the ball for the kick off. Opponents must be at least 10yd away.
From a kick off the ball must travel at least 10yd toward the opponents' goal line, unless touched by an opponent. It must not be kicked out of play.
After the kick off the receiving team may interfere with its opponents, but the kicking team must recover the ball before interfering with the opposition.

The ball is an inflated rubber bladder enclosed in a leather case.
Length 11–11¼in.
Long circumference 27¾–28½in.
Short circumference 20⅞–21⅛in.
Weight 14–15oz.

11—11¼in
28—28.6cm

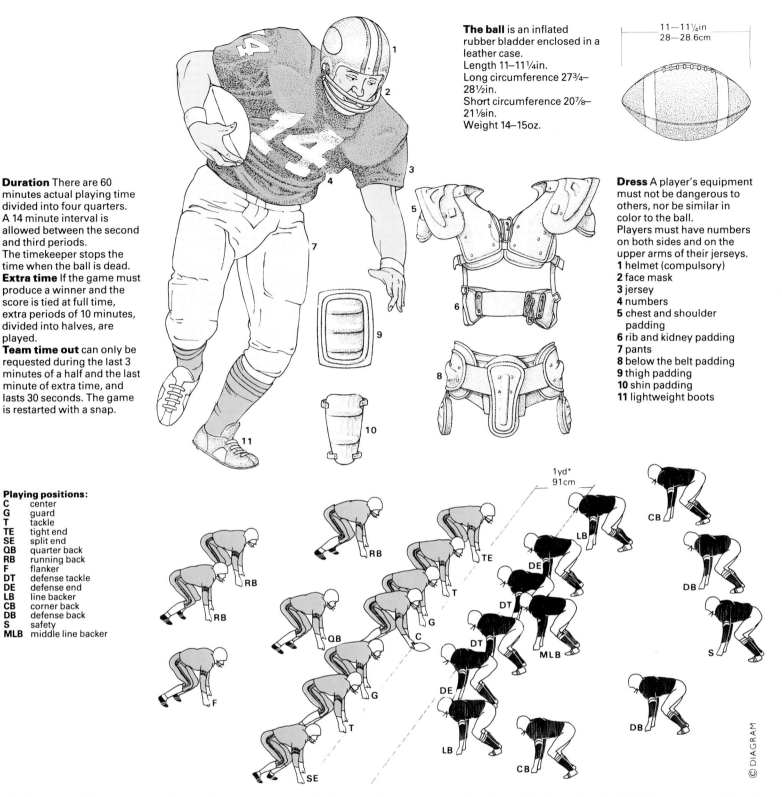

Duration There are 60 minutes actual playing time divided into four quarters. A 14 minute interval is allowed between the second and third periods.
The timekeeper stops the time when the ball is dead.
Extra time If the game must produce a winner and the score is tied at full time, extra periods of 10 minutes, divided into halves, are played.
Team time out can only be requested during the last 3 minutes of a half and the last minute of extra time, and lasts 30 seconds. The game is restarted with a snap.

Dress A player's equipment must not be dangerous to others, nor be similar in color to the ball.
Players must have numbers on both sides and on the upper arms of their jerseys.
1 helmet (compulsory)
2 face mask
3 jersey
4 numbers
5 chest and shoulder padding
6 rib and kidney padding
7 pants
8 below the belt padding
9 thigh padding
10 shin padding
11 lightweight boots

Playing positions:
C	center
G	guard
T	tackle
TE	tight end
SE	split end
QB	quarter back
RB	running back
F	flanker
DT	defense tackle
DE	defense end
LB	line backer
CB	corner back
DB	defense back
S	safety
MLB	middle line backer

Playing the ball Players may kick, carry, strike, and throw the ball, with certain exceptions.
A player has possession if the ball is firmly held by a hand, arm, or leg, or under the body.
If two opponents have possession, the ball is awarded to the player who gained it first or, if possession was simultaneous, to the team that last touched it.
If the player with the ball touches the ground with any part of his body except for his hands or feet, the ball is dead.
If a player gains possession in his own goal area and is held or kneels on the ground, the ball is dead. The team in possession is allowed 20 seconds to put the ball in play.

Moving with the ball
When a team has possession it is allowed three downs to gain 10yd. If it gains the 10yd, it is allowed another three downs. If it does not gain the 10yd, the ball is awarded to the opposition from the position in which it became dead.
A down is measured by the forward point of the ball. If it is necessary to measure the distance gained, the ball is rotated so that its long axis is parallel to the sidelines. A down starts from when the ball is put in play at a scrimmage.

Scrimmage The teams are separated by the scrimmage zone, which is the area between the sidelines that extends on each side of the scrimmage line.
The scrimmage line is an imaginary line, parallel to the goal line, through the point of the ball farthest from the goal of the team in possession.
The players of the team in possession must be either clearly in the line (within and behind the scrimmage line) or in the backfield (clearly behind the line players). There must be at least seven line players, five of them in a continuous line and ineligible for a pass. The two end players and all backfield players may receive a pass. The opponents must be at least 1yd behind their side of the scrimmage line until the ball is in play.

The snap One of the line players (the center) facing the opposition goal snaps the ball back in one continuous action. He may not handle the ball again until it has been played by another player.
No player is allowed to move so as to draw an opponent offside deliberately. No line player may move at all after adopting his stance, until the ball is snapped. If a team is in possession within a yard of the goal line the scrimmage occurs 1yd from that goal line.

Offside A player is offside if the ball has last been touched by one of his own team behind him, except when onside, hand off, and forward pass rules apply. A player in an offside position is played onside if the ball touches an opponent or if a teammate carries the ball past him. If a player moves across the line of scrimmage before the ball is put into play, he is also offside.

© DIAGRAM

Scoring

Touchdown (6 points) is made when the ball is in the possession of a player who is in his opponents' goal area, or who crosses or touches their goal line.

Convert (1 point or 2 points) After a touchdown the scoring team is allowed to attempt to add to its score by a scrimmage between the hash marks on or outside its opponents' 5yd line. 1 point is scored by kicking a field goal and 2 points are scored by scoring a touchdown by ball carrying or passing play.

Field goal (3 points) Scored by a drop kick or a place kick (except at kick off) when the ball goes over the crossbar without touching the ground after being kicked.

Safety touch (2 points) Scored when a team plays the ball into its own goal area and the ball becomes dead in the team's possession or touches or crosses the dead line or sideline in goal.

Rouge or single point (1 point) Scored when the ball is played into the opposition goal area and becomes dead in the opponents' possession or it touches or crosses the boundary lines or touches the ground, player or any other object beyond those lines.

If a team, having played a ball in its own end zone, makes an offside pass in its goal area and retains possession, the opposition may claim 2 points or the "option." If a team gains possession in its area from an opponent's kick or fumble and makes an offside pass, the opposition gains 1 point or the option.

Out of bounds The ball is out of bounds if it or the player in possession touches a sideline (in front of or beyond the goal), dead line, the ground, or any object beyond those lines. Generally the ball is put into play at a scrimmage between the hash marks opposite the place it went out. When the ball is carried off the field or is thrown out by a forward pass, that team retains possession, except on the third down when no yards have been gained. When the ball is kicked out of bounds the opposition is awarded possession, except at a kick off. If it is kicked out from a kick off, the kick off is

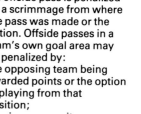

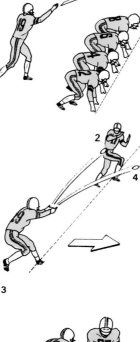

repeated or an option is awarded. If it is not touched and goes into the opposition's goal area or hits the goal, the ball is dead and the opposition puts it into play at its 25yd line. When on any play the ball is fumbled out of bounds or touches a player before going out, the team that last touched the ball has possession. It is scrimmaged either where the ball went out of bounds or where the ball was last touched in the field of play, whichever is nearest to the goal line of the team entitled to possession. A player who goes off the field, except as a result of bodily contact, must remain out of that play.

Passing

Forward pass (1) Only one forward pass is allowed in any one down. It is thrown from behind the scrimmage line toward the opponents' dead line and to any eligible receivers. The ball must not touch the ground, goalposts, crossbar, officials, or other object.

Onside (or lateral) pass (2) occurs when the ball is thrown, handed, knocked, batted, or fumbled by a player parallel to, or in the direction of, his own dead line. The place where the ball strikes the ground, a player, or an official, or is caught or goes out of play determines whether it is an onside or offside pass.

Hand off pass (3) occurs when the ball is handed, not thrown, to another player behind the scrimmage line. There are no restrictions on the number of hand off passes during a play, but the player receiving the ball must not occupy a lineman's position.

Offside pass (4) occurs when the ball is passed from in front of the scrimmage line toward the opponents' dead line, or when it is knocked

Fouls Players may not:
hold an opponent, other than the one with the ball, with their hands or arms;
tackle an opponent, other than the one with the ball, from the rear (clipping);
kick an opponent;
strike an opponent with the fist, heel of the hand, knee, or elbow;
charge or fall on a player with the ball when it is dead (piling);
trip an opponent;
tackle an opponent off the field;
grasp an opponent's face guard;
combine together or give assistance, by direct contact, to the rear of the ball carrier **(5)**;

with the hand or arm toward the opposition dead line. An offside pass is penalized by a scrimmage from where the pass was made or the option. Offside passes in a team's own goal area may be penalized by:
the opposing team being awarded points or the option of playing from that position;
a scrimmage on its own 25yd line, if it intercepts an opponent's forward pass and then makes an offside pass from within its own goal area.

use the body of another player to rise up in an attempt to play the ball **(6)**;
hold hands or lock arms at a scrimmage **(7)**;
touch the kicker when he is kicking from a scrimmage;
contact an opponent in any other unnecessarily rough or unfair manner;
abuse opponents, officials, or spectators.

Penalties Infringements are penalized by any one or combination of the following:
loss of a down, when the team loses that one of the permitted number of downs;
loss of yards, when the team concedes 5, 10, or 25yd but it cannot also lose that down;

Tackling is grasping the ball carrier with hands or arms.

Interference is when a player obstructs, blocks, or charges an opponent in order to prevent his approach to the ball carrier, potential ball carrier, or the ball.

Screening is interference without direct contact.

Defensive players may only tackle the player with the ball, although they may interfere with opponents who are attempting to shield him and who are penetrating their defense for a forward pass.

Offensive players, except when the ball has been thrown forward or kicked across the scrimmage line, may interfere with any opponent in order to protect the player with the ball. After a forward pass across the scrimmage line, only the eligible receivers may interfere with opponents.

loss of the ball;
an option, when the non-offending team may choose between the penalty or the advantage of the position;
a first down, awarded automatically to the team in possession when the other team commits certain offenses;
removal of a player, with substitution permitted.
A team will be penalized on the field for offenses by its officials, who may also be disqualified.

COMPARISON OF CANADIAN AND AMERICAN FOOTBALL
A summary of the major differences between the two North American football games.

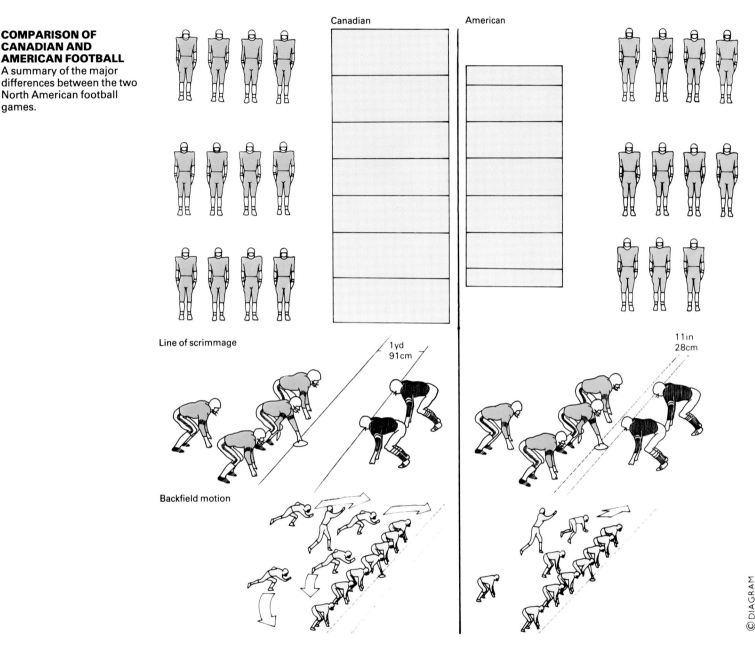

Canadian

American

Line of scrimmage

1yd 91cm

11in 28cm

Backfield motion

Field The Canadian field is larger than the American field. Canadian goalposts are on the goal line; American goalposts on the end line.

Teams Canadian football allows 12 players on the field. American football allows 11.

Ball into play in Canadian football time is allowed for lining up and substitution, and the attackers then have 20 seconds in which to put the ball into play.
In American football the attackers have 30 seconds to put the ball into play.

End of a period In Canadian football there is a further complete play if any time remains when a play ends.

In American football there is no further play if a period ends before the ball is returned to play.

Punt returning In Canadian football there is no fair catch. Tacklers may not approach within 5yd of the receiver until he has touched the ball; the punter or a player "onside" to the punter, however, may legally recover the ball if he gets to it before the receiver. The punt returner concedes a rouge if he fails to run or kick the ball out of the end zone. In American football punts may be allowed to roll dead; be received for a fair catch; or be returned with the aid of blocking by the returning team. If the receiving team touches or fumbles the ball,

the kicking team may legally recover it.
There is a touch back if the punted ball crosses the goal line.

Downs Three downs are needed in Canadian football to make 10yd.
Four downs are needed in American football to make 10yd.

Scrimmage line In Canadian football the offensive line is at the forward point of the ball and the defensive line 1yd beyond it.
In American football the offensive and defensive lines are at each end of the ball before it is put into play.

Backfield motion In Canadian football all backfield players may move in any direction at a snap.
In American football only one attacking back may move backward or parallel to the line of scrimmage at the snap.

Scoring One point is scored for a single or rouge in Canadian football.
There is no equivalent in American football.

Penalties Canadian football has 5, 10, 15 and 25yd penalties, and penalties are the same for attackers and defenders.
In American football there are 5, 10, and 15yd penalties, and differences between offensive and defensive penalties.

© DIAGRAM

Rugby union

Rugby Union is an amateur game played by two teams of 15 players, who are allowed to carry, kick and throw the ball. Players attempt to score points by placing the ball on or over the opponents' goal line (a try) or by kicking it over the crossbar (a goal).

The pitch must be of grass, or clay or sand provided the surface is not dangerous. The touchlines are not part of the playing area.
Officials The referee (1) is in charge of the game, but he may take the advice of the touch judges in matters of time and, in certain games, players' misconduct. He uses a whistle to indicate the start and end of play, scores and infringements. Players must not dispute his decisions and must obtain his permission to leave or reenter the pitch during play. The two touch judges (2) remain off the playing area except when standing behind the posts to judge a kick at the goal. They indicate touch and other decisions with a flag.

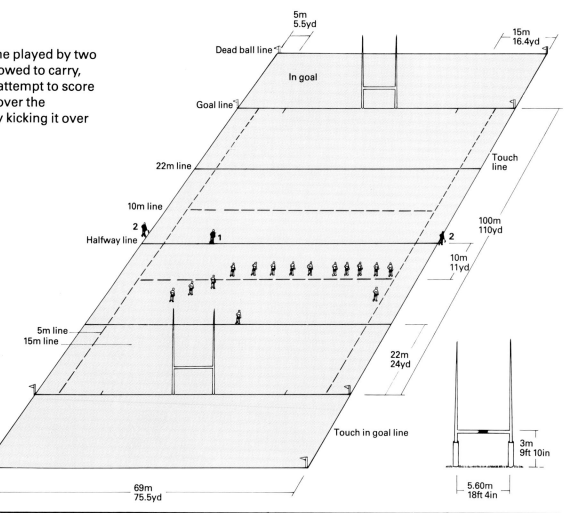

Rugby league

Rugby league is similar to the union game, from which it developed, but it has its own procedures and a different style of play. The game is played by amateurs and professionals and there are 13 members in each team.

The pitch conforms to the measurements shown in the diagram. The touch lines are not part of the playing area.
Officials The referee (1) controls the game and its timing, and signals with a whistle.
Two touch judges (2) assist the referee. They stand on either side of the pitch, except when judging kicks at goal. Each has a flag to signal when the ball goes out of play.

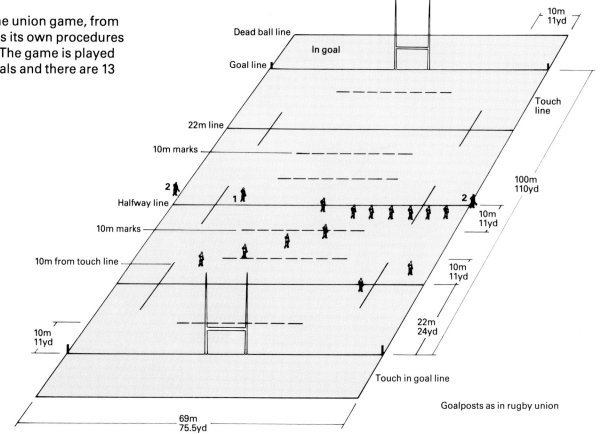

The ball is oval in shape, of four panels and made of leather or other approved material. It weighs 400–440g.
A rugby league ball is slightly shorter and thinner than a rugby union ball.

28cm
11in

RUGBY UNION
Starting play Captains toss for kick off, which is a place kick (**1**) from the center spot. A place kick is also taken by the conceding team after a goal and a drop kick (**2**) after an unconverted try. Opponents must stand on or behind their 10m line, which the ball must reach unless first touched by an opponent. If the ball goes into touch (crosses the touchline) without bouncing, opponents may accept the kick, have it retaken or scrummage in the center. If the ball goes into touch in goal, over the dead ball line, or after some touch downs, defenders restart with a drop out (a free drop kick) on or behind the 22m line.
If the ball does not cross the

22m line, the opposition may choose to form a scrum or to retake the kick. If the ball pitches directly into touch, they may also accept the kick. Opponents may not cross the 22m line until the kick is taken.
Scoring
A try (**3**) (4 points) is scored by grounding the ball in the opponents' in goal area. The player must be touching the ball as it is grounded. A penalty try may be given, if a foul prevents a try.
Conversion (2 points) A place kick or drop kick at goal follows a try. It is taken on a line through where the try was scored except after a penalty try, when it is taken as if the try was scored between the posts.

1 Place kick

2 Drop kick

3 Try

4 Goal

RUGBY LEAGUE
Starting play Captains toss for ends and the losing team kicks off with a place kick from the center spot. A place kick is also taken by the conceding team after a try or a goal.
Defenders restart the game with a tap penalty from the center of the 22m line after an attacker:
sends the ball into touch in goal or over the dead ball line; infringes in the goal area; is tackled in goal before he grounds the ball. The game is restarted by the defending team with a drop kick from the center of the goal line after a defender:
sends the ball over the dead ball line or into touch in goal;
breaks the law accidentally;

touches down, is tackled or kicks straight into touch from his own goal area. The kicker must not cross the appropriate line, kick the ball straight into touch or send it less than 10m. Opponents must allow the ball to travel 10m before touching it.
Scoring
A try (3 points) is scored by grounding the ball in the opponents' in goal area or if opposing players simultaneously ground the ball in the in goal area. It is also scored if the ball touches the ground in front of the goal line, but the player's momentum then carries him over the line. A penalty try may be awarded if a foul prevents a try.

The kicker's team must be behind him; opponents must remain behind the goal line until the kicker runs at the ball, when they may charge or jump.
A dropped goal (3 points) is scored during play when the ball is dropped from the hands and kicked over the crossbar on the half volley.

Headband
Scrum cap
Shin guard

Conversion (2 points) must be a place kick.
A drop goal (3 points in England, 1 point elsewhere).
A penalty goal (2 points) may be drop kicked.

A penalty goal (3 points) is scored from a penalty kick awarded for an infringement.
(Goals are valid if the ball strikes the crossbar or posts, or is blown back after passing correctly through the posts.)

UNION/LEAGUE
Duration There are two halves of 40 minutes each. Teams change ends at half time after a five-minute interval. The referee adds on any time lost by stoppages.
Replacements Union allows replacement of a maximum of three injured players. In games played by under 21's up to six replacements are allowed. Replaced players may not rejoin the match.
League allows two substitutes for any reason, but only with the referee's permission during a stoppage or when the ball is out of play.
Playing the ball A player may run with the ball and kick it in any direction, but he may not throw or knock it toward his opponents' dead-ball line.
Any player holding the ball may be tackled.
Touch down In both league and union a defender may ground the ball in his own in goal area.
In league, defenders restart the game with a drop out from the goal line.
In union, it is restarted by a scrum 5m from the goal line, if a defender carries the ball over it, or a drop out from the 22m line if an attacker puts the ball into in-goal.

Dress Players wear jerseys, shorts, socks, and boots. Headbands or scrum caps may be worn. Shin guards are optional, and league players may also wear other protective clothing, provided it is not rigid.

Rugby boots Studs on the boots must be circular and securely fastened. The wearing of a single stud at the toe is prohibited. A molded rubber multi-studded sole is acceptable.

©DIAGRAM

RUGBY UNION

Scrummage Players are formed into a scrummage, usually by their own forwards, at or near the place of the infringement and parallel to the goal lines. The team not responsible for the stoppage puts the ball in. If there is doubt as to who is responsible, the ball is put in by the team moving forward or by the attacking team.

Scrum positions and numbers in rugby union are usually:
1 prop forward
2 hooker
3 prop forward
4 lock forward
5 lock forward
6 flank forward
7 flank forward
8 No. 8 forward
9 scrum half back
10 stand off or outside half back
11 left wing threequarter back
12 left center threequarter back
13 right centre threequarter back
14 right wing threequarter back
15 full back

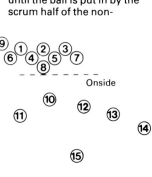
Onside

There must be at least three players in each front row. The front rows interlock leaving a clear tunnel between them. Other forwards bind with at least one arm onto a teammate. Other players remain behind the line of the rear foot of their pack.

The scrum should be steady until the ball is put in by the scrum half of the non-offending team. He stands 1m away, midway between the front rows, holding the ball in both hands between his knee and ankle. He aims it to hit the ground just beyond the width of the near prop's shoulders. If the ball runs straight through the scrum, it must be put in again.

The two hookers strike for possession; they must not be lifted off their feet.

Front players must not raise a foot until the ball touches the ground. All players may try to play the ball but they must keep one foot on the ground. No player may handle the ball.

A ruck occurs in free play when one or more players from each team close around the ball when it is on the ground between them. Players must be on their feet and must bind with at least one arm around a teammate.

Players may not:
return the ball into the ruck;
handle it or pick it up except to handle a try;
jump on other players;
make the ruck collapse;
fall on or over the emerging ball.

A maul occurs in free play when one or more players from each team closes around a player who is carrying the ball. It ends:
when the ball is on the ground;
the ball or player carrying it emerges from the maul;
when a scrummage is ordered.

Fair-catch (mark) A player makes a fair-catch when, being stationary with both feet on the ground in or behind his 22m area, he cleanly catches the ball direct from a kick, knock-on or throw-forward by one of his opponents and at the same time he exclaims, "Mark!"

A fair-catch may be obtained even though the ball on its way touches a goal post or crossbar and can be made in in goal.

A free kick is awarded for a fair-catch.

The kick must be taken by the player making the fair-catch, unless he is injured in so doing. If he is unable to take the kick within one minute a scrummage shall be formed at the mark. His team shall put in the ball.

Line-out If the ball or the player carrying it touches or crosses the touchline, the ball is "in touch" and in union play is restarted by a "line-out." The ball is thrown in at right angles to where it went into touch and between players of both

Ruck   Maul

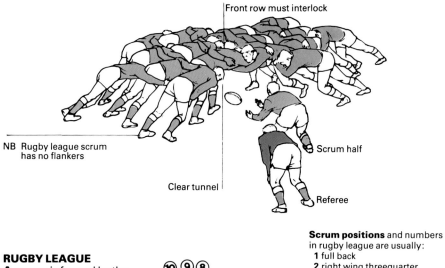

Front row must interlock

NB Rugby league scrum has no flankers

Clear tunnel

Scrum half

Referee

RUGBY LEAGUE

A scrum is formed by the forwards of each side to restart play whenever the game is not restarted by a kick off, a penalty kick, a drop out or a play-the-ball. It is normally formed where the infringement occurred, but it must be at least 10m from the touchline and 5m from the goal line. The six forwards pack into a three-two-one formation. Once the scrum is correctly established, the forwards may push to gain an advantage.

The ball is played straight into the center of the tunnel by the scrum half of the non-offending team.

The front row forwards may not raise a foot until the ball is put in and may not strike

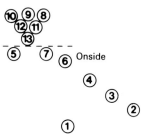
Onside

the ball before the hookers. No players may handle the ball. If a ball goes into touch, play is restarted by a scrum 10m infield from that point. If a forward ball goes straight into touch, a scrum is formed where contact with the ball was made. If a penalty kick is sent straight into touch, the kicking side restarts with a place kick

Scrum positions and numbers in rugby league are usually:
1 full back
2 right wing threequarter
3 right center threequarter
4 left center threequarter
5 left wing threequarter
6 stand off half
7 scrum half
8 front row prop forward
9 hooker
10 front row forward
11 second row forward
12 second row forward
13 loose forward

10m infield from that point.
Tackling A player is tackled when he:
is held by one or more opponents and the ball or his arm holding the ball touches the ground;
is held so that he can make no progress;
is lying on the ground and an opponent lays a hand on him.

The play-the-ball

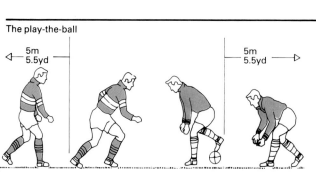
5m 5.5yd   5m 5.5yd

He must not move from the place where he is tackled.

The play-the-ball In rugby league, a tackled player is allowed to be released immediately he indicates that he wishes to play-the-ball.

He must then without delay stand up, face forward and drop or place the ball on the ground in front of his foremost foot. Once on the ground the ball may be kicked or heeled in any direction and from that contact the ball is in play. One opponent may mark the tackled player and a player from each side may support these two players; each other team member must stand at a distance of at least 5m behind his teammate in the play-the-ball.

The team in possession is allowed five successive play-the-ball, but at the sixth, providing an opponent has not touched the ball in this period, play is restarted by handing the ball over to their opponents for them to play-the-ball.

teams, who line up to receive the ball. Players other than the scrum half and the player throwing in must be 10m away from the imaginary line bisecting the two lines of players. The thrower is from the team that did not touch the ball last. After an improper throw opponents choose to throw in or scrummage. If the ball pitches straight into touch, a line-out occurs opposite to where the ball was kicked or where it went into touch, whichever is nearer the kicker's goal.

This does not apply to penalty or free kicks or if the ball is kicked from within the player's 22m area.

Unless jumping or peeling off from a scrummage, players must stay at the line at least 1m from the next player in their team and 500mm from an opponent, until the ball touches the ground or another player. Peeling off in order to catch the ball from a teammate in the line may only occur after the ball has left the thrower's hands.

Players must not push, charge, bind or lift until the ball has touched the ground or has been touched by a player. Any consequent scrum or penalty must be 15m infield.

The line-out ends when;
a ruck or maul is taking place and all feet of players in the ruck or maul have moved beyond the line-of-touch;
a player carrying the ball leaves the line-out;
the ball has been passed, knocked back or kicked from the line-out;

Line out

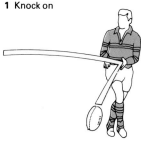

the ball is thrown beyond a position 15m from the touch line;
the ball becomes unplayable.

Fouls Players may not:
strike, hack, kick or trip an opponent;
make a dangerous tackle or tackle with a stiff arm;
willfully charge, obstruct or grab an opponent who does not have the ball, except in a ruck or maul.

Obstruction and deliberate time wasting are penalized by a penalty kick or a penalty try.

A deliberate knock-on or forward throw is punished by a penalty kick at the place of infringement.

If the knock-on or throw-forward is unintentional, a scrummage shall be formed either at the place of infringement or, if it occurs at a line-out, 15m from the touch line along the line-of-touch unless:
a fair catch has been allowed;
the ball is knocked on by a player who is in the act of charging down the kick of an opponent but is not attempting to catch the ball;
the ball is knocked on one or more times by a player, who

is in the act of catching or picking it up or losing possession of it, and is recovered by that player before it has touched the ground or another player.

Offside A player is offside if he is in front of the ball when a teammate is playing it. He will be penalized if he then plays the ball or obstructs or tackles an opponent or if he approaches within 10m of an opponent waiting for the ball.

An offside is penalized by a penalty kick at the point of infringement or, in free play, the option of a scrum at the place the offenders last played the ball.

A player in an offside position may be made onside if a teammate carries the ball past him or kicks the ball past him or pursues it. No penalty will be given if the player's position is unavoidable and he retires immediately and without interfering with an opponent. If he cannot avoid contact he is "accidentally offside" and a scrummage is formed.

Penalties The referee may caution and dismiss players and award penalty kicks and tries. A dismissed player is

reported and may not rejoin the match. A penalty kick may be taken by any player, but he must indicate if he is making a shot at goal.

Advantage The referee does not whistle for an infringement during play which is followed by an advantage gained by the non-offending team. An advantage must be either territorial or such possession of the ball as constitutes an obvious tactical advantage. The referee has wide discretion as to what constitutes an advantage and is sole judge of whether an advantage has been gained.

The occasions when advantage does not apply are:
when the ball or player carrying it touches the referee; when the ball emerges from either end of the tunnel at a scrummage not having been played; when a players is "accidentally" offside.

---

1 Knock on

2 Knock on

5 Offside interference

6 Offside tackle

Fouls It is forbidden to:
deliberately trip, strike, or obstruct a player:
attack unnecessarily an opponent's head;
drop knees-first on to a grounded opponent;
use a dangerous throw in a tackle;
deliberately break the laws;
use obscene language;
argue with the referee;
reenter the play without the referee's permission;
abuse the spirit of the game.

A knock on occurs when the ball is propelled forward from a player's hand (**1**) or his arm (**2**). An accidental knock on will not be punished if the player kicks the ball before it hits the ground. Charging down a kick does not count as a knock on.

3 Foward pass

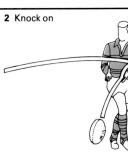

4 Obstruction

© DIAGRAM

A forward pass (3) occurs when the ball is deliberately thrown or passed toward the opponents' goal line.

Obstruction It is forbidden to impede an opponent who does not have the ball (**4**).

Offside Unless in his own goal area, a player is offside when the ball is played or held by a member of his own team behind him.

An offside player must make no attempt to join in the play (**5**), nor must he encroach within 5m of any player who is waiting for the ball (**6**). He must move 5m from any opponent who gains possession.

He may be placed onside if:
an opponent carries the ball more than 5m;
an opponent touches the ball without holding it;

a teammate runs in front of him with the ball or chases a kick forward;
he retires behind the point where the ball was last played by a teammate.

Penalties The referee may caution or dismiss offenders and award penalty kicks for misconduct, unless this acts to the offending team's advantage.

In the professional game players may be sent to the Sin Bin for 5 or 10 minutes. There is no Sin Bin in the amateur game.

The penalty kick is taken from or behind where the offense occurred by punting, drop kicking or place kicking the ball. The kicker's team must remain onside. Opponents must retire 10m or to their goal line.

If a defender, who scores a try, is fouled by a defending player, a penalty is awarded at the center line 10m from the goal line.

This penalty is a kick at goal only and is taken after the attempted conversion of the try and in addition to the conversion. Alternatively a 7 point try could be attempted.

Soccer

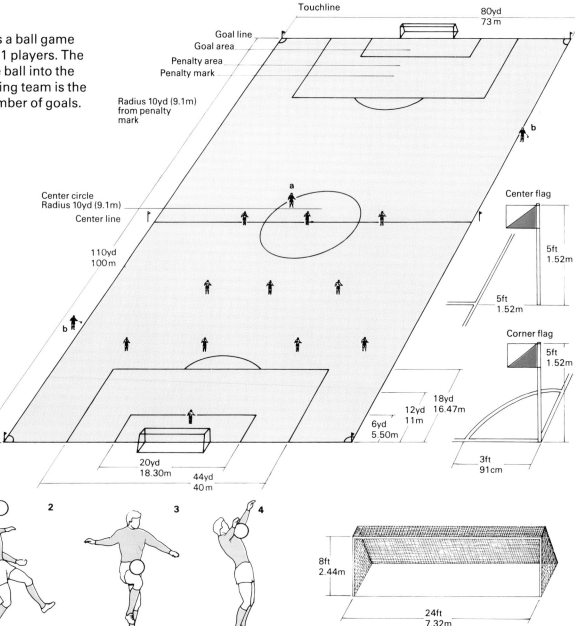

Soccer (Association football) is a ball game played by two teams, each of 11 players. The object of the game is to put the ball into the opponents' goal, and the winning team is the one that scores the greater number of goals.

Touchline

Goal line
Goal area
Penalty area
Penalty mark

80yd
73 m

Radius 10yd (9.1m)
from penalty
mark

b

Center flag

5ft
1.52m

5ft
1.52m

Center circle
Radius 10yd (9.1m)

Center line

110yd
100 m

a

Corner flag

5ft
1.52m

b

18yd
16.47m

12yd
11 m

6yd
5.50m

3ft
91cm

20yd
18.30m

44yd
40 m

The field is rectangular and must be 50–100yd wide and 100–130yd long.
At either end there is a goal and a goal area enclosed in the larger penalty area. The posts and crossbar of the goals must be of equal width and of the same width as the goal line.
The touchlines and the goal lines are part of the playing area.
At each corner of the field is a flag on a post that is at least 5ft high and must not have a pointed top. Flags on either side of the center line are optional, but must be set back at least 1yd from the touchline.

Playing the ball   1   2   3   4

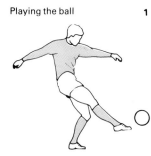

8ft
2.44m

24ft
7.32m

Officials A referee (a) controls the game and is assisted by two linesmen (b). The referee:
acts as timekeeper and keeps a record of the game;
enforces the laws;
stops the game at injuries, infringements, etc, and restarts it appropriately;
cautions or sends off offenders;
may end the game because of bad weather, interference by spectators, etc.
The linesmen, one on each touchline, indicate when the

ball is out of play, and which side has the right to put the ball into play again with a throw in, corner kick, or goal kick. They raise their flags to indicate any infringement, and the referee may choose whether or not to act on this signal.
Teams Each team has 11 players, one of whom is the goalkeeper.
Substitutes A maximum of two substitutes is permitted, depending upon the competition and for any

reason. They may have to be named before the game. Once substituted, a player may not return to the game. The referee must be informed of any substitution.
A player, who has been ordered off after play has started, may not be replaced.
In the event of an injury an outfield player may become the goalkeeper, provided he obtains the referee's permission and wears a distinctive jersey.

Duration The game is played in two halves of 45 minutes each; the teams change ends at half time. The half time interval may not exceed five minutes, except by consent of the referee.
The referee adds on time for moments lost through injuries, time wasting, etc. Time is also extended to allow a penalty kick to be taken at the end of either period.

Playing the ball Except at throw ins, the goalkeeper is the only player allowed to play the ball with his hands or arms, and he may only do so within his own penalty area.
A player may, however, use any other part of the body in order to stop, control, or pass the ball, move with it, or score. He may use his:
1 feet
2 head
3 thigh
4 chest

The ball is made of leather or other approved material. At the start of a game, it must weigh 14–16oz and should be inflated to a pressure of 0.6–1.1 atmosphere (=600–1100gr/cm^2) at sea level.

Its circumference should be 27–28ins.
The ball may not be changed during the game without the referee's permission.

Dress The goalkeeper (**1**) must wear different colors to distinguish him from the other players and the referee. All other players in the team (**2**) must wear uniform jerseys or shirts, shorts, socks and footwear. Shin pads (**3**) are a recommended protection. Boots (**4**) may be studded or have bars of leather and rubber across the soles. Studs must be of solid leather, rubber, plastic, aluminum, or similar material, but they must be rounded and not less than ½in in diameter or more than ¾in long from the mounting. Studs that are molded as part of the sole must be of a soft material. Provided that there are at least 10 studs on each sole, the minimum diameter of each stud may be ⅜in. Gloves (**5**) are frequently worn by goalkeepers. Numbers (**6**) are usually worn on the back of the jersey.
Players may not wear anything, which could injure another player, particularly faulty studs. Any player wearing dangerous equipment will be expelled from the game until it is replaced.

Scoring

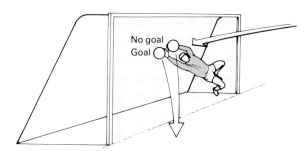

No goal

Goal

No goal
Goal

Scoring A goal is scored when the whole of the ball has crossed the goal line under the crossbar and between the posts, provided that the attacking team has not infringed the laws.
Result The team scoring the greater number of goals wins. If the number of goals scored is equal, the result is a draw. In some competitions draws are resolved by:
replays;
a period of extra time (usually two halves of 15 minutes each) immediately after the 90 minutes;
taking of kicks from the penalty mark;
the toss of a coin.

Starting and restarting the game The two captains toss a coin for choice of ends or for the right to kick off. On the referee's whistle the team kicking off shall play the ball from a stationary position on the center spot into the opponents' half of the field. This is known as a place kick.
At that moment every player must be in his own half and no opponent may come into the center circle until the ball is played.
Once played the ball must travel its own circumference and the player taking the kick off must not kick it again until it has been touched by another player.

After a goal is scored play is restarted the same way by the team that has conceded the goal. The second half is begun with a kick off by the team that did not start the first half.
If during play the referee stops the game when the ball is in play and there is no reason to award a free kick to either team, the referee may restart the game by dropping the ball at the place where it was when play was stopped. A player may not place the ball until it has touched the ground.

Out of play The ball is out of play when it completely crosses the boundaries of the pitch, or when the game has been stopped by the referee. Play is restarted by a throw in when the ball has crossed the touchlines, or by either a goal kick or a corner kick when it has crossed the goal line.

A throw in is taken along the touchline at the point where the ball went out of play. It is awarded against the team that last touched the ball before it went out of play.

The ball must be thrown into play with both hands, from behind and over the head (**1**). The thrower must face the play (**2**). As he releases the ball, part of each foot must be on the ground either behind (**3**) or on (**4**) the touchline. If these rules are infringed the throw in passes to the opposition. No goal can be scored from a throw in, and the thrower may not play the ball again until it has been touched by another player.

A goal kick is awarded to the defending team when the ball crosses their goal line after having been last touched by an opponent. The kick may be taken by any player of the defending side, including the goalkeeper.

The ball is placed within the half of the goal area nearer the point where it crossed the goal line (**1**). The kick must send the ball out of the penalty area (**2**) and the kicker may not touch the ball again until it has been played by another player. All opponents must retreat outside the penalty area until the kick is taken (**3**). No goal can be scored directly from a goal kick.

A corner kick is awarded to the attacking team if the ball crosses the goal line having been last played by one of the defending team.

It is taken from the quarter circle by the corner flag on the appropriate side of the pitch (**1**). The flag must not be moved to help the kicker. Opponents (**2**) must remain at least 10yd away until the kick is taken (until the ball has travelled its circumference). A goal can be scored direct from a corner kick (**3**), but the kicker must not play the ball again until it has been touched by another player.

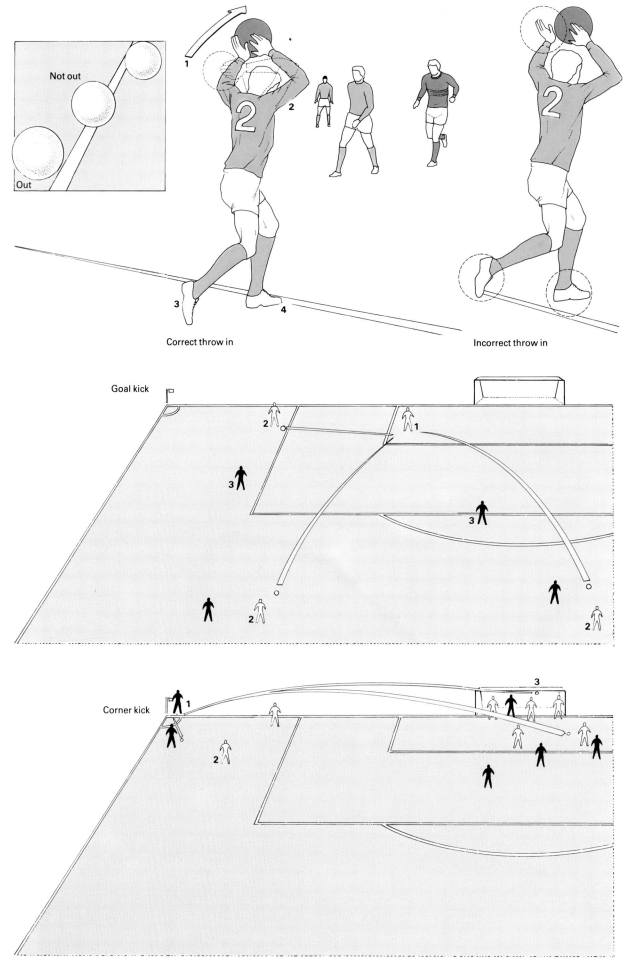

Correct throw in   Incorrect throw in

Goal kick

Corner kick

A free kick is either direct or indirect and is taken from where the offense occurred. **A direct free kick** is one from which the player taking the kick can score direct (**1**). **An indirect free kick** is one, from which a goal cannot be scored until the ball has been touched by another player (**2**). At any free kick all opponents must be at least 10yd from the ball (**3**), except at an indirect free kick less than 10yd from the goal, when they may stand between the goal posts. If the defending side is given a free kick in its own penalty area, the ball must be kicked out of the area and no opponents may enter the area until the kick is taken. The ball must be stationary at a free kick and the kicker may not replay the ball until another player touches it.

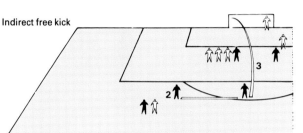

Direct free kick

Indirect free kick

Penalty kick Any offense that incurs a direct free kick is punished by the award of a penalty kick to the opposing team when it is committed by a defending player in his own penalty area.
A penalty kick is taken from the penalty mark. All players except the goalkeeper and the player taking the kick must stand outside the penalty area at least 10yd from the penalty mark. The player taking the kick must propel the ball forward and he may not play it a second time until it has been touched by another player. The goalkeeper must stand on the goal line without moving his feet until the ball is kicked.

The kick is retaken if:
the defending team breaks the law and a goal is not scored;
the attacking team, with the exception of the kicker, infringes and a goal is scored;
there are infringements by players of both sides.
If the kicker breaks the law, for instance by kicking the ball twice, the defending side is awarded an indirect free kick.

Offside

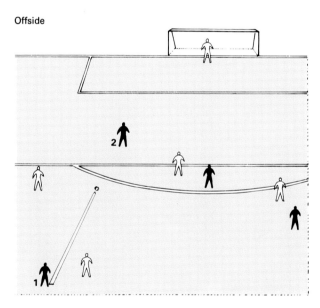

1 Tripping

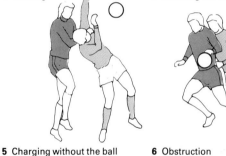
2 Holding

3 Handling the ball

4 Dangerous play

5 Charging without the ball

6 Obstruction

© DIAGRAM

Offside An attacking player is offside if, when the ball is played (**1**), he is nearer the opposing goal than two opponents and the ball (**2**), unless:
he is in his own half of the pitch;
an opponent was the last player to touch the ball;
he receives the ball direct from a goal kick, a corner kick, or a throw in.
Although a player may be technically in an offside position, he is not penalized unless in the opinion of the referee he is interfering with play or with an opponent, or is seeking to gain an advantage by being in an offside position.

Fouls and misconduct
A direct free kick (penalty kick) is awarded for the following intentional fouls if they are committed by a defender in his penalty area:
1 tripping an opponent;
2 holding an opponent;
3 playing the ball with a hand or arm (except for the goalkeeper in his penalty area);
kicking or attempting to kick an opponent;
jumping at an opponent;
charging in a violent or dangerous manner at an opponent;
charging from behind (unless the opponent is guilty of obstruction);
striking or attempting to strike an opponent;
spitting at an opponent;
pushing an opponent.

An indirect free kick is awarded:
4 for dangerous play;
5 for charging fairly, with the shoulder, but when the ball is not within playing distance;
6 for intentionally obstructing an opponent while not attempting to play the ball, in order to prevent him reaching it;
for charging the goalkeeper, unless the goalkeeper is holding the ball, obstructing an opponent, or has gone outside his goal area;
when a goalkeeper takes more than four steps while holding the ball, throwing it in the air and catching it, or bouncing it, or if he touches the ball again with his hands after releasing the ball and before it has been played by

a teammate outside his penalty area or by an opponent anywhere;
when the goalkeeper wastes time;
for offside;
when a player taking a kick off, throw in, goal kick, corner kick, free kick or penalty kick plays the ball a second time before another player has touched it;
after the game has been stopped to caution a player.

Cautioning and sending off The referee must caution a player if he:
enters or leaves the game without the referee's permission;
continually breaks the laws;
shows dissent from any of the referee's decisions;
is guilty of unsporting conduct.
The referee has the power to send a player off the field for the rest of the game if he:
commits acts of violence or serious foul play (including spitting);
uses foul or abusive language;
continues to break the laws after a caution.

Baseball

Baseball is played by two teams, each of nine players, who attempt to score more runs than their opponents. In each batting period the players attempt to make the circuit of the bases as many times as possible. However, when the fielding team has put out three opponents, the whole of the batting side is out and becomes the fielding side.

Area The playing field is composed of the infield and the outfield. The infield is the area bounded by the four bases. The outfield is the area beyond this section bounded by the extension of the two foul lines.
Home base is a five-sided slab of whitened rubber, while the other three bases are marked by white canvas bags. The pitcher's plate is a rectangular slab of whitened rubber usually set on a raised mound of earth.

Fielding positions
1 pitcher
2 catcher
3 first baseman
4 second baseman
5 third baseman
6 shortstop
7 left fielder
8 center fielder
9 right fielder

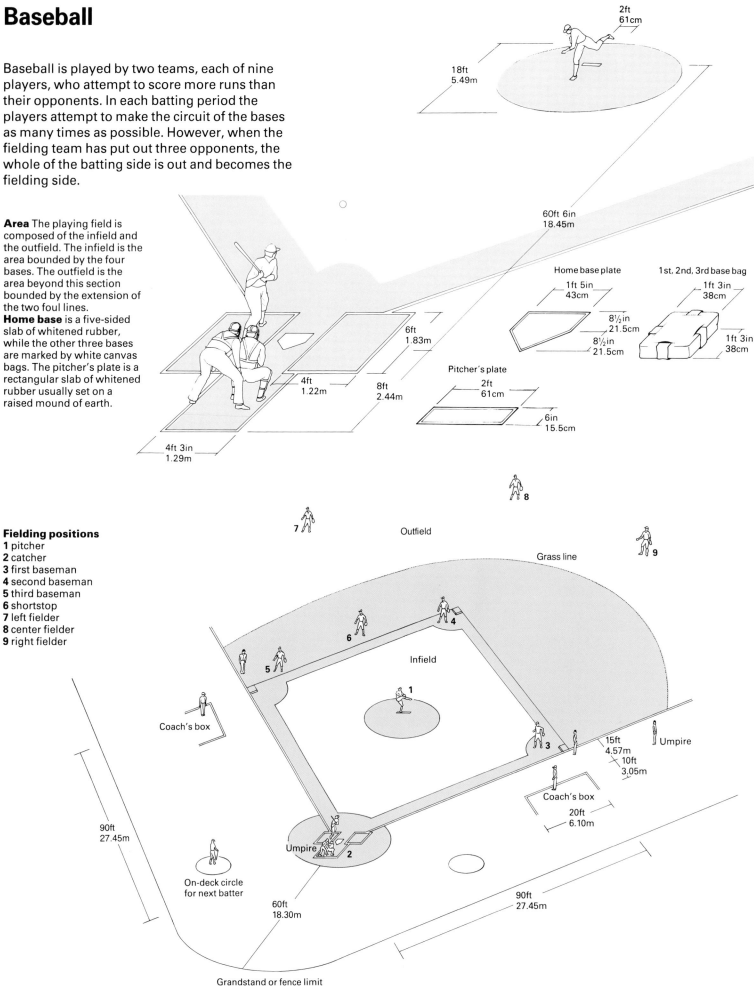

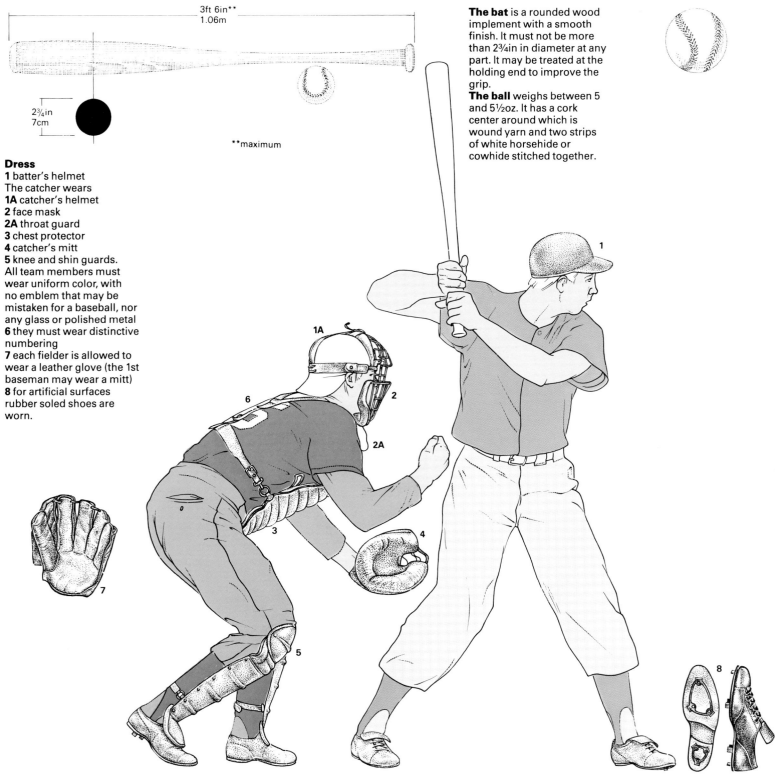

3ft 6in**
1.06m

2¾in
7cm

**maximum

Dress
1 batter's helmet
The catcher wears
1A catcher's helmet
2 face mask
2A throat guard
3 chest protector
4 catcher's mitt
5 knee and shin guards.
All team members must wear uniform color, with no emblem that may be mistaken for a baseball, nor any glass or polished metal
6 they must wear distinctive numbering
7 each fielder is allowed to wear a leather glove (the 1st baseman may wear a mitt)
8 for artificial surfaces rubber soled shoes are worn.

The bat is a rounded wood implement with a smooth finish. It must not be more than 2¾in in diameter at any part. It may be treated at the holding end to improve the grip.
The ball weighs between 5 and 5½oz. It has a cork center around which is wound yarn and two strips of white horsehide or cowhide stitched together.

Officials Where possible there are four umpires. The umpire-in-chief, wearing protective equipment, stands behind the catcher specifically to judge on strikes, but he is also the overall judge on all decisions.
The other umpires stand near the first, second, and third bases to judge whether a runner safely reaches the bag. For each game an official scorer is appointed to record the statistical details of the play.

Umpire-in-chief

Starting play The visiting team bats for the first half of an inning (the top).
(The second half of an inning is termed the bottom.)
Before the players take the field, the umpire must check that the playing area is correctly marked and that the players' equipment conforms to the regulations.
The umpire must also receive from the home club a number of new baseballs for use in the game.
The manager of the home team is the sole judge if the weather conditions make play doubtful, but once the game is under way, it is the umpire who decides in bad weather if play should be stopped, restarted, etc.

When the umpire suspends play he calls "time;" when he restarts, he calls "play."
Five minutes before play is due to start, the umpire must receive each team's batting order in duplicate. He keeps one copy for himself and passes the other to the opposing manager.
The players of the home team then take their defensive positions, the batter takes up his position, and on the call of "play," the game begins.
The batting team must have two coaches in the coaches' boxes during their half-inning.

© DIAGRAM

Batting Each member of the batting side takes his place in the batter's box according to the order decided by the team manager.

The batter must stand with his feet within the box. He attempts to score runs by striking the ball as it is pitched to him.

The strike zone is the area over home plate, the upper limit of which is a horizontal line at the mid-point between the top of the shoulders and the top of the uniform pants, and the lower level is a line at the top of the knees. The strike zone shall be determined from the batter's stance as the batter is prepared to swing at a pitched ball.

A strike is called by the umpire when the batter does not swing at a pitch in the strike zone, or swings at any pitch and misses, or hits the ball into foul territory with fewer than two strikes against him.

A ball is a pitch delivered outside the strike zone that is not struck at by the batter. After four balls the batter may walk to first base.

Running The batter becomes a runner when he

Strike zone

Strike

Ball

has hit the ball into fair territory, walked on four pitched balls, is hit by a pitch, or (though sometimes not enforced for younger youth baseball) if the catcher drops a third strike.

A force play is when the batter runs to first base and forces any runner on that base to move to second base;

if there are runners on the first and second base, both runners must run.

A runner is "safe" at a base if he touches the bag before the fielder with the ball touches him or the base. He may stay there until he is dismissed or until he is forced to move on by the arrival of another runner.

A steal is when a runner gains a base without the help of a hit, walk, or error, usually by running to it while the pitched ball is going toward the batter.

The runner is out if he is tagged out by an opposing player with the ball.

Tagging up A runner may vacate a base on a caught fly only after the ball is touched by a fielder. If he has left the base he must return and tag up before he may advance. If the ball is returned to the base ahead of him, he is out.

Force play

Steal

Duration A game lasts a specified number of innings; professionals play nine.

Each side has a turn at bat to complete an inning. A half-inning is completed when three of the batting side are out.

With a tie scored after the specified innings, extra innings are played until one team is ahead at an inning's end.

Scoring The team that scores most runs is the winner.

A run is scored when a player completes a circuit of the bases, touching each in turn.

1 If a batter hits the ball away from the fielders into the distant outfield, he may make a home run (ie get around all the bases in one

turn). It is also awarded if he hits a fly ball (one that does not touch the ground) over a boundary fence that is more than 250ft from home base and in fair territory.

(A grand slam home run is a home run hit when the bases are loaded, ie when three men are on base. It scores four runs, the maximum possible from one hit.)

2 If a fair ball bounces over the fence, the batter may go to second base. Most often when he hits the ball he will reach first base and then continue around as following batters take their turns.

Whenever a batter hits the ball into the field of play, he must run to first base.

Substitutes may be introduced at any time when the ball is dead. A substitute takes the replaced player's position in the batting order; once substituted for that player may not return to the game.

A substitute may take the place of any player on the field, providing the umpire is informed.

No player whose name is on the batting order may become a substitute runner. Relief pitchers usually warm-up in the "bull-pen" before they come into the game. The use of substitutes is at the manager's discretion, as are all decisions on the strategy of the game.

Fielder's misconduct If a fielder stops a batted ball by throwing his glove or cap at it when it would have gone out of the playing area, the batter is awarded extra bases according to the rules.

1
2

Fair territory

Foul territory

 Set position

 Wind-up position

 illegal pitch

illegal pitch

Pitching The pitcher is allowed no more than eight practice pitches before he starts play or takes over from another pitcher.
He may deliver the ball only from either the set position or the wind-up position.
At any time before he pitches, he may throw the ball to a base, providing he steps in that direction.

He may only rub the ball between his hands; any attempt to shine it on his clothing, apply saliva or any foreign substance to it, or rub it on the ground, is an offense.
Any violation leads to disqualification.
The pitcher must not pitch the ball directly at the batter;

he must not delay the game and must pitch the ball 20 seconds after receiving it.
A balk The pitcher concedes a no pitch (called a balk):
for an illegal pitch with runners on base, when his foot is not in contact with the pitcher's plate;
if he pretends to pitch and does not do so;

if he fails to step directly toward a base when he is throwing to that base;
if he pitches when not facing the batter;
if he makes any sort of feinting movement;
if he drops the ball while in the pitching motion;
if he pitches when the catcher is not in position.

A balk allows all baserunners to advance to the next base.
A base runner may also advance bases: when a wild pitch or a throw from the pitcher to a base goes beyond a base;
when a pitch gets past the catcher and lodges in the umpire's clothing.

1 Caught

2 Bunt to foul territory

3 Tag

4 Not out

4 Out

Putting out batters and runners More than one of the batting side may be out between consecutive pitches.
 A batter is out:
1 if he hits the ball and it is caught "on the fly" by a fielder, even if it is caught in "foul" territory;
2 when he attempts to bunt (tap) the ball down in front of him on a third strike and it goes into foul territory; if he fails to make contact on the third strike (providing the catcher catches the third strike);
if he hits a fly ball so that it can be caught in the infield when there are less than two out and runners on first and second or on first, second, and third (infield fly rule);
when he is touched by the

Double play

ball as he tries to hit a third strike;
when a runner is hit by a batted ball in fair territory;
when the umpire judges that a spectator has prevented a fielder from catching a fly ball;
if he deliberately strikes the ball twice;
if he interferes with or obstructs a fielder.

A runner is out:
3 if a fielder tags (touches) him with the ball when he is not in physical contact with a base;
if a batted ball hits him as he runs between bases;
if he runs more than 3ft off a straight line to avoid being tagged;
4 if a fielder with the ball tags a base at which a force

exists before the forced runner reaches the base.
A double play occurs when two outs are recorded between consecutive pitches such as a runner from first forced at second and the batter forced at first on the same ground ball.

A triple play occurs when three outs are recorded between consecutive pitches such as when a fly ball is caught and two runners are forced before they can tag up.

© DIAGRAM

Softball

Since first being played as an indoor version of baseball in Chicago in 1888, softball has grown into a major outdoor team game. Softball is played by both men and women. There are two types of softball, fast pitch (FP) and slow pitch (SP) with several rules differences between the two.

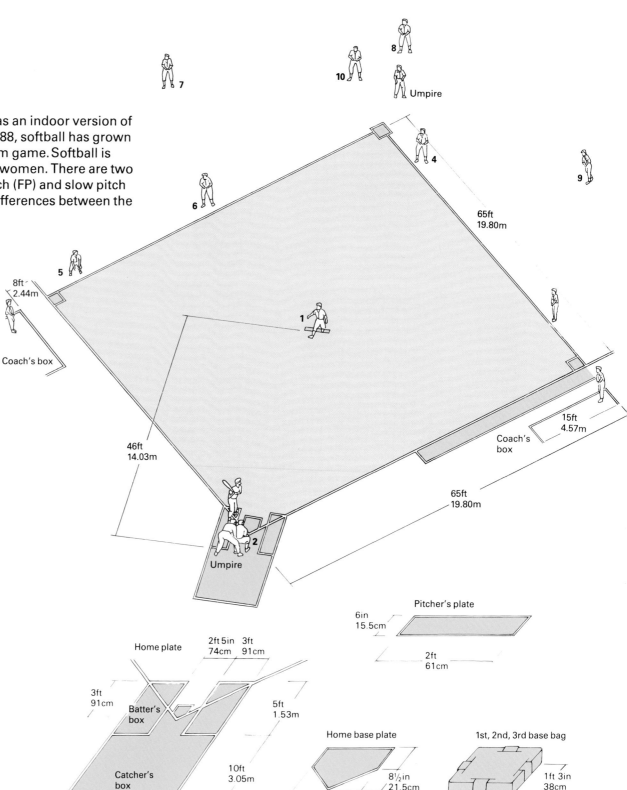

The field Bases are 60ft apart (FP) and 65ft (SP). In fast pitch the pitching distance is 40ft for women and 46ft for men; in slow pitch it is 46ft for all players. The outfield fence is 200ft for women and 225–250ft for men in fast pitch; the outfeild fence is 250ft for women and 275–300ft for men in slow pitch.

The home plate is made of rubber or other suitable material.

The pitcher's plate is made of rubber and the top of the plate is level with the ground.

The bases are made of canvas or other suitable material and must be securely fastened in position.

Officials Matches are controlled by:
a) the plate umpire, who judges batting, appeals, and forfeited matches; and
b) the base umpires, who take up different positions on the playing field from where best to render base decisions. The umpires share equal authority to: judge illegal pitches and stealing bases; expel players or team officials; and suspend play.

Fielding positions
1 pitcher
2 catcher
3 first baseman
4 second baseman
5 third baseman
6 shortstop
7 left fielder
8 center fielder
9 right fielder
10 short fielder (SP)

Teams A team consists of nine players (FP) or ten (SP), who must all be present to start or continue a game. Pitchers and catchers must stand in their prescribed positions. Other players may be stationed anywhere on fair ground.

Substitutes All players may be substituted at any time. All starting players can re-enter one time. A substitute may not return to the game after being removed.

Starting play Teams toss a coin to determine the order of play.

Duration A game consists of seven innings. A full seven innings need not be played if the second batting team scores more runs before the third player is out in the last half of the seventh inning. A tied game continues for additional innings until one side has scored more runs at the end of a completed inning, or until the side batting second scores more in their half of an inning before their third dismissal.

A game that the umpire ends prematurely is considered finished if five or more completed innings have been played.

Scoring The winning team is the one that scores the greater number of runs.
A run is scored when a player completes a circuit of the bases, touching each in turn.
A player may not score a run ahead of a preceding runner.

If the batter hits a ball into the air (fly ball) over the boundary fence a home run is scored. If, on an unfenced field, however, that fly ball, or any other fair ball, passes out of the field less than 200ft from the home base, the batter and runners are only allowed to proceed two bases.
A forfeited game scores 7-0 in favor of the team not at fault.

Dimensions at top:
2ft 10in
86.5cm

The bat is round in cross-section, and made of hard wood or metal. All bats must have safety grips of cork, tape, or composition material.

The ball is made of kapok, polyurethane or of a mixture of cork and rubber. It is covered in horse or cow hide or has an artificial surface. The cover is cemented to the ball and sewn with waxed thread. Circumference 11⅞–12⅛in; weight 6¼–7oz. Special rubberized balls are available but usually the ball is not soft.

1

2

3

Dress Uniforms are similar to those worn for baseball. Gloves may be worn by any player, but mitts (**1**) may only be worn by the catcher and first baseman.
Shoes (**2**) may have metal plates with spikes a maximum of ¾" long. Catchers and plate umpires must wear masks (**3**) (FP). Body protectors (**4**) may be worn and are compulsory for women catchers (FP).
Batting Players bat in the order listed on the scoresheets.
If a player has not completed a turn when the team's half of the inning at bat is ended, that player becomes the first batter in its next inning at bat.
The batter must stand within the lines of the batter's box.
The strike zone is:
that space over any part of home plate which is between the batter's armpits and top of the knees when a natural batting stance is assumed (FP); or
that area between the top of the shoulder and the bottom of the knee (SP).
A strike is a ball pitched into the strike zone at which the batter either does not swing, or swings and misses.
A ball landing in foul territory (foul ball) is also a strike. In fast pitch a batter cannot be declared out on such a hit, but in slow pitch each foul ball counts as a strike – so the third strike hit foul is out.
A batter is allowed three strikes.
A ball is a ball pitched outside the strike zone and

not swung at by the batter. In slow pitch if the pitch is not swung at or hit by the batter the ball is dead, and no play can take place.
In fast pitch the ball is live. After four balls the batter may walk to first base.
Running The batter becomes a runner:
upon hitting the ball into fair territory;
after four balls;
after interference by the catcher;
when a fair ball strikes the person or clothing of an umpire on foul territory.
A runner may move to the next base while the ball is in play;
when the ball reaches home plate or is batted (SP)
when the ball leaves the pitcher's hand on a pitch or if it is dropped during the wind-up or backswing (FP);
when the ball is overthrown;
when the ball is batted into fair territory.
The runner may also move to the next base without threat of dismissal:
when the batter is awarded a base and preceding bases are occupied;
when a fielder obstructs a runner;
when a fielder illegally stops the ball;
when the ball is overthrown into foul territory and is ruled out of play.
Runners must return to their bases:
when a ball is legally caught on the fly;
when the ball is batted illegally;
after interference by a batter or runner;

when the batter is hit by a pitched ball.
Pitching Pitchers are allowed up to 1 minute in which to pitch a maximum of five balls at the start of an inning or when one pitcher relieves another (FP); 3 pitches (SP).
1 The pitcher must stand: with both feet on the pitcher's plate;
facing the batter and with his shoulders in line with the first and third bases;
holding the ball with both hands in front of his body. This position may be kept for 1–10 seconds. The catcher must be in position before the pitcher assumes the pitching position.
2 The delivery starts when the pitcher removes one hand from the ball. It must be delivered underhand, and the hand must be below the hip, and the wrist no further from the body than the elbow.
3 The pitcher may take one step forward, but this must be in the direction of the batter and simultaneous with delivery.
The release of the ball and the follow through of the hand and wrist must be in a forward direction, past the straight line of the body. Any type of wind-up is allowed, provided:
the ball is pitched immediately after the pitching motion;
one hand is not removed from the ball and returned to the ball after the swing;
there is no halt or reverse in the forward motion;
there is not more than one

revolution in a "windmill" pitch (FP only);
the ball must be released the first time pass the hip (SP);
the wind-up does not continue after stepping forward.
In slow pitch no "windmill" action is allowed and the ball must travel through an arc of between 6 and 12ft to the plate.
A no-pitch occurs if the pitcher:
pitches during a halt in play;
attempts to pitch before the batter has taken up position, or is off balance after the previous pitch;
pitches when a runner is out for leaving a base too soon.
Dismissals (outs)
A batter is out if:
a ball is legally caught on the fly;
a fly ball is hit in the infield when there are fewer than two teammates out and runners on the first two or three bases (infield fly rule);
a fielder deliberately drops an infield fly or line drive (an aerial ball batted sharply and directly into the playing field) with any of the bases occupied and fewer than two players dismissed;
the preceding runner interferes with an attempt to field the ball – the runner is then also dismissed.
There are three strikes against the batter when fewer than two teammates are out and the first base is occupied (FP);
the third strike is caught by the catcher (FP);
the batter misses the third strike and is hit by the ball (FP);

the batter bunts (taps) the third strike into foul territory (FP).
A runner is out when:
forced to the next base and the fielder touching the base receives the ball before the runner reaches or returns to it;
before reaching or returning to a base the runner is legally touched with the ball by a fielder;
having left a base before a fly ball is caught, the runner fails to return to that base before it or the runner is tagged by a fielder with the ball;
running more than 3ft from a direct line between the bases to avoid being touched with the ball by a fielder;
overtaking a preceding runner;
deliberately kicking the ball;
deliberately interfering with an attempt to field the ball or with a thrown ball;
hit by a fair ball off base before the ball has touched or passed a fielder;
A force-out occurs when the runner loses the right to a base because the batter has become a runner and the fielder on the next base is holding the ball.
A runner is not out if, after touching 1st base, the runner overruns it and is clearly about to return to it.
Misconduct by players or team officials is punishable by a warning for a first offense and expulsion from the game for a second offense.

Rounders

Rounders is an English game similar to baseball and softball. A batter attempts to strike a ball and run around an area marked by posts to score a "rounder." The team that scores the most rounders wins the match. It is usually played by women and children, though the majority of leagues are formed from mixed clubs.

The pitch Four vertical posts, supported in bases, are set at the corners of the running track. The lines of the batting and bowling squares are considered part of those squares.

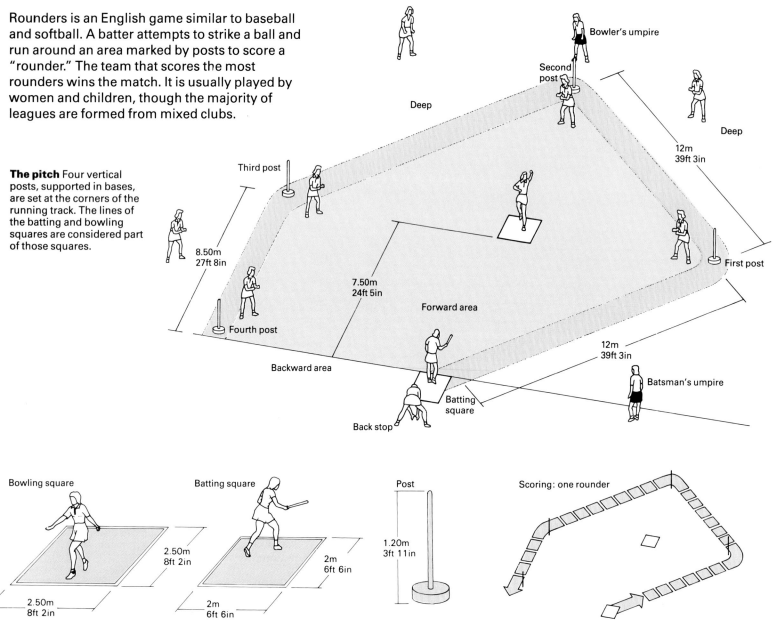

Teams Each team consists of a maximum of nine players or a minimum of six. Only five males are allowed in a mixed team.
Substitutes Two substitutes nominated prior to the start of the game may be used at any dead ball situation after first informing the umpires and the other team.
Numbers All players, including substitutes, are clearly numbered.

Officials A match is controlled by the batter's umpire, who must be able to see both the batting square and the first post without turning the head; and by the bowler's umpire. The umpires' decisions are final. They may consult each other and both record the scores. They exchange positions after both first innings have been completed.

Start of play Captains toss for choice of inning. A team must retain the same batting order throughout an inning.
Duration Each team has two innings. An inning ends when all the batters are out. A team leading by five or more rounders has the option of requiring the other team to follow on. A team enforcing this option forfeits its second inning (unless their opponents level or lead the first inning's score) and the game is deemed to have finished.

Scoring
One rounder is scored if a batter hits the ball and runs around the track to touch the fourth post before another ball is bowled – unless the batter is dismissed or the next post is "stopped" (touched by a fielder holding a ball).
A half rounder is scored if the batter completes the track as for a rounder but without hitting the ball.

A penalty half rounder is awarded to the batting team when the bowler delivers two consecutive no-balls to the same batter, or if a batter is obstructed by a fielder. It may be awarded in addition to a rounder if a batter scores a rounder despite either of these offenses. Two penalty half rounders are awarded if a batter scores a rounder despite both offenses. A penalty half rounder may be awarded to the fielding team if the waiting batting side obstructs the fielders.

17cm
6¾in

Batting

1 After a good ball, the batter must move to the first post.
2 The batter's feet must be within the batting square until the ball leaves the bowler's hand. The batter must keep both feet behind the front line until the ball has been hit or it has passed by.
3 A backward hit occurs if the ball is hit directly into the backward area.
4 A batter may take a no-ball and score in the usual way. The batter is deemed to have accepted the ball when coming within reach of, making contact with, or passing first post. When only one player in a team remains to be dismissed, the batter may have one minute's rest between rounders and is allowed a choice of three good balls at each turn.

The stick is round in cross-section. It must be no more than 17cm around the thickest part. The maximum length is 46cm.

Running A batter must pass outside, or halt at, each of the first three posts in order to reach the fourth, carrying the bat. The batter must touch the fourth post by hand or bat. When waiting (even temporarily) at a post, the batter must maintain contact with it – either by hand or bat – until the ball has left the bowler's hand. The batter may run on whenever the bowler is not in possession of the ball and is in the bowling square. The batter must not overtake another runner, nor stay at the same post as another batter.

The ball weighs 70–85g. Its circumference should be 17–19cm. It should be leather, preferably white.

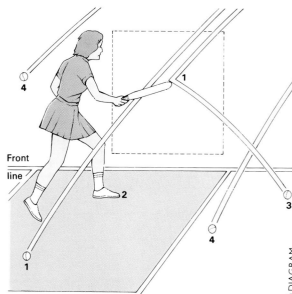

Front line

© DIAGRAM

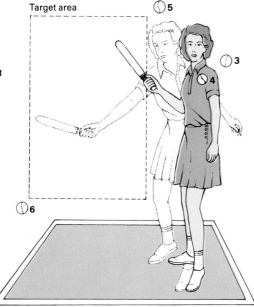

Dismissing the batters

More than one batter may be out between consecutive balls.
A batter is out when:
1 one or both feet are over the front or back line of the batting square before the ball has been hit or passed by;
2 running on the inside of a post – unless it is a result of obstruction;
3 run-out by a fielder who touches (with the ball or the hand holding the ball) the post to which the batter is running;
4 obstructing a fielder or deliberately deflecting the ball;
overtaking another batter;
leaving a post before the ball has left the bowler's hand.

Side out When there is no batter waiting to bat, all the running batters can be out simultaneously if any fielder throws full pitch or places the ball directly into the batting square before any batsman reaches fourth post (**5**).

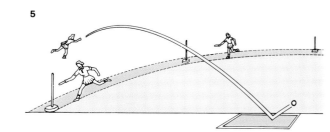

Target area

Bowling A bowler may be changed only afer delivering a good ball. The bowler may leave the bowling square in order to field the ball.
No-balls A ball is considered a no-ball if:
1 it is not bowled with a continuous and smooth underarm action;
2 the bowler fails to keep both feet within the bowling square until the ball is released;
3 it is bowled on the wrong side of the batter;
4 it is aimed at the batter's body;
5 it is bowled higher than the batter's head, or
6 lower than the batter's knee;

7 it hits the ground before it reaches the batter;
8 it is bowled "wide" (out of reach of the batter).
Obstruction is caused if:
1 a fielder in any way impedes the batter's stroke or run;
2 a batter deviates from the running track, thereby impeding a player fielding the ball.
The batting side, while waiting to bat, must stand behind the marked line in the backward area away from the backstop (the fielder positioned behind the batter) and the fourth post fielder.)

Cricket

Cricket is a ball game played by two teams of eleven players. It is played on a pitch with two wickets placed 22yd apart. Each team bats (takes its innings) in turn. The object of the batting side is to make runs, while the bowling and fielding side tries to dismiss the batsmen. The winning team is the one that scores more runs.

The pitch is the area between the two bowling creases and extending 5ft in width on either side of a line joining the center of the wickets. The pitch, of grass (or approved matting), is prepared before the game to be level and with the grass trimmed short. In first-class cricket, regulations govern when and how often the pitch is to be rolled, mown, watered, or covered.
The rest of the playing area is enclosed by a boundary line.
The wicket at each end of the pitch is composed of three vertical stumps on top of which are placed two horizontal bails.
The return and popping creases are unlimited in length.
Teams There are eleven players in a team.
Fielding positions (for a right-handed batsman):
1 bowler
2 wicket keeper
3 slips
4 leg slip
5 backward short leg
6 square short leg
7 forward short leg
8 silly point
9 gully
10 silly mid off
11 silly mid on
12 mid wicket
13 square leg
14 backward point
15 point
16 cover
17 short extra cover
18 extra cover
19 deep extra cover
20 mid off
21 deep mid off
22 mid on
23 deep mid on
24 short fine leg
25 deep fine leg
26 short third man
27 third man
28 long leg
29 deep square leg
30 deep mid wicket
31 long on
32 long off

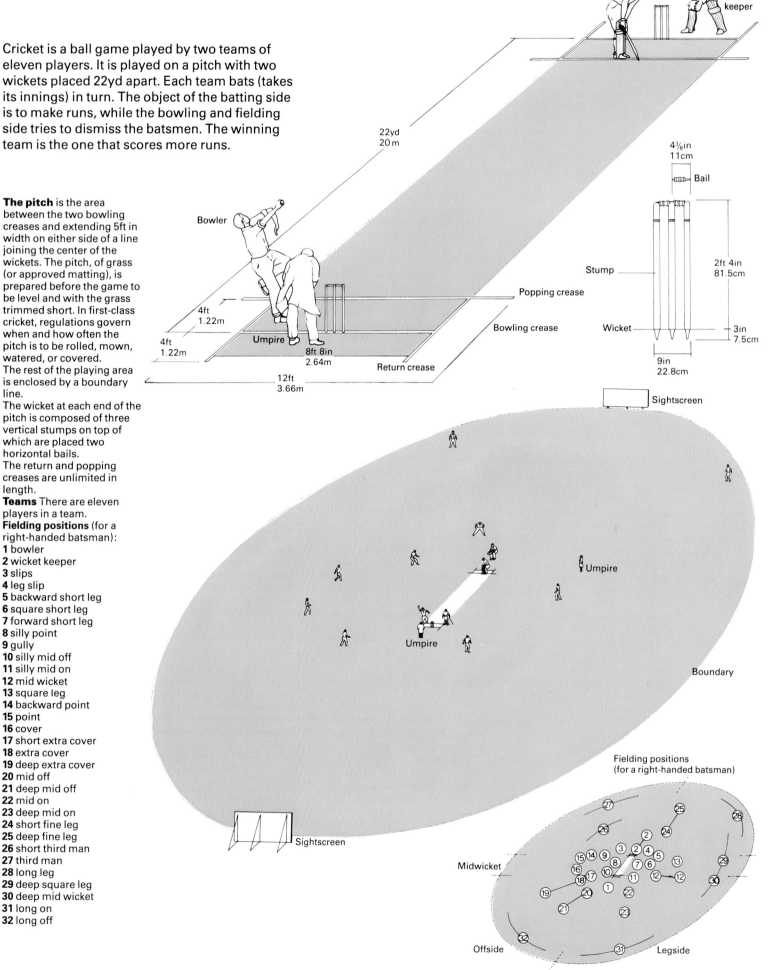

Batsman

Wicket keeper

22yd
20m

4³⁄₈in
11cm

Bail

Stump

2ft 4in
81.5cm

Wicket

3in
7.5cm

9in
22.8cm

Bowler

Popping crease

Bowling crease

4ft
1.22m

4ft
1.22m

Umpire

8ft 8in
2.64m

Return crease

12ft
3.66m

Sightscreen

Umpire

Umpire

Boundary

Sightscreen

Fielding positions
(for a right-handed batsman)

Midwicket

Offside

Legside

3ft 2in
96.5cm

4¼in
10.8cm

Bat Wood with rubber grip. Maximum dimensions are shown. Usual weight is about 2lb 10oz.
Ball Red leather with a stitched seam. Circumference 8¹³/₁₆–9in. Weight 5½–5¾oz. If the ball is lost during a game, a similar replacement should be found.
Each innings usually starts

with a new ball, and in top-class cricket the fielding side may demand a new ball after a stipulated number of overs.

Dress White or cream shirts and trousers, possibly a sweater and a peaked cap. Also:
1 batsman's gloves
2 wicket keeper's gloves
3 white padded leg guards
4 abdomen protector
5 cricket boots may be spiked or have rubber soles
6 protective helmet

Substitutes are permitted to field for any player who is ill or injured during a match. Exceptionally the umpire may allow a substitute for a player for any other reason providing that the opposing captain gives his permission. Substitutes may field, but not bat or bowl.
Duration varies with the standard of the match. There may be a limited playing time, or a specified number of overs. In both cases play ends before time if a result is obtained.
Test Match cricket (between national teams) is played over five six-hour playing days, and first-class cricket over three or four days. One-day matches are played at both international and first-class level. At other levels, two-day, one-day, and afternoon matches are played.
Innings Matches consist of one or two innings per team. An innings is completed when: ten of a team's batsmen have been dismissed: the batting captain "declares" (voluntarily ends the innings): or
a specified number of overs have been bowled.
Intervals are allowed for meals (usually 40 minutes for lunch and 20 for tea) and between innings (10 minutes).
Not more than two minutes is allowed for an incoming batsman to take his place at the wicket, or he is out.

© DIAGRAM

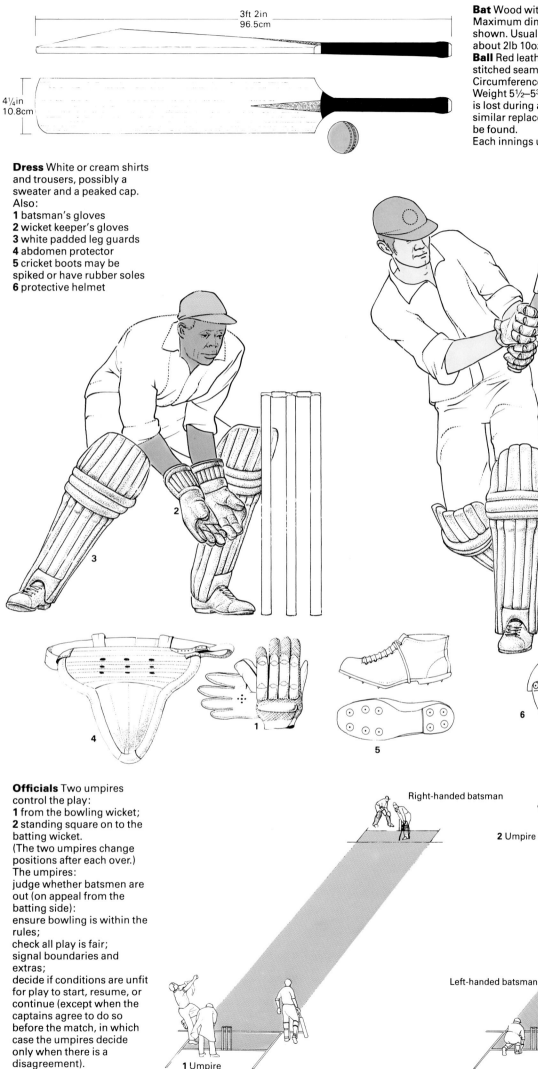

Officials Two umpires control the play:
1 from the bowling wicket;
2 standing square on to the batting wicket.
(The two umpires change positions after each over.)
The umpires:
judge whether batsmen are out (on appeal from the batting side):
ensure bowling is within the rules;
check all play is fair;
signal boundaries and extras;
decide if conditions are unfit for play to start, resume, or continue (except when the captains agree to do so before the match, in which case the umpires decide only when there is a disagreement).

Right-handed batsman

2 Umpire

1 Umpire

1 Umpire

Left-handed batsman

1 Umpire

2 Umpire

Starting play Each team bats in turn. The choice of batting or fielding first goes to the captain who wins the toss of a coin.

Two members of the batting team take up their positions, one at each wicket. A member of the fielding side bowls from one end to the batsman defending the opposite wicket. The rest of the fielding side is positioned to stop runs and to help dismiss the batsmen. The umpire calls "play" at the start of a day or an innings, and "time" at the close of play.

The follow on In a two-innings match, each side takes its innings alternately unless it is forced to "follow on" (to take its second innings immediately after its first).

A team batting second may be asked to follow on by the opposing captain if it scores: 200 less than the opposition in a five-day match: 150 less in a three-day or four-day match; 100 less in a two-day match; 75 less in a one-day match.

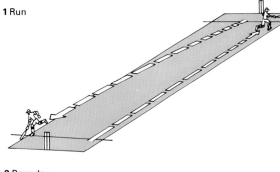

1 Run

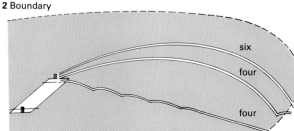

2 Boundary

Scoring is in runs.
1 A run is scored when both batsmen, after a hit or at any time the ball is in play, pass each other and reach the opposite popping crease. The run does not count if a batsman runs short or is run out. If the batsman is out caught, no runs are scored.
2 When the ball crosses the boundary on the full pitch, it counts six runs; if it touches the ground first it counts four. After a boundary the batsmen resume their original positions. Normally, only the boundary score counts, not any runs made between the wickets at the same time.

Extras are runs scored without hitting the ball with the bat. They may be scored from a wide (**3**), a bye (**4**), a leg bye (**5**), or a no ball.

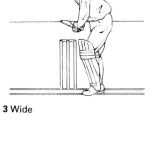

3 Wide   **3** Wide

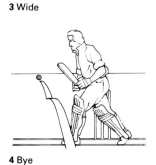

4 Bye   **5** Leg bye

Result The match is won by the team with more runs after both teams have completed the required number of innings. If any innings is incomplete, the match is a draw. If scores are equal when the innings are completed, the match is a tie.

In limited-over cricket, the match is won by the team

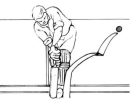

scoring more runs in the overs allowed. Draws are possible only when the weather interferes with play. The result of a won match is expressed as a win by the numbers of runs by which one team beat the other, or as a win by the number of wickets still to fall if the last side to bat exceeds the other's total of runs.

Fair ball

No ball: throw

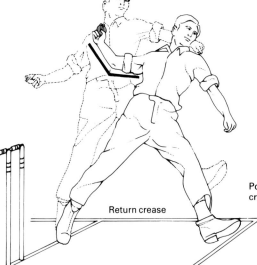

Bowling is in "overs" of six or eight balls (as in the agreed conditions and consistent throughout the match).

Overs are delivered from alternate wickets.

A bowler must bowl a complete over unless he is injured or suspended.

Bowlers may change ends as often as they wish, but must not bowl two successive overs in one innings.

They may bowl from either side of the wicket provided they inform the batsman. The umpire at the bowling end shall call "over" after the sixth or eighth ball, once he sees that both sides have ceased to regard the ball as in play.

A no ball is called if the bowler:

Return crease

Popping crease

throws instead of bowls the ball;
in his delivery stride has no part of his front foot grounded behind the popping crease;
does not ground his back foot within the return crease or its forward extension. Either umpire may call and signal "no ball" immediately on delivery.

The receiving batsman may

hit a no ball and make runs from it, but he can only be dismissed by being run out, handling the ball, hitting the ball twice, or obstructing the field.

If the batsman fails to make any runs from a no ball, one run is added to his team's total score.

A wide is called if the bowler sends the ball so

Fair ball

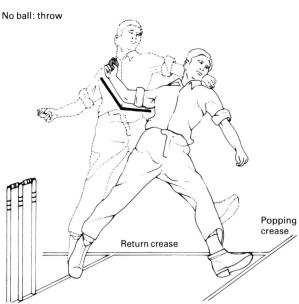

Fair ball

Fair ball

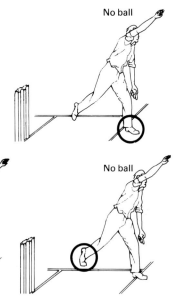

No ball

No ball

high over or so wide of the wicket that it passes out of the batsman's reach.

The umpire shall signal the wide as soon as the ball has passed the line of the striker's wicket and one run is added to the team's score. Batsmen may be out stumped, run out, handled the ball, or obstructing the field and hit wicket.

A bye is a run taken when the ball has not touched the batsman's bat or any part of his person.

A leg-bye is a run taken when the ball touches but is not deliberately deflected by any part of the batsman's body except his hands. (Runs scored when the ball comes off the batsman's gloves are added to his own score.)

Dismissing the batsman

The umpire will not decide that a batsman is out unless the other team makes an appeal of "How's that?" The appeal must be made before the bowler begins his run up or bowling action for the next ball.

A batsman may be out in the following ways:

Leg before wicket (lbw) If any part of his body, dress or equipment intercepts a ball that would have hit the wicket, provided that:
the ball has not previously touched his bat or a hand holding the bat;
the ball pitched or would have pitched in a straight line between the wickets or on the offside;
the point of impact is in a straight line between the wickets, even if above the bails.

Caught When a fielder within the playing area catches the ball before it touches the ground after it has come off the batsman's bat or gloves (holding the bat), the catch is considered fair if: the ball is hugged to a fielder's body or lodges in his clothing or in a wicket keeper's pads, but not if it lodges in a protective helmet; the ball is caught after it has touched a person on the field, but not if it has touched a protective helmet; the ball is caught off an obstruction within and not part of the boundary; the hand holding the ball touches the ground but the ball does not.

Hit wicket If the batsman breaks the wicket with his bat or body while playing a shot or while setting off for a first run.

Run out If the batsman has his wicket broken by the opposition when he is out of his ground going for a run or for any other reason when the ball is in play.

Stumped If in receiving a ball the batsman moves out of his ground, other than to attempt a run, and the wicket keeper, without another fielder's intervention, breaks the wicket.

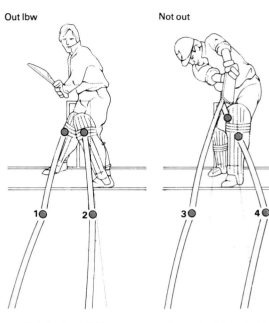

Out lbw   Not out

1 Ball pitched on offside
2 Ball pitched straight before wicket
3 Player first hits ball with bat or hand
4 Ball pitched outside leg stump

Bowled When the ball delivered by the bowler hits the wicket and dislodges a bail, even if the ball touches the bat or the batsman's body first, or if he breaks the wicket by hitting or kicking the ball onto it.

Handled the ball If the batsman, without his opponents' consent, touches the ball with his hand when it is in play unless the hand is holding the bat.

Hit the ball twice If the batsman strikes or stops the ball with any part of the bat or his person and then willfully hits it again unless he is protecting his wicket.

Obstructing the field If the batsman willfully obstructs any member of the opposition.

Retiring A batsman may retire at any time, but may only resume his innings with the consent of the opposing captain.

Fielding A fielder may stop the ball with any part of his body, but if he uses any other means (eg his cap) the batting side is awarded five runs.

Not more than two fielders may field behind the popping crease on the leg side; if they do, the umpire will call a no ball.

The wicket keeper must stay behind the stumps until the ball passes the wicket or touches the striker's bat or body, or until the batsman attempts a run.

Bowled   Hit wicket

Run out   Stumped

Caught

Dead ball

The ball is "dead" when:
it settles in the hands of the wicket keeper or bowler;
it goes over the boundary;
it lodges in the clothing or equipment of a batsman or umpire;
a batsman is out;
a penalty is awarded for a lost ball or a fielding infringement.

The umpire may call "dead ball" at his discretion:
in the case of serious injury;
if the striker is not ready;
if the bowler drops the ball.
The ball is not dead if:
it strikes an umpire;
a wicket is broken (unless the batsman is out);
an unsuccessful appeal is made.

The ball is in play the moment the bowler starts his run.

Misconduct The umpire will intervene if:
players lift the ball's seam to obtain a better grip;
bowlers use wax or resin to shine the ball, though they may dry the ball with sawdust or a towel;

the fielding side attempts to distract the receiving batsman or tries to help its own bowlers by damaging the pitch;
bowlers persistently bowl "bouncers" (short, fast deliveries);
batsmen attempt to "steal" runs during a bowler's run up.

Last over The last over before an interval or close of play will be started if the umpire arrives in position at the bowler's end before time is called. It will be completed unless a batsman is out or retires within two minutes of the interval, or at the captains' request even if a wicket falls after time.

© DIAGRAM

Lacrosse

Two versions of lacrosse are played internationally; the 12-a-side game for women, and the 10-a-side men's game. The major differences, apart from team size, are in the pitch and the amount of body contact and stick checking allowed. In both versions the ball is caught, thrown, and carried using sticks fitted with nets; and play is allowed behind the goals.

Pitch Women's pitches have no boundaries. An area of 110m×60m (120yd×70yd) is desirable.

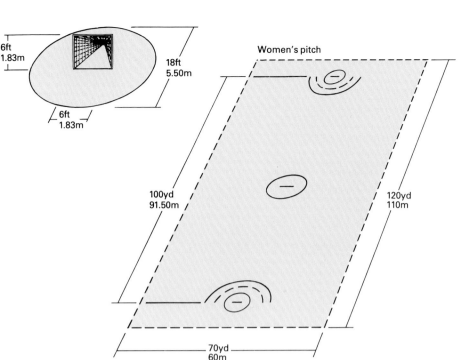

Women's pitch

WOMEN'S LACROSSE

Teams In women's lacrosse teams may consist of up to sixteen players. Four line up changes (4 players) may be substituted in each half, with unlimited substitution at half time. One player counts as one line up change and any player substituted off, may return to the field of play at a later time, unless she has been sent off. If, after the fourth substitution, a team loses a player for whatever reason, that team must play short for the remainder of that half.

Officials 3 field umpires. Two umpires act as lead umpires at their respective end of the pitch and as a trail umpire on their side at the other end of the field. The third umpire administers all the center draws and acts as a trail umpire on the opposite side of the field to the lead umpires at both ends of the pitch. The three umpires act as a team, calling fouls in their domain and also those that may be unsighted by the other umpires.

Duration The women's game consists of two halves, of 25 minutes stop-clock duration. During the first 23 minutes of play, the clock is stopped after each goal is indicated. Play is restarted by a center draw. In the last 2 minutes of play, the clock is stopped on every whistle. A yellow flag is dropped at the scorer's table to indicate two minutes' playing time remains and a red flag is dropped to indicate 30 seconds of playing time remains.

Starting play The team captains toss for choice of ends. The women's match begins with a "draw." It restarts in the same way after a goal has been scored.

Playing the ball Women players may pass, throw, catch, or carry the ball in their sticks; and roll it. But they may not kick it. A player must be gripping her stick with at least one hand before she can play the ball or become involved in the game in any way. A goalkeeper may catch the ball with her hand but must place it in her stick immediately and clear the ball within 10 seconds.

Scoring A goal is scored when the ball passes completely over the goal line. It may be conceded by a defender, but it cannot be deflected by the foot or leg of an attacker, or by a non-player. A goal cannot be scored: after an official has whistled; after the period has ended; if any part of the attacker is inside the goal crease; or when the attacking team has too many players on the field.

Neutral throw In women's lacrosse, the game may be restarted with a throw: if two players are equidistant from the ball when it goes out of bounds or play is stopped; when the ball lodges in a stick or clothing; when two opposing players foul simultaneously; when the ball goes into the goal off a non-player; when an unintentional incident has stopped play;

when the game has been stopped for any other reason.
Sticks and bodies must be 1m apart for a throw. The umpire stands with her back to the center of the field, 5–10m from the players, and throws the ball with a short high throw so that the players take it as they move in.
Play may not resume within 8m of the crease line or 4m of the agreed boundaries. No throw is permitted within 4m of the agreed side boundary, or 8m of the goal crease.

Out of bounds The boundaries are agreed by the umpires and captains before a match. If a ball goes out-of-bounds it is given to the nearest player to the ball regardless of the last team in possession, except for deliberate running of the ball out of bounds, when a minor foul is awarded to the opposing team. The player gaining possession of the out-of-bounds must be given 1m of clear space.

Goal crease fouls Only the goalkeeper or someone deputizing for her may enter the goal crease. The goal crease extends upward in an imaginary cylinder. Only one player may be inside the goal circle at any one time. Penalty for infringement – minor foul – 8m from the goal crease to the side. Should the goalkeeper's stick extend outside the goal crease, her stick may be checked by an opponent. The maximum time the ball may be inside the goal circle is 10 seconds.

Fouls A two tier system of dealing with fouls exists depending on the severity of the infringment. For major fouls such as body contact, dangerous play, severe misconduct and repeated minor fouls, a "free position," with the offender placed 4m behind the ball-carrier is given. For a minor foul, eg tackling a stick when the opponent is about to receive the ball, playing with an illegal stick and kicking the ball, a "free-position" is awarded to the innocent team. A player sent-off may be replaced by another team-member, but the oncoming player may not re-enter the field of play until three minutes have elapsed.

Penalties In women's lacrosse a "free position" is awarded for all fouls: the player who has been fouled is given the ball, and all other players must be at least 4m away. On the whistle, the player with the ball may pass, run, or shoot.

The draw is used to start the game. The two center players stand each with one foot toeing the center line. They hold their sticks in the air, about hip level, wood to wood, plastic to plastic, parallel to the center line, so that each stick is between the ball and the player's goal. No other player may be within 10m.
All other players must be outside the center circle until the umpire has called "ready, draw." The two players then draw their sticks up and away from each other. A player may turn her stick under the ball as the stick is swept away. A left-handed player may swing her stick behind her head instead of in front of it.

Stand rule Except after a goal, when the whistle blows all players must "stand" and retain their relative position on the field. No player may move until the umpire calls play.

The draw

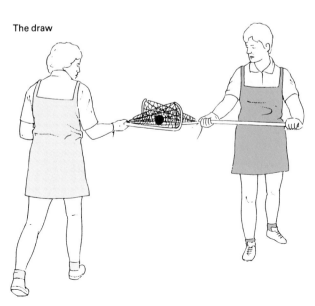

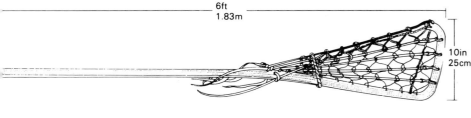

6ft
1.83m

10in
25cm

The stick is strung so that the ball should not become lodged in it, and shaped so that it cannot be used to hook an opponent or his/her stick. Metal is allowed on the handles of sticks.

Women's lacrosse
length: 91–112cm (36–44in); width: 18–23cm (7–9in).

Men's lacrosse
length 101.6–182.8cm (40–72 in);
width: 10.1–25.4cm (4–10in) although the goalkeeper's stick may be up to 38.1cm (15in) wide.

The ball India rubber, colored yellow, white or black. In women's lacrosse an orange ball denotes a low bounce indoor ball. It should weigh 142–149gm (5–5¼oz) and bounce 1.1m–1.3m (44–51in) when dropped from 1.8m (72in) onto concrete. Its circumference is 20–20.3cm (7¾–8in).

Dress Women goalkeepers are allowed to wear helmets and/or facemasks and throat protectors. Gloves and padding on the arms and legs are permitted, as long as they do not overly increase the size of the hands, arms and legs of the player.
All players must wear numbers differing from others on their shirts. Markings on the back must be at least 20cm tall and 10cm on the front. Close-fitting gloves, noseguards, eye guards and mouth guards may be worn by all players.

Dress
Men players wear:
1 shirt numbered front and back;
2 helmets and face-guards;
3 shorts or tracksuit trousers;
4 elbow pads;
5 gauntlets;
6 shin guards.
Goalkeepers may also wear:
7 body pad;
8 thigh pads.

© DIAGRAM

MEN'S LACROSSE
Teams The 10 players in a men's team are the goalkeeper, three defenders, three midfielders, and three attackmen. Each team must at all times keep four players in its own half, and three in the opposing side's half. For international events, men's teams may have up to 13 substitutes and substitution may be made at any stoppage of play and "on the fly" (some countries have more restrictive substitution laws).
Each team has a playing captain, and only he may appeal to officials.
Officials
3 referees on the field;
a chief bench official;
a timekeeper;
a scorer, who records goals and fouls;
2 penalty time-keepers.

Duration Men play four "quarters" each of 25 minutes playing time. Teams change ends after each quarter. There is a 10-minute interval at half time, and there are 2 minutes between 1st and 2nd quarters, and 3 minutes between 3rd and 4th quarters.
A team is allowed two time-outs per half, of up to 90 seconds each. They may be called only when the ball is dead, or when the ball is in the possession of that team and in the opponents' half.

Pitch For men's lacrosse the dimensions of the pitch are as follows:
width: 54.86m (60yd);
wing area line to side line: 9.14m (10yd);
wing area line to center spot: 18.29m (20yd);
center line to goal area line: 18.29m (20yd).

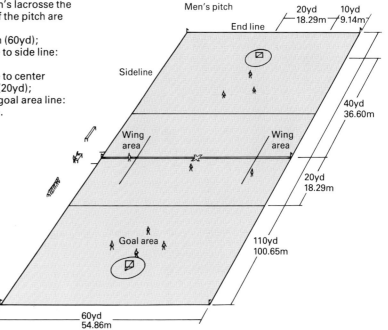

Men's pitch

End line

20yd
18.29m

10yd
9.14m

Sideline

40yd
36.60m

Wing area

Wing area

20yd
18.29m

Goal area

110yd
100.65m

60yd
54.86m

Overtime If the scores are equal at full-time, then two 4-minute overtime periods are played, each team being allowed one time-out per overtime period. The teams change ends between the periods.

If the scores are still tied at the end of the two overtime periods, then the match continues for 4-minute periods, no more times-out allowed, until a goal is scored, thus deciding the winner. The teams change ends between these "sudden death" overtime periods.

Starting play The team captains toss for choice of ends. The match begins with a "face." It restarts in the same way after intervals, goals, and some stoppages.

Playing the ball Players may pass, throw, catch, or carrry the ball in their sticks and roll or kick it.

A goalkeeper may touch the ball with his hand, but only to deflect a shot within his goal crease – he must not catch or throw it.

A player must be gripping his stick with at least one hand before he can play the ball or become involved in the game in any way.

Scoring A goal is scored when the ball passes completely over the goal line. It may be conceded by a defender or by a non-player. A goal cannot be scored: after an official has whistled; after the period has ended; if offside applies; if part of the attacker is inside the goal crease; or when the attacking team has too many players on the field.

A goal may be kicked.

Out of play The ball is out of play if it, or the player in possession of it, passes over a boundary line (**1**). Possession is given against the team that last touched the ball – except for "out of play" after a shot at goal, when the ball is awarded to the player of either side nearest to the ball when it went out. The game is restarted by a free play. All other players must be at least 2.74m from the team member taking the play (**2**).

Entering the goal crease The goal crease is the circle surrounding each goal area. No attacking player is allowed within the crease at any time. If he touches the ground within the crease with any part of his body (**3**), his side loses possession. But he may reach into the crease to catch the ball or play a loose ball (**4**).

If the goalkeeper gains possession of the ball while within the crease, his stick may not be checked by an opponent. But the goalkeeper, or any defender with the ball, may only remain within the crease for 4 seconds. No defender in possession of the ball may enter the crease.

Offside If a men's team does not have its players properly distributed in the two halves, it is offside. If a team has four or more players off the field in the penalty box, it will not be penalized for having fewer than four players in its own half, provided it keeps three players in the opponents' half and the rest in its own.

The face The ball is placed on the ground between the backs of the sticks of two opposing players, who crouch with their backs to the goal they are defending. Their sticks must be parallel to and touching the ground and 25.4mm apart. Their hands must be on the handles of their sticks, not touching the stringing of the stick. The ball is rested between the backs of the sticks.

When the referee blows his whistle, the two players attempt to direct the ball with sticks or feet.

No other player may stand within 9.1m.

A face may be used after a stoppage in any part of the field, except within 18.2m of the goal line or 6m of a boundary line. A face at the center spot is used at the start of a quarter or after a goal is scored.

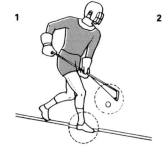

1

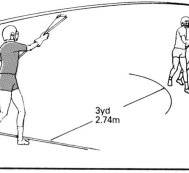

2
3yd
2.74m

3

4

Tackling Men players may charge an opponent. A player may "take out" an opponent, usually done by hitting him with the shoulder, provided that the opponent has possession of the ball, or is within 2.7m of a loose ball. The contact must be above the knees and below the neck, and not from the rear (**1**). A player may check an opponent's stick with his own if the opponent has possession of the ball, or is within 2.7m of a loose ball (**2**).

1

2

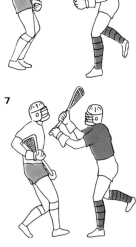

3

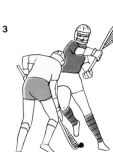

4

5

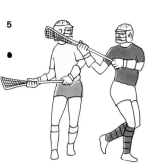

6

7

Fouls A player may not: charge an opponent in a reckless or dangerous manner (**3**); hold or trip an opponent (**4**); interfere with an opponent's stick, except by a legal stick check; strike an opponent with the stick (**5**); obstruct or impede an opponent (**6**), except by a legal body check or a legal hold (an opponent does not have to move from an opponent's path); throw the stick; wave or hold the stick in front of an opponent (**7**).

Penalties Time penalties are awarded for fouls. For "technical" (ie minor) fouls: the ball is either given to the other team, or the offending player is suspended for 30 seconds.

For "personal" fouls, players are suspended for 1–3 minutes. For "expulsion" fouls (flagrant offenses against other players or officials), a player may be suspended for the rest of the game.

Roller hockey

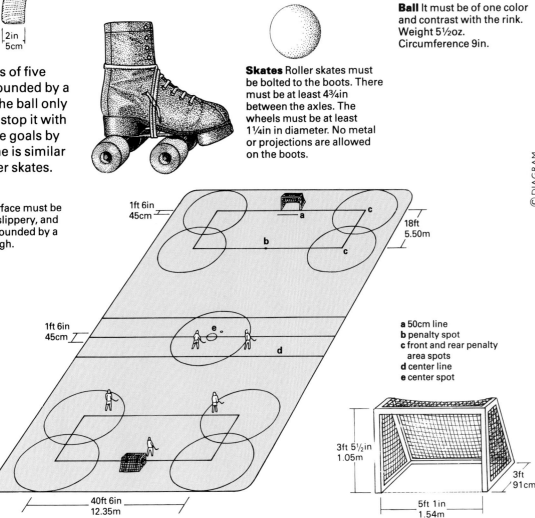

The stick must be of the dimensions shown and must not weigh more than 18oz. It is made of wood and must have no metal parts. Binding is allowed. The blade must be curved, and flat on both sides.
Ball It must be of one color and contrast with the rink. Weight 5½oz. Circumference 9in.

3ft—3ft 9in
91—114cm

2in
5cm

Skates Roller skates must be bolted to the boots. There must be at least 4¾in between the axles. The wheels must be at least 1¼in in diameter. No metal or projections are allowed on the boots.

Roller hockey is played by two teams of five players on a firm and level rink surrounded by a barrier. Players are allowed to play the ball only with their sticks, although they may stop it with any part of their bodies. Teams score goals by hitting the ball into the net. The game is similar to ice hockey, but it is played on roller skates.

1ft 6in
45cm

18ft
5.50m

1ft 6in
45cm

40ft 6in
12.35m

a 50cm line
b penalty spot
c front and rear penalty area spots
d center line
e center spot

3ft 5½in
1.05m

3ft
91cm

5ft 1in
1.54m

© DIAGRAM

Dress Players wear protective padding including knee pads. Only goalkeepers may wear pads on their legs outside their clothing. Goalkeepers are allowed to wear helmets, face masks, and gloves.

Teams Each team has five players, including a goalkeeper. It must have a further additional goalkeeper and may have four substitutes. There must always be at least three players on the rink.
Substitution Players can be substituted during the game; goalkeepers only during a stoppage.
Officials include a referee who controls the game, assisted by:
two goal judges;
two timekeepers;
an official to keep a record of the match.
Starting Captains toss for choice of ends or the right to commence play. If the winning captain chooses ends, then the losing team commences play. The game then starts at the center.
Face-off Two opponents face each other, with their backs to their own goals. Their sticks must be before them, the blades touching the floor and 9in behind the ball. They play the ball when the referee whistles.
Duration In international matches a game consists of two periods, each of 20 minutes playing time. Otherwise, a half varies from 10—25 minutes. There is an interval of 3 minutes.
Extra time If both sides are equal at the end of the regular playing time, a 3-minute rest is allowed. Then the teams begin a play-off, with the first team to score a goal winning. If neither team has scored after 10 minutes, they are given another 3-minute rest, then change ends, and begin another 10-minute period. This system is continued until a winner is determined.

Rink The surface must be firm but not slippery, and must be surrounded by a barrier 8in high.

Playing the ball A player may only play the ball with his stick, which may not be raised above his shoulders. He may stop the ball with his skates or any part of his body provided it is not knocked forward to his team's advantage.
He is not allowed to kick, pick up, carry, push, or drag the ball with any part of his body or his skates.
When shooting, it is forbidden to hit the ball with the acute edge of the blade (chopping);
the ball may be hit only with the flat part of the blade. The ball must not rise above 5ft, except when it ricochets off two sticks outside the penalty area.
(Inside the penalty area a face-off is awarded from the nearest base spot.)
The goalkeeper is allowed to play the ball within his penalty area with any part of his body, including his hands, even if he is on the ground. If the ball lodges in his clothing or in the external netting of the goal, a face-off is awarded from the nearest base spot in the penalty area.

Players are not allowed to interfere with play:
if a skate is damaged or removed from the boot;
if the wheels of a skate are not running freely;
without a stick;
when holding the barrier or the goal cage (the goalkeeper is allowed to hold onto his goal cage).
Scoring The whole of the ball must cross the line between the posts.
Out of play If the ball is played out of the rink, the opposition is awarded an indirect free hit. It is taken 2½ ft from where the ball crossed the barrier. A face-off is awarded: if the ball ricochets off two sticks out of play; if it was deliberately played to obtain a free hit; or if the referee is uncertain which team last played the ball.
Fouls Players are not allowed to:
play the ball illegally;
charge unfairly;
obstruct deliberately;
fight, trip, kick, throw, hold an opponent, use the stick against an opponent;
tackle unfairly.

Penalties Violations of the rules may be penalized as follows.
An indirect free hit, usually called a free hit, may be awarded. The ball must be stationary for the hit. Opponents must be at least 9ft away. The player taking the hit may not play the ball again until it has been touched by another player. A goal may not be scored direct from an indirect free hit.
A direct free hit is awarded for more serious fouls. All players, except the one taking the hit and the goalkeeper, must be 15ft behind the ball; they must not move until the ball is played. The goalkeeper must be behind the crease line, but his stick may be in front of it. A goal may be scored direct, but a direct shot is not necessary.
A penalty shot is a direct shot from the penalty spot, awarded for grave or serious infringement of rules within the penalty area. All players, except the one taking the penalty shot and the goalkeeper, must be behind the center line. The

goalkeeper must be behind the 50cm line. The player taking the penalty may shoot directly toward the goal mouth, or he may bring the ball by skating. No player, including the goalkeeper, may move until the ball is played and the referee has sounded his whistle. The striker may not play the ball again unless it has hit the goalkeeper or the outside of the goal or has been played by another player. The player who takes a shot directly toward the goal mouth may not replay the ball if this has been rebounded off the barrier without any player replaying the ball.
Expulsion A player may be sent off for any period up to 5 minutes' playing time, or for the rest of the game. He can be replaced by a substitute. For a second offense, a player must be sent off for the rest of the match.
A player shown a red card cannot be replaced by a substitute.

Field hockey

Hockey is a field game played by both men and women. Each team has 11 players, who use a stick with a hook which forms the head to hit the ball along the ground. The object of the game is to send the ball into the opponents' goal, and the team to score the greater number of goals wins.

The pitch conforms to the measurements shown. The field is rectangular, 100yd long and 60yd wide. The boundaries are clearly marked out with lines.

Officials Two umpires (**1**) and one or two timekeepers. Each umpire supervises play in his/her own half of the field, without changing ends, for the whole of the game and controls the game with a whistle. An umpire may not enforce a penalty when by doing so an advantage would be given to the offending team.

Duration There are two periods of 35 minutes each. Teams change ends at half time, when there is an interval of 5–10 minutes. In the event of an injury, the game is suspended and lost time is added to the second half.

Playing the ball Players may only control the ball with the flat side of their sticks, but within his own circle the goalkeeper may kick or propel the ball with his own feet or pads unless the propelled ball is considered dangerous.

Starting play Team captains toss for choice of start. The winner of the toss has either: the right to choose which end his team will attack in the first half; or the right to have possession of the ball at the start of the game.

The opposing side will automatically have the second option. The team not having started the game has possession of the ball for re-starting the game after half-time.

The pass back is made at the center of the field to start the game (also after half-time and after each goal is scored).

The ball, which may be pushed or hit, must not be directed over the center line. All players of the opposing team must stand at least 5yd from the ball and all players of both teams, other than the player making the pass-back, must be in their own half of the field.

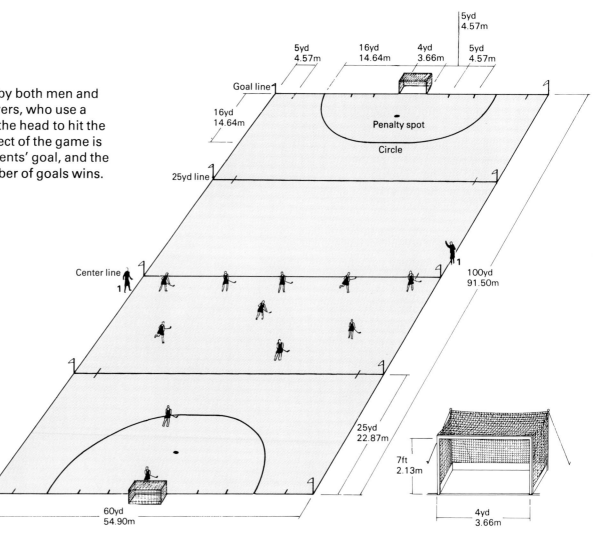

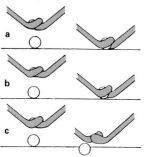

Shinguard

Scoring A goal is scored when the whole ball has passed over the goal-line between the posts and under the crossbar, provided it has been played by an attacker from within the striking circle. (It is valid if the ball is deflected off a defender.) If the posts or bar are displaced, the umpire decides if the goal is valid.

The bully To restart the game after an incident or after an accident, a bully is played on the spot where the incident or accident occurred.

One player from each team stands squarely facing the sidelines, with his own goal-line to his right. The ball is placed on the ground between the two players, and each then taps his stick first on the ground on his own side of the ball, then – with the face of the stick – his opponent's stick above the ball. This is done three times, after which one player must strike the ball.

A bully must not be played within 16yd of the backline or goal-line.

Teams Teams have a maximum of 11 players including a captain. Each team is allowed to substitute up to three players during the game, during any stoppage of play other than following the award of a penalty corner or penalty stroke.

Dress Shirt, shorts (or skirt). No dangerous objects or boots with metal studs, spikes, or nails may be worn.

Goalkeepers The following equipment is permitted: faceguard (**1**), gauntlet gloves (**2**), pads (**3**), kickers, headgear and elbow pads.

The bully

a

b

c

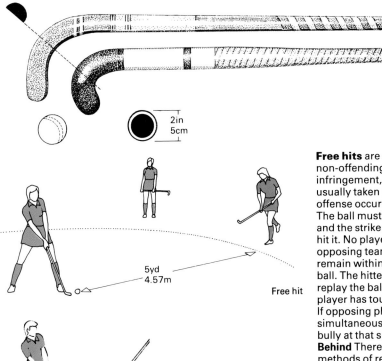

The stick has a flat face on its left-hand side. The head is made of wood, and must have no metal fittings, sharp edges or splinters. The total weight of the stick must not exceed 28oz nor be less than 12oz. It must be narrow enough to pass, inclusive of any covering, through a ring having an interior diameter of 2in.

The ball is traditionally white but a ball of any other color may be used. It weighs 5½–5¾oz and has a diameter of 8¹³⁄₁₆–9¼in. The ball which is hard may be solid or hollow. The ball often has a core of rubber and cork covered with man-made materials such as PVC and Porvair.

2in
5cm

Free hit

Hit in

Free hits are awarded to the non-offending side for infringement, and are usually taken where the offense occurred.
The ball must be stationary and the striker must push or hit it. No player of the opposing team should remain within 5yd of the ball. The hitter may not replay the ball until another player has touched it.
If opposing players foul simultaneously, they take a bully at that spot.
Behind There are three methods of restarting play if the ball crosses the goal-line without scoring.
A free hit occurs from 16yd opposite where the ball

crossed the line if the ball was last played by an attacker, or if a defender unintentionally hit it over the line from at least 25yd away.
A corner is awarded to the attacker if a defender plays the ball unintentionally over the line from less than 25yd away.
A penalty corner is given if a defender intentionally plays the ball over the goal-line.
Ball passes the side-line
If the ball passes completely over the side-line, it is placed on the line at the spot at which it crossed the side-line. A player of the opposing team may push or hit the ball.

5yd
4.57m

1 Dangerous play

2 Tripping

3 Charging

A corner hit is taken by an attacker on the back-line within 5yd of the corner flag nearer to the point where the ball crossed the back-line. The player taking the penalty corner may hit or push from the back-line but may not, after striking the ball, approach or remain within playing distance of the ball until it has been touched or played by another player of either team.
Fouls A player must not: raise any part of his stick above the shoulder when playing or attempting to play the ball (**1**); trip (**2**), shove, charge (**3**), strike, or handle an opponent:
obstruct an opponent with the body or stick;

play the ball with the rounded side of the stick; interfere in the game without a stick; stop the ball with his hand or catch it; undercut or play the ball in a potentially dangerous way; stop or deflect the ball on the ground or in the air with any part of his body (except for the goalkeeper); deliberately raise the ball so that it will fall into the circle; use the foot or leg to support the stick in order to resist an opponent; or kick, pick up, throw, carry or propel the ball except with the stick.

Penalty corners are awarded against defenders for:
deliberately playing the ball over the back line;
offenses within the circle (unless a penalty stroke is taken);
after a deliberate foul within the 25yd line;
after an infringement at a corner.
It is taken anywhere on the goal-line, at least 10yd from the goalpost. The rest of the attacking team must be outside the circle. Not more than five of the defending team are permitted to stand behind their own goal-line or back-line. The rest of the defending team must be beyond the center-line.

© DIAGRAM

Offside A player (**1**) is off-side if he is within his opponents' half when the ball is played by a teammate (**2**) further from the goal-line than he is, and when there are fewer than two opponents nearer the goal-line than he is. An offside player is only penalized if he gains an advantage.

An offside is penalized by a free hit to the opposition at the spot where it occurred.
Ball outside the field of play When the ball passes completely over the back line and no goal is scored, or over the side-line, it is out of play and the game is restarted.

A penalty stroke is awarded against defenders in the circle for an intentional foul, an unintentional foul that prevents a goal, or persistent and deliberate positioning infringements at penalty corners.
It is taken from a spot 7yd in front of the center of the goal by an attacker, who may take one step forward to push, flick or scoop the ball. Thereafter, he may not replay the ball or approach the goal. The goalkeeper must stand on the goal-line. After the player taking the stroke and the goalkeeper are in position and the umpire has blown his whistle, the goalkeeper must not leave the goal-line or

move his feet until the ball has been played. All other players must stand beyond the 25yd line.
If the goalkeeper illegally prevents a goal, it is still awarded unless the attacker induced the offense. If the ball should come to rest inside the circle, be lodged in the goalkeeper's pads, be caught by the goalkeeper, or pass outside the circle, the penalty stroke is ended. If no goal is scored, or if an attacker commits an offense, the game restarts with a free hit 16yd in front of the center of the goal-line.

Hurling

Hurling is a Gaelic field game played by two teams of 15 players. The ball may be struck with or carried on the hurley and, when off the ground, may be struck with the hand or kicked. The object is to score most points. A goal (3 points) is scored when the ball passes between the posts and under the crossbar; one point is scored when it passes between the posts and over the crossbar.

Pitch The minimum size is 130m by 80m; the maximum 145m by 90m.

Teams Each team has 15 players and may have three substitutes. Substitution is permitted only during a stoppage.

Officials The game is controlled by a referee (**1**). He is assisted by two linesmen (**2**), who change sides at half time, and four goal umpires (**3**), who stand one outside each goalpost and do not change ends at half time.

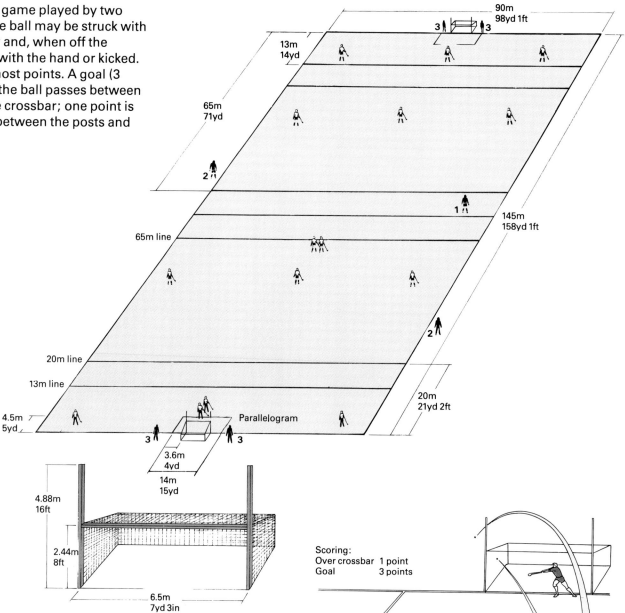

90m
98yd 1ft

13m
14yd

65m
71yd

145m
158yd 1ft

65m line

20m
21yd 2ft

20m line

13m line

4.5m
5yd

Parallelogram

3.6m
4yd

14m
15yd

4.88m
16ft

2.44m
8ft

6.5m
7yd 3in

Scoring:
Over crossbar 1 point
Goal   3 points

Start The captains toss for choice of ends. Two players from each side then line up at the center and the other players position themselves behind their own 65m line. The referee then throws the ball along the ground between the players.

Duration Playing time is 70 minutes, with a maximum interval of 10 minutes at half time, after which the teams change ends.

Scoring The team scoring most points wins.

A goal (3 points) is scored when the entire ball passes between the posts and under the crossbar, except when thrown or carried by a member of the attacking team.

A point is scored when the ball passes between the posts and over the crossbar, except when thrown by a member of the attacking team.

Scores are disallowed if an attacking player enters the parallelogram before the ball. They are valid if the ball returns to the parallelogram before an attacker can leave the area, providing he is not involved in the play, or if the ball is too high to be reached by players in the parallelogram. Goals and points may be awarded at the referee's discretion if the posts or crossbar are displaced.

Playing the ball The ball may be kicked or struck with the hand when off the ground; it must not be carried or thrown except on the hurley. The ball may not be touched on the ground with the hand. Carrying is taking more than three steps while holding the ball. A player may catch the ball only twice before hitting it.

Throw in The referee throws the ball between opponents to restart play after half time, simultaneous fouls by opposing players, and in certain instances when play has been interrupted.

The hurley is a curved stick with a broad blade. It is 4in at its widest and tapers to each end. Its weight is 567–680g.

The ball generally has a cork center with a cover of horsehide.
Circumference 23–25in.
Weight 100–130g.

3ft
91cm

Dress Players wear:
1 shirt
2 shorts
3 socks
4 boots
5 helmet (optional)

Penalties

A free puck is awarded for infringements. It is taken where the offense occurred unless:
a) the offense was committed by a defender in the 20m area (when it is taken from the opposite point on the 20m line);
b) a player is fouled after delivering the ball (when it is taken where the ball lands, unless a goal is scored or the ball goes out of play, in which case the free puck is taken where the ball went out). Except for sideline pucks, the ball must be on the ground or lifted with the hurley and struck above the ground. The ball may not be transferred from the hurley to the hand at a free puck. The player may not play the ball again until it has been touched by another player. If it hits a non-player direct from the free puck, the free puck is retaken.
If a player stands within 20m or illegally charges a free puck, the opposing team is awarded a free puck from where he stood or charged.

A puck-out is awarded to the defenders when an attacker hits the ball across the end line. It is taken from within the parallelogram.
The ball may be held, but must be hit on the first stroke; if missed, it may not be held again but may be raised or pucked off the ground.
The player may hit the ball more than once before another player touches it. All opponents must be beyond the 20m line. If the opposition encroaches into the 20m area, the defense takes a free puck on that line opposite where the offender stood.

A 65m free puck is awarded to the attacking team when the ball is played over the end line by a defender. It is taken on the 65m line, opposite where the ball crossed the line.
If a player stands within 20m or charges before it is taken, a free puck is awarded from where he charged or stood.

A side puck is awarded against a player who plays the ball over the sideline. It is taken as a free puck where the ball crossed the line. The linesman positions the ball; the player may not move it before striking it.
All other players must be at least 13m away; a free puck is awarded after an offense.

Tackling A player may charge an opponent shoulder to shoulder. A player is not fouled if he turns deliberately to make a fair charge come from behind.
A goalkeeper may not be charged within the parallelogram, unless he has the ball or is obstructing an opponent.
A player may strike another player's hurley only if both are striking the ball.

Fouls A player may not:
push, kick, trip (**1**), hold, strike, or jump at an opponent;
obstruct a player with his hand or arm, even if not holding him;
reach from behind a player who has the ball;
charge a player from behind (**2**), or charge or interfere with an opponent who is not playing the ball or moving to play the ball;
deliberately touch a player with the hurley;
reach for the ball with the hurley over another player;
throw the hurley.

Interference If anyone but a player prevents the ball crossing the sidelines, a side puck is awarded against the last player to hit the ball. A goal, point or 65m puck is awarded if the ball is similarly prevented from scoring or from crossing an end line.

Expulsion The referee may send off any player guilty of violent or threatening conduct. A whole team may be disqualified and suspended for rough play. Players may also be cautioned.

1 Foul – tripping

2 Foul – barging in the back

© DIAGRAM

Shinty

Shinty is a Gaelic field game of Scottish origin, played by two teams of 12 men each. A caman (club) is used to hit a ball, and the object is to score goals in a match lasting 90 minutes, divided into two halves.

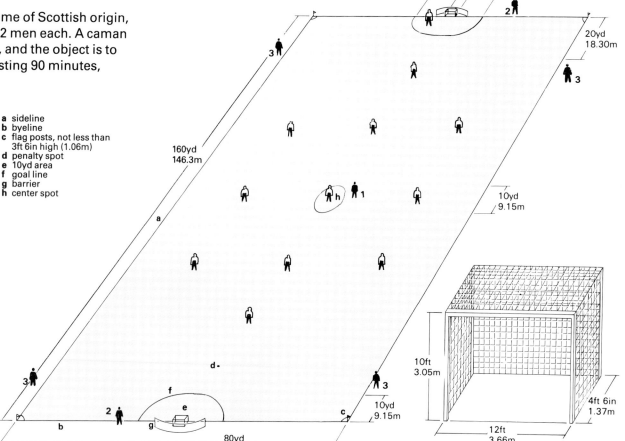

The field is rectangular as shown in the diagram. The size of the field may be as follows:
length: 140yd (128m) – 170yd (155m);
breadth: 70yd (64m) – 80yd (73m).
Most fields are 80yd (73m)×160yd (146m).
The front of the goalposts are white. Only at the top may the front and back goalposts be connected by a bar, strut, or board.
The byelines and sidelines should be fenced.
Alternatively, both goals should be protected by a barrier of wood, wire, or rope a minimum distance of 15ft from either side of the goalposts. All fences, posts, etc, except corner flags, are at least 6ft from byelines and sidelines.

a sideline
b byeline
c flag posts, not less than 3ft 6in high (1.06m)
d penalty spot
e 10yd area
f goal line
g barrier
h center spot

Players Each team has 12 players. A team may substitute any two players during a match.
Dress Players wear jerseys, shorts, socks, and boots without spikes or tackets (hobnails or studs). The goalkeeper must wear a jersey of a different color.
Officials The referee (**1**) controls the game. He is assisted by goal judges and linesmen, who do not change ends at half time and report only at the referee's request. Goal judges (**2**) observe goal scoring, fouls in the 10yd area, when the ball crosses the goal line and who last hit it, and whether an attacker is in the 10yd area when the ball enters it. Linesmen (**3**) are responsible for one half of a sideline each. They observe when the ball crosses the sideline and who hit it.
Duration Games last 90 minutes, with an interval of at least 5 minutes at half time. Extra time is allowed for a penalty hit to be taken. The ball must be in play when each half ends.

The start Play is begun and restarted after a goal and half time with a throw up in the center.
The throw up The referee blows his whistle and starts the game by throwing up the ball to a minimum height of 12ft between two opposing players standing on the center spot.
The two players must stand at least 3ft apart, with camans crossed. They shall not move away until the ball is hit in the air or touches the ground.
If the two center players are one left-handed and one right, each has choice of his side in the throw up for half the match.
No other player is allowed within 5yd of the center spot until the ball is played.
Playing the ball Players may use both sides of the caman to hit the ball.
Only the goalkeeper may use his hands to stop or control the ball.
Kicking the ball is not allowed.
The ball may be passed without touching the ground.

A throw up

A player within striking distance of the ball is allowed to hook an opponent's caman.
Scoring For a goal to be scored, the ball must pass wholly over the goal line between the posts and under the crossbar.

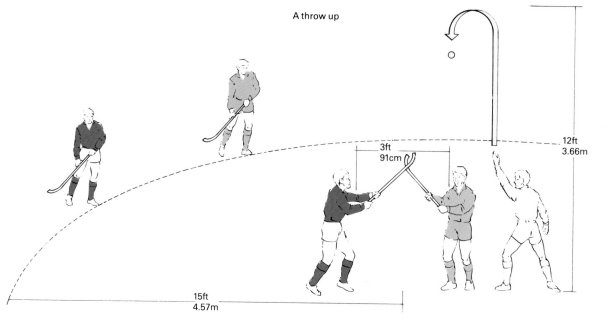

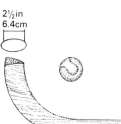

2½in
6.4cm

The caman (club) is wooden, without metal attachments. It should not stand higher than hip level. The "bas" (head) must pass through a 2½in diameter ring. The "bas" is triangular, the "cas" (shaft) cylindrical. Leather or tape binding is used to give a good grip.

The ball is made of cork and worsted, with a leather covering.
Weight: 2½–3½oz.
Circumference: 7½–8in.

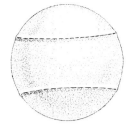

Out of play

A 10yd hit is awarded from anywhere within the 10yd area to the defending side if an attacker sends the ball across the byeline without a goal being scored.

A corner hit is awarded from the 2yd quarter circle to the attacking side if a defender hits the ball across his own byeline. A goal may be scored directly from a corner hit.

A hit in is awarded to the opposition if the ball is accidently hit across the sideline.

The hit is taken where the ball crossed the line. The player faces the pitch with both feet on the ground. No player may be within 5yd of the striker before the ball is in the air. The ball is returned to the field by an overhead hit with the back of the caman.

If the player misses the ball completely, he may not retake the hit. If he does not take the hit correctly, it is awarded to the opposition. If he hits the ball more than once, a set blow is awarded to the opposition. After the hit, the striker may not participate again until another player has hit the ball. A goal may be scored directly from a hit in.

Offside An attacker can only be offside if he is in the 10yd area when the ball enters it.

A set blow to the opponents is the penalty imposed for infringements, including offside, unless it would give an advantage to the offender. The ball is placed on the ground where the infringement occurred and is struck with the club in any direction.

No other player may be within 5yd of the striker until the blow is taken, or the referee may order a retake. If the player misses the ball completely, the blow is retaken.

After the blow, the striker may not participate again until the ball has touched the club, body, or clothing of another player. A goal may not be scored directly from a set blow.

A hit in

A set blow

Offside

Fouls No player shall: kick (**1**), catch (**2**), or throw the ball (though the goalkeeper inside his 10yd area may stop and slap the ball with his open hand); use his hands, arms, legs, knees, or club to hold, obstruct, push, charge, trip, hack, jump at, or throw an opponent; deliberately throw his caman at the ball, or join play without his caman, or part of it, in his hand (**3**); deliberately hinder another player while not himself playing the ball (he is penalized for obstruction) (**4**); deliberately put the ball over the sideline (a set blow is awarded to the opposition at the point of striking); cleek (hook) an opponent's caman when the player is not himself within striking distance of the ball (**5**); Hooking when within striking distance of the ball is allowed (**6**).

Cautions and suspension

The referee may caution or expel a player for: rough or reckless play; misconduct; wilful infringement of the rules; or unsporting speech or behavior on the field. A suspended player may not be replaced.

Penalty hit A penalty hit is awarded against a defender for an infringement in the 10yd area.

The ball is hit direct at goal from the penalty spot. Until the hit is taken, all players except the striker and defending goalkeeper, who shall remain on his goal line, must stand behind and not closer than 5yd to the ball. The referee may order a retake if players are out of position. If the ball fails to reach the goal line, the hit is deemed a bye and the ball is played by a defender. If the ball strikes the goalposts or crossbar and rebounds onto the field, it shall be in play.

The striker may not hit the ball again until another player has touched it. A goal may be scored directly from a penalty hit.

1

2

3

4

5

©DIAGRAM

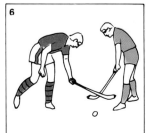

6

Ice hockey

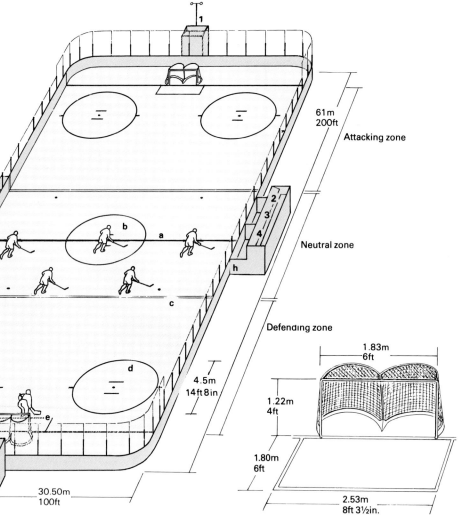

Ice hockey is played by two teams on an ice surface known as a rink. Five players and a goalkeeper from each team are allowed on the ice at any time. The object is to score points by hitting the puck with the stick into the opposing team's goal.

61m 200ft

Attacking zone

Neutral zone

Defending zone

4.5m 14ft 8in

30.50m 100ft

1.83m 6ft

1.22m 4ft

1.80m 6ft

2.53m 8ft 3½in.

Rink Maximum dimensions are shown. Rinks for international matches have:
a center line;
b center circle;
c zone marking;
d face-off circle;
e goal crease;
f goal judge's box;
g team benches;
h penalty bench;
i boards.
Boards must be:
without obstruction on the side facing the rink;
white in color;
uniform in height, from 1.1–1.2m (40–48in).
Goals must be of approved design and materials, and placed so as to remain stationary during the game. Posts, crossbar and framework must be red.

Team benches, one for each team, should hold 19 persons. Only players in uniform, managers, coaches, doctors and trainers are allowed on the benches. The coach must stay within an area the length of his bench.
Penalty bench with space for eight players (two areas with room for four players from each team) and extra seating for the timekeepers, scorer and announcer.
Officials There must be:
one referee and two linesmen;
two goal judges (**1**);
game timekeeper (**2**);
penalty timekeeper (**3**);
official scorer (**4**).

Players A team may have 18 players and a regular and spare goalkeeper in uniform at the start of a game. Players must wear numbers and a list of final names and numbers must be given to the referee or scorer before the start.

A team may have only six players, including a goalkeeper, in play at any time; a bench minor penalty is imposed for an offense.

Goalkeeper A team may have only one goalkeeper on the ice at any time. Another player may be substituted for the goalkeeper, but without goalkeepers' privileges.

Starting line-up The visitors' manager or coach shall when asked:
give his starting line-up to the referee or scorer before the start of a game and place a playing line-up on the ice. A minor penalty is imposed if the starting line-up is changed.
Failure to play If a team in the dressing room fails to appear on the ice with 0.00 remaining on the intermission clock, a minor penalty is imposed. If the team fails to start play within five minutes of being so ordered, it shall forfeit the game and be reported to its federation.
If a team fails to appear because of accidental or unforeseen circumstances, the referee shall allow a

further 15 minutes, after which the game shall be canceled and the incident reported to the authorities. If a team withdrawn from the ice fails to return and play when the referee orders, it shall receive a bench minor penalty after one minute and forfeit the game after 2 minutes.
The official responsible shall be suspended and reported to his federation.
Ends The home team has choice of ends at the start. Teams change ends after each period.
Start The game begins with a face-off at the center of the rink.

Playing line-up
1 goalkeeper
2 right defense
3 left defense
4 center
5 right wing
6 left wing

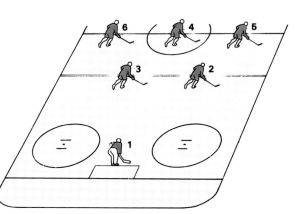

Duration Three 20-minute periods of actual playing time, with 15 minutes break between.
If any unusual delay occurs within 5 minutes of the end of the first or second periods, the referee may order the next intermission to be taken at once and the balance of that period to be added to the next one. The ice is usually flooded between periods.
Result The team scoring most goals wins. In general, if the score is equal after the three regular periods, the game is a tie (subject to national regulations).

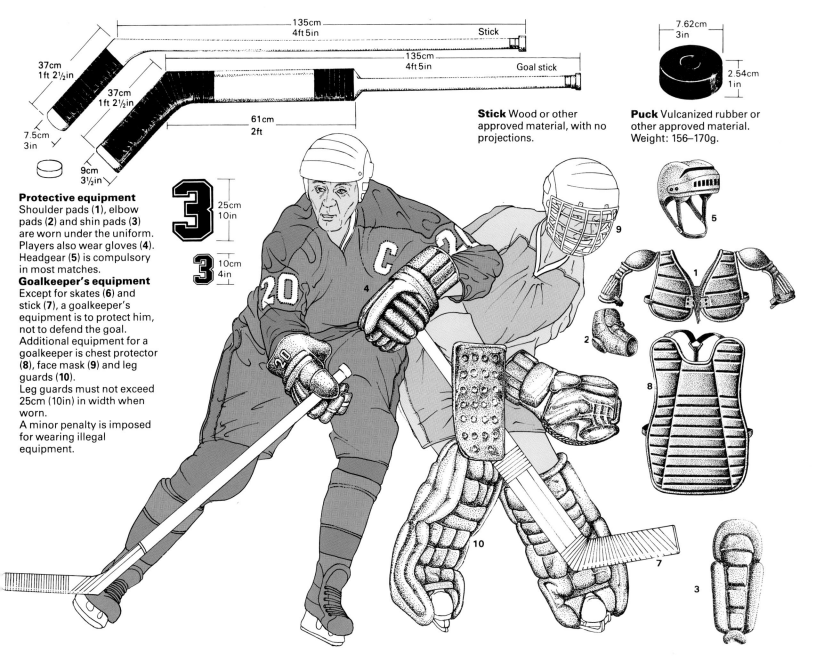

135cm
4ft 5in — Stick

135cm
4ft 5in — Goal stick

61cm
2ft

37cm
1ft 2½in

37cm
1ft 2½in

7.5cm
3in

9cm
3½in

7.62cm
3in

2.54cm
1in

25cm
10in

10cm
4in

Stick Wood or other approved material, with no projections.

Puck Vulcanized rubber or other approved material. Weight: 156–170g.

Protective equipment
Shoulder pads (**1**), elbow pads (**2**) and shin pads (**3**) are worn under the uniform. Players also wear gloves (**4**). Headgear (**5**) is compulsory in most matches.

Goalkeeper's equipment
Except for skates (**6**) and stick (**7**), a goalkeeper's equipment is to protect him, not to defend the goal. Additional equipment for a goalkeeper is chest protector (**8**), face mask (**9**) and leg guards (**10**).
Leg guards must not exceed 25cm (10in) in width when worn.
A minor penalty is imposed for wearing illegal equipment.

Captain A team must appoint a captain and up to two alternate captains, none of whom may be a goalkeeper or playing coach. Their names and numbers must be given to the scorer before play begins. Captains wear a "C" and alternate captains an "A" on their sweaters.

Only one captain or alternate captain, on the ice at the time, may question the referee; a misconduct penalty is imposed if a captain or alternate captain approaches the referee from the bench.

Change of players
Changes from the team bench are allowed at any time, provided any player leaving the ice is out of play. A penalized player who is to be changed when his penalty expires shall, before the change, go by way of the ice to his team bench.
A bench minor penalty is imposed for any offense.

Skates must be of an approved design; speed or fancy skates are prohibited. Players and referees, but not goalkeepers, must wear skate heel guards.

Face-off procedure
The referee or linesman (**1**) "faces" the puck by dropping it on the ice between the sticks of the two players facing.
The facing players (**2**) stand opposite their opponents' end, about a stick-length from the face-off spot (**3**), with feet together behind the face-off line (**4**) and parallel to the rinkside.
No other player may enter the face-off circle (**5**) or come within 4.5m (14ft 10in) of the two players facing. They must be onside.
The facing players' sticks must be full blade on the ice, entirely clear of where the puck will drop and on each player's own side of the face-off spot.

Players must not touch the puck until it reaches the ice.
If after a warning a facing player fails to take up his position promptly, the referee or linesman may face the puck without waiting.
If a facing player touches his opponent's body with his own stick or body, except in playing the puck when the face-off is completed, he is removed from the face-off. The referee shall re-face the puck after a violation during a face-off. He may order the replacement of a facing player who does not immediately take up his proper position.
For a second violation during a face-off the referee or linesman shall throw the player out of the face-off.

Location of face-offs
1 At the center of the rink at the start of play.
2 At the point of stoppage: after an infringement by players from both teams; after a stoppage caused by a defender in his team's defending zone; after a stoppage in the neutral zone; after any stoppage not specifically described in these rules.
(Unless play stopped within 6m (19ft 8in) of the boards, when the face-off shall be on an imaginary line between the face-off spots in each defending zone.)
3 At the nearest face-off spot in the neutral zone if a stoppage was caused by an attacker in his team's attacking zone.

4 At the nearest end face-off spot after a stoppage between the end face-off spots and that end of the rink.

© DIAGRAM

Scoring A team scores one point for each goal. For a goal the puck must legally and completely cross the goal line, between the goalposts and below the crossbar. A maximum of two assists may be awarded.

A goal and assist(s) are scored when:
a) an attacker legally puts the puck into the goal with his stick;
b) the puck is deflected into the goal from the shot of an attacker off the stick, person or skates of a teammate (provided it was not deliberately kicked, thrown or otherwise directed into the goal).
In case a) the goal is credited to the scorer (**2**) and an assist to the player (**1**) or players who took part in the play preceding the shot.
In case b) the goal is credited to the deflecting player and the assist to the shooting player.

A goal but no assist is scored when the puck is shot into the goal by a defender (except as under "inteference"). The goal is credited to the last attacker.

Awarded goals A goal is awarded to the attackers if, when the goalkeeper has been removed from the ice, an attacker with the puck is beyond the center line with no opponent between himself and the goal and is then interfered with by an opponent who:
illegally enters the game;
throws his stick;
fouls him from behind.
A goal is also awarded to the attackers if a goalkeeper throws his stick at the puck or an attacking player at a penalty shot.

Passing Rules govern the passing of the puck from zone to zone. In all cases the position of the puck, not the passing player's skates, determines the zone from which the pass is made.
A pass is completed when the puck touches the body, stick or skates of a teammate who is legally onside.
a) Any player may pass to a teammate in the same zone.
b) A player who was in the zone from which a pass was made may follow and play the puck in any zone, or over his opponents' goal line if the "icing" rule does not apply.
c) A defending team may make and take forward passes from their defending zone to the center line, but the pass must be completed by a player who is onside at the center line or follows the puck over that line.
d) If an attacker passes the puck back from his attacking zone, an opponent who was not in the zone where the pass was made may play the puck anywhere, provided the puck precedes him into his own attacking zone.

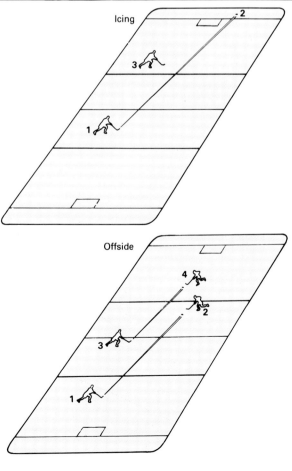

After all other types of pass, a face-off is held where the pass was made.

Icing the puck The puck is iced when a player (**1**) shoots the puck from behind the center line to beyond his opponents' goal line (**2**). The linesman will call "icing" if the player attempted to pass the puck to a teammate who failed to touch it (**3**).
The puck is not iced:
if it enters the goal, in which case the goal counts;
if, from a face-off, it goes beyond the goal line at the other end of the ice;
if the referee considers that an opponent other than the goalkeeper was able to, but did not, play the puck before it passed his goal line;
if an opponent's person, skates or stick touched the puck before it crossed the goal line.
The puck must be touched by a member of the team retrieving the puck after it has crossed his goal line for icing to be called.
If the referee wrongly calls "icing," the puck is faced in the neutral zone at center ice.

Offside A player is offside if both his skates are completely beyond the relevant line when the puck is passed:
from the defending zone (**1**) to beyond the center line (**2**) from the neutral zone (**3**), across the center line, and into the attacking zone (**4**). A player who is offside may stop the puck before it crosses the line, return to his own side of that line, and then hit the puck over it.
If the linesman considers that offside play was deliberate, a face-off is held at the end face-off spot in the offender's defending zone (except when the offender's team has fewer players than its opponents, in which case the face-off is from where the pass was started).

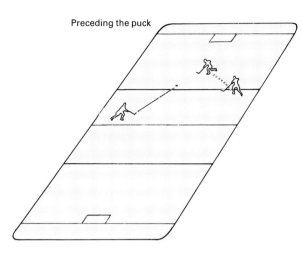

Preceding the puck

© DIAGRAM

Preceding the puck into the attacking zone is obligatory except:
when a player actually propelling the puck was first in possession of the puck with both feet in the neutral zone;
when the puck is cleanly intercepted by a defender and carried or passed into the neutral zone by the defenders;
when the player legally carries or passes the puck back from the neutral zone into his defending zone while an opponent is in the latter zone.
After an offense, a face-off is held in the neutral zone at the face-off spot nearest the offender's attacking zone.

Advancing the puck A minor penalty is imposed if a player, other than a goalkeeper and unless checked by an opponent, deliberately holds the puck against the boards or goal.

Unplayable puck The puck is out of play if it:
a) leaves the playing surface;
b) hits an obstacle above the surface other than the boards, glass, or netting;
c) becomes lodged in the netting on the outside of a goal.
In cases a) and b), if the puck was accidentally put out of play, a face-off is held where the puck last touched a player (except when the rules state otherwise). If the puck was deliberately put out of play, a face-off is held where the offense occurred (except when the rules state otherwise) and a minor penalty is assessed for delay of game. Goaltenders are assessed a minor penalty when they shoot the puck directly over the glass without deflection.
In case c), if the puck was put out of play by a defender, a face-off is held at either end face-off spot. If an attacker was responsible, the face-off is at the nearest face-off spot in the neutral zone.

Puck out of sight If the referee is unable to see the puck in a scramble or under a fallen player, play is stopped and resumed in the same place with a face-off.

Illegal puck If during play another puck appears on the ice, play continues with the legal puck until the end of the play then in progress.

Puck striking referee Play continues if the puck strikes the referee.

Injuries An injured player other than a goalkeeper may be replaced by a substitute without the teams leaving the ice.
An injured goalkeeper shall be replaced by the spare goalkeeper, unless both a team's goalkeepers are injured, in which case the players may leave the ice and the team has 10 minutes to prepare another goalkeeper.
An injured penalized player may go to the dressing room if a substitute sits on the penalty bench. If the injured player returns to his team bench before his penalty expires, he may take his place on the penalty bench when play next stops.
If an injured player is unable to go to his bench, play stops:
a) at once if his team had possession, though they may first shoot if in a shooting position;
b) after the opposing team loses possession if they had possession at the time of the injury, though the referee may stop play at once if an injury is serious.

Broken stick A player may play without a stick, but not with a broken stick.
A new stick must not be thrown to him; he must collect it from his team bench.
A goalkeeper may play with a broken stick until a stop in play, or until he obtains a new stick. A goalkeeper may receive a new stick from a teammate without going to his team bench.
A minor penalty is imposed for any offense. If the goalkeeper illegally receives a stick, the minor penalty is served by a player then on the ice.

Leaving the benches A player who leaves his team bench during a disagreement on the ice shall receive a game misconduct penalty.
A player who leaves the penalty bench except at the end of a period or when his penalty expires is penalized with:
a minor penalty if he does not enter a disturbance on the ice;
a minor penalty plus a game misconduct penalty if he does enter such a disturbance (the penalties to be served at the end of his unexpired penalty).
If a penalty timekeeper's error causes a player to return prematurely to the ice, he shall serve only his unexpired time.
If a player is illegally on the ice (whether by his own error or not):
any goal scored by his team is disallowed;
any penalty imposed on either team is to be served.

Interference A minor penalty is imposed if a player:
interferes with or impedes the progress of an opponent not in possession of the puck;
deliberately knocks the stick from an opponent's hands, or prevents an opponent who has lost his stick from retrieving it;
by means of his stick or body interferes with or impedes the movements of the goalkeeper by actual contact while the goalkeeper, but not the puck, is in the goal crease;
when on either bench, uses his stick or body to interfere with the puck or an opponent on the ice.
A gross misconduct penalty is imposed if a player on either bench:
throws any article on to the ice;
molests or interferes with an opponent or official.
Unless the puck is in the goal crease, a goal will be disallowed if an attacker not in possession stands or holds his stick in the goal crease or stands on the goal crease line – except when he is forced into that position by the interference of an opponent. (A face-off at the nearest face-off spot in the neutral zone is held after a disallowed goal.)

Spectators' interference The referee will stop play if:
play is interfered with by objects thrown onto the ice;
a player is interfered with by a spectator (if that player's team has a scoring position, the referee will first allow the play to be completed).
Play will resume with a face-off where the stoppage occurred.

Delaying the game A bench minor penalty is imposed for deliberately delaying the game.
A minor penalty is imposed if a player leaves his team bench to instruct a teammate, unless he remains on the ice as a substitute.
If a player deliberately moves the goal, a minor penalty is imposed, except that a penalty shot is awarded if the minor penalty would not have expired before play ends.

FOULS

Charging into an opponent (**1**). It is a charge if a player takes more than two normal steps.

A minor penalty is imposed; a major penalty is imposed if injury is caused or if the charge is against an opponent from behind or against a goalkeeper within his crease.

High sticks (**2**) is carrying the stick above shoulder height.

A minor penalty may be imposed at the referee's discretion and in some competitions a major penalty is assessed if the fouled player is cut with the stick.

Hitting the puck with a high stick is penalized by a face-off, unless the offending side loses possession or scores against itself.

A goal scored from a high stick is disallowed, but a body deflection into goal while the stick is high is allowed.

Kneeing and elbowing (**3**) A minor penalty is imposed, or a major penalty if injury is caused.

Spearing, butt ending, or cross checking Spearing (**4**) and butt ending (**5**) are poking with the point or butt end of the stick.

In a cross check (**6**) both hands are on the stick and no part of the stick is on the ground.

A minor penalty is imposed except in the case of spearing, which always incurs a major penalty; and a major penalty is imposed if injury is caused or if the offense is against a goalkeeper in his crease.

Tripping (**7**) may be with the stick, knee, foot, arm, hand or elbow.

A minor penalty is imposed, except when a puck carrier is tripped from behind when in the attacking zone with only the opposing goalkeeper to beat. In the latter case a penalty shot is awarded. No penalty is imposed if a player obtains possession by hook-checking.

Roughing, boarding (**8**), **and slashing** (**9**) may be penalized by a minor or a major penalty even when no injury is caused.

Boarding is causing an opponent to be thrown violently into the boards. Slashing is swinging the stick to impede or scare an opponent.

1 charging

2 high sticks

4 spearing

5 butt ending

6 cross checking

Hooking (**10**) A minor penalty is imposed on a player who impedes or seeks to impede the progress of an opponent by hooking with his stick.

Holding (**11**) A minor penalty is imposed on any player who holds an opponent with his stick or in any other way.

Clipping is falling and sliding into a puck carrier's path so that he loses possession.

A minor penalty is imposed on any player who clips an opponent. No penalty is imposed if the puck is hit from the opponent's possession before the player falls.

Kicking a player or deliberately injuring or attempting to injure any person are offenses penalized by a match penalty.

Fighting is penalized as follows:
starting a fight, a major and minor instigator penalty; fighting back, major penalty; third player to enter a fight, major penalty and a game misconduct.

Throwing the stick is penalized as follows:
if a defender throws his stick or any article at the puck in his defending zone, a penalty shot is awarded to the attackers if they have not scored when that play is completed;
any other incident in the playing area incurs a major penalty.

Handling the puck A minor penalty is imposed if a player other than the goalkeeper closes his hands on the puck, or picks it up while play is in progress.
A penalty shot is awarded if a defending player other than the goalkeeper picks up the puck within the goal crease area.

A minor penalty is imposed if a goalkeeper:
deliberately drops the puck into his pads; or deliberately throws or bats it out of the playing area.

All players are permitted to stop or bat the puck in the air with the open hand, or to push it along the ice using the hand, but if another player of the same team plays the puck next, a face-off is held.

If a puck is knocked into the goal by the hand of an attacking player directly off a defender, the goal is disallowed, but a puck sent into the goal by the hand of a defender is allowed as a goal.

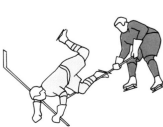

7 tripping

8 board checking

9 slashing

10 hooking

3 elbowing

11 holding

Falling on the puck A minor penalty is imposed if any player other than a goalkeeper falls on or gathers the puck to his body in any way while standing or lying.
A penalty shot is awarded if a defender commits these offenses when inside his goal area.

Misconduct toward officials A misconduct penalty is imposed on any player who:
uses obscene, profane, or abusive language;
persists in disputing, or shows disrespect for, the referee's rulings;
intentionally knocks the puck out of the referee's or linesman's reach when he is retrieving it;
bangs his stick on the ice to show disrespect;
refuses to go at once to the penalty bench when penalized;
unnecessarily enters or stays in the referee's crease while he is consulting with a game official;
persists, after a warning, in any conduct designed to incite an opponent into incurring a penalty;
molests an official.
If the referee cannot identify the culprit, a bench minor penalty is imposed on the offending team.
If a manager, coach, or trainer is guilty of any such misconduct, a bench minor is assessed.

PENALTIES

Minor penalty For a minor penalty the offender is ruled off the ice for 2 minutes actual playing time.
No substitute is allowed unless the player receiving the penalty is injured or removed from the game.
If a team scores while the opposing team is shorthanded (has fewer players on the ice) following one or more minor (or bench minor) penalties, the first of these penalties automatically ends provided that the goal was not scored from a penalty.

A bench minor penalty is imposed when an offense is by a team or when the actual offender is unknown. A bench minor penalty lasts for 2 minutes and is served by a team member designated by the coach through the captain.

Major penalty For his first major penalty in a match, an offender is ruled off the ice for 5 minutes. For his third major penalty he is ruled off the ice for the rest of the match. A substitute is allowed after 5 minutes of a major penalty.
When a player receives a major and a minor penalty at the same time, the major penalty is served first.

Misconduct penalty For a misconduct penalty the player is sent off the ice for 10 minutes; a substitute is allowed immediately. After the penalty, the player may rejoin the game only at a stoppage of play.

Match penalty The offender is sent off for the rest of the game, and excluded from future games until his case has been dealt with. (See **Fouls** for details of when substitutes are permitted.)
A 10-minute penalty without substitute is imposed.

Penalty shot

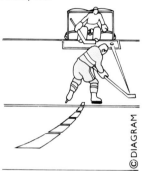

Penalty shots The puck is placed on the center face-off spot. The coach chooses any player not serving a penalty to play the puck, unless the attacker is tripped from behind. Then he must take the penalty shot himself.
Except for the opposing goalkeeper, all other players must withdraw behind the center line.
The opposing goalkeeper must remain in his goal crease until the puck crosses the blue line. He may then try to stop the puck or player in any legal way.
For the shot, the puck must be kept in motion toward the goal; a goal cannot be scored from a rebound.
If a player awarded a penalty shot is penalized in the same incident, he takes the shot before serving his penalty.
If a shot fails because an opponent distracts the player or a spectator interferes, the shot is retaken (the opponent receives a misconduct penalty).
Time for a penalty shot is not counted as playing time or overtime.
If a goal is scored, the puck is centered; if not, it is faced-off at either spot in that zone.

Game misconduct penalty For a game misconduct penalty the player is sent off for the rest of the game. A substitute is allowed at once. A second misconduct penalty by a player is automatically a game misconduct penalty.

Goalkeeper's penalties No goalkeeper can be sent to the penalty bench for a minor, major, or misconduct penalty. These penalties are served by a teammate then on the ice and chosen by the coach. For a third major penalty a goalkeeper receives a game misconduct penalty. If given a game misconduct or match penalty he is replaced by the substitute goalkeeper.
A goalkeeper leaving his crease to enter an altercation incurs a bench minor penalty for his team.

Delayed penalties If a player is penalized while two teammates are serving penalties, he goes to the bench at once and his penalty time begins only when that of one of the other two players ends. A substitute may take his place on the ice until his penalty time begins.
In such a case, any player whose penalty expires can return to the ice only if play is stopped or the substitute is removed (except that if two teammates' penalties expire together, one may return immediately).

Calling of penalties Following a minor, major, or match penalty offense by a player of a side in possession, play is stopped at once.
If a minor penalty is signaled against a shorthanded team and a goal is scored by the other side before the whistle is blown, the goal is allowed and the delayed penalty forgotten. The player serving a penalty may return to the ice.
All fouls before or after the referee stops play are penalized, even if they are by the same player.

Bandy

Bandy is related to ice hockey, but there are certain basic differences between the two games. Bandy is played on a larger ice rink and there is no play behind the goals; 11 players from each team may be on the ice; they play a ball with curved sticks. The aim, as in ice hockey, is to score a greater number of goals than the opposing team.

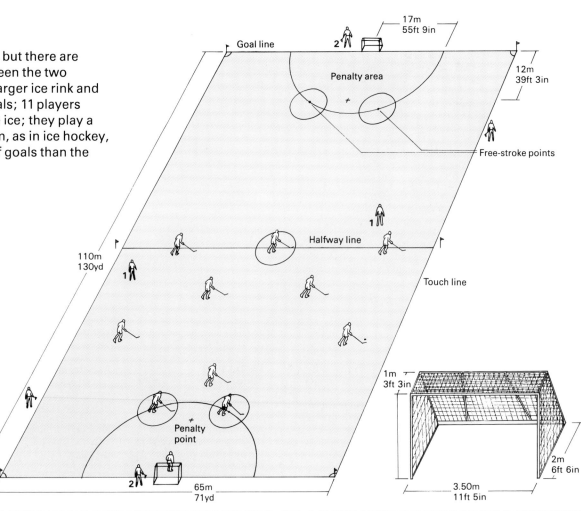

Rink This is rectangular and is 60-110m long and 45-65m wide. The rink is surrounded by a movable border which is made of wood, plastic, aluminum or some other approved material. The border stops at least 1m from each corner.
If the border shifts more than 1m and the ball touches a part of the rink that has moved, play is stopped and restarted by a stroke-in or a face-off.

Officials are:
two referees (or three for major matches) in control of the game and responsible for timekeeping (**1**);
two goal referees (**2**), who judge incidents on the goal line;
match secretary, to assist the referee with timekeeping and to be responsible for penalized players.

Teams Each team has fourteen players (including two goalkeepers), of whom eleven may be on the ice at any time.

Substitutes In addition to eleven players each team is allowed three (four in international games) substitutes. These may be used at any time, provided that the players they replace have left the rink before the substitutes enter it. Replacement must always be made at the same spot: across the touchline close to the halfway line. (In international matches the replacement of the goalkeeper may take place by the goal.)

Duration There are two halves of 45 minutes each, with a 10-minute interval at half-time when the teams change ends.
If there is a tie, extra time of two 15-minute halves is sometimes played, and this may be repeated until one team wins.
Starting play The teams toss for stroke-off or choice of ends.

A stroke-off from the center begins each half and restarts play after a goal.
Players remain in their own half and must be at least 5m away from the ball, until the ball is passed. The player stroking-off plays the ball into the opponents' half, and may not play the ball again until another player has touched it.
A stroke-in is awarded to the opposition if the ball is played over the touchline. The ball is placed on the ice within 1m of where it crossed the line. All opponents must be at least 5m away.

Face-off After an accidental stoppage, play restarts with a face-off at the point where the ball was when play stopped.
Two players, one from each team, face each other with their backs to their own goal line. Their sticks must be parallel and on either side of the ball, which is played in at the referee's signal. All other players must be at least 5m away.
If play stopped within the penalty area, the face-off is taken at the nearest free-stroke point.

A goal throw is awarded against an attacker who plays the ball over his opponents' goal line. The goalkeeper fetches a ball from one of the ball baskets outside the end-line and starts play by a direct throw. Before a goal-throw the goalkeeper must not move more than 5m on the ice, or if he does not move, he is allowed to hold the ball for 5 seconds at the most. The goalkeeper may not play the ball again until another player has touched it.

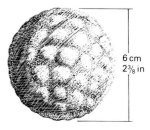

1.20m
3ft 11in

The stick is made of wood or similar material, without metal fittings or a handstrap. Maximum length: 120cm. Maximum width: 6cm.

The ball is made of colored plastic or other approved material. When dropped on the ice from a height of 1.5m it should bounce 15-30cm. It weighs 58-62g.

6 cm
2⅜ in

© DIAGRAM

Dress

Skates (**1**) must not have sharp points or projections. All players and officials on the ice should wear approved helmets (**2**). The goalkeeper wears a distinctive costume, with padded gloves and leg pads (**3**). The goalkeeper should use a face mask.

Players also wear exterior mouthguards (**4**) or approved face masks and padded gloves (**5**). Players also wear shin pads.

Goalkeepers

A goalkeeper must not use a stick. He may only be challenged when he has the ball or is impeding an opponent.

Within his own penalty area he may use his skates or any part of his body to play the ball. After catching the ball he may carry it in one or both hands. He may not bounce or release it on the ice and then hold it again. He must release the ball back into play as soon as possible and may only hold it for up to 5 seconds without moving.

When he throws the ball, it must touch the ice, the border or a player before crossing the halfway line. If he is unable to release the ball, the referee may award a free stroke to the defending team.

Outside his own penalty area he may use any part of his body other than his arms or hands to play the ball.

Playing the ball

A player may:
play the ball with his stick;
kick the ball;
control the ball with his body, provided he has both skates on the ice;
jump off the ice, provided he does not endanger other players.

A player may not:
play without a stick nor play with a broken stick;
use his arms, hands, or head to control the ball;
play the ball when kneeling or lying on the ice;
play or attempt to play the ball with his stick above shoulder height;
play the ball above the illuminated area when the game is under artificial lighting.

Tackling

A player may physically challenge an opponent who has the ball or is challenging for it. He may not:
kick, trip, push, grasp, or impede an opponent or his stick;
throw his stick at the ball.

A penalty is awarded against a defender in the penalty area for dangerous or violent play against an opponent or for illegally preventing a goal.

The player taking the penalty must hit the ball forward from the penalty spot; if no goal is scored he may not play the ball again before it has been touched by another player.

The goalkeeper must stand still behind the goal line. No other players are allowed in the penalty area or behind the goal line.

Time is extended to allow a penalty to be taken.

If the attacking team commits an offense and the ball enters the goal, the penalty is retaken; if the ball missed, play continues. If the defending team commits an offense and no goal is scored, the penalty is retaken.

Expulsion A player guilty of severe or repeated infringements or misbehavior may be expelled from the rink for 5 minutes, 10 minutes, or the entire game.

An expelled player may not be replaced by a substitute.

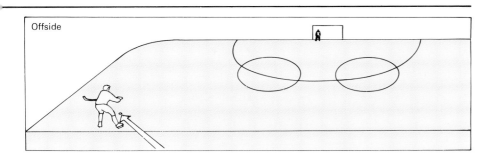

Offside

A corner stroke is awarded against a defender who plays the ball over his own goal line.

An opponent plays the ball in from within 1m of the nearest corner angle. He may not play the ball again until it has been touched by another player.

Defending players must be behind their own goal line and at least 5m from the ball. Although their sticks may touch the ice across the goal line, they may not cross the line until the ball has been played. Attacking players must be outside the penalty area.

Offside A player is offside if, when the ball is played or touched by a teammate, he is in front of the ball within his opponents' half, unless there are at least two opponents nearer their goal line than he is.

A player may stand offside as long as he does not interfere with the game and the ball is not passed to him directly or indirectly. He is not offside if the ball has last been played by an opponent.

A free stroke is awarded against offenders for most infringements outside the penalty area, but the referee must not deprive the offended side of a chance to score.

The free stroke is taken from where the offense occurred unless it took place in the penalty area, when it is taken from the nearest fixed free-stroke point.

The player who makes the stroke may not touch the ball again until it is played by another player. Opponents must be at least 5m away.

Scoring A goal is scored when the whole of the ball crosses the line between the goal posts and under the crossbar.

It cannot be scored directly from a stroke-off, corner stroke, goal throw, stroke-in, face-off, or direct throw by the goalkeeper.

It may be scored directly from a free stroke or penalty. The team that scores the greater number of goals wins.

Swimming

Swimming is both an individual and a team water sport. Participants compete in races and the first swimmer to cover a predetermined distance is the winner. Competitions are held in four major categories of swimming stroke – freestyle, breaststroke, butterfly, and backstroke.

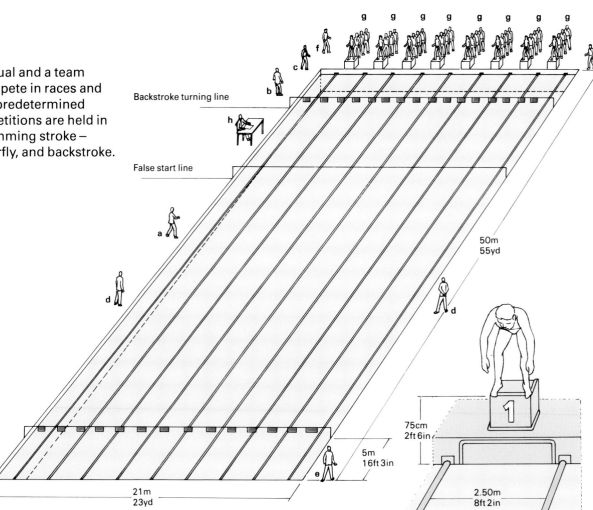

Backstroke turning line

False start line

50m
55yd

21m
23yd

5m
16ft 3in

75cm
2ft 6in

2.50m
8ft 2in

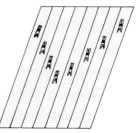

The pool Competitions are held in pools of varying lengths, but in the Olympic Games, where swimming is the second largest sport, a 50m pool is used.
The pool is divided into eight lanes, numbered one to eight from right to left. Each swimmer must remain in his own lane.
In all events except the backstroke, swimmers begin the race by diving in from starting blocks.
Dress Costumes of all competitors should be in good moral taste and be non-transparent. The referee has the sole authority to exclude any swimmer whose costume does not comply with this rule.

Officials Minimum international requirements are a referee, a starter, at least two placing judges, two stroke judges, two turning judges, and when electronic timing devices are not being used a minimum of two or preferably three timekeepers per lane plus additional timekeepers to take the times of the first and second in each race.
The referee (a) has overall control, ensuring that the rules are obeyed, inspecting the course, and adjudicating in any disagreements between officials or competitors.
The starter (b) controls the competitors until the race has begun. He must ensure that each swimmer is in his correct lane, and he and the referee are the sole judges of whether the start is valid.
Placing judges (c) decide the order of finish and may act as turning judges at the finish end.
Stroke judges (d) observe whether the swimmer's stroke mechanics conform to the approved pattern for each race. They report to the referee any swimmer who

fails to comply with the stroke rules.
Turning judges (e) observe all turns and relay take-overs. They report to the referee any swimmer who fails to comply with the turning rules of any particular stroke.
The chief timekeeper (f) Lane timekeepers (g) record the time for the competitor swimming in their lane on cards to be reviewed by the chief timekeeper.
For Olympic events electronic timing must be used.
The recorder (h) keeps a complete record of the race results.
Marshals ensure that the swimmers behave in a safe and orderly manner. The clerk of the course arranges the swimmers in their proper heats and lanes.
The start Except in the backstroke the competitors step up to the back of the starting blocks at the referee's call. Then on the starter's command, "Take your marks", they step forward to the front of the blocks and assume a starting position. Only when they are

all quite stationary will the starter give the signal for the race to begin. The starting signal may be a shot, klaxon, whistle or the word "go."
False start In international competition the starter may call two false starts, but must then warn the competitors that, if a third false start occurs, a swimmer who breaks before the signal will be disqualified. The swimmers are recalled after a false start by the starter repeating the starting signal and by the lowering of a false start rope onto the water. In US competitions a single false start disqualifies a swimmer.
Backstroke races The swimmers line up in the water, facing the edge of the pool. They may grip the pool

edge or rail with their hands, but their feet must be on the wall under the water but not curled over the edge of the pool or the gutter. On the starting signal they push away from the wall.
The spearhead principle In each event the competitor with the fastest entry time is assigned the center lane or; in pools with an even number of lanes; the lane on the right of center. The other swimmers are placed alternately left and right of him in descending order of speed, so that the slowest swimmers are in the two outside lanes.
If the entry times are a true indication of form, the swimmers will fan out into a spearhead formation during the race.

The spearhead

Starting position
for forward strokes

Front crawl stroke

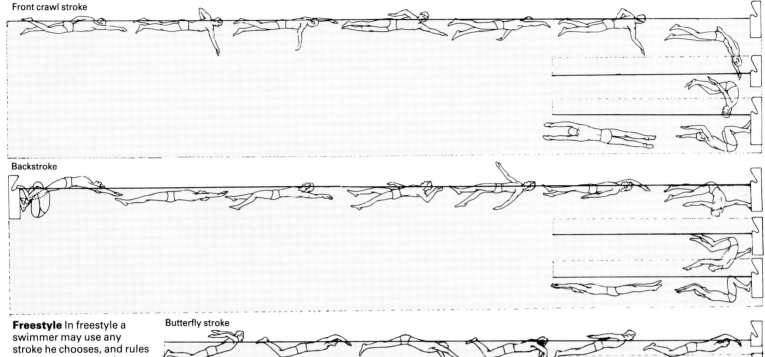

Backstroke

Butterfly stroke

Breaststroke

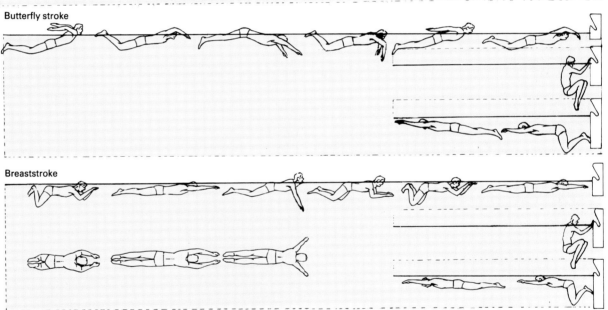

Freestyle In freestyle a swimmer may use any stroke he chooses, and rules relating to breaststroke, butterfly and backstroke do not apply.
In turning and finishing, the swimmer must touch the end of the pool; he may do so with any part of his body. The stroke generally chosen is the front crawl.

Front crawl In this stroke each arm is alternately brought over and then into the water, while the legs perform a kicking action. The swimmer generally breathes on one side in the trough made by the arm pull.

Backstroke Competitors must swim on their backs throughout the race. They are permitted to use a somersault turn, but any swimmer turning beyond the vertical before he touches the end of the pool will be disqualified. A swimmer will also be disqualified for changing from his back before his head or hand touches the finishing line.

Butterfly The arms in this stroke are brought forward at the same time to enter the water at some point in front of the shoulders and are then pulled backward under the water. No alternating movement of the arms is permitted. The shoulders must at all times be parallel to the surface of the water. Simultaneous up and down movements of the legs and feet are permitted but alternating movements of the legs are not permitted.

Breaststroke The body must at all times be parallel to the surface of the water. The hands must be pushed forward together from the breast and then brought back on or under the surface of the water.
In the leg kick the feet must be turned outward in the backward movement; a dolphin kick is not permitted. During each complete cycle of one arm stroke and one leg kick, some part of the head of the swimmer must break the surface of the water, except that after the start and after each turn the swimmer may take one arm stroke completely back to the legs and one leg kick while wholly submerged before returning to the surface.

At the turn and on finishing the race, the touch must be made with both hands simultaneously either at, above, or below the water level.

Medley events In individual events competitors swim an equal distance of four strokes; the sequence is butterfly, backstroke, breaststroke and freestyle. In medley relays each swimmer swims one stroke for the set distance; the order is backstroke, breaststroke, butterfly and freestyle.

Disqualification A competitor is liable to disqualification for:
impeding or obstructing the progress of another swimmer (including swimming out of lane);

appearing at the starting blocks after the swimmers have been called to the start;
permitting any misconduct, using abusive language, or failing to follow directions;
walking on the floor of the pool;
finishing a race in a lane other than the one in which he started;
entering the water while a race is in progress;
using any equipment such as fins to aid his performance.

Olympic events (for men and women except where specified):
50m freestyle
100m freestyle
200m freestyle
400m freestyle
800m freestyle (women)
1500m freestyle (men)
100m breaststroke
200m breaststroke
100m butterfly
200m butterfly
100m backstroke
200m backstroke
200m individual medley
400m individual medley
4 x 100m freestyle relay
4 x 200m freestyle relay
4 x 100m medley relay.

© DIAGRAM

Synchronized swimming

In synchronized swimming, competitors are judged on their performance of set swimming movements. Competitors perform compulsory figures and swimming routines to musical accompaniment. There are competitions for solos, duets and team routines.

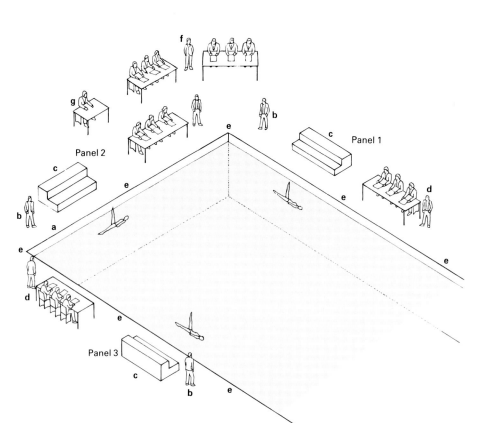

Pool The pool area must be at least 12m (13.1yd) square. For compulsory figures it must be at least 3m (9.8ft) deep, for routines at least 1.7m (5.6ft) deep. The area may be extended but the 1.7m (5.6ft) depth must be maintained for a further 8m (26.2ft). The water must be clear enough for the bottom of the pool to be visible. The minimum permitted water temperature is 24°C.

Equipment Competition organizers are responsible for providing suitable equipment for the reproduction of accompaniment. This must include underwater speakers conforming to national safety standards.

Dress For the compulsory figures a white cap and a dark costume must be worn. For routines competitors may choose any design provided it is in good moral taste and is non transparent.

Officials International requirements: **a)** a referee; **b)** an assistant referee for each panel of judges in the figures competition; **c)** 5 or 7 judges in each panel; **d)** a clerk of the course and 3 scorers for each panel.
In the figure competition there would be a swimmer in front of each set of judges. The referee moves around the pool during the routines, possibly beginning at the deep end.

The diagram above gives a sample layout. Positions of officials vary according to the figures drawn for the competition, and depth of water required. The judges must be in a position to see at all times.
For the routine competition:
e) 7 judges positioned around the pool;
f) 2 to 3 timekeepers, 1 clerk of the course and 3 scorers;
g) controller of music.
In the figure competition the assistant referee instructs the swimmers when to start and the judges when to show their marks.
In the routine competition the referee signals the start, when to show the marks and he also imposes any penalties, informing the scorers of these, and approves the marks.
The scorers record and compute the marks for both sections.
The clerk of the course ensures that the swimmers

are in position for the start. In the routines the timekeepers record the time of deckwork and overall times, and inform the referee of any discrepancy.
The competition consists of two parts, the figure competition and the routine competition.

THE FIGURE COMPETITION
A group of 6 figures is performed. The draw for the group is made in public 18 to 36 hours before the start of the figure competition from the 6 groups of compulsory figures set by FINA, the international governing body. These groups are changed every 4 years. Figures have an official degree of difficulty, 3 in each group are 1.8 or under and the remainder are 1.9 or over, at least one figure being from each category and no more than 2 from any one category. Half the figures are of a difficulty of

1.7 or less and half of a difficulty of 1.8 or more.
Judging figures Figures are judged on whether they are performed slowly, high and controlled with each section clearly defined and in uniform motion (unless otherwise specified in the description). Where there is more than one panel of judges, an equal number of figures is judged at each panel.
Execution of figures Most movements are executed in a stationary position unless travel is mentioned in the description.
Scoring figures Each figure is marked with scores from 0 to 10 in ½ point increments by each judge. The marks are recorded by the scorers. The highest and lowest marks are then canceled and the remaining marks are totaled and divided by the number of judges minus 2 and multiplied by the degree of

difficulty. The resultant marks for each figure are totaled and any penalties deducted, giving the final figure score for each swimmer.
Penalties 2 point penalties are incurred if:
a) a competitor performs the wrong figure and then performs the correct one (a repetition of the error results in no score being awarded for the figure);
b) a competitor stops voluntarily and asks to do the figure again.

Examples of basic positions

1 Ballet leg
2 Ballet double leg
3 Bent knee
4 Knight or castle
5 Vertical
6 Tuck
7 Front pike
8 Back pike
9 Split

THE ROUTINE COMPETITION

Competitors may enter one solo, one duet and one team. International teams consist of eight members.

The figure score added to the routine score is:

1) solo – the sum of the figure marks as reached above;

2) duet – the average of the figure marks of the two competitors involved;

3) team – the average of the scores of each team member.

For the routine competition there are two marks, one for technical merit and one for artistic impression; both are awarded by the judges using 1/10th points. The judges' marks in both cases are recorded, the highest and lowest canceled and the remainder totaled. The technical merit mark is multiplied by 6 and divided by the number of judges minus 2, and the artistic impression mark is multiplied by 4 and divided by the number of judges minus 2. The total of the figure score, artistic impression and technical merit marks is the final score for the routine.

Penalties in routines A one point penalty is deducted from the score for the following:

a) exceeding the time limit of 20 seconds for deck movements;

b) deviating from the time limit for a routine;

A 2 point penalty is incurred:

c) for deliberate use of the bottom of the pool to execute a figure or to assist another competitor during the routine.

d) if a routine is interrupted by a competitor during deck movements and a new start is allowed.

If one or more competitors leaves the pool during a routine, the routine is disqualified unless the departure is caused by circumstances beyond the control of the competitor(s).

Times for routines:

solos 3½ min;
duets 4 min;
teams 5 min.

There is a time allowance of 15 seconds minus or plus the allotted time. The time includes a maximum of 20 seconds for deckwork (movements on the side of the pool). The time allowance is because there can be a slight variation in the speed at which musical equipment plays the tape. In routines preliminary rounds may be swum, if needed, to select the number of swimmers to take part in finals.

Examples of selected figures

Ballet leg single (degree of difficulty 1.5)

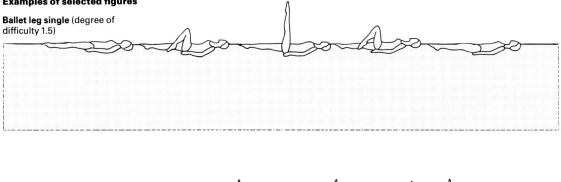

Catalina (degree of difficulty 1.9)

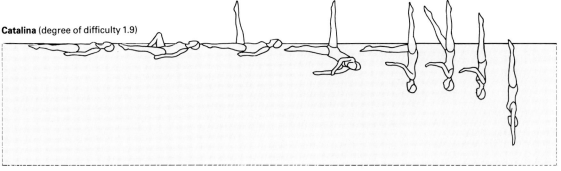

Dolphin bent knee (degree of difficulty 1.5)

Barracuda back pike somersault (degree of difficulty 1.9)

Walkover front (degree of difficulty 1.5)

© DIAGRAM

Water polo

Water polo is a team game played by two teams of up to 13 a side, only seven of whom may be in the water at the same time. The ball may be propelled one-handed, but not punched by any player other than the goalkeeper. Each team attempts to score by putting the ball into its opponent's goal.

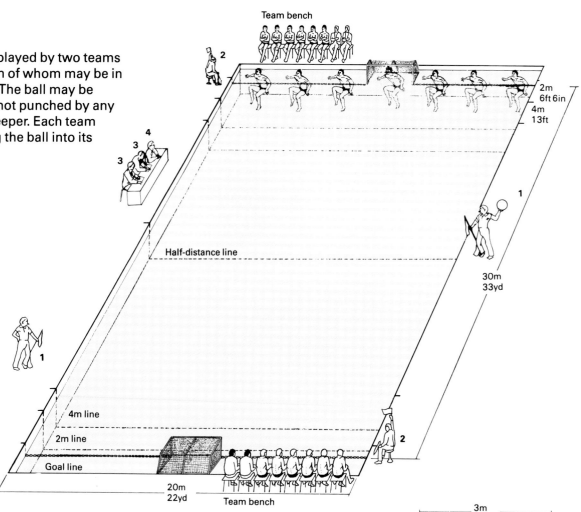

Team bench

2m
6ft 6in
4m
13ft

Half-distance line

30m
33yd

4m line

2m line

Goal line

20m
22yd

Team bench

Playing area Uniform dimensions are illustrated. The minimum depth for major competitions is 1.80m. All lines must be visible throughout the game. Suggested colors are: goal line and half-distance line, white; 2m line, red; 4m line, yellow. There must be sufficient room for the referees to walk along the edge of the pool. Goals must be painted white and fixed firmly.

Dress Players wear trunks. One team must wear blue caps, the other white. Goalkeepers wear red caps. All caps must be tied under the chin. If a player loses his cap, he must replace it at the next stoppage. Caps are numbered on the sides – the goalkeeper being number 1 and the other players 2-13. No dangerous articles may be worn. No player may grease or oil his body.

Officials The game is controlled by between five and seven officials.

1 Two referees who use a whistle and a stick, fitted with a white flag on one end and a blue flag on the other. They stop and start the game, decide fouls, goals and throws. They also apply an advantage rule by not declaring a foul, if the offending team would benefit from the stoppage. They have the power to order any player out of the water.

2 Two goal judges who each have a white flag to signal goal throws and a red flag to signal corner throws. They raise both flags for a goal. They are positioned

opposite the referee at each end of the pool directly level with the goal line.

3 Timekeepers, who record the time when the ball is actually in play. They use a whistle to indicate the end of a period of play and an audible signal to indicate that a team has been in possession of the ball for 35sec without a shot at goal.

4 Secretaries, who record major fouls and signal with a red flag when any player is awarded a third personal fault. They also control players' periods of exclusion by signaling when an excluded player may re-enter the game.

Teams A team comprises 13 players of whom six are substitutes.

Substitution Except in case of injury or accident, a substitute may only enter the game: during the interval after a goal; before extra time; after a teammate has been excluded from the rest of the game for showing disrespect, wearing oil or committing a third personal fault.

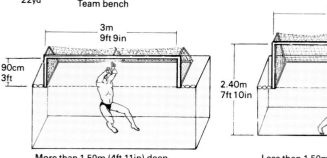

More than 1.50m (4ft 11in) deep

3m
9ft 9in

90cm
3ft

Less than 1.50m (4ft 11in) deep

3m
9ft 9in

2.40m
7ft 10in

The team captain must inform a referee of all substitutions. No substitutes are allowed in cases of brutality.

Duration Play lasts for four periods of seven minutes' actual playing time. There is a two-minute interval between each period for changing ends. Players in the water may only leave at an interval when injured or with the referee's permission. For an accident or injury the referee may suspend play for up to three minutes.

If there is a tie and a definite result is required, there is a five-minute break, then two periods of three minutes' play with one-minute interval between. This pattern is continued until a decision is reached.

Start of play Players take up position on their own goal lines about 1m apart from either goal post (only two players are allowed between the posts). One referee then blows his whistle and throws the ball into the center of the pool.

Restarting play
a) After a goal, players may take up any position in their own half. The team conceding the goal restarts play, when one referee whistles, by one player passing the ball to a teammate, who must be behind the half-distance line when he receives the ball.
b) After a stoppage, for injury, etc, or after a simultaneous foul by two opponents, one referee throws the ball into the water giving both teams an equal chance of gaining possession.

The ball A water polo ball must be round and fully inflated. It must be completely waterproof. Its circumference must be 68–71cm and its weight 400–450g.

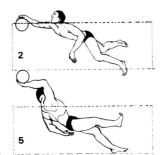

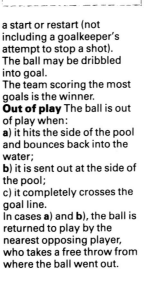

Playing the ball

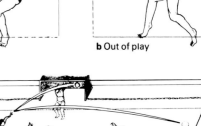

a Out of play   **b** Out of play

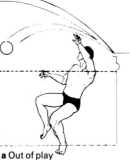

Corner throw

© DIAGRAM

Playing the ball Apart from the goalkeeper players are not permitted to:
touch the ball with both hands simultaneously;
strike the ball with a clenched fist.
They are permitted to:
dribble with the ball (**1**);
seize the ball (**2**);
lift the ball out of the water (**3**);
remain stationary with the ball (**4**);
pass or shoot the ball (**5**);
play the ball, when it is in the air.
A team must concede a free throw, if it fails to shoot at goal within 35sec of gaining possession of the ball.

Goalkeepers A goalkeeper may stand, jump from the floor of the pool, walk, use both hands and punch the ball.
He must not go or touch the ball beyond the half-distance line, but may shoot at his opponent's goal as long as he is still within his own half of the pitch. He must not hold the bar, rail or trough at the end of the pool.
Scoring A goal is scored when the ball completely crosses the goal line between the posts and under the crossbar, providing it has not been punched and at least two players have touched it after

a start or restart (not including a goalkeeper's attempt to stop a shot). The ball may be dribbled into goal.
The team scoring the most goals is the winner.
Out of play The ball is out of play when:
a) it hits the side of the pool and bounces back into the water;
b) it is sent out at the side of the pool;
c) it completely crosses the goal line.
In cases **a)** and **b)**, the ball is returned to play by the nearest opposing player, who takes a free throw from where the ball went out.

If an attacker sends the ball out of play over the goal line, a goal throw is awarded.
If the defender sends the ball over his own goal line, a corner throw is awarded.
A corner throw is taken by the attacker nearest where the ball went out of play. It must be taken from the 2m

mark on the side of the pool where the ball went out. Only the defending goalkeeper may be in the 2m area when the throw is taken.
A goal throw is taken by the defending goalkeeper. It must be taken from the goal line between the goal posts.

Fouls

Free throw

Fouls and misconduct
Offenses are classified as ordinary fouls (penalized by a free throw to the other team) and major fouls (penalized by personal faults and periods of exclusion).

Ordinary fouls It is an ordinary foul to:
take or hold the ball under water when tackled (**1**);
swim beyond the goal line before the referee's signal to start the game;
assist a player at the start;
hold onto or push off from the goal posts or the sides of the pool, or hold onto the rails except at the start or a

restart;
stand or walk on the floor of the pool;
punch the ball;
touch a referee's neutral throw before it reaches the water;
jump from the floor of the pool;
deliberately impede an opponent unless he has the ball;
play the ball with both hands at the same time;
push an opponent;
be within 2m of the opposing goal line except when behind the line of the ball;
waste time (including having possession for more than 35sec without shooting);
take a penalty throw incorrectly.
Major Fouls It is a major foul to:
kick or strike an opponent (**2**);
commit any brutal act (**3**);
illegally stop a goal inside the 4m area (**4**);
hold, sink or pull back an opponent not holding the ball;
interfere with the taking of a free throw;
re-enter the water improperly when an

excluded player or substitute;
intentionally splash water in an opponent's face;
continually commit ordinary fouls with intent.
After a major foul the offending player is awarded a personal fault and is ordered out of the water for 35sec, until a goal is scored or when the defending team retake possession of the ball, whichever is the sooner.
A player is excluded from the game when he has three personal faults or penalties recorded against him.
Only when the penalized player is to be permanently excluded from the game may a substitute take his place. He may be replaced by a substitute immediately if the third foul is punished by a penalty throw or otherwise replaced as outlined above for a personal foul.
Free throw The player may:
a) throw the ball;
b) drop the ball into the water and dribble it before passing.
The throw must be made in such a way that other players can see the ball leave the thrower's hand.

At least two players must touch the ball before a goal can be scored.
Any free throw awarded for a foul in the 2m area must be taken from the 2m line opposite where the foul occurred.
Other free throws are taken from where the offense occurred.
A penalty throw is awarded for the following major fouls within the 4m area: holding, sinking, or pulling back an opponent not holding the ball;
kicking or striking an opponent;
committing any foul that prevents a probable goal.
A penalty throw is also awarded for an act of brutality anywhere in the pool.
Any player except the goalkeeper may take the penalty throw from any point along the 4m line. He must throw directly at goal.
All players except the defending goalkeeper must leave the 4m area, and no player may encroach within 2m of the thrower.
The goalkeeper must remain on his goal line.

Diving

Competitive diving is separated into men's and women's springboard and platform (highboard) events. Competitors perform a set number of dives, each of which is marked, and the competitor with the most marks in the final is the winner.

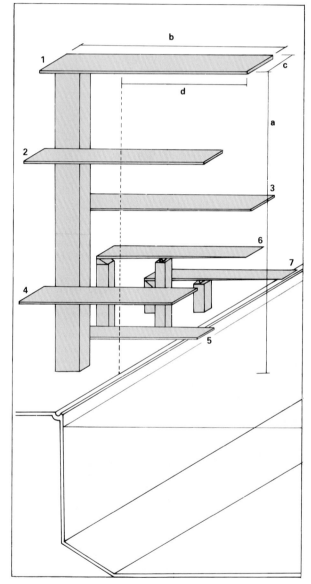

Type of board	a height	b length	c width	d to pool edge
1 Platform competition	10m	6m	2m	1.5m
2 Platform competition	7.5m	6m	1.5m	1.5m
3 Platform competition	5m	6m	1.5m	1.25m
4 Platform training	3m	5m	1.5m	1.25m
5 Platform training	1m	5m	0.6m	0.75m
6 Springboard competition	3m	4.88m	0.6m	1.8m
7 Springboard competition	1m	4.88m	0.6m	1.8m

Diving apparatus Diving platforms and springboards may be provided at the heights shown. They should be approved by the technical diving committee before a contest. They must be rigid and the surface and front edge of the platform covered with an approved resilient non-slip surface.
Springboards shall be at least 4.8m long and 0.5m wide and normally made of aluminum extrusion and covered with a non-slip surface.
Mechanical agitation to the water surface aids the divers. Illumination must not cause glare.
Officials Competitions are judged by a judging panel consisting of the referee and judges.
The referee controls the competition and supervises the judges.
The judges (usually five or seven in major international competitions) are positioned separately on both sides of the diving board or, if that is not possible, together on one side of the board. After each dive each judge gives his mark when the referee signals.
Marks are recorded by two secretaries, who also record the minutes of the competition.
Preliminary contests In the Olympic Games and world championships there is always a preliminary and final competition. In other competitions preliminary

contests are held, at the discretion of the meet director, when there are more than twelve competitors. In springboard events a preliminary contest consists of eleven dives for men and ten for women. In platform events ten dives are required for men and eight for women.
The twelve divers with the most points in the preliminary contest qualify for the final dive in reverse order of their placings as determined by their total score in the preliminary rounds.
There is no carry over of points and the twelve divers perform another complete list of dives. The diver with the highest points in the final is declared the winner.
Events
Men's springboard events consist of eleven different dives; five dives each selected from a different group, the total degree of difficulty of which shall not exceed 9.5, and six dives without limit of the degree of difficulty, of which one dive shall be selected from each group, plus an additional dive, which may be selected from any group.
Women's springboard events consist of ten different dives; five dives each selected from a different group, the total degree of difficulty of which shall not exceed 9.5; and five dives without limit of degree of difficulty, of which

one dive shall be selected from each group.
Men's platform events consist of ten different dives; four dives each selected from a different group, the total degree of difficulty of which shall not exceed 7.6, and six dives without limit of degree of difficulty, each selected from a different group. The dives may be performed from either the intermediate or 10m platform except in Olympic Games or world championships, when only the 10m board may be used.
Women's platform events consist of eight different dives; four dives each selected from a different group, the total degree of difficulty of which shall not exceed 7.6, and four dives without limit of degree of difficulty, each selected from a different group. The dives may be performed from the 5m, 7.5m or 10m platform except in Olympic Games or world championships, when only the 10m board may be used.

Notification of dives
Before the competition, not less than 24hr, each competitor must give the diving secretaries a complete statement of the dives selected.
A dive can be performed in three positions: straight, indicated with an (a); piked (b); and tuck (c). Twist dives are indicated with a (d) and may be performed in any position.

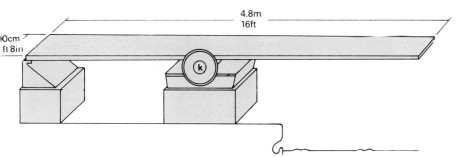

4.8m
16ft

Ocm
ft 8in

Springboards are 1m or 3m high, with a fulcrum (**k**) that may be adjusted by the competitors.
Dive groups There are six official groups of dives;
1 forward dives (body facing the water);
2 backward dives (body facing the platform);
3 reverse dives (body facing the water);
4 inward dives (body facing platform);
5 twist dives;
6 armstand dives (from the platform only).

© DIAGRAM

1   2   3   4   5   6

Starting positions Divers may take off from a forward (**1**), backward (**2**) or armstand (**3**) position. Forward take-off dives may be performed either standing or running.
Standing dives The starting position for a standing dive is assumed when the diver stands on the front end of the board or platform.
The body must be straight, head erect, arms straight and to the sides, above the head or in any sideways position. The arm swing commences when the arms leave the starting position.
Running dives The starting position for a running dive is assumed when the diver is ready to take the first step of his run.
The run must be smooth, straight and without hesitation and must consist of at least four steps, including the take-off.
The take-off from a springboard must be from both feet. The take-off from a platform can be from one or both feet.
The take-off must be bold, reasonably high and confident.
In a standing dive the diver

must not bounce on the board before take-off.
In an armstand dive there must be a steady balance in the straight position.
Points may be deducted for loss of balance, restarting, touching the end of the board, diving to the side of the direct line of flight and for lifting both feet from the board when preparing for a backward take-off.
The flight During the flight (passage through the air) the body may be straight, with pike or with tuck. The position of the arms is the choice of the diver.
Straight (**4**) The body must not be bent at the hips or the knees; the feet must be together and the toes pointed.
With pike (**5**) The body must be bent at the hips, the legs straight at the knees and the toes pointed.
With tuck (**6**) The whole body must be bunched, with the knees together, the hands on the lower legs and the toes pointed.
Flying somersault dives A straight position should be clearly held for approximately half a somersault.

Dives with twist The twist must not be manifestly made from the board. In pike dives with twist, the twist must follow the pike. In somersault dives with twist, the twist may be performed at any time. The twist must be within 90° of that announced or the dive will be declared a failure.
The entry The body must always be vertical or near vertical on entering the water. The body must be straight and the toes pointed.
Head-first entries (**7**) The arms must be stretched above the head and in line with the body; the hands must be close together.
Feet-first entries (**8**) The arms must be close to the body; there must be no bending at the elbows.
Finish The dive is considered finished when the whole body is completely under the surface of the water.
Judging dives The judges, without communicating with one another, consider the technique and grace of: the starting position, the run, the take off, the flight through the air and the entry.

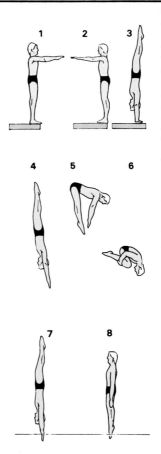

1   2   3

4   5   6

7   8

Scoring Each judge awards a mark in points and half points from 0-10 for each dive in accordance with the following table:
completely failed 0;
unsatisfactory ½–2;
deficient 2½–4½;
satisfactory 5–6;
good 6½–8;
very good 8½–10.
The secretaries cancel the judges' highest and lowest marks, total the remainder and multiply by the degree of difficulty to give the score for the dive for a five judge competition. For a seven judge competition the result is multiplied by three fifths for comparison purposes with a five judge event.
A dive other than that announced is a failed dive and scores no points.
A dive performed in a position other than that announced is deemed unsatisfactory and scores a maximum of 2 points.
A dive spoiled by exceptional circumstances may with the referee's permission be repeated.
Result An event is won by the competitor scoring most points in the final. A tie is declared if two divers have equal points.

Surfing

A surfer's basic equipment is a board, normally made to his individual specifications, with which he attempts to ride waves as they approach the shoreline. In competitions surfers may be required to ride a number of waves. Each performance is scored separately, and the points from the best waves are totaled to give a final score.

Officials The number of officials depends on the size of the competition and may include judges, a referee, a starter, and an official supervising the event.

Starting On the starter's signal the competitors enter the water and paddle out to their appropriate positions.

Duration Heats will be of 15–25 minutes duration, whilst finals will be of 30–45 minutes. Heat times depend upon surf conditions. Surfers may catch as many waves as they wish in the allocated heat time. Depending on number of competitors in the heat the final total of waves counted for determining heat position will be 3 or 4, with 5 waves counted in the final.

Scoring Competitors are awarded points for each wave they ride. They score between 0.1-10 (with 0.1 increments) on the following criteria. Riders will be given maximum points for performing in the most difficult part of the wave, selected for quality and size, for the longest time at the fastest speed using the widest range of functional maneuvers involving the highest degree of difficulty.
1 making the wave
2 beating sections
3 tube rides
4 turns, cut backs and reentries
5 nose walking (longboard – over 9ft – category only).
Points may be lost for interference or other offenses.

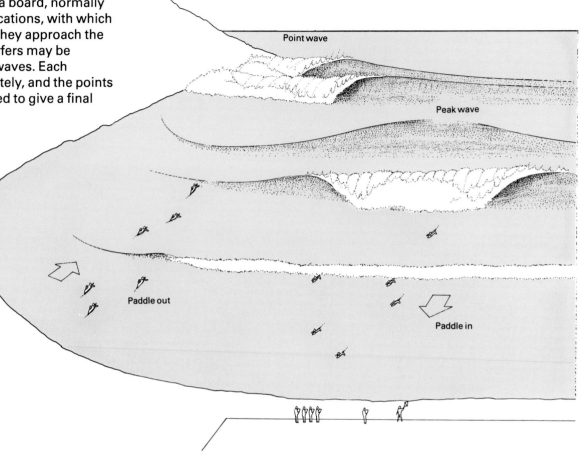

Point wave

Peak wave

Paddle out

Paddle in

Interference A competitor must not:
interfere with a rider who has wave possession (left);
interfere with the previous heat when paddling out;
surf in the contest area unless actually competing. After a heat competitors must return at once, either kneeling or prone.

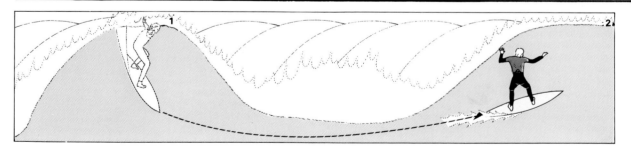

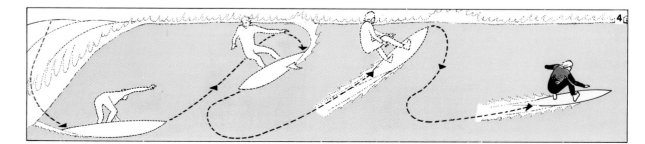

6ft-7ft 6in
1.83-2.28m

Typical performance board

Single fin board ideally suited for the novice

Boards are usually made to the surfer's individual requirements, according to his weight, experience and the type of surf. Most modern competition boards are tri-fins (ie 3 fins on the tail).

Dress Depending on the climate surfers wear: baggies (surf shorts); a full wetsuit with long arms and legs or with short arms and legs, made of neoprene rubber.

Contest singlets of different colors are worn for identification purposes in competitions.

© DIAGRAM

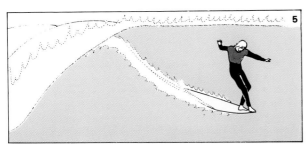

Wave possession
Whenever possible, a wave should only be ridden by one competitor.
A competitor is entitled to priority on a wave if he:
is closest to the curl (**6**);
stands up before any other competitor paddles towards that wave;
is nearest the peak on a peak wave. Should there be a contestant on either side of a peak wave (**7**) then each surfer has possession of his own side.

Penalties Offenses are penalized by loss of points or disqualification from the competition.

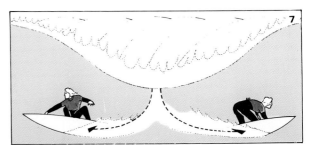

Water skiing

Water skiing as a competitive sport is divided into three distinct sections – jumping, slalom, and trick riding. The winner of a championship is the best overall performer in the three events.

Slalom course

27m
29yd

68m
75yd

82m
90yd

82m
90yd

259m
283yd

82m
90yd

82m
90yd

68m
75yd

27m
29yd

23m
25yd

1·80m**
6ft

6·40–6·70m
21–22ft

30cm
1ft

**maximum

3·70–4·30m
12–14ft

Courses Separate courses are marked out for each of the three events.
Jumping The ramp is an inclined plane, 1.65–1.80m high for men and 1.50m high for all other classes. It has an apron on the right-hand side and a flat surface.
The boat must take a parallel course to the ramp on its right-hand side.
Slalom The boat passes down the center of the slalom course, while the skier swings across its wake to pass six buoys on their outside. The skier must then follow the boat through the central gate at the end of the course.
Trick riding is performed on a straight course with entrance buoys at either end.

Officials Large championships are controlled by a chief judge, who appoints individual judges for each event (usually five per event).
Judging
Jumping A referee rides in the boat to check speeds and to ensure that the boat takes the correct path. Judges watch the jump to ensure that it is correct.
Slalom One judge rides in the boat while the others, from the shore or from judging towers, judge how many buoys are scored.
Trick riding The judges assess whether each trick has been performed within the rules.
The judges have the authority to award re-rides if the boat's speed or path is irregular.

Jump course

19m
62ft 3in

15m
49ft

100m
110yd

100m
110yd

82m
89yd

150m
164yd

50m
55yd

Towing Boats must have sufficient power and conform to official dimensions.
The towing line must be fixed at the center line of the boat.
Inboard or outboard power may be used, and the boats should be fixed with adequate speedometers and two-way radios.
Drivers for the boats are selected from the appointed officials.
Tow lines must have:
12 strands with 60 yarns per strand;
a diameter of 6.3mm at 5.5kg load;
a weight of 16–18.5g/m;
a minimum breaking load of 590kg.

Skis Various types of ski are used for each event, but no ski must be wider than 30% of its length.
Any type of foot binding or fixed fin may be used.
Every care must be taken to ensure that the skis are safe, with no dangerous splinters, chippings, etc.
In jumping events competitors use two skis, in slalom one and in trick riding either one or two.

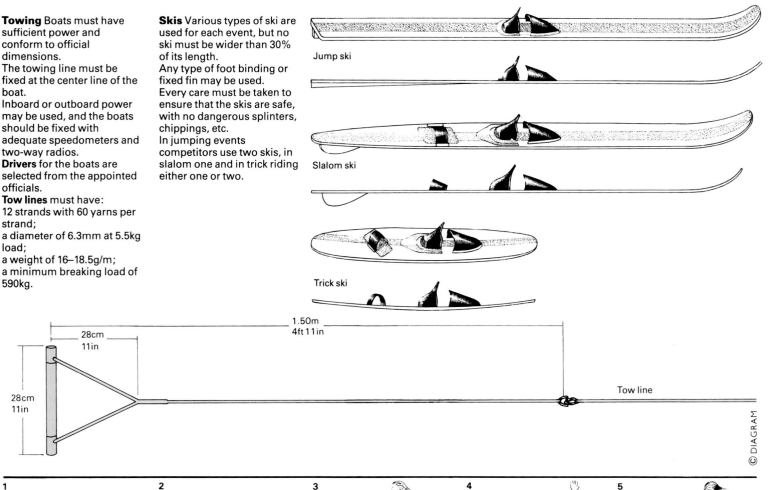

Jump ski

Slalom ski

Trick ski

1.50m
4ft 11in

28cm
11in

28cm
11in

Tow line

© DIAGRAM

Duration In major competitions there are two rounds for each event – a preliminary round and a final round for those leading after the preliminary.
Rounds
Jumping Each competitor has 2 jumps in the first round and 3 jumps in the final round.
Slalom Each competitor continues to negotiate the course at increasing speeds up to specific maxima and then with the line shortened by predetermined increments until he misses a buoy or falls.
Trick riding Each competitor makes two passes down the course (ie travels the length of the course twice); a pass

must not last more than 20 seconds.
Scoring
Jumping For a jump to score, the skier must pass over the ramp, land on the water, and then ski to the ride-out buoy that marks the end of the course.
A competitor's longest jump gives his score for the round.
Slalom To complete a successful pass the skier must follow the boat out through the finishing gate.
1 Each buoy passed scores one point. (The score counts if the skier successfully passes outside the buoy and also crosses back into the wake before passing the level of the next buoy.)

2 A competitor finishes, if he sinks a buoy, but not if he "grazes" a buoy.
Trick riding Examples of tricks are:
3 side slide;
4 backward, toe 180°;
5 wake turn.
Each trick successfully completed inside the course has a tariff value according to its difficulty. These scores are totalled for both passes to give the score for the round.

Result In major championships the placings for each event are determined by adding together each competitor's scores for the two rounds. Placings for the championship as a whole are determined as follows. The winners of the jumping, slalom and trick riding are each given 1000 points. The other competitors are each given a proportion of 1000 depending on the proportion of their own score to that of the winner. The competitors' three scores are then aggregated to give the overall placings for the championship.

Speed
Jumping The boat for men may travel up to 57kmh; for women up to 51kmh.
Slalom The boat must proceed at a specified speed timed by the judge in the boat.
Trick riding The skier informs the boat driver of the speed he requires.

Rowing

Rowing is divided into two basic types of competition. Regatta events are knock-out competitions, ending with a race between two or more finalists. Head of the river races (which are not used in international championships) are processional; boats set off at intervals and the result is decided by their times over the course.

Courses

Regattas are held over a stretch of river, lake, coast or artificial course.

For major international competitions the courses should be straight, current-free and divided into lanes. International races are over 2000m, except for veteran races, which are over 1000m.

Head races are held over a stretch of river of variable length.

Officials A regatta committee is responsible for the overall control and organization. A race committee controls the racing.

Supervisors, at embarking and disembarking points, check the composition of crews and the specification of the boats.

Umpires follow the race in a launch. There is a judge at the start, a starter and an aligner.

Competitors Within each class of boat competitors may be divided into categories by experience, age or weight. By winning certain events rowers graduate from novice status through divisions of the senior class to achieve open status.

Dress Rowers and scullers wear singlets or T-shirts and shorts (or one-piece outfits); shirts bear club or national colors or other insignia.

Breakages A race may be stopped and re-rowed if there is a breakage of equipment from whatever cause within 100m of the start. After that a breakage will not lead to a re-row except in some cases where a collision has occurred. If an accident is caused by an outside agency, a re-row may be ordered.

Substitutes are allowed for up to half the number of the crew and for the coxswain until one hour before the first race. (Substitutes may be allowed later in cases of serious illness.) No substitutes are allowed in single sculls events.

REGATTA RACES

The start Crews must be at the start at least 2min before the race. The aligner indicates, by raising a white flag, when all the crews are aligned correctly. To aid alignment the boats may be held by officials in moored stake boats.

The starter says, "attention", followed by "are you ready", at which time he shall raise a red flag and then lower the flag quickly to one side with the command, "go".

After a false start the boats may be recalled (within 100m) by ringing a bell and waving a red flag.

The race Each boat should keep within its own lane (if marked). It may be excluded if it interferes with another boat or its course.

No outside advice is allowed, eg by electronic means.

An umpire may warn a boat about its steering only if it is about to impede or collide with another boat that is on a correct course.

If collision occurs, or any interference after a warning, the umpire may exclude the offending crew or crews. He may order a restart.

The finish A crew has finished when the bow of the boat crosses the finish line. If an oarsman or sculler falls out, the boat can still be placed, but not if the coxswain falls out.

When all crews have finished, the umpire raises a white flag if the race is in order and there is no protest; otherwise he raises a red flag.

The judges decide the finishing order using photographs, if necessary. If two or more boats finish simultaneously, a re-row can be arranged.

HEAD RACES

There are no lanes or stations. The overtaking crew has the right of way. The organizing committee must draw up the race regulations.

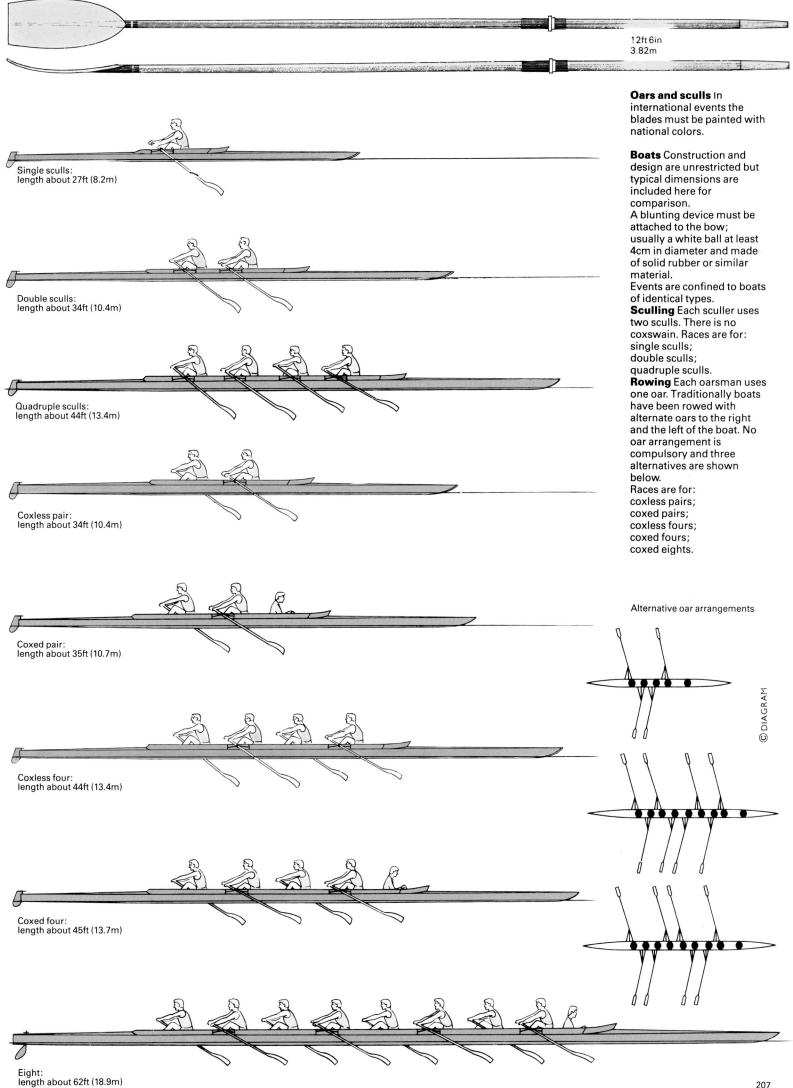

12ft 6in
3.82m

Oars and sculls In international events the blades must be painted with national colors.

Boats Construction and design are unrestricted but typical dimensions are included here for comparison.
A blunting device must be attached to the bow; usually a white ball at least 4cm in diameter and made of solid rubber or similar material.
Events are confined to boats of identical types.
Sculling Each sculler uses two sculls. There is no coxswain. Races are for:
single sculls;
double sculls;
quadruple sculls.
Rowing Each oarsman uses one oar. Traditionally boats have been rowed with alternate oars to the right and the left of the boat. No oar arrangement is compulsory and three alternatives are shown below.
Races are for:
coxless pairs;
coxed pairs;
coxless fours;
coxed fours;
coxed eights.

Single sculls:
length about 27ft (8.2m)

Double sculls:
length about 34ft (10.4m)

Quadruple sculls:
length about 44ft (13.4m)

Coxless pair:
length about 34ft (10.4m)

Coxed pair:
length about 35ft (10.7m)

Coxless four:
length about 44ft (13.4m)

Coxed four:
length about 45ft (13.7m)

Eight:
length about 62ft (18.9m)

Alternative oar arrangements

© DIAGRAM

207

Canoe sprint racing

Canoe sprint races are held on still water courses over 500m, 1000m and 10,000m for men and 500m and 5000m for women. International events are held for one-man, two-man and four-man kayaks and for one-man, two-man and four-man Canadian canoes.

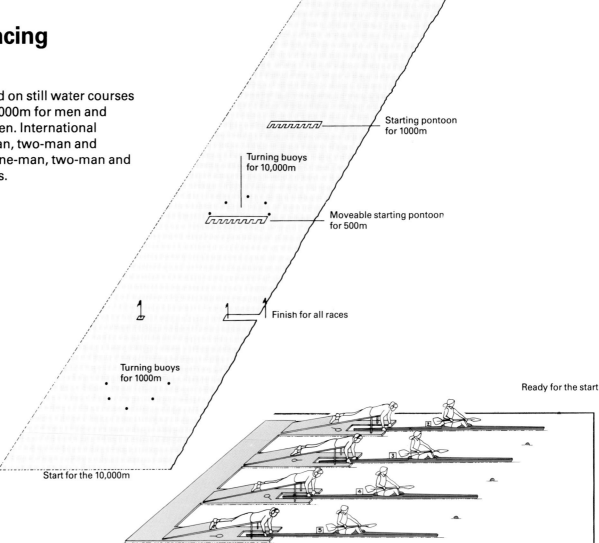

Turning buoys for 10,000m

Starting pontoon for 1000m

Turning buoys for 10,000m

Moveable starting pontoon for 500m

Finish for all races

Turning buoys for 1000m

Ready for the start

Start for the 10,000m

Courses should be through flat water and be as still and windless as possible.
They are marked by buoys with flags.
Courses for 500m and 1000m races are straight, covered once only and, if possible, are marked from start to finish. Courses for more than 1000m may be divided into straights and turns (marked by red and yellow flags).
Courses with turns are raced in anti-clockwise direction.
Start and finish lines are marked by two red flags.
There must be at least 5m width for each boat at the start and 45m total width at the finish.
Distance of straights for more than 1000m are as follows:
a) maximum 1850.5m between starting line and 1st flag of 1st turning point;
b) maximum 1750.5m between last flag of 1st turning point and flag of 2nd turning point;
c) maximum 500m between last flag of 2nd turning point and 1st flag of 3rd turning point.
The specification for all other stretches shall be in accordance with (c).
The radius of each turn shall be at least 40.5m.

Approaching a turn (C 1)

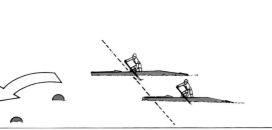

Approaching a turn (K 1)

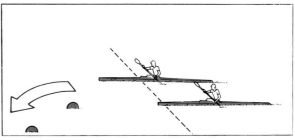

Entries for championships and Olympic events are limited to one per nation for each event.
Substitutes are permitted in all events, but a crew may not be changed after it has begun to compete in an event.
Officials International competitions shall be held under the supervision of the following officials:
chief official; technical organizer; competition secretary; starters; aligners; 25m umpires; course umpires; turning point umpires; finishing line judges; timekeepers; boat controller; announcer; press official.
A competition committee (made up of the chief official, technical organizer and one other) hears protests, settles disputes and decides disqualifications.
For championships, a jury of seven, headed by the president or a leading member of the ICF (International Canoe Federation), receives any appeals against competition committee decisions.
Start Lots are drawn for starting positions. Boats line up with their bows on the starting line. The aligner raises a white flag when all the boats are level and stationary. (In championships the boats are held by officials so that their sterns touch starting pontoons.)
The starter calls "attention please" and, if satisfied, shall give the starting signal by a shot. The shot can be replaced by the word "go". It is a false start if a competitor begins paddling after the words "attention please" and before the shot. A crew is disqualified for two false starts.
If a competitor breaks his paddle within 25m of the start, there is a recall and a new start after the paddle has been replaced. (Flags indicate the 25m distance.)
Race procedure
Races up to 1000m Boats must keep to their lanes from start to finish and approach not nearer than 5m to another craft.
Races over 1000m Boats may leave their lanes, provided they do not impede other competitors. This allows wash-hanging: positioning a canoe so that it is sitting on an opponent's bow wave.
At turns, the outside boat must give room to an inside boat if the bow of the inside boat is level with:
the front edge of the outside boat's cockpit (K1);
the forecockpit (K2, K4);
the competitor's body (C1);
the body of the foremost competitor (C2).
Otherwise, boats must follow the course as closely as possible at turning points. Boats are not disqualified for touching when turning, except when an advantage is gained.
An overtaking craft must keep clear at all times, but the overtaken craft must not alter its course to cause difficulties for the other craft.
The finish A canoe finishes when its bow passes between the red finishing flags.
When all the canoes have finished, the umpire shows a white flag if no rule has been infringed or a red flag if there has been an infringement.
Boats qualifying for a next round, or the first four boats in a final, are then re-measured and weighed.

Paddles are usually made of glass fiber or wood and are designed for speed and lightness. The blade is spoon-shaped to give a clean entry into the water. Kayak paddles have two blades. Canadian canoe paddles have one.

Canoes Dimensions are limited according to class. Sections and longitudinal lines must be convex and uninterrupted.
Kayaks may have steering rudders.
Canadian canoes must be symmetrical upon axis of length, have no steering gear, and be open for prescribed proportions of their length.
Events Men's, women's and junior (15-18 years) events are held for:
one-man, two-man and four-man kayaks (K1,K2, K4); one-man, two-man and four-man Canadian canoes (C1, C2, C4).
World and Continental championships are held every year except Olympic years. Championship and Olympic events are given in the table at the foot of the page.
Heats and finals For the 10,000m there are no heats, but boats may be started at intervals, if necessary.
For the 500m and 1000m heats may be held.
Heats and the final must be on the same stretch of water and none may include more than 9 canoes.
Allocation to heats and lanes is decided by lot.
The heat system should allow three canoes in each heat to proceed to the next stage and finishing positions not times are the deciding factor.
For championships intervals between stages must not be less than 1 hr for 500m and 1½ hr for 1000m events.

K 1

Length 5.20m (17ft)**
Beam 51cm (1ft 9in)*
Weight 12kg (27lb)*

K 2

Length 6.50m (21ft 4in)**
Beam 55cm (1ft 10in)*
Weight 18kg (40lb)*

K 4

Length 11m (36ft)**
Beam 60cm (1ft 11½in)*
Weight 30kg (66lb)*

C 1

Length 5.20m (17ft)**
Beam 75cm (2ft 6in)*
Weight 16kg (35lb)*

C 2

Length 6.50m (21ft 4in)**
Beam 70cm (2ft 4in)*
Weight 20kg (44lb)*

C 4

Length
Beam 75cm (2ft 6in)*
Weight 30kg (66lb)*

*minimum
**maximum

Numberplates These must have black numbers on a yellow background and measure 18×20cm. They are carried on the afterdeck of kayaks and foredeck of Canadian canoes.
Dress Undershirts bear national colors or insignia for international events. All competitors wear black starting numbers on a white background.

Disqualification
Competitors are disqualified for breaking racing rules or attempting to compete by dishonest means (including taking pace or receiving help or encouragement from boats not in the race). Colliding with or damaging another boat (including an opponent's paddle) makes a boat liable to disqualification. A competitor withdrawing from one event without valid reason may be disqualified from any other event in the same meeting.

©DIAGRAM

		Events			500m and
		500m	1000m	10,000m	1000 Olympic
Men		K1	K1	K1	K1
		K2	K2	K2	K2
			K4	K4	K4
		C1	C1	C1	C1
		C2	C2	C2	C2
		C4	C4		
Women		500m		5000m	500m Olympic
		K1		K1	K1
		K2		K2	K2
		K4			

209

Canoe slalom racing

Canoe slalom is a sport testing canoe control under difficult conditions. Competitors negotiate a rapid river course with natural and artificial hazards. Gates must be negotiated in the correct order. There are individual and team events for one-man kayaks for men and women and for one-man and two-man Canadian canoes for men only.

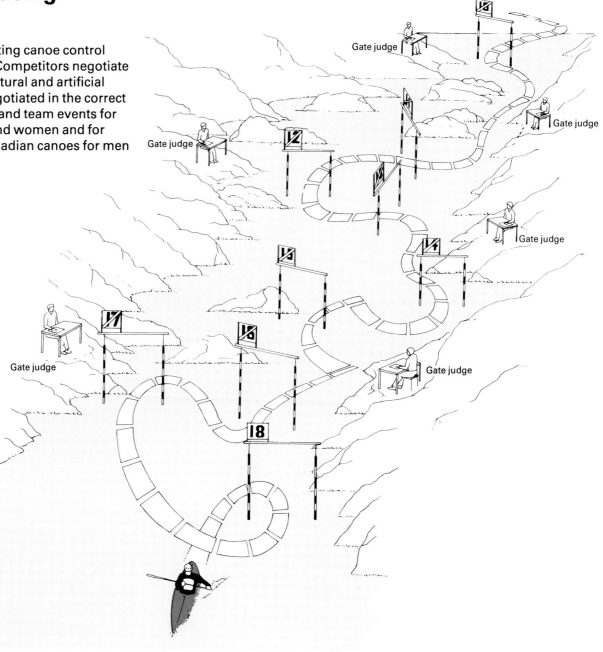

Gate judge

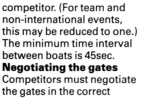

Courses are on mountain rivers, below weirs or on special artificial streams. The water flow must be torrent-like and the current at least 2m/sec.
The stretch of water should include natural and artificial hazards, current, counter current, rapids and rocks. Courses are marked by "gates", which are pairs of poles strung over the river and dangling down to the water. Canoes must pass through the gates in a prescribed order, given a course up to 600m length and graded I to VI according to difficulty. (Major competitions are on grades IV or V.)
Courses must be navigable throughout (with a depth for world championships of at least 40cm).
Gates Courses should have 20–25 gates, including at least six upstream gates. All gates are numbered in order. Gates with two green poles are downstream gates and gates with two red poles are upstream gates.
The bottom of gate poles should hang approximately 15cm above the water. The finish line should be clearly marked on both sides.

Officials
1 chief official
2 technical organizer
3 chief judge
4 section judges
5 starter
6 pre-start controller
7 finish judge
8 timekeepers
9 chief of scoring
10 course designer
11 boat scrutineer
12 safety officer
In addition, at international competitions, a jury of three to seven international slalom experts controls events.
Competitors may only take part in one individual and one team event.
For senior world championships (held every other year) each nation may enter four boats in each

individual category.
For the Olympic Games each nation may enter three boats.
For junior world championships each nation may enter three boats. (A reserve boat may be taken to the competition.)
Events Individual and team events:
men, K1, C1, C2;
women, K1.
Procedure After a demonstration run by at least one non-competitor, final acceptance of the course is agreed by the managers and certain officials. Each competitor is then allowed one training run over the course.
The competition usually takes the form of two timed runs over the course by each

competitor. (For team and non-international events, this may be reduced to one.)
The minimum time interval between boats is 45sec.
Negotiating the gates
Competitors must negotiate the gates in the correct order.
Competitors must pass between the poles without either pole being touched by boat, paddle or competitor's body.
In team events all a team's boats must cross the finish line within 15sec.
Penalties Gate judges signal penalties with yellow discs marked with numbers.
0 Point Penalty:
correct negotiation without a fault.
5 Point Penalty:
correct negotiation of the

gate, but with a touch of one or both poles (repeated touching of the same pole is only penalized once).
50 Point Penalty:
a) touch of a gate (either 1 or 2 poles) without correct negotiation;
b) intentional pushing of a gate to allow negotiation (it is not judged an intentional push, when the body and/or the boat of the competitor was already in a position in which it would have ideally negotiated the gate);
c) the body (in C2 one of the two competitors) crosses the gate line upside down;
d) negotiation of the gate in a different direction from that indicated on the course plan (during any negotiation no part of the body, trunk and head must at any time cross

the gate line in the wrong direction);
e) gate left out (gate left out is determined to have occurred when negotiation of the next gate begins);
f) a team failing to cross the finish line within 15 seconds.
Undercutting of a gate without a touch is not penalized.
Repeated attempts at a gate without touching the poles is not penalized if the body of the competitor has not passed the line between the poles.
50 penalty points is the maximum obtainable on any gate.
At all times the benefit of the doubt must be given to the competitor.

Paddles Kayak paddles have two blades. Canadian canoe paddles have one.

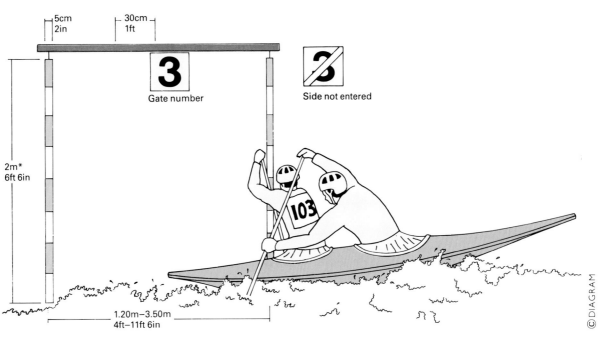

5cm 2in
30cm 1ft

3
Gate number

Side not entered

2m* 6ft 6in

1.20m–3.50m 4ft–11ft 6in

Equipment Safety helmets and buoyancy aids are required.
Starting numbers are worn (by the front man only in C2).
Capsize An Eskimo roll (a complete roll-over under water) is not considered to be a capsize.
In team races teammates may help each other roll up. If a competitor leaves his boat, he is disqualified for that run (as is his whole team in a team event). Crossing the finish line upside down results in disqualification for that run.
Lost or broken paddle Only a spare carried on the boat may be used (or a teammate's spare paddle in a team event).
Clearing the course A competitor caught up by another boat must give way, if the gate judge gives repeated short blasts on his whistle.
The chief judge may permit a competitor impeded by another boat to repeat his run.
Results In individual events a boat's result equals the time in seconds (from starting line to finish line) plus any penalties.
In team events the result also includes any penalty for the finish line.
Only the better run by a boat (or team) counts for its final position, except that ties are broken in favor of the boat with the better time on its other timed run.

K1
Length 4m (13ft 1½in)*
Beam 60cm (2ft)*
Weight 9kg*

C1
Length 4m (13ft 1½in)*
Beam 70cm (2ft 3½in)*
Weight 10kg*

C2
Length 4.58m (15ft)*
Beam 80cm (2ft 7in)*
Weight 15kg*

*minimum

Canoes Dimensions are limited according to class. Canoes must be rudderless, unsinkable and fitted with handholds at the stem and stern (loops or toggles, or a cord running the length of the craft).
Competitors must be able to free themselves immediately from their boats.

Protests against the right of a competitor to participate or against official decisions must be made by team leaders.
Any appeal against the jury must be to the ICF board via the national federation, except at world championships, where the jury is the final arbiter.
Disqualification occurs for breaking racing rules, receiving outside assistance or trying to win by irregular means.
If a competitor is compelled to break any rule by the action of another competitor, the jury decides what action it will take.

Wild water racing

K1
Length 4.50m (14ft 9in)**
Beam 60cm (2ft)*
Weight 10kg*

C1
Length 4.30m (14ft)**
Beam 70cm (2ft 3½in)*
Weight 11kg*

C2
Length 5m (16ft)**
Beam 80cm (2ft 7in)*
Weight 18kg*

*minimum
**maximum

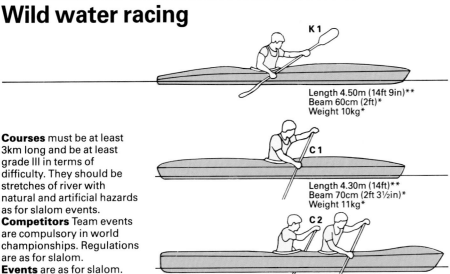

Courses must be at least 3km long and be at least grade III in terms of difficulty. They should be stretches of river with natural and artificial hazards as for slalom events.
Competitors Team events are compulsory in world championships. Regulations are as for slalom.
Events are as for slalom. (There is no Olympic wild water event.)

Officials are as for slalom, but there is no chief of scoring or course designer.
Canoes Dimensions are limited according to class. Rudders are not allowed. General safety regulations are as for slalom events.
Preliminaries The course is inspected and ratified before the race by delegates of the participating nations. Official training runs must be held on the day before the meeting and under the same technical conditions that will prevail during the competition.

Races Each race consists of one run down the course. Starting intervals depend on the difficulty of the course and the number of competitors.
No portage (carrying of boats) is allowed.
At dangerous passages the correct channel is marked by gates.
Any competitor who is overtaken must give free passage to the overtaking craft.
Results Individual results are based on the time from start to finish. Team results are based on the time from the start of the first boat to the finish of the last.
Protests, appeals, disqualifications Rules are as for slalom.

©DIAGRAM

Canoe polo

Kayaks:
Length: 2-3m;
Width: 50-60cm;
Ends: in plan, a curve not less than 10cm radius at any point;
Bow and stern profiles a curve not less than 5cm radius at any point;
Dry weight: 7kg min.

The ball should be an official water polo ball, or of similar material, with a 68.5-71cm circumference and 400-500g mass.

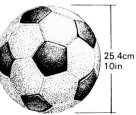

25.4cm
10in

Canoe polo is a competitive ball game between two teams, each of five players. Players paddle polo kayaks on a well defined area of water attempting to score goals against the opposition. The winning team in the game is the one which scores most goals.

Playing area must be rectangular and have, where possible, a length to width ratio of 3:2. Water must be still and at least 90cm deep. Open framed goals lie over the center of each goal line.

Officials First referee, second referee (umpire), timekeeper, scorekeeper, 2 goal linesmen and a scrutineer.

Duration Two 10-minute periods with a 3-minute half time period. Extra time is in two periods of 3 minutes.

Teams Each team consists of a maximum of 8 players, only five of whom are allowed on the playing area at one time.

Dress Players must wear safety helmets and buoyancy aids. All team members must have the same color of kayak, body covering and helmets. Each player wears a number on his body and helmet.

Play At the start of each period, all players will line up with the back of their kayaks on their own goal line. The referee blows a whistle and throws the ball into the center of the playing area.
Only one player from each team may make an attempt to gain possession of the ball.

Scoring A goal is scored when the whole of the ball passes through the plane of the front of the goal frame. After a goal is scored the team that has conceded the goal will take the restart throw from the center of the playing area and the referee will blow his whistle to restart play. All players of both teams must start in their own half.

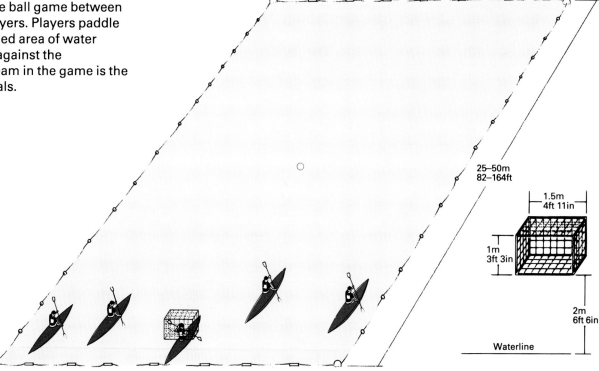

25–50m
82–164ft

1.5m
4ft 11in

1m
3ft 3in

2m
6ft 6in

Waterline

20m
65ft 7in

Paddles Each paddler has one double bladed paddle; each blade no more than 50×25cm in plan with no part of the edge less than 3cm radius in plan.
They must have no sharp or dangerous features.
The paddle may be used to stop the ball in the air or move it over the water. It is not permitted to strike the ball with the paddle.

Substitution is allowed at any time.

Ball out of play If the ball is put over the side line, touches the vertical plane of the goal line or any overhead obstacle, the team not last to touch it with their paddle, kayak or person is awarded the throw as follows:
side line throw (signal 5): the ball must not be thrown in the direction of attack;
goal line throw (signal 6): taken anywhere along the goal line;
corner throw (signal 7).
Type of throw depends upon whether the last player to touch the ball was attacking or defending and is indicated by the referee by hand signals.

A free throw may not be direct at goal.

Tackles A hand tackle is when a player with open hand pushes an opponent's side or arm. The player being tackled must have sole possession of the ball.
A kayak tackle is a player with his kayak pushing an opponent's kayak. This tackle must not make contact with the tackled player's body. The tackled player must be competing for the ball and within 3 meters of it.

Fouls Illegal play includes: obstruction, holding, illegal possession, dangerous use of paddle, illegal tackles, and unsportsmanlike behaviour.

Possession A player must pass the ball within 5 seconds.

Penalties Sanctions available to the referees are: free throw; free shot; goal penalty; player sent off for two minutes; player sent off for rest of game; player reported to the National Federation Canoe Polo Committee.

Advantage The referees can play advantage if neither has blown his whistle.

Canoe sailing

Canoe sailing is a sport more related to yacht racing than to other forms of canoeing. Sailing is under International Canoe Federation rules and International Yacht Racing rules. World championships are held at three-year intervals.

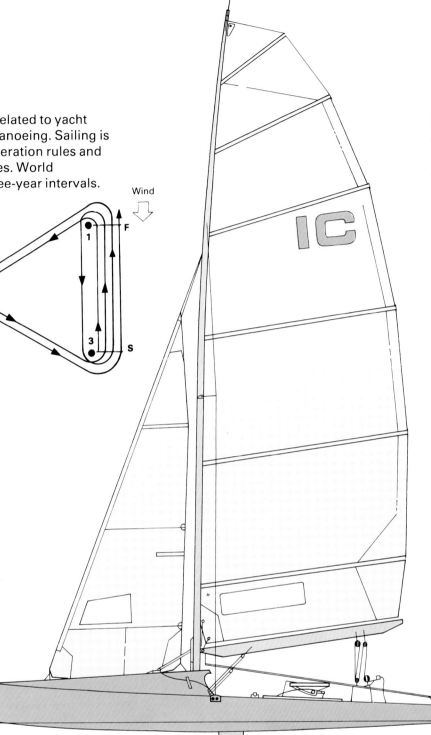

Wind

The course An equilateral triangle marked by three buoys. Sailed in the order: start, 1, 2, 3, 1, 3, 1, 2, 3, finish. The number 1 buoy is always set to windward of the start. Each leg of the course is about 1⅛ nautical miles, giving a total distance of about 10 nautical miles.
Start and finish lines are between the buoys and the foremast of the race committee boat (which flies a blue flag when it is on station).
If the course is shortened, the race usually finishes at the number 1 buoy, giving a total distance of about 6½ nautical miles.

Officials Jury, race committee, protest committee and measurement committee.
Protests and appeals Protests are made as in the IYRU rules. Appeals against decisions by protest or measurement committees are decided by the ICF jury.
Wind speed Normally races are not started in winds faster than 10 meters per second.
Time limits Races are void if the first canoe fails to complete:
the first round within 1 hour 20 minutes;
the whole course within 4 hours.
Scoring system 1st place, ¾ point; 2nd place, 2 points; 3rd place, 3 points and so on.
Retirement, maximum plus one point. Non-starter, maximum plus 2. Disqualification, maximum plus 3. (Maximum is the number of competitors attending the championships after withdrawals.)
The lowest scorer wins.
If six or seven races are held, each competitor may discard his score for one race. If less than five races are held, the championship is annulled.

10sq m canoe
Length: 5.180m (17ft)
Beam: 1.018m (3ft 4in)
Minimum weight: 63kg (139lb)

Class rules All boats must be officially measured and receive certificates of conformity to class rules. These aim to make hull shapes and sail areas as uniform as possible. There are no restrictions on deck layout or sail plan. Remeasurement is required after extensive modifications or repairs.

Sliding seat Maximum extension: 1.525m either side of the canoe.
Weight: 9–12kg, including moving parts.
Carriage must not extend beyond the sheerline.
Hull Any material or method of construction can be used. Must be to drawn design, within tolerances allowed for minor errors and aging.

Mast, boom rigging Rotating masts: maximum thickness at least 2/3 of the depth at the same position. No sail may be set more than 6.36m above the underside of the hull. (Maximum height of the foretriangle: 4.73m above the underside of the hull, where the line of the forestay meets the forward surface of the mast).
Sails Total area: maximum of 10sq m.
Mainsail area: maximum of 8.5sq m.
Sails must pass through a hoop of internal diameter of 300mm.
Letter IC in red, national letter and registered number must be carried on the mainsail.

Crew One person.
Dress Personal buoyancy aid must be worn or carried ready for use.
Hull buoyancy: 75kg minimum with hull flooded. Must be at least two tanks or flexible bags.

Centerboard must not project more than 1m from the underside of the hull. It must be fixed in case of capsize and be capable of being raised so as not to project beyond the keel.

Measurements are checked with templates. The hull is completely decked and unswampable. Protective strips on the keel and centerboard are not included in measurements. Rubbing bands at the gunwales must be of certain dimensions. Stripped weight to be at least 63kg (maximum of 5kg correcting weights).

©DIAGRAM

Yacht racing

Using sail power only, competitors aim to complete a prescribed course in the shortest time. Races are organized by race committees, who issue sailing instructions on starting, sailing the course, finishing, and scoring. The rules given here are from those of the International Yacht Racing Union, and govern yacht maneuvers when racing in daylight.

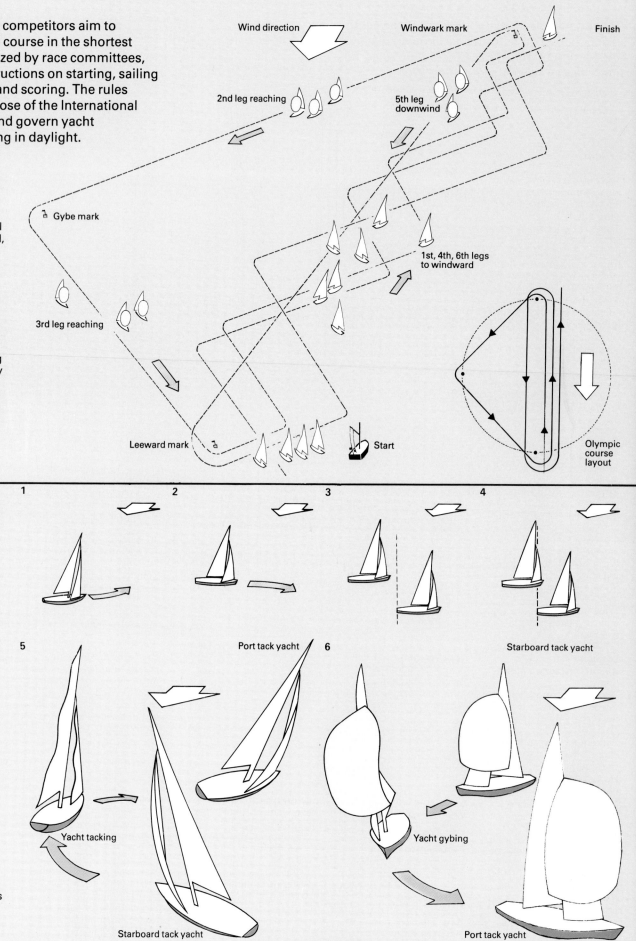

Wind direction Windwark mark Finish

2nd leg reaching

5th leg downwind

Gybe mark

1st, 4th, 6th legs to windward

3rd leg reaching

Leeward mark Start

Olympic course layout

The course Marks (usually buoys) must be rounded or passed in the correct order and on the required side. If necessary, because of foul weather or insufficient wind, flag signals are used to denote that the course is shortened or reversed, or that the race is canceled, postponed, or abandoned.

The start The starting line may be between two marks (usually buoys), a mark and a sighting post, or an extension from two sighting posts. The starting area may be marked by buoys.

The finish The line is marked in the same way as the starting line. There may be a time limit for finishing a race.

Racing A yacht is "racing" from her preparatory signal until she has either finished or retired, or until the race has been canceled, postponed, or abandoned. Yachts that are racing must fly a rectangular flag at the masthead.

1 2 3 4

Definitions

1 Luffing is altering course toward the wind until head to wind.

2 Bearing away is altering course away from the wind until the yacht begins to gybe.

3 Yacht clear astern.

4 Overlapping yacht.

5 Tacking is altering course from port to starboard tack, or vice versa, with the wind ahead. A yacht is tacking from the moment she is beyond head to wind until she has borne away to a close-hauled course on the new tack.

6 Gybing A yacht begins to gybe when, with the wind behind, her mainsail crosses her center line. The gybe ends when the mainsail has filled on the other tack.

5 Port tack yacht 6 Starboard tack yacht

Yacht tacking

Yacht gybing

Starboard tack yacht Port tack yacht

Starting procedure Three flag signals are given at five-minute intervals:
1 Warning signal, when the class flag is "broken out" (hoisted);
2 Preparatory signal, when the "blue peter" is broken out;
3 The starting signal, when both flags are lowered. Sound signals are given with a gun or hooter, but the flag signal is used for timing purposes. Yachts maneuver in the starting area to be in a position to cross the line at the starting signal.

Starting prematurely Any yacht over the line at the starting signal must recross the line.

An individual premature start (**4**) is usually signalled by displaying the code flag "X" and by one shot or one other sounded signal; the responsiblity for returning rests with the helmsman concerned.

A general recall, if several unidentified yachts are over the line, is signalled by the code flag "First Substitute" and by two shots or other sound signals.

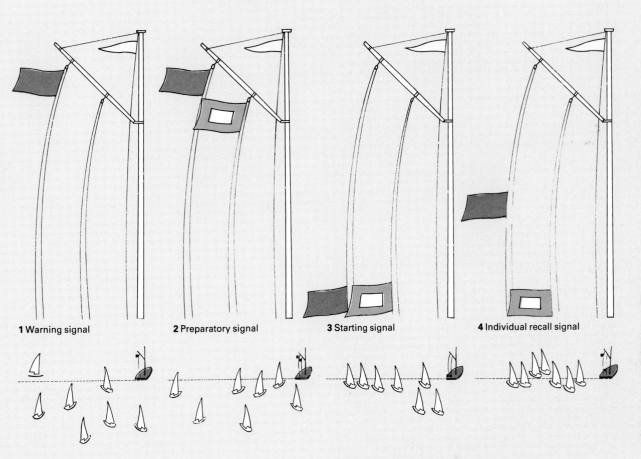

1 Warning signal   **2** Preparatory signal   **3** Starting signal   **4** Individual recall signal

---

Rounding a mark
1 If a yacht passes a mark on the wrong side, she must return by that side and then round or pass the mark on the correct side.
2 If a yacht touches a mark, she must either:
retire at once;
protest against another yacht for causing her offense;
or absolve herself by sailing clear of all other yachts and remaining clear while making two complete 360° turns.

Giving room at a mark
Provided an overlap exists at least two lengths from a mark or obstruction, an outside yacht must give room to inside to:
overlapping yachts on the same tack (**3**);
overlapping yachts on the same or opposite tacks going downwind (**4**).
This includes giving room for the inside yacht to tack or gybe, if that is an integral part of the maneuver; the inside yacht must tack or gybe at the first reasonable opportunity. (Modified rules apply before the starting signal.)

Yachts meeting If two yachts are on collision courses, the one that does not have the right of way must keep clear; if that yacht fails to take avoiding action the other yacht must also try to avoid collision.

A yacht with the right of way does not have complete freedom of maneuver; she must not alter course so that she prevents another yacht from keeping clear, nor obstruct a yacht that is keeping clear.

A yacht that breaks a rule should retire immediately or observe such other penalty as may be imposed in the sailing instructions. If she fails to do either, then other yachts must still observe racing rules towards her.

1   **2**

3   **4**

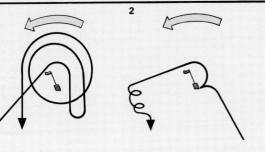

Two boat-lengths

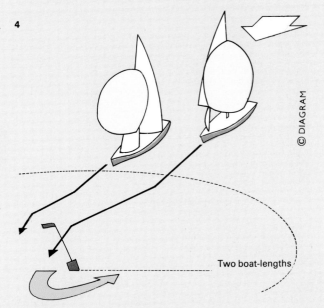

Two boat-lengths

© DIAGRAM

Right of way Several basic rules apply:

1 When yachts are on opposite tacks, the port tack yacht keeps clear.

2 When yachts are on the same tack, the windward yacht keeps clear.

3 When yachts are on the same tack and one is overtaking, the yacht clear astern keeps clear.

4 When one yacht is changing tacks, that yacht keeps clear.

5 When both yachts are changing tacks, the yacht on the other's port side keeps clear.

6 When one yacht is anchored, aground or capsized, the yacht underway keeps clear.

Exceptions

1) When close-hauled, a yacht may hail a yacht on the same tack for room to tack to clear an obstruction.

2) If a yacht is on the wrong side of the starting line at the start signal, the yacht that is sailing incorrectly must keep clear of all boats sailing correctly.

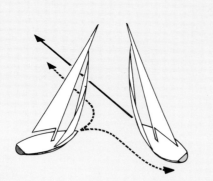
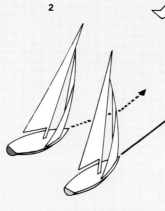
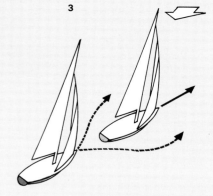
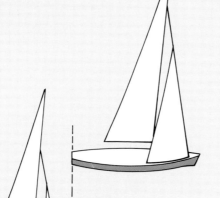
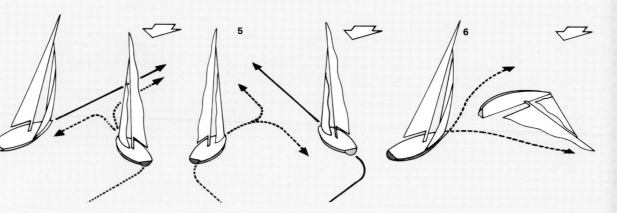

Overtaking Rules that apply when an overtaking yacht establishes an overlap from clear astern and is within two lengths' distance are as follows:

1 If the overtaking yacht tries to pass to leeward, the yacht ahead must keep clear after the overlap is established and the overtaking yacht must give her room to do so. The overtaking yacht may not luff toward the windward yacht until she has gone clear past.

2 If the overtaking yacht tries to pass to windward, the overtaking yacht must keep clear. The yacht ahead may luff the overtaking yacht. A leeward yacht may carry a windward yacht to the wrong side of the sailing mark, provided that she also sails the wrong side.

A yacht may luff another only if she has the right to luff all the yachts that might be affected by her action, in which case they must all respond, even if an intervening yacht would not otherwise have had the right to luff.

3 All these rights cease as soon as the overtaking yacht's helmsman is ahead of the other yacht's mast. (Overtaking rules are modified before the start.)

Within two lengths

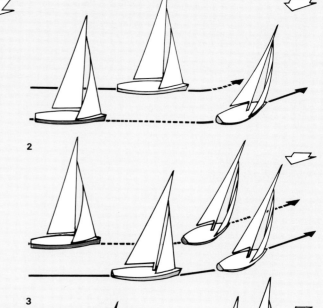
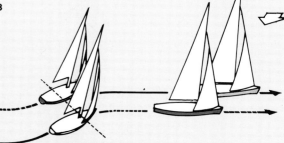

216

Sailing the boat A yacht may be propelled only by wind and water to increase, maintain or decrease her speed, with her crew adjusting the trim of sails and hull and performing other acts of seamanship. Prohibited are: "pumping" (frequent rapid trimming of the sails to fan the air like a bird's wing); "ooching" (lunging forward and stopping abruptly); "rocking" (persistently rolling a boat from side to side); "sculling" (repeated movement of the helm, not necessary for steering); repeated gybing or tacking unrelated to tactical considerations. Permitted when suitable wave conditions exist is initiation of surfing or planing by pumping the sheet of any sail, but only once for each gust of wind.

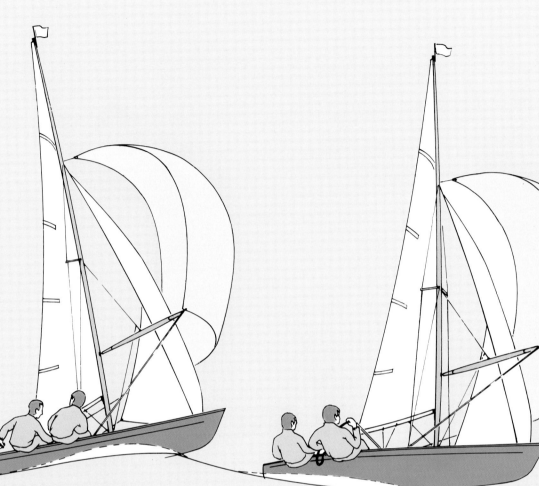

Planing

Yacht rides on wave, crew move forward with sails eased

Sails hauled on, yacht planes in front of wave, crew move back

© DIAGRAM

Infringements and protests

The conditions of yacht racing do not permit referees or umpires, other than in special match races, and competitors therefore should acknowledge their own rule infringements and enter protests about those of other yachts within a time limit. (Before making a protest he must usually have flown a "protest flag" and should have tried to inform the offending yacht that a protest would be made.) When a yacht infringes rules or instructions or causes another yacht to do so, she must retire at once or obey sailing instructions on penalization. Causing a collision always requires retirement.

In national events, protests are heard by the race committee or a subcommittee; appeal is to the national authority. In international events, when protests are heard by an IYRU jury, there is no appeal.

Committees and juries may also instigate hearings where no protest has been made. The outcome of a hearing may penalize a different yacht or invoke a different rule from those in the original protest. If the finishing position of a yacht is "materially prejudiced" by rendering assistance, being damaged when having the right of way or by act or omission of the race committee, the yacht may be granted redress or the race may be cancelled or abandoned, or other arrangements made. In the Olympics a yacht so prejudiced receives points equal to her average points (to the nearest one-tenth) for the other races that count.

Penalties for acknowledged infringements

1 During the race the penalty may be two full turns (720°) clear of other yachts and as soon as possible after the infringement.
2 After the race the penalty may be to score for finishing in a place worse than the actual finishing place by 20% of the number of starters (minimum of three places lower, maximum of one place more than the number of starters).

Penalties after a hearing

(ie for unacknowledged infringements) are:
1 usually disqualification from the race;
2 exclusion from the series;
3 for a gross infringement the owner or helmsman or crewman in charge may be disqualified from racing for a period of time.

Olympic scoring system

(used for major competitions):
first place, 0 points
second place, 3 points
third place, 5.7 points
fourth place, 8 points
fifth place, 10 points
sixth place, 11.7 points
seventh place and below, place plus 6 points.
A yacht that does not finish or that finishes and thereafter retires or is disqualified is scored points for the finishing position one more than the number of yachts entered in the series.

TEAM RACING

Matches are held between two or more teams of two or more yachts each.
A match consists of two races between the same two teams.
During races yachts maneuver to aid teammates and hinder opponents.
Right of way rules may be waived between teammates provided there is no collision.
If there is contact between teammates, one yacht must acknowledge infringement by displaying a green flag. (Certain additional sailing rules apply for team racing.)

Scoring In team racing the first yacht to finish receives ¾ point, the second receives 2 points, the third 3 points, the fourth 4 points and so on.
Penalty points are added to a yacht's score as follows:
For infringement acknowledged by displaying a green flag, 2.5 points;
For an unacknowledged infringement, 6 points.
For serious damage, 10 points.

Result The team with the lowest total of points wins the series.
Ties between two teams will be broken in favor of the winner of the match or race when the two teams met or, failing this, the winner of the second race of that match. Ties between three or more teams will be broken in favor of the team or teams scoring the lowest aggregate points when the tied teams met or, failing this, the lowest points in the series. Failing this the tie will be broken by drawing lots.

OLYMPIC YACHT CLASSES

In the Olympic Games there may be events for the following ten yacht classes: Three person keelboat, Soling; two person keelboat, Star; two person catamaran, Tornado; two person high performance dinghy, Flying Dutchman; two man dinghy, 470; two woman dinghy, one man dinghy, Finn; one woman dinghy, International Europe Class; one man sailboard, one woman sailboard, Lechner 390. There are seven races for each class and each yacht counts her best six results for her total score.

Soling
Keel yacht
Length: 26ft 9in (8.16m)
Waterline: 20ft (6.10m)
Beam: 6ft 3in (1.91m)
Draft: 4ft 3in (1.30m)
Sail area: 250sq ft (23.22sq m)
Spinnaker carried
Weight: 2200lb (998kg)
Construction: fiberglass
Crew: three

Star
Keel yacht
Length: 22ft 9in (6.92m)
Beam: 5ft 8in (1.73m)
Sail area: 280sq ft (26sq m)
Construction: plywood or fiberglass
Crew: two

Tornado
Catamaran
Length: 20ft (6.096m)
Beam: 10ft (3.048m)
Sail area: 235sq ft (21.83sq m)
Minimum weight: 295lb (133.8kg)
Construction: plywood or fiberglass
Crew: two

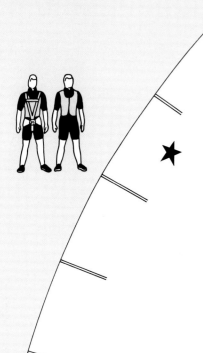

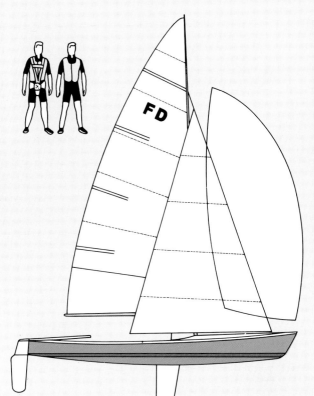

Flying Dutchman
Centerboard dinghy
Length: 19ft 10in (6.04m)
Beam: 5ft 10½in (1.79m)
Sail area: 202sq ft
(18.76sq m)
Spinnaker: 144sq ft
(13.37sq m)
Minimum weight: 384lb
(174kg)
Construction: molded
plywood or fiberglass
Crew: two (one trapeze)

470
Centerboard dinghy
Length: 15ft 4¾in (4.70m)
Waterline: 14ft 9in (4.50m)
Beam: 27ft 7¾in (8.44m)
Sail area: 145sq ft
(13.48sq m)
Spinnaker carried
Weight: 260lb (118kg)
Construction: fiberglass
Crew: two (one trapeze)

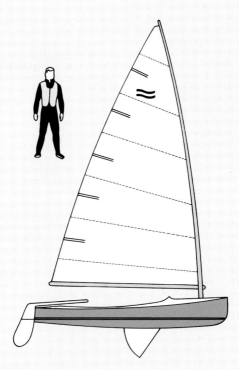

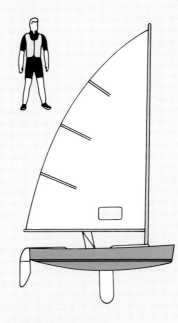

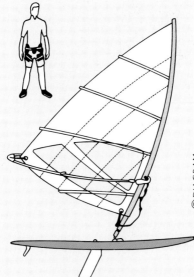

Finn
Centerboard dinghy
Length: 14ft 9in (4.50m)
Beam: 4ft 11½in (1.51m)
Sail area: 107sq ft (9.94sq m)
Minimum weight: 319lb
(145kg)
Construction: molded
plywood or fiberglass
Crew: women; two
    men; one

International Europe
class
Centerboard dinghy
Length: 11ft (3.35m)
Beam: 4ft 6in (1.37m)
Draft: 3ft 3in (1m)
Sail area: 75sq ft (7sq m)
Crew: one

Lechner 390
Sailboard
Length: 12ft 10in (3.9m)
Beam: 2ft 1in (0.63m)
Sail area:
men; 79sq ft (7.3sq m)
women; 73sq ft (6.8sq m)
Construction: fiberglass
Crew: one

©DIAGRAM

Yacht classes All yachts are either keel boats, dinghies, or catamarans. Keel boats and dinghies are further divided into classes. Class rules may govern the measurements, shape, weight, buoyancy, and equipment of member yachts; and every yacht must have official certificates of conformity to class rules.

There are many internationally recognized classes, but all are one of three kinds.

1 In a "one design" class, all boats must be identical.

2 A "development" class allows stated variations, which may be considerable.

3 A "formula" class (for keel yachts only) does not govern individual measurements; instead a number of measurements (such as overall length, draft, sail area) are inserted into a mathematical formula and the result must not exceed a given limit.

Prohibitions A yacht must not eject or release from a container any substance (such as polymer) that might reduce the frictional resistance of the hull to the water.

Unless prescribed in a yacht's class rules or in the sailing instructions, a yacht must not use any device, such as a trapeze or plank, to project a crewman's weight outboard. Nor shall any crew member station any parts of his torso outside a yacht's lifelines, other than temporarily.

Only manual power may be used except for a power winch or windlass for weighing anchor or after running aground or fouling any object or a power pump in an auxiliary yacht.

Only when prescribed in the class rules may a crewman wear extra clothing or equipment to increase his weight.

Required equipment for yachts is prescribed in class rules and sailing instructions.

Generally included are: an anchor; protest flags; specified identifying inscriptions on the sails; life-saving equipment.

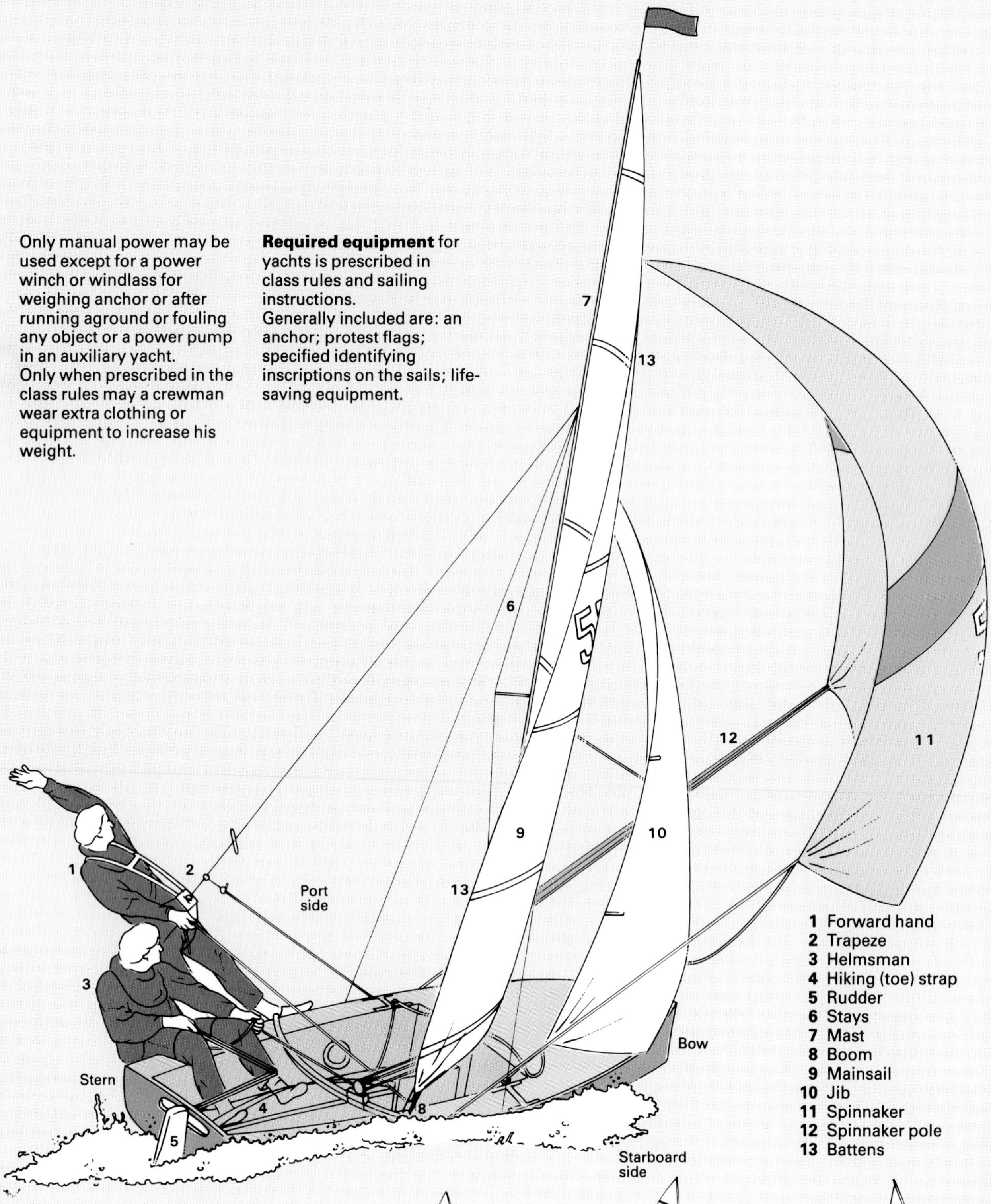

Port side

Stern

Starboard side

Bow

1 Forward hand
2 Trapeze
3 Helmsman
4 Hiking (toe) strap
5 Rudder
6 Stays
7 Mast
8 Boom
9 Mainsail
10 Jib
11 Spinnaker
12 Spinnaker pole
13 Battens

Sailing rigs

Standing tugsail rig:
junior racing/training

Sliding gunter rig:
family sailing/racing

Bermudan cat rig:
one-man racing

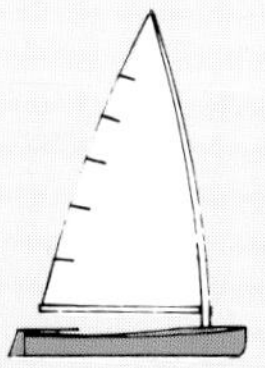

Unstayed cat rig:
one-man racing

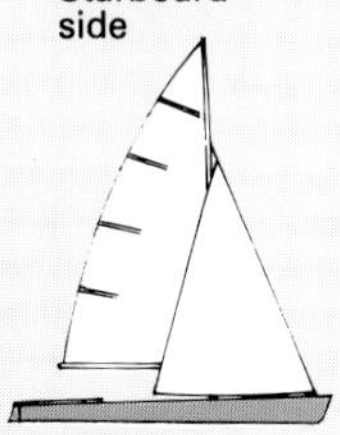

Bermudan rig sloop:
two-man racing

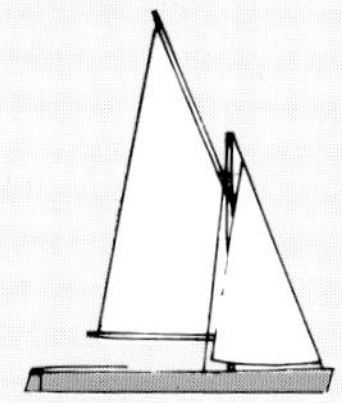

Gaff rig sloop:
two/three-man racing

Una-rig:
international A-division
catamaran racing

Fully battened mainsail:
international sloop B-
division catamaran

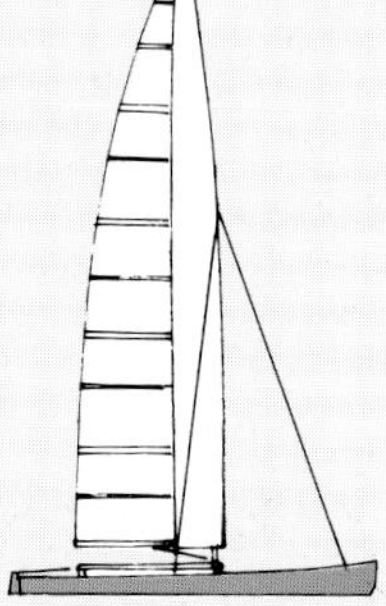

Wing mast rig: C-division
catamaran: international
"Little America's Cup" racing

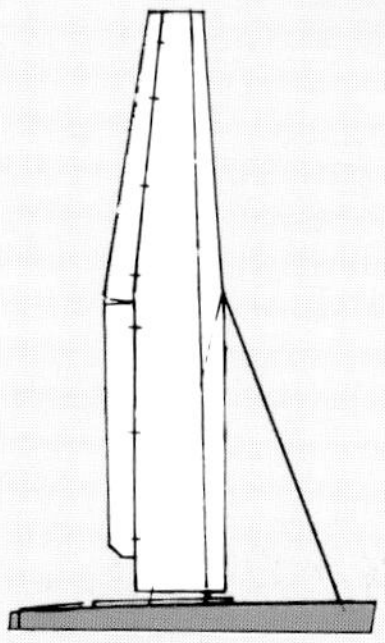

Solid wing rig:
C-division catamaran
racing

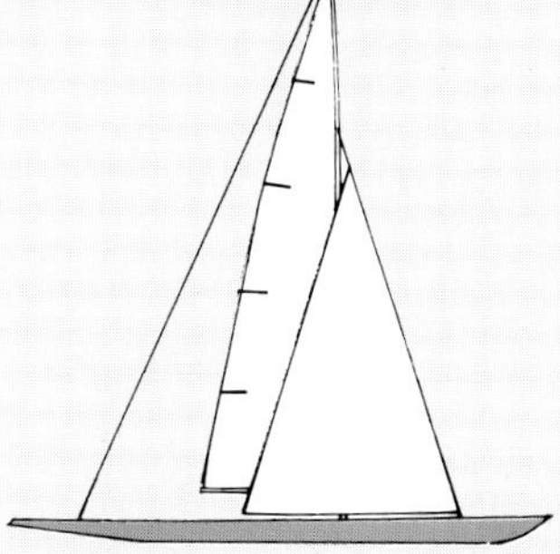

Bermudan sloop high aspect
ratio:
inshore racing

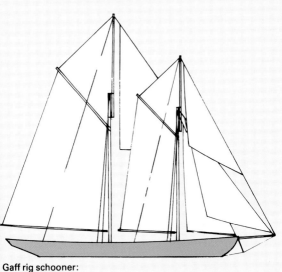

Gaff rig schooner:
non-racing type

Bermudan rig staysail
schooner:
division 1 ocean racing

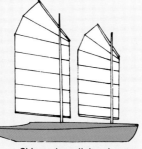

Chinese lugsail rig schooner:
single-handed ocean racing

Gaff rig ketch:
non-racing type

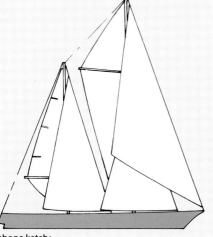

Wishbone ketch:
division II ocean racing

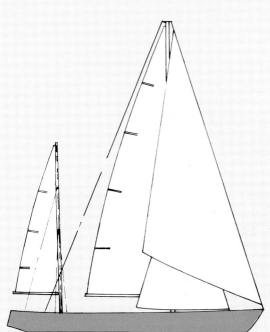

Bermudan ketch rig:
maximum size ocean racing

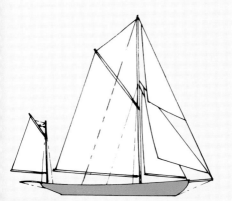

Gaff rig yawl:
non-racing type

Bermudan rig yawl:
division III ocean racing

Mast head sloop Bermudan
rig:
division IV ocean racing

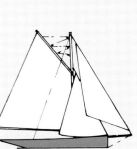

Gaff rig cutter:
non-racing type

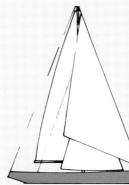

Mast head cutter Bermudan
rig:
division III ocean racing

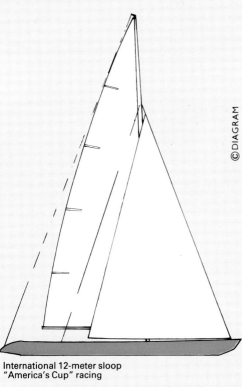

International 12-meter sloop
"America's Cup" racing

© DIAGRAM

Offshore yacht racing

Competitors race sea-going keel yachts over offshore courses. Yachts are divided into classes, and races range from short afternoon events to great round-the-world races lasting seven or eight months.

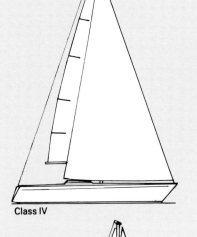

Class IV

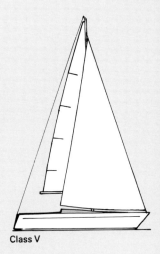

Class V

Class III

Class I

Class II

Yacht classes Yachts are divided according to their ratings into offshore classes. The five largest ones are:
I (33–70ft)
II (29–32.9ft)
III (25.5–28.9ft)
IV (23–25.4ft)
V (21–22.9ft)

Organization The international body for the sport is the Offshore Racing Council, and most offshore races are run under its International Offshore Rule and special safety regulations.

Race categories There are four categories, according to the course's distance from the shore.

Category 1 races are of long distance and are well offshore. Yachts must be completely self-sufficient for extended periods, capable of withstanding heavy storms, and prepared to meet serious emergencies without outside assistance.

Category 2 races are of extended duration, along or not far from the shoreline or in large unprotected bays or lakes. A high degree of self-sufficiency is required, but with the reasonable probability of outside aid in a serious emergency.

Category 3 races are across open water, most of it relatively protected or close

to the shoreline. This category includes races for small yachts.

Category 4 races are short, close to the shore in relatively warm or protected waters.

Race awards Prizes are generally awarded:
a) to a winner in each class (based on corrected times – calculated from the yachts' ratings and race times);
b) to the first boat to finish the course.

Yacht ratings Each yacht has a rating, obtained by inserting its measurements (length, beam, depth, girth, sail area, and many others) into a complex formula (the International Offshore Rule). Measurement is in two stages: hull measurements when the yacht is ashore during building or in winter; freeboard and some other measurements when afloat in full commission.
Ratings are expressed in feet or meters and are used to divide yachts into offshore racing classes.
Rating certificates are compulsory and must be renewed after alterations or a change of ownership.

Owner's responsibility The safety of a yacht and her crew is the sole responsibility of the owner. He must do his best to ensure that the yacht is thoroughly seaworthy, properly equipped, and manned by an experienced crew who are physically fit to face bad weather.
It is the sole responsibility of each yacht to decide whether or not to start or continue in a race.

Inspection A yacht may be inspected at any time. If she does not comply with official specifications her entry may be rejected, or she may be disqualified or subjected to some other penalty prescribed by the national authority or sponsoring organization.

Basic standards The hulls and equipment of offshore racing yachts must meet certain basic standards.
Hulls must be self-righting, strongly built, and fully watertight. They must be properly rigged and ballasted, and completely seaworthy.
Equipment must function properly and be readily accessible. Specifications vary according to the type of yacht and the category of course. They cover:
a) structural features such as hatches, cockpits, and lifelines;
b) accommodation, such as bunks, galley, and the provision of drinking water;
c) navigation equipment, such as compass and spare compass, charts, piloting equipment, radio direction finder, lead line or sonar, log, and navigation lights;
d) general equipment, such as fire extinguishers, bilge pumps, anchors, first aid kits, foghorns, radar reflectors, and fuel shutoff valves;
e) safety equipment, such as life jackets, whistles, safety harnesses, life rafts, life buoys, distress signals, heaving lines, ship's dinghy, and white flares;
f) emergency equipment, such as spare navigation lights and power source, storm sails, emergency steering equipment, tools and spare parts, portable sail numbers, and radio receiver.

Electronic aids Permitted electronic aids are: speedometer and log; sonar; wind speed and direction indicator; radio receiver; radio direction finder (but not automatic or self-seeking); radio transmitter (for private business, emergencies, or for race reporting when included in the sailing instructions); repeating compass. The only permitted links are between radio receiver and direction finder, and between compass and compass repeaters.

Average crew of 6/8 aboard 37ft yacht

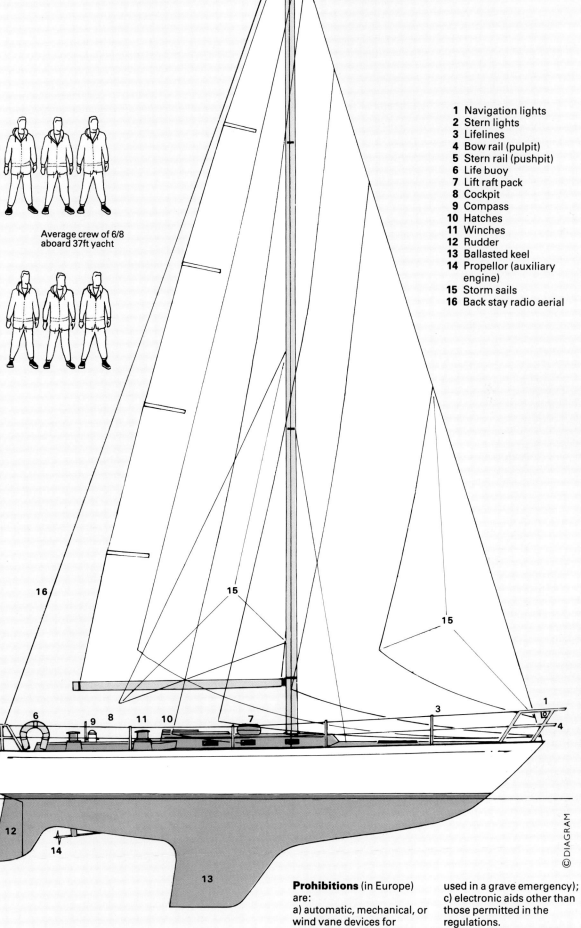

1 Navigation lights
2 Stern lights
3 Lifelines
4 Bow rail (pulpit)
5 Stern rail (pushpit)
6 Life buoy
7 Lift raft pack
8 Cockpit
9 Compass
10 Hatches
11 Winches
12 Rudder
13 Ballasted keel
14 Propellor (auxiliary engine)
15 Storm sails
16 Back stay radio aerial

© DIAGRAM

Prohibitions (in Europe) are:
a) automatic, mechanical, or wind vane devices for steering;
b) engine or power pump, except for charging batteries, pumping bilges, or supplying power for weighing anchor or heaving off (full details must be reported if the engine is used in a grave emergency);
c) electronic aids other than those permitted in the regulations.
(If a yacht has any prohibited devices, these must be sealed inoperable before a race.)

9

Windsurfing

Windsurfing is one of the "new generation" sports, having only developed in the last 20 years. In that time the competitive arena has increased immeasurably, with the combination of board, sail, mast and boom becoming more and more technologically advanced.

The sport has developed into many different sections, each requiring its own specialist equipment, skills and expertise.

Disciplines There are three basic disciplines of competition:
course racing;
slalom;
wave performance.
Additional sections are:
speed;
freestyle;
one design racing.

COURSE RACING
The courses traditionally used have been the Olympic Triangle courses; but with the advent of "funboards" it was considered that a more testing layout was required. The "M" course has evolved as a result (see diagram).

The start The start sequence is a six minute warning, three minute, one minute, then "go." Racers start together, crossing an imaginary line set from a start boat to a buoy, usually around 100–200m (109.3–218.7 yd) away. Any racer crossing the start line before the start is allowed to "re-start" or may be disqualified, depending on the signals given by the race officer.
The minimum wind limit is 11 knots.

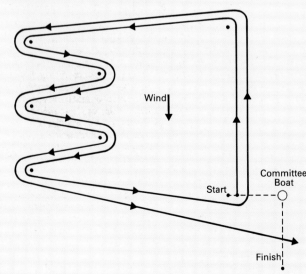

Type of board Any board and sail may be used. In one design racing every sailor races on the same equipment provided by one manufacturer.
The Lechner 390 is the racing board chosen for use by competitors in the Olympic Games.

Scoring The first place finisher scores 0.7 of a point, the second 2 points, third 3 points, and so on. In a series of races the winner is determined by the lowest totaled points after discard. The table shows an example of this. Racer C, who obtains first position in races 2 and 4, wins overall as he has the best score after discarding the worst result in race 3. Competitor B is second and competitor A is third overall after discard.

The reason for this discard is to average out the results in the event of a racer having an equipment breakage or being in collision with another racer and unfairly stopped.
The usual number of races in the course section is five to seven. When four races are completed, one discard is allowed. When seven races are completed, two discards are allowed.

Result	Race 1	Race 2	Race 3	Race 4	Total	Discard	Final total
Racer C	3.0	0.7	4.0	0.7	8.4	−4.0	4.4
Racer B	2.0	3.0	0.7	2.0	7.7	−3.0	4.7
Racer A	0.7	2.0	3.0	4.0	9.7	−4.0	5.7

SLALOM RACING

This is a knockout contest, run in heats of eight to ten racers at one time, with the first four or five competitors to finish advancing through to the next round, and so on up to the final.

A total of 34 heats is needed to complete a full slalom round of 64 racers with the final and losers' final deciding the top 16 places. However, in strong winds a complete round of slalom, depending on the size of the course, can be finished in as little as 3 to 4 hours by a good race team, with one heat starting as another finishes.

Course Two types of course are normal for slalom, depending upon the prevailing conditions. In very large surf it is usual to set only two buoys, one close to the shore, the other outside beyond the waves. Racers then have to round each mark in a "figure of eight" at least twice before finishing.

Occasionally, up to six buoys may be set in a "downwind" pattern; each competitor rounds each mark once only, as shown in the diagram. This course is usually used for flat water slalom, where the speed and maneuverability is much greater.

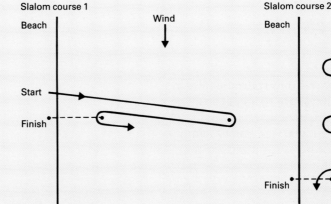

Slalom course 1
Beach
Wind
Start
Finish

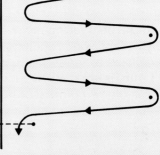

Slalom course 2
Beach
Wind
Finish

The start can either be a "Le Mans" type running start with racers lined up on the beach, who then run into the water and launch all together, or a water borne start across an imaginary line between marks on the water.

Type of board The fast moving and fast gybing small boards have become standard for this discipline with a minimum wind limit of 12 knots being required in professional racing.

Protests A protest may be made against other racers for collisions and right of way infringement, but these are dealt with quickly by the jury immediately after each heat.

Slalom racing is generally held very close to the shore and is enjoyed by both racers and spectators alike for the thrills, falls and close finishes.

WAVE PERFORMANCE

Wave performance demands highly tuned skills and is regarded as the most spectacular of all.

The contest is "man-on-man," a surfing term for one racer against another, the best advancing into the next round.

Scoring A minimum of three judges score each move in the contest area in three categories:
jumps;
transitions;
surfing.

Throughout each section, the more difficult, innovative and varied the moves are, the higher the scores awarded will be.

Competition only takes place in waves, though no minimum or maximum wave size is specified. The minimum wind limit is 12 knots.

Heats are usually five to six minutes in duration. When the heat finishes, the judges' scores are taken and the highest three moves scored in each section are added together to give a grand total. The winner advances to the next round.

Factoring When a particular wind or wave condition prevails, the scores may be factored, so that one category may be factored higher than another if that category proves more difficult.

For example, jumps could be a factor of 3, transitions a factor of 2 and surfing a factor of 5, when the wind makes surfing very difficult.

Therefore the total score for surfing would be multiplied five times, the score for transitions twice and the score for jumps three times. The race director first decides and then announces factoring levels before the start of the contest.

Moves The moves are becoming more daring with jumps getting higher and higher and heights of 10–15m (32.8–49.2ft) are often safely achieved and landed. Transitions are becoming more intricate, and the surfing and riding of waves is continually reaching new levels.

Loops, forward rolls and killer-loops are now common place. The double loop is now a possibility in competition.

FREESTYLE

This is another specialist section, which was very popular in the early 1980s, before the smaller boards came into use. The format is simple: each competitor finds as many different ways of sailing a board as possible.

The windsurfer may sail: inside the boom;
a railride on the edge;
with the board upside down;
a pirouette; or
a combination of all of these.

Judging is by a panel of experts and the most consistent performer with the most varied tricks wins.

Speed sailing A windsurfer is the fastest sailing craft in the world.

Freestyle move: railride

Types of board Top speed competitors use the smallest and narrowest boards possible with the most efficient sailing rigs. Racers now wear crash helmets when sailing, such are the speeds, and the idea of specially built courses in the windiest locations appears to be the future format for the 45 knot barrier.

Record attempts Each record attempt must be observed and ratified by an officially appointed representative of the International World Speed Sailing Committee. Video timing cameras are often used at each part of the course to verify the speeds.

© DIAGRAM

Powerboat racing

Powerboat racing divides into sportsboat racing on inland water, and offshore racing at sea. Each division includes a variety of boat classes. Courses are marked out with buoys or racing markers. A points scoring system is used to determine the winner in races with two or more heats.

Events Competitive events are divided into:
international events open to competitors holding an international license issued by their national powerboat racing authority;
national and open invitation events open to competitors holding a national license;
club events open to members of the organizing club only, or to members of one other club in inter-club races;
basic competitive events open to members of the organizing club who hold basic licenses and taking place on a restricted course as laid down by the national powerboat racing authority.
Control
Competitors must have a valid license and third-party insurance issued by the national authority.
Organizing clubs must be affiliated to the national authority and have third-party insurance cover.
All boats entered are subject to the directions and control of the race committee, but it is the sole responsibility of each entrant to decide whether or not to start or continue in a race.

Dress
Lifejackets are compulsory for all persons on board.
Helmets are compulsory except in the cabin category of classes I and II.

Scrutineering Pre-race scrutineering shall be carried out by national officials for international and national events, and by clubs for club and basic events.

Officials In addition to the organizing race committee, independent observers are required as follows.
For national and international sportsboat races there must be one observer representing the powerboat racing authority of the country of the race.

For national offshore races there shall be three, and for international offshore races five, independent observers. The chairman of this jury of observers is appointed by the powerboat racing authority of the country of the race, the others by the organizing club.

For international events, both sportsboat and offshore, one extra observer may be appointed to the jury by each national authority taking part.
Officers of the day must not participate in any event at which they are officiating.

COURSES
Sportsboat races are held on stretches of inland water. The maximum number of boats allowed in a race depends on the course's dimensions. It is recommended that boats be divided into heats according to speed.
Offshore races range from long-distance races for powerboats in classes I and II, to basic offshore races for smaller boats. Basic offshore races may not exceed 40 miles in total length and are held within an area extending not more than 2 miles offshore and not more than 8 miles from end to end.
Start Boats making a premature start are not

recalled but may be penalized at the discretion of the race committee.
Finish A boat finishes when her stem crosses the finishing line.
After finishing, a driver must withdraw from the circuit without hindering other boats.
Racing flag code
Yellow flag held stationary signals caution;
yellow flag waved means extreme danger;
red flag signals that the race is stopped;
black flag with a number requires the boat with that number to withdraw from the race;
black and white checkered flag signals the end of the race.

Lap scoring and timekeeping The usual system is operated by four officials, sometimes with assistants.
A caller calls out the number of each boat as it passes the start/finish line. This is recorded by the lap scorer.
A timekeeper reads the time at which each boat crosses the line. This is noted by the recorder.
(The use of a second watch is recommended for checking the race time.)
Point scoring A point scoring system is used for races with two or more heats. The usual one is: 400 points for 1st place, 300 for 2nd, 225 for 3rd, 169 for 4th, 127 for 5th, 95 for 6th, 71 for 7th, 53 for 8th, 40 for 9th, 30 for 10th, 22 for 11th, 17 for

12th, 13 for 13th, 9 for 14th, 7 for 15th, 5 for 16th, 4 for 17th, 3 for 18th, 2 for 19th, 1 for 20th.
Publication of results
In any international, national, open invitation, or inter-club meeting with more than one heat, results are to be prominently displayed before the next heat begins.
Rescue craft must stand by for all races.
For sportsboat races, rescue craft must carry: two good swimmers, signal flags, an efficient fire extinguisher, ropes, a boathook, adequate first aid equipment. An ambulance must also be in attendance.
For hydroplane races, a rescue craft must be capable of planing at 20mph. It must

be manned by at least two experienced crew and carry first aid equipment and a boarding ladder.
Hazards A boat may anchor during a race, but must weigh and recover her anchor and not slip.
A boat that grounds or fouls a buoy, vessel or other obstruction may clear herself with her own anchors, warps, or other gear.

Powerboat classes

Sportsboat racing is divided into:
classes SJ to SZ;
classes S1 to S∞;
national stock outboard series;
junior sportsboats;
classes OF, OI, ON, and OZ.

Hydroplane racing is a subdivision of sportsboat racing. It is divided into:
classes OJ to OD;
racing inboards.

Offshore racing is divided into:
class I (28–45ft)
class II (20–28ft)
class III (over 14ft)
class IV (standard production boats over 12ft).

Eligibility All boats taking part in international or national events must conform to the appropriate class rules issued by the UIM or the national authority. All craft complying with these classes must, where required, be measured and registered with the national authority.
In club and basic events, at the discretion of the organizing club, craft may be admitted which do not comply with UIM or national rules.

Sportsboat handicapping

International and national races are not run to an individual handicap system. No class may be handicapped in a series behind another class of greater capacity.
A percentage disqualification clause may only be introduced to classes with three or less starters and then only in the second and subsequent heats.
For international and national events where group handicapping is used, clubs set handicap times on the fastest known boat starting in each class.
New classes may be handicapped separately or together with existing classes, depending on the entries in each race.
Classes OI and ON shall be handicapped separately from existing sportsboat classes. Mercury BP and Johnson and Evinrude GT engines in the I and N classes are handicapped separately, regardless of a boat's hull design.

Records World and national records are subject to UIM (Union Internationale Motonautique) record rules. Any person proposing to attempt a record must give at least four weeks' notice to the national authority.

Classification

1 class I offshore powerboat
2 class III offshore powerboat
3 ON class circuit powerboat
4 hydroplane
5 class IV offshore powerboat
6 national class cruiser

© DIAGRAM

Right of way When two boats are approaching in risk of a collision, one shall keep out of the way as follows:
1) When two boats are turning a buoy alongside each other, the boat on the outside must keep clear.
2) When two boats are crossing, the one with the other boat to her starboard must keep clear.
3) If two boats meet end on, each must alter course to starboard.
4) Every boat overtaking any other must keep clear of the overtaken boat.

5) An overtaking boat cannot set course for a turning mark until clear ahead of the overtaken boat.
A boat that is directed by these rules to keep clear shall:
slacken her speed, stop, or reverse as necessary;
avoid crossing ahead of the boat with right of way.

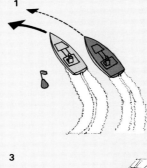

Protests A protest regarding the qualification of a boat, engine, driver, or owner, or against the validity of an entry or of the rules must be made before the start. Such a protest made after the race can only be considered if the driver can prove that the relevant facts were unknown to him before the start.
Race protests can only be made by drivers who took part in the race. Such protests must be made within the time given in the program.
Protests against a result must be made within an hour of the official results being posted.
All protests must be in writing and accompanied by the appropriate fee.

Appeals Ten days after receiving the race committee's decision, the appeal, grounds for appeal, and a deposit must be sent to the race committee, who will forward it to the secretary of the national authority.

Penalties All infringements of general racing and safety rules, or any attempt by an owner or driver to gain unfair advantage over other competitors will be penalized. Clubs will be penalized if they cancel a national event without giving proper notice.
Clubs will be fined for permitting infringements of licensing and insurance rules.

Speed skating

In speed skating two skaters at a time race in a counterclockwise direction around a track. Races for both men and women are held over varying distances. Points are given in relation to the skater's time in each event and the distance winner is the skater who achieves the fastest time. The overall winner is the skater who has the lowest total of points.

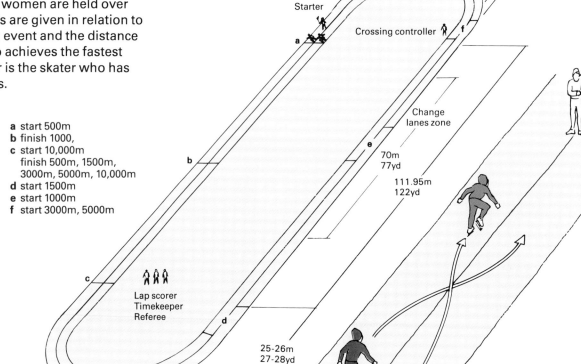

The track An international speed skating track is a closed, two-lane circuit 333¼m or 400m long. There must be two curved ends each of 180°, the radius of the inner curves being between 25 and 26m. The width of each lane must be at least 4m, preferably 5m. The lanes are divided by snow, or by painted lines and blocks of rubber or other suitable material.
The crossing line is the whole length of the straight from the end of the curve. Pre-start lines are marked 1m behind the starting lines. The start of a 1000m race on a 400m standard track is marked in the middle of the front straight (the crossing zone) and the finishing line is marked in the center of the opposite, or finishing, straight.
Every meter of the last five meters before the finishing line is marked.
Races of distances in excess of 10,000m do not have to be held on a standard track.
Officials include a referee and assistant referee; starter and assistant starter; judge; timekeepers; lap counter; and two corner judges.

Events
Men: 500m, 1000m, 1500m, 5000m, 10,000m;
Women: 500m, 1000m, 1500m, 3000m, 5000m.
Events take place in a specified sequence over two days.
Competitors Skaters are not allowed to compete over single distances, but they may have at least 30 minutes' rest between events.
Teams In the Olympic Games each country may enter a maximum of 12 male competitors and eight female competitors.
Men: Each country may enter only four racers in the 500m, 1000m and 1500m events and three racers in both the 5000m and 10,000m events.

a start 500m
b finish 1000,
c start 10,000m
   finish 500m, 1500m, 3000m, 5000m, 10,000m
d start 1500m
e start 1000m
f start 3000m, 5000m

Women: Each country may enter only four racers in the 500m, 1000m and 1500m events and three racers in both the 3000m and 5000m events.
The number of racers in an event may be reduced.
Lanes are decided either by: a draw, the skater drawn first skating in the inner lane; or performance in the preceding distance, the skater with the lower total of points skating in the inner lane.
Skaters must stand still in an upright position between the pre-start line and the starting line. Their skates may not be over the starting line.
On the command of "ready" they adopt their starting positions, and are started by a shot or a whistle.
A skater at fault in two false starts is disqualified for that distance.

Starting In some competitions the starting order for each event is decided by the racers' performances in the previous events. In the Olympic Games there is a draw for the starting order in each event.
Competitors race in pairs in a counterclockwise direction.
Restarts A race may be restarted:
after a false start;
if a starter is interfered with;
if a competitor or any obstacle other than a broken skate prevents a skater from finishing the race.
A skater is allowed 30 minutes' rest before a restart. He starts the second race in the same lane as the first race. If two skaters are allowed a restart, they draw for lanes.

Changing lanes Skaters must change lanes each time they reach the crossing straight, except in the first straight of the 1000m or 1500m race on a 400m track. It is the responsibility of the skater leaving the inner lane to avoid collision.
Skaters may not change lanes or cross the lines when entering, skating on, or leaving a curve.
Overtaking A skater may only overtake if he does not impede the leading skater. When a skater has been overtaken and passed, he must remain at least 5m behind his opponent.
Any form of pacemaking – in front, alongside, or behind the other skater – is forbidden.
Finishing Skaters finish when one skate reaches the finishing line.
Penalties Skaters may be disqualified from an event, from further events, or from events already run for:
deliberate fouls;
collisions caused when moving from the inner lane;
two false starts;
changing lanes on a curve.

Scoring Points are scored on the basis of the skaters' times:
in 500m races each second equals one point;
in 1000m races the points are half of the number of seconds;
in 1500m races the points are a third of the number of seconds;
in 3000m races the points are a sixth of the number of seconds;
in 5000m races the points are a tenth of the number of seconds;
in 10,000m races the points are a twentieth of the number of seconds.
Results The skater who achieves the best time for a distance is the winner. If more than one skater has the same time, each of them is the winner.
The overall winner is the skater with the lowest total of points.
In some competitions the overall winner must have competed in all distances.

Dress The skater who starts in the inner lane wears a white armband; the skater starting in the outer lane wears a red armband.
Skates Speed skates have long, thin, straight blades, reinforced with steel tubing for lightness and strength. The shoe is made of thin leather for lightness.

Short track speed skating

There are three types of race in short track speed skating; individual races over varying distances, relay races with teams of four skaters and pursuit races between two skaters.

The track must be at least 5.71m wide in the straights. The distance between the apex of the semi-circular end and the board must not be less than 5.77m.

Officials include: a referee; at least five judges; starter; timekeepers; lap counter; recorder; two track stewards; competitors' steward.

INDIVIDUAL RACES
Events
Short-distance: 500m, 1000m;
Long-distance: 1500m, 3000m.

Heat system A maximum of four skaters race together in short-distance events and a maximum of six skaters in long-distance events. Skaters may qualify for further rounds by either:
winning a heat;
being among a specified number of skaters with the fastest times;
or being among the fastest runners-up.
The race winner is the first skater to finish in the final.

Elimination system A maximum of eight skaters competes. After four laps the skater in last position is eliminated. Another skater is eliminated after the next two laps and after each successive two laps until only the winner remains.

Overtaking The leading competitor has the right of way and may be passed on the outside, providing he/she keeps to the inside of the track or may be passed on the inside if he/she keeps to the outside of the track. The responsibility for any collision or obstruction is with the skater who is overtaking.
A skater who has been, or is being, lapped may be instructed by the judges to move to the outside of the track to allow the oncoming skaters the right of way. The judges may signal to the skater to move to, and remain on the track without impeding other competitors.

Offenses A skater may not:
deliberately impede another competitor with any part of the body;
slow down unnecessarily, so causing another competitor to slow down or collide;
deliberately cross the track or in any way interfere with another competitor or with the result of the race.

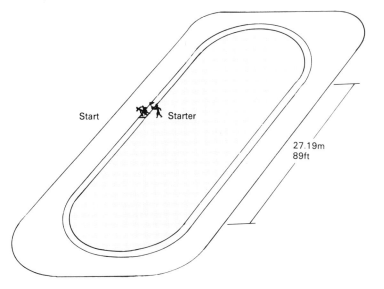

Start   Starter

27.19m
89ft

© DIAGRAM

Penalties Offenses may be penalized by disqualification, and a skater can be disqualified during a race.
A skater who is disqualified is not allowed to compete in the rerun.

RELAY RACES
Competitors Teams have four members, each of whom must take part. Only one competitor at a time from each team may skate in a race until relieved.

Substitutes may be allowed if a skater is injured during a race or contest.
If the substitution occurs during a heat or semi- or quarter-final, the substitute must remain in the team for the rest of the contest.

Relaying A skater may be replaced by another member of the team at any time except during the last two laps.
The incoming team member is not in the race until he has touched, or is touched by, the skater who is being replaced.
The replaced skater must leave the track without impeding any of the other skaters.
A pistol signals the beginning of the last three laps and a bell the beginning of the final lap.

Offenses Skaters may not impede, obstruct, or interfere with opponents, either on or off the track. Offenses may be penalized by disqualification of the whole team.

Result The team of the first skater to reach the finishing line wins the race.

PURSUIT RACES
Competitors Each race is between two skaters.
Starting The skaters start opposite each other, each in the middle of the straight.
Duration Each race lasts a maximum of 10 laps.
Result The winner is the skater who overtakes the other one or who finishes in the faster time.
Heat winners qualify for the next round, in which the fastest qualifier is matched against the slowest qualifier and the second fastest against the second slowest, and so on, until the winner is determined.

Figure skating

There are three types of figure skating competition: single skating, pair skating, and ice dancing. Competitors perform compulsory movements and movements of their own choice. Marks are awarded for technical merit (composition) and artistic impression (presentation). Judges mark each competitor individually and the winner in each part is the skater or pair or dance couple placed first by the majority of judges.

Rink The rink area for free skating and short programs should be rectangular. Maximum size: 60x30m. Minimum size: 56x26m. There must be a music reproduction system.

Music In both single and pair skating the music is selected by the competitors.

Officials There must be two referees, a maximum of nine judges for both figure skating and ice dancing; one announcer; two secretaries; one timekeeper; and supplementary officials as necessary.

Duration In both single and pair skating, the original programs and the free skating sections have specified time limits. For original programs the maximum time is two minutes and forty seconds. Skaters may finish in less time if they have attempted all the stipulated moves; no extra marks may be obtained for extending the program to the maximum time or repeating moves that have failed.

For free skating the maximum times are: women, four minutes; men, four and one half minutes; pairs, four and one half minutes.

The skater must finish within ten seconds before or after the specified time. The end of the time is signaled by a gong or whistle.

Sequence The compulsory dances are skated first, followed by the original program or dance and then the free skating or dancing. There is a draw to decide the starting order in the compulsory section. The starting order in subsequent sections is decided by the competitors' performances in the previous sections.

Restarts If a competitor is interfered with the referee may allow the program to be restarted. Such restarts occur after all the other competitors in the same group have performed. Any previous score is disregarded.

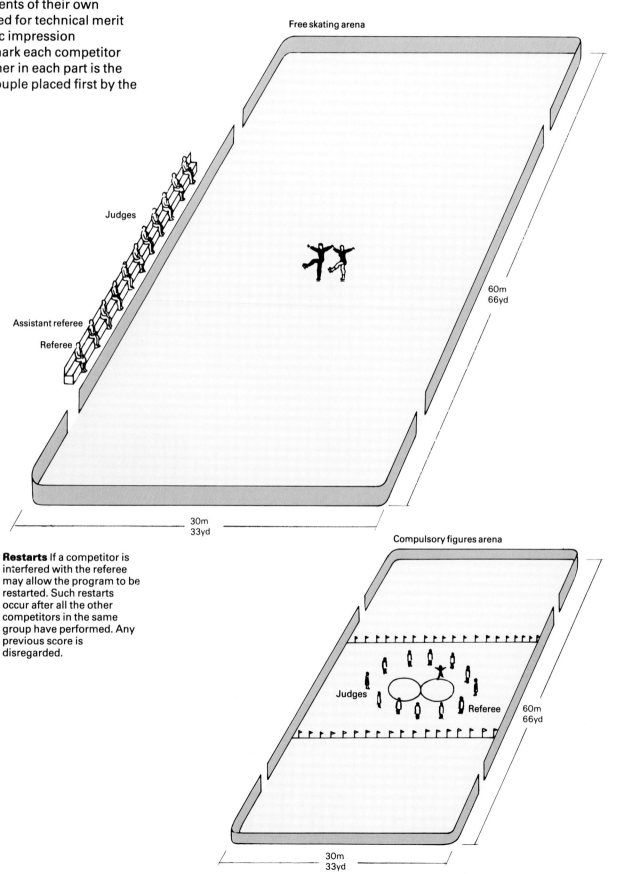

Free skating arena

Judges

Assistant referee

Referee

60m
66yd

30m
33yd

Compulsory figures arena

Judges

Referee

60m
66yd

30m
33yd

Dress Costumes for ISU (International Skating Union) championships must be modest, dignified and appropriate for athletic competition.

Skates usually have a single steel blade about 3mm wide. The blade is hollow-ground on the bottom to give two skating edges; figures are skated on the inside or the outside edge.

© DIAGRAM

ICE DANCING

Ice dancing consists of:
a) compulsory dances;
b) original dance;
c) free dancing.
The dance couple must consist of one woman and one man.

Compulsory dances

Competitors skate two dances drawn from the following groups of dances:
1) Westminster Waltz, Viennese Waltz, Starlight Waltz, Ravensberger Waltz;
2) Kilian, Quickstep, Paso Doble, Yankie Polka;
3) Blues, Rhumba, Argentine Tango, Tango Romantica.

The original dance is treated as a separate part of an event. Each couple chooses its own music, tempo, and composition but the rhythm is announced annually by the ISU Ice Dance Committee.
The dance is to be composed of sequences consisting of one complete circuit of the ice surface. The choice of steps, connecting steps, turns and rotations is free, provided the movements conform to ISU rules.

Free dancing The free dance consists of non-repetitive combinations of dance movements composed into a 4-minute program displaying the dancers' personal ideas in concept and arrangement. Competitors choose their own music. All steps, turns, and changes of position are permitted, as are certain free skating movements appropriate to the rhythm, music, and character of the dance. Competitors are marked for their general knowledge and ability in dancing as well as for the originality and concept of their ideas.

SINGLE SKATING

Single skating consists of:
a) an original program that includes compulsory movements (this section is omitted from some competitions);
b) free skating.

The original program consists of eight prescribed free skating elements with connecting steps. It lasts for a maximum of two minutes and forty seconds. The connecting steps are also marked and should be kept to a minimum. Marks are deducted if unprescribed or additional elements are included.

PAIR SKATING

This consists of:
a) an original program that includes compulsory moves;
b) free skating.

The pair must consist of a man and a woman. They need not perform the same movements or always remain in contact with each other, but they must give a united, harmonious performance.

Forbidden movements: swinging the lady while holding her hand or foot; jumping toward the other partner; rotating with one partner gripping the other's leg, arm, or neck.

Lifting is permitted only with the hands; it is forbidden to hold the partner's legs. The partner may not be carried for more than three complete revolutions. The lifting arm must be fully extended. It is forbidden to turn the lifted partner in a horizontal position.

The original program consists of eight compulsory elements with connecting steps. Marks are deducted if unprescribed or additional elements are included.

Spins
1 Sit spin
2 Camel spin
3 Upright spin

FREE SKATING

The skater selects movements, jumps, spins, steps and other linking movements. This program should be executed with a minimum of two-footed skating, in harmony with the music.

Scoring

The scale of marks for each performance runs from one to six (to one decimal place).

Ice dancing The score from each judge is obtained as follows:

the marks for the compulsory dances are added;

the marks for the composition and presentation of the original dance are added.

Original program: two marks for required elements and presentation.

Original dance: two marks for composition and presentation.

Free skating Each judge awards two marks for each program: one for technical merit and the other for artistic impression.

The judges simultaneously display the marks they have awarded, using black numbers for whole marks and red numbers for decimals.

Results

At the end of each part of the competition each judge places the competitors according to the total points he has awarded.

The competitor or pair placed first by the absolute majority of judges is the winner; the other places are similarly decided.

If two or more competitors or pairs have obtained a majority for the same place, the higher-placed will be the one who has been awarded

that place by the greater number of judges. If such majorities are equal, the lowest total of place numbers of those judges forming the majority decides between them.

After the result in each part of the competition has been determined, the placing obtained by each competitor in each part of the competition is multiplied by the appropriate factor as follows:

Dance	Factor	
Compulsory dances	20%	(0.4)
Original/ set pattern	30%	(0.6)
Free dance	50%	(1.0)

Singles	Factor	
Original program	33%	(0.5)
Free skating	50%	(1.0)

Pairs	Factor	
Original program	33%	(0.5)
Free skating	67%	(1.0)

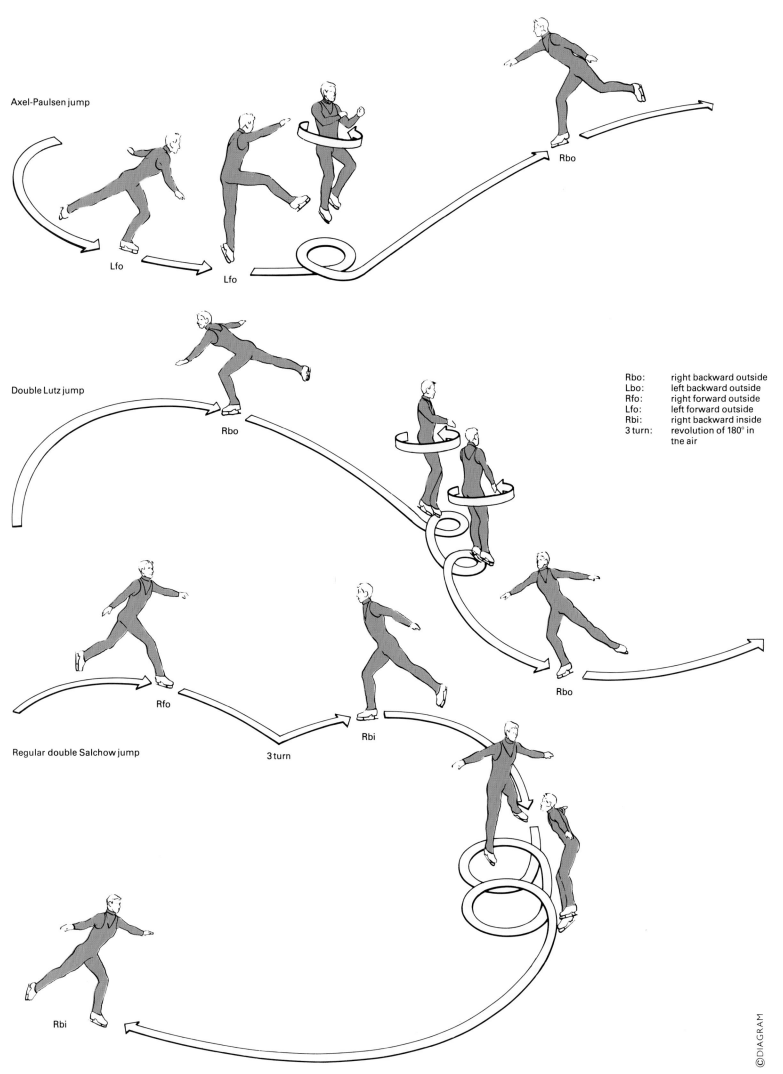

Axel-Paulsen jump

Lfo

Lfo

Rbo

Double Lutz jump

Rbo

Rbo: right backward outside
Lbo: left backward outside
Rfo: right forward outside
Lfo: left forward outside
Rbi: right backward inside
3 turn: revolution of 180° in
the air

Regular double Salchow jump

Rfo

3 turn

Rbi

Rbo

Rbi

©DIAGRAM

233

Skiing

Skiing sports are divided into three basic groups: Alpine, Nordic, and biathlon. Alpine skiing includes downhill, slalom, giant slalom and Super-G races, and the Alpine combined event. Nordic skiing includes cross-country, ski jumping, and the Nordic combined. Biathlon combines cross-country skiing with rifle shooting. All these skiing sports are included in the Winter Olympics.

Skis are made of synthetic materials which have largely replaced wood and metal. Alpine skis have steel edges; the length and weight of the skis differ according to the intended use, height of the competitor and personal preferences.
Downhill skis are heavier and stiffer than skis for other alpine groups.

Slalom skis are shorter and easier to turn.
Giant slalom skis have more flexibility and camber than downhill skis and their width is between that of downhill and slalom skis.
Super G skis are just as heavy as downhill skis.
Ski-jumping skis are heavier, wider and longer than the others.

Cross-country skis are narrow and light and have a toe fastening to allow freedom of movement for the heels.
Sticks (poles) are used for balance, to help in climbing and to give impetus at starts and turns.
They are made of steel or aluminum tubing.
Handles are usually plastic,

and there is an adjustable strap.
The basket, about 8cm from the end, prevents the stick from sinking too deep into the snow.
The length of sticks used varies with the skier's size and preference; the top usually reaches between the waist and armpit when the arm is hanging normally and

the tip of the stick is on the ground.
In cross-country the stick reaches the armpit when the tip is placed on the ground, but the stick is much shorter for downhill racing.

Officials Skiing competitions require a large number of officials. Each event is supervised by a committee. The duties of officials and their assistants include setting and maintaining the course, starting, gate-keeping (in Alpine events), supervising the finish, and timing.
Many events require officials, who are not competitors, to make the track by skiing on the course before the competition begins.
There is a jury to decide protests, disputes, and other problems.

Boots must fit to give maximum control over the ski edges and support for the ankles.
Racing boots are stiffer and fit higher than cross-country boots, which are lighter and lower-fitting for extra comfort.

Bindings hold the boots firmly to the skis. They also release the skier from the skis in case of a fall.
Waxing Racers wax the under surface of their skis to increase their speed. The type and amount of wax used varies according to temperature, snow conditions, etc. Waxing is

particularly important on cross-country skis.
Dress must be warm, waterproof, and tight-fitting (to reduce wind resistance). Goggles may be used as protection from glare, wind, and snow spray, and to improve visibility in some conditions.

Downhill racers must wear crash helmets.
Penalties Competitors may be disqualified for not complying with regulations. Offenses include:
receiving unauthorized assistance;
not following the proper course (eg missing out a gate in racing events);

not giving way to an overtaking skier at the first demand.

©DIAGRAM

235

Alpine skiing

Alpine skiing includes four types of race: downhill, slalom, giant slalom and Super-G. There are also combined events comprising several races, either downhill, slalom, or both. There are races for men, women, and teams. General rules apply to all Alpine events.

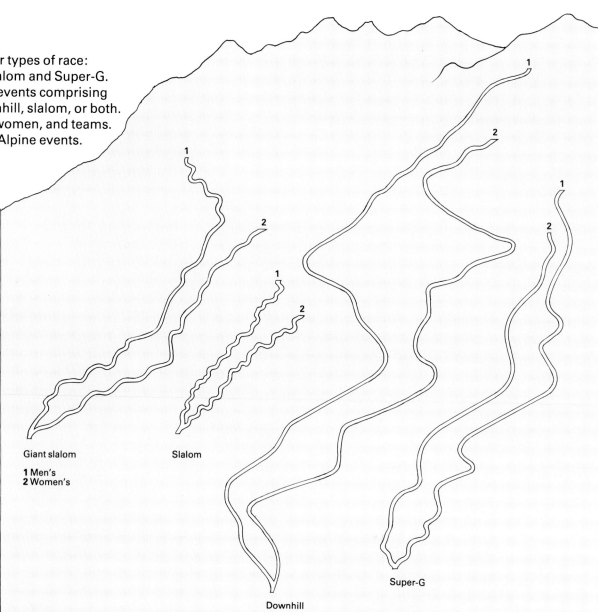

Giant slalom

1 Men's
2 Women's

Slalom

Super-G

Downhill

Courses The snow must be as smooth and compact as possible.
Snow banks, straw, nets, etc, should be used for protection against hazards. Smaller obstacles should be removed from the course. There must be direct communication between the start and finish.

Competitors The starting order of the competitors in all alpine competitions is determined by their points (downhill, slalom, giant slalom and Super-G). The first group comprises the 15 best competitors present, regardless of nationality. All remaining competitors start in order of their points. All competitors without points are drawn in the last group. If, in the first 15 competitors present, the point difference between one and the following competitor is too great, the jury has to decide the number of competitors in the first group. If the number without points is too great the jury divides them into several groups. In this case, each nation announces the group to which it wishes to belong. Each group is then separately drawn.

Timing For all international competitions, electronic timing provided with a printer and with communication between start and finish, which will allow measurements of the times to 100ths of a second must be used. The starting gate must be placed in such a way so that starting is impossible without it opening.
For all competitions, the hand timing must be totally separate and independent of the electronic timing at the start and finish. It must record to a full tenth of a 10th second.
With electronic timing, the time is taken when a competitor crosses the line between the finish posts with any part of his body or equipment. With hand timing the time is taken when the competitor's foot crosses the line.

Re-runs A skier may appeal for a re-run because of:
obstruction;
objects on the course;
a missing gate;
a timing failure;
any other circumstances beyond his control that interfered with his performance.
In the case of fixed start intervals the competitor may start the re-run at the fixed interval, after he has reported to the start referee. With non-fixed start intervals, the chief of timing and calculation or his special assistant tells the starter that each competitor should start. As soon as the starter has received the order for the next start, he gives the competitor the warning "Ready" and a few seconds later the start signal. The competitor must start within 10 seconds of this order. The time for the re-run is the

one recorded, even if it is longer than the competitor's original time.
A skier may be disqualified if he makes an unjustified appeal.

Team races Unless special conditions apply, a team consists of five competitors, of which the three best count for the result. The placings of the teams is determined by addition of the race points of the three best competitors of each team. In case of a tie, the placing is determined by the result of the best individual competitors. For combined placings, the team score for each discipline is calculated. In case of a tie, the best team is determined by the team placing in the order of downhill, giant slalom or slalom.

Start The starting area is reserved for the starting competitor and officials. A

special roped off area must be provided for trainers, team captains, service personnel, etc, in which they may take care of the waiting competitors without being interrupted by the public. An adequate shelter must be prepared for the competitors waiting for the call to start. The start is prepared in such a way that the competitors can stand relaxed on the starting line and can quickly reach full speed after leaving the start. All outside help is forbidden. By order of the starter, the competitor must plant his poles in front of the start line, or where indicated. The starter must not touch the competitor at the start. Pushing off from the start posts or other aids is forbidden and the competitor may start only with the help of his ski poles. Skiers are warned 10 seconds before the start of

the race, and in races other than the slalom the last 5 seconds are counted out by the starter before he gives the command to start. Alternatively, an automatic audible signal is used.
A competitor who, without just cause, is not ready to start at the appointed time will be disqualified. A competitor who starts more than 3 seconds early in a race with fixed starting intervals will be disqualified for a false start. When a competitor crosses the start line more than 3 seconds after the official start time, his time is taken as if he had started 3 seconds after the official start time.

Finish
In downhill and Super-G races, the finish must be no less than 15m wide and in slalom and giant slalom no less than 10m wide.

Downhill skiing

Skiers in downhill events race down the course as quickly as possible. Control gates are used to direct competitors over the course and to reduce the average speed. The winner is the skier who legally completes the course in the fastest time.

Course It must be possible to slide down the length of the course without using ski poles.
There must be no convex outward curves and no sharp, hard ridges or ledges. Competitors must not be forced to travel too far or too high in the air.
The course must increase in width as the speed increases.
Sections through wooded terrain must be at least 30m wide; other sections may be narrower since sun and wind can damage a snow surface that is too wide.
There must be a wide, gently sloping, and unobstructed run-out at the finish. Communication must be arranged between the start and finish.
A course must not be used if sections in full sun are immediately followed by sections in deep shadow.
At least three fore-runners (not competitors) must ski the course at racing speed before the race in order to indicate a line and test the setting of the gates.
Men's courses must have a drop of 800–1000m. In Olympic and world ski championships, the best time for the course must not be less than two minutes.
Women's courses must have a drop of 500–700m. In Olympic and world ski championships, the best time for the course must not be less than 100 seconds. If possible, women's downhill courses should be separate from the men's.

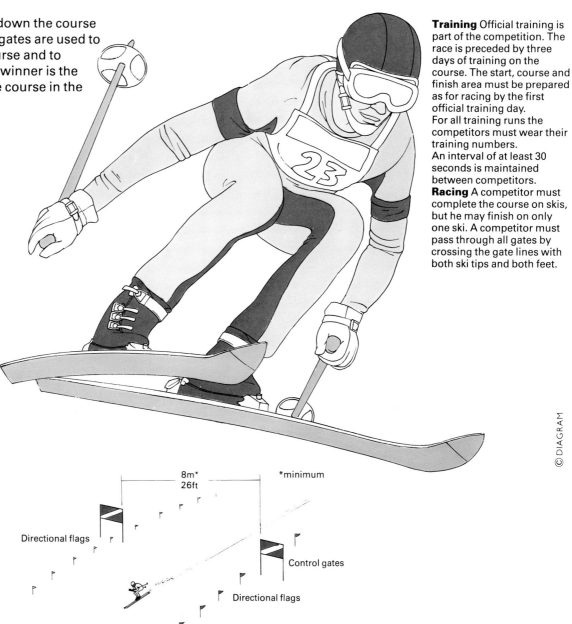

8m*
26ft

*minimum

Directional flags

Control gates

Directional flags

Training Official training is part of the competition. The race is preceded by three days of training on the course. The start, course and finish area must be prepared as for racing by the first official training day.
For all training runs the competitors must wear their training numbers.
An interval of at least 30 seconds is maintained between competitors.
Racing A competitor must complete the course on skis, but he may finish on only one ski. A competitor must pass through all gates by crossing the gate lines with both ski tips and both feet.

© DIAGRAM

Control gates are used to direct competitors over the course, keep them away from dangerous areas and, to reduce the average speed for the run.
A downhill gate consists of 4 slalom poles. Rectangular cloth panels are fastened on the poles so that they can be easily recognized from a distance. Gates must be at least 8m wide. With the exception of the start and finish, gates are numbered consecutively down the course. Men's courses are marked by red gates and women's courses are marked either with alternating red and blue gates or only red gates.

Direction flags are set on each side of the course: red flags down the left side and green flags down the right.

Results Unofficial times (taken by timekeepers) and disqualifications are announced on the official notice board and also at the finish.
Official results are determined from the times of those competitors who have not been disqualified.

Alpine combined

The alpine combined event comprises two races: downhill and slalom. Points are awarded for each race according to official tables. These points are added together to give the final classification.

Sequence The slalom race usually precedes the downhill race.
The starting order for both the downhill and slalom are decided by a draw.
Results The combined results are calculated by adding the points which correspond to the results of the various races.

Slalom

Competitors in the slalom follow twisting courses defined by pairs of flags (know as gates). A competition is decided by two runs down different courses. The winner is the competitor with the fastest aggregate time for the two runs.

Courses should test a wide variety of ski techniques. Traverses across the slope are interspersed with runs down it, and courses must include turns that allow maximum speed, precision, and neat execution. The snow must be as hard as possible.
The course must be at least 40m wide, if two runs are set on the same slope.
In world and Olympic championships the course must be set on slopes with a gradient of 20 to 27 new degrees (= 33 to 45%).
Vertical drop
World and Olympic championships
men: 180–220m; women 130–180m.
Other international races
men: 140–220m; women: 120–180m.

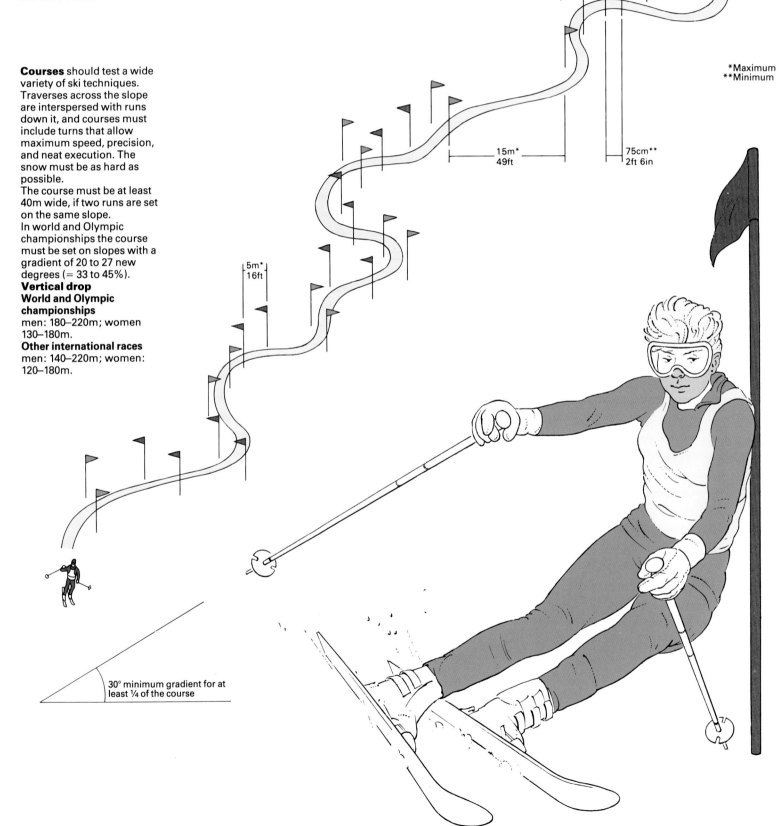

*Maximum
**Minimum

15m*
49ft

75cm**
2ft 6in

5m*
16ft

30° minimum gradient for at least ¼ of the course

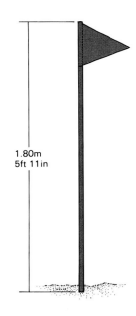

1.80m
5ft 11in

Gates Slalom gates consist of two solid, uniform poles, which must be 3–4cm in diameter and extend 1.8m above the snow.

The gates must be alternately blue or red, with flags matching the color of the pole.

The distance between any two gates must be at least 0.75m, and not more than 15m.

Each gate must be between 4m and 6m wide.

In a hairpin gate the distance between the two verticals must be 0.75m.

The course must contain open and vertical gates, and two or three vertical combinations (consisting of between three and five gates) and at least four hairpin combinations.

For men's courses there are between 55 and 75 gates; for women's courses between 40 and 60 gates.

Except for the starting and finishing gates, the gates are numbered down the course, with the numbers on the outside of the poles.

Gates must not be set in monotonous combinations; nor must they spoil the fluency of a run by forcing sudden braking.

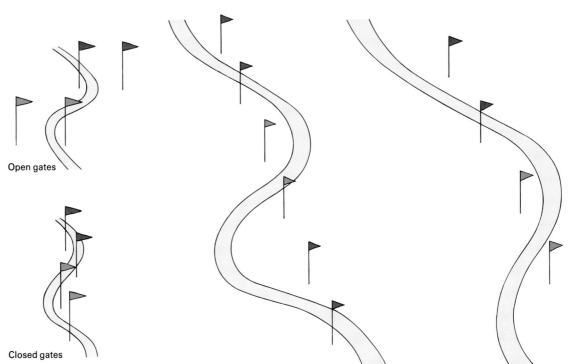

Open gates

Closed gates

Combination

Hairpin

Starting Competitors start irregularly, by official decision, and may begin before the previous racer has finished.

Racers are divided into groups. In the first round they start according to their starting numbers.

In the second round, the starting order for the second run is determined by the result list of the first run except for the first fifteen. The fifteenth in the result list starts first; and the first in the result list starts fifteenth. A competitor who is not at the start at the appropriate time may be disqualified. Each competitor must start at the starting point.

Starting gate

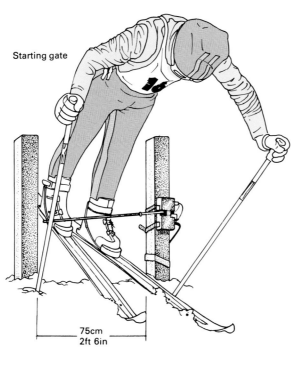

75cm
2ft 6in

Execution of the slalom
A slalom must always be decided by two runs on two different courses. Both courses must be used one after the other, in the order decided by the jury. The race committee may reduce the number for the second run, provided competitors have been told beforehand.

Racing The course must be completed on skis, but a competitor may finish on one ski.

Racers must pass through all gates.

They must wear their starting numbers.

They may not receive any form of assistance.

They must cross the finish line with both feet.

Result The winner is the competitor with the fastest aggregate time for both runs.

Giant slalom and Super-G

The courses used in giant slalom and Super-G are longer than the slalom course and the gates are placed farther apart. A giant slalom competition is decided after two runs, Super-G after one.

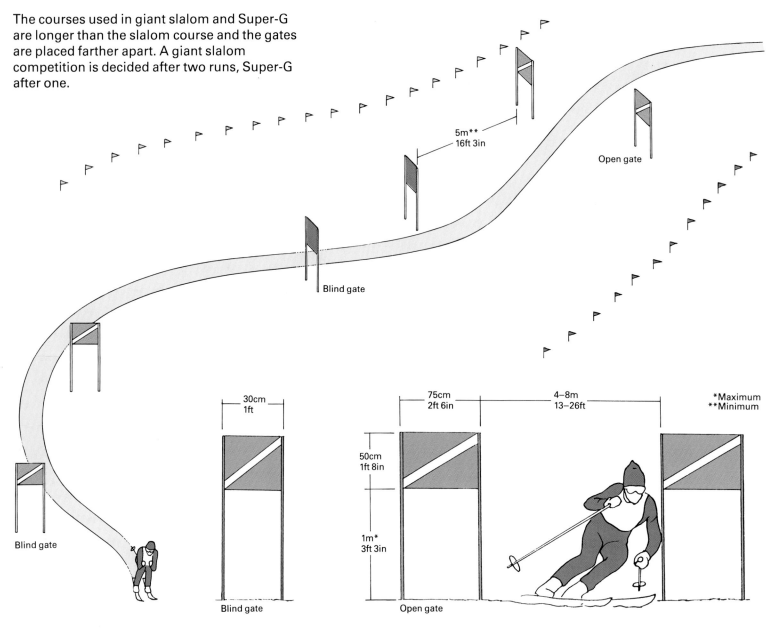

5m**
16ft 3in

Open gate

Blind gate

30cm
1ft

Blind gate

75cm
2ft 6in

4–8m
13–26ft

*Maximum
**Minimum

50cm
1ft 8in

1m*
3ft 3in

Blind gate

Open gate

Courses for both giant slalom and Super-G races are prepared as for downhill races. The parts of the course where gates are set and where competitors have to turn are prepared as for a slalom.
Courses should be at least 30m wide, preferably on hilly and undulating terrain. The full width of the hill should be used wherever possible.
Vertical drop: giant slalom
men: 250–400m; women 250–350m.
Vertical drop: Super-G
men: 500–650m; women: 350–500m.
(Some competitions are allowed where the minimum vertical drop is not possible.)

Slalom poles and banners
Ordinary slalom poles are used. The banners are 75cm wide and 50cm high. They are fastened between the poles so that the lower edge of the banner is at least 1m above the snow. The gates must be alternately red and blue. In bad visibility, red direction flags should be placed down the left side of the course facing downhill and green flags on the right.
Setting the gates
The gates must be set so that the competitors can distinguish them clearly and quickly even at high speed.
Giant slalom The gates must be at least 4–8m wide. The distance between the nearest poles of two successive gates must not

be less than 10m.
12–15% of the vertical drop in meters = number of gates.
The first run is set the day before the race. Both runs can be set on the same course but the second run must be re-set.
Figures are less important than for a slalom. Most of the gates are single with figures being set mainly on uninteresting terrain.
A giant slalom should present a variety of long, medium and small turns.
Super-G The gates must be 6–8m wide from inner pole to inner pole for open gates and 8–12m for vertical gates. 10% of the vertical drop = maximum number of gates. A minimum of 35 gates is set

for men and 30 for women. The distance between the turning poles of two successive gates is 25m. The course must be set on the day before the race. A Super-G should contain a variety of long and medium turns.
In both giant slalom and Super-G the competitor should be free to choose his own line between the gates, which must not be set down the fall-line of the slope.

Start
Competitors start at 60 second intervals for both the giant slalom and Super-G.
Result
An event with two runs is won by the competitor with the fastest aggregate time. An event comprising only one run is won by the fastest competitor.

Freestyle skiing

Freestyle skiing has become popular in recent years and now features prominently in the international FIS calendar. It comprises three events – ballet, aerials and moguls (currently only moguls features as an Olympic event).

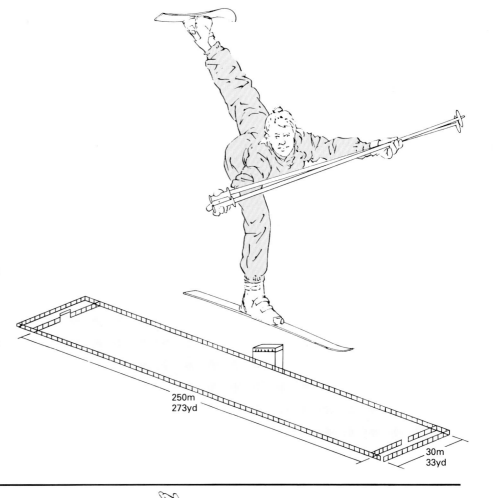

BALLET
This event consists of a 2-minute routine of spins, jumps, steps and acrobatic maneuvers, choreographed and set to music of the skier's choice.
The course The ballet site should be a constant pitch with one continuous fall-line.
The course must be groomed as smoothly as possible.
The course must be adequately covered with snow and all obstacles removed.

The start is anywhere on the course.
The ballet starter checks with the competitor and then orders the music to begin.
Scoring Marks are awarded for technical difficulty (50%) and composition and style (50%).
The finish area for the ballet event must be equal to the width of the course. The ballet skier may finish the run at any point on the course.

250m
273yd

30m
33yd

AERIALS
Skiers launch themselves off specially constructed snow jumps or "kickers" performing single, double or triple somersaults with a variety of twists, and landing on a steep slope of softened snow. Two different acrobatic jumps are performed.
The course must be free of all hazards.
Scoring Marks are awarded for quality of take-off and height in the air (20%), form (50%) and accuracy of landing (30%).

The start is anywhere on the course, but cannot exceed the maximum start line established as the safety precaution for the jump hill. The aerial start begins with the starter confirming that the jump is clear, then informing the competitor to proceed. The competitor has 15 seconds in which to start.
The finish area for the aerial event must be large enough to allow the competitor to stop safely. Safety fences and barriers must be in place.

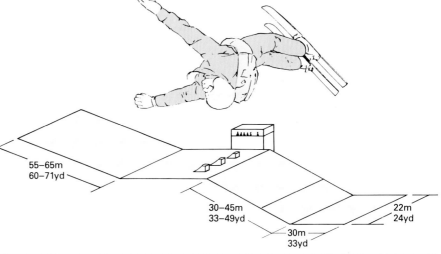

55–65m
60–71yd

30–45m
33–49yd

30m
33yd

22m
24yd

MOGULS
The skier performs an individual descent of high speed turns down a steep slope, covered in large bumps or "moguls". The skier follows the fall-line and executes two jumps during the run.
Course The mogul site is a constant pitch with one continuous fall-line and is evenly covered in "moguls". Four control gates are located on the course at equally spaced intervals, with gates measuring 8–10m.
Scoring Marks are awarded for the technical quality of turns (50%), the speed of the run (25%) and the form of the jumps (25%).

The start A start gate with the electric timing device attached is located where the competitor can quickly reach full speed after leaving the start.
The start signal begins with a warning 10 seconds before the start. The starter counts "3, 2, 1" and gives the start command.
Finish With electric timing, the time is taken when a competitor crosses the line between the finishing posts with any part of his body or equipment.

200m
219yd

30m
33yd

©DIAGRAM

Ski jumping

◯◯◯◯◯

Ski jumping requires strength, grace, and courage. Competitors make two jumps from a specially constructed hill, and points are awarded for style and technique as well as for the distance achieved.

The jumping hill is constructed according to officially approved specifications.
Before training and competitions the hill must be smooth and hard from the in-run to the out-run, and must be tested to confirm its safety.
Before the start of competitions, trial jumps are performed by non-competitors; these help determine the starting place and the length and inclination of the take-off. Conditions must be consistent for all competitors.
The norm point (**P**) marks the ski-jumpers' expected landing point, extending to the table point (**TP**). The critical point (**K**) marks the maximum safe landing distance. These points vary according to the dimensions of the hill.
In some competitions two hills are used and the difference between their norm points must be at least 15m.
In some international competitions the norm point may not exceed 90m.
On hills with a norm point of over 80m, instruments for measuring the in-run speed and wind conditions must be used.
Point **P** is marked on the hill by a board, and on the snow by a blue line about 2m long on each side of the landing slope;
point **TP** is similarly marked by a board and green lines; and point **K** by a board and red lines.

Officials In international competitions five jumping judges must be appointed, each of whom makes an independent assessment of the jumps.

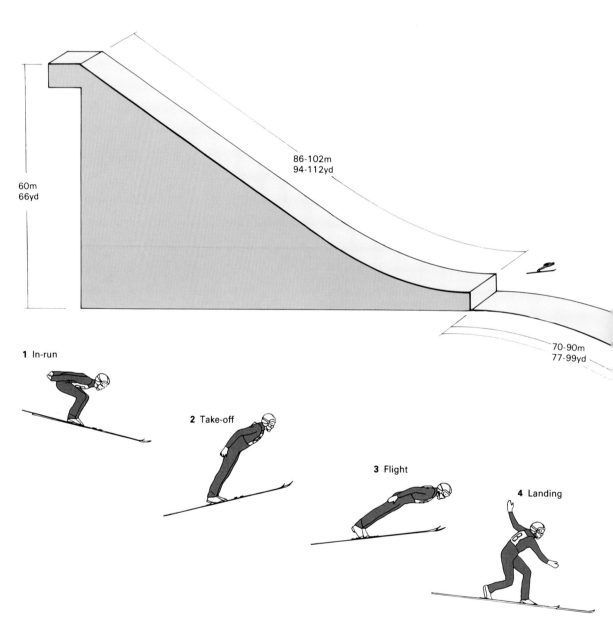

60m
66yd

86-102m
94-112yd

70-90m
77-99yd

1 In-run

2 Take-off

3 Flight

4 Landing

Jumping Competitors are divided into four groups. Each competitor has two jumps; a jump in the trial round is optional. Competitors in the same class must begin from the same starting point.
The in-run (**1**) The ski-jumper adopts a relaxed crouched position adapted to the in-run. Ski poles or other aids for increasing speed are forbidden.

The take-off (**2**) must be a powerful action (varying according to the speed and profile of the hill), and made with boldness and precision. The knees must be straightened and the body stretched in a fast, rhythmic, and aggressive movement.
During the flight (**3**) the skis should be kept almost horizontal until just before landing. The skis should be parallel and in the same plane. The body should lean

well forward and be as straight as possible at the hips. The legs and the upper part of the body should be taut, and the feet together. Arm movements must be controlled.
The landing (**4**) must be made with flexible but controlled movements and should not be too low. The ski-jumper should not prepare prematurely for the landing. Skis must be together (not more than a

ski's width apart), with one foot in front of the other. Knees and hips are bent into the *telemark* position to counter the force of the landing. The arms are spread for balance.
The ski-jumper then straightens up and continues to the out-run in a normal downhill position, holding himself as upright as the gradient and condition of the surface allow.

Judging Scores are given in points and half points. The ideal jump is one executed with power, boldness, and precision, while giving an impression of calmness, steadiness, and control. The personality of the ski-jumper plays an important role, and individuality of style is permissible as long as basic requirements are met.
The general impression of the entire jump determines the award of style points. Judging begins at the moment of take-off. Any faults made at take-off are not penalized, however, as they will in any case influence the flight and the distance achieved.
Faults are less heavily penalized if they are immediately rectified.
A standing jump is one in which the skier travels from landing to the out-run in full balance. Any fall in the out-run is irrelevant. The standing jump scores between 6 and 20 points.
Falls A fall on the in-run loses 20 points; between 0 and 12 points are deducted for any other falls.

If a competitor touches the snow or his skis with both hands to maintain balance before reaching the out-run, this counts as a fall.
If a competitor has no control over the cause of the fall, he may be allowed to repeat the jump, or the jump may be declared a standing jump.
Results Distances are marked out before the competition, and boards are placed at 1m intervals on the sides of the landing slope.

Distances jumped are measured to the nearest ½m. They are taken from between where the feet land. Each jump receives a total point score for style, and a total point score for distance.
The style score is reached by eliminating the highest and lowest of the judges' scores and adding the remaining three scores.
The distance score is calculated according to an official table, varying with the norm point of the hill. The competitor with the highest total of points from his two jumps is the winner.

Judges' tower

Norm point (P)

Table point (TP)

Critical point (K)

Out-run
80-100m
88-110yd

© DIAGRAM

Ski flying

Each year the FIS (Fédération International de Ski) grants permission for the hosting of two ski flying competitions, including the World Ski Flying Competition. Competitors are entered by their own national ski organization.

The number of days and jumps Ski flying events take place over 3 days, with each competitor taking three jumps on each of the days. The first day is a training day.
Results Distances are measured in full meters. Style points are awarded as for ski jumping.

In-run speed and wind speed are required.
On the second and third days, the best two of three jumps counts in the results. The winner is selected by the addition of total points from both days of jumping; the highest cumulative score wins.

Nordic cross-country

Cross-country races are held over a variety of distances and terrain. Men's races cover 10, 15, 30, and 50km, and women's races 5, 10, 15, and 30km.

The courses run up and down hills as well as on undulating and flat ground, and gradients vary according to the distance of the race. Skiers usually start at intervals, and the winner is the competitor who finishes in the shortest time. Some races are started as mass starts and some as pursuit starts. Two different techniques are used in cross-country skiing – the classical technique and the freestyle or skating style.

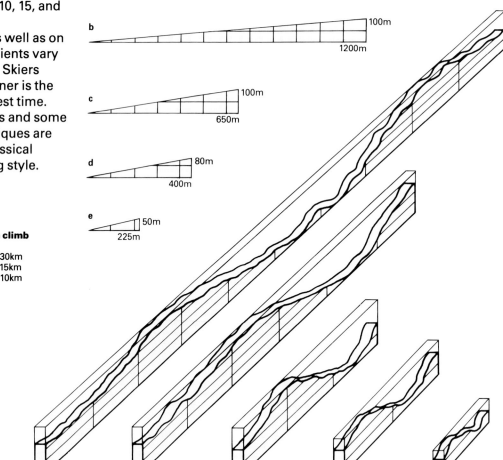

The maximum climb
a Men 50km
b Men/women 30km
c Men/women 15km
d Men/women 10km
e Women 5km

Event	men	men/women	men/women	men/women	women
Distance	50km, 31mi	30km, 18.6mi	15km, 9.3mi	10km, 6.2mi	5km, 3.1mi
Maximum height	200m, 656ft	200m, 656ft	200m, 656ft	150m, 492ft	100m, 328ft

The course should ideally be one third undulating, one third uphill, and one third downhill. It should be laid out as naturally and with as much variety as possible, preferably through woodland.

Courses should be designed to test the skier's technical, tactical, and physical abilities.

Short-distance and relay courses are usually the most arduous. The degree of difficulty should relate to the level of the competition. The most strenuous climbs should not occur within the first 2 or 3km, nor should there be long downhill runs in the final stretches.

The rhythm of the course should be broken as little as possible by sharp changes in direction or steep climbs. Downhill sections must be laid out so that they can be negotiated without danger, even on a particularly fast or icy track.

Course measurements
Length
Men: 10, 15, 30, 50km;
Women: 5, 10, 15, 30km.
Height In world championships the maximum highest point for a cross-country course is 1800m.
The maximum differences in height between the highest and lowest parts of a course are:
5km course: 100m
10km course: 150m
15km+ course: 200m.
The maximum climb (the difference in height of a single climb, without a break of at least 200m) must not exceed:
5km: 50m
10km: 80m
15km+: 100m.

The maximum total climb should be within:
5km: 150–225m
10km: 250–450m
15km: 400–650m
30km: 800–1200m
50km: 1400–1800m.
Marking The course is marked after every 5km, and at every 1km along the last 5km.
The direction of the race is marked by boards, arrows, flags, and ribbons. Each race is indicated by a different color.
Women: 5km blue; 10km violet; 15km red/yellow; 30km green/orange; 5km relay blue/orange.
Men: 10km yellow; 15km red; 30km green; 50km orange; relay violet/yellow.
Starting Starts may be single or double, at intervals of 30 seconds. Group and mass starts are only

permitted by special authorization.
Electronic timing with an audible starting signal may be used. If hand timing is used, the starter warns the competitor 10 seconds before the beginning of the race, and counts out the last 5 seconds.
The competitor must start with both feet behind the starting line, but with the poles in front of it.
Early starts If hand timing is used, the competitor is recalled. If electronic starting is used, the competitor is allowed 3 seconds before his appointed starting time; alternatively, he is recalled to start outside the electronic starting gate.
Late starts A competitor who starts late must not interfere with the start of other competitors.

Racing Competitors must follow the marked course and pass through all the controls. Only the skier's own propulsion may be used, and pacemakers are not allowed.
Both poles may be exchanged during the race but skis may not; changes must be made without assistance.
Skis must be marked immediately before the start in order to prevent unauthorized changing of skis during the race. The course must be completed on two marked skis for individual races and at least one for relay races.
Skis may be waxed by the competitor during the race. When a competitor is overtaken he must give way at the first request, even if the course has two tracks.

Any accidents, or any skiers who have retired from the race, must be reported at the next control or at the finish.
Finishing The competitor's finishing time is taken when his first foot crosses the line between the finishing posts or with electronic timing, when the contact is broken. The finish referee records the order in which the competitors complete the course.
Results Competitors are placed according to the difference between their starting and finishing times. Times are measured in full tenths of a second.
If two or more competitors have the same time they are awarded the same placing, the competitor with a lower starting number being listed first.

Competitors In world championships each country may enter four competitors, who are distributed separately into four groups. The team leader may decide on the distribution of his skiers. The group starts, beginning with group one. In international competitions competitors are divided into three groups:
Group A: international competitors;
Group B: a maximum of 20 other competitors from the organizing country;
Group C: remaining competitors.
They start in the order, B, A, C.

Reserves are only allowed to replace competitors after the draw in the event of illness or injury.
Competitors are permitted to train on and inspect the course prior to the race.
Timing Electronic timing should be used whenever possible, together with hand timing as a check.
Competitors are timed along the course: once during a 10km course: twice during 15 and 30km courses, and at least three times during a 50km course.

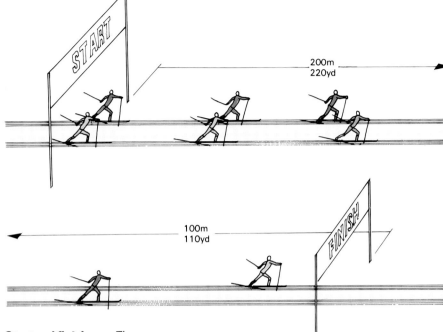

200m
220yd

100m
110yd

Start and finish area The start and finish should be situated in the same area. This area should contain: loudspeakers and scoreboards;
a temperature board, showing air and snow temperatures at intervals before and during the race; rooms for medical treatment;
general and official facilities. For a double start there must be two parallel tracks for at least 200m, and two parallel tracks at least 100m long at the finish.
Refreshment stations are provided at the start and finish, and along the course in races of more than 15km: two stations for races up to 30km in length, and four stations for races up to 50km.

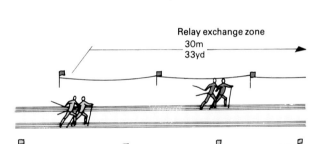

Relay exchange zone
30m
33yd

The hand-over

Relay races are organized according to the rules for cross-country skiing, with the following additions. Separate colors are used for the start numbers for each relay section. In world championships these are: first section, red; second, green; third, yellow; fourth, blue.
Skis are marked in the same colors as the relay sections.
Start There is a mass start, with competitors aranged in one or more arcs.
Skiers begin 2m apart, and each one has the same starting conditions.
The tracks must be parallel for the first 100–200m and then converge into three separate tracks during the next 100m. There must be no sharp bends or corners in the first kilometer.
The relay exchange zone is a clearly marked area 30m long. The last 200m before the exchange zone must be at least double-tracked, and without sharp bends or corners.
The hand-over must take place within the relay exchange zone, when the racer touches his teammate. If the hand-over is illegal, the skiers may be recalled to perform a proper exchange.
Finish The last 200m must be at least double-tracked, and without sharp bends or corners.
A racer does not have to give way in the last 100m.
Teams consist of three or four racers. Each may run only one section.

Nordic combined

The Nordic combined competition consists of ski-jumping and cross-country skiing. Competitors take part in both events, and points are given for their performances. The winner is the competitor with the highest total of points.

70m
77yd

Duration The competitions take place on consecutive days. The ski-jumping normally precedes the cross-country.
Competitors There is a separate draw for the jumping event.
Competitors are drawn in four groups. Group 1 starts first.
The combined cross-country

competition is carried out using the Gunderson method. The winner of the combined jumping competition starts first with the other competitors following according to the converted time difference.
The cross-country course is 15km in length. Technical difficulties must be less than for specialized

cross-country events. The total climb must be between 400 and 550m. The course is indicated by red and blue markers.
The jumping hill has a norm point of between 60 and 70m, and in world championships the norm must be 70m. Other installations and requirements are the same

as for independent jumping competitions.
Jumping Each competitor has three jumps. Each jump is awarded points for distance and style, and the lowest total is eliminated.
The final result is the order of finishing the cross-country event.
Team competition The competition consists of team

ski jumping and a 3 × 10km relay competition. A team consists of three competitors.
Sprint competition The competition consists of team ski jumping and a 15km cross-country competition run over short laps. A team consists of two competitors.

Biathlon

Biathlon is a combined sport of cross-country skiing and rifle shooting that was first included in the Winter Olympics in 1960. World championships are held every year. There are a number of individual and team events. The shooting is conducted with small bore rifles.

The course must be laid out naturally and should vary as much as possible. It should be set over undulating country within prescribed limits and differences in height.

It should be a true test of the competitors' strength, endurance, tactical knowledge and ski technique.

The most strenuous part of the course should be around the halfway point.

Preparation All trees and stumps are cut down to ground level before the snow falls.

On the day of the race at least ten members of the tracking patrol ski over the course to ensure that weather conditions have not made it dangerous.

Marking The course is clearly marked with flags and every fifth kilometer is indicated by boards at the side of the track.

Shooting ranges The start, shooting and finish are generally at the same place. The range is 50m, and the firing points should be even, firm and clearly numbered. Near the range is a test range so that competitors can have a trial shoot before the competition.

Shooting areas are marked off from spectators.

Organization Competitions are organized by the organizing committee, competition committee, jury and officials.

The jury is responsible for arranging medical examinations, imposing penalties and ensuring that competitions are carried out according to the rules.

Officials include the chief of the course, the chief of shooting, the chief of timekeeping and calculation, a doctor and as many assistants as are necessary to man the butts and ensure adequate communication along the course.

Dress may be strengthened and protected on both elbows and on the right or left shoulder. Padded material may be used to alleviate the pressure of the sling used to carry the rifle.

Equipment A competitor may have only one pair of marked skis and one marked rifle.

If a ski or binding breaks one ski may be replaced, as may broken sticks and slings. A spare weapon may be handed to the range officer for use if needed.

Weapons All non-automatic weapons with a caliber up to 5.6mm may be used, but magnifying optical sights are not allowed. The minimum trigger pressure is 0.5kg. During the course there must be no round in the rifle.

Ammunition All ammunition, including reserves, must be carried by

the competitors from the start.

Food and refreshments are provided for the competitors.

Procedure on the course Competitors follow the flagged track, using no other means of propulsion than skis and sticks and with no pacemaker.

Although competitors may wax their skis and repair equipment, no assistance is permitted beyond providing wax and handing over repair equipment.

If a competitor is overtaken, he must give way.

Competitors who observe any accident should report it at a control point.

Procedure at the firing range When the competitor arrives at the firing point he/she goes to the allocated firing position. There the competitor loads the rifle with five rounds, which are

fired in his/her own time, with the skis either on or off. The competitor fires five rounds from each of four firing points and between the bouts of shooting there must be at least 3km of skiing.

The first and third shoots are in a prone position, when the rifle may be supported only by hands and held against shoulder and cheek, not propped on the ground. The second and fourth shoots are in a standing position. Again, any support is forbidden and the rifle must be held against shoulder and cheek, but not supported on the chest.

In both shooting positions the supporting arm may be supported by a sling as long as the rifle itself does not touch it behind the grip of the hand.

Penalties Serious offenses, such as taking short cuts,

using means of propulsion other than skis and sticks, or changing the trigger pressure of the rifle, are penalized by disqualification.

Time penalties are issued for other offenses. For example, two minutes are added to the time of anyone who carries his rifle loaded around the course and also for each shot not fired.

Types of competition The are four types of competition:

Individual competition: men 20km race; junior men and women 15km race; junior women 10km race.

Sprint competition: men and junior men 10km; women and junior women 7.5km.

Relay competition: men and junior men 4x7.5km; women and junior women 3x7.5km.

Team competition: men 20km race; junior men and

Scoring The running time from start to finish (including the shooting) plus all penalty minutes equals the competitor's total time. There is a 1 minute penalty for misses.
In relays, sprints and team events a penalty loop is skied for each miss.

©DIAGRAM

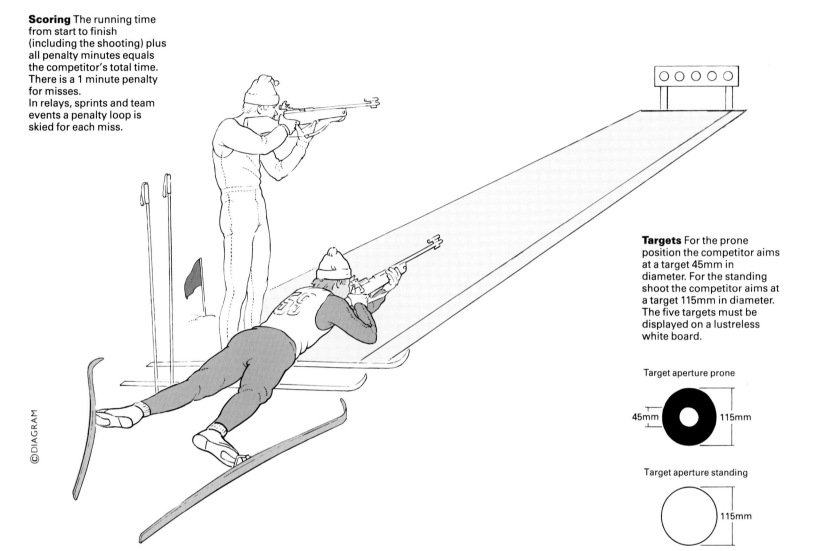

Targets For the prone position the competitor aims at a target 45mm in diameter. For the standing shoot the competitor aims at a target 115mm in diameter. The five targets must be displayed on a lustreless white board.

Target aperture prone

45mm　115mm

Target aperture standing

115mm

women 15km race; junior women 10km race.
Individual competition
Individual events take place over 20km, 15km and 10km (see *below*). Competitors start at 1 minute intervals and must complete a specified number of bouts between certain distances on the course.
The competitor fires over a distance of 50m at mechanical targets. The competitor is penalized with 1 minute for each missed target.
20km (men)
4 bouts of shooting which take place between 4km and 18km with at least 3km between two successive bouts.
15km (junior men)
3 bouts of shooting between 4km and 13km with a minimum distance of at least 3km between two successive bouts.

15km (women)
4 bouts of shooting between 3km and 12km.
10km (junior women)
3 bouts of shooting between 2km and 8km with a minimum distance of 2km between two successive bouts.
Sprint competition
Competitors are started at 1 minute intervals either individually or in groups. Competitors fire over a range of 50m at the same targets as in the individual race. For each target the competitor misses he must cover 150m handicap circuit taking approximately 20 seconds.
10km sprint competition (men)
2 bouts of shooting take place at approximately 2.5km and 7.5km.
The first firing session is 5 rounds prone after approximately 3.5km of

cross-country. The second is after 7.0km when 5 rounds are fired from a standing position.
7.5km sprint (women)
2 bouts of shooting take place between 2.5km and 5.0km in the sequence prone/standing. Other sprint conditions are as for the men's event.
Relay competition
Each team comprises:
4 members (men's events);
3 members (women's events).
Each team member has to ski 7.5km with two bouts of shooting, one prone and one standing. The team covers a total distance of 30km (men's events) 22km (women's events).
There is a mass start by all the first skiers in the respective teams. The first firing session takes place at 2.5km. Each competitor has 8 rounds of ammunition for

5 targets. If he hits all targets with the first 5 rounds he can continue to ski. If not he must continue firing until he has either hit all 5 targets or fires all 8 rounds. If he fails to hit 5 targets he must cover one 150m handicap circuit for each missed target.
The competitor then fires in the standing position at 5km. In the handover area the next man is sent on his way with a pat on the back.
Team competition
A team comprises 4 biathletes who race in a serried formation for:
20km (men's events);
15km (women's events).
There are four shooting bouts per team: one for each team member who fires five rounds.
Teams start at 2 minute intervals. A team may be overtaken by another team only in serried formation. The biathlete who is to shoot

does so whilst the other 3 team members race to a waiting area in front of the handicap loop.
If the biathlete hits all 5 targets the team may continue. If not the team has to race a 300m long handicap loop for each target missed.
The team must cross the finish line in a serried formation.

The penalty course for relay and sprint races is an oval loop 150m long, laid out on even ground near the shooting range.
Competitors who incur penalties through missing targets or not having fired their round of ammunition are responsible for running the correct number of penalty circuits before the handover or crossing the finishing line.

247

Skibob racing

Competitors on skibobs attempt to cover a marked course as rapidly as possible. International events include downhill, Super G, giant slalom, slalom and parallel slalom.

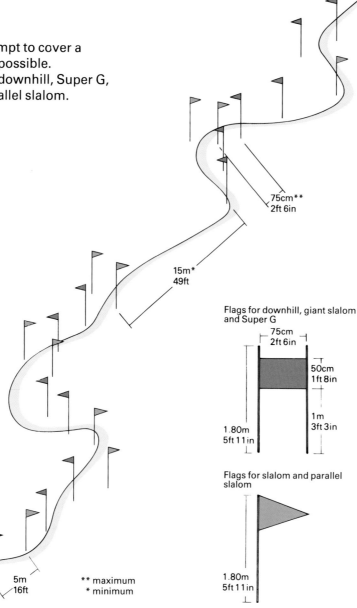

Section of slalom course

75cm**
2ft 6in

15m*
49ft

5m
16ft

** maximum
* minimum

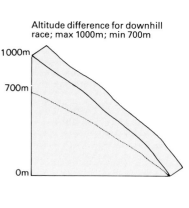

Altitude difference for downhill race; max 1000m; min 700m

1000m
700m
0m

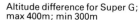

Altitude difference for Super G; max 400m; min 300m

400m
300m
0m

Altitude difference for giant slalom: 400m

400m
0m

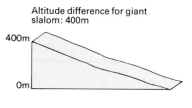

Altitude difference for slalom; 200m

200m
0m

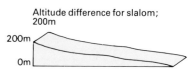

Altitude difference for parallel slalom; max 100m; min 80m

100m
0m

Flags for downhill, giant slalom and Super G

75cm
2ft 6in

50cm
1ft 8in

1m
3ft 3in

1.80m
5ft 11in

Flags for slalom and parallel slalom

1.80m
5ft 11in

Competitions Downhill, slalom and Super G events are held under the surveillance of the FISB (Fédération Internationale de Skibob).
Timing Electronic timing apparatus is used, with additional hand timing in case electronic timing fails.
Result In single races, the order of placing is based on the time taken to cover the course. If two competitors record the same time, they are placed together. In combined events, comprising more than one race, points are scored for each separate performance.

DOWNHILL RACES
Courses The altitude difference between the start and finish is normally 700–1000m (765.5–1093.6yd) for races.
The length of all downhill courses should be such that the best competitor achieves a time of about 2 minutes. Downhill courses must be completely ready and the sticks placed at least one day before the beginning of the competition.
The terrain must be free of stones, branches, roots, etc, and any parts of the course in wooded terrain must be at least 20m (21.8yd) wide. Any obstacle against which a competitor might be thrown must be covered with snow, straw, or catch-nets.
There must be an obstacle-free space at the outside of curves to safeguard competitors who leave the course.
All gates must be arranged to protect the competitors against accidents, and the last two gates before the finish must be open.
Courses must be equipped with easy means of transport to the start.

Markings Gates consist of two red/blue alternating unbreakable vertical poles with rectangular flags.
Official training is an integral part of the competition and must last at least one day.
The race cannot take place if there have been no perfect training conditions. The course is closed to the public during official training.
Non-stop training Official training must include a non-stop training run down the course.
Competitors must wear starting numbers and begin training within 15 minutes of receiving the order to start.
Competitors may make only one run during non-stop training.
Official timing apparatus is in action.

Start Starting times are fixed under the best conditions of snow and visibility.
The starting area is under cover, and a competitors' shelter provided.
Competitors start the race at 60-second intervals. Ten seconds before each competitor starts, the starter gives the command: "attention." Five seconds before the start, he counts down from five to one before giving the starting command: "ab," "allez," or "go." Competitors must be allowed to look at the clock. A competitor who is not ready to start at his given time will be disqualified by the starter unless the delay was caused by circumstances over which he had no control.

A competitor will be disqualifed if his steering gear crosses the starting line more than one second before his official starting time. A competitor whose steering gear crosses the starting line more than one second after his official starting time is timed as if he had started one second after his official time.

The race A competitor is liable to disqualification if he accepts outside help or makes use of a pacemaker; fails to clear the way when requested by an overtaking competitor; fails to cross between the gates; takes a short cut; fails to observe safety regulations; fails to cross the finishing line on his skibob. (A competitor is not disqualified for losing his foot skis.)

SUPER G

Course The altitude difference between the start and finish for Super G races is 400m (437.4yd) for men and 300m (328.1yd) for women.

A Super G course should have large medium turns with reasonable changes. The run must be positioned on the day before the race so that it can be inspected.

Gates are 6–8m (6.6–8.7yd) wide. Flags are alternately red and blue.

10% of altitude difference = maximum no of gates on the course.

It is not permitted to set the gates of a Super G in the line of descent only.

Skibob Competitors must use a single-track guidable skibob. It may be of any material – such as wood, metal, or plastic. Its total length must not exceed 2.30m (2.5yd) when the front ski is followed in its trace by the rear ski.

Competitors must be amateurs. All entries for international events must be made through national associations.

Dress Competitors wear:
1 crash helmets (compulsory for races and official training);
2 ski boots
3 foot skis, 50–55cm (19.7–21.6in) in length
4 starting number
5 goggles

Officials for a skibob event are a race director, FISB judge, chief judge, start judge, finish judge, gate judges, course chief, course tracer, race secretary, starter and assistants, chief timekeeper and assistants, umpire, equipment officer, medical officers, chief and assistant stewards, press officers.

© DIAGRAM

GIANT SLALOM

The giant slalom is longer than the slalom, the gates are farther apart, and competitors choose their own line between gates. The event is usually only one run.

Courses are prepared as for downhill races, except at controls and turning sections, where they are prepared as for slalom races. The altitude difference between the start and finish is 400m (437.4yd). The course must be at least 20m (21.8yd) broad, and of such a length that the best competitor achieves a time of about 2 minutes.

The course must have edges and slight undulations, but no ascending or flat stretches.

Gates consist of two unbreakable poles, with rectangular flags. Poles must be placed on a level, and 6–8m (6.5–8.7yd) apart. Red-flagged gates alternate with blue-flagged gates; starting and finishing gates always have red flags. All gates are numbered. The last two gates must be open. Snow near the gates must be stamped or rolled to avoid deep furrows when skibobbers change direction.

Result The event is won by the competitor with the fastest time.

Training and inspection
The gates are put in position two hours before the start of the race, and competitors may familiarize themselves with the course by descending alongside the gates. They are forbidden to pass through the gates or practice direction changes alongside the course (with start numbers on).

SLALOM

Courses The altitude difference between the start and finish is 200m (218.7yd). The gradient must be fairly steep, but sufficient to allow several clear changes of direction.

The snow must be stamped hard to avoid furrows during the competition.

Gates There must be 50 to 75 gates at least 1.80m (2yd) above ground. Gates consist of single poles and triangular flags.

Gates are alternately red and blue and the sticks as well as the flags are colored. All gates are numbered. The first two gates must be open.

Training and inspection
The gates must be in position at least 1½ hours before the race, and competitors may familiarize themselves with the final course by ascending alongside it, either on foot or on the skibob. They must not go on the course itself.

Start Starting intervals for slalom races may be different. Competitors must start after receiving the starting order.

Racing The course must be completed on the skibob. Racers must pass through all gates.

They must wear their starting numbers.

They may not receive any form of assistance.

They must cross the finish with skibob.

Result The winner is the competitor with the fastest aggregate time over two runs.

PARALLEL SLALOM

Courses Two courses are positioned side by side in parallel slalom racing. The altitude difference between the start and finish for both men's and women's races is 80–100m (87.4–109.3yd).

The run is marked by a succession of flags indicating the curves. Both courses must be set by the same official and they must be parallel.

The course setters must consider the fluidity of the run, changes in curves and the essential change in rhythm. The division between the two runs must be clear to the contestants.

Gates Flags are red for the left hand course and blue for the right hand course.

The first marker flag must be at least 8m (8.7yd) and not more than 10m (10.9yd) from the start of the run. The distance between marker poles must 6–7m (6.6–7.6yd).

Luge tobogganing

Competitors on luge toboggans make four runs down a purpose-built course. There are individual events for men and women, and a doubles event for men. Events are won by the competitors with the best aggregate times for the four runs. Speeds are similar to those achieved in bobsleigh events, though the courses are usually much more twisted and labyrinthine.

Course All courses are artificial with a cement infrastructure. They are artificially refrigerated. Length of course: men's singles 1000m–1250m; women's singles, men's doubles and juniors 800m–1050m. The gradient must not exceed 10%. The course should feature a left-hand bend, right-hand bend, hairpin, S bend, and labyrinth as well as straight sections. A starting ramp must be provided, and provision made for starting the shorter races. Control towers linked by telephone with the start and finish are compulsory, as are means for transporting toboggans, competitors, and officials to the starting line. Many courses are floodlit.
The race consists of:
4 runs for singles and 2 runs for doubles in the Olympic Games;
3 runs for singles and 2 runs for doubles in world cup events;
2 runs for all categories and a team competition in the world championships.

Competitions The main competitions are the Olympic Games, world cup, world championships, European championships and the world and European junior championships. Other international and national competitions are also held under the auspices of the FIL (Fédération Internationale de Luge de Course).
Events in major competitions are:
men's individual race;
women's individual race;
men's doubles race;
team event (world championship and European championship).
Women's and doubles races are run over four-fifths of the men's individual course.
Competitors must be amateurs and members of a national association affiliated to the FIL.
Teams for the Olympics may have a maximum of three men and three women entered for the individual events, and two men's doubles. For other events teams may include twice these numbers.
Substitution is not permitted once a race is in progress. If a team member is injured during training, another team member may be nominated to take his place.
Officials The race director, starting and finishing officials and timekeepers ensure the smooth running of races. Control is exercised by the jury (three persons drawn from national associations affiliated to the FIL), the chairman, technical delegates, and the FIL representative.
Training Both systematic and non-stop training are compulsory.
Systematic training comprises a tour of the course under the guidance of the race director, training runs on a shortened start and a thorough step by step study of the course's bends and curves.
Non-stop training ideally involves at least four runs for each competitor. Under adverse conditions every competitor must have made at least one run for the race to take place.
For Olympic races at least two training runs by each competitor must be timed and published.

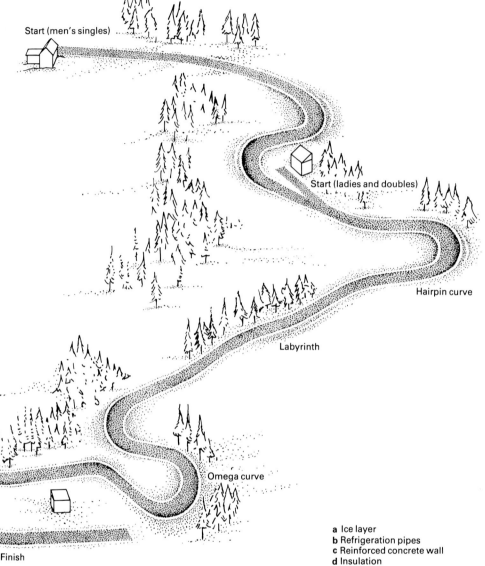

Start (men's singles)

Start (ladies and doubles)

Hairpin curve

Labyrinth

Omega curve

Finish

a Ice layer
b Refrigeration pipes
c Reinforced concrete wall
d Insulation
e Height of curve
f Radius of curve

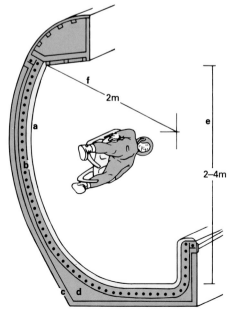

Toboggan may be of any type but must:
have room for one or two riders to sit safely;
have only one pair of runners;
not exceed 22kg (48.5lb) if an individual toboggan or 25kg (55lb) if a doubles toboggan (ballast may be used to bring it up to this weight, but must be firmly attached so that it cannot be jettisoned during a race);
not exceed the prescribed track dimensions;
be without braking or steering mechanisms of any kind.

The distance between the inside edges of the two runners may not exceed 45cm (17.7in).
Once entered in a race competitors may alter, adapt, or exchange toboggans provided they do not breach any of these rules.
A temperature check of toboggans is made at the top and bottom before and at the end of each run. Toboggans are weighed at the finish.

Dress Competitors wear aerodynamic speed suits and booties. Crash helmets are compulsory.
Further protective clothing, such as elbow and knee pads, are optional and must not enhance the aerodynamics of the competitor's body.

The start A sitting start is compulsory for all events. Starting order is decided by lot and varied over the four runs to ensure that conditions for all competitors are as equal as possible.
Only one toboggan may be on the course at a time. Once the "track is clear" signal is given the competitor has 30 seconds (singles) or 45 seconds (doubles) in which to push-off from the start handles. A clock which is clearly visible to the competitors is positioned at the start.

False start If the false start was due to a technical error a new start is compulsory. If the competitor is at fault he/she is disqualified.
Timing Electronic timing apparatus, accurate to 1/1000 of a second, is compulsory for Olympic and international races. At least two hand stopwatches are used as a check in case of a failure of the electronic apparatus. Competitors must repeat their runs after a timing failure.

Steering The competitor lies flat, with his body from the waist upward over the back of the toboggan.
Slight shoulder, hand and foot pressures on the respective parts of the sled transmit steering force through the bridges and runners to the steels.

Offenses Competitors will be penalized for:
failing to wear a crash helmet;
warming toboggan runners before a race;
adding ballast to bring the toboggan over the allowed weight;
wearing weighted clothing (eg lead belts);
leaving the toboggan voluntarily during a race;
pushing, or allowing another person to push, the toboggan either at the start or during a race (except after a spill when the toboggan

may be pushed if it would otherwise be impossible to start moving again);
acting in a dangerous manner during training or a race;
training outside the approved hours;
failure to train;
infringing amateur status;
acting in a way deemed to be damaging to the sport or to the FIL.
Penalties vary from exclusion from a particular race to total disqualification, depending on the gravity of the offense.

© DIAGRAM

251

Bobsleigh racing

Competitors on bobsleighs attempt to cover a specially built course as rapidly as possible. Teams consist of either two or four men.

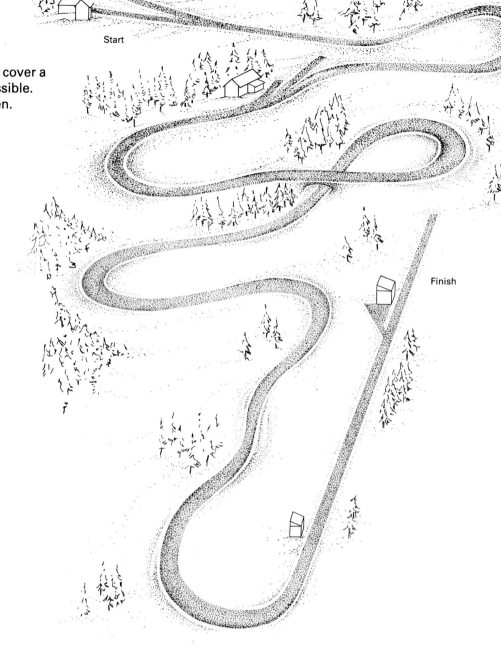

Start

Finish

The course Most bobsleigh tracks are of an artificial construction, formed from concrete with refrigeration pipes passing below the surface. Ice is formed by spraying a fine film of water over the course; this layer of ice must be at least 19mm (¾in) thick before racing can take place.
Natural tracks (constructed from blocks of solid ice) are now in the minority.
In order to qualify for championship events a course must be at least 1200m (1312yd) in length with a gradient of 8–15%. It must have a minimum of 14 banked curves of a concave construction and straights with walls high enough to keep the bobs in the track and prevent serious injury in the event of a crash.

Timing Electronic timing equipment is used to time the bobs during a run. Timing points are placed at strategic positions along the track giving start time, intermediate times and finish time. These timings indicate the progress of the bobs and are often used by drivers and coaches to evaluate each run. In the event of equipment failure during a run, the affected team are allowed to go again when ready.

Start area Before the start clock there is an area of at least 15m (49.2ft) in length which is used by the teams to build up momentum; this is the start area and is marked by a length of wood frozen into the ice but protruding 7.6–10cm (3–4in) above it. This block of wood is used by the brakemen (and side pushers in a 4-man bob) as a back-stop for the initial start effort.

The braking straight is an area after the finish clock and is used by the brakemen to slow down the bob before coming to a standstill at the finish exit.

Control stations at critical points on the course are connected by telephone and radio to the control building. Control station personnel ensure that the run is clear before each heat and keep the spectators informed, over a loudspeaker system, of a bobsleigh's progress. Video systems are also used and cameras are permanently sited at various points along the track.

Competitions The allocation of competitions to tracks and the judicial running of these events is controlled by the FIBT (Fédération Internationale de Bobsleigh et de Tobogganing). Events include: Olympic Games; World Cup events; and international and junior international competitions. All competitions include a two-man and a four-man event.

Results Events usually consist of four runs, or heats, for each team. Two runs are made on two consecutive days. The winner is the team with the lowest aggregate of times. Times are taken to the nearest 1/100th of a second. In the event of a tie, joint placings are allocated.

The team The two-man team consists of a driver and brakeman, who provide the initial impetus at the start before mounting the bob; once in the bob they work together transferring their bodyweight when cornering and keeping as low as possible in order to achieve maximum aerodynamic performance. In addition, the driver will attempt to take the fastest line from top to bottom with the use of steering ropes attached to the runner-bearing front axle. The brakeman slows the bob down by the use of a harrow type brake which digs into the ice.
A four-man team consists of two side pushers in addition to the driver and brakeman.

Because of this extra weight, a four-man bob is approximately two seconds faster than a two-man.

Training For world championships, teams train for four days on the track with two training runs per day; this is for both two- and four-man events. Teams must achieve three good runs (ie three runs without crashing, though not necessarily consecutively) to qualify for the competition itself. Teams that have not had sufficient training may not be allowed to compete. A thorough knowledge of the course is essential for a fast and safe run.

Two-man bob

Competitors must be amateur. All entries for international events must be made through national federations. Competitors must also hold an up-to-date FIBT licence.

Dress Crash helmets (**1**) are compulsory. In addition, goggles (**2**), elbow guards and gloves should be worn. For racing, teams usually wear skintight racing suits.

Officials Race officials are appointed by the FIBT and normally consist of a jury, president and a minimum of two jury members. They ensure that competitions are strictly controlled under FIBT rules.

©DIAGRAM

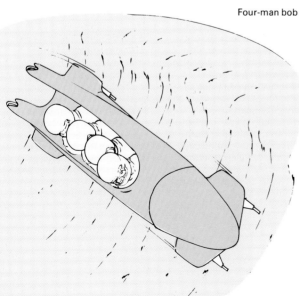

Four-man bob

Bobsleighs are constructed of steel and fitted with an aerodynamic cowling, molded from fiberglass and other composite materials. Steering is achieved by pulling on ropes which are connected to a centrally pivoted front axle. Attached to both front and rear axles are runner carriers onto which are bolted steel runners; the rear axle is fixed.

Maximum weight for a two-man team and bob is 390kg (860lb).

Maximum weight for a four-man team and bob is 630kg (1389lb).

If the permitted weights are not reached, ballast may be added to the bob.

The start The bobs are lined up in their running order, fixed by a draw, keeping the starting area clear. A team not in position when its starting number is called is disqualified unless the delay is caused by circumstances over which it has no control. Green and red lights, together with an audible tone, signify to teams when they may or may not start. When the track is clear the lights will change from red to green and at the same time a buzzer will sound. Teams then have one minute in which to start. Failure to start within this time frame will result in disqualification. Teams must start under their own efforts and must not use any other form of assistance, either

mechanical or additional persons. Teams are permitted to wear special start shoes for the start phase.

The race Teams must achieve all competition runs in order to gain a placing in the overall race. Teams will be disqualified if:
a) they fail to arrive at the start on time;
b) they fail to start in the allotted one minute time frame;
c) on reaching the finish they are minus a team member or any piece of equipment with which they started the run;
d) they fail to produce a finish time as the result of a crash;
e) they contravene FIBT rules concerning the race;
f) they are caught cheating.

Pigeon racing

In pigeon racing all birds start from a single point, but each finishes in its own loft. The winning pigeon is the one that returns home in the fastest time, and this requires a complex timing system to ensure accurate results.

Procedure
1 Pigeons are taken to the race point in purpose-built vehicles.
2 Each pigeon flies home to its loft over an officially measured distance.
3 Times of arrival are recorded by the owners and sent to the organizers.

Pigeon loft

Pigeons There are races for young and for older birds. Each bird has a registration ring that it wears for life. Pigeons are trained to return to their lofts from an early age. Both cock and hen birds are used for racing.

Equipment Pigeon owners require a loft, pigeon crates, rings, and officially approved clocks.

Officials To organize and supervise pigeon racing many officials and assistants are required, including: race conveyors and assistant conveyors; liberators; marking officials; and a clock committee.
Starting the race An owner submits his pigeons to the race marking committee. After the birds have been marked with racing rings they are kept in sealed enclosures until the race starts.
All the birds are conveyed together to the starting point from which they are liberated.

Distance Both young and older pigeons begin a season racing over about 60 miles. Later on, older birds will race over distances of up to 600 miles, but young pigeons are normally restricted to distances of up to 250 miles.
Timing For each race, officials place a rubber racing ring on one leg of each bird. The number on this ring and the bird's registration number are recorded. The racing ring also has an additional number on its inner side, which is secret.

The owners are officially informed of the liberation times of the birds. When a bird returns home its racing ring is removed and inserted into the clock, recording the time of arrival.
The clock is then returned to the race officials and checked against a master timer to calculate each pigeon's flying time.
Each owner's clock will have been submitted to the clock committee for 14 days before the race. The clocks are set by officials, and returned to their owners just before the race.

Returning home A pigeon is trained to return to its loft as quickly as possible and to enter the loft immediately it arrives home. The direction from which it approaches the loft will be dictated by the force and direction of the wind at the time.
To attract pigeons back to their loft, coopies (decoy birds) are sometimes used. These only fly around the loft and are trained to attract the racing birds to the loft landing board.
Stray birds that fail to return home are traced back to the owner by their rings.

Results The exact distance and flying time are divided by 60. Velocity, expressed in yards per minute, is then obtained by dividing distance by time.
The fastest pigeon wins the race.
Speeds may be combined over a season to calculate the best average speed.
Penalties Any bird that is raced without complying with the rules is disqualified.

Sled-dog racing

Sled-dog races are between harnessed dog teams, each controlled by a driver. Teams start at intervals, and the team with the shortest elapsed time wins. The number of dogs in a team varies with race distances and terrain.

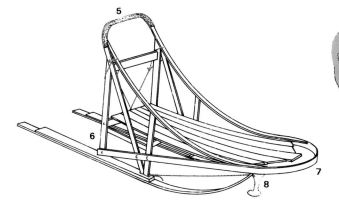

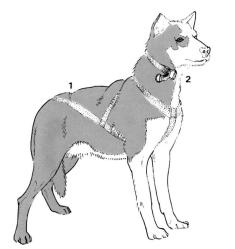

Dress Starting-position numbers must be worn each day. All numbers must be returned at the end of each heat.

Equipment used is:
1 harness;
2 collar;
3 whip
4 sled bag;
5 sled, with sufficient space to carry a dog;
6 sled brake;
7 sled brushbow.
8 snubline
The sled bag of canvas or similar material is needed to carry any badly injured dog.

Harnessing All dogs except lead dogs must be harnessed with neck lines; lead dogs must also be harnessed, but may be run without neck lines.
No muzzles may be used, nor collars hooked as full choke collars.
The snubline is only to be used for hitching.

© DIAGRAM

Competitors One driver ("musher") per team. Drivers often have a dog handler to assist them.
Officials Chief judge, judges, and course manager.

Procedure Each team with its equipment must be ready for inspection near the starting line ten minutes before its start time.
Any dog becoming unfit after departure must be carried on the sled.
Red markers indicate turns; green markers beyond an intersection or around a turn indicate a straight ahead.
Team and driver must run the full marked course and all original dogs must return.

Start and finish Sleds start at intervals, usually every two minutes.
Timing is from when the sled's brushbow crosses the starting line until the first dog reaches the finishing line.
Starting order for the first day is drawn before the race. Starting order for succeeding days is determined by the elapsed time, the fastest team leaving first.

Racing rules A team coming within 20ft of the team ahead has right of way. The following team can require the team to make way; or, if requested, to come to a full stop, but not when repassing or within a half mile of the start or finish lines.
Teams may not be assisted by pacing.
Outside assistance is only allowed in order to stop an unmanageable team; and then only by holding the sled unless race officials indicate otherwise.
Out of bounds If a team leaves the race trail, the driver must return to the point of deviation and continue from there.

Fouls Use of the whip other than for snapping is prohibited, except when dogs become unmanageable.
No interference with competing teams is allowed. Drivers can be disqualified for:
failing to attend the first day's drivers' meeting;
using any equipment not carried at the starting line;
administering any forbidden drugs to the dogs or allowing anyone else to do so.
Cancellation In case of cancellation of the race after the first day, full prize money is still awarded.

Greyhound racing

A greyhound race is between a usual maximum of eight, or in some places nine, greyhounds over any distance between 230yd and 1200yd. The dogs are released from traps and chase a motorized lure around the track. Prizes are awarded and betting is a prominent feature. There is no international governing body, but the following rules and procedures apply fairly generally.

Registration All greyhounds racing on officially approved courses must be registered with the national governing body for the sport. They must also fulfill all race entry qualifications.

Identification Registered greyhounds have identity books or cards, giving details which can vary from country to country but which can include:
sufficient details of physical characteristics to distinguish that greyhound from all others;
the name of its current trainer;
details of inoculations;
details of a bitch coming into season, whelping a litter, or being spayed;
details of all trials, races, withdrawals and disqualifications for fighting.
Age The age of a greyhound is calculated from the first day of the month in which it was whelped. (In the USA it is from the day it was whelped.)
Name A greyhound's name must be registered. Any change of name must be registered and entered in the stud book. The copying of names relating to any person, living or dead, past famous greyhounds or to any organization for advertising purposes is strictly controlled and may be forbidden by the governing body.

Muzzles All greyhounds must wear approved safety muzzles, when racing. In the USA these are white plastic and are used for photo finishes.
Racing jackets Each greyhound must race wearing an approved jacket with the trap number on each side.
Jackets are colored according to trap number: the colors used vary from country to country.
Owners National rules vary, but in general:
no owner may be under a minimum age;
a greyhound must be registered and run in the true or approved assumed name of the *bona fide* owner;
an owner may appoint and register an authorized agent to act for him;
any change of ownership of a greyhound that is to race again must be notified and registered;
all rules apply also to any part-owners or lessees.
Disqualification Any person may be disqualified for conspiring in any corrupt or fraudulent practice

concerning greyhound racing – including the improper administering of drugs to greyhounds, offering or receiving bribes, willfully entering a disqualified greyhound for a race, making a false statement about a greyhound's documents or identity, or selling information about a greyhound with which he is connected.
Persons are also liable to disqualification for cruelty to a greyhound; and for acting in any official capacity or entering, owning, or having charge of a greyhound at any unauthorized course.
Race cards provide information on the racecourse, meeting, and officials, and give details of each race and each dog competing.
Categories of race These vary from country to country. Some countries have a grading system: greyhounds of the same grade compete, winners advance to the next grade, repeated losers fall a grade. Other countries have a race system based on the

greyhounds' training, with:
open races, for greyhounds in the charge of any licensed trainer;
races for greyhounds trained by trainers licensed at the racecourse concerned;
kennel races, for greyhounds trained at courses with the same executive.
Other entry categories in the training-based system are:
inter-racecourse races, between two or more teams representing different courses;
private matches, between greyhounds with different owners and usually different trainers.
Special entry categories are:
invitation races, for specified greyhounds;
produce races, which are restricted to greyhounds whelped in a particular year.
In many countries any race may be declared:
a sweepstake, with the entry fees or other payments by the owners being returned as prize money;
a selling race, when one or more of the runners is to be offered for auction afterwards.

Finally, any of the above may be held as:
a normal race;
a handicap race, with one greyhound having to run the full distance and others starting at the same time from traps that give them a number of yards start;
a hurdles race, over three or four sets of hurdles.
In the USA all races are graded. Experienced greyhounds are graded from A to E, A being the highest grade. Greyhounds are promoted or relegated between grades according to their performance. There is also a mixed grade S which includes stakes and special races, and the maiden classification grade M for greyhounds that have not won a race.
No-race is declared only if:
there is mechanical or other defect of the lure equipment or the starting traps;
the lure is not kept within a reasonable distance from the leading greyhound;
no greyhound completes the course within a reasonable time;
there is any outside interference with the race.

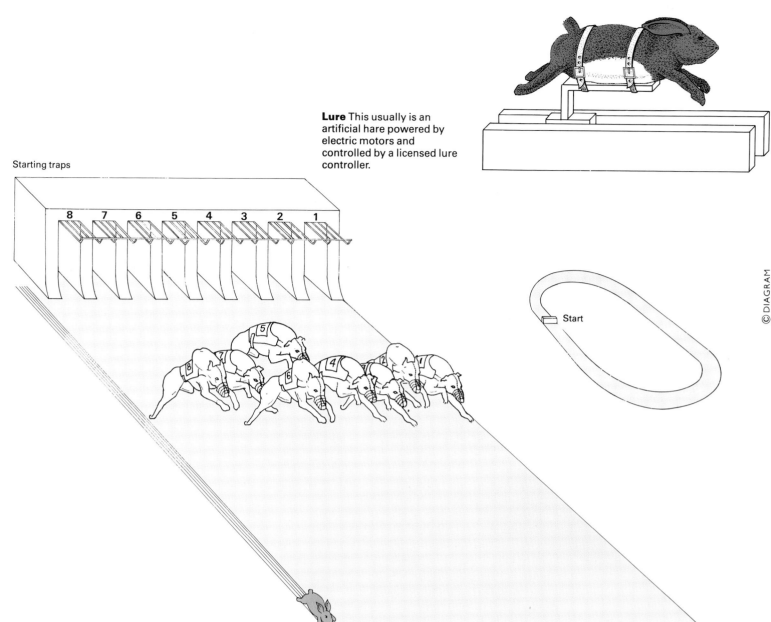

Lure This usually is an artificial hare powered by electric motors and controlled by a licensed lure controller.

Starting traps

Start

© DIAGRAM

Rerun A no-race may be rerun at the same meeting after a minimum time lapse. Whether a greyhound competes in a rerun is the option of the owner or, in his absence, his agent or trainer. In the USA races are not rerun.

Racecources Approved courses have a track with starting traps, a motorized lure and a finish line with photo or ray-timing apparatus; an enclosed paddock with racing kennels; public enclosures; and in some countries, a mechanical/electrical totalizator for betting.

Officials for an approved course are: racing manager or secretary; stewards; judge(s); paddock judge; clerk of the scales; starter; lure operator; security officer; veterinarian; racecourse trainer. Officials' titles vary from country to country.

Traps usually are numbered from 1 to 8 from the inside trap outward.
Each greyhound wears the number of the trap, to which it is allocated, and this number is given on the race card.
There may be reserves to take the place of any withdrawals. In non-handicap races greyhounds are allocated by draw to traps from the inside outward, except that in some countries greyhounds classified as wide runners may be separately allocated to inside traps. In handicap races the greyhound(s) running the full distance start(s) from the trap(s) nearest to the side of the track, on which the lure passes the start. Runners benefiting from the handicap are placed in ascending order across the course from that side.

Paddock admission is limited to racecourse officials, holders of temporary appointments, stewards, licensed trainers and kennelhands (lead-outs in the USA) in charge of any greyhound running at that meeting, owners of any greyhound running, and any person specifically authorized by the course authorities.

Kenneling procedure This takes place before the first race of the meeting. Greyhounds are officially identified and are weighed by a licensed official. Any greyhound varying more than a certain amount from its last running weight must be withdrawn.
After being inspected by the course veterinarian, greyhounds are put in individual kennels and are locked in for security purposes.

Paddock procedure
Before a race, greyhounds about to run are taken from their kennels and reidentified. They are then fitted with the correct racing jackets and muzzles and reexamined by the veterinarian.
After being paraded in front of the public enclosures, they are led to the starting traps and placed inside.

The start When all the greyhounds are in the traps, all persons other than the starter and his assistants must retire. The starter then gives the public signal for the lure to be started and the traps are opened, when the lure is approximately 12yd in front of them.
If a starting trap fails to open, the lure is stopped as quickly and safely as practicable – if possible, out of sight of the greyhounds. Failure of a greyhound to start after his trap opens is not in itself a reason for declaring "no-race."

Fighting Any greyhound that fights during a race is disqualified and its owner forfeits all rights in that race. (In the USA the first time fighter is not disqualified.) There are procedures for reinstating disqualified greyhounds, but repeated fighting will lead to permanent exclusion.

Out of bounds A greyhound that runs out of the defined course, whether it returns and crosses the finish line or not, is regarded as not completing the course.

Timing is by photo or ray-timing apparatus. Often the time for the first greyhound to finish is checked against a handheld stopwatch. Timing is from when the starting trap's front reaches 45° to the perpendicular until the winning greyhound's nose reaches the finish line.
For handicap races, although the winner is still the first greyhound to reach the finish line, its race time is calculated by adding to its actual time a prescribed amount (0·60 of a second in some countries, 0·80 in others) for each yard of distance benefit received under the handicap.

Prizes A disqualified greyhound forfeits all rights in a race, and any prize already awarded must be returned.
In case of a tie, prizes are, if possible, divided equally. Otherwise they are allocated by the mutual agreement of the owners; or, failing this, on the decision of the course authorities.

Horse racing

There are two basic forms of horse racing: flat racing and races over jumps. In the latter the horses jump fences (in steeplechases) or hurdles placed around the course. A meeting includes either flat races or steeplechase and hurdle races. Entrance qualifications, race distances, and types of prize vary considerably.

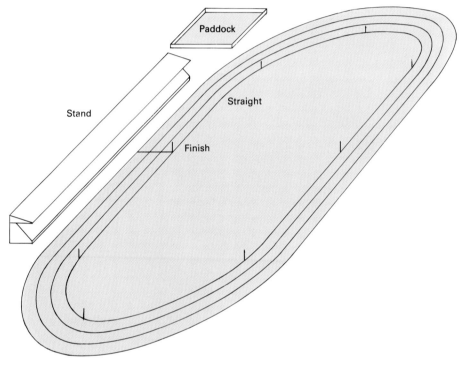

The course Styles vary between countries. The surface may be grass, dirt, or packed snow; the layout a simple oval or a complex pattern with a number of possible starting points; the length ⅝ mile–2½ miles or more. Some courses provide for both flat and steeplechase/hurdle racing.

Steeplechases All fences except water jumps are at least 4½ft high. In the first two miles there are at least 12 fences and at least 6 fences in each succeeding mile. In each mile there is at least one ditch, 6ft wide, on the take-off side of the fence, guarded by a bank and rail not more than 2ft high. There is a water jump at least 12ft wide, guarded by a fence not more than 3ft high.

Hurdles All hurdles are at least 3½ft high from bottom bar to top bar. In the first 2 miles there are at least 8 flights of hurdles, with another flight for each complete ¼ mile after that. As hurdles are made so that they are easily knocked over, a horse that hits a hurdle can usually keep going.

Fence — Water jump — Ditch — Hurdle

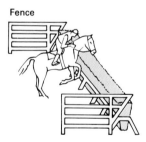

Officials who supervise meetings are known as stewards. Other officials include:
the racing secretary or "clerk of the course," in charge of the course and meeting arrangements;
the weighing officer or "clerk of the scales," who controls weighing out and weighing in;
the handicapper, who arranges the weights for the handicap races;
paddock judge and patrol judges;
the judge, who witnesses the finish and declares the result, after consulting photographs if necessary;
the camera patrol, who film crucial points of the race to help the stewards

decide objections;
the starter.
Types of races Races vary according to distance, type of horse entered, prize and weighting system.
Race distances for flat races vary from ⅝ to 2¾ miles. Some countries (eg UK and Australia) concentrate on the longer races (1¼ miles and more), others (eg USA) on short races of 1 mile or less. Distances for steeplechases are 2–4½ miles and for hurdles 2–3½ miles.
Special categories include: novice races for horses, that have not won a race of the type concerned at the start of the current season; maiden races, for horses that have never won; auction plates, for horses bought in public auction as

yearlings (weight allowances may be given in relation to purchase price); selling races, in which the winner is auctioned afterwards; claiming races, in which horses may be claimed for purchase for not less than the price stated in the conditions of the race. (In countries in which claiming races are frequent, all horses in a race are listed for the same claiming price and the system provides a way of grading horses, since the successful are moved up to higher price races.)
Weighting system The normal load a horse carries (rider and equipment) can be altered by the addition of lead weights to give an overall "weight" to be

carried. This allows four types of race:
open races, in which every horse carries the same weight;
weight for age races, in which younger horses receive the benefit of a lighter weight;
condition (or allowance) races, in which basic weight allowance for age and sex of horse is varied by added weight penalties for past successes (measured in prize money terms);
handicap races, in which the weights are adjusted to try to give horses an equal chance of winning.
In all races weight allowances are given to apprentices and jockeys with limited winning experience, providing that the prize

money involved is below a certain amount.
Weighing-out Before a race all riders must be weighed. The trainer is responsible for his horse carrying the correct weight, which includes hood and blinkers (if these have been declared for the horse), number cloth, martingale, breastplate, saddle and clothing as well as the jockey himself.
Lead weights may be added to the jockey's saddle to give the correct weight.
Crash helmet, whip, bridle, rings, plates or anything worn on the horse's legs are not included in the weight.
The start Before the race begins the horses are ridden in front of the stand. They must be at the starting post at the correct time. No

Dress Jockeys wear:
1 crash helmet or "skull cap," which is compulsory;
2 shirt in the owner's colors and trousers;
3 boots;
4 spurs;
5 jockeys carry a whip.
In steeplechases, hurdle races and national hunt flat races, riders must wear body protectors.
The saddle is the rider's responsibility, unless he is an apprentice, when the trainer is responsible.
It consists of:
6 saddle;
7 girth and surcingle;
8 stirrup irons;
9 leathers or webs;
and a number cloth.
If a rider is weighed out with visor, hood or blinkers, the horse must wear them for the race.
Blinding hoods or any kind of shutter hood are forbidden.

Jockeys A jockey must be licensed. He may operate independently, unless he is an apprentice, or he may be retained by an owner.
A substitute jockey is allowed either before or after the weigh-out, providing there is no unreasonable delay.

Horses The age of a horse is taken from January 1 in the year it was foaled.
Male horses are known as colts to the age of five, and horses thereafter; females as fillies to five and mares thereafter. A gelding is a castrated colt or horse.
For flat races, a horse must be a two year old before it can race; for hurdles, a three year old; and for steeplechasing, a four year old.
In general, long races favor older horses; young horses dominate sprints.

Horse's age In flat racing a race may be restricted to a certain age group: two year olds; three year olds; or four year olds and older.
Horse's sex Some races are for horses of one sex only: fillies only, or colts and geldings only.

preliminary jumps are allowed before a steeplechase or hurdle race, except in Germany. The start is usually from starting stalls, but sometimes from a starting gate or flag, with the horses started in a straight line as far as possible.
In flat races the horses are drawn for starting positions with number 1 on the inside. An unruly horse may be withdrawn by the starter. No horse, when stalls are used, may start from outside the stalls or be held inside the stalls, except in the USA where, when necessary, a horse's head is steadied in the stall.
A horse is considered to have started once it has come under starter's orders. A false start may be declared and the race restarted if there is a fault in the starting mechanism. In steeplechase or hurdle races, if the horses fail to return after the recall signal, the race is void. If only one horse returns, it is awarded a walkover.
The race Each jockey must try to give his horse the chance to do as well as it can. If a rider is dismounted, he may remount, but the horse must be remounted where the rider fell. The rider may be assisted in catching and remounting the horse.
A horse will be disqualified, if it receives assistance from anyone except its jockey in jumping a fence or a hurdle that it has refused.
If a horse misses a fence or hurdle, or passes the wrong side of a direction marker, it must return and ride the course correctly, or be disqualified.
A horse will also be disqualified if its rider, by reckless riding or by intention jeopardizes another horse's chances.
A horse may be disqualified or its placing altered:
if, in steeplechase or hurdle race, it crosses and interferes with another horse at, or in the home run from, the last fence or hurdle;
if, in a flat race, it crosses and interferes with another horse in any part of the race.
Weighing-in After a race all the riders are weighed again.
If a jockey's weight exceeds his weigh-out by more than a permitted amount, it is reported to the stewards, but the horse is not disqualified. If it falls below by more than a permitted amount, the horse is disqualified.
When the weigh-in reveals no infringements, the stewards confirm the result.
The finish The first horse past the post wins, except in the case of a disqualification. If two or more horses finish together, the judge's decision is based on the order in which their noses pass the post. In this the judge is assisted by the photo-finish camera.
Dead heat If two horses run a dead heat for first place, each is judged a winner and prize money for the first two places is divided equally between them. This applies in dividing all prizes, whatever the number of horses involved.
If two horses run a dead heat for second place and the first horse is disqualified, these horses become joint winners.
Walkover In a walkover a horse need only be ridden past the judge's box to be declared the winner.
The prize The race may be:
a stakes or sweepstake, with prize money made up from the fees of entrants together with "added money" paid by the course;
a cup with a prize made up of a trophy and prize money;
a private sweepstake with no "added" money;
a match between the horses of two different owners on terms agreed by them.

© DIAGRAM

Harness horse racing

In harness racing, horses are driven from a light, two-wheeled "sulky." Horses are trained to "trot" or "pace," and separate races are held for the two gaits. Horses race for purse money, and bets are placed by the public. (The rules given here are those of the United States Trotting Association. Similar rules apply in other countries.)

Colors Distinguishing colors are compulsory for drivers. Judges may bar from a race anyone they consider to be improperly dressed.

Protective helmets (1) with a hard shell and adequate padding must be worn by drivers. Chin straps must be used.

Whips (2) must not exceed 4ft 8in. Excessive use of the whip and whipping under the arch of the sulky are prohibited. A crop is the only other permitted goading device.

The sulky (3) It is the responsibility of the owner and trainer to ensure that all sulkies used in the races have wheel discs of an approved type. The use of mudguards may be ordered by the presiding judge.

TROTTERS

Shoes (4) Trotters usually wear level shoes in front and swedge shoes behind. The swedge is a creased shoe providing traction when the horse's hind foot hits the ground. Shoes for trotters usually weigh 8oz each.

Toe weights Trotters often have toe weights (5) clipped to each hoof. Weighing 2–4oz, they are used to extend a horse's stride.

Trotting A high-stepping diagonal gait. Right front and left hind legs are brought forward in unison, followed by left front and right hind legs.

Trotting

PACERS

Shoes (6) Pacers usually wear flat or half round shoes in front. Behind they usually wear a combination shoe, half round inside and half swedge outside. The half round portion is to reduce risk of injury, while the half swedge portion increases traction. Pacers' shoes weigh about 5oz each.

Hopples (or hobbles) (7) are leather straps encircling the front and hind legs on the same side to help the horse maintain its gait.

If a horse wears hopples, it must wear them throughout a race. If a horse usually races hoppled, it needs the judges' approval to race free legged; if it usually races free legged, it needs approval to race hoppled. Any person attempting a fraud by removing or altering a horse's hopples, either before or during a race, is liable to be suspended or expelled.

The head pole (8) is a cue to keep the horse's head straight. Fastened alongside the head and neck, it must not protrude more than 10in beyond the horse's nose.

The gaiting strap (9) is fastened inside the shafts of the sulky to prevent the horse swinging the rear and traveling sideways on its gait.

Pacing A swaying, lateral gait. Right front and hind legs are swung forward in unison, followed by left front and hind legs.

Pacing

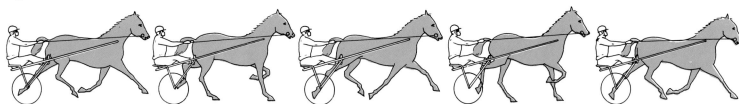

261

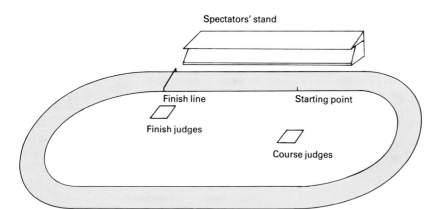

Spectators' stand

Finish line

Starting point

Finish judges

Course judges

The track is oval in shape. Lengths vary from ½–1mi.
The starting point is marked on the inside rail. It must be at least 200ft from the first turn.
The wire (finish) is the real or imaginary line from the center of the judges' stand to a point immediately across and at right angles to the track.

A horse will only be placed if the driver is mounted in his sulky at the finish.
The winning horse is the one whose nose reaches the wire first. In a dead heat both horses count as winners. Where two horses tie in a summary, the winner of the longer dash or heat wins the trophy. If lengths are the same and horses tie in the

summary and the time, both horses are the winners.
Timing Using an approved electric device or three official timers, times are taken from when the first horse leaves the starting point to when the winner's nose reaches the wire. Times must be publicly announced or posted, and are recorded in minutes,

seconds, and fifths of seconds.
In a dead heat the time is recorded for each winner.
Officials include: program director, presiding judge, paddock judge, starter, patrol judge, finish wire judge, timers, clerk of the course.
Length of races As stated in the conditions for the meeting, and given in units of not less than 1/16mi.
Number of heats As stated in the conditions for the meeting, usually one or three to a race.
There must be at least 40 minutes between the heats in a race.
A dash is a race decided by a single heat.

Paddock rules Except for paddock officials, the only persons authorized to enter the paddock are the owners, trainers, drivers, grooms, and caretakers of horses waiting to compete. Horses must be in the paddock at least one hour before competing. Having entered the paddock, horses and the persons associated with them may only leave the paddock before the race for the purpose of warming up.

Starting gate

Post positions Post (or starting) positions are determined by lot for a dash or first heat. Post positions for subsequent heats, unless the published conditions state otherwise, are determined as follows:
the winner of the previous heat takes the pole (or inside position) and the others are positioned according to their placings. Positions are settled by lot in the case of a dead heat.
Tiered starts A maximum of two tiers of horses, allowing 8ft per horse, is permitted to start in any race. Whenever a horse is withdrawn from a tier, horses on the outside move in to fill the vacant position.

Withdrawing a horse that has drawn or earned a position in the front tier does not affect the position of the horses in the second tier.
The starting gate must have arms perpendicular to the rail, and a screen or shield in front of the position for each horse.
The starter The horses are brought to the start by the starter, who controls them from the formation of the parade until he gives the word "go" at the starting point.

Starting procedure Horses are brought to the gate as near as possible ¼mi before the starting point. The starting gate is then brought to the starting point with graduated speed:
for the first ⅛mi, not less than 11mph; for the next 1/16mi, not less than 16mph; from that point to the starting point, the speed is gradually increased until the starting point is reached.
Only in the case of a recall may the speed be decreased in the course of a start.
The starter gives the word "go" when the gate reaches the starting point.
Unless dismissed before the word "go," all horses that are not prevented by injury or accident must complete the course.

Recalls The starter may sound a recall only if:
a horse scores ahead of the gates;
there is interference;
a horse has broken equipment;
a horse falls before the word "go" is given;
a horse refuses to come to gate before the gate reaches the pole ⅛mi before the starting point.
No recall is possible after the word "go" has been given.
Recall signal A recall is sounded by the starter and signaled to the drivers by flashing lights. The starting gate proceeds out of the horses' path.

Starting violations Drivers will be fined and/or suspended for:
delaying the start;
failing to obey the starter's instructions;
rushing ahead of the inside or outside wing of the starting gate;
coming to the starting gate out of position;
crossing over before reaching the starting point;
interfering with another driver during the start;
failing to come up into position.
Hearings are held before any penalty is imposed.

Age The age of the horses is reckoned from January 1 of the year of foaling, except for foals born in November and December, whose age is reckoned from January 1 of the succeeding year.

Race categories

Classified races are between selected horses, regardless of money won.

Conditioned races have specific entrance conditions, such as age, sex, or success over a given period.

Claiming races are those in which all starters may be purchased in conformity with the rules.

Handicap is a race in which performance, sex, or distance allowance is made. Post positions may be determined by claiming price.

Matinee is a race with no entrance fee, in which the premiums – if any – are other than for money.

Futurity is a race in which competing horses are nominated before being foaled.

Stake is a race for which entries close the year before the race and in which all nominating and starting fees are added to the purse.

Early closing races are those for which entries close at least six weeks before the race.

Late closing races are those for which entries close less than six weeks before the race.

Overnight events are those for which entries close not more than three days before the race (not including Sundays).

Coupled entry When a race includes two or more horses owned or trained by the same person, or trained by same stable or management, they are normally coupled as an "entry." A wager on one of the horses counts as a wager on all horses in the entry. In special events horses under separate ownerships but with the same trainer may be permitted to race as separate betting entries.

Money distribution

Dashes Unless conditions state otherwise the distribution is 45%, 25%, 15%, 10%, 5%.

Every heat a race As for a dash, with nothing set aside for the winner.

Two in three A horse must win two heats to win the race, and 10% is set aside for the race winner. The remainder is divided between the heats and distributed as if each heat were a dash. If the race is not decided after three heats, the heat winners or horses making a dead heat for first usually run in a fourth heat for the winner's 10%.

Placing system As for a two in three, a horse must win two heats to win the race. Other race placings are decided by a summary of heat placings. The summary is decided along the lines that a horse with a clear first place is higher than a horse with a tied first place or no place higher than second. Unless the conditions state otherwise, the money is divided 50%, 25%, 15%, and 10%.

Violations of driving rules

No driver may:

change to the right or left if this would compel another horse to shorten its stride or be pulled out of its stride by its driver;

jostle, strike, hook wheels, or interfere in any way with another horse or driver;

endanger other drivers by crossing sharply in front of the field;

swerve in or out or pull up quickly;

crowd a horse or driver by "putting a wheel under him";

help another horse by causing confusion or interference among horses then trailing;

let any horse pass needlessly, or lay off normal pace to leave a hole that

could easily be kept closed; in any way impede the progress of another horse or cause it to break from its gait;

change course after selecting a position in the home stretch, or by swerving or bearing in or out cause another horse to change its course or hold back;

drive in a reckless or careless manner;

shout loudly during a race, or use any goading device other than an ordinary whip or crop;

remove either foot from his stirrups from the word "go" until the race ends.

Breaking rules A horse that breaks from its gait must, where clearance exists, be taken to the outside and

pulled back to gait. It is a violation if a driver: does not attempt to pull his horse to gait;

fails to take the outside where clearance exists;

fails to lose ground by the break.

Drivers are then penalized as for a violation of a driving rule.

If there has been no violation, a horse is only set back if, at the finish, a contending horse on its gait is lapped on the breaking horse's hind quarter.

Complaints Any complaint by a driver must be made to the judges immediately the heat ends, unless he is prevented by accident or injury.

Action after violations An offending horse may, for that heat or dash only, be set back in the placings behind any horse with which it interfered.

If an offense prevents another horse from finishing, the offending horse may be disqualified from receiving any winnings and its driver fined, suspended, or expelled. In case of an offense by a horse coupled in an "entry," both horses may be set back if the judges consider that the finish was affected. Otherwise, horses in an "entry" are penalized separately.

Failing to finish Horses must contest every heat in a race. A horse failing to finish a heat will be ruled out,

unless the failure was caused by broken equipment or interference.

Inconsistent driving Deliberately preventing a horse from winning, driving inconsistently, and racing to perpetrate or aid a fraud are offenses punishable by fine, suspension, or expulsion. The judges may at any time substitute another driver.

Doping Blood, urine, and saliva tests may be used to determine the presence of forbidden drugs. Any person administering such drugs to a horse, or influencing or conspiring with another person to do so, will be fined and/or suspended, or expelled.

Impede by crossing sharply

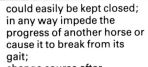

Hook wheels

Impede by slowing down

Remove foot from stirrup

Strike an opponent's horse

© DIAGRAM

Show jumping

A jumping competition is one in which the horse's jumping ability and the rider's skill are tested under various conditions over a course of obstacles. Certain defined errors are faulted, and, depending on the type of competition, the winner is the competitor with either the lowest number of faults, the fastest time, or the highest number of points.

A typical Grand Prix course:

1 brush and rails;
2 hog's back;
3 post and rails;
4 narrow stile;
5 double-triple bar, planks and poles;
6 fancy gate;
7 treble vertical parallels
8 white gate;
9 narrow stile;
10 water jump;
11 double-parallel poles;
12 oildrums and poles
13 poles over a bank;
14 double-oxer, post and rails;
15 stone wall.

Examples of straight obstacles

Stone wall   Gate   Brush and rails   Hog's back

Examples of spread obstacles

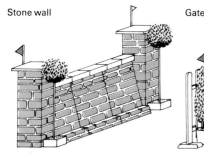

Types of competition
Grand prix
Nations Cup
Puissance
Hunting
Six bars
Baton relay
Fault and out relay
Accumulator
Derby
Doubles and triples
Hit and hurry
Knock-out
Relay
Take your own line
Top score
Two phases
Two rounds

Team competitions For CSI0 competitions an official team is composed of a maximum of a team captain, 6 riders and 15 horses. Teams for the Olympic Games and Nations' Cup have 4 riders and 4 horses, of which only the best three scores are counted.

Individual competitions
For Olympic competitions riders may ride only one horse and not more than three riders may ride for the same nation in the final individual competition. For other events competitors may enter a maximum of 3 horses, but must declare at the beginning of the competition which one or two they intend to ride.

Officials include:
judges;
course designers;
timekeeper;
arena and collecting ring stewards;
veterinary commission;
appeal committee.

Result Depending on the type of competition, the winner is the competitor or team with either the lowest number of faults, the fastest time with fewest faults or the highest number of points.

The arena is enclosed, and while a horse is jumping all entrances and exits are shut. Once the competition has started, competitors are not allowed to enter the arena on foot, exercise their horses, or jump any of the fences, unless actually taking part.

The course From the starting line to the finishing line the maximum length of a course in meters is the number of obstacles in the course multiplied by sixty. The starting and finishing lines and all obstacles are marked with red flags on the right and white flags on the left.

Plan of the course A plan showing the general layout of the course is posted for the competitors' benefit. It shows:
the positions of the start and finishing lines;
the relative positions of obstacles, their type and numbers;
any compulsory passages or turning points;

the length of the course;
the track to be followed (a continuous line means that it must be followed precisely and a series of arrows indicates only the direction from which each obstacle is to be jumped);
the marking system to be used;
the time allowed and the time limit, if any;
the obstacles to be used in any jump-off, and the length of course and time allowed for the jump-off.

Horses For CSIO championships and Olympic Games horses must be: owned by a member of the same national federation; registered with that federation; ridden by a person of the same nationality as the owner.

Riders before the year of their 18th birthday cannot take part in a Nations' Cup, a Puissance, Grand Prix, Power and Speed, Derby, Championships or Games for Seniors. A card of authorization from their national federation is compulsory for each show in a foreign country.

Dress Civilians are required at international events to wear the uniform of a riding club recognized by their national federation, hunt uniform, a red or black coat, white breeches, hunting cap, black boots or black top boots. Ladies are allowed to wear light fawn breeches and bowler hat or a hunting cap. A hunting stock is recommended for international events, otherwise a white shirt and tie must be worn.

Saddlery There are no restrictions on saddles or bridles, but blinkers and hoods are forbidden. Only a running martingale is allowed. Whips exceeding 75cm or weighted at one end are also prohibited.

Triple bars   Double oxer   Parallel poles

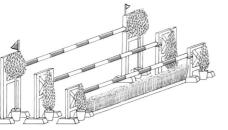

© DIAGRAM

Obstacles are numbered consecutively in the order in which they are to be jumped. Multiple obstacles carry only one number, but each element has a different letter (for example 3A, 3B, 3C). As far as possible, fences resemble natural hazards, but they are not absolutely fixed.

Except in Puissance, Power and Skill Competitions or in a High Jump Record, obstacles must never exceed 1.70m in height or 2m in width. The water jump never exceeds 4.50m width.

Types of obstacle:

A straight obstacle is one where the elements are placed vertically one above the other in the same plane, for example gates, walls, posts and rail(s).

Multiple obstacles are composed of two, three, or four obstacles and are taken in successive jumps. The distance between any two parts is a minimum of 7m and a maximum of 12m. Banks, slopes and ramps with or without fences are counted as multiple obstacles.

A spread fence is one that requires the horse to jump both height and width, for example triple bars, double-oxer and hog's back.

The water jump is a spread fence with a small guardrail or hedge on the take-off side (about 50cm high) and a ditch full of water between 4m and 4.50m in width. The limit of the jump is clearly marked on the landing side at CSIs with a white strip of

wood, at CSIO and Olympic Games with a strip of white rubber approximately 5cm wide.

Fences for Nations' Cup competitions There are 12 obstacles with heights varying between 1.30m and 1.60m. The course is normally about 600m and has to include at least one double or one treble obstacle, six fences not less than 1.40m high, two straight obstacles not less than 1.50m high and a water jump with a minimum width of 4m. Spread obstacles may vary between 1.50m and 2.0m in width with a height in proportion to their width, with the exception of triple bars, which may have a maximum spread of 2.20m.

Fences for puissance competitions There are between four and six obstacles, of which straight fences must be at least 1.40m high. There may be a maximum of four jump-offs over a reduced number of fences, which may be raised and/or increased in width.

Olympic Games

Team final competition For round A the length of the course and the number and measurements of the obstacles are the same as for the individual event.
In round B all teams may participate. The jump-off is held over six obstacles 1.40–1.70m high. Spread obstacles are increased to between 1.60m and 2.20m.

Individual final competition For round A the course does not exceed 900m, with between 12 and 15 obstacles varying in height from 1.40m to 1.60m. Spread obstacles vary from 1.50m to 2.0m in width and the water jump is at least 4.30m wide.
In round B the height of the obstacles may be raised from 1.40m to 1.70m and the width increased to 2m, but there may not be more than 10 obstacles.

Knocking down an obstacle

Failure at the water jump

Procedure

Walking the course Before the start of the competition the rider is permitted to inspect the course and fences on foot.

The order of starting is decided by a draw.

Starting When his number is called, the competitor enters the arena already mounted. He does not cross the starting line until the judge gives the starting signal, normally a bell.

The first round is not normally against the clock, but subsequent rounds may be.

Once he has passed the starting line, the competitor must jump the fences in the correct order and will be penalized for any errors, such as knocking over a fence, refusing a fence (in which case the fence must be taken again) or losing his way. If a horse knocks down a fence on a refusal, the rider must wait until it has been rebuilt before retaking it and continuing with the rest of the course.

At the end of the course the rider must leave the arena still mounted.

Penalties

Obstacles knocked down

An obstacle is considered to be knocked down when any part of it is knocked down or dislodged, even if the falling part is arrested by another part of the obstacle.

Touches and displacements are not counted, nor is an obstacle considered to be knocked down if it falls only after the competitor has crossed the finishing line.

Knocking down the top element is only penalized, when an obstacle or part of an obstacle is composed of several elements in the same vertical plane.

When an obstacle has several elements not in the same vertical plane, a competitor is penalized for only one mistake, irrespective of the number of separate elements knocked down.

Any element of a knocked-down obstacle that prevents a competitor from jumping another obstacle, or part of a multiple obstacle, must be removed before the competitor continues.

Falls A rider is considered to have fallen if he is separated from his horse, which has not fallen, in such a way that he has to remount or vault into the saddle.

A horse is considered to have fallen when its shoulder and quarters have touched the ground or the obstacle and the ground.

Any fall is penalized wherever it takes place and whatever the cause. A competitor will be eliminated, if he fails to continue the course from the point, where the fall occurred.

When a horse or rider falls in knocking down or refusing an obstacle or after any other disobedience, the penalties for both faults are added together.

A loose horse that falls, jumps an obstacle, goes to the wrong side of a flag or passes through the starting or finishing line is not penalized.

A loose horse that leaves the arena is eliminated.

Disobedience Penalized as disobedience are:
a rectified deviation from the course;
a refusal, run-out or resistance;
circling, except after a run-out or refusal;
crossing the track first taken between any two consecutive obstacles, except when specifically allowed by the course plan; passing the obstacle and then approaching it sideways.

Refusal It is a refusal if a horse stops in front of an obstacle to be jumped, whether or not the fence is knocked down or displaced. It is not a refusal if a horse stops at an obstacle without knocking it down or reining back and then immediately makes a standing jump.

It is a refusal if the stop is prolonged or if the horse steps back even a single pace, voluntarily or not, or if it takes more room to jump.

A competitor is eliminated if he knocks down an obstacle while stopping and then jumps the obstacle before it is re-erected.

If a horse slides through an obstacle, the judge decides whether it is to count as a refusal or as an obstacle knocked down.

A competitor is eliminated after three refusals, or if he shows an obstacle to his horse after a refusal.

Running out A horse is considered to have run out if:
it is not fully under its rider's control and avoids an obstacle it should have jumped;
it jumps an obstacle outside the boundary flags.

The rider is eliminated if he fails to bring his horse back to jump the obstacle.

Resistance A horse is considered to offer resistance if at any time it fails to go forward.

A horse is eliminated if:
it resists its rider for 60 consecutive seconds;
it takes more than 60 seconds to jump an obstacle except in the case of a fall;
it fails to pass the starting line within 60 seconds of the signal to start.

Deviation A deviation from the course occurs when a competitor:
does not follow the plan of the course;
goes the wrong side of a flag;
jumps obstacles out of order;
jumps an obstacle outside the course, or misses the jump.

In order to correct a deviation, the competitor must return to the course at the point where the error was made.

If a deviation is rectified before the next obstacle is jumped, it is penalized as a disobedience.

If a deviation is not so rectified, the penalty is elimination.

Competitors will be eliminated for receiving unauthorized assistance if any person in the arena draws their attention to a deviation in an attempt to prevent elimination.

Scoring There are two different tables for scoring show jumping. Most competitions are decided under table A.

Table A

First disobedience, 3 faults; knocking down an obstacle or failure at the water jump, 4 faults;
second disobedience, 6 faults;
fall by horse or rider, 8 faults;
disobedience and knocking down an obstacle, 3 or 6 faults plus 6, 8 or 10 seconds;
third disobedience and other offenses stated in the rules, elimination;
exceeding the time allowed, $\frac{1}{4}$ fault for each second or part of a second.

Faults for disobedience are cumulative, whether they are made at the same obstacle or not.

Faults are added together to give the competitor's score for the round(s).

The time taken by the competitors may be used to decide cases of equality for first and other places, according to the conditions of the competition.

In cases of equality of faults for first place, there may be one or more compulsory jump-offs against the clock or not, according to the conditions of the competition.

Refusal at an obstacle   Fall by horse and rider

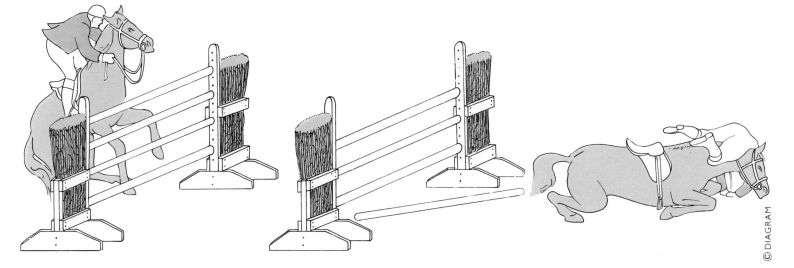

© DIAGRAM

Table B
This table is used for hunting competitions. Penalties are scored in seconds and added to the time of the round. The number of penalty seconds for each jumping mistake is calculated in relation to the length of the course and the number of times a horse is required to jump in the round.

Time and speed The timing of a round begins at the exact moment when the mounted rider passes the starting line, and ends when – still mounted – he crosses the finishing line.
Time allowed For international competitions the time allowed for each round is calculated from the length of the course and the following speed limits:
Normal: minimum 350m per minute;
Puissance: 1st round, 300m per minute; jump-off, no limit;
Hunting: minimum 350m per minute (outdoor); 325m per minute (indoor);
Six bars: no limit;
Nations' Cup: 400m per minute (outdoor); 350m per minute (indoor);
Olympic Games: 400m per minute.
The time limit is twice the time allowed in all competitions.
Recording time Time is recorded in seconds, tenths of seconds and hundredths of seconds. Automatic timing devices are used in all international competitions.
Interrupted time The clock must be stopped when, for example, a rider knocks down a fence, which his horse refuses to jump. It is not started again until the fence is rebuilt, at which point the rider is given the signal to recommence.

Time penalties are incurred as follows:
1) for knocking down an obstacle as a result of a disobedience:
6 seconds penalty for a single obstacle or the first part of a multiple obstacle;
8 seconds for the second part of a multiple obstacle;
10 seconds for the third or subsequent parts.
2) For knocking down part of a multiple obstacle and refusing or running out at the next part without knocking it down:
the clock is stopped as for a knock down resulting from a disobedience, and penalties of 8 to 10 seconds are imposed, depending on whether the disobedience was at the second, third, or subsequent parts.
Elimination Competitors are eliminated if they:
fail to enter the arena when called;
jump an obstacle in the arena before the starting signal, even if it is not in the course;
start before the signal, or fail to start within 60 seconds after it;
have three disobediences in a round, or show any obstacle to a horse after a refusal;
enter or leave the arena dismounted, except with the jury's permission;
have more than 60 seconds of resistance from their horse in any one round;

take more than 60 seconds to jump an obstacle (except in the case of a fall);
jump an obstacle without having corrected a deviation from the course;
jump an obstacle that is not in the course;
jump an obstacle in the wrong order;
pass the wrong side of a flag and fail to rectify the error;
exceed the time limit;
jump a knocked-down obstacle before it is rebuilt;
restart after an interruption before the signal is given;
jump an optional obstacle in a jump-off either more than once or in the wrong direction;
fail to jump the whole obstacle after a refusal;
fail to jump out of a closed obstacle in the correct direction, or interfere with a closed obstacle;
fail to jump each part of a multiple obstacle separately;
fail to cross the finishing line mounted before leaving the arena or their horses leave the arena before finishing the round;
accept a whip during a round or any other unauthorized assistance at the jury's discretion;
enter the arena on foot after the start of the competition at the jury's discretion;
commit any other offense that the rules specifically state is penalized by elimination.

A jump-off takes place to decide the winner among competitors who are tied for first place after earlier rounds.
Unless the rules state otherwise, the number of obstacles is reduced and individual fences may be raised or widened. For the first jump-off (except in Puissance or Nations' Cup) not less than half the original fences are retained, and for the second jump-off not less than six fences.
There are never more than two jumps-off unless the rules state otherwise. Either the first, or the first and second jumps-off may be against the clock. The jump-off may be decided by the number of faults plus the time taken to complete the round.
Special rules apply to Puissance jumps-off, in which the fences are made progressively higher until the winner is determined.
In the Nations' Cup the jump-off is timed and is over six obstacles. The winning team is decided by adding together jumping and time faults; if there are still teams with equal faults, the time taken is the decisive factor.

Dressage

Dressage competitions test the harmonious development of the horse's physique and ability, and demand a high degree of understanding between horse and rider. Competitors carry out official tests incorporating a variety of paces, halts, changes of direction, movements and figures.

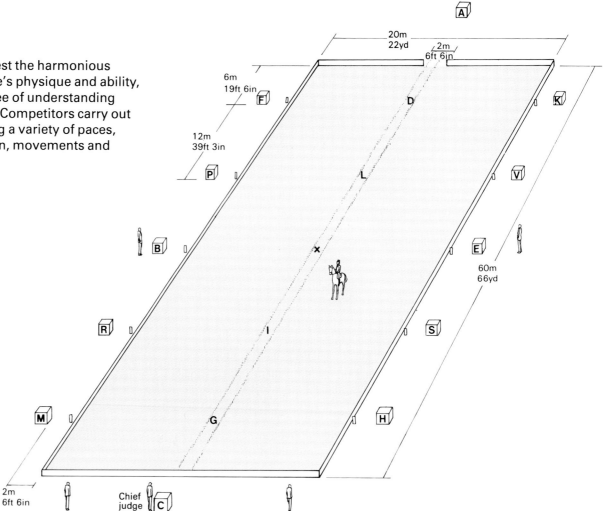

Arena International competitions must be in a sand arena measuring 60m×20m.
(An arena 40m×20m may be used for less advanced tests.)
Arenas must be perfectly level.
There must be 20m between the arena and the public. Indoor arenas must be at least 2m from any wall.
The center line is marked by raking or rolling it in a suitable way. Outer markers have letters in black or white and are placed about 0.5m outside of the approximately 0.3m high fence of the arena. Center letters are marked smaller underneath the outer letters. The entrance is marked by the letter A.
Officials International events are judged by a jury of five members: three on one short side of the arena and one on each of the long sides.
Tests The FEI (Fédération Equestre Internationale) issues the following tests for use at international level:
The Grand Prix (also team competition), The Grand Prix Special (individual competition) both Olympic standard: Intermediaire II (advanced standard); the Intermediaire I and Prix St. Georges (medium standard).
The FEI also issues:
the Concours Complet (for use at three-day-events);
the free style test on Intermediaire I and Grand Prix level; the junior tests and the young riders tests.
Horses must:
be currently registered with a national federation; be owned by a member of that federation; exceed 14.2 hands; fulfill entry requirements for specific competitions.
Saddlery Compulsory are an English hunting-type of saddle and a double bridle. Prohibited are martingales and bearing, side or running reins of any kind, bandages, boots and any form of blinkers.

Schooling No horse may take part in an official international event (CDIO) if, in the town where the competition takes place, it has been schooled or mounted in the three days before the event or during the event by anyone except the competitor.
(Training in hand may be undertaken by persons other than the competitor.)
Riders For all official events riders must:
be members of a national federation;
be at least in the year of their 16th birthday in order to take part in senior events;
be the same nationality as the horse's owner;
hold a card of authorization from their national federation for any show abroad.
Dress Service dress may be worn. Civilians wear a dark coat and white breeches, top hat, hunting stock and spurs. No whip is carried.

Procedure At the judges' signal the competitor enters the arena in collected trot or canter, whichever is asked for in the corresponding test, halts and salutes.
The test is then carried out entirely from memory and all movements must follow in the order laid down in the test sheet.
If the test requires a movement to be carried out at a certain point in the arena, it is to be executed when the rider's body is over that point.
A change of pace at a marker should occur when the rider's body passes that marker.
A bell is rung whenever the competitor departs from the direction or pace given in the test sheet. The test must then be restarted from the point at which the error occurred.

A fall by horse and/or rider does not result in elimination. The competitor is penalized by the effect of the fall on the execution of the movement and in the collective marks.
The test ends with a final salute, after which the competitor leaves the arena at point A.
Penalties For every error, whether rectified or not, every omission and every movement taken in the wrong order the competitor is penalized:
the first time by the loss of 2 points;
the second time by the loss of 4 points;
the third time by the loss of 8 points;
the fourth time by elimination, although he may continue the test to the end.

Marking Competitors receive two kinds of mark from each judge:
1) Movements and transitions are grouped into categories, which are given a mark from 0–10 by each judge. A mark of 0 means that a competitor performed nothing that was required.
2) Collective marks from 0–10 are awarded by each judge for the paces, impulsion, submission, and the rider's seat and use of aids.
(The collective marks and marks for certain movements can be given increased influence on the final result by using a coefficient fixed by the FEI.)

Test requirements Official tests include the following halts, paces, and movements.

The halt The horse should stand attentive, still and straight, with weight evenly distributed over all legs. The transition from any pace to the halt should be made progressively in a smooth, precise movement.

The walk is a marching pace, with the four legs following one another in well marked four time. Walks are collected, medium, or extended according to the length of the stride.

There is also a free walk in which the horse is allowed complete freedom of the neck and head.

The trot is a two-time pace on alternative diagonals (near fore and off hind and vice versa) separated by a moment of suspension. Steps should be free, active and regular. The trot should always be entered without hesitation. Recognized trots are collected, medium and extended. (The collected trot is replaced by the working trot in tests below St. Georges level.)

The canter is a three-time pace. In the right canter the sequence is left hind leg, left diagonal (right hind and left fore leg), right fore leg, followed by a period of suspension with all four legs in the air. Recognized canters are collected, medium and extended. (The collected canter is replaced by the working canter in tests below St. Georges level.)

The counter (false) canter is a suppling movement on the circle. The horse remains bent to the leading leg.

Change of leg at the canter In a simple change of leg the horse is brought into a walk for one or two well-defined steps and then restarted into a canter with the other leg leading.
In a change of leg in the air the change is executed in close connection with the suspension that follows each canter stride.

Walk

Trot

Canter

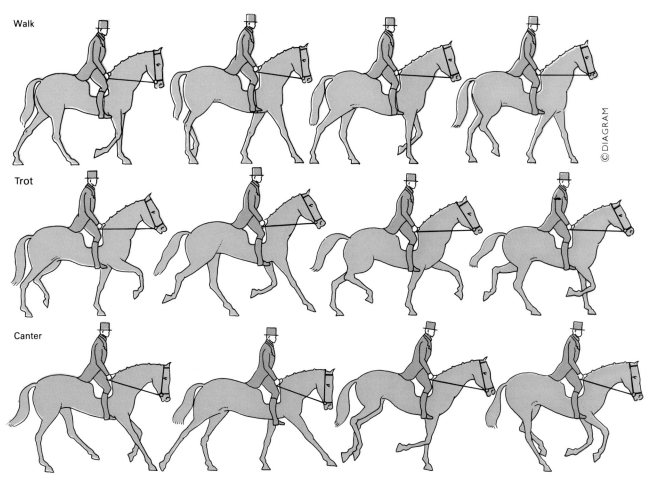

©DIAGRAM

The collected paces The horse's quarters are lowered with all the muscles and joints acting as springs. This enables the horse to develop its impulsion in a forward and upward direction.

The rein back is a retrograde movement with backwards steps, in which the legs are raised and set down almost simultaneously by diagonal pairs. The horse must be ready to halt or move foward without pausing at the rider's demands.

The submission is shown by a light acceptance of the bridle, soft but clear transitions, suppleness and flexibility, the possibility of lengthening the frame in medium and extended paces, the suppleness in the neck and the lightness of the forehand.

Transitions All changes of pace and speed should be quickly made but smooth. The same is true of transitions between passage and piaffe.

Changes of direction The horse should adjust the bend of its body to the curvature of the line followed, remaining supple and following the indications of the rider without any resistance or change of pace.

Riding corners At collected paces, the horse must describe a quarter of a circle of approximately 3m radius. At other paces, the circle's radius should be approximately 6m.

The passage is a measured, very collected, very elevated and very cadenced trot. Each diagonal pair of legs is raised and put to the ground alternately, gaining ground with an even cadence and a prolonged suspension.
In principle the height of the toe of the raised foreleg should be level with the middle of the cannon bone of the other foreleg. The toe of the raised hind leg should be slightly above the fetlock joint of the other hind leg. The neck should be raised and gracefully arched with the poll at the highest point and the head close to the perpendicular.
Crossing the forelegs or swinging the forehand or the quarters from side to side are serious faults.

The piaffe is a movement resembling the very collected trot on the spot. The neck is raised, the poll supple, the head perpendicular, the mouth maintaining light contact on a taut rein. The alternate diagonals are raised with even, supple, cadenced and graceful movement, the moment of suspension being prolonged.
In principle the height of the toe of the raised foreleg should be level with the middle of the cannon bone of the other foreleg. The toe of the raised hind leg should be just above the fetlock joint of the other hind leg. The body of the horse should move up and down with a supple, harmonious movement without any swinging of either the forehand or the quarters from one side to the other. Although executed strictly on the spot and with perfect balance, the piaffe must always be energetically executed.

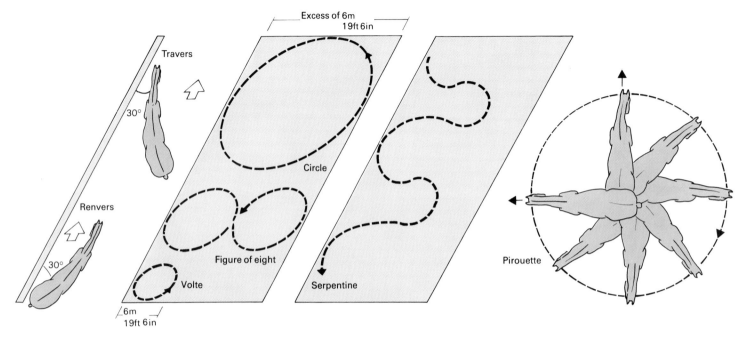

Travers

Renvers

30°

30°

6m
19ft 6in

Excess of 6m
19ft 6in

Circle

Figure of eight

Volte

Serpentine

Pirouette

Lateral movements (work on two tracks) comprise two suppling movements, the leg yielding and the shoulder-in as well as the classical movements, travers, renvers and half-pass. The aim is to improve the obedience, to supple the horse in his shoulders and the quarters and to develop and increase the engagement of the quarters and thereby also the collection.

In all but the leg yielding the horse is bent uniformly from poll to tail and moves with the forehand and quarters on two different tracks.

The pace remains always regular, supple and free. The forehand should always be slightly in advance of the quarters.

Leg yielding The horse's body is quite straight except for a slight bend at the poll. The horse looks away from the direction in which it is moving.

Shoulder-in The horse is slightly bent around the inside leg of the rider. The outside shoulder is placed in front of the inside hind quarter. The inside legs pass and cross in front of the outside legs. The horse looks away from the direction in which it is moving. The horse should not be at an angle of more than 30° to the direction in which it is moving.

Travers (head to wall) in which the horse moves along the wall with its head at an angle of 30° to the wall. The horse is slightly bent

around the inside leg of the rider and looks in the direction in which it is moving.

Renvers (tail to wall) is the inverse position of the travers, with the tail instead of the head to the wall. The horse looks in the direction in which it is moving.

On two tracks: the half-pass: The horse's head, neck and shoulders are always slightly in advance of the quarters.

The horse is bent slightly and looks in the direction in which it is moving. The outside legs (on the side from which the horse is moving) pass and cross in front of the inside legs.

Counter-change of hand in half-pass (zig-zag). The judges concentrate on the changes in position of the horse, the movement of its legs and the precision, suppleness and regularity of its movements.

Figures:

The volte is a circle of 6m diameter.

The circle has a stated diameter in excess of 6m.

The serpentine The first loop is started by moving gradually away from the short side and the last loop is finished by moving gradually toward the opposite short side.

The figure of eight is executed following the same rules as for the serpentine inside a square with a designated point on the center line as the center. The rider changes the bend of his horse at the center of eight.

The half-pirouette is a half turn on the haunches executed in walk or in canter. The forehand commences the half-turn, tracing a half circle around the haunches without pausing at the moment the inside hind leg ceases its forward movement. The inside hindfoot, while forming the pivot, should return to the same spot each time it leaves the ground. The horse moves forward again without a pause on completing the half-turn.

The pirouette (executed in walk, canter or, if in a free style test, in piaffe) is a small circle on two tracks with a radius equal to the length of the horse, the forehand moving around the haunches. The forelegs and the outside hind leg move around the inside hind foot, which forms the pivot. The pace is not considered to be regular, if the pivot foot is not raised and returned to the ground in the same way as the other hind foot. The pivot foot should always return to the same spot.

Position of the rider All the movements should be obtained without apparent effort by the rider. He should be well-balanced, with loins and hips supple, thighs and legs steady and well stretched downward. The upper part of the body should be easy, free and erect with arms close to the body. Riding with both hands is compulsory in the ordinary tests but optional in the free style tests.

Use of the voice is strictly forbidden and involves the deduction of at least two marks from what would otherwise have been scored for a movement.

Only women riding side-saddle are permitted to carry a whip.

Elimination Grounds for elimination are:
failure to obey judges' signals;
leaving the arena before completing the test;
a horse leaving the arena out of control;
a horse entering the arena when not actually competing;
a fourth error of course;
doping;
a horse going lame;
resistance (failing to enter the arena within 60 seconds of the starting bell, or refusing to continue the test for a period of 60 consecutive seconds).

Classification After each performance and after each judge has given his collective marks, which must be done with due consideration, the judges' sheets pass to the scorers. The marks are multiplied by the corresponding coefficients where applicable, and then totalled. Penalty points for errors in the execution of the test are then deducted on each judge's sheet. The total score for the classification is obtained by adding the total points on each of the judge's sheets.

The individual classification is decided as follows.

In all competitions with the exception of Grand Prix Special the winner is the competitor having the largest total points, the second the one with the next highest total and so on. In case of equality of points the relevant competitors are given the same placing.

In Grand Prix Special, subsequent to a Grand Prix, the classification is decided as above. However, in case of equality of points for the first, second and/or third places there will be a ride-off, using the same test and the same order of starting, to decide the final classification. In case of equality of points for places other than the first three the competitors concerned are given the same placing.

The number of competitors/horses to take part in a Grand Prix Special is limited to and compulsory for the best one third. However, there is a minimum 12 and maximum 18 including those who tie for the 18th place of the total number of the competitors in the initial Grand Prix.

Order of starting For the order of starting the organizer has the option to use the reverse order of the placings in the Grand Prix or the riders placed 13th to maximum 18th in the Grand Prix will start first, followed by the group of riders placed 7th to 12th and then by the group placed 1st to 6th. The order of starting within these groups is determined by draw.

Three-day event

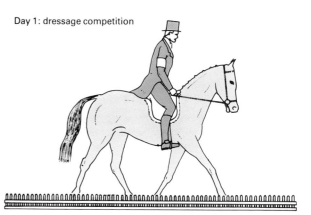

Day 1: dressage competition

The three-day event consists of three distinct equestrian competitions – dressage, endurance, and show jumping. They are held on three consecutive days, and each rider must ride the same horse throughout. The event is designed to test the harmonious development, speed, endurance, obedience, and jumping ability of the horse, and requires a perfect understanding between horse and rider.

Horses competing at international level must:
exceed 15.0 hands;
be at least 6 years old;
be owned by a member of a national federation;
be registered with that federation;
must have an international passport.

Saddlery For the dressage, an English saddle and a snaffle or simple double bridle are compulsory. Various nosebands are permitted, provided they are made of leather and used with a snaffle.
Blinkers, bandages, martingales and bearing and side or running reins are all prohibited.
For the endurance and jumping, a running martingale is allowed. Blinkers or hoods are not allowed.

Riders competing at international level must be in at least their 18th year and must possess an amateur license. They may take part only as nationals of their native countries and as members of a national team.

Dress Military dress with a helmet or hard hat is permitted for all stages of the event.
For the dressage and jumping competitions civilians are expected to wear hunting attire, for cross-country a polo-necked sweater or shirt, white breeches and black boots. They must wear protective headgear, secured by a harness.
Spurs are compulsory for the dressage competition. Whips must not be carried.

Officials A ground jury made up of a president and two judges, appeal committee, technical delegates, a course designer, veterinary officials, timekeepers, stewards and jump judges.

International categories are:
CCI, or international three-day event;

CCIO, or official international three-day event;
World three-day event;
Olympic three-day event.
All have the same three stages of competitions, dressage (day 1 and an extra day, if required by the number of entries); endurance (day 2); show-jumping (day 3).
All have team and individual classifications.

Team competitions There are normally four members in a team, but only the marks of the best three are counted. A team of three may enter, but all three must complete the competition. In CCI competitions the number of teams entered by a nation is at the discretion of the organizers. The teams are unofficial.
In CCIO and Olympic competitions only one team per nation may enter.
There must be at least three teams for a competition to be valid.

Individual competitions All team members are automatically considered as individuals. (They compete only once with their scores considered in both classifications.) Additional individual competitors may also be entered up to a maximum stated in the event rules.

Results The three competitions affect the final result in the ratio: dressage 3; endurance 12; jumping 1. Competitors acquire penalty points in all competitions. The individual winner is the rider with the least penalty points.
The winning team is that with the lowest total penalty points, after adding together the scores of the best three members.

Order of starting is fixed by draw at the start of the event. It is the same for each competition. Team captains decide starting order within teams.

Day 2: endurance competition

Examination of horses Horses are examined for fitness:
before the dressage competition;
after phase C and before the cross country on day two;
before the jumping competition.

Weight The minimum weight to be carried in the endurance is 75kg. There is no weight restriction for the dressage test and jumping competition.
Competitors are weighed at the start and end of the endurance competition. If necessary, they may be weighed with all the equipment to be carried (bridle excepted). After the endurance competitions riders must not dismount before reweighing. The bridle may be included in these reweighings.

DRESSAGE: DAY 1

The object is to test the harmonious development of the horse's physique and the degree of understanding between horse and rider.

Rules are generally as for other dressage competitions, with specific exceptions.

Type of test An officially approved (FEI) three-day event dressage test is used for CCIs and CCIOs. The degree of difficulty depends on the difficulty of the whole event.

Markings Each judge awards a competitor collective marks and 1–10 marks for each of the test's numbered movements. The judges' marks are next averaged and the competitor's average mark converted into a penalty score by subtracting from

Day 3: jumping competition

the maximum marks obtainable. Penalties for course errors are added and the final penalty score is multiplied by a factor calculated to give the dressage competition its correct importance relative to the whole event. There is no casting vote or ride-off in the event of equality of marks. In the event of equality between competitors, the classification is decided by the best cross-country score. If there is still equality, placings will be decided by the best steeplechase score and, if there is still equality, the best will be the competitor whose cross-country time was closest to the optimum time.

ENDURANCE: DAY 2

The object is to prove the speed, endurance, and jumping ability of the fit, well-trained cross-country horse and to test the rider's knowledge of pace and riding across country.

Phases The endurance competition has four phases:
A) Roads and tracks
B) Steeplechase
C) Roads and tracks
D) Cross-country

Speeds and distances

CCIs are divided into 3 different levels, indicated by a star system according to the severity of the endurance course as follows:
one star (CCI*) for horses just reaching international standard;
two stars (CCI**) for horses with some international experience;
three stars (CCI***) for experienced international horses.

Phase A and C:
10,000–16,000m at 220m/min (CCI *, **, ***);
16,000–19,800m (CCIO).

Phase B:
2560–2760m at 640–690m/min (CCI*);
2640–3105m at 660–690m/min (CCI**);
3100–3450m at 690m/min (CCI*** and CCIO).

Phase D:
5200–6270m at 520–570m/min (CCI*);
5500–6840m at 550–570m/min (CCI**);
6840–7410m at 570m/min (CCI***);
7410–7980m at 570m/min (CCIO).

Course markings All courses are marked with yellow direction flags or signs, with the letter of the particular phase superimposed. Roads and track sections are marked at 1km intervals with numbered posts.
Red and white flags indicate compulsory sections, obstacles, compulsory changes of direction and the start and finish of each phase.
Riders must keep the red flags to their right and the white flags to their left.

Obstacles There are an average of three obstacles to every 1000m for phase B and four to every 1000m for phase D.
Obstacles must be fixed. They must not exceed the prescribed dimensions. Steeplechase obstacles are similar to those used on regulation steeplechase courses.
Cross-country obstacles should be imposing in shape and left as far as possible in their natural state. No obstacle may have a drop on its landing side greater than 2m from its highest point. Artificial obstacles must not demand an acrobatic feat of jumping for the horse nor give the rider an unpleasant or unfair surprise.
Obstacles are consecutively numbered. Each separately numbered obstacle is judged independently. Multiple obstacles have elements separately lettered (3A, 3B, 3C) and are judged as one fence.

The penalty zone is marked out with sawdust, chalk or pegs. It extends 10m in front of, 20m beyond and 10m to either side of each obstacle.

Start Competitors are normally started at intervals of less than 5min for phase A. Starting times for other phases are based on the time allowed for the preceding phase. There is a compulsory halt of 10min between phases C and D. Phases A, B and D must be started from a halt.

Pace Riders may choose their own pace. Phases A and C are normally ridden at the trot or slow canter; phases B and D at the gallop.

Dismounting Riders may walk beside their horses for phases A and C, provided they are mounted when passing the finishing post. In phases B and D they are penalized for dismounting (voluntarily or not) in the penalty zone;
outside the penalty zone they are not penalized, provided they remount and continue from where they dismounted. Riders must not dismount until they have been weighed after phase D.

Timing The time allowed for each phase is the set distance divided by the set speed. Timing is from the moment the horse's chest passes the starting post. Time lost or gained in any one phase does not affect the time allowed for the next phase.
The time limit for phases A and C is one-fifth more than the time allowed. The time limit for phases B and D is double the time allowed.

Scoring Time penalties and faults at obstacles are taken into account.

Time penalties For every second over the time allowed competitors lose:
for phases A and C, 1 penalty point;.
for phase B, 0.8 of a penalty point;
for phase D, 0.4 of a penalty point.

Faults at obstacles For a first refusal, 20 penalties; second refusal, 40 penalties; fall of horse/rider, 60 penalties. (Included as refusals are running out, circling, dismounting, and entering or leaving the penalty zone without jumping the obstacle.)

Elimination Grounds for elimination are:
arriving late at the start or starting before the signal;
willfully obstructing a competitor, who is overtaking;
receiving assistance from a third party, except to catch a horse, adjust saddlery or remount after a fall;
failing to obey red or white flags;
removing or altering flags;
any act of cruelty;
doping;
rapping a horse;
wearing spurs capable of wounding a horse or excessively spurring an exhausted horse;
failing to carry the minimum weight or dismounting before being weighed after phase D;
exceeding the time limit for any phase.

Penalty zone elimination The following faults cause elimination if they occur within the penalty zone:
third refusal at the same obstacle (phases B and D);
second fall of horse/rider in phase B;
third fall of horse/rider in phase D;
error of course not corrected;
missing an obstacle or flag;
retaking an obstacle already jumped;
jumping obstacles in the wrong order.

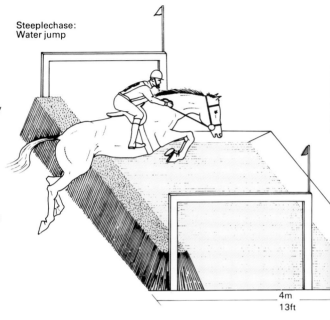

Steeplechase: Water jump

4m
13ft

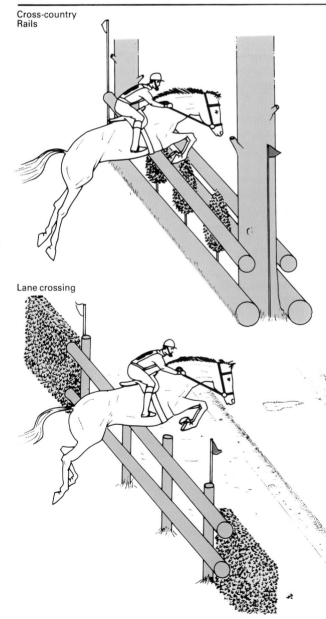

Cross-country Rails

Lane crossing

Fence

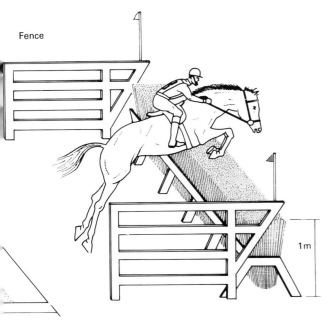

1m

Elephant trap

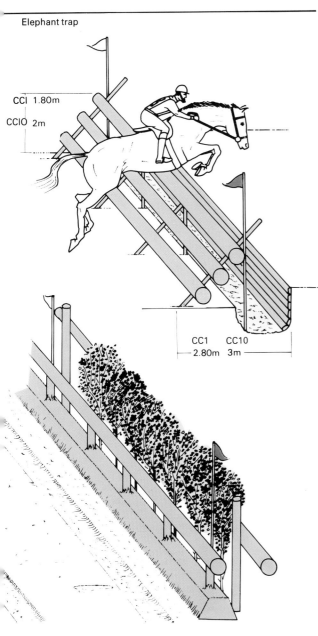

CCI 1.80m
CCIO 2m

CC1   CC10
2.80m 3m

JUMPING: DAY 3

Object The jumping competition is intended to test whether the horses can continue in service after the endurance competition.

The type of course depends on the difficulty of the whole event and on the intended influence of the jumping competition on the final result.

The track will be irregular and have changes of direction to test the horse's handiness. No acrobatic feat of jumping or turning will be required and no compulsory passage included.

Obstacles There will be 10–12 obstacles, 15 efforts maximum. All will be massive, imposing in shape and appearance, almost fixed and set with wings or extensions.

They will include a double resembling a road crossing, two fly fences (with both height and spread) and, where possible, a ditch or water jump.

No obstacle will be higher than 1.20m; at least a third will be this height. Obstacles with spread only may not exceed 3m in spread for CCI or 3.50m for CCIO competitions.

Fly fences will not exceed a spread of 1.80m (CCI) or 2m (CCIO) at the highest point and 2.80m (CCI) or 3m (CCIO) at the base.

Speed and distance For CCI competitions the requirement is 600–800m at a speed of 350–400m/min. For CCIO it is 750–900m at 400m/min.

Penalties For a first disobedience, 10 penalty points;
knocking down an obstacle or a foot in the water, 5 penalty points;
a second disobedience in the entire event, 20 points;
a third disobedience in the entire event, elimination;
a fall by horse and/or rider, 30 penalty points;
jumping an obstacle in the wrong order, elimination;
an error of course not rectified, elimination;
exceeding the time allowed, ¼ mark for every second or part of a second;
exceeding the time limit (twice the time allowed), elimination.

Classification Penalties at obstacles are added to those for exceeding the time allowed.

Show jumping: Fancy gate

Wall and rails

Hog's back

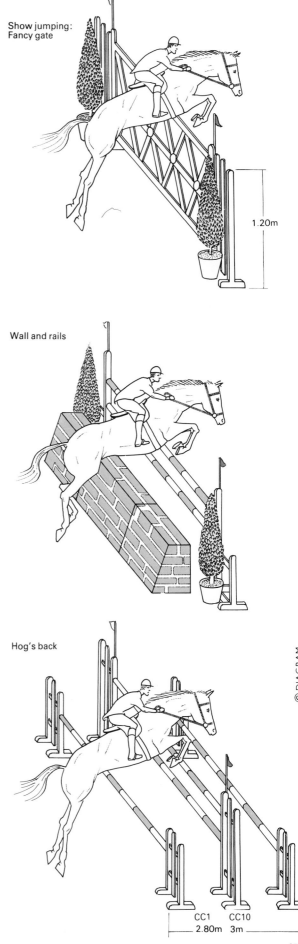

1.20m

CC1   CC10
2.80m 3m

© DIAGRAM

273

Polo

Polo is played by two teams of four players mounted on horseback. Each team attempts to score goals by striking a ball with its sticks between the opponents' goalposts. Players must control their ponies with the left hand, as the stick may be held only in the right hand. The winning team is the one to score the greater number of goals.

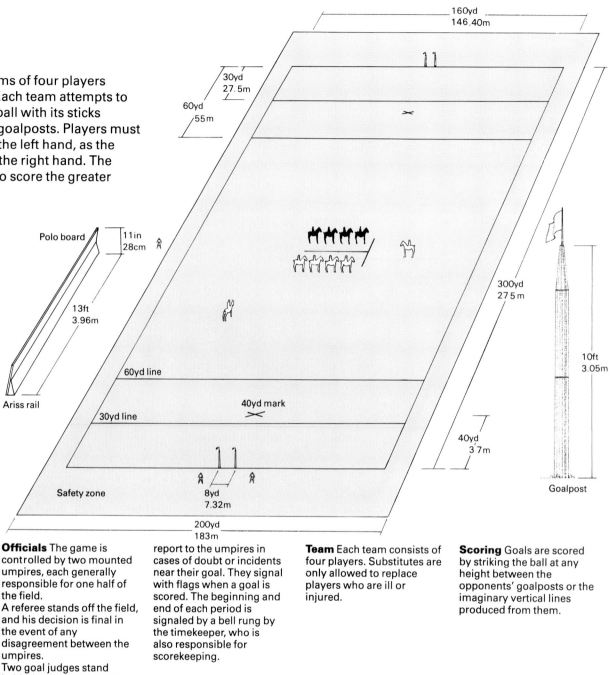

The ground comprises the playing area and a safety zone around it. No one other than officials and players' assistants may enter this zone during play.

The boards extend along either length of the playing area and are secured by iron pegs. They are designed to direct low balls back into play and are constructed in short sections, which may be easily replaced if damaged during a game. The numbers 30, 40, and 60 are marked on the inside face of the boards at the appropriate lines on the ground. A mark is also made at the ends of an imaginary center line.

Where boards are not used, flags with the appropriate numbers are used to mark the ends of the lines, but they are fixed well beyond the sidelines to minimize the risk of collision.

Goalposts are of light construction, designed to break if collided with.

Officials The game is controlled by two mounted umpires, each generally responsible for one half of the field.

A referee stands off the field, and his decision is final in the event of any disagreement between the umpires.

Two goal judges stand behind each goal area and report to the umpires in cases of doubt or incidents near their goal. They signal with flags when a goal is scored. The beginning and end of each period is signaled by a bell rung by the timekeeper, who is also responsible for scorekeeping.

Team Each team consists of four players. Substitutes are only allowed to replace players who are ill or injured.

Scoring Goals are scored by striking the ball at any height between the opponents' goalposts or the imaginary vertical lines produced from them.

The right of way is one of polo's most important principles. Right of way is held by the player(s) following the ball on its exact line, or at the smallest angle to it, and taking it on the offside. It is a foul for another player to cross or pull up in the right of way, thereby making a player with the right of way check his pace.

Examples of right of way:
1) Player A hits the ball to X, follows its line, and assumes the right of way.
If player B can reach the ball at X without interfering with A's play, then B assumes the right of way and may strike the ball at B1. B must pull up if he can reach X only at the risk of fouling A. Provided he keeps out of A's way throughout, B may then swerve and take a nearside backhander at B2.
2) Opposing players A and B share the right of way. No other player may enter it, even if he is meeting the ball on its exact line.
3) Player A is riding in the general direction of the ball, but at a slight angle to it. He will have the right of way, provided he adjusts his course slightly in order to take the ball on his offside. After A has thus assumed the right of way, player B would not obstruct the right of way if he took the ball on his own offside at point X. If A fails to adjust his course, intending to take the ball on his nearside, he loses the right of way by endangering B, who is approaching with the ball on his offside.
4) Player A hit the ball to X. Player B, riding to meet the ball on its exact line on his offside, is the player with the right of way. Player C, riding in at an angle, must not cross B's right of way. Player A may ride on and attempt to take the ball on his offside, since this would not obstruct B's right of way.
5) Player A hits the ball to X and assumes the right of way. B rides for the ball, accompanied by A's partner C. It is a dangerous foul if C forces B across A's path, or causes him to pull up to

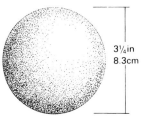

Sticks Polo sticks are made in varying lengths to suit the individual, and are fitted with a grip. The mallet heads are covered in sycamore, ash, bamboo, or vellum.
The ball is made of ash or bamboo, and weighs 4¼–4¾oz.

3¼in
8.3cm

Duration A match is divided into eight seven-minute periods or "chukkas," amounting to 56 minutes' actual playing time. This may be reduced by the match organizers by cutting the number of periods, their duration, or both.
There is a three-minute interval between each period, and a five-minute interval when half the periods have been played. If the scores are equal at the end of the match, the last period is extended until the ball goes out of play, hits the boards, or a goal is scored. If no goal is scored, the match continues after a five-minute interval. The lengths of periods and intervals are the same as before.
Ends are changed at half time: after the fourth period in a seven-period match, and after the third period in a five-period match. Periods are started and stopped by the timekeeper's bell. When it rings for the end of a period, the game stops as the ball goes out of play or hits a board.
A second bell is rung 30 seconds after the first: if the ball is still in play, the game stops wherever the ball may be.
If the losing side is awarded a penalty within 20 seconds of the end of the game, the timekeeper will allow 20 seconds from the time the penalty is taken before ringing the final bell. If a goal is scored, the bell is rung immediately.

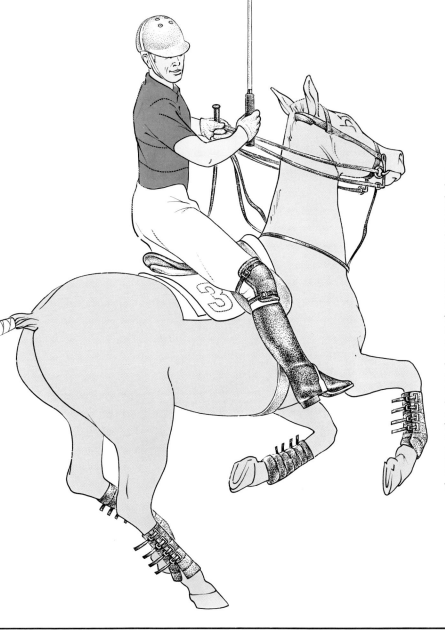

Dress A polo helmet or cap with a chinstrap must be worn by all players.
Polo boots and knee pads must be free of any buckles or studs that might damage another player's equipment. Sharp spurs are forbidden. Distinguishing colors must be worn by both teams.
Ponies may be of any height, but must be calm in temperament. They must be able to see with both eyes, and blinkers or any form of noseband that restricts their vision are not allowed. Frost nails and screws on the shoes are forbidden, but a calkin (a small, spur-like projection) may be used on the hind shoes only. Rimmed shoes are permitted, but only if the rim is on the inside of the shoe. Bandages or boots must be worn on all four legs.

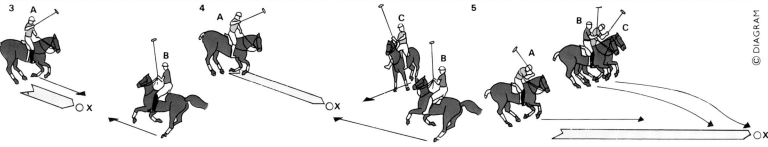

avoid being sandwiched between A and C.
6) A player does not gain the right of way merely by striking the ball, since another player might be following closer to the line of the ball.
7) If two players are following a ball hit by a third player, the player closer to

the line of the ball has the right of way.
8) If two players are at equal angles from either side of the line of the ball, the player with the ball on his offside has the right of way.
9) Two players approaching the ball from exactly opposite directions should approach with the ball on

their offsides. If a collision seems likely, the player who actually gets the ball on his offside has the right of way.
10) If the line of the ball changes suddenly, by glancing off a player, for example, the right of way will almost inevitably change. The player who had the right of way may

continue for a short distance along his original course without obstruction.
11) If a player misses a dead ball when trying to hit it back into play, the line of the ball for the purpose of defining the right of way is taken to be the same as the direction in which the player was then riding.

12) If the ball comes to a dead stop at any time, its line is considered to be the direction in which it was traveling before it stopped.

© DIAGRAM

Starting play The opposing sides line up facing the umpire in the center of the ground, each team being on its own side of the half-way "T" mark.

The umpire bowls the ball underhand between the two ranks of players at a distance of not less than 5yd. The players must remain stationary until the ball has left the umpire's hand.

Ends are changed at half time and after every goal, unless the goal was awarded as a penalty for a dangerous or deliberate foul in an attempt to prevent a goal. If a foul occurs after the first note of the bell in any but the last period, the game stops and the next period begins with the penalty for that foul being put into play as if there had been no interval.

If the ball hits the boards at the end of the previous period, it is treated as if it had gone over them.

Out of play The ball is out of play when:
a) it is hit over the boards or sidelines, the umpire bowls the ball in from the spot where it crossed the board or line, parallel to the back line (**1**);
b) it is hit over the back line by the attacking side, the defender hits the ball in from the point where it crossed the line, but not nearer than 4yd to the goalposts, boards, or sidelines (**2**);

c) it is hit over the back line by the defending side; the attackers take a penalty hit from the 60yd line opposite the point at which the ball crossed the line (**3**);
d) the ball becomes damaged or lodged in a player's clothing; the ball is bowled toward the nearer side of the ground at the point of the incident, but at least 20yd from the goalposts, boards, or sidelines (**4**).

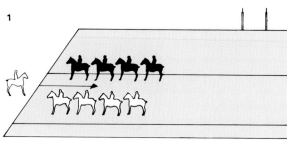

1

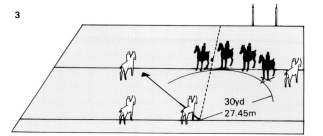

3

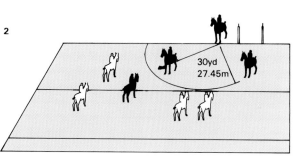

2

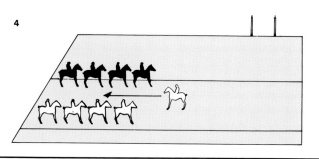

4

Misuse of the stick
It is forbidden to reach across or under an opponent's pony to strike the ball (**1**).
A player may not hit into the legs of an opponent's pony (**2**). A player may only hook an opponent's stick if both he and the ball are on the same side of the opponent's pony, or in a direct line behind it. The stick may only be hooked when the opponent is about to strike, and not above shoulder height (**3**).
A player must not use his stick dangerously or hold it in such a way as to interfere with another player or pony. If a player rides into the backhand stroke of an opponent in the right of way, he does so at his own risk, and without foul.

1

2

Penalty goals The umpire may award a penalty goal if he considers that a goal would have been scored but for a foul by the defending side.

Ends are not changed after a penalty goal, and the umpire restarts the game by bowling the ball between the ranks of players 10yd from the offending team's goal.

Penalty hits The umpires decide on the gravity of an offense and award penalty hits at appropriate distances. Where the hit results from the ball going out of play, the distances are fixed by the rules.

a) A free hit from a spot 30yd (or alternatively 40yd) from the offending team's back line, opposite the middle of the goal. The offending side must remain behind the back line until the ball has been hit, and may not stand behind the goal nor ride out between the goalposts where the hit is taken (**5**).

If the captain of the non-offending side wishes, the hit may be taken from the spot where the foul occurred, in which case no member of the other side may be nearer than 30yd to the ball. The players in the side taking the free hit must not be nearer the back line than the ball (**6**).

b) A free hit from a spot 60yd from the offending team's back line, opposite the middle of the goal.

The offending team must be at least 30yd away from the ball; the players in the team taking the hit are free to place themselves where they wish (**7**).

c) A free hit from the spot where the foul occurred (**8**). Positioning is as for (b), and the ball must be at least 4yd from the boards or sidelines. Free hits are also taken from the center spot, with positioning as for (b).

Failure to carry out penalty hits correctly may result in:
a penalty goal;
allowing the non-offending team members to position themselves where they wish;

retaking the hit unless a goal was scored or awarded.

If, having hit the ball over their opponents' back line, the attacking side does not allow the resulting free hit to be taken correctly, the hit is retaken from the 30yd line. Unnecessary delay in taking a free hit may result in the umpire bowling the ball in from the same spot.

5

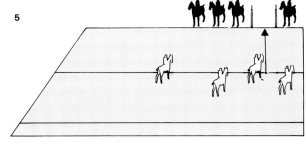

7

6

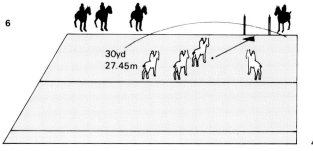

8

"Riding off" or bumping between players riding in the same direction is permitted. Players must not:
bump at angles which may be dangerous to other players or their ponies;
strike with the head, hand, forearm, or elbow (although pushing with the upper arm is permitted);
attempt to seize another player, his equipment, or his pony;
zig-zag in front of another player when galloping, if doing so causes him to check his pace to avoid a fall;
ride across a pony's legs in an attempt to trip it;
ride at an opponent so as to intimidate him into pulling up or checking his stroke, even if no actual foul or crossing of the right of way took place.

3

Accidents and loss of equipment The umpire stops the match if a player is injured or a pony goes lame. He will also stop the match if he considers that a pony's equipment is so damaged as to be a danger to other players and ponies.

If a player loses his helmet, the game will be stopped to allow him to recover it, but only when neither side will be favored by a stoppage.

If a player falls from his pony without injury, the match will not be stopped. While dismounted, the player may not touch the ball or interfere with the game.

If a player is injured, 15 minutes are allowed for his recovery. If he is unable to continue after that interval, the game is restarted with a substitute player. Should the injury have been caused as a result of a foul by the opposing team, the injured player's captain may call on one of the opposition to retire, and the game will then continue with three players on either side.

© DIAGRAM

Speed skates are light with a long, low wheelbase.

Roller skating (speed)

There are speed roller skating events for men, women and relay teams. Indoors competitors race counterclockwise around an oval track or outdoors on smooth surfaced pathways. Procedures are similar to those of speed skating on ice.

22yd
20m

Starter

Timekeeper

44yd
40m

Judges
Lapscorer

34ft 8in
10.50m

Track (indoors) The width of the straights limits the number of skaters in a heat. Minimum widths are:
8ft for two skaters;
15ft for three skaters;
18ft for five skaters;
20ft for six skaters;
Races are always counterclockwise around the track.

Courses Outdoor races are held on available traffic free smooth, hard surfaces such as footpaths and cycleways, sometimes utilizing cycle race tracks.

Distances Men and women skate over the following distances:
300m, 500m, 1500m, 3000m, 5000m.
Men only skate the following distances:
10,000m, 20,000m.
Relay races are held over the following total distances:
5000m, 10,000m, 20,000m.

Officials At least twelve officials must be in attendance. These include a minimum of three judges, a starter, timekeeper(s), a lap scorer, a recorder, two track stewards, and a competitors' steward.

Dress Competitors must wear numbers on their backs and left hips.

Start At the start of a race no part of the competitor's skates may be across the starting line, the tips of the skates may be on the line. A competitor who deliberately starts before the starter's pistol or causes a false start is warned. For a third offense the skater is penalized usually by having to start 5yd behind the other competitors.

Overtaking The leading competitor has the right of way and may only be overtaken on the outside as long as he keeps to the inside of the track.

The responsibility for any obstruction or collision is with the overtaking skater unless the leading skater deliberately fouls.

Lapping A skater who has been or is being lapped will be ordered to give way. The judges will signal him with a yellow flag and the skater must then go to the outside of the track without impeding any other competitor. In most races when a competitor is lapped he or she is eliminated from the race. The judges will signal with a blue flag and the skater must then leave the track without impeding any other competitor.

Offenses A skater must not: deliberately cross the inside of the track with either skate; impede another competitor; touch another competitor with any part of his body; lose speed and so cause another competitor to slow down; improperly cross the track; conspire to produce an unfair result.

Penalties Offenses may be penalized by disqualification. A black flag is used to disqualify an offender during a race. The skater must immediately leave the track without impeding any other competitor.

A skater who is disqualified may not compete if a race is rerun, and is suspended for 1 month or longer.

Result The winner of an individual race is the first skater to reach the finishing line with one of his skates.

RELAY RACES Every team member must take part in a race.
One skater from each team skates until a teammate relieves him. Takeovers are by touch and are permitted at any point in the race except during the last two laps.
Substitutes are allowed in cases of injury or damage to a skate, but they must remain in the team for the rest of the competition.

Roller derby

Roller derby is a speed roller skating sport for teams of men and women. Competitors race around the track and gain points by lapping opponents. By contrast with conventional speed skating events, a good deal of body contact is permitted between competitors.

The track is oval, and usually 100–200ft around. The skating surface is usually hardwood coated with a thin veneer of plastic.

Teams Each team includes five men and five women.

Duration The men skate for a period of 12 minutes, and then the women skate for a similar length of time.

Procedure All the men skate together and then all the women. Competitors are not required to keep in lane. Tripping is prohibited, but pushing and jostling are both allowed.

Scoring Points are accumulated by lapping opponents.

Roller skating (artistic)

As in ice skating, there are international, national, and club championships in figure, pair, and dance skating. Figure events include compulsory figures and free skating, and dance events comprise compulsory dances and a program of free dancing.

Rink The skating surface is usually asphalt, asbestos, cement, or hardwood.

Dress Freedom of movement is a major requirement.
Costumes are similar to those used for ice skating.

FIGURE SKATING
Events for single skaters comprise compulsory figures and free skating.

Compulsory figures for roller skating include circles, loops, rockers, counters, threes, and brackets.
All figures are performed on circles marked on the rink surface.
Each figure must be repeated three times consecutively.
Skaters must start, at rest, from the point where the circles intersect.
Every stroke must be made with the four wheels, never with the toe-stop.
No impetus is allowed from the foot that is about to become the tracing foot.
Circles must be traced continuously except for a brief interruption to change the tracing foot.
Turns must be skated with a clean edge, without skids, scrapes, noise, or lifting of the wheels.

Execution The head should be upright, relaxed, and held naturally.
The body should be upright, but not stiff nor bent at the hips.
The arms should be held gracefully.
The hands should not be carried higher than the waist;
the palms should be parallel to the floor and the fingers neither extended or clenched.
The tracing leg should be flexible and slightly bent at the knee.
The free leg should also be slightly bent at the knee.
The free foot should not be too near the tracing foot and should be carried slightly above the rink surface with the toe pointing downward and outward.
All exaggerated positions should be avoided.
A consistent speed, rhythm, and even flow should be maintained; jerky, abrupt, and angular movements should be avoided.
Skaters may make only moderate use of their arms and free leg during the execution of compulsory figures.

Judges

Free skating Skaters perform unspecified movements to music of their own choice.
The length of program varies with the competition; competitors may finish up to 5 seconds before or after the time limit.

Falls A fall does not eliminate a skater from the competition.
A skater who falls through no fault of his own may be allowed to restart, possibly after an interval.
A skater who falls through his own fault will have his marks adjusted accordingly. He must continue from where he fell.

Scoring The scale of marks for each performance is from 1 to 6, with intermediate decimal places.
Compulsory figures Each judge gives a mark for each figure. Taken into consideration are:
good edge running, without flats or sub-curves;
superimposition;
clear turns made in the correct position;
maintenance of a consistent speed;
style, carriage, and movement;
the size of the figure.

Free skating Each judge awards two marks: one for the content of the program (difficulty and variety); the other for the manner of the performance.
Result A competition is won by the skater placed first by the majority of judges.
Second and third places are similarly decided.
Subsequent places are decided by the lowest totals of judges' placings.
PAIR SKATING
The two partners must give the impression of unison, though they do not have to perform all the same movements and may separate occasionally. They are always judged as a pair, never as individuals.

DANCE SKATING
Events comprise two, three, or four compulsory dances, followed by a program of free dancing to music of the competitor's own choice.
Compulsory dances One of the official groups of dances is chosen by the organizers before the competition begins.
Execution Basic head, body, and leg positions are the same as for figure skating.
Further requirements for dance skating are that competitors should:
raise and lower their bodies only by bending their tracing knees;
execute the dance with ease, avoiding all angular and stiff movements;
skate close together and execute all movements in unison;
keep footwork neat and make all steps accurately;
keep edges and turns smooth and clean;
pay careful attention to the time and rhythm of the music;
coordinate all movements with the music, and express the music's character in the dancing.

Free dancing consists of a non-repetitive performance of novel movements, which can include variations of known dances or parts of dances, combined into a program with originality of design and arrangement.
All recognized movements are permissible, as are other movements appropriate to the rhythm, music, and character of the dance.
Unnecessary feats of strength or skating skill are counted against the dancers.
The separation of partners must not exceed the time needed to change positions.
Spins must not exceed 1½ revolutions.
Jumps and lifts where the man's hands are higher than waist level are not permitted.
Toe-stops may be used in the interpretation of the music, but their use must be strictly limited.

Scoring Each compulsory dance is marked from 0 to 6, to one decimal point.
Two marks from 0 to 6 are awarded for the free dancing: the first for the contents of the program based on its harmonious composition, conformity with the music, variety, originality, beauty, and difficulty; the other for the manner of the performance based on the dancers' sureness, timing, rhythm, style, and carriage.
Result Marks for compulsory dances and for free dancing are given equal importance in the final result.

© DIAGRAM

Cycle racing

Cycle racing is broadly divided into track and road racing. Both categories include a variety of different events at national and international level. Indoor events include special track races and stationary "races" on sets of rollers.

Dress Competitors must be completely clothed from the neck to just above the knees in a sleeved jersey and shorts or a one-piece costume resembling this. Club members must wear club colors except in time trials. Racing numbers are worn to identify competitors. A crash helmet must be worn for road races and for training or racing on circuits and tracks. Socks and gloves or mitts are optional, but generally worn. Goggles must be non-splinterable.

Machines For road racing any kind of cycle is allowed, provided it is propelled only by human force, has no streamlining and does not exceed specified dimensions. For track racing free-wheel gears, brakes and quick release wheels are usually prohibited. Tandems and multicycles must conform to general regulations.

Equipment For track racing a cycle must be fitted with a fixed wheel and all unnecessary accessories removed. For road racing a cycle must have brakes and, if ridden at night, lights and reflectors and for long rides a pump, a spare tube and one or two feeding bottles mounted in "cages" attached to the frame.

Competitors must be licensed by their clubs in accordance with national regulations.

Banned substances Any competitor found to be taking banned substances, ie any substance likely to affect his performance, is liable to suspension. A rider is also barred from competition if he is taking banned substances in the course of medical treatment.

Officials include a chief judge (a referee in the USA) with one or more assistants, timekeepers, machine examiners, lap scorers and starters, if needed. A chief commissaire (referee) and at least one assistant commissaire are necessary at a road race meeting.

Starts for road races are at the drop of a flag and may be made either standing or rolling. Riders may be given a short untimed distance in which to settle down or clear a built up area.

Finishes are determined by crossing a finishing line, at which point the riders are timed. On circuit races the riders may be timed for each circuit.

Dismounting A rider who has dismounted may complete the course carrying, dragging or wheeling his machine, but must not receive assistance.

Refreshments Competitors may accept food and drink that are handed to them at specified feeding stations.

Sanctions against offenders may include, in order of severity, a warning, a reprimand, a fine, relegation, disqualification, suspension and withdrawal of licence. Amateurs may not be fined.

Appeals over the results The results of races are settled at road meetings by the commissaires. At track and roller meetings the chief judge acts as the chief official and deals with claims and disputes.

ROAD RACES

Road races must be run in conformity with the law of the country in which they are run and with regard to the local traffic regulations. Riders may take pace from each other but not from any other vehicle and may exchange machines equipment, food and drink.

Stage races Competitors race over a number of stages. The best known stage race is the Tour de France, in which competitors cover 3400km in 24 one-day stages.

Circuit races, called criteriums, consist of several laps over a circuit of roads. Races may vary in length up to 100km.

Control points, called pits, are set up on long events for feeding and repairs.

Pacing by another rider is not allowed in individual time trials, but is permissible in other road races and team time trials.

Illegal riding includes pushing another rider (**1**), and crossing in front of another rider to prevent him from moving on (**2**).

1

2

1

2

Box (1) A tactic by which a rider rides just behind and to one side of another and thus prevents a third rider from overtaking without swinging right out.

Break-away (2) getting clear of the field.

Course des primes A race with intermediate prizes called primes, at specified laps or other points along the course.
Demi-fond A middle distance paced track event.
Domestique A team rider in road racing, whose job is to help his team leader to win.
King of the mountains The title given to the winner of most points in hill climbs as part of a road, circuit or stage race.
Lanterne rouge (red lantern) A booby prize for the last man in a stage race.
Maillot jaune (yellow jersey) worn by the current leader of the Tour de France and some other major events.

Musette A cotton bag in which food is handed up to a rider in a road race.
Omnium A track event where the competitors ride in several races of different kinds.
Peleton The main bunch of riders in a road race.
Repechage A kind of "second chance" race to allow losers from the heats an additional opportunity to qualify for the next round of the series in a progressive race.
Sag wagon One of the last following vehicles in road events used to pick up riders who have dropped out.
Stayer A track rider in a motor paced race.

TRACK RACES

There are many different kinds of races held on tracks and on closed circuits (roads that are closed to the public). Tracks are usually hard surfaced but may be on grass.
Track markings include lines to mark handicap starts, finishing lines and starting points for various standard distances.
The sprinters line is a red line 90cm from the inside edge of the track. No overtaking is allowed inside this line if the rider ahead is on or inside this line.
Sprints are races between 2 or more riders over one or more laps of a track (preferably less than 500m) up to 1000m, timing is over the last 200m only, the earlier part of the race is devoted to tactical maneuvering.
Handicap races are over short distances generally not more than 1000m. At the start riders are positioned on the track according to their handicaps, held upright and given a push-off.
Individual pursuit Two riders start on opposite sides of the track and race over the following world championship distances: 3000m women and junior men; 4000m amateur men; 5000m professionals. If one rider does not catch the other rider the rider with the faster time wins.

Team pursuit is similar to individual pursuit over 4000m but with two teams of four riders. Victory is decided on the time of the first three riders to finish from each team.
Australian pursuit is similar to an individual pursuit with up to eight riders on the track. The race may be set over a number of laps or for a stated time; riders caught are eliminated.
Italian pursuit is between two or more teams of up to five riders. The leading rider from each team drops out after each lap and the finishing time of the last rider of each team decides the race.
Point to point is a bunch race in which points are awarded for the highest placed riders in each lap or group of laps.
The winner of the most points is the overall winner, even if that rider never finishes first on any point scoring lap.
Scratch races are bunch events in which all competitors start together but the term generally means longer races over distances from 5–100km. Variants include: "devil-take-the hindmost" (Miss and Out in the USA), in which the last rider over the line each time is eliminated; and "unknown distance" in which the riders do not know the total distance they have to ride until the bell sounds for the last lap.

Madison racing is a form of relay racing in which a pair of riders race with one in the race and one slowly circling the track and resting. The relays are effected by the outgoing rider pushing his partner into the racing group of riders.
Human pacing may be allowed in track events, but only one pacer may be on the track for each competitor except during a changeover. Pacers must wear normal racing dress with crash helmets. Men may pace women.
Motor pacing Track events of over 10km may be motor paced with each rider, called a stayer, preceded by a motor-cyclist who sets the pace and affords some shelter from the wind. The pacer must be a licensed rider and men may pace women.
Motorcycles used in motor pacing must be between 500cc and 1000cc. Each machine must carry a roller supported on a frame projecting behind the rear wheels to international specifications. The purpose of the roller is to prevent the following rider from getting too close to the pacer.
Motorcyclists acting as pacers must wear pacing leathers and specified undergarments and may not wear extra clothing or padding to compensate for differences in physique. Loose or flapping garments that might give an unfair advantage as windbreaks for the stayer are not allowed.

1

2

Cyclo-cross (1) events take place in winter over open country. A course should include some woodland and fields as well as paths and roads. It should not contain hazards such as flights of steps. The maximum recommended distance is 24km. If a circuit is used each lap should be at least 3km.
Hill climbs generally do not exceed 5km and may be much shorter depending on the gradient of the hill.
Time trials Competitors set off at 1 minute intervals and race against the clock to cover a set distance in the least possible time. Each rider must ride alone and unpaced. Distances for time trials are short distances up to 50km, middle distances up to 160km and long distances 12 and 24 hours.

Roller races (2) These "stationary races" take place on sets of rollers, two close together to support the rear wheel and a third spaced out to support the front wheel. The rollers are geared to dials that indicate the "distance" covered by the rider. In general, there can be up to four competitors. Each rider may be supported by an attendant. In some races the attendants leave go when the riders have covered 200m. The end of the event is signaled by an audible signal such as a pistol shot, and a bell is rung for the last lap. Gears for roller racing are restricted to give all competitors a fair chance. Crank lengths are also controlled and gears and cranks are inspected before each event.

© DIAGRAM

Motorcycle racing

There are many types of competition for motorcycles, with a wide variety of machines competing on various types of course. Road racing – on specially built circuits or sometimes on ordinary roads – has the largest following at international level. Races are held for several classes of motorcycle, and may be of any length.

The track should have a non-skid surface if possible. Ideally, yellow or white lines should be painted along the edges of the track if there is danger of the rider leaving the course.
Warning signs should be placed in advance of any corners on the course. The start line must be on a flat part of the track.

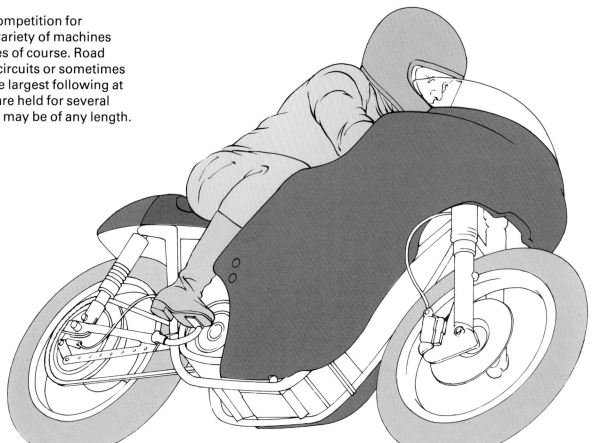

Dress Riders must wear protective leathers or an approved substitute. Clothing must form a complete covering. The boots must not have metal studs. In the past the rider's "leathers" were usually black, but now colored leathers have become popular.

Helmets must conform to current safety standards and be in sound condition. The all-enveloping full-face style helmet is most popular. If an open-face type helmet is used, goggles or visors of a non-splintering material must be worn.

Classes The usual classes are for motorcycles with an engine capacity of:
125cc (single cylinder)
250cc (twin cylinder)
350cc (twin cylinder)
500cc (four cylinder)
750cc (four cylinder)
Unlimited (501–1300cc)

Brakes At least one break must be fitted on each wheel. They must be capable of controlling the machine independently.

Tires must be fitted to a rim of at least 16in diameter. In national and international events there are no restrictions on the type of tire.

Number plates must be fitted to both sides of the machine to the rear of the rider and on the front. They may be made of a rigid material or painted on the streamlining. In many countries different colors are used to indicate the various capacity classes.

Handlebars must not be less than 400cm in width.

Clutch and brake levers must have an integral ball-end of at least ¾in diameter.

Footrests must be fixed.

Guard An adequate guard must be fitted to prevent the drive chain or shaft being touched accidently.

The exhaust pipe must not project behind the machine or its bodywork. Exhaust gases must not foul the tires or brakes or raise dust so as to inconvenience a following rider. Waste or surplus oil must not be discharged onto the track.

Fuel must be of a standard grade as supplied from normal commercial pumps.

Oil drain plugs must be tightly locked in position.

Permitted modifications The frame of the machine must be that unit originally supplied by the manufacturer. Different categories of the sport allow different modifications. In most cases certain items must be removed, such as license holders, club badges (except transfers), center stands, stop light/rear light bulbs, indicator bulbs, stalk mirrors. Any additional item of non-original equipment not necessary for the racing event may be removed, except where otherwise specified. The regulations for different events are made to ensure that equipment may be removed but nothing may be added or otherwise modified unless specified in the regulations for the individual event.

Scrutineering Before the start of a race all machines will be carefully scrutineered to ensure they conform to the required legal and safety standards.
A machine may be barred from racing if it is found to be defective during scrutineering.
The organizers may also ask for a machine to be stripped and scrutineered after a race.

Types of meeting
International meetings are held under the jurisdiction of the FIM (Fédération Internationale Motocycliste). National, regional and local organizations hold their own meetings, governed by rules and class specifications, which may differ slightly from those issued by the FIM.

Officials Stewards, up to five in number, are responsible for supervising a meeting. It is their duty to adjudicate any protests that might arise.
The clerk of the course is responsible for the actual meeting and organizes the events. He supervises the entries, starters, judges, timekeepers and scrutineers.

Flag signals Riders must respond to all flag signals. Flags should measure 800mm by 600mm. Officially recognized flag signals are:
national flag, start;
checkered flag, finish;
black flag with rider's number, that rider to stop;
white flag, ambulance or other vehiclé on the course;
yellow flag, motionless, danger;
yellow flag, waved, slow down, prepare to stop, no overtaking;
green flag, course clear;
blue flag, rider behind;
blue flag, waved, rider behind wishes to overtake;
red with vertical yellow stripes, oil on the course.

1

Sidecars The passenger platform may be attached to either side.

Classes Sidecar racing events are usually divided into 350cc, 500cc and 1300cc.

Sidecar starts (1) In international sidecar racing events clutch starts are made with the engine running.

The wheels of the motorcycle must be at least 400mm diameter, measured over the outside of the tire, of 100mm width.

The engine must not protrude beyond a longitudinal line drawn midway between the tracks formed by the rear wheel of the motorcycle and the sidecar wheel.

Streamlining and bodywork is optional but, if fitted, must have a ground clearance of at least 75mm. Streamlining must be easily detachable for scrutineering.

© DIAGRAM

2

3

4

Starters The maximum number of riders in a solo machine race is determined by the type of course.

Starting positions may be arranged by means of a grid. Positions may be allocated by the organizers of the meeting according to the rider's known ability or, in the case of a final preceded by heats, according to the rider's total time for the respective heats.

The position at the front of the grid on the inside of the track is given to the fastest rider. This is called the pole position.

The start is signaled by the lowering of the flag.

Bump start (2) In races for solo machines the riders begin to push their machines when the flag drops and jump on as the engine fires.

Clutch start (3) The riders line up on the grid with their motors already running. Shortly before the flag drops, first gear is engaged and the machine is held on the clutch. As the flag drops, the clutch is released and the machine rapidly accelerated.

Le Mans start (4) The rider is required to run to his machine, parked on the opposite side of the track, mount and then kick-start his engine before accelerating away.

A false start occurs when a rider moves forward from his position before the starting signal is given, even though, as in a grid start, he may not cross the actual start line. A 1-minute penalty is usually added to the offending rider's total time for the race.

Riding conduct The clerk of the course will immediately exclude any rider, who is in his opinion guilty of riding in a foul, unfair or dangerous manner. The offending rider is shown the black flag and a black disc with his number. He must then leave the track as soon as possible.

The finish is signaled by the waving of the checkered flag as the leading rider completes his last lap. All riders are flagged off the track at the finish line, even though they may not have completed the required number of laps.

SPECIAL RULES
Among the classes with differing rules are the Superbike class and the Production Motorcycle class.

Superbikes In order to qualify a machine must be of a type that is in production and on sale to the general public. The engine capacity must be between 501cc and 750cc.

Engines over 500cc and up to 1000cc have a maximum of 2 cylinders.

Engines over 400cc and up to 750cc have a maximum of 3 or 4 cylinders.

Production Motorcycle class The rules of "Proddie" racing, as it has become known, vary from country to country, but generally machines should be standard. Skill and inexpensive maintenance are emphasized.

Drag racing

Motorcycle drag racing is similar to drag car racing. Riders on specially prepared machines race in pairs over a straight 440yd track. A competition proceeds by a process of elimination – with the faster rider in each pair going into the next round.

Track The drag racing track, or "strip," is 440yd long and at least 50ft wide. There must be a braking area at least 800yd long at the end of the track.

Burn-out (1) Competitors preheat and clean out their tires before the race.
Start The "Christmas tree" light system is used (as described under drag car racing).
Race procedure is generally the same as for drag car racing.

Classes There are two main divisions: street solo and competition solo. Both are further divided into classes: Pro Stock; Super Street; Funny Bike; Competition; Ultimate Street-bike.

Sprint

Sprints are popular in the UK, Australia and parts of Europe. They are races from point to point in a straight line on an approximately level, metalled surface. They are less than one mile in length and are held between two or more competitors or individually against time. There are races for solo machines and for sidecar combinations.

Dress Protective clothing must be worn during practice and racing. It consists of full leathers, boots, gloves and an approved helmet.
Scrutineering All machines must be presented to the scrutineer before a meeting in order to ensure they conform to regulations.
The start is made from a stationary position with the engine running and the foremost part of the motorcycle behind the start line.

Streamlining The only restriction on streamlining is that there must be a clearance of at least 2in between the streamlining and the extremities of the handlebars.
Throttle All machines must have a self-closing throttle.
Fuel There is usually no restriction on the type of fuel used.
Superchargers are permitted for sprint racing.
Brakes Solo machines require at least one brake operating independently on each wheel.
Tires may be of any type.
Mudguards are optional.

Classes For solo machines, the classes are:
up to 125cc;
125cc to 250cc;
250cc to 350cc;
350cc to 500cc;
500cc to 750cc;
750cc to 1000cc;
1000cc to 1300cc.

Speedway

Speedway racing is a highly specialized form of motorcycle sport. Riders on special speedway machines race around an ash or shale surfaced oval track. A special riding technique is needed as the machines have no brakes and riders are forced to broadside their machines through the bends at speeds of up to 70mph.

The track Speedway tracks are oval, usually with a lap length of 350yd. They are usually loosely surfaced with either ash or shale.

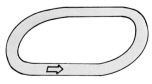

Races are usually over four laps. They are always ridden in a counterclockwise direction.

Speedway championships in order of priority are: the individual speedway championship of the world; the team speedway championship of the world; the pairs speedway championship of the world; approved international test matches; national speedway championships; any other approved international fixtures; league fixtures; any other speedway fixtures.
Championship meetings consist of 20 races, with four competitors in each race. Meetings are organized so that each competitor rides in five races and competes against each of the other competitors during the course of the meeting.

Scoring is 3 points for first place, 2 points for second, and 1 point for third.
Competitors Teams consist of four riders plus a reserve.
The start is made from a stationary position, with the engine running and the foremost part of the motorcycle right up to the starting tape.
A ballot is held beforehand to determine starting grid positions. Any rider who puts a wheel outside his grid before the start will be excluded.

Ice racing

Ice racing is similar to speedway. There are both individual and team events, and the riders race around an ice track. Motorcycles have steel spikes attached to their wheels to grip the ice surface. Events are divided into heats, and points are awarded for the first three places in each heat.

The track is 300–400m in circumference. The minimum width for three drivers is 9m and four riders 12m. The track must be surrounded by a snow safety wall at least 1.20m high.
Pits are not heated. At least 8sq m per rider must be covered.

Meetings International ice race meetings are normally open to 16 drivers and consist of 20 heats. There are individual and team competitions. Points are normally awarded to the first three riders in a heat.

Teams normally have seven or eight riders. Each team is distinguished by its colors.
Starting positions are determined by ballot.

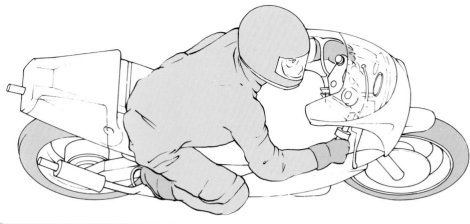

Street solo Normal road-going bikes, but with any motorcycle-type engine and any modifications. The frame must be of the original type. Any gearbox may be fitted.

Competition solo The frame may be altered. Any engine or engines may be used. The engine can run on any fuel except hydrazine.

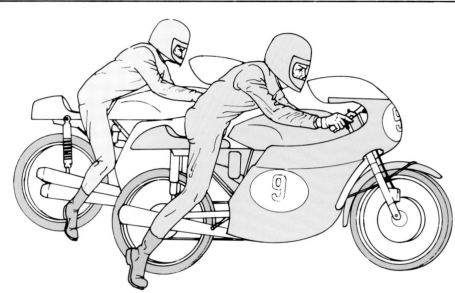

Sidecar combinations All the rules for solo machines apply to sidecar events. Other rules also apply.
Classes are usually:
up to 500cc;
500cc to 1300cc.

Wheels The three road wheels may be arranged to give either two or three tracks.
One of the wheels may be replaced by two wheels provided the distance between the vertical center lines does not exceed 8in.
Engine position is optional.
Passenger protection The passenger must always be protected from the road wheels and from the primary and final drive.
Ballast may be carried in addition to or in place of a passenger. If a passenger is replaced by ballast, it must weigh not less than 132lb and must be securely fixed.

© DIAGRAM

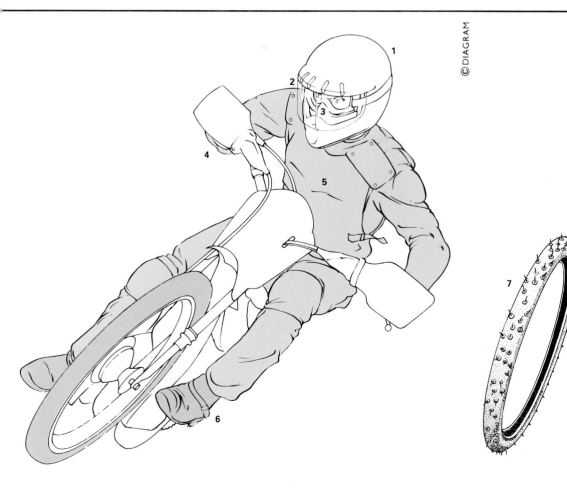

Machines Specialized motorcycles of not more than 500cc. They consist of little more than a simple frame, an engine (single-cylindered), two wheels, and a seat.
Brakes are prohibited.
The fuel used is methanol.
Dress Team members wear distinguishing colors. Competitors in individual competitions wear numbers. Padded body protection is worn under the clothing.
1 approved helmet
2 goggles or visor
3 facemask
4 gloves
5 team uniform
6 steel-shod boots

Machines The referee will disqualify any motorcycle that he considers to be dangerous.
Brakes are prohibited as in speedway racing.
Tires have non-slipping anti-skid steel spikes (**7**), which must not exceed 28mm in length.

Moto cross

Moto cross takes place on cross-country courses without prepared surfaces. Events are generally for solo motorcycles, although sidecar races are popular in Europe.

Dress Protective clothing must be of the approved type and consists of riding jeans, gloves, knee length boots and long sleeved riding shirt. Helmets are compulsory and must be in a sound condition.

The course may be of any length and generally includes steep hills, extremely rough ground and water hazards. Most courses are between one and three miles in length. Races can be held over a set distance, for example, five laps, or a set time, for example, 20 minutes. The starting stretch must be long enough for safety.

The course should be clearly marked with flags and other indicators as to width and direction of travel. It is forbidden to ride in the opposite direction to the race.

Starters The maximum number of riders in a race for solo machines is determined on the basis of the track characteristics.

The start is signaled by a starting gate.

The start is made with the engines running.

Leaving the course If a rider leaves the course, he must return to it at the point at which he left it.

If a rider decides to retire, he must remove himself and his machine from the course as soon as possible.

Conduct Riders are prohibited from dangerous or unfair conduct in general, and from cutting across other riders in particular. A rider who is about to be overtaken must not knowingly impede the progress of the overtaking rider.

The finish is signaled by the waving of a checkered flag as the first rider crosses the finish line.

Fuel must be of standard grade as supplied from normal commercial pumps.

Solo machines Events are usually for the following classes: 125cc, 250cc and 500cc.

Handlebars must be rounded or otherwise protected.

Clutch and brake levers must have an integral ball-end at least ¾in in diameter.

The throttle must be self closing.

The engine of any machine may be examined after the race to check conformity to class regulations.

The gearbox is modified and strengthened.

A chain guard must be fitted to the primary chain.

Exhaust No exhaust pipe must project behind the machine.

Suspension is modified to give extra strength.

Tires Special knobby tires are used to improve traction. They may of any type allowed in the regulations. Chains and non-skid devices are not permitted.

Mudguards are compulsory.

Sidecars All the rules for solo machines apply to sidecar events. Other rules also apply.

The wheels of a scrambles combination must be at least 16in in diameter. They may be arranged to give two or three tracks. The distance between the tracks must be at least 32in.

The single sidecar wheel may be replaced by two wheels, provided that the distance between their tire centers does not exceed 8in at their closest point.

Passenger protection Adequate provision must be made to protect the passenger from the road wheels and from any other driven parts.

Trials

In trials the emphasis is on riding skill rather than speed. Trials are held in stages, partly on surfaced roads and partly on extremely rough ground. Competitors are started at intervals and the one who incurs fewest penalty points is the winner. There are events for solo machines and for sidecar combinations.

The course Trials are held partly on surfaced roads and partly on extremely rough ground.
The onus of following the marked course rests entirely with the rider.
A rider who leaves the course must rejoin it at the same point.
Penalties A rider is penalized if:
he dismounts;
he touches the ground with any part of his body;
he or his machine receives any outside assistance;
his machine ceases to move in a forward direction (UK only);
any part of his machine crosses an artificial boundary;
his machine travels outside the boundary marker;
he breaks or removes a tape or support.

Sidecar penalties are the same as for solo trials events, together with penalties incurred if the passenger touches the ground or receives outside assistance in maintaining his balance.
Trials machines are lightweight motorcycles designed to overcome the toughest terrain. They must comply with all the legal requirements for use on public roads.
Clutch and brake levers must have an integral ball-end of at least ¾in in diameter.
Tires must be of a type approved by the governing body. It is forbidden to cut the threads or to fit chains or spikes.
A number plate must be fitted at the rear.

Lights must be a permanent fitting and the use of torches or flashlights is forbidden.

Grasstrack racing

Grasstrack racing is popular in the UK, Australia and parts of Europe. Grasstrack meetings are broadly speaking speedway on grass with riders broadsiding on special machines.

Courses Grass track courses are laid out in fields. They are plain ovals. The length of the course is 450–1300m.
Conduct The referee will exclude any rider who in his opinion is guilty of foul, unfair or dangerous riding.
Fuel Pure methanol is used.
Machines are similar to those used in Speedway, but use twin shocks.
There are events for solo machines and for sidecar combinations.
Throttle All machines must be fitted with a self-closing throttle.

Brakes It is recommended that solo machines have a brake on the front wheel. Three-wheelers must be equipped with a brake on the driving wheel.
Tires There are no restrictions on the type of tire, but chains and other non-skid devices are prohibited.

Chain guards Adequate chain guards must be fitted to prevent the chain from fouling.
Sidecars must be rigidly fixed to the motorcycle. There are classes for 500cc and 1000cc and for right hand sidecars as well as left hand.

Passenger protection must be provided on side-car combinations from the rear wheel, the primary and final drive and from the sidecar wheels.
Wheels The three road wheels, which may be disposed to give either two or three tracks, shall be each of at least 400mm in diameter measured over the

outside of the tire.
One of the wheels may be replaced by two wheels, provided the distance between the vertical center lines of those two wheels does not exceed 200mm. Where wheels are not wire spoked, they shall be enclosed in discs.

©DIAGRAM

Motor racing

Cars are raced in many ways, but the best-known is circuit racing around specially prepared tracks. Single-seater racing cars, sports cars, production sedans, "stock" cars, and veterans all have their own circuit events. Races may run for a set number of laps or last for a specified time.

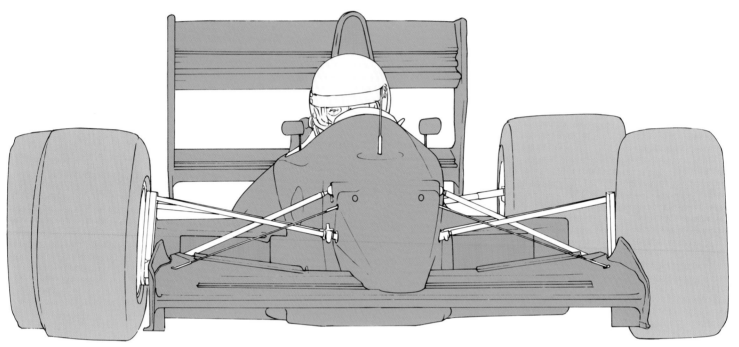

CIRCUIT RACING
Circuits vary from banked speedways, lapped in under a minute, to 14-mile circuits with tight hairpin bends. All must comply with strict safety regulations, providing for marshals' posts, fire equipment and safety barriers.
Officials of the appropriate governing body inspect circuits before awarding a racing license and lay down the maximum number of cars allowed to start in a race.
Under FIA (Fédération Internationale de l'Automobile) regulations, tracks must be at least 30ft wide with starting grid space of at least 2m by 8m for each car.

Vehicles All cars must:
have not more than four road wheels;
be of sound construction and mechanical condition;
have a full diameter steering wheel;
have a protective bulkhead between engine and driver's compartment;
have a complete floor;
have all doors hinged and detachable parts securely fastened;
be fitted with sprung suspension between the wheels and the chassis.
Other requirements are listed under the various formulae.
Each car is checked before a race by official scrutineers to ensure that it complies with regulations.

Officials at a race meeting include: clerk of the course; secretary of the meeting; stewards; timekeepers; scrutineers and assistants; pit observers; track observers; flag marshals; finishing judges; handicappers and starters.
Competitors must have a competition license.
Dress Drivers must wear: an approved crash helmet, properly fastened;
goggles or visors (unless the car has a full-width windshield);
protective, fire-resistant clothing covering arms, legs and torso.
Practice Before a race cars are tested on the circuit to make them as competitive as possible.
Each lap is officially timed to determine the cars' starting positions.

Starting All cars start together; their positions on the starting grid are determined by their performance in practice. The fastest are placed at the front, with the fastest car in pole position (the position in the front row which will give the driver most advantage going into the first corner). The race is started when the lights change from red to green.
Some races use a rolling start. A pace car leads the field, in their grid order, around one lap. It then drives off the circuit and the race begins.
A car moving off before the official signal incurs a time penalty.
Duration Circuit races last for a set number of laps or length of time (eg Le Mans 24-hour race).
Formula One races (which are over a set number of laps) are arranged to give either 2 hours or 200 miles racing, whichever is the shorter.

Flags are used during races to gives instructions to drivers. Internationally recognized signals include:
blue, motionless: another car following;
blue, waved: another car trying to overtake;
yellow: danger;
yellow with red stripes: slippery surface;
white: official non-racing vehicle on course;
red: stop race;
black: car indicated to stop.
The race Although drivers attempt to improve their race position, they are not allowed to drive dangerously and must reduce speed or stop if ordered to do so.
They may receive advice and mechanical assistance.
A car may be ordered to withdraw if it becomes unfit to race.
Result The winning car is the one that completes the distance first or is leading when the set racing time ends.

Single-seater racing

Helmets All motor racing competitors must wear helmets of an approved design.

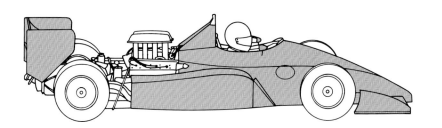

International Formula One Up to 3500cc; no forced induction permitted. These cars compete for the World Driver's Championship and the World Constructors' Championship. Specifications govern bodywork and equipment. Tuning of the engine is unlimited. Maximum of 12 cyclinders.

Formula Atlantic A formula for single seater cars, powered by production-based 1600cc racing engines. Raced in the Antipodes as Formula Pacific. Now defunct in the UK.

Formula Ford 2000 Developed from Formula Ford 1600, using two-liter Ford pinto engine. Aerodynamic devices, eg wings, are permitted.

Formula Vee US and European formula similar to Formula Ford, but using Volkswagen 1300cc engines. No more than a specified amount of money may be spent on tuning.

Formula Super Vee As Vee but using 1600cc Volkswagen engines that may be highly tuned.

Formula Libre This is an unrestricted formula. The organizers of the race establish their own classes and handicap certain cars, if necessary.

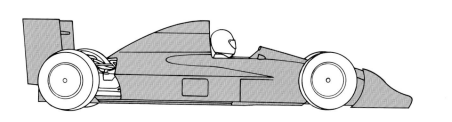

Formula 3000 Introduced in 1985 to replace Formula Two as the final rung on the ladder to F1 racing. Engines must be normally aspirated, up to 3000cc and with a maximum of 12 cylinders.

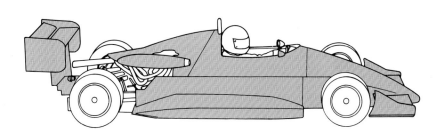

Formula Three Up to 2000cc with engines derived from 4-cylinder production engines.
All cars are fitted with an air restrictor over the induction system, limiting their power and speed.

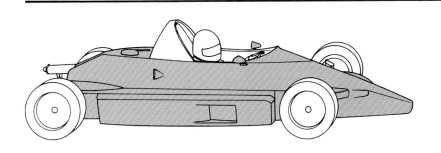

Formula Ford 1600 This uses production 1600GT Cortina (Kent) engines with only minimum modifications allowed (such as removing the air cleaner and changing carburetor jets). In Europe tires must be of standard road type on 5½in wide wheels. Slicks are used in the USA.

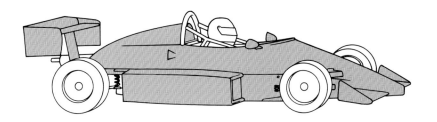

Formula Vauxhall Lotus European single seater formula for identical Reynard-built chassis, powered by two-litre, 156bhp GM engines.

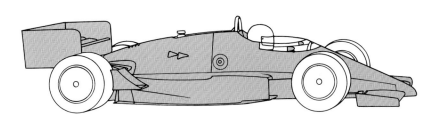

CART
Indianapolis type cars
Up to 2999cc supercharged or 4490cc unsupercharged. Otherwise unrestricted.

Sedan and sports car racing

In addition to single-seater formulae, circuit racing has many classes for sedan and sports cars.

Group C World Sports-Prototype Championship formula for closed, two-seater sports cars. From 1991, competing cars must deploy 3.5 liter engines similar to those used in Formula One Grand Prix racing. In the USA, the IMSA GTP series caters for similar chassis, although engine regulations differ.

Sports cars Apart from the internationally regulated Group C for long distance cars, sports and saloon (sedan) car racing is largely run on national or even club basis and recognized categories vary greatly from country to country. In general terms there are opportunities for: unmodified production cars; modified production cars; regulated hybrids built up from production engines and/or chassis; cars built up from kits and plans of small-scale manufacturers; unregulated specials. Cutting across these are engine-capacity categories, and races at local level often throw together a wide assortment of sports and even sedan cars racing together in classes based on engine size.

US sedan racing For American production sedan cars, with only limited modifications allowed. Cars are grouped into classes based on estimates of their capabilities.

US production car racing For production cars of mainly foreign origin, grouped into eight classes according to estimated potential performance.

Vintage racing Many countries have races held especially for vintage and thoroughbred cars. They are split up into various classes according to size and age.

Drag racing

The object of drag racing is to record the fastest time over a short straight track only 440yd long. Cars compete in pairs, and competitions are won by a series of elimination rounds against cars of the same category.

The track or "strip" must be 440yd long with a braking distance of a further half mile. The width of the track must be at least 50ft. There is a separate road along which cars return to the starting area.

Vehicles are of various classes, from mass-produced cars to highly specialized racing machines. The most specialized cars have engines capable of producing up to 1500hp. Two engines may be permitted, but in US drag racing there is a restriction of 800cu in on engine capacity.
Some braking systems include special parachutes. "Funny cars" are also raced: dragsters fitted with fiberglass replica sedan bodies.

Starting Cars compete in pairs.
They line up on the starting line and are started by the "Christmas tree" system. In the center of the track is a pole with a vertical series of yellow, green, and red lights. These operate in sequence, starting from the top of the "tree." When the green light comes on, the cars can move off.
If a car moves before the green light, a red light comes on automatically and the car is disqualified.

Group A Series production touring cars, of which 5000 examples must be built in a 12 month period to ensure homologation. Limited engine modifications are permitted and there are various capacity classes.

Group N Series production touring cars, outwardly almost identical to the cars you might see in a dealer's showroom window. Limited tuning is allowed as are full racing tires.

The race If both cars start cleanly, it is a direct race to the finishing line.
If a car crosses into the opponent's lane, it is disqualified.
In every race cars are timed for both the elapsed time and terminal speed.
As each car starts, it breaks a timing light that is linked to another set of lights at the finish. As the car crosses the finishing line it breaks another light beam to record the elapsed time.
After it has crossed the finishing line the car passes through another light beam, connected to the finishing line, that records the car's terminal speed.

The elapsed time is the factor that decides the winner, though this may be modified by a time handicap system. It is possible for the losing car to record the faster terminal speed.

The result Time handicapping is not used in professional drag racing, but may be used in the amateur categories.
When handicapping does not apply, the first car to break the light beam at the finish wins. Otherwise the elapsed time is adjusted to include the time advantages given to the slower cars within the class.
Racers compete in a series of elimination races against cars in a similar category to produce the ultimate winners. There may also be awards for the fastest terminal speeds and the quickest times at a meeting.

© DIAGRAM

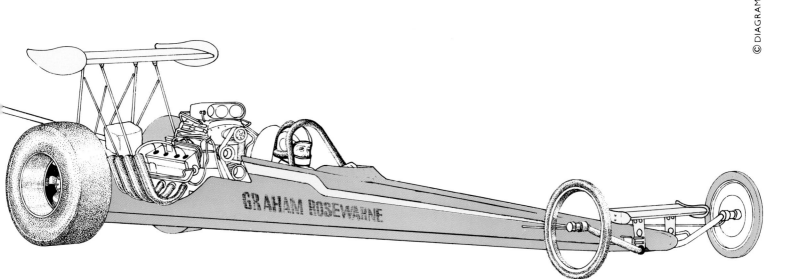

Stock car racing

Stock car racing in the USA is for cars that in outside appearance are the stock production models available to the general public. They are, however, highly modified for racing and can achieve very high speeds. Stock car racing in the United Kingdom is much less streamlined – with stripped-down and modified cars racing and crashing on small oval tracks.

US STOCK CAR RACING
Track Usually an oval circuit with banks, but occasionally road race tracks are used.
Vehicles Of the several categories, the Grand National Championship division is the most famous. It has the following two classes:
Standard size cars Limited to cars with a minimum wheelbase of 119in, a maximum engine size of 430 cubic in (7 liters), and standard bodies complying with weight requirements.
Intermediate size cars Limited to cars with a wheelbase of 115–119in and a maximum engine capacity of 430 cubic in (7 liters).
Weight All GN cars must weigh at least 3800lb ready to race.

Races begin with a rolling start and may be up to 600 miles long.
UK STOCK CAR RACING
Competitions Cars begin in a massed start. Contact between cars is allowed but deliberate attempts to force other drivers off the track are forbidden.
Vehicles are divided into classes. Each class is governed by specific regulations. In some the shape of the car body has to be altered, the glass is removed and roll bars or cages have to be installed. Cars are numbered and brightly painted with the color of the roof denoting the driver's status.

STADIUM RACING
Cars compete in groups around a loose-surfaced oval track ¼–½ mile long. There are various classes of car, from "banger" sedans to midget racers with 5 liter V-8 engines.

Rallying

Cars compete over a course divided into a number of stages. Each stage is timed individually and at the end of an event competitors' aggregate times are totted up. The winning car is the one to have taken least time to complete all the stages.

Competitors Each car is crewed by a driver and a navigator.
The route This can comprise private land such as forestry roads, closed off sections of public highway, purpose-built motor racing circuits and sometimes a combination of all three. It is the navigator's job to plot the route on a map and to warn his driver of likely

hazards. The two will communicate by means of an intercom system during the event. If a car needs repairs in between stages, they may be carried out without penalty at a pre-determined service point. If a car breaks down on a stage, it may be repaired but the time taken to effect this is added to the driver's time for the stage. If he fails to

complete the stage within a given time, he will be excluded from the event.
Vehicles Cars complying with FIA Group A and Group N regulations are eligible for international championships. National series may cater for cars from outside these classifications.

HILLCLIMB

Competition In hillclimb competitions each car competes singly and makes two attempts to complete the course in the fastest time. Results are based on each car's better attempt. There is an overall winner as well as individual class winners.

Vehicles are organized in classes according to the number of entrants.
The course is on a hill, tarmac-surfaced, and at least 12ft wide. Lengths vary: in some countries ¾–1 mile is usual, in others the average is much longer.

SPRINTS
Sprint competitions are similar to hillclimbs, but the course is over a flat section of track. Events may be held on racing circuits or airfields.

SLALOM

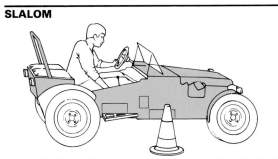

Competition Slalom, or autotest, competitions are a test of maneuverability. Cars attempt the course singly. Each car starts with 0 points and receives 1 point for each second taken and 10 points for each marker touched. The winner is the driver with the fewest points at the finish.

Vehicles Many countries have three classes: production open, production closed, and specials. (Specials include such features as separate handbrakes for each rear wheel, or steering from front or back.)

The course is laid out with markers. It includes sections to be completed in reverse and competitors are also required to back in and out of garages, represented by marker cones.

AUTOCROSS

Competition Cars compete against the clock over courses that do not include ordinary roads. Cars may race alone, or be started in pairs or threes. There are individual class winners and an overall competition winner.

Vehicles International regulations cover classes for production cars, buggies, and special cars. Nationally decided classes make further divisions according to engine capacity, engine position, and for cars with front- or rear-wheel drive.
The course is over grass or some other rough surface.

Lengths are usually 500–800yd. The first corner must be at least 50yd from the start, and no straight may exceed 200yd. There is a 5-second penalty for touching a marker, and cars are automatically disqualified for crossing an imaginary line between any two markers.

RALLYCROSS

Competition Heats are usually between four to eight cars and are held over three laps of the course. Times are recorded and the fastest drivers progress to the finals, which are decided by a straight race, rather than against the clock.

Vehicles Competitions are for sedan or production sports cars, which are often highly modified.
The course combines rough surfaces and tarmac but does not include public roads.

HILL TRIALS

Competition Cars attempt to climb farthest up a steep hill. Measuring is to the point where the car fails to maintain unassisted motion. Cars are penalized for touching markers.
Vehicles Sporting trial cars may use any engine up to 1650cc and feature independent braking on each rear wheel. There are also competitions for production sedans, from which 4wd cars are banned.

Passengers Each car is allowed one passenger. Passengers may "bounce" the car to increase traction, but must keep their arms and legs within the car.
The course is marked out on a very steep, rough hill.

GRASSTRACK
All cars start together and race over an unsealed or grass course. The cars are put in classes by the organizers, but are usually sedans with tuned engines and special safety devices.

©DIAGRAM

Karting

In karting, competitors race around one of three types of approved track: permanent, round-the-houses, or temporary. Karts are classified according to engine capacity.

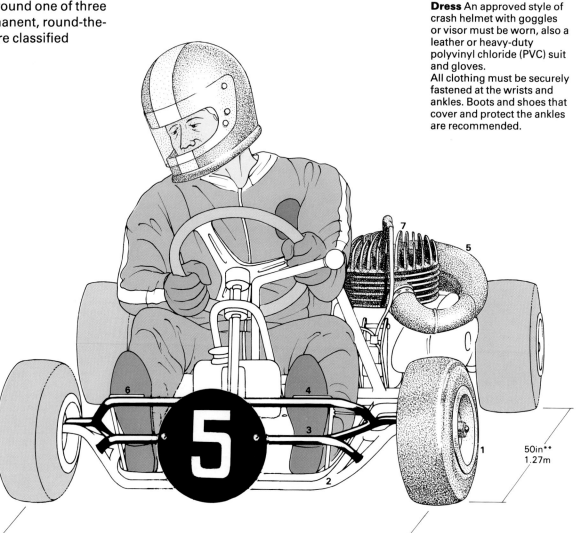

Dress An approved style of crash helmet with goggles or visor must be worn, also a leather or heavy-duty polyvinyl chloride (PVC) suit and gloves.
All clothing must be securely fastened at the wrists and ankles. Boots and shoes that cover and protect the ankles are recommended.

Eligibility to race
Chassis and engine Every kart must comply with national automobile club regulations and be in a sound mechanical condition. It is the responsibility of competitors to keep their karts in eligible condition throughout the competition.
Scrutineering Competitors must make their karts available for inspection at any time required by the organizers.
The officially nominated driver is the only person eligible to drive a kart on the track during racing or practice.

Kart specifications
Chassis dimensions: wheelbase, track, and height must comply with official specifications.
1 Tires Pneumatic tires are obligatory, and are 9–17in in diameter.
2 The frame must be of sound construction.
3 Bumpers are compulsory at both front and rear.
4 Brakes are foot operated, either drum or disc type. Four-wheel brakes are compulsory for all gearbox karts.
5 Exhaust systems must comply with official regulations. Mufflers are compulsory.
6 The throttle must be foot operated.
7 The engine must be officially homologated (a standard production two-stroke engine). Supercharging is prohibited. 100cc engines may have only one cylinder; larger engines only two. Engines must have suppressors. There are price limits on engines for certain classes.
Drive Karts must be chain driven.
Weight Each kart class has a combined minimum weight for kart and driver.

50in** 1.27m

40in** 1.01m

Overall length 6ft 6in** 2m

**maximum

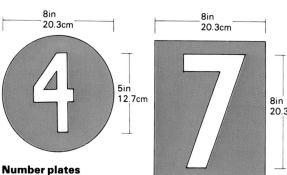

8in 20.3cm

8in 20.3cm

5in 12.7cm

8in 20.3cm

Number plates
Rectangular plates must be fitted to the front, rear, and sides; circular plates only to the front and rear. Restricted kart license holders must use black number plates with white numbers. International kart license holders use number plates according to class.

Types of event
Closed events, confined to members of the organizing club.
Restricted events, confined to the organizing club and up to 12 invited clubs.
National events, open to holders of a current international kart license.
International non-priority events, open to any holder of an appropriate competition license issued by a national automobile club that is a member of the FIA.
Entries are to be approved by competitors' own national automobile clubs.
International priority events are classified as such by the FIA, and are open to competitors under the same conditions as international non-priority events.

Classes
Kart racing is divided into four classes:
Juniors for drivers aged 12–16, karts as Class 100 National, motors 100cc, no gearbox.
Class 1 is in two sections: Class 100 National and Class 100 International, motors 100cc, no gearbox.
Class 4 is in three sections: Class 210 Villiers, Class 250 International and 125 International. Karts have manual gearboxes.
Cadet Karting for drivers aged 8–12.

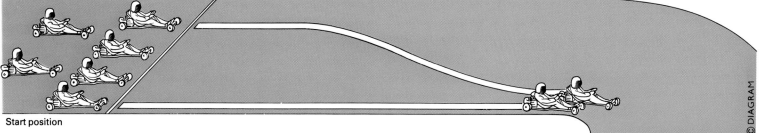

Start position

Administration Karting is organized by national automobile clubs that are members of the FIA.

Tracks National automobile club track licenses are issued to approved venues. Track regulations include the following:
tracks must have a minimum width of 20ft;
chicanes (where the track narrows) are not encouraged, but where essential must not exceed certain limits;
the track surface must be similar throughout;
track edges must be marked in an approved manner, and track markings must not constitute a hazard;
spectators must be protected by barriers and safety precautions.
There are three types of track:
Permanent, where shape can be determined at any time and all protective barriers are permanently in position;
Round-the-houses, tracks using public roads;
Temporary, other tracks.

Officials All officials should be present during practice and racing.
Officials include:
kart steward;
club steward(s);
meeting secretary;
clerk of the course;
medical officer;
kart scrutineer;
chief timekeeper;
chief lapscorer and judge;
chief flag marshall starter;
chief course marshall with four or more assistants;
chief paddock marshall with two or more assistants;
general officials.

Signals are displayed to the drivers by flags or signal boards. Drivers are penalized for disobeying signals.
National flag A race with a rolling start begins at the moment the flag is raised. A standing start race begins the moment the flag is lowered.
Blue flag A stationary flag signals that another competitor is following close by. A waved flag signals that another competitor is trying to overtake.
White flag A service car is on the circuit.
Yellow flag A stationary flag signals danger and no overtaking. A waved flag signals serious danger and the need to be prepared to stop.
Yellow flag with red stripes Stationary, signals oil on the road ahead. Waved, signals that oil on the road is imminent.
Green flag Proceed, the hazard has been removed.
Red flag Complete and immediate stop for all karts.

Black and white warning board bearing a competitor's number indicates that the offending competitor will be flagged down, if he repeats an offense.
Black flag with white number The driver of the kart with that number must report to the clerk of the course.
Black and white multi-checkered flag Finish.
Competitors The maximum number of starters is determined according to the track license at individual circuits.

Practice Before racing a definite period is allowed for practicing. Drivers leave the paddock one at a time for the start; otherwise racing rules apply. Each driver must complete at least three laps' continuous running before racing.

Race procedure
Handicaps are based on an allowance of time or distance determined by either a timed performance in practice or a previous race, or by an assessment of performance by the organizers.
Handicaps are displayed on the official notice board not less than 15 minutes before the start of the race.
Starting positions are displayed before the race on the chief paddock marshall's board. The number 1 position is on the side of the track that is on the inside of the first corner. This position is taken by the competitor with the best preliminary performance.

Rolling start: for non-gearbox karts. Karts go round the course at a steady pace while awaiting the signal.
Standing start: for karts with a gearbox. Karts take up their position on the starting grid, with their engines running. Any driver unable to start raises his left hand and stays still.
Finish To be classed as finished, a kart must cross the finish line under its own propulsion not more than two minutes after the winner and having completed at least half of the race.
The first three finishers are weighed to check that they are not below the specified minimum weight limits for driver and kart combined.

Conduct Official instructions must be obeyed. These include:
karts must be driven in an orderly manner;
a driver who is forced to leave the track must rejoin it at the nearest practicable point to where he left it;
refuelling during the race is forbidden.
Penalties In order of severity, the penalties that may be inflicted are:
reprimand;
fine or a time or point penalty;
exclusion;
suspension;
disqualification.

Protests Any protests must be made in accordance with the general competition rules of the national governing body.
A protest as to the validity of an entry must be made within two hours of the end of the official examination.
A protest against a handicap, the composition of a heat, etc, must be made immediately upon notification.
A protest against a scrutineer must be made immediately.
A protest against any irregularity during a competition must be made within half an hour of the finish.
A protest against a result must be made within half an hour of announcement.

Appeals Any competitor may appeal against a decision affecting him. He must do so in writing to the stewards, enclosing the appropriate fee. Such an appeal must be made within one hour.

Gliding

In gliding, aircraft without engines are used. The gliders are towed into the air, and the pilots locate thermals (currents of warm air rising from the ground), using them to gain height before gliding downward to the next thermal. Competitors may be judged on altitude, distance, or speed.

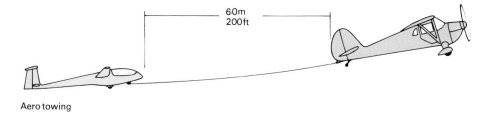

60m
200ft

Aero towing

Gliders Most gliders are monoplanes with long slender wings, able to make the best use of air currents. Gliders have a low sinking speed and can glide at very flat angles. Motor gliders, with an engine used only for takeoff, may be used.

Preparations for flight
There is a recommended cockpit check that must be made before takeoff. Controls must be working freely and instruments must be checked and set as required.
Ballast may be used to make up the correct cockpit load. The pilot and crew must be fastened in safety straps. The trim is set for takeoff, and the canopy locked shut. On motor gliders, additional checks should be made to ensure that there is sufficient fuel, that the propeller is free, and that people are clear of the takeoff path.

360m
1200ft

Auto launching

Bungee launching

Release point

Cumulus cloud

Prevailing wind

Aero tow takeoff

Thermal

Lake

Launching Gliders may be launched by aero towing, by car and winch, or by "bungee" launch.

Aero towing The glider is towed into the air by an airplane or "tug." The tug pilot is in command of both aircraft so as to avoid a collision. He is responsible for ensuring that the tow rope is suitable and that signals are fully understood, although the glider pilot chooses the moment to release the tow rope.
Once the glider pilot has released the tow rope, he should turn away so that it is fully clear to the tug pilot that the glider is free. The rope should not be released under tension, and it should fall only in the designated area of the airfield.

Auto and winch towing may be used on any flat ground, such as an airfield runway.
If there is any jerking or hesitation at the start of the launch, the car or winch driver must stop and await further signals before restarting. Should the glider pilot suspect power failure during the launch, he should release the rope at once while there is still room ahead to land.

Bungee launching is sometimes used to launch a glider from the top of a steep hill. A rubber rope is attached to the front of the glider and is pulled out into a "v" shape by about six people in either side of the "v." They walk or run as appropriate, stretching the rope until the glider leaves the ground.

Ground handling The glider should not be moved without crew on the windward wingtip and at either the tail or the nose. If the glider is moved into the wind, the nose must be held down and the tail up. If it is moved downwind, care must be taken to prevent the control surfaces from slamming. When the wind is strong, the airbrakes should be opened and the crew increased.
The crew runs with the glider to steady it until take-off, and if the launch point slopes downhill, the crew can prevent the glider from overrunning by holding it back until the takeoff starts.

Flying Once the tow rope has fallen away, the pilot soars upward if he is in a rising air current, or glides downward toward a thermal. The pilot judges the location of thermals by the lie of the land and cloud shapes.

Equipment Gliders have many of the same instruments as airplanes. Gliders have a control stick that operates the elevator and ailerons, and pedals to operate the rudder. Equipment includes altimeters, air-speed indicators, variometers (showing the rate at which the glider is rising or falling), maps, refreshments, and extra clothing. Each crew member must have his own parachute.
Gliders flying above heights of 3600m (12,000ft) should carry an oxygen supply system with a contents gauge. This should automatically be used above 4500m (15,000ft) or at any other time needed.

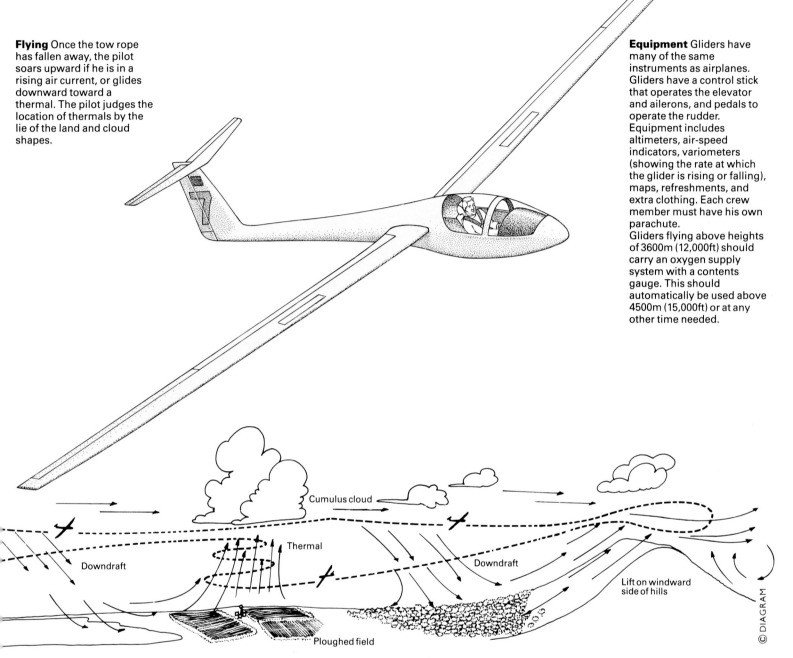

Cumulus cloud

Thermal

Downdraft

Downdraft

Lift on windward side of hills

Ploughed field

© DIAGRAM

Locating thermals Warm air, and consequently updrafts, can be expected over open fields and over houses, particularly above cities. Upcurrents are indicated by cumulus clouds; a pilot who flies into a thunderstorm may be quickly carried up to 9000m (30,000ft). Geographical features such as ridges produce upward rising waves.
Cold air, and consequently downdrafts, can be expected over woodland and lakes; down currents also flow over valleys.

Climbing Thermals are narrow, and the glider must turn in tight circles in order to stay within the effective area.
A glider joining another in a thermal must circle in the direction established by the first glider.
A pilot should not change direction abruptly if there is another glider anywhere nearby, and he should ensure that he remains in full visibility of other pilots.

Right of way Airplanes must give way to aero tows and gliders, and gliders must give way to balloons; at all times it is each pilot's responsibility to avoid collision.
When two aircraft are converging at about the same height, the aircraft that has the other on its right must give way. If a headlong collision seems imminent, both aircraft must swing to the right.
When landing, the lower-flying aircraft has the right of way.
Air space is controlled by air traffic rules according to local conditions, to ensure safety both in the air and on the ground.

Weather Gliders should not be left out in winds of 37kph (20 knots) or more, as the risk of being blown over and damaged is high.
Lightning can strike down the winch wire, and car or tow launching should be suspended if a storm is imminent.
Low cloud may be hazardous to inexperienced pilots.
Launching should not take place in wet weather if the air temperature is below freezing, as ice on the wings can adversely affect efficiency and stalling speed.

Parking Gliders must be parked in such a way as to avoid being blown over or damaged in poor weather. If parked across wind, the windward wing should be weighted down, and the tail skid should be anchored on the side away from the wind. When unparking in strong wind, the pilot should be in the cockpit with crew at each wingtip, and the tail must be up before turning into the wind.

297

Competitions Many countries hold an annual competition, and world gliding championships are held every two or three years. Competitions may be judged on distance or speed. There are three categories of record: world, national, and local; each category contains single-seater, two-seater, and women's classes.

Badges are awarded to solo pilots for proficiency tests. The simplest test requires the pilot to know the basic air rules, and to carry out three solo flights of a circuit and a turn in each direction, with normal landings. The Commission Internationale de Vol à Voile lays down international standards for the following badges:

Silver badge The requirements for this include a duration flight of at least five hours, a distance flight of at least 50km (approximately 31mi), and a height gain of 1000m (approximately 3300ft).

Gold badge The requirements for this include a distance flight of at least 30km (approximately 186mi) in a straight line or around a triangular course (which need not necessarily be completed provided that 300km is exceeded), and a height gain of 3000m (approximately 9900ft).

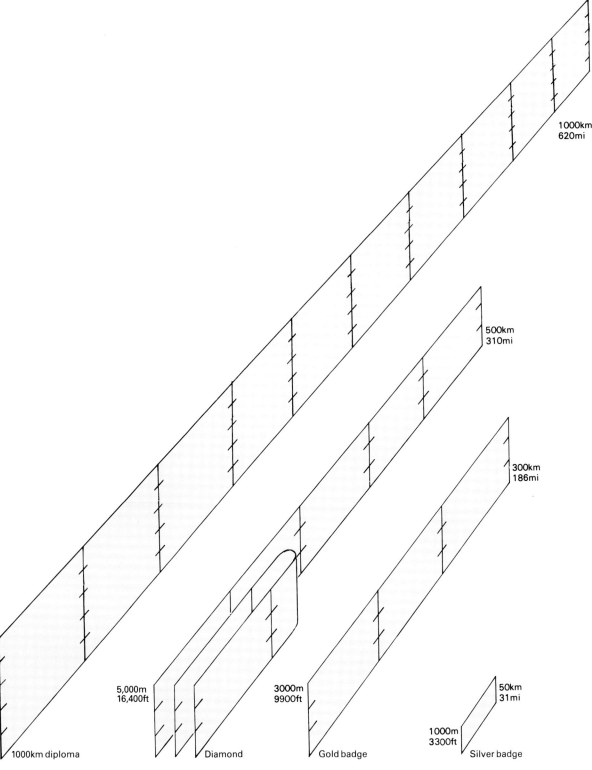

1000km
620mi

500km
310mi

300km
186mi

5,000m
16,400ft

3000m
9900ft

50km
31mi

1000m
3300ft

1000km diploma

Diamond

Gold badge

Silver badge

Diamonds These may be added to gold or silver badges. They are awarded for a completed triangle or an out-and-return flight of 300km (186mi); a distance flight of at least 500km (approximately 310mi), and a height gain of at least 5000m (16,400ft).

1000km diploma This is awarded for a distance soaring flight of 1000km (approximately 620mi) or more.

Evidence Proof that the flights have achieved the necessary standards is supported by correctly calibrated barographs (showing the height attained), and photographs of the turn points taken from the glider on distance flights.

Signals It is essential that signals between the person in charge of the launching and the winch or tow car driver or tug pilot be clearly understood.
Unless there is a radio or telephone system in operation, one of the following methods may be used:
signaling with one bat;
signaling with two bats;
signaling with lights;
hand signals;
movement of aircraft controls.

Airfield signals Many airfields have signals, some of which are as follows:
A red and yellow striped arrow pointing in a clockwise direction indicates that a right-hand circuit is in force. A white double cross indicates that glider flying is in progress.
A white dumbbell indicates that aircraft and gliders are confined to paved surfaces. A dumbbell with black bars indicates that takeoffs and landings must be made on the runway, but taxiing on the grass is permitted.
A red L displayed on the dumbbell indicates that light aircraft may fly from the runway.

A large white L indicates that a part of the airfield shall only be used by light aircraft.
A white T indicates that takeoffs and landings shall be parallel to the shaft of the T and toward the cross arm.
A white disc at the head of the landing T indicates that the direction of landings and takeoffs may not be the same.
A red panel with a yellow bar indicates that the landing area is in a poor condition.
A red panel with a yellow cross indicates that the airfield is unsafe and that landing is prohibited.

Hang gliding

Hang glider pilots launch and land the aircraft using their legs. The pilots, who are in a harness attached to the wing, use thermals or ridge lift (rising air produced when the wind blows over a hill or mountain) to remain aloft and often land back on the launch point. Competitors are judged on distance and speed.

1 cross tube
2 battens
3 control frame
4 parachute
5 rigging wires
6 leading edge tube
7 sail
8 keel pocket
9 keel tube
10 hang point
11 harness

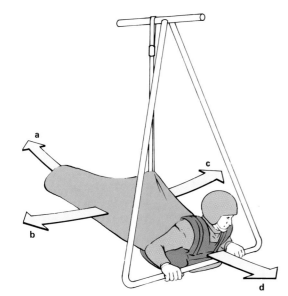

a Pilot moves aft to decrease speed
b Pilot's weight right to turn right
c Pilot's weight left to turn left
d Pilot moves forward to increase speed

Hang gliders Most are made with dacron sails and aluminum frames. The sail is made more rigid by battens ("flexwings") which are controlled by the movement of the pilot's weight. Some hang gliders are made from rigid materials such as wood and glass fiber. These are usually controlled by more conventional types of control such as ailerons, elevators and rudders. Both types have low sinking speeds but the glide angle is not as flat as that of a cockpit glider. Hang gliders can be turned much tighter than cockpit gliders and so use smaller thermals.

Equipment such as air-speed indicators, variometers, maps, compasses, harness, parachute, refreshments and radios are also used by hang gliders. Pilots flying in mountainous areas often carry oxygen.

Preparations for flight After rigging the glider and before every launch the pilot thoroughly checks each portion of the aircraft.

Launching Most hang gliders are launched off hill or mountain sides. Some are towed into the air. Once airborne the pilot places his feet on a stirrup which then allows his body to lie flat in line with the airflow. Some pilots fly in a sitting position. Heights of 10,000ft (3048m) have been attained by some hang gliding pilots flying in mountainous areas.

Flying Just as with cockpit gliders, hang glider pilots fly from thermal to thermal to make distance across the ground. Because of the lower speed of a hang glider, however, the greatest distances are usually made by flying downwind. Otherwise all the rules of cockpit flying regarding rights of way, thermal flying and weather conditions apply equally to hang gliders.

Competitions Many countries hold national championships and the world championships are held every two years. Competitors are usually judged on distance or speed around a course. The record categories and badges in cockpit gliding are also used by hang gliders. The requirements are the same. Many hang glider pilots have achieved the Silver Badge and several have attained the Gold Badge. Cameras and barographs are used as evidence for these flights.

Airfields Although not used very much by hang gliders, airfield rules and regulations apply and are followed by hang gliding pilots.

Air racing

Formula air racing is designed to encourage low-cost racing and aircraft development while maintaining maximum safety. The most popular class is Formula One, but four other classes also race in the United States.

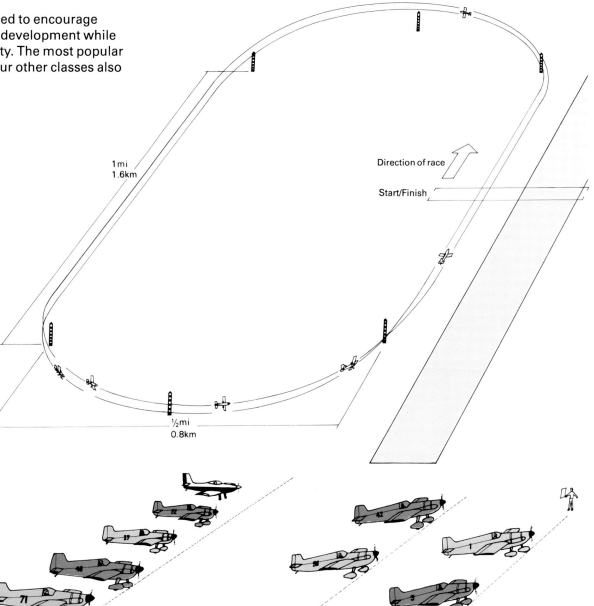

1 mi
1.6km

½ mi
0.8km

Direction of race

Start/Finish

Air start

Racehorse start

Racecourse The dimensions of the course are laid down in the rules for each class.
For Formula One racing, the course should be as near as possible to 3 miles (4.8km) in length. The course is six-sided, the corners being marked by six pylons about 30ft (9m) high. It has two straights, each 1 mile (1.6km) long. The pylons are painted conspicuous colors, and are placed so that a pilot can see at least the next two pylons while flying around the course.

Officials
Stewards Each racing event is controlled by at least three stewards. They interpret and enforce the rules, and may fine competitors or ban pilots or aircraft for any infringements.

Other officials include the clerk of the course, the chief timekeeper, the chief starter, the chief judge, and members of the technical committee.
This committee must include at least two pilots with racing experience. The committee inspects the aircraft and checks on the qualifications of the pilots.

Briefing The clerk of the course holds a briefing every day of the event on which practice, qualifying trials, or racing take place. All pilots must attend all briefings, or have a complete individual briefing before being allowed to compete.
Winning The winner of a race is the aircraft that crosses the finish line first, provided it has completed the required number of laps and has not incurred any penalties.
After crossing the finish line all aircraft must gain height and prepare to land.

Flags are used to signal to aircraft:
red and white flag, signals the start of a race or qualifying run;
white flag, signals the start of the last lap;
black and white checkered flag, signals the end of the race;
black flag, directs one or more aircraft to leave the course;
yellow flag, signifies an emergency.
Starts The number of aircraft starting is normally limited to eight.
There are two kinds of start: air starts and racehorse starts.

Air starts The competing aircraft take to the air individually and then take up formation on a pace aircraft. The pace aircraft crosses the starting line and then pulls up, releasing the racing aircraft. If no pace aircraft is available, the competitors take up formation on the aircraft drawn nearest the number 1 pylon.

Racehorse starts The aircraft line up on the take-off grid at one end of the runway, and are started by the drop of a flag. The order in which the aircraft line up is decided by their performance in the trials, the fastest qualifying aircraft having first choice, and so on.
The race begins when the starter lowers his flag, but the starting time is taken from the moment the first aircraft crosses the start line in flight after one preliminary lap. Any aircraft that does not take off within 30 seconds of the first aircraft will be excluded.

Reserves The first alternate (reserve) aircraft should be ready for takeoff, as it will be eligible for the race if any of the qualifying aircraft fails to reach the start line. Alternate pilots must prove their eligibility in the same way as other pilots.

Formula Class	Power unit	Horsepower	Speed		Racecourse length	
			mph+	km/h	mi	km
1 Unlimited	Any piston engine	any power	400+	643.7+	9–10	14.4–16
2 Formula One	Any stock 201cu in engine	100	190–230+	306–370	3	4.8
3 T6 Harvard	Stock Pratt & Whitney 1340	600	180–235	290–378	5	8
4 Sports biplane	Stock Lycoming	180	160–210	257–338	3	4.8
5 Formula V	Stock 1600cc Volkswagen	65	140–180	225–290	2–3	3.2–4.8

Formula One racing airplanes have a wingspan of approximately 15–22ft (4.5–6.7m). They must comply with the following rules:

Engine Any stock aero engine with a capacity of not more than 201cu in (3277cu cm).

Propellor must be fixed in pitch.

Airframe must weigh at least 500lb (approximately 230kg) when empty, with a wing area of at least 66sq ft (approximately 6sq m). It must have a fixed undercarriage and brakes.

Cockpit must comply with field of vision requirements.

©DIAGRAM

Aircraft qualification To qualify for a race, aircraft must complete two laps of the course at full speed before the race. The speed of the second lap is used to decide qualification.

Pilot qualification Pilots must have flown at least 10 hours in their particular type of aircraft. They must have flown at least 500 hours as pilot in charge of an aircraft, or alternatively a minimum of 100 hours plus 10 hours in the particular type for every 100 hours short of 500 hours in charge.
They must have taken off and landed the type of aircraft at least five times during the 90 days before the race, and must have flown that type for 2 hours or any aircraft for 10 hours during the previous month.

Aircraft eligibility Aircraft must comply with their class specifications and must arrive at the course in time for inspection.
Class specifications prescribe design and structural standards for aircraft, the test program required before they are allowed to compete, and the modifications which are permissible on the engines. All Formula Class racing aircraft are fully aerobatic.

Aircraft documents to be inspected before the race include:
entry form;
certificate of airworthiness or a permit to fly;
logbooks for engine and airframe; propeller maintenance record;
valid insurance certificate.

Aircraft equipment includes seat belts and shoulder harness, and may also include parachutes, protective helmets, fire-protective clothing, radio, and oxygen, according to the rules for the particular class.

Demonstrations Pilots must demonstrate their ability to take off safely in formation or fly in formation, and must fly five laps of the course (one at full power) before they may compete.
Pilots new to racing must fly 10 laps, including two at full power.

Safety No open containers of fuel are allowed in the pit area where the aircraft are prepared, and fire fighting equipment must be provided there. No smoking is allowed within 50ft (15m) of aircraft, and no alcohol is allowed in the pit area. All aircraft must carry enough fuel for the race, plus one lap at full power and 20 minutes at cruising speed. They must keep a safe distance apart while racing.

Pylon turns Aircraft must fly outside the pylons when cornering. Flying inside (known as "cutting a pylon") will lead to penalties. Flying over the top of the pylon also constitutes a "cut."

Altitudes Aircraft must race at not less than 25ft (7.5m) above the ground, and not higher than 500ft (150m), unless a greater altitude is necessary for reasons of safety. In emergencies they must fly at not less than 300ft (90m).

The typical formula race consists of two or more preliminary heats which qualify pilots for the consolation and championship heats.

Overtaking Aircraft must keep a safe distance apart during a race. The pilot of an overtaking aircraft is responsible for the safety of the maneuver, but the slower aircraft must keep to its course to avoid impeding the faster one. An aircraft must never overtake between another plane and a pylon, unless the slower aircraft is flying extremely wide.

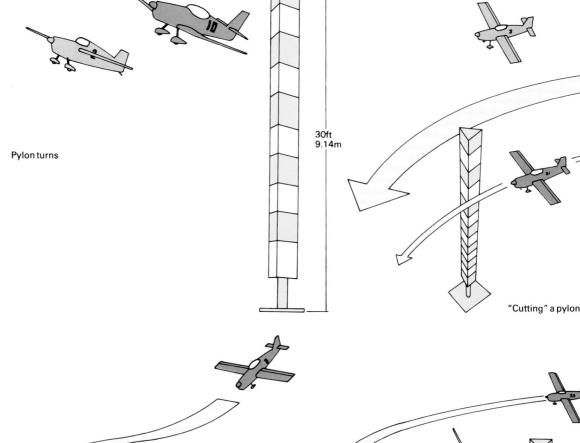

Pylon turns

30ft
9.14m

"Cutting" a pylon

Overtaking plane keeps clear

Emergencies An emergency is signaled by flying a yellow flag, and by radio from the air traffic control if radio is available in the aircraft. The lead aircraft must climb to at least 300ft (90m), giving way to any aircraft in difficulties, and other aircraft must follow suit. Aircraft must remain at the safety height until signaled by radio or by a red and white flag that the emergency is over.

Protests may be made as to the eligibility of an aircraft or its pilot, or the manner in which it is flown. Pilots, officials, or individuals entering aircraft may make protests, which must be in writing and handed in to the stewards within half an hour of the end of the race.

Penalties The stewards may exclude any aircraft or competitor for breaking the rules, or may fine them. The fines are deducted from prize money, and do not exceed the total prize money an offender has won.

Exclusion This penalty may be imposed for dangerous flying, unsafe condition of the aircraft or its pilot, unruly or unsportsmanlike behavior, or fraudulent description of an aircraft or its pilot.

Appeals An appeal may be made against any decision of the stewards. These appeals are made to the governing body of formula air racing in the country concerned.

Cancellation The stewards may cancel or postpone a race if they think the conditions are unsafe for spectators or contestants. If a race is stopped after the lead aircraft has completed half the course, the event is deemed to have been completed.

Weather A race is postponed or canceled if any of the following conditions prevail:
visibility less than 1.8 mile (3km);
cloud lower than 330ft (100m);
surface wind greater than 25 knots (46kph);
excessive turbulence, cross winds, rain, or snow.

Aerobatics

Competitive aerobatics includes a large variety of maneuvers designed to test the skill of the pilots and the versatility of their aircraft. Pilots fly compulsory and free programs and are generally marked for each maneuver. The competitor with the highest score after the contest programs have been flown is the winner.

Aircraft types Single engined light aircraft are usually used. World championships and most international competitions are open to piston-engined aircraft only, which must be fully capable of performing the required maneuvers. They are usually 180-360hp and may be biplanes or monoplanes.

Replacements An aircraft may be replaced by another aircraft at any time during the contest, provided the change is officially recommended by the technical commission and approved by the jury. If an aircraft is damaged during flight, the flight may be repeated if the jury agrees.

Radio sets may only be used for safety reasons in international competitions.

Teams vary according to the rules of each competition. Solo entries are also allowed. Competitors may be substituted only before the contest begins.
For world championships a team comprises not more than five pilots; there may be women's and men's teams. Other team members may include: chief delegate, team manager, judge, two assistants, trainer, doctor, not more than three mechanics and an interpreter.

Jury For world championships there is an international jury consisting of seven members elected by the international aerobatics commission of the FAI (Fédération Aéronautique Internationale) plus the chief judge, who has no vote. The jury is responsible for ensuring that the championships are conducted in accordance with the regulations.

Judges For world championships and international competitions there is a board of judges consisting of a chief judge, a minimum of seven and a maximum of ten international judges with their assistants, four positioning judges, and an administrative secretary. The positioning judges are placed at each corner of the performance zone. If electronic tracking equipment is used, they operate it and record its indications.

The technical commission is responsible for inspecting competing aircraft and certifying them airworthy. At world championships the commission comprises three to five engineers.

Briefing Daily briefings are held, which competitors, officials, judges and jury members must attend.

Training flights Each competitor may make one training flight in order to familiarize himself or herself with local conditions in the performance zone.
This flight is limited to 15 minutes.

Weather conditions For world championships the cloud base must be at least 165ft (50m) above the maximum height at which competing aircraft will fly, and visibility must be at least 3mi (5km). If the conditions are worse than this or there are adverse winds the jury may halt flying.
If a majority of team managers agrees, the jury may decide to continue in slightly worse conditions than normally required, in order to complete the championships. If a competitor thinks that weather conditions are not sufficiently good, he or she can discontinue a flight and may, with the jury's agreement, repeat the flight later.
At other competitions, the minimum weather conditions required for contest flights may be determined by regional weather patterns.

Performance zone All competition flights must be performed within a zone of 1000m by 1000m (approximately 1100yd by 1100yd), which must be clearly marked on the ground.

Height In world championships and most international competitions, competitors must not fly lower than 100m or higher than 1000m (approximately 330ft and 3300ft).
Each competitor is allowed 15 minutes from takeoff to complete the flight program. In other competitions, especially those that include less experienced pilots, the minimum height specified will often be between 300m and 500m (990ft and 1650ft).

© DIAGRAM

World championship programs Pilots fly three programs:
a known compulsory program;
a free program of the competitor's choice;
and an unknown compulsory program.
The highest-placed third of the men competitors and the highest-placed half of the women competitors may then compete in a fourth program, which carries a separate championship title (the freestyle championship). Each program has a draw to determine the competitors' starting order.

Program 1 The known compulsory program is published in advance for all competitors. It is composed of figures in both normal and inverted flight, performed continuously in the specified order.

Program 2 The free program may consist of up to 18 figures, which must be selected from the aerobatic catalogue within given criteria governing versatility and repetition.

Program 3 The unknown compulsory program consists of at least 15 figures chosen by the heads of delegations, and arranged by the jury into a sequence.

Competitors are informed of details of the program at least 24 hours before they are due to fly, although they are not permitted to train for the program.
The score for each figure is multiplied by a difficulty coefficient for that figure.
In the freestyle program each judge rates the total performance, taking into account the difficulty and versatility of the complete sequence, rather than marking individual figures.
The final score in each program for each competitor is found by means of a computer program which has the effect of averaging the judges' scores.

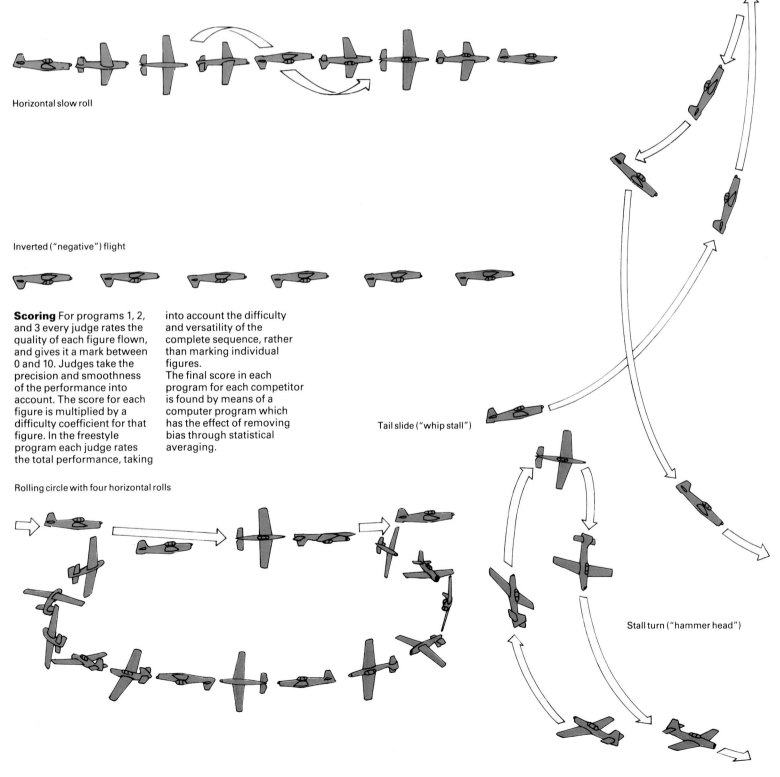

Horizontal slow roll

Inverted ("negative") flight

Scoring For programs 1, 2, and 3 every judge rates the quality of each figure flown, and gives it a mark between 0 and 10. Judges take the precision and smoothness of the performance into account. The score for each figure is multiplied by a difficulty coefficient for that figure. In the freestyle program each judge rates the total performance, taking into account the difficulty and versatility of the complete sequence, rather than marking individual figures.
The final score in each program for each competitor is found by means of a computer program which has the effect of removing bias through statistical averaging.

Rolling circle with four horizontal rolls

Tail slide ("whip stall")

Stall turn ("hammer head")

Program 4 The freestyle program lasts for four minutes only, and any number of figures may be flown within that limit.
Other programs Most international competitions have a similar pattern to the world championships. Some competitions may consist of only two programs: possibly a known compulsory and a free program, each of between 15 and 18 figures.
Penalties Penalty points are incurred for various infringements. Any figures flown after the time limit of 15 minutes in the first three programs are not marked. Any deviation by more than five seconds from the four minutes allowed for program 4 is penalized by 10 penalty points per second. Penalties are incurred for flying too high or too low or outside the performance zone. Pilots are also penalized for interrupting the program to correct their course, or for climbing to regain height.
Results vary according to the rules of each competition. In the world championships there are winners (men and women) who do best in each of the four programs. The overall champions are the man and woman who gain the highest total number of points in the 3 qualifying programs. There are also men and women team champions and a male and female freestyle champion.

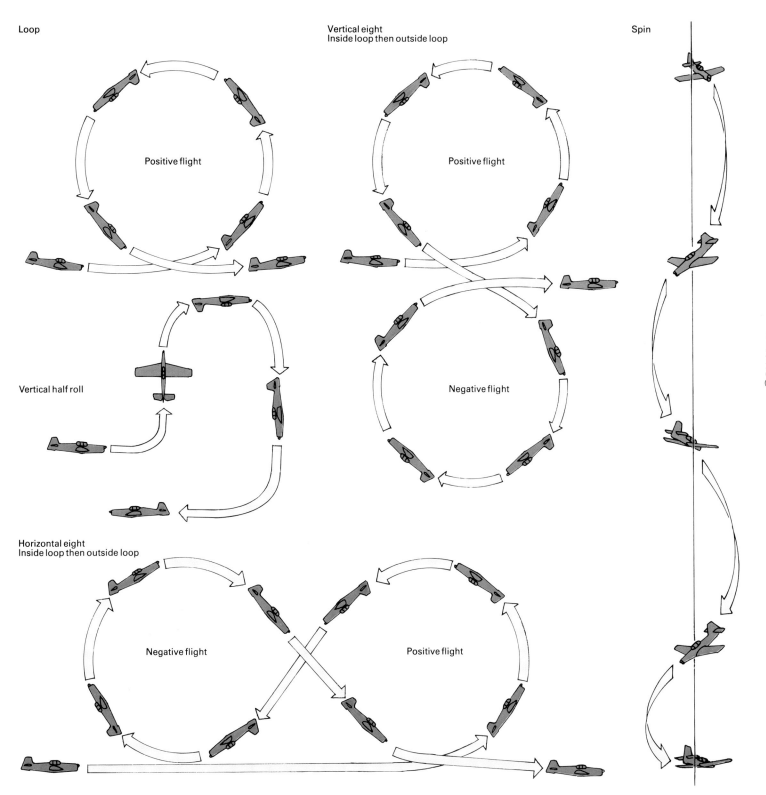

Loop

Positive flight

Vertical half roll

Horizontal eight
Inside loop then outside loop

Negative flight

Positive flight

Vertical eight
Inside loop then outside loop

Positive flight

Negative flight

Spin

© DIAGRAM

305

Sport parachuting

Sport parachuting is a comparatively modern development, the first world championships having been held in 1951. Parachute jumping is controlled by a special division of each country's national aero club.

Clothing Each competitor must wear a protective helmet, and if the jumps are made over or near water, the parachutist must have suitable life-saving equipment. Generally competitors wear one-piece coveralls (jumpsuits), goggles and gloves.

Other equipment For jumps from heights above 4500m (approximately 14,750ft) oxygen equipment must be carried. For any fall involving a delayed opening of 10 seconds or more, competitors must have an altimeter worn where it can easily be read.

Parachutes may be of any type approved by a national authority. Competitors must wear a reserve parachute in addition to the main parachute.

Aircraft may be of any type including lighter-than-air craft, but they must be suitably prepared for the purpose. Each country has its own regulations governing such preparation. Pilots must be experienced in solo flying and must undergo special training in dropping techniques.

Competitors Only qualified parachutists registered with a national aero club may take part in international or world championships. They must be of age and certified medically fit.

Drop zone (DZ) All competitive parachuting is carried out over a drop zone, an area of ground into which parachutists may be safely dropped. This is surrounded by an over-shoot area, which is largely free of major hazards.

A windsock indicates the wind direction at ground level. It must be able to indicate the wind direction when the wind speed is 2m/sec (6.5ft/sec) or more.

Weather Wind at ground level must not exceed 9m/sec or 7m/sec (29.5ft/sec or 23ft/sec) for accuracy jumps. For accuracy events the judges determine the position of the windsock which is located approximately 50m (164.1ft) from the target.

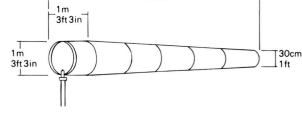

1 pilot chute
2 nylon slider (to ensure gradual inflation of the canopy)
3 toggle (to operate brake line)
4 harness
5 brake or steering line
6 suspension lines
7 cells or openings which hold air

8 parachute container
9 reserve parachute
10 main parachute
11 safety helmet
12 goggles
13 gloves
14 jump suit

The speed of the wind is indicated in m/sec by an anemometer which is installed in the most appropriate position in the drop zone.

Briefing All parachutists must attend a briefing before the start of a competition.

Jump and opening altitude The minimum jump altitude above ground level for free fall jumps is 700m (2296.5ft) for an individual jump and 800m (2624.7ft) for a team jump.

For all jumps, the parachute must be fully open at 400m above ground level.

Training jump Competitors may make at least one training jump before a championship begins, either as an individual or in a group.

Events vary, and may be carried out by teams or individuals. They include accuracy jumps onto a target, style jumps, free-fall jumps and canopy contact jumps.

Awards World championships are awarded for each event and in style and accuracy for men and women separately. There is also an overall champion with the best score for both individual events.

Officials consist of a drop zone controller, an international jury and a panel of judges.

The drop zone controller must keep the target area free of hazards, personally watch all descents, and keep a check on wind and weather conditions.

Should these become unsuitable, he may halt the competition.

The international jury must consist of at least three members of the CIP (the international parachuting committee of the FAI).

Judges A panel of international judges is nominated by competing aero clubs. The CIP decides the number of judges and the host nation chooses the chief judge and his assistant. At least seven judges must judge each event in world championships, and at least five in international championships.

Ground to air communication Communication between the judges on the ground and the competitors on board the aircraft is by two-way radio.

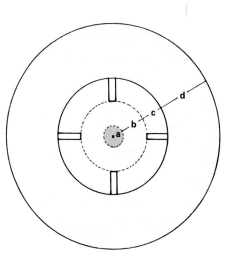

Target area
a 5 cm disc on 16cm electronic pad in sand or fine gravel (3m circle)
b clearly marked circle (5 m)
c rounded gravel (5 m)
d clearly marked circle (35 m)

Accuracy events
Individual parachutists or teams attempt to land on, or as close as possible to, the center of a target. Performance is based on the number of consecutive landings on the central disc, plus the distance of the next jump not on the disc.
Individual accuracy jumps are made from an altitude of 800m (2624.7ft).
Team jumps are made from an altitude of 1100m (6309ft). The team must jump from the same aircraft during one passage of the aircraft over the target.
Style events Individuals perform a series of individual maneuvers in free fall.
Each round consists of a style series of maneuvers. The style jumps are made from an altitude of 2200m (7218ft) or 2000m (6562ft) if meteorological conditions do not allow.

Relative work Teams perform a formation of sequences in free fall. Each round consists of a sequence of scoring formations.
4-way event The teams consist of 4 jumpers including the team captain. The exit altitude is 2,950m (9,500 ft). The working time is 35 sec.
8-way event The teams consist of 8 jumpers including the team captain. The exit altitude is 3,500m (11,500ft). The working time is 50sec.
Canopy relative work events Teams perform a canopy formation or a sequence of canopy formations during descent under open canopy.

Formation All parachutists are connected by legal grips. All parachutes are fully open and under control.
8-way speed formation event The exit altitude is 1,800m (6,000ft) with a working time of 120 sec.
4-way rotation event The exit altitude is 1,8000m (6,000ft) with a working time of 120 sec.
4-way sequential event The exit altitude is 2,000m (6,600ft) with a working time of 180 sec.
Rejumps may be allowed if a malfunction of the main canopy creates a control problem in an accuracy event. In canopy relative work, a canopy malfunction is also sufficient grounds for a rejump.

Disqualification may be ordered for misconduct, or for failing to have the parachute open by at least 400m (1310ft) above the ground.
Scoring Once any jumper has left the aircraft, the jump is official and is scored.
Determination of the winner In accuracy events the competitor/team with the lowest aggregate score for the rounds completed is the winner.
In style events the competitor with the lowest total time, including penalties, for all jumps is the winner.
In relative work and canopy relative work the winners in both the 4-way event and the 8-way event are the teams that accumulate the highest number of points in the completed round.

Ground signals The following signals from the ground are commonly used; they are made with colored panels in red, orange, yellow, or white and are supplemented by radio signals.
Full cross: conditions are safe.
T: conditions are unsafe for any but experienced parachutists.
I: all parachuting is temporarily suspended.
L: parachuting is suspended and aircraft must land.

Some free fall formations

Zigzag

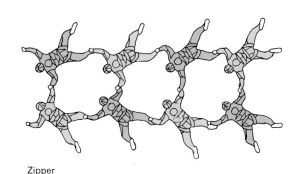

Zipper

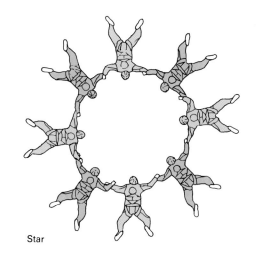

Snowflake

Star

Canopy formation

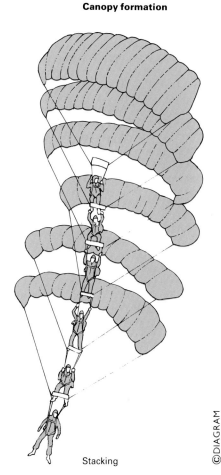

Stacking

©DIAGRAM

307

Ballooning

Hot air balloons are maneuvered by regulating the temperature of the air within the envelope by means of a burner, thus causing the balloon to gain or lose height. Competitions are based on precision navigation of the balloon using the available winds. World records have been established in the various size categories of balloons for flight duration, altitude, and maximum distance.

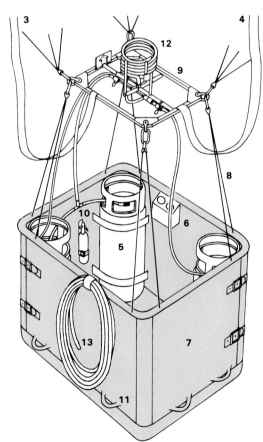

Balloons Most hot air balloons vary in size between 793–6797cu m (28,000–240,000cu ft). For special events (such as world record attempts) much smaller and much larger balloons have been made.

The envelope is made of light, high-tenacity nylon or polyester fabric, specially treated for impermeability and resistance to sunlight. It has one or two controls, depending on the design. The maneuvering or cooling vent, which can be opened in flight to release hot air to stop an ascent or initiate a descent, is often combined with the deflation port which releases the hot air at the top of the balloon to completely deflate the balloon.
Some balloons have rotation vents which are vertical openings that allow a release of lifting air or gas and which may be opened or reclosed in flight: these may be used to position the basket for landing.
The envelope is connected to the basket by stainless steel wires, which keep the fabric at a safe distance from the flame.

The basket is usually woven from rattan or willow and incorporates a suspension system that may consist of rope, stainless steel cables or aircraft aluminum tubing.

The dropline is 30–45m (100–150ft) long. It is deployed whenever the pilot wishes landing assistance from the crew on the ground.

Cylinders Gas is carried in lightweight cylinders strapped inside the basket. The cylinders are operated by an on-off valve. Only one cylinder is used at a time, although they are connected in series.

The burner assembly is positioned above head level and is fed by liquid propane from the cylinders. More than one burner may be incorporated into the assembly.

1 envelope
2 rotation vents
3 control
4 rip control panel
5 propane cylinder
6 altimeter, variometer, compass and pyrometer
7 basket
8 suspension cables
9 load ring, plate, or frame
10 fire extinguisher
11 carrying handles
12 burner
13 drop line
14 throat
15 crown
16 equator
17 vertical rotation vent

Equipment includes: an altimeter, a rate of climb indicator (variometer), an envelope temperature indicator (pyrometer) and fuel tank gauges.

Auxiliary equipment may include: air-to-ground radio, aircraft radio, compass, maps, helmets, inflation fan, spare fuel cylinders.

Crew A small balloon may carry only the pilot, while a large balloon may carry up to 12.

Starting procedure The balloon fuel system and burner is assembled and a pre-flight test of the fuel pressure and burner performance is made. The balloon is spread out with the basket on its side and the envelope is spread out with the crown downwind. The basket is tied off to the chase vehicle for safety.
The throat of the balloon is held open while an inflation fan blows cold air into the envelope. Once the envelope has been completely cold air inflated, the burner is ignited. Using successive bursts of flame, the air within the envelope is warmed causing it to rise to the vertical position. Further heating lifts the balloon from the ground.

Maneuvering The balloon's movements are determined by the atmospheric conditions. Winds vary according to the altitude, and the balloon can only be steered by changing altitude by regulating the burner. More fuel is burned to gain height, less to lose it. The maneuvering vent may be used to release hot air and cause a more rapid descent. Balloons normally fly about 300m (1,000ft) above the ground. Oxygen is needed for flight above 3,800m (12,500ft). The world record for a hot air balloon is over 9800m (65,000ft).

Landing A landing site must be in downwind, as the balloon can be steered only to a limited degree depending on the winds. The approach is controlled by using the burner and maneuvering vent.
When becalmed over unsuitable terrain, the pilot may deploy the drop line so that the ground crew can maneuver the balloon to an open area for landing.

Deflation On completion of the flight, the fuel system is shut down, and the envelope's deflation port is opened. This releases all the remaining hot air in the balloon and it will collapse to the ground. The crew gather it into a long cylinder for packing into the envelope carry sack.

© DIAGRAM

Sports information bodies

There are many international sports organizations that exist primarily to promote a greater understanding of sports between nations. Some of these are listed below along with other major national sports information bodies for America, Canada, UK and Australia. On the following pages the names and addresses of many national and international governing sports bodies for sports described in **Rules of the Game** are given. The list is arranged alphabetically by sport.

Amphora (of olive oil) awarded by the Athens Panathenaic Games' organizers (c575–390 BC) to a victorious boxer.

USA

American Alliance for Health, Physical
    Education, Recreation and Dance
1900 Association Drive
Reston
Virginia 22091
USA

International Council on Health, Physical
    Education and Recreation
1900 Association Drive
Reston
Virginia 22091
USA

UK and Commonwealth

Australian Council for Health, Physical
    Education and Recreation
PO Box 1
Kingswood
South Australia 5062
Australia

British Olympic Association
1 Church Row
Wandsworth Plain
London
SW18 1EH

Canadian Association for Health, Physical
    Education and Recreation
10th Floor
333 River Road
Vanier City
Ontario K1L 8B9
Canada

Centre for International Sports
    Management
PO Box 1168
Station B
Ottawa
Ontario K1P 5R2
Canada

International Assembly of National
    Confederations of Sport
Francis House
Francis Street
London
SW1P 1DE

The Sports Council Information Centre
16 Upper Woburn Place
London WC1H 0QP

International

Comité International Olympique
Chateau de Vidy
CH-1007 Lausanne
Switzerland

General Association of International Sports
    Federations
Villa Henri
7 Bvd de Suisse
MC 98000
Monte Carlo

International Association for Sports
    Information
Clearing House
Galerie Ravenstein 4–27
B–1000 Brussels
Belgium

International Association for the History of
    Physical Education and Sport
Carl-Diem-Weg
Postfach 450327
D5000 Köln 41
Federal Republic of Germany

Major national and international governing sports bodies

	USA and Canada	UK and Eire	International organizations
Aerobatics	National Aeronautic Association of USA 1763 R St, NW Washington DC 20009 USA	British Aerobatic Association Gracious Pond Farm Gracious Pond Road Chobham Surrey GU24 8SW England Royal Aero Club of the United Kingdom Kimberley House 47 Vaughan Way Leicester LE1 4SG England	International Aerobatics Commission Wittman Airfield PO Box 3086 Oshkosh W1 54903 USA
Aikido		Martial Arts Commission 1st Floor Broadway House 15/16 Deptford Broadway London SE8 4PE England British Aikido Association 25 Hey Road Huyton Liverpool Merseyside L36 5SW England	Aikido World Headquarters 17-18 Wakamatsu-cho Shinjuku-ku Tokyo 162 Japan
Air racing		Formula Air Racing Association Merrie Oak Warmlake Sutton Valence Maidstone Kent ME17 3JA England	International Formula One 926 Rawhide Place Newbury Park California 91320 USA
American football	National Football League 350 Park Avenue New York NY 1022 USA		
Archery	National Archery Association of the United States 1750 East Boulder Street Colorado Springs CO 80909-5778 USA The National Crossbowmen of the USA PO Box 1615 Easton PA 18044 USA National Field Archery Association Rt 2, Box 514 Redlands CA 92373 USA	The Grand National Archery Society 7th Street National Agricultural Centre Stoneleigh Kenilworth Warwickshire CV8 2LG England IAU Field Division TK 9 Manor Street Tattenhall Wolverhampton WV6 8RA England	Internationale Armbrustschützen Union IAU Central Body Schlösslirain 9 CH 6006 Luzern Switzerland Fédération Internationale de Tir à l'Arc Via Cerva 30-20122 Milano Italy
Athletics	Athletic Congress of the USA PO Box 120 Indianapolis Indiana 46206/0120 USA	British Amateur Athletic Association Amateur Athletic Association Edgbaston House 3 Duchess Place Hagley Road Edgbaston Birmingham B16 8NM England	International Amateur Athletic Federation 3 Hans Crescent Knightsbridge London SW1X 0LN England
Australian rules football			Victorian Football League (VFL) VFL House 120 Jolimont Road Jolimont Victoria 3002 Australia
Badminton	United States Badminton Association (USBA) 501 West Sixth Street Papillion Nebraska 68046 USA	Badminton Association of England National Badminton Centre Bradwell Road Loughton Lodge Milton Keynes MK8 9LA England	The International Badminton Federation 24 Winchcombe House Winchcombe Street Cheltenham Gloucestershire GL52 2NA England
Ballooning	Balloon Federation of America PO Box 400 Indianola Iowa 50125 USA	British Balloon and Airship Club PO Box 1006 Birmingham B5 5RT England	
Bandy			Svenska Bandyförbundet (Köpmannagatan 19) Box 78 S-641 21 Katrineholm Sweden
Baseball	National Baseball Congress PO Box 1420 Wichita Kansas 67201 USA	British Baseball Federation East Park Lido Hull HU8 9AV England	International Baseball Association Pan American Plaza Suite 490 201 South Capitol Avenue Indianapolis IN 46225 USA
Basketball	National Basketball Association, USA Olympic Tower 645 Fifth Avenue New York NY 10022 USA	English Basketball Association Calomax House Lupton Avenue Leeds LS9 6EE England	Fédération Internationale de Basketball (FIBA) PO Box 70 06 07 Kistlerhofstrasse 168 D-8000 Munich 70 West Germany

	USA and Canada	UK and Eire	International organizations
Biathlon	US Biathlon Association Box 5515 Essex Junction UT 05453 USA	British Ski Federation Brocades House Pyrford Road West Byfleet Surrey KT14 6RA England	Internationale de Pentathlon Moderne et Biathlon Werdenfelser Straße 19, D-8105 Farchant Federal Republic of Germany
Billiards, snooker and pool	Billiard Congress of America 1901 Broadway Street Suite 310 Iowa City Iowa 52240 USA	The Billiards and Snooker Control Council Coronet House Queen Street Leeds LS1 2TN England	
Bobsleigh racing		British Bobsleigh Association Ltd Springfield House 7 Woodstock Road Coulsdon CR3 3HS England	Fédération Internationale de Bobsleigh et de Tobogganing Via Piranesi 44/B 20147 Milan Italy
Boules			Fédération Francaise du Sport Boules 11 Cours Lafayette 69006 Lyon France
Bowling		*Crown Green Bowling* British Crown Green Bowling Association 14 Leighton Avenue Maghull Liverpool L31 0AH England *Flat Green Bowls* English Bowling Association Lyndhurst Road Worthing West Sussex BN11 2AZ England	
Boxing		Amateur Boxing Association of England Francis House Francis Street London SW1P 1DE England British Boxing Board of Control 70 Vauxhall Bridge Road London SW1V 2RP England	International Amateur Boxing Association (AIBA) Postamt Volkradstrasse postlagernd GDR Berlin 1137
Canadian football	Canadian Football League 1200 Bay Street 12th Floor Toronto M5R ZA5 Canada		
Canadian 5 pin	Canadian 5 Pin Bowlers Association 1475 Star Top Road Unit 3 Gloucester Ontario KIB 3W5 Canada		
Canoe sports	American Canoe Association 8580 Cinderbed Road Suite 1900 PO Box 1190 Newington Virginia 22122–1190 USA	British Canoe Union Mappereley Hall Lucknow Avenue Nottingham NG3 5FA England	International Canoe Federation 1124 Budapest Koszta Jozsef u 3 I 3 Hungary
Court handball	United States Handball Association 930 North Benton Avenue Tucson AZ 85711 USA		World Handball Council Croke Park Dublin 3 Eire
Cricket		Marylebone Cricket Club Lord's Ground London NW8 8QN England	
Croquet		The Croquet Association Hurlingham Club Ranelagh Gardens London SW6 3PR England	
Curling	US Curling Association Box 248 Poynette WI 53995 USA	Royal Caledonian Curling Club 2 Coates Crescent Edinburgh EH3 7AL Scotland	
Cycle racing	US Cycling Federation Inc 1750 East Boulder Street Colorado Springs CO 80909 USA	British Cycling Federation 36 Rockingham Road Northants NN16 8GH England	Union Cyclist International 6 Rue Amat 11202 Geneva Switzerland

	USA and Canada	UK and Eire	International organizations
Darts		British Darts Organisation Limited 2 Pages Lane Muswell Hill London N10 1PS England	
Diving	United States Diving Pan American Plaza 201 South Capitol Avenue Suite 430 Indianapolis IN 46225 USA	Amateur Swimming Association Harold Fern House Derby Square Loughborough LE11 0AL England	Fédération Internationale de Natation Amateur (FINA) 425 Walnut Suite 1610 Cininnati Ohio 45202 USA
Dressage	American Horse Shows Association 202 East 42nd Street 4th Floor New York NY 10017–5806 USA	BHS Dressage Group British Equestrian Centre Stoneleigh Kenilworth Warwickshire CV8 2LR England	Fédération Equestre Internationale Bolligenstrasse 54 Boite postale CH-3000 Berne 32 Switzerland
Fencing	United States Fencing Coaches Association 118 Fayette Street Ithaca NY 14850	Amateur Fencing Association The de Beaumont Centre 83 Perham Road West Kensington London W14 9SP England	Fédération Internationale D'Escrime 32 Rue La Boétie 75008 Paris France
Field hockey		The Hockey Association 16 Northdown Street London N1 9BG England	Fédération Internationale de Hockey Avenue Des Arts 1 Bte 5 – 1040 Bruxelles Belgium
Gaelic football		Cumann Luthchleas Gael Parc an Chrocaigh Ath Cliath 3 Dublin 3 Eire	
Gliding	Soaring Society of America PO Box E Hobbes NM 88241 USA	British Gliding Association Kimberley House 47 Vaughan Way Leicester LE1 4SG England	Fédération Aéronautique Internationale 6 Rue Galilee F-75782 Paris CEDEX 16 France
Golf	Professional Golfers Association of America Box 109601 Palm Beach Gardens Florida W3418 USA		
Greyhound racing	American Greyhound Track Operators Association 1065 N E 125th St Suite 219 North Miami FL 33161-5832 USA	The National Greyhound Racing Club Ltd 24-28 Oval Road London NW1 7DA England	
Gymnastics	US Sports Acrobatics Federation PO Box 2602 Durango CO 81301 USA	British Amateur Gymnastics Association Ford Hall Lilleshall National Sports Centre Nr Newport Shropshire TF10 9NB England	Fédération Internationale de Gymnastique Juraweg 12 Case postale 405 3250 LYSS Switzerland
Hang gliding		British Hang Gliding Association Cranfield Airfield Cranfield Bedfordshire MK43 0YR England	
Harness horse racing			Harness Horsemen International 1800 Silas Dean Highway Suite 220 Rocky Hill CT 06067 USA
Horse racing	The Jockey Club 40 East 52nd Street 15th Floor New York NY 1022	The Jockey Club of Great Britain 42 Portman Square London W1H 0EN England	International Racing Bureau Ltd Rookery House Newmarket Suffolk CB8 8EQ England
Horseshoe pitching	National Horseshoe Pitchers' Association of America Box 278 Munroe Falls OH 44262 USA		
Hurling		Gaelic Athletic Association (Eire) Croke Park Dublin 3 Eire	
Ice hockey	National Hockey League 33rd floor 650 Fifth Avenue New York NY 10019 USA		International Ice Hockey Federation 12 Prinz Eugene Strasse 1040 Vienna Austria

	USA and Canada	UK and Eire	International organizations
Jai alai (pelota)	National Association of Jai Alai Frontons Highway US-92 PO Box 2630 Daytona Beach FL 32015 USA US Amateur Jai Alai Players' Association 1935 N E 150th Street North Miami FL 33181 USA		
Judo		British Judo Association 9 Islington High Street London N1 9LQ England Martial Arts Commission 1st Floor Broadway House 15/16 Deptford Broadway London SE8 4PE England	International Judo Federation 50 Gamhoria Street Cairo Egypt
Jiu Jitsu		British Jiu Jitsu Association 5 Avenue Parade Accrington Lancashire BB5 6PN England Martial Arts Commission 1st Floor Broadway House 15/16 Deptford Broadway London SE8 4PE England	
Karate		Marshall Arts Commission 1st Floor Broadway House 15/16 Deptford Boradway London SE8 4PE England	World Union of Karatedo Organizations Headquarters Senpaku Shinko building 1-15-16 Toranomon Minato-ku Tokyo 105 Japan
Kendo		British Kendo Association 36 Finn House Bevendon Street London N1 6BL England Martial Arts Commission 1st Floor Broadway House 15/16 Deptford Broadway London SE8 4PE England	Zen Nihon Kendo Renmei c/o Budokan 2-3 Kita-no-maru koen Chigoda-ku Tokyo Japan
Korfball	US Korfball Federation 11017 Bell Air Place Oklahoma City OK 74132 USA	British Korfball Association PO Box 179 Maidstone Kent ME14 1LU England	International Korfball Federation Woudenbergseweg 56 PO Box 1000 3700 BA Zeist The Netherlands
Lacrosse	United States Women's Lacrosse Association Inc 20 East Sunset Avenue Philadelphia PA 19118 USA US Inter Collegiate Lacrosse Association PO Box 928 Washington and Lee University Lexington VA 24450 USA	English Lacrosse Union 70 High Road Rayleigh Essex SS6 7AD England All England Women's Lacrosse Association Francis House Francis Street London SW1P 1DE England	International Lacrosse Federation PO Box 1149 Piscataway NJ 08854 USA
Lawn tennis	US Tennis Association 51 East 42nd Street New York NY 10017 USA	Lawn Tennis Association Barons Court West Kensington London W14 9EG England	The International Tennis Federation (ITTF) Palliser Road Barons Court London W14 9EN England

Luge tobogganing	Canadian Amateur Bobsleigh and Luge
	  Association
	1600 James Naismith Drive
	Gloucester
	Ontario KIB 5N4
	Canada
			Fédération Internationale de Luge de Course
			  (FIL)
			Secrétaire Général
			56 Chemin du Vallon de Toulouse
			F 13009 Marseille
			France

Modern pentathlon	United States Modern Pentathlon Association PO Box 8178 San Antonio Texas 78208 USA	The Modern Pentathlon Association of Great Britain Q8 Baughurst Road Baughurst Basingstoke RG26 5JF England	Union Internationale de Pentathlon Moderne Limastrasse 1 1-Berlin 37 Federal Republic of Germany
Motor cycle racing	American Motorcyclist Association (AMA) PO Box 6114 Westerville OH 43081–6114 USA	Auto Cycle Union (ACU) Miller House Corporation Street Rugby Warwickshire CU21 2DN	Fédération Internationale Motocycliste (FIM) 19 Chemin William-Barbey CH–1292 Chambésy Geneva Switzerland

	USA and Canada	UK and Eire	International organizations
Mountain running			International Committee for Mountain Racing (ICMR) Hallsteads Gosforth Seascale Cumbria England
Motor racing		RAC Motor Sports Association Ltd Motor Sports House Riverside Park Colnbrook Slough SL3 0HQ England	Fédération International du Sport Automobile 8 Place de la Concorde 75008 Paris France Union International Motornautique (UIM) Nouveau Stade 11 2 Avenue Prince Hereditaire Albert MC 98000 Monaco
Netball		All England Netball Association Ltd Francis House Francis Street London SW1P 1DE England	The International Federation of Netball Associations 99 Awaba Street Mosman New South Wales 2088 Australia
Orienteering	US Orienteering Federation PO Box 1444 Forest Park GA 30051 USA	British Orienteering Federation 'Riversdale', Dale Road North Darley Dale Matlock Derbyshire DE24 2HX England	International Orienteering Federation Box 76 S–191 21 Sollentuna Sweden
Paddleball	National Paddleball Association (USA) PO Box 91 Portage MI 49081 USA		
Pigeon racing		Royal Pigeon Racing Association The Reddings Near Cheltenham Gloucestershire GL51 6RN England	
Polo	United States Polo Association 4059 Iron Works Pike Lexington KY 405111 USA	The Hurlingham Polo Association Ambersham Farm Ambersham Midhurst West Sussex GU29 0BX England	
Powerboat racing	American Powerboat Association National Headquarters 17640 East Nine Mile Road PO Box 377 East Detroit MI 48021–0377 USA	Royal Yachting Association RYA House Romsey Road Eastleigh Hampshire SO5 4YA England UK Offshore Boating Association 16a Station Approach West Byfleet Surrey KT14 6NF England	Union International Motornautique Nouveau Stade 11 2 Avenue Prince Hereditaire Albert MC 98000 Monaco
Roller hockey		National Roller Hockey Association of England 528 Loose Road Maidstone Kent ME15 9UF England	Fédération Internationale de Roller Skating 1500 South 70th Street PO Box 6579 Lincoln Nebraska 68506 USA
Roller skating		National Skating Association of Great Britain 15–17 Gee Street London EC1 2RU England	Fédération Internationale de Roller Skating 1500 South 70th Street PO Box 6579 Lincoln Nebraska 68506 USA
Rounders		National Rounders Association 110 Broadmead Road Woodford Green Essex 1G8 7EH England	
Rowing	The United States Rowing Association 201 South Capitol Avenue Suite 400 Indianapolis IN 46225 USA	Amateur Rowing Association 6 Lower Mall London W6 9DJ England	Fédération Internationale des Sociétés d'Aviron (FISA) Talstrasse 65 Case Postale 4822 CH-8022 Zurich Switzerland
Rugby		Rugby Football Union Rugby Road Twickenham London TW1 1DZ England The British Amateur Rugby League Association (BARLA) West Yorkshire House 4 New North Parade Huddersfield HD1 5JP England	International Rugby Football Board (IRFB) 180 Whitton Road Twickenham Middlesex TW2 7RE England

	USA and Canada	UK and Eire	International organizations
Rugby fives		Rugby Fives Association 1 Kennington Road London SE1 7QR England	
Shinty		Camanachd Association Algare Badabrie Banavie Fort William PH33 7LX Scotland	
Shooting	National Skeet Shooting Association (USA) PO Box 680007 San Antonio Texas 78268 USA Amateur Trapshooting Association (USA) 601 West National Road Vandalia Ohio 45377 USA National Rifle Association of America 1600 Road Island Avenue North West Washington DC 20036 USA	National Rifle Association Bisley Camp Brookwood Woking Surrey GU24 0PB England The Clay Pigeon Shooting Association 107 Epping New Road Buckhurst Hill Essex IG9 5TQ England The National Small-Bore Rifle Association Lord Roberts House Bisley Camp Brookwood Woking Surrey GU24 0NP England	International Shooting Union UIT Bavariaring 21 D-8000 München 2 Federal Republic of Germany
Show jumping	American Horse Shows Association 202 East 42nd Street 4th Floor New York NY 10017-5806 USA	The British Show Jumping Association British Equestrian Centre Stoneleigh Kenilworth Warwickshire CV8 2LR England	Fédération Equestre Internationale Bolligenstrasse 54 Boite postale CH-3000 Berne 32 Switzerland
Skating	Canadian Amateur Speed Skating Association 1600 James Naismith Drive Gloucester Ontario KIB 5N4 Canada	National Skating Association of Great Britain 15-27 Gee Street London EC1V 3RE England	International Skating Union Promenade 73 Postfach CH-7270 Davos Platz Switzerland
Skibob racing		Skibob Association of Great Britain Marwood House Colville Road Acton London W3 8BJ England	Fédération Internationale de Skibob Lutherstraße 27 D4100 Duisburg 1 Federal Republic of Germany
Skiing	United States Ski Association PO Box 100 1500 Keans BLVD Park City UT 84060 USA	The British Ski Federation Brocades House Pyrford Road West Byfleet Surrey KT14 6RA England	Fédération Internationale de Ski Worbstrasse 210 CH-3073 Gümligen bei Bern Switzerland
Sled dog racing			International Sled Dog Racing Association Inc PO Box 446 Nordman Idaho 83848 USA
Soccer	United States Soccer Federation United States Olympic Complex 1750 East Boulder Street Colorado Springs CO 80909 USA	The Football Association Ltd 16 Lancaster Gate London W2 3LW England	Fédération Internationale de Football Association (FIFA) PO Box 85 CH-8030 Zurich Switzerland
Softball	Amateur Softball Association of America 2801 NE 50th Street Oklahoma City Oklahoma 73111 USA	National Softball Federation PO Box 1303 London NW3 5TU England	
Sport parachuting	United States Parachute Association 1440 Duke Street Alexandria VA 22314 USA	British Parachute Association Wharf Way Glen Parva Leicester LE2 9TF England	
Squash	United States Squash Racquets Association Incorporated PO Box 1216 Bala-Cynwyd PA 19004 USA	The Squash Rackets Association Francis House Francis Street London SW1 England	International Squash Rackets Association 93 Cathedral Road Cardiff Wales
Surfing	US Surfing Federation 7104 Island Village Drive Long Beach California 90803 USA	British Surfing Association Burrows Chambers East Burrows Road Swansea SA1 1RF England	International Surfing Association PO Box 617 Umtentweni 4235 Natal South Africa
Swimming and Synchronized swimming	United States Swimming 1750 East Boulder Street Colorado Springs Colorado 80909 USA	Amateur Swimming Association Harold Fern House Derby Square Loughborough LE11 0AL England	Fédération Internationale de Natation Amateur (FINA) 425 Walnut Suite 1610 Cincinnati Ohio 45202 USA

	USA and Canada	UK and Eire	International organizations
Table tennis	United States Table Tennis Association Olympic Complex 1750 East Boulder Street Colorado Springs CO 80909 USA	English Table Tennis Association Queensbury House Havelock Road Hastings East Sussex TN34 1HF England	The International Table Tennis Federation 53 London Road St Leonards-on-Sea East Sussex TN37 6AY England
Team handball	US Team Handball Federation 1750 East Boulder Street Colorado Springs CO 80909 USA	British Handball Association Bridgefield Forum Leisure Centre Cantbridge Lane Halewood Liverpool L26 6LH England	Internationale Handball Federation Lange Gasse 10 CH-4052 Basel Switzerland
Ten pin bowling	American Bowling Congress 5301 South 76th Street Greendale Wisconsin 53129 USA	British Tenpin Bowling Association 114 Balfour Road Ilford Essex IG1 4JD England	Fédération Internationale des Quilleurs Yrjo Sarahete Linnustajantie 6 i 49 02940 Espoo Finland
Three-day event	American Horse Shows Association 202 East 42nd Street 4th Floor New York NY 10017–5806 USA	The British Horse Society British Equestrian Centre Stoneleigh Kenilworth Warwickshire CV8 2LR England	Fédération Equestre International Bolligenstrasse 54 Boite postale CH 3000 Berne 32 Switzerland
Trampolining		The British Trampoline Federation Ltd 152A College Road Harrow Middlesex HA1 1BH England	Fédération Internationale de Trampoline Otzbergstrasse 10 6000 Frankfurt 71 Federal Republic of Germany
Triathlon	Triathlon Federation USA PO Box 1010 1604 East Pikes Peak Avenue Colorado Springs CO 80909 USA	British Triathlon Association PO Box 29 Wakefield WF1 1ZU England	International Triathlon Union 1154 W 24th Street N Vancouver V7P 2J2 Canada
Volleyball	United States Volleyball Association 1750 East Boulder Street Colorado Springs Colorado 80909–5766 USA	English Volleyball Association 27 South Road West Bridgford Nottingham NG2 7AG England	Fédération Internationale de Volleyball (FIVB) Avenue de la Gare 12 CH-1001 Lausanne Switzerland
Water polo	United States Water Polo 1550 East Boulder Street Colorado Springs CO 80909 USA	Amateur Swimming Association Harold Fern House Derby Square Loughborough LE11 0AL England	Fédération Internationale de Natation Amateur (FINA) 425 Walnut Suite 1610 Cincinnati Ohio 45202 USA
Water skiing	American Water Ski Association PO Box 191 Winter Haven Florida 33882 USA	British Water Ski Federation 390 City Road London EC1V 2QA England	International Water Ski Federation (IWSF) 66 Ansanther Road Edgbaston Birmingham B15 3NP England
Weightlifting	The United States Weightlifting Federation Inc 1750 East Boulder Street Colorado Springs Colorado 80909 USA	British Amateur Weightlifters' Association 3 Iffley Turn Oxford OX4 4DU England	International Weightlifting Federation 137 4 Budapest PF 614 Hungary
Windsurfing	US Boardsailing Association (USBA) PO Box 978 Hood River OR 97031 USA	Professional Boardsailors Association (PBA) No 1 Barn Cottages Albany Park Colnbrook Slough SL30 0HS England	
Wrestling	United States Amateur Wrestling Foundation Amateur Athletic Union 3400 West 86th Street Box 68207 Indianapolis IN 46268 USA	English Olympic Wrestling Association 16 Choir Street Cambridge Industrial Estate Salford M7 9ZD England British Amateur Wrestling Association 16 Choir Street Cambridge Industrial Estate Salford M7 9ZD England	Fédération Internationale de Lutte Amateur Avenue Ruchonnet 3 CH-1003 Lausanne Switzerland
Yacht racing	US Yacht Racing Union (USYRU) 8516 Sand Point Way NE Seattle WA 98115 USA	Royal Yachting Association RYA House Romsey Road Eastleigh Hampshire SO5 4YA England	International Yacht Racing Union 60 Knightsbridge Westminster London SW1X 7JX England

Index of sports

Aerobatics 303
Aikido 58
Air racing 300
Alpine combined event 237
Alpine skiing 236
American football 144
Archery, crossbow 69
Archery, field 68
Archery, target 66
Association football 160
Asymmetric bars,
   gymnastics 32
Athletics 10
Australian rules football 140
Autocross, motor racing 293

Badminton 116
Ballooning 308
Bandy 192
Baseball 164
Basketball 124
Beam, gymnastics 32
Biathlon 246
Billiards, carom 82
Billiards, English 80
Bobsleigh racing 252
Boules (boccie) 98
Bowls, crown green 97
Bowls, flat green 94
Bowling, Canadian 5 pin 92
Bowling, tenpin 90
Boxing 48

Canadian 5 pin bowling 92
Canadian football 152
Canoe polo 212
Canoe sailing 213
Canoe slalom 210
Carom billiards 82
Circuit racing, automobile
   282
Circuit racing, motorcycling
   288
Circuit racing, sedan and
   sports car 290
Circuit racing, single-seater
   288
Clay pigeon shooting 76
Court handball 108
Cricket 172
Croquet 102
Crossbow archery 69
Cross-country running 24
Cross-country skiing 244
Crown green bowls 97
Curling 101
Cycle racing 280

Darts 65
Darts cricket 65
Darts football 65
Decathlon 23
Discus 18
Diving 200
Down-the-line shooting 79
Downhill racing, skiing 237
Drag racing, automobile 290
Drag racing, motorcycle 284
Dressage 268

English billiards 80
Equestrianism 266

Fencing 62
Field archery 68
Field hockey 180
Figure skating 230
Fives, rugby 110
Flat green bowls 94
Flat racing 258
Floor exercises, gymnastics
   (men) 36
Floor exercises, gymnastics
   (women) 34
Football, American 144
Football, Association 160
Football, Australian 140
Football, Canadian 152
Football, Gaelic 138
Free pistol shooting 75
Freestyle skiing 241

Gaelic football 138
Giant slalom, skiing 240
Gliding 296
Golf 104
Grass-track racing, motor
   racing 292
Grass-track racing,
   motorcycling 287
Greyhound racing 256
Gymnastics 30

Hammer 19
Handball, court 108
Handball, team 132
Hang gliding 299
Harness horse racing 260
Heptathlon 23
High jump 20
Hill climb, motor racing 293
Hill trials, motor racing 293
Hockey, field 180
Hockey, ice 186
Hockey, roller 179
Horizontal bar, gymnastics
   42
Horse racing 258
Horse vault, gymnastics
   (men) 39
Horse vault, gymnastics
   (women) 31
Horseshoe pitching 64
Hurdles, athletics 14
Hurdles, horse racing 258
Hurling 182

Ice dancing 230
Ice hockey 186
Ice racing, motorcycling 284
Ice skating 228

Jai alai 111
Javelin 16
Jujitsu 60
Judo 52

Karate 54
Karting 294
Kendo 56
Korfball 130

Lacrosse 176
Lawn tennis 118
Long-distance running 12
Long jump 22
Luge tobogganing 250

Marathon 14
Middle-distance running 12
Modern pentathlon 26
Motocross (scrambles) 286
Motor racing 288
Motorcycling 282
Mountain running 24

Netball 128
Nordic combined event 245
Nordic skiing 234

Offshore yacht racing 222
Olympic athletics events 10
Olympic trench shooting 76
Orienteering 25

Pacing, harness horse racing
   260
Paddleball 114
Parachuting, sport 306
Parallel bar exercises,
   gymnastics 40
Pelota 111
Pigeon racing 254
Pistol shooting 74
Pole vault 21
Polo 274
Pommel horse, gymnastics
   40
Pool 86
Powerboat racing 226

Rallycross, motor racing 293
Rallying 292
Rapid fire pistol shooting 74
Relay events, athletics 12
Rhythmic gymnastics 43
Rifle shooting 70
Rings, gymnastics 38
Roller derby 278
Roller hockey 179
Roller skating, artistic 279
Roller skating, speed 278
Rounders 170
Rowing 206
Rugby fives 110
Rugby league 156
Rugby union 156
Running, cross-country 24
Running game target
   shooting 73
Running, mountain 24

Scrambles, motorcycling
   286
Sedan and sports car racing
   290
Shinty 184
Short-track speed skating
   229
Shot put 17
Show jumping 264
Skating, ice figure 230
Skating, ice speed 228
Skating, roller artistic 279
Skating, roller speed 278
Skeet shooting 78
Ski flying 242
Ski jumping 242
Skibob racing 248
Skiing 234
Skittles 89
Slalom (autotest) 293

Slalom, canoe 210
Slalom, skiing 240
Sled-dog racing 255
Snooker 84
Soccer (Association football)
   160
Softball 168
Speedball 135
Speed skating, ice 228
Speed skating, roller 278
Speedway, motorcycling 284
Sport parachuting 306
Sports car racing 290
Sports acrobatics 44
Sprint, athletics 12
Sprint, canoeing 208
Sprint, cycling 280
Sprint, motor racing 293
Sprint, motorcycling 284
Squash 112
Steeplechase, athletics 14
Steeplechase, horse racing
   258
Stock car racing 292
Super-G skiing 240
Surfing 202
Swimming 194
Synchronized swimming 196

Table tennis 120
Target archery 66
Team handball 132
Tennis, lawn 118
Tennis, table 120
Tenpin bowling 90
Three-day event 271
Trampolining 45
Trials, motor racing 292
Trials, motorcycling 287
Triathlon 28
Triple jump 23
Trotting, harness horse
   racing 260

Volleyball 122

Walking events 15
Water polo 198
Water skiing 204
Weightlifting 46
Wild water racing 211
Windsurfing 224
Wrestling 50

Yacht racing 214
Yacht racing, offshore 222

General index

A

Accuracy parachute jump 307
Acrobatics, sports acrobatics 44
Aerobatics 303–305
Aero-tow 296
Aikido 58–59
Air racing 300–302
Air rifle 70–71
Alley, skittle 89
Alpine combined event 237
Alpine skiing 236–240
Altimeter 297, 308
American football 144–151, 155
Ammunition 71, 73–75, 77–79, 246
Archery, crossbow 69
   field 68
   target 66–67
Arena, athletics 10–11
   dressage 268
   show jumping 264
Arrows 66–67, 68
Artistic gymnastics 30–42
   men's 36–42
   women's 31–45
Association football 160–163
Asymmetric bars 30, 32–33
Athletics 10–23
Australian rules football 140–143
Autocross 293
Autotest 293
Auto-tow 296
Axel-Paulsen jump 233

B

Backboards 124–125
Backstroke 194–195
Badges, gliding 298, 299
Badminton 116–117
Baguette 99
Balk, baseball 167
   English billiards 80
Ball, American football 145, 151
   Australian football 141
   bandy 193
   baseball 165
   basketball 125
   billiard 81, 83
   Canadian 5-pin 93
   Canadian football 153
   canoe polo 212
   court handball 109
   cricket 173
   croquet 103
   field hockey 181
   Gaelic football 139
   golf 105
   hurling 183
   korfball 131
   lacross 177
   lawn tennis 119
   netball 129
   paddleball 115
   polo 275
   pool 87
   roller hockey 179
   rounders 171
   rugby 157
   rugby fives 110
   shinty 185
   skittles 89
   snooker 85
   soccer 161
   softball 169
   speedball 135
   squash 113
   table tennis 121
   team handball 133
   tenpin bowling 91
   volleyball 123
   water polo 199
Ballet leg 196–197
Ballooning 308
Bandy 192–193
Barebow 68

Barracuda 197
Baseball 164–167
Basket, balloon 308
Basket, basketball 124–127
   korfball 130–131
   netball 128–129
Basketball 124–127
Bat, baseball 165
   cricket 173
   softball 169
Baton, relay 12–13
Beam 30, 32–33
Behind 140–143
Biathlon 246–247
Bigbore rifle shooting 70–71
Billiards, carom 82–83
   English 80–81
Blackguard 110
Block 86–87
Blocking 123
Blue Peter 215
Boats, canoes 208–213
   powerboats 226–227
   rowing 206–207
   sculls 207
   water skiing 205
   yachts 214–223
Bobsleigh racing 252–253
Bolt, crossbow 69
Boule pointée 98–100
Boule portée 98–100
Boule tirée 98–100
Boules (boccie) 98–100
Bounce off 140
Bout, boxing 48–49
   fencing 62–63
   wrestling 50–51
Bow 67, 68
Bowler, cricket 172–175
Bowling, Canadian 5-pin 92–93
   tenpin 90–91
Bowls, crown green 97
   flat green 94–96
Boxing 48–49
Break shot, pool 86
Breaststroke 194–195
Broom, curling 101
Bull 65
Bully 180–181
Bungee, launch 296
Bunker 106
Buoy 204–205, 213–214, 224–227
Burner 308
Butterfly stroke 194–195
Bye 174

C

Caddie 104
Cage 18–19
Caman 184–185
Canadian 5-pin bowling 92–93
Canadian football 152–155
Cannon 80–81
Canoe, Canadian 208–211
Canoe polo 212
Canoe sailing 213
Canoe slalom 210–211
Canoeing 208–211
Canter 269
Capsize 211
Carom billiards 82–83
Catalina 197
Cesta 111
Chalk 89
Cheese 89
Chukka 275
Circle, discus 18
   dressage 270
   hammer 19
   shot 17
Circuit racing, automobile 288–291
   motorcycle 282–283
   sedan and sports car 290–291
   single-seater 288

Clay pigeon shooting 76–79
Clean and jerk 46–47
Club, golf 104–107
Cockpit 301
Collected paces 269
Compass, orienteering 25
Conversion, rugby league 157
   rugby union 157
Convert 154
Coopies 254
Count-out 48
Counter-canter 269
Course, air racing 300
   bobsleigh 252
   canoe sailing 213
   canoe slalom 210–211
   cross-country running 24
   downhill racing 236–237
   endurance 272–273
   giant slalom 236, 240
   grass track racing 287
   greyhound racing 257
   horse racing 258
   luge tobogganing 250–251
   motocross 286
   mountain running 24
   Nordic cross-country 244–245
   offshore yacht racing 222
   orienteering 25
   powerboat racing 226
   show jumping 264, 273
   skibob racing 248–249
   slalom 236, 238–239
   sprint canoeing 208–209
   super-G 236, 240
   trials 287
   windsurfing 224–225
   yacht racing 214
Court, badminton 116
   basketball 124–125
   court handball 108–109
   jai alai 111
   lawn tennis 118–119
   netball 128–129
   paddleball 114
   rugby fives 110
   squash 112
   team handball 132–133
   volleyball 122–123
Court handball 108–109
Cricket 172–175
Cricket, darts 65
Croquet 102–103
Cross-country running 24
   modern pentathlon 26–27
Cross-country skiing 244–245
Crossbar, Gaelic football 138
   high jump 20
   pole vault 21
   rugby 156–157
   soccer 160–161
   speedball 135–137
   team handball 132
Crossbow archery 69
Crosse 176–178
Crown green bowls 97
Cue, carom billiards 82–83
   English billiards 80–81
   pool 86–88
   snooker 84–85
Cue ball, carom billiards 82–83
   English billiards 80–81
   pool 86–88
   snooker 84–85
Curling 101
Cushion, English billiards 80–81
   pool 86–88
Cycle racing 280–281
   triathlon 28–29
Cyclo-cross 281

D

Dash 262–263
Darts 65
Darts cricket 65
Darts football 65

Decathlon 10–11, 23
Demi-fond 281
Deuce 118
Discus 10–11, 18
Diving, platform 200–201
   springboard 200–201
Dolly 101
Dolphin 197
Double 65
Double Lutz jump 233
Double-rise shooting 79
Double Salchow jump 233
Down-the-line shooting 79
Downdraft 297
Downhill racing 236–237
Draw, lacrosse 176
Draw-weight 67
Dressage 268–271
Dribble, basketball 125
   speedball 136
Drive, golf 105
Drop zone 306

E

Endurance 272–273
English billiards 80–81
Epée 27, 62–63
Equestrianism 264–273
Eskimo roll 211
Expedite system 121

F

Face-off, bandy 192
   ice-hockey 187
   roller hockey 179
Facing 178
Fair-catch 158
Fall, wrestling 50–51
Fédération Aéronautique Internationale 303, 306
Fédération Equestre Internationale 268, 271
Fédération Internationale d'Escrime 27
Fédération Internationale de Luge de Course 250
Fédération Internationale Motorcycliste 282
Fencing 62–63
   modern pentathlon 26–27
Field archery 68
Field events 10–11, 16–23
Field hockey 180–181
Field round 68
Figure skating 230–233
Figures, synchronized swimming 196
Finn 219
Fives, rugby 110
Flat green bowls 94–96
Flat racing 258–259
Flèche 62
Flight, ski-jumping 242–243
Floor exercises 30, 34–37
Floorer 89
Flying Dutchman 219
Foil 62–63
Follow-on 174
Football, American 144–151, 155
   Association (soccer) 160–163
   Australian rules 140–143
   Canadian 152–155
   darts 65
   Gaelic 138–139
   rugby 156–159
Footer 97
Formula cars 287–288
Frame, Canadian 5-pin 92–93
   English billiards 80
   skittles 89
   tenpin bowling 90–91
Free pistol shooting 75

Decathlon 10–11, 23
Demi-fond 281
Deuce 118

Freestyle, field archery 68
   swimming 194–195
   windsurfing 224–225
Frontis 111
Fronton 111
Fumble 147, 148, 151

G

Gaelic football 138–139
Gates, canoe slalom 210–211
   downhill racing 237
   giant slalom 240
   skibob 248–249
   ski slalom 238–239
   super-G 240
Gauntlet and V-attack 60–61
Giant slalom 240
Gliding 296–298
   hang gliding 299
Go-karting 294–295
Goal, American football 144, 148, 151
   Australian football 140–141
   bandy 192–193
   basketball 124, 126
   Canadian football 154
   canoe polo 212
   field hockey 180
   Gaelic football 138
   hurling 182–183
   ice hockey 186–191
   korfball 130–131
   lacrosse 176–178
   netball 128
   polo 274–277
   roller hockey 179
   rugby 156–157
   shinty 184–185
   soccer 160–161
   speedball 135–137
   team handball 132–134
   water polo 198–199
Gold, archery 66
Golf 104–107
Grass-track racing, motor racing 293
   motorcycling 287
Green, crown green bowls 97
   flat green bowls 94–96
Greyhound racing 256–257
Grip, tenpin bowling 91
Gybing 214, 217
Gymnastics 30–44

H

Hachimaki 57
Hajime 52–54, 56, 58, 60–61
Hakama 57
Halt 269
Hammer throwing 10–11, 19
Handball, court 108–109
   team 132–134
Hang gliding 299
Hare 257
Harness horse racing 260–263
Hash marks 152–154
Hazard 80–81
Head of the river races 206
Heel calk 64
Heptathlon 10–11, 23
High house 78
High jump 10–11, 20
Hikiwake 56, 58, 60
Hill climb 293
Hill trials 293
Hockey, field 180–181
   ice 186–191
   roller 179
Hole, golf 104–107
Home base 164, 168
Home run, baseball 166
   softball 168
Hoop, croquet 102–103
Horizontal bar 30, 42
Horse racing 258–259
   harness 260–263

Horse vault 30, 31, 39
Horseshoe pitching 64
House, curling 101
Hunters' round 68
Hurdles, athletics 14–15
    horse racing 258–259
Hurley 183
Hurling 182–183
Hydroplane racing 226–227

I

Ice dancing 230–233
Ice hockey 186–191
Ice racing 284–285
Ice skating, dance 230–233
    figure 230–233
    short track speed 229
    speed 228–229
Individual demonstration
    (gauntlet and V-attack) 60–61
Infield 164
In-run 242–243
International Amateur Athletic
    Federation 23
International Amateur Boxing
    Association 48
International Curling Federation
    101
International Europe Class 219
International Yacht Racing
    Union 213, 214, 217
Ippon, aikido 58–59
    jujitsu, 60–61
    judo 52
    karate 54–55

J

Jack, boules 98–100
    crown green bowls 97
    flat green bowls 94–96
Jai alai 111
Javelin 10–11, 16
Jerk 46–47
Jujitsu 60–61
Jockey 259
Judo 52–53
Judogi 53, 61
Jump ball 125
Jump, long 10–11, 22
    high 10–11, 20
    ski 242–243
    triple 10–11, 23
    water ski 204–205

K

Karate 54–55
Karate-gi 55
Karting 294–295
Kata 58
Katamewaza 52
Kayak 208–212
Keikogi 57
Kendo 56–57
Kiss shot 83
Knockdown, boxing 48–49
Knock-on, rugby 159
Korfball 130–131

L

Lacrosse 176–178
Lagging, carom billiards 82
    pool 86
Landing area, long jump 22
    ski jumping 242–243
    triple jump 23
Lanes, athletics 10–15
    Canadian 5-pin 92–93
    speed skating 228–229
    swimming 194–195
    tenpin bowling 90–91
Lateral 111
Lawn tennis 118–119
Lechner 390 219, 224
Leg before wicket 175
Line-out 159
Long-distance running 10–13

Long jump 10–11, 22
Loop, aerobatics 305
    roller skating 278
Low house 78
Luffing 214, 216
Luge tobogganing 250–251
Lure 257

M

Madison racing 281
Maillot jaune 281
Mallet 102–103
Map, orienteering 25
Marathon 10–11, 14
Mark, Australian football 142
    crown green bowls 97
    rugby 158
    yacht racing 214–217
Mat, flat green bowls 94–96
    gymnastics 30, 34–37
    judo 52–53
    wrestling 50–51
Match play 104–107
Maul 158–159
Medley, swimming 195
Middle-distance running 10–13
Modern pentathlon 26–27
Motocross 286
Motor racing 288–293
Motorcycle racing 282–287
Mountain running 24
Muzzle 256

N

Nagewaza, jujitsu 60–61
    judo 52
Nations' Cup 264–265
Net, badminton 116–117
    lawn tennis 118–119
    table tennis 120–121
    volleyball 122–123
Netball 128–129
Ne-waza, jujitsu 60–61
    judo 53
Ninidori 58–59
Nordic combined event 245
Nordic skiing 234–235, 242–247
Norm point 242–243

O

Oars 207
Obi 61
Obstacles, endurance 272–273
    horse racing 258–259
    show jumping 264–267, 273
Offshore yacht racing 222–223
Olympic sports, archery 66–69
    athletics 10–23
    basketball 124–127
    biathlon 246–247
    bobsleigh 252–253
    boxing 48–49
    canoeing 208–211
    cycling 280–281
    diving 200–201
    equestrianism 264–273
    fencing 62–63
    gymnastics 30–43
    handball (team) 132–134
    hockey (field) 180–181
    ice hockey 186–191
    judo 52–53
    luge 250–251
    modern pentathlon 26–27
    rowing 206–207
    shooting 70–79
    skating (ice) 228–233
    skiing 234–245
    soccer 160–163
    swimming 194–195
    synchronized swimming 196–197
    volleyball 122–123
    water polo 198–199
    weightlifting 46–47
    windsurfing 224–225

wrestling 50–51
    yachting 214–221
Olympic trench shooting 76–77
Orienteering 25
Outfield 164

P

Pacing, cycling 281
    harness horse racing 260–263
Paddle, canoe 209, 211, 212
    paddleball 115
Paddleball 114–115
Parachuting, sport 306–307
Parallel bars 30, 41
Parallelogram, Gaelic football
    138–139
    hurling 182–183
Parry 62
Passage 269
Pass back 180
Peg, croquet 102–103
Pelota 111
Pentathlon modern 26–27
Piaffer 269
Pigeon loft 254
Pigeon racing 254
Pike, diving 201
    synchronized swimming 196–197
    trampolining 45
Pins, tenpin bowling 91
    Canadian 5-pin 93
Pirouette, dressage 270
Piste 62–63
Pistol shooting 74–75
    modern pentathlon 26–27
Pitch, American football 144–145, 151, 155
    Australian football 140
    boules 98–100
    Canadian football 152–155
    cricket 172–175
    field hockey 180–181
    Gaelic football 138
    hurling 182–183
    korfball 130
    lacrosse 176–178
    rounders 170–171
    rugby 156–159
    shinty 184–185
    soccer 160–163
    speedball 135–137
Plate, baseball 164
    softball 168
    skittles 89
Play-the-ball 158
Pocket, English billiards 80–81
    pool 86–88
    snooker 84–85
Pole vault 10–11, 21
Poles, athletics 21
    skiing 234–245
Polo 274–277
Pommel horse 30, 40
Pool 86–88
Post, rounders 170–171
Powerboat racing 226–227
Puck 186–191
Puck-out 183
Puissance 264–265
Punt, speedball 136
Punt returning 155
Pursuit races, cycling 281
    short track speed skating 229
Putting 107
Pylon turn 302

Q

Queensberry, Marquess of 48
Quiniela 111
Quiver 67

R

Racing, air 300–302
    bobsleigh 252–253
    downhill ski 236–237
    go-kart 294–295
    greyhound 256–257
    harness horse 260–263
    horse 258–259
    motor 288–293
    motorcycle 282–287
    offshore yacht 222–223
    pigeon 254
    powerboat 226–227
    skibob 248–249
    sled dog 255
    yacht 214–221
Racket, badminton 116–117
    lawn tennis 118–119
    squash 112–113
    table tennis 120–121
Rallycross 293
Rallying 292
Randori kyoghi 58–59
Range, archery 66–69
    biathlon 246–247
    down-the-line shooting 79
    Olympic trench shooting
    76–77
    pistol shooting 74–75
    rapid fire pistol shooting 74
    rifle shooting 70–73
    skeet shooting 78
Rebote 111
Regatta races 206
Rein back 269
Relays, athletics 12–13
    biathlon 246–247
    roller skating 279
    short track speed skating 229
Renvers 270
Rest, English billiards 80
    snooker 85
Rhythmic gymnastics 43
Riding, dressage 268–270
    modern pentathlon 26–27
    polo 274–277
    show jumping 264–267
    three-day event 271–273
Riding off 277
Rifle shooting 70–73
Rigs, sailing 220–221
Ring, boxing 48
Ringer 64
Rings, gymnastics 30, 38
Rink, bandy 192–193
    curling 101
    flat green bowls 94–96
    ice hockey 186–191
    ice skating 230–233
    roller hockey 179
    roller skating 278–279
Riposte 62
Road racing 280–281
Roll, aerobatics 304–305
Roller derby 279
Roller hockey 179
Roller races, cycling 281
Roller skating, artistic 278
    speed 279
Ropes, boxing 48–49
Roquet 103
Rouge 152–155
Rounders 170–171
Routines, synchronized
    swimming 197
Rowing 206–207
Ruck 158–159
Rugby fives 110
Rugby league 156–159
Rugby union 156–159
Running 12–13
    cross-country 24
    mountain 24
    triathlon 28–29
Running game target shooting
    73

S

Sabre 62–63
Safety shot 83
Sailboards 219, 224–225
Sailplane 296–299
Scratch shot 86–88
Scrimmage, American football
    146–149, 155
    Canadian football 153–155
Scrum 158–159
Sculls 207
Seconds, boxing 48
Sedan and sports car racing
    290–291
Serpentine 270
Serve-out 115
Setter-up 89
Shinai 56–57
Shiaijo 52
Shinty 184–185
Short-track speed skating 229
Shot put 10–11, 17
Shotgun 76, 78–79
Show jumping 264–267, 273
Shuttle 116–117
Sidecars 283–285
Signals, air racing 300
    gliding 298
    kendo 56
    parachuting 307
Single-rise shooting 79
Single-seater racing 288
Skates, bandy 193
    ice figure 231
    ice hockey 186–191
    ice speed 228–229
    roller artistic 278
    roller hockey 179
    roller speed 279
Skating, ice 228–233
    roller 278–279
Skeet shooting 78
Ski flying 243
Ski jumping 242–243
Skibob racing 248–249
Skiing, Alpine 234, 236–241
    biathlon 246–247
    Nordic 234–235, 242–245
Skis 234–247
    water 205
Skittles 89
Slalom, autotest 293
    canoe 210–211
    giant 240
    ski 238–239
    super-G 240
    water ski 204–205
    windsurfing 224–225
Sled-dog racing 255
Smallbore rifle shooting 70–71
Snap, American football
    146–148
    Canadian football 153–155
Snatch 46–47
Snooker 84–85
Snubline 255
Soccer (Association football)
    160–163
Softball 168–169
Soling 218
Somersault 45
Spare, Canadian 5-pin 93
    tenpin bowling 91
Speed sailing 225
Speed skating, ice 228–229
    roller 279
Speedball 135–137
Speedway 284–285
Spin, aerobatics 305
    ice skating 233
Sport parachuting 306–307
Sports acrobatics 44
Sports car racing 290–291
Sportsboat racing 226–227
Spotters 45

Spring, athletics 12–13
  canoeing 208–209
  cycling 281
  motor racing 293
  motorcycling 284–285
Sprint canoeing 208–209
Squash 112–113
Stadium racing 292
Stake 64
Standing count 49
Star 218
Starting blocks 13
Starting trap 257
Steeplechase, athletics 14–15
  horse racing 258–259
Stick, bandy 192–193
  field hockey 180–181
  ice hockey 186–191
  lacrosse 177
  polo 274–277
  roller hockey 179
  rounders 171
  skiing 234
Stock car racing 292
Stone, curling 101
Strike, Canadian 5-pin 93
  tenpin bowling 91
Stringing 80–81
Stroke play 104–107
Stumping 175
Style parachute jump 307
Super-G 240
Surfboard 203
Surfing 202–203
  windsurfing 225
Swimming 194–195
  modern pentathlon 26–27
  synchronized 196–197
  triathlon 28–29
Synchronized swimming
  196–197
Synchronized trampolining 45

T
Table, carom billiards 82
  English billiards 80
  pool 86
  snooker 84
  table tennis 120
Table point 242–243
Table tennis 120–121
Tachi-waza 60–61
Tacking 214
Tackling, American football 149
  Australian football 143
  bandy 193
  Canadian football 154
  Gaelic football 139
  hurling 183
  lacrosse 178
  rugby 158
Take-off, diving 201
  long jump 22
  ski jumping 242
Tanto randori 58–59
Target, clay pigeon shooting
  76–79
  crossbow archery 69
  field archery 68
  parachuting 306–307
  pistol shooting 74–75
  rifle shooting 70, 73
  target archery 66–67
Target archery 66–67
Team handball 132–134
Tee, curling 101
  golf 104–105
Tennis, lawn 118–119
  table 120–121
Tenpin bowling 90–91
Three-day event 271–273
Throw in, soccer 162
Throw off, korfball 131
  team handball 132
Throw up, korfball 131

shinty 184
Throwing events, discus
  10–11, 18
  hammer 10–11, 19
  javelin 10–11, 16
  shot put 10–11, 17
Tie-break 118
Time-out, American football
  145
  basketball 126
  speedball 136
  volleyball 123
Tip off 136
Tir 98–100
Toboggan 250–251
Toe calk 64
Tomiki aikido 58–59
Tornado 218
Touchback 137
Touchdown, American football
  148
  Canadian football 154
  rugby 157
  speedball 136–137
Toucher 96
Tour de France 280
Tow lines 205
Tow rope 296–297
Track, athletics 10–11
  drag racing 284, 290
  harness horse racing 262
  ice racing 284
  motorcycle racing 282
  roller derby 279
  roller skating 279
  running 12–13
  short track speed skating 229
  speed skating 228–229
  speedway 284
  stock car racing 292
Track events 12–15
Track racing, cycle 280–281
Trampolining 45
Trap 76–79
Travers 270
Trials, hill 293
  motorcycling 287
Triathlon 28–29
Trick riding, waterskiing
  204–205
Triple jump 10–11, 23
Trot 269
Trotting 260–263
Try 157
Tuck, diving 201
  trampolining 45

U
United States Trotting
  Association 260

V
Variometer 297, 299, 308
Volleyball 122–123
Volte 270

W
Walk, dressage 269
Walking events 10–11, 15
Walkover 197
Water hazard, golf 105
Water jump, athletics
  steeplechase 15
  horse racing 258
  show jumping 264, 266
  three-day event 272
Water polo 198–199
Water skiing 204–205
Wave performance 224–225
Wave possession 202–203
Waza-ari, aikido 58–59
  jujitsu 60–61
  judo 52
  karate 54–55
Weightlifting 46–47

Weights 47
Wicket 172–175
Wild water canoeing 211
Windsock 306
Windsurfing 224–225
Wire, harness horse racing 262
World Boxing Council 48
Wrestling, freestyle 50–51
  Greco-Roman 50

Y
Yacht racing 214–221
  offshore 222–223